PEACE AND FAITH

FOR WILLIAM HARTER

1936-2020

PEACE AND FAITH

CHRISTIAN CHURCHES AND THE ISRAELI-PALESTINIAN CONFLICT

EDITED BY

CARY NELSON & MICHAEL C. GIZZI

PRESBYTERIANS FOR MIDDLE EAST PEACE
Distributed by Academic Studies Press

Philadelphia & Boston

The paper used in this publication meets the minimum requirements of the American National Standard for Information Sciences—Permanence of Paper for Printed Library Materials, ANSI Z39.48-1992.

Cover photograph: The interior of the Church of the Holy Sepulchre in Jerusalem.
Photo Credit: IAN

Manufactured in the United States of America.

IN PRAISE OF *PEACE AND FAITH*

All Christians will be informed by *Peace and Faith*'s exploration of current engagements with Israel, ranging from so-called "Christian Zionism" to the BDS (Boycott-Divestment-Sanctions) movement. All church members will be challenged by its case studies of ecclesial responses to the state of Israel and the Israeli-Palestinian conflict. Israel and the Church, Judaism and Christianity, synagogues and churches, Jews and Christians—all reflect a complex relationship with a two thousand-year history. *Peace and Faith*'s nineteen essays by Christian and Jewish scholars bring historical, theological, ecclesiastical, and political perspectives to bear on this complex relationship. Centuries of anti-Jewish thought and action have led the Church to diminished reception of the gospel, restricted apprehension of God's faithfulness, and a distorted sense of its own nature and purpose. All readers will benefit from the book's thoughtful analysis of anti-Semitism's enduring history and current manifestations. By avoiding slogans, clichés, and exaggerations, *Peace and Faith* deepens Christian faith and strengthens hope for peace.

> **—Joseph D. Small, University of Dubuque Theological Seminary, author of *Flawed Church, Faithful God: A Reformed Ecclesiology for the Real World* and other books; former director of Theology, Worship, and Educational Ministries for the Presbyterian Church(USA)**

3

An essential volume for anyone interested in Christian churches and the Israeli-Arab conflict. Brings together between two covers the essential historical data, theological positions, church pronouncements, and intellectual arguments that define denominational debates, thereby setting the stage for informed dialogue.

> **—Jonathan D. Sarna, Brandeis University; Director, Schusterman Center for Israel Studies, author of *American Judaism: A History* and other books**

Debates about Israel-Palestine often involve slogans and caricature, and so seldom lead to genuine dialogue or a deeper understanding of the conflict. The essays in *Peace and Faith* challenge some of the truncated or overly simple views that many Christians have of Judaism, Zionism, and Israel—and so invite readers to a better informed and more humane conversation.

> **—David Heim, former editor-in-chief, *The Christian Century*; editor of *How My Mind Has Changed***

Peace and Faith should be required reading for those concerned about "Christian churches and the Israeli-Palestinian conflict," as the subtitle puts it. It brings perspective and understanding to a conversation that has been often been foolish and shortsighted.

> **—Mark Galli, former editor-in-chief, *Christianity Today*; author of *When Did We Start Forgetting God?: The Root of the Evangelical Crisis and Hope for Our Future* and other books**

This is a much needed and highly welcome volume. Most literature has been theological or polemical in nature, and has given voice mostly to post-colonial, pro-Palestinian views. While that is, of course, a legitimate point of view, the editors and writers of the proposed volume have wished to add a more even-handed and empirical study of the realities of Christian groups and the Israeli-Palestinian conflict. The volume includes highly informative essays, some of which are absolute gems.

> **—Yaakov Ariel, University of North Carolina at Chapel Hill, author of *Evangelizing the Chosen People* and other books.**

BDS has misled many good-willed people. This volume by scholars and leaders unveils the reality behind the myth.

> **—Gerald McDermott, Beeson Divinity School, editor of *The New Christian Zionism***

This book is a long overdue addition to the discussion of Christian engagement with the Israel-Palestinian conflict. Its greatest strength is the clear-eyed, comprehensive treatment, always with a steady aim toward justice and reconciliation. The contributors have long been engaged with the issues at hand. Those in the Presbyterian tradition will especially appreciate the careful historical and theological analysis of the recent struggles and the reasons for them. Nothing is easy about this subject. The book provides a fresh starting point for all future discussions. I highly recommend it.

> —**Roy W. Howard, Pastor, Saint Mark Presbyterian Church, North Bethesda, Maryland**

In recent years, an aggressive anti-Israel agenda has begun to permeate a number of Christian churches in the United States. Despite the disturbing rise of Christian anti-Zionism, we still don't have a good grasp of how the campaign to delegitimize Israel took root or how it can best be combated. *Peace and Faith* fills this void. Including perspectives of scholars alongside those who work and worship within the churches, the book provides a set of thoughtful and nuanced assessments of the battles over anti-Israel divestment and the materials that have been produced and disseminated to drive them. Readers will learn about the key theological and political issues that currently inform church debates on Israel and Christian-Jewish interfaith relations. All who seek a just and sustainable resolution to the Israeli-Palestinian conflict will benefit from reading Peace and Faith, which concludes with a compelling framework for a Christian-articulated reconciliation between the Israeli and Palestinian peoples.

> —**Miriam F. Elman, Syracuse University; co-editor of** *Jerusalem: Conflict and Cooperation in a Contested City*; **Executive Director, Academic Engagement Network**

Peace and Faith is a great achievement, a carefully chosen collection of thoughtful essays about the Israeli-Palestinian conflict authored by both Jews and Christians. It will be an essential resource for anyone concerned with these issues, especially North American Protestants and Jews. The voices gathered here are diverse in interest, experience, expertise, and religious identity. What unites them is the willingness, indeed the eagerness, for informed, respectful dialogue, along with a shared dismay about such hostile voices as those of the BDS movement. *Peace and Faith* thus clearly reflects a point of view. But one need not share it to find the book highly informative and helpful for discussion among a wide range of partners. I thank the editors and contributors. The book will be a critical resource for people with a wide range of views who share a desire for dialogue.

—Dr. Heidi Hadsell, president emerita, Hartford Seminary

This book makes an invaluable contribution to what are often contested conversations about the future of Israel and Palestine. The topic remains a central point of debate both between Christians and Jews and among Christians themselves. While *Peace and Faith* gives special emphasis to the Presbyterian Church, the issues raised there in various official statements and throughout the book's other essays concern the Christian churches at large and their Jewish partners in dialogue. Having all this readily available in a single volume provides an essential resource for continuing discussions of these ethical and political challenges.

—Rev. John T. Pawlikowski, Professor Emeritus of Social Ethics and director of the Catholic-Jewish Studies Program, Catholic Theological Union; author of *Jesus and the Theology of Israel* and other books

Peace and Faith cogently explores how the complicated Israeli-Palestinian conflict has been used to draw apart the parties to the conflict and those who support them. We learn about the political and theological divides that have been deepened by these battles. And—unique to this book alone—we learn how to chart a better course forward. Jews and Christians deserve much better than has been given to them in the past; if we agree that we need to foster reconciliation for the parties and ourselves, this book's important lessons and strategies make it necessary reading.

—Rabbi Yehiel E. Poupko, Rabbinic Scholar, Jewish Federation of Metropolitan Chicago; author of *Chana: A Life in Prayer*

Peace and Faith lays essential and original groundwork for any further church discussion of boycott, divestment, and sanctions against Israel (BDS). Any such discussion will be self-reflective and self-critical, given the heritage of Christian anti-Judaism that remains unresolved and too often unaddressed in our churches. These essays model the kind of approach we need, while also challenging the record of BDS advocacy to date as one-sided and blinkered. The ecumenical and interreligious set of authors that Nelson and Gizzi have assembled include first-rank scholars and front-line church leaders. Their long experience and intellectual integrity sets their work apart from the more common fare offered by apologists—whether for Israel or for BDS. Lay and clergy readers alike will find effective resources here to move beyond the ignorance, sympathy, and frustrated indignation that leave us vulnerable to manipulation. Peace and Faith is a call for responsible dialogue about the challenge that the church faces in engaging modern-day Israel and the Palestinian community on gospel grounds. No one will be able to claim an informed place in that dialogue who has not wrestled with and learned from the masterful presentation of key issues in this volume.

> **—Peter A. Pettit, Teaching Pastor, St. Paul Lutheran Church; former director, Institute for Jewish-Christian Understanding, Muhlenberg College**

Peace and Faith is a brilliant, empowering treasury of information, fair perspectives, essential background revelations, and historic wisdom. It takes up what is perhaps the world's most misunderstood struggle—typically "explained" with conflicting sets of "facts" and Biblical interpretations—and substitutes thoroughly researched and profound essays that consistently shed light on the topic. The Israeli-Palestinian conflict looks no less tragic as a consequence, but the abundant ideological fog that so often clouds understanding is dissipated by these well-crafted essays. For decades I have participated in political and church discussions on the subject, and this is the best contribution I have seen to this critical sphere for faith, compassion, and public policy engagement.

> **—Rev. Paul H. de Vries, PhD; President, NY Divinity School; Founder and Evangelical Convener of the NY Jewish-Evangelical RoundTable**

There are great riches here, including the introduction, which is quite a resource in itself.

> **—Adam Gregerman, Saint Joseph's University; author of *Building on the Ruins of the Temple: Apologetics and Polemics in Early Christianity and Rabbinic Judaism***

CONTENTS

LIST OF ILLUSTRATIONS

ACRONYMS & ABBREVIATIONS

ACJ—American Council of Judaism
ACPC—American Christian Palestine Committee
ACSWP—Advisory Committee on Social Witness Policy
ADL—Anti-Defamation League
AFME—American Friends of the Middle East
AFMEP—Americans for Middle East Peace
AFSC—American Friends Service Committee
AIPAC—American Israel Public Affairs Committee
AJC—American Jewish Committee
AMIDEAST—America-Mideast Educational and Training Services
ARZA—Association of Reform Zionists of America
AZEC—Jewish American Zionist Emergency Council
BCE—Before the Common Era
BDS—Boycott, Divestment, and Sanctions
CATC—Christ at the Checkpoint
CCAR—Central Conference of American Rabbis
CCI—Christians Concerned for Israel
CCJR—Council of Centers on Jewish-Christian Relations
CE—Common Era
CIPAC—Christian Israel Public Action Campaign
CIA—Central Intelligence Agency
CMEP—Churches for Middle East Peace
CPT—Christian Peacemaker Teams
CUFI—Christians United for Israel
ECLA—Evangelical Lutheran Church in America
ECO—Evangelical Covenant Order
EPC—Evangelical Presbyterian Church
EPF—Episcopal Peace Fellowship
EWIG—Ecumenical and Interreligious Work Group
FDR—Franklin Delano Roosevelt
FOSNA—Friends of Sabeel North America

GA—General Assembly
HILC—Hispanic Israel Leadership Coalition
HP—Hewlett Packard
ICCJ—International Council of Christians and Jews
IDF—Israel Defense Forces
IHRA—International Holocaust Remembrance Association
IJCIC—International Jewish Committee on Interreligious
    Consultations
IPMN—Israel Palestine Mission Network
JCPA—Jewish Council for Public Affairs
JFK—John Fitzgerald Kennedy
JLC—Jewish Leadership Council
JVP—Jewish Voice for Peace
KJV—King James Version
KKK—Ku Klux Klan
KPD—*Kairos Palestine Document*
LBJ—Lyndon Baines Johnson
LGBTQIA+—lesbian, gay, bisexual, transgender, queer or
    questioning, intersex, and asexual or allied, and
    others not included (+)
MCC—Mennonite Central Committee
MC USA—Mennonite Church USA
MENA—Middle East North Africa
MennoPIN—Mennonite Palestine Israel Network
MESC—Middle East Study Committee
MRTI—Mission Responsibility Through Investment
NCC—National Council of Churches
NGO—Non-Governmental Organization
PA—Palestinian Authority
PCA—Presbyterian Church in America
PCJCR—Presbyterians Concerned for Jewish Christian Relations
PCUSA—Presbyterian Church USA
PFMEP—Presbyterians for Middle East Peace
PIEF—Palestine Israel Ecumenical Forum
PLO—Palestine Liberation Organization
PNS—Presbyterian News Service

PPF—Presbyterian Peace Fellowship
RSV—Revised Standard Version
Sabeel—Sabeel Ecumenical Liberation Theology Center
UCC—United Church of Christ
UK—United Kingdom
UMC—United Methodist Church
UMKR—United Methodists Kairos Response
UN—United Nations
UNRWA—United Nations Relief and Works Agency
URJ—Union for Reform Judaism
USAID—United States Agency for International Development
WCC—World Council of Churches
YMCA—Young Men's Christian Association
ZU—*Zionism Unsettled*

PREFACE

PEACE AND FAITH: Christian Churches and the Israeli-Palestinian Conflict, composed of new essays, is the first collection to bring together writers from different faith communities to discuss the Boycott, Divestment, and Sanctions movement's impact on one of the more fractious topics addressed by Christian denominations: the Israeli-Palestinian conflict. In so doing, it builds on interfaith projects under way for decades. Theology and politics intermingle in debates taking place in local churches, Christian NGOs, and national church meetings that define official policy. The debates revive and reframe the most basic values of Christianity and the questions church members seek to resolve: How do Christians today hew to the principles Jesus articulated? How can justice be pursued in the context of competing national narratives and historical understandings? What bearing do or should centuries of Christian violence against Jews and Muslims have on contemporary theology and ethics? Is it ethical, or even possible, to set aside millennia of Christian anti-Semitism in judging Israel's conduct? What Christian values should be honored in pursuing Jesus's mission of reconciliation today? How may the pursuit of truth be corrupted by passionate social witness? Can advocacy cross the line into hatred? These are among the critical questions this collection poses and attempts to address.

A number of people deserve our thanks and gratitude for sharing their expertise with us as we worked on this project, including David Heim, Gerald McDermott, and David Fox Sandmel, as well as several current or former staff members from Israel Action Network: Paulina Carey, Ethan Felson, Stephanie Hausner, Geri Palast, Zachary Schaffer, and Avi Weinryb. In addition to helping us to find factual information and managing the publication process, they joined others, among them David

Fox Sandmel and Raeefa Shams, in reading and commenting on one or more chapters in detail. Adam Gregerman and Dexter Van Zile each provided exceptionally detailed comments on the entire manuscript. Edward Moran pointed us toward several relevant documents. Ethan Felson read the entire manuscript and made numerous comments and suggestions; he also lent us a box of church publications, answered a number of factual questions, shared his experience of religious meetings, and assisted with moving the publication process forward. Sandmel helped us research several questions and put us in touch with other members of the interfaith community. An earlier version of Cary Nelson's essay "A Critical Reading of *Zionism Unsettled*, Its Antecedents, and Its Legacy" appeared in the Summer 2019 issue of *Religions*. It incorporates a review of *Why Palestine Matters* first published in *Fathom*. A version of "A Reconciliation Roadmap" was published as "What Peace Would Require" in the January 29, 2020, issue of *The Christian Century*. A portion of the introduction was presented at an Indiana University webinar series organized by Alvin Rosenfeld on behalf of the Institute For The Study of Contemporary Antisemitism.

Our partner, Presbyterians for Middle East Peace (PFMEP) has been active in the denomination for over a decade. Its membership ranges across conservative, centrist, and progressive lay members and clergy, all unified by the search for peace and reconciliation. PFMEP supports a two-state solution, seeking justice for both Israelis and Palestinians. It neither endorses nor opposes political candidates. PFMEP's many publications are cited throughout the book. Its roots go back at least to the early 1970s; indeed, some of its current leaders, among them the late William Harter, co-authored Presbyterian Church publications from the 1970s discussed in detail in the introduction to this book.

Publication of the book has been supported by a foundation grant covering several interfaith projects.

Finally, a note on style. The question of whether *anti-Semitism* or *antisemitism* is the preferred spelling continues to be debated in the scholarly literature. We have considered it to be a choice protected by academic freedom. Thus, rather than impose uniformity, we have allowed each author to choose how to spell the term.

INTRODUCTION

CARY NELSON

THE POLITICAL AND THEOLOGICAL FOUNDATIONS OF CHRISTIAN ENGAGEMENT WITH THE JEWISH STATE

Among the many ways to fracture a congregation, talking about Israel is one of the most dependable. Intersecting claims about justice, biblical prophecy, national identity, historical legacies, personal allegiances, geographical dynamics, confessional commitments, and headline-grabbing crises run through the topic and deep into bedrock convictions.

—Peter A. Pettit, "How New is the New Christian Zionism?" 20

The God to whom the witnesses of Jesus' resurrection attributed the event was antecedently present in their consciousness as the God who had called Abraham to be the father of his people, who had chosen Jacob and not Esau, who gave the Law at Sinai, who fought for Israel and sometimes against her, who sent prophets with messages of judgment and salvation, who could be angry—and could also be funny, given to pranks like ambushing Jacob in the guise of a river god, or making a donkey a prophet . . . . We are separated by just one question: Did the God of Israel in fact raise his servant Jesus from the dead or did he not?
— Robert W. Jenson, "Afterword" *Covenant and Hope* 286-87
The relationship between Judaism and Christianity has implications for the church's self-understanding that must be addressed if the church is to know fully who it is . . . . Apart from understanding both biblical Israel and the ongoing life of the Jews, the church cannot fully understand itself.
—Joseph D. Small, *Flawed Church, Faithful God* 153

Peace and Faith is an interfaith project designed to bring the long history of Christian-Jewish relations to bear on perhaps the most vexing of contemporary topics, one which combines religion and politics in a volatile mix: the Israeli-Palestinian conflict and the role that debates within religious communities can or should play in the pursuit of reconciliation and conflict resolution. We have brought together contributors from several faith communities—Catholic, Episcopalian, Jewish, Mennonite, and Presbyterian—to address both recent debates within the churches and the often fraught history that underlies them. In our invitations to potential contributors we made clear that we sought several kinds of essays—formal academic studies addressing historical topics; close textual analyses of key documents, statements, and publications; and personal testimony and analysis from participants in church debates. All three categories of writing, spanning both academic and nonacademic work, are necessary to gain an adequate understanding of the book's subject. They are also essential as part of a book directed toward all educated readers interested in Jewish-Christian relations and the Middle East, including those active in the organizational debates over the status of the Jewish state. We hope to have produced a companion to those debates that can be of both practical and conceptual use to debate participants.

The Case Against Academic Boycotts of Israel (2015) was intended not only for people at universities but for all those involved in the controversies over academic boycotts. We thus see *Peace and Faith* as a comparably dual use or "crossover" volume. You can read Susan Andrews's essay to learn about an example of church/synagogue collaboration or you can use it as a model of how to conduct such a relationship. You can read Michael Gizzi's guide to Jewish/Arab reconciliation projects in Israel mainly to learn about them or you can consider participating in or donating to one of the projects he summarizes. You can read the several personal narratives about engagement in church debates—among them those by John Kampen, Michael Gizzi, and John Wimberly and William Harter—to learn more about the content of church policy statements and about how they were negotiated, or you can use the same essays as a handbook to guide your own denominational work. You can read the several exceptionally detailed readings of key church documents as part of a quest for understanding and you can use them as guides to how to analyze texts being debated at meetings you attend. The several essays offering historical background have not only disinterested intellectual and political value but also insight into the underlying conditions of ongoing controversies, thereby empowering more informed personal participation.

The repeated efforts by our authors to encourage their denominations to reject hostility and embrace reconciliation—from Amy-Jill Levine's rereading of the Gospels, through C. K. Robertson's account of Episcopalian debates, Robert Cathey's description of interfaith work in Chicago, and Michael Gizzi, John Wimberly, and William Harter's detailed history of a conflicted Presbyterian Church—once again combine informative history with model proposals to guide future conversations. The section on reconciliation, Part Three of the book, represents the culmination of the theme. The three essays in that section are notably intertwined. Andrews's story about a US-based reconciliation project cannot be immediately applied to the entire Israeli-Palestinian conflict, but it has direct application to the local reconciliation projects that Gizzi describes. The "Reconciliation Roadmap" that follows describes multiple actions and policy changes that would make still more such projects possible.

The long historical context that continues to influence church and synagogue policy, sentiment, and conviction is a topic so large that it has accumulated its own substantial library of books, essays, and statements of principle. We make no claim to treat the topic comprehensively, but we do want to make the key figures, concepts, and moments of that history available to our readers. For that reason, the book opens and closes with resources to help our readers frame current religious discussions within that larger and much longer historical context. Although this introduction will highlight key features of the essays that follow, its larger purpose is to acquaint readers with the historical, political, and theological issues that undergird church engagement with the Israeli-Palestinian conflict and the history of Jewish/Christian relations.

The introduction is thus the opening essay in the book; it provides essential background for the chapters that follow. The first part of the introduction, "Christian Theology and the Status of Israel," opens with a discussion of evangelicalism, the largest and most politically powerful Christian denominational movement engaged with the Israeli-Palestinian conflict. An overview of the relevant history of the Mennonites, perhaps the least widely understood Christian denomination, though one quite vocal about the conflict, follows. Given the continuing influence of supersessionist assumptions among Mennonites, it makes sense for a general discussion of supersessionist convictions to follow—beliefs embodying the theological principle that Christianity superseded or "replaced" Judaism, thus constituting a "replacement theology." It is paired with sections on the long-vexed theological topics that are very much intertwined with supersessionism: first, the status of the divine covenant with the people of Israel; second, the concept and status of being "chosen" as the covenantal people.

The second part of the introduction, "Christianity and the Boycott Movement," analyzes the anti-Zionist political agenda that has roiled so many churches for a generation. It includes a detailed summary of the main action item, the proposal to divest from investments in Israel, that has been debated in various forms at numerous annual denominational meetings. The introduction's third part, "The Structure of the Book," covers the chapters that follow. The concluding section, "Dialogue and Reconciliation," identifies the book's aspirational and practical agenda.

Debates over the Israeli-Palestinian conflict present substantial challenges for everyone, but religious groups face special burdens. Unlike secular political constituencies, it is not (and perhaps should not be) as easy for people of faith to settle for demonizing one side or the other. Nor can they as easily ignore the need to diminish hatred and to encourage reconciliation—while still insisting on the recognition of each side's needs, fears, and historical perspectives—and the need to find solutions to the conflict that can actually work. Peace groups have learned that the competing "narratives" of two peoples can coexist; they do not have to be reconciled, because collective reconciliation can proceed even without mutually agreed upon narratives.

That said, the anti-Zionist movements within Christian churches and much of the international political left share a series of arguments, strategies, and tactics that constitute one of the great moral failures in recent history: the refusal to compare human rights abuses against Palestinians in Gaza and the West Bank with the vastly more serious crimes committed in Iraq, Syria, Yemen, and other countries in the region, as well as in Bosnia, Cambodia, China, North Korea, and Rwanda, among other places worldwide. "Where are the Israeli atrocities capable of standing with those committed by, to name a few, the Pol Pot regime in Cambodia, the Assad regime in Syria, ISIL in Iraq and Syria, or the Nazis, first in Germany and later throughout Europe between 1933 and 1945?" (Harrison 148). When religious groups combine hostility toward the Jewish state with indifference to human rights abuses by other far more repressive regimes, they have violated the ethical imperatives that should, at least in theory, guide their politics. When checkpoint delays loom larger than mass murder, our moral compass has lost its way. We may no longer expect secular political constituencies to recover their capacity to compare, contrast, and evaluate the actions of nation-states or violent mobs objectively, but we believe people of faith can still be challenged and indeed are expected to do so.

In partnership with Presbyterians for Middle East Peace (PFMEP) and its umbrella group Pathways for Middle East Peace, we give special attention to developments within that denomination. Protestant denominations do a great deal of political, cultural, and theological work at their annual meetings, often generating contentious document archives in the process. Reports and recommendations may precede the meetings, but the debates among representatives attending and subsequent votes are often what actually dictate national church policy. The number of reports about Middle East conflicts and the sheer number of pages devoted to the Israeli-Palestinian conflict by Presbyterians are remarkable. Indeed, it would be entirely possible to publish a separate book collecting these documents and reflecting on Presbyterian perspectives. We have been able nevertheless to cover much of the relevant denominational history and recent debates here and in the second part of the book.

In contrast to Protestant denominations, the Catholic Church creates theological and policy consensus largely from the top down. Nonetheless, as Yaakov Ariel reminds us, "the Church does not always speak in one voice" ("Contemporary" 302), neither historically nor in a given period. Catholic doctrine evolves over time, with some beliefs acquiring greater authority than others. "Doctrines give rise to further doctrines. Doctrines are fecund" (D'Costa vi). The highest truths are represented by the magisterium, the Church's teaching authority that is vested in the pope and the bishops in communion with him. Not all Church statements about Jews and Judaism carry that much weight. Some are binding on Catholics, others merely advisory.

As Giovanni Matteo Quer shows in his chapter, there are a number of Catholic NGOs and Catholic-allied groups, especially in Europe, that have supported anti-Israel boycott initiatives, and some that have helped fund them.[1] Others have joined in creating or signing documents highly critical of Israeli policies. Those Catholic organizations that endorse boycotts of Israel, such as the Catholic pacifist organization Pax Christi and the Italian Associazione Papa Giovanni XXIII, also often see them as perfectly compatible with the peace process, a disabling contradiction that they typically fail to confront. Despite the hierarchical structure of the Catholic Church in terms of theology and liturgical practice—and despite the progress made on these fronts—Rome has not chosen to enforce political conformity on its constituent and allied organizations. Some Catholic organizations, like Pax Christi and its branches, are quite independent of central control, while others, like Caritas, are fundamentally Vatican operations. At this point, one can reasonably conclude that the Vatican will only intervene to impose its views on Catholic organizations if they exhibit explicit anti-Semitism.

As with the Vatican's relations with the Jewish state, in this case socio-political concerns trump theological ones. Some estimate that some 150,000 Christians, including 55,000 Roman Catholics, were among the 750,000 Arabs who fled Israel in the 1948-49 war of independence. The Christian community in Palestine and in Arab countries generally has declined from twenty percent to four percent of the overall population, but the Vatican is still concerned with the safety of the small Catholic community. Some church properties are now in Palestinian territory, so the Vatican professes political neutrality to protect its ownership and access. As D'Costa reports, the Middle Eastern Synod has clung to hard supersessionism. At a 2010 Vatican press conference, Cyril Salim Bustros, the archbishop of the Melkite Greek Catholic Archeparchy of Beirut, declared "We Christians cannot speak of the 'promised land' as an exclusive right for a privileged Jewish people. This promise was nullified by Christ" (125).

In a July 2020 webinar organized by the American Jewish Committee (AJC), Archbishop Paul Gallagher, Secretary of Relations with States of the Holy See (effectively the Vatican's foreign minister), justifiably referred to the "sea change" in Catholic/Jewish relations initiated by the Church's historic 1965 declaration *Nostra Aetate*.[2] Yet the Church has not adopted the International Holocaust Remembrance Association's (IHRA) influential definition of anti-Semitism. As recently as 2020, Jews involved in high level interfaith dialogue have urged the Vatican to do so without success. Gallagher argued that definitions tend to be either too loose or too restrictive to be applicable to changing historical conditions, though the usefulness of the IHRA definition in identifying instances of anti-Semitism and formulating legislative actions has been clear. And the pledge of joint action between the Vatican and the Israeli state to fight anti-Semitism has yet to be fulfilled. Despite his deeply felt opposition to anti-Semitism, Pope Francis has yet to convene a major interfaith event devoted to the topic. Meanwhile, Rabbi David Rosen, the American Jewish Committee's (AJC's) Director of International Jewish Affairs, observes that he meets bishops who do not even know the content of *Nostra Aetate*. Lisa Palmieri-Billig, AJC's representative in Italy and Liaison to the Holy See, remarks that she meets many Christians who are shocked when told that Jesus was a Jew: "How can that be?" If *Nostra Aetate* was a miraculous transformation at the Olympian Heights, after more than half a century it has yet to fully penetrate to the grass roots.

Focused chapters on other denominations are included in the book's first section, and there will be sections on Methodism and Mennonism in this introduction. We have included viewpoints by people from within those churches alongside analyses by scholars from outside the church. However, we do not attempt to cover all denominations, in part because the arguments raised for and against Israel are often similar. Among the groups that do not receive treatment are the "dissenting denominations within Protestantism, among them Jehovah's Witnesses, the Seventh-Day Adventists, and the Mormons" (Ariel "Contemporary" 297). As Ariel notes, "Jehovah's Witnesses believe they alone are fulfilling God's will and reject all other religious expressions. Likewise, they anticipate the kingdom of God as the only legitimate political entity . . . . They have no use for Israel, the state or the land, and, considering the Jews to be a legitimate object of missionary activity, have made hundreds of converts in Israel" (298). Seventh-Day Adventists have for the most part maintained "the traditional Christian belief that the Jewish role in history ended with Jesus's death on the cross" (298), but in the past twenty years have begun to embrace reconciliation projects. Yaakov Ariel provides an overview of relevant Mormon history:

> Mormon interest in the prospect of the Jewish return to Palestine goes back to Joseph Smith, the Book of Mormon and the tour of the Mormon elder Orson Hyde to Palestine in 1841, in which he "dedicated" the land for its Jewish inhabitants. Smith and his followers have viewed themselves as members of the tribe of Joseph and understood America to be the Promised Land. Mormon sacred scriptures speak about Judean refugees making their way from

Jerusalem to America at the end of the First Temple period and of Jesus blessing America. Likewise, they speak about America in messianic terms, and cast their experiences in their first generation in biblical terms, as the sons of Israel crossing the desert towards the Land of Zion-Deseret.

While identifying America with Zion and themselves as Israelites, Mormons have not made supersessionist claims in relation to Jews and Judea. They recognize the Jews as the Children of Judah and the Land of Israel as a second Zion, the gathering place of the Jews at the end of the era, when they accept Christianity in its rightful Mormon version. Mormon prophets and elders have looked favorably upon the Jewish return to Palestine. . . . In the 1970s Brigham Young University established an academic center near Jerusalem, in Kibbutz Ramat Rachel, where hundreds of Mormon students came to take courses, mostly about Israel, the Bible and the Middle East. Wishing to encourage the Mormon involvement with Israel, [Jerusalem Mayor] Teddy Kollek facilitated the allocation of a large piece of land on the Mount of Olives for building a permanent compound. Brigham Young University raised tens of millions of dollars and built a magnificent center, designed by the Israeli architect David Reznik, overlooking the old city of Jerusalem. The Jerusalem center has opened its doors to Israelis, conducting series of concerts. Likewise, the Mormon Tabernacle Choir has visited Israel and included "Hatikvah" and "Jerusalem of Gold" in its repertoire.

The project caused a controversy in Israel, with Orthodox Jews protesting the allocation of land to a religious group known for its extensive evangelism. Consequently, the Mormon Church and the Israeli government signed an agreement, according to which Mormon students who come to study at the Brigham Young campus in Jerusalem would not evangelize during their stay in Israel. Both the building of the campus, the only one outside of Utah and Hawaii, and the agreement not to evangelize have been outstanding in Mormon global policies. While Mormon attitudes towards Israel have, on the whole, been supportive, since the 1980s, the Mormon Church has forged a balanced policy in relation to the Israeli-Arab conflict. The Brigham Young center in Jerusalem has played a role in implementing this policy. Among other ventures, it asks its students to study and spend time in the Palestinian community, as well as among Israelis. Attitudes towards the Middle East are not a matter of dogma, and while many Mormons are overtly supportive, there are other voices too. (Yaakov "Contemporary" 298-299)

C. K. Robertson in his chapter here recounts and reviews the history of the Episcopal Church's engagement with the Israeli-Palestinian conflict. John Kampen concentrates on a key 2017 Mennonite resolution, supplying an analysis not only of the text and the debates surrounding it but also of the relevant church history over the preceding generation. Jonathan Rynhold covers the large and highly influential evangelical movement in an essay grounded in detailed statistical evidence. Evangelicals represent the single largest Christian group in the US, and they have both a distinctive understanding of Christian history and a unique relationship with successive Israeli governments. Israeli governments have often welcomed the radical—though by no means universal—evangelical view that Israel, as the living embodiment of a theological prophecy, is essentially beyond reproach. Yet, as Daniel G. Hummel documents in detail, the evangelical movement has evolved over time and has long been fissured by theological differences; it has never been one thing. Nonetheless, their influence on US policy toward Israel is considerable. "They frequently report major events in Israel and the Middle East in their vast network of traditional and digital media, often visit Israel and the holy places, organize gigantic pro-Israel conventions, and lobby on behalf of Israel in Congress and at the White House" (Gilboa 10). The paradox inherent in evangelicalism in fact helps clarify the divisions that define mainline Protestant denominations as well. As Ethan Felson wrote in 2008, "Our Evangelical Protestant neighbors are often friends of our national identity, as demonstrated by their support for the State of Israel, but are at times less than friendly to our faith identity as Jews. Our Mainline Protestant neighbors are often friends of our faith identity, but at times this friendship does not extend to our national identity" ("Evangelical").

PART I: CHRISTIAN THEOLOGY AND THE STATUS OF ISRAEL

EVANGELICALS

Premillennialists believe in a literal reign by Christ on earth for a thousand years (millennial) before (pre) the end of history. Premillennial dispensationalism is a reading of the Bible that views God as dealing differently with his people in different eras or dispensations. They focus on eras of end-time events that are punctuated by the coming of Jesus Christ called "the rapture." The rapture involves Jesus Christ taking Christians off the earth, sometimes followed by a great battle. In the final days, the end times, there will be a mass conversion of Jews who will follow Jesus as messiah. Postmillennialists usually believe that Jesus Christ will appear after the faithful establish the kingdom of God through the power of the Spirit and a widespread living of gospel values. (D'Costa 66)

Despite the movement's internal differences, there are key points of convergence in what remains a decentralized evangelical constituency. Hummel calls Genesis 12:3 "the organizing of the modern Christian Zionist movement" (5). The New International Version that most evangelicals use translates the verse, which is the core of God's covenantal declaration to Abraham, as "I will bless those who bless you, and whoever curses you I will curse; and all peoples on earth will be blessed through you." Robert Alter's slight revision concludes "those who damn you I will curse, and all the clans of the earth through you shall be blessed." Alter's use of "clans" arguably gives the passage a more national or ethnic-specific edge, but both versions serve now to "cast Christians as covenantal partners in the pursuit of Israeli security" (Hummel 101). Dispensationalists were among the first to read Genesis 12:3's command to bless Israel as a political mandate (58). But there were differences among evangelical communities. Jerry Falwell, whose Moral Majority seemed to define evangelicalism for several years in the

1980s, emphasized the punitive side of 12:3, "I will curse those who curse you," and was among those who saw anti-Semitic states like Nazi Germany or the Soviet Union as having been punished for their views, whereas John Hagee, Texas megachurch pastor, televangelist, and founder of Christians United for Israel in 2006, has, since the 1990s, moved toward an affirmative reading. Those who support Israel will gain God's favor and with it wealth and prosperity.

Although we do not address what amounts to a nascent politically significant denominational impact on Israel's status in the world, that development embodies the same prosperity-oriented theology. The key example is that of the remarkable growth of spirit-centered Christianity in Africa, Asia, and Latin America. More focused on testifying to the personal experience of the Holy Spirit's presence than on biblical interpretation, spirit-centered Christians emphasize the blessings that flow from adherence to Genesis 12:3. Their increasing numbers constitute what Hummel characterizes as "a seismic shift in Christianity's center of gravity" (223). The Catholic Church has experienced a similar geographical shift in membership, but it remains a hierarchical, not a decentralized, Church. Even if Rome increasingly turns its attention toward members in Africa and Latin America, the Vatican remains the Church's center. Europe and North America, however, could see their impact on Protestant politics diminish.

It is difficult to imagine the conviction that the health of a nation state depends on its policies toward Israel actually triumphing over the powerful anti-Zionist constituency in, say, South Africa, though there are pro-Zionist spirit-centered religious leaders there. At the same time, spirit-centered evangelical Christianity has "a network of more than six million followers with church branches throughout central and northern Brazil" (Hummel 225). Brazil has long voted against Israel in the United Nations, but Christian Zionists in Brazil are gaining political power and trying to get that practice changed; President Jair Bolosonaro supports them and supports Israel. Evangelicals in Brazil have built a huge, enlarged replica of Solomon's Temple in São Paulo. Brazil did vote against a 2016 UN resolution denying Israel's connection to the Western Wall and the Temple Mount/Haram al-Sharif, and that was before Bolosonaro became president in January 2019. Some read the prosperity-oriented theology that defines so much of global Christian Zionism as crassly materialistic, but it has nevertheless had an undeniable impact on Christian Zionism worldwide.

More problematically, as Jonathan Rynhold explains in Chapter Five here, the scenario many evangelicals still embrace actually celebrates the founding of the Jewish state as a step toward the abolition of Judaism as such:

> It proclaimed there will be seven years of natural disasters and terrible wars in which two-thirds of humanity will perish. Meanwhile, the Jews will return to their ancient homeland. They will establish a state there ruled by the Antichrist posing as the Messiah. The Antichrist will inflict a reign of terror. The arrival of Jesus at the end of the Great Tribulation will end the Antichrist's rule and establish the millennial kingdom. Only those Jews who accept Jesus as their personal savior will survive. Jesus will then rule, with the Jews inhabiting David's ancient kingdom.

Most Jews and many Christians find it unsettling or unacceptable to lay out an "end of days" scenario and timeline and promote it as an unquestioned truth. As Emil Fackenheim writes, "all attempts to link the precarious present with the absolute future are themselves precarious and cannot be otherwise" ("The Holocaust" 206). Peter Ochs makes much the same argument: "the only 'end time' we can talk about concretely is one that we can reach within historical time." Some evangelicals specify that a third of Jews will participate in a mass conversion to Christianity and be saved, while the other two thirds will perish and be damned. That obviously embodies a decisive, if partly deferred, supersessionism in which Judaism only serves a subservient, instrumental relation to the true revelation in Christ. Advocacy of the mass conversion of Jews at the end of time, meanwhile, recalls the violent pressure to convert that caused thousands of Jews to meet with torture or death in earlier historical periods.

Two recent surveys of evangelicals and born-again Christians in the US—one initiated by Joel C. Rosenberg in 2017 and one initiated by Motti Inbari and Kirill M. Bumin in 2018—give additional statistical grounding to our understanding of evangelicals' relationship to Israel. Both surveys were administered by LifeWay Research, the first reaching

2,000 and the second reaching 1,000 respondents. Rosenberg reports that "Those age 65+ are the most likely age group to indicate they have a 'Positive' view of Israel Today (76%), followed by age 50-64 (69%), age 35-49 (64%), and age 18-34 (58%)" (3). Inbari and Bumin add that this is not because millennials are less religious; indeed, millennials have a higher rate of church attendance than older evangelicals. But the younger group is also both more sympathetic to Muslims and more likely to criticize Israeli government policy. When combined with decreasing support for Israel among young people aligned with the Democratic Party, this trend should trouble Israel, at least if the government wants to avoid an increasingly politicized relationship with the US. There are ten times as many evangelicals in the US as there are Jews. Moreover, despite anti-Semitic bombast about the "Jewish lobby," treating it as a uniquely sinister and powerful force rather than a lobby like any other, it is evangelicals by far, not a Jewish lobby, who put the decisive weight behind political and military support for Israel. Moreover, as Robert O. Smith concluded in a study of the roots of Christian Zionism,

> popular American affinity for the State of Israel draws from the taproot of apocalyptic hope informing American identity and national vocation from the revolutionary era to the present . . . . Given this Judeo-centric tradition's direct contribution to American popular Christianity and civil religion—through varying degrees of national-covenantalism, premillennial dispensationalism and cultural fundamentalism—claims that American popular affinity for the State of Israel is generated primarily by external manipulations or lobbies strain the bounds of credulity (185).

It was only in the 1960s, however, that evangelicals began to develop a sense of obligation to Israel. There were as yet no evangelical political action groups in 1970. A decade later, American evangelicalism began to be fundamentally politicized. More than mainline Protestant groups, moreover, they found it very hard to give up the mission to convert Jews, a commitment seriously at odds with Israeli society, "where the continuity of the Jewish people was an overriding priority" (Hummel 20). "Christian mission has come to imply the extinction of Jewish religious culture to Jewish people" (D'Costa 144). Faced with proselytizing tactics like handing out pamphlets urging Jews to repent, and particularly offensive campaigns focused on converting children, Israelis responded with anger; a minority chose violence, while others proposed legislative prohibitions. Billy Graham, the single most influential evangelical voice in mid-twentieth-century America, in the 1970s disavowed the notion that Jews should be a special focus of missionary campaigns, even though he was torn between his commitments to evangelize and to reconcile. As late as 1989, however, some evangelical leaders called for increased efforts to convert Jews. It was not a pragmatic decision. Success in converting Israeli Jews was virtually nonexistent. Like other Christians, evangelicals had a choice to make in Israel: exercise American-style freedom to proselytize or seek religious peace in Israel. For evangelicals, the choice was part of a larger theological configuration, a choice between rapture and fire or covenantal solidarity (Hummel 238).

Covenantal solidarity instead provided them with both theological warrant and practical options. Overall, Inbari and Bumin report in "Why Evangelicals Support Israel" that now US "evangelical support for Israel is driven by respondents' beliefs rooted in evangelical Christian theology and by their feeling of cultural and religious affinity with Jews. Hypotheses regarding geopolitical/security concerns, feelings of guilt for historical persecution of Jews at the hands of Christians, or feelings of commonality on the basis of political/democratic institutions were not supported by the data." They also offer strong evidence that socialization plays a major role: "being around other Evangelicals who talk about Israel and about its importance to the evangelical community is one of the most significant predictors of support for Israel." Indeed, socialization plays a much stronger role among both supporters and detractors of Israel than most researchers realize, as even theology is reinforced by social interaction. A stunning 83.94 percent of respondents to the 2018 survey support "the notion that the State of Israel is connected to the idea of the Second Coming of Jesus." A strong seventy-two percent responded affirmatively to the question "Do you believe God's covenant with the Jewish people is eternal?" Inbari and Bumin thus conclude that "the majority of Evangelicals do, indeed, reject supersession theology."

Evangelical support for Israel has helped make evangelicalism a regular target of the BDS movement in mainline Protestant churches, where anti-Zionist publications give special attention to condemning it. The anti-Zionist and BDS-allied Presbyterian Israel/Palestine Mission Network's *Steadfast Hope* (2009, 2011) includes a subsection on "Christian Zionism's flawed theology" that claims it "makes God a party to Israel's breach of international law" (13) and "elevates the rights of Israeli Jews while denying human and civil rights to Palestinians" (14). In addition to scattered comments elsewhere in the book, Israel Palestine Mission Network's (IPMN's) *Zionism Unsettled* (*ZU*) (2014) includes a chapter on "Evangelicals and Christian Zionism." The chapter opens by reporting that "For decades the Presbyterian Church (U.S.A.) has opposed the evangelical blend of dispensationalism and Christian Zionism because it fuses religion with politics, distorts faith, and imperils peace in the Middle East" (45). Of course, *ZU* itself arguably displays all these characteristics. The section proceeds by detailing what Gary Burge identifies as "five problematic theological convictions of evangelical Christian Zionists," beginning with the belief "that God's promises of land to Abraham in Genesis 12, 15, and 17 are valid today" and continuing with the claim that "any criticism of the state of Israel is not only anti-Semitic but also against God's will" (46). The argument goes on to fault evangelicals for rejecting "the New Testament teaching that spiritualizes and universalizes the Old Testament land promises by treating them as spiritual metaphor, not literal land grants in perpetuity" (47). The edge of sarcasm in the last phrase is enhanced by the cinematic "blockbuster" language used to characterize the belief "that *history is coming to its close*": "God's final blockbuster" will be "the destruction of all unbelievers" (46). Mainline Christian anti-Zionism also draws on and is allied with Palestinian Christian activist hostility to evangelicalism.

THE MENNONITES

Along with the Amish, the modern Mennonite church traces its roots to the Anabaptist movement of the 16th century. Anabaptists argued that baptism is only valid when it embodies an adult confession of faith in Christ and a consequent adult baptism ceremony. Infant baptism is rejected because it entails no such conscious decision. Because of this practical and theological difference, Anabaptists were aggressively persecuted at the time by both Protestants and Catholics. Torture and execution were common. Despite this parallel history of persecution, Mennonites never developed any identification with or sympathy for the Jews, instead adopting a supersessionist value system that retains its influence today.

Mennonite supersessionism in Germany and elsewhere also acquired strongly anti-Semitic and racist components, the latter culminating in tens of thousands of Mennonites' involvement with Nazism and participation in the Holocaust. As Ben Goosen writes, "A great gulf looms between the image of Mennonites as a peaceful Christian denomination engaged in humanitarianism and peace building around the world, including in the Middle East, and what historians have begun to reveal about the entanglement of a substantial minority of Mennonites with National Socialism during the 1930s and 1940s" ("Real History"). At the height of the Third Reich's power, about a quarter of the world's Mennonites were in Nazi territory. Mennonite theologians advocated a racialized theology. That legacy was reinforced when Mennonite Nazi sympathizers and allies fled Europe for Canada and South America, joining substantial colonies in Brazil and Paraguay. The Mennonite Central Committee worked hard to portray postwar Mennonite refugees as victims of Nazism, claiming that "Mennonites were fundamentally 'an un-Nazi and unnationalistic group'" ("Real History"). In reality, for years, both wartime and postwar Mennonite publications in both areas echoed Nazi sentiments. "Leading Mennonites helped finance the *German Paper for Canada*, a pro-Nazi organ. And in the United States, Herald Publishing House of Newton printed the rabidly anti-Semitic *Defender*, whose monthly circulation reached 100,000" (Goossen "Mennonites and the Holocaust"). Some Mennonites who helped save Jews have been recognized by the Yad Vashem Holocaust Memorial in Jerusalem as Righteous Among the Nations, among them forty Dutch Mennonites, but they are overshadowed by the far larger number who collaborated with the Nazis. Moreover, as Mennonite scholar Lisa Schirch writes, "Mennonite Nazi connections and theologies of racial superiority continue to have impact today." As Goossen points out, "Even among well-meaning and respected church members, anti-Semitic tropes continue to circulate. In 2017, Mennonite periodicals carried pieces that alternately excused genocidal killings by invoking Jewish communists, and [falsely] denied that Jews were murdered near Mennonite colonies" ("Mennonites and the Holocaust"). Convincing documentation has established that the latter claim is false. Gerhard Rempel adds detail about Mennonite use of slave labor in farms and factories near concentration camps.

Goossen, a scholar who grew up in a Kansas Mennonite town, takes note of "white Mennonites' fear that spreading the gospel among people of color might erase their own privileged position—that helped produce the notion of Mennonite ethnicity. Without a foil, this term would be toothless" (*Chosen* 211). Since the 1990s, nonetheless, Mennonite missionary activity has enrolled many people of color in the global south. That has finally promoted among some a concept of Mennonite peoplehood that is racially diverse.

For centuries, Mennonites have embraced a principle of "nonresistance," essentially a comprehensive form of pacifism. They regarded this as central to Jesus's teaching and "an inalienable Tenet of Christianity" (Goossen *Chosen* 2). In the US, that led them to become conscientious objectors in both World Wars, a choice the US treated brutally in World War I but finally accommodated in World War II. The Third Reich, however, had no tolerance whatsoever for pacifists. German Mennonites and those in Nazi-occupied countries consequently abandoned pacifism and accommodated to the requirement for military service.

Mennonites in the Ukraine, numbering about 35,000, had suffered persecution by Stalin and shared the Nazi construction of "Jewish Bolshevism" as their great enemy. They thus greeted the Nazis as liberators and benefitted from the shared belief in their purported Aryan racial identity. "Many Mennonites viewed Hitler as a kind of 'German savior' and as part of a "divine plan"'" (Schirch, "Mennonite, Nazism"). Goossen documents a Mennonite perpetrator of war crimes and subsequent apologist who "saw Jews and Bolshevism as being part of a single evil cabal that threatened his ethnic and faith communities" ("Real History").[3] When the Nazis relocated Mennonites to the Ukraine, "the arrivals' limited possessions had to be supplemented with spoils from

Auschwitz" (Goossen *Chosen* 154). Some Mennonites collaborated in the Nazi death squads and wore the German uniform. The mobile killing units that carried out genocide across Eastern Europe included Mennonite members. Benjamin Goossen, Mark Jantzen, and others are beginning to provide specific examples of Mennonite participation. Thus, for example, "Beginning in October 1941, one to two dozen Mennonites from Chortitza [a Mennonite colony in the Ukraine], along with another fifty volunteers, reportedly joined Einsatzgruppe C, helping to massacre the area's remaining 30,000 Jews" (Goossen *Chosen* 159). There was a Mennonite Waffen SS squadron in the Ukraine's Molotschna Colony (Goossen "Mennonites and the Holocaust"). Notably, there were also Waffen SS cavalry units composed mostly of Mennonites, including the 700-member regiment in the Habstadt colony in Nazi-occupied Ukraine. As Goossen writes, "cavalry members were expected to kill any Jews remaining in the colony or encountered elsewhere" ("Waffen-SS"). When the Third Reich's Eastern Front began to collapse in 1943, Mennonite settlements were among those who retreated west with the Wehrmacht and the SS. This history places a special burden on contemporary Mennonite supersessionism and hostility to Israel, a burden not only to document the past but also to expunge its lingering anti-Semitic impact.

Over the last twenty years, Mennonites both individually and collectively have instead worked extensively to promote the BDS cause and the delegitimization of Israel. Thus, in his 2001 book *Hebron Journal*, Mennonite activist Arthur Gish writes that "The national symbol of Israel should be a gun . . . . Guns are their gods" (68). Several short films from the Mennonite Central Committee were well publicized and influential. They included "The Dividing Wall" (2004), a 23-minute video that questions whether security concerns in fact motivated the construction of the security barrier, and "Children of the Nakba" (2005), which questions the legitimacy of Israel's existence (Van Zile "The Mennonite's Mission"). In the leadup to the 2017 meeting vote on the resolution that John Kampen discusses in his chapter, the Mennonite Church coordinated with the Mennonite Central Committee to offer a series of three anti-Zionist webinars. The first of these was a presentation endorsing *Kairos Palestine* featuring Dr. Munther Isaac of Bethlehem

Bible College on the West Bank. The concluding event, first aired in June 2017 and made available online, included a speaker who declared that Israel within its pre-1967 boundaries meets the international definition of apartheid.

MITIGATING SUPERSESSIONISM

On January 26, 1904, Theodor Herzl met with Pope Pius X to seek the Pope's support for the establishment of a Jewish state in Palestine. Cardinal Merry del Val, the Vatican Secretary of State, attended as well. According to Herzl's account in his diaries, which is not disputed, the Pope's reply was blunt:

"We cannot give approval to this movement. We cannot prevent the Jews from going to Jerusalem—but we could never sanction it. The soil of Jerusalem, if it was not always sacred, has been sanctified by the life of Jesus Christ. As the head of the Church I cannot tell you anything different. The Jews have not recognized our Lord, therefore we cannot recognize the Jewish people." After Herzl elaborated on his argument, asking that the religious issue be set aside in face of the rise of anti-Semitism, the Pope added that "The Jewish religion was the foundation of our own; but it was superseded by the teachings of Christ, and we cannot concede it any further validity" (Herzl *Diaries* 1602-4).

Over a hundred years later, Pope Benedict XVI on his 2009 visit to the Holy Land would not only endorse the Jewish state's right to exist ("Let it be universally recognized that the State of Israel has the right to exist, and to enjoy peace and security within internationally recognized borders.") but also commend the two-state solution and gave the form of peace providing two states for two peoples something like biblical status by invoking Isiah 42:6: "let peace spread outwards from these lands, let them serve as a 'light to the nations.'"

Benedict's statement is fundamentally aspirational, a contextual prayer, rather than a theological declaration. In one of the little recognized features of what remains a substantially hierarchical church, even a Pope's statements in and of themselves do not necessarily possess the ultimate doctrinal authority. But they obviously carry practical weight in encouraging how Catholics worldwide are urged to think. And the

Catholic Church still has the capacity to influence world opinion and how some Protestant denominations see religious issues. Papal statements carry inertial, incremental force when they build on, amplify, or reinforce central elements of evolving theology.

Benedict's prayer most centrally reinforces the impact of 1965's *Nostra Aetate*, widely regarded as the single most positively transformative document in Jewish/Christian relations in centuries. To understand how we got from Pius X to *Nostra Aetate* and Benedict's prayer requires some history. We need particularly to review the distinction between hard and soft supersessionism. And we need to recognize that supersessionism returns in several different ways, most of them grounded in fundamental attacks on the existence of the Jewish state, though not in warranted critiques of Israeli policy. The return or revival of supersessionism—I add revival because it never really went away—is partly in the replication of supersessionism's structural features and partly in its echoing of anti-Semitic tropes. Thus, when Rutgers faculty member Jasbir Puar revives blood libel accusations by saying Israelis are harvesting Palestinian organs or deliberately stunting the growth of Palestinian children, she helps facilitate a structural and temporal claim that the Jewish state's covenantal and moral authority have been superseded (Nelson *Israel Denial*). Christian BDS advocates tend to make the moral and theological arguments in tandem. That is apparent in the Presbyterian publications analyzed later in this book. Part of what I am going to do here is give readers the arguments and tropes that will prepare them for the correspondences between supersessionism and the demonization of the Jewish state that are detailed in subsequent chapters.

Within a few hundred years of the establishment of the Christian church, a temporal narrative coalesced to define Christianity's relationship with its Jewish sources. R. Kendall Soulen summarizes this story in which the church supersedes or replaces Judaism:

God's abiding commitment to creation passes through the flesh of the people Israel in the Old Covenant and ultimately lodges with irrevocable finality in the one Jewish man, Jesus of Nazareth. But with that the vocation of the people Israel reaches its foreordained goal and comes to an end. In the process, God's commitment to

Israel's flesh is revealed as only a passing stage on the way to god's truly abiding commitment, which is to Christ and the community of salvation in its spiritual form. (54)

"God had always foreseen, even intended, this development, and he has now provided himself with a people drawn from the Gentiles who would be worthier of their election" (Nicholls 173). This encapsulates "hard" supersessionism, the theological position that largely defined the church until the mid-1960s, when formal efforts to moderate supersessionism in an alternate theology began to emerge, producing what has come to be known as "soft" supersessionism. In "The Covenant in Rabbinic Thought" and again more recently in "Supersessionism Hard and Soft," David Novak distinguishes between the two versions of supersessionism. Eugene Korn has summarized the difference:

"Hard" supersession (i.e., the doctrine that the new covenant replaced the Jewish covenant and that, after Jesus, God rejected the Jews in favor of the church) was the longstanding Christian teaching regarding Judaism and the Jews. The "new Israel" has invalidated the "old Israel," and the new covenant of the spirit rendered the Mosaic covenant limited temporally, i.e., during the time the Jerusalem Temple stood. The concurrent validity of the Mosaic covenant and the new covenant (i.e., "soft" supersessionism, the doctrine that the church has grafted onto the living tree of the Jewish people, that the new covenant is the ultimate fulfillment of the still-living Jewish covenant) with its implication that there could be concurrent validity to both the Mosaic and the new covenants, was entertained by only a few early Christian thinkers, but ultimately rejected by early normative Christian theology, which was so heavily shaped by Augustine's hard supersessionist understanding of covenantal history. With the advent of the new covenant of the spirit, the Mosaic covenant became meaningless, even an obstacle to future salvation history . . . . according to hard supersessionism, if Christianity is true, post-Temple Judaism must be false—or at least dead. ("The People Israel" 163)

Because supersessionism developed gradually, it cannot be given a definitive starting point. Nonetheless, as Steven McMichael writes, "by the time we get to the end of the Middle Ages, the standard theological position was that only the moral commandments of the old covenant were to be observed and everything else of the old covenant was null and void in terms of its religious and salvific efficacy" (58). "The old covenant is not simply inferior to the new: it is no longer in force and has been canceled and abrogated by God himself" (Nicholls 169). "The Old Testament plays a role purely to point (usually in a way that erases itself after pointing through allegory and typology) to what is known in the New" (D'Costa 24). "The Torah and Jewish tradition," Novak adds, "are now past memories rather than living norms" ("Covenant" 67). "For hard supersessionism," he explains, "the old covenant is dead. The Jews by their sins, most prominently their sin of rejecting Jesus as the Messiah, have forfeited any covenantal status" (66). Indeed, from this perspective, the failure to embrace Jesus as the Messiah led to the Jews being cast out of the land of Canaan. "Hard supersessionists," he continues more bluntly, "treat Jews who are not Christians as if they were dead. To hard supersessionists, it is almost accidental that Christianity came out from the Jewish people and their Judaism at all . . . . Whereas hard supersessionists look to Christianity as emerging ex nihilo, as it were, soft supersessionists look to Christianity as emerging de novo " (67). "Ex nihilo" suggests Christianity has no predecessor; "de novo" implies Christianity emerged from a preexisting reality, namely Judaism. Yet even soft or minimal supersessionism aims to displace Judaism by negating the covenantal promise through its spiritualization, thereby erasing the value of Jewish attachment to the Holy Land and transferring its sacrality to Christianity. The effect is "to spiritualize the meaning of the term Israel so that it loses this-worldly political reality" (Nicholls 381). "The 'land' of Israel is only a symbolic pointer towards a very different land, a 'heavenly homeland'" (D'Costa 92). Abraham Heschel counters: "The Hebrew Bible is not a book about heaven—It is a book about the earth." In the process of promoting its exclusive version of spirituality, Christianity promotes a corrupting self-aggrandizement: "imagining that it has replaced Israel, the church becomes susceptible to distorted, idealized images of itself" (Small 136).

The church's self-aggrandizement is facilitated by a carnality/spirituality binary imposed on the opposition between Judaism and Christianity, with the church "declaring itself the 'new spiritual Israel'

that had superseded the old carnal Israel in God's election and design"
(Soulen ix). In that model, "the old carnal Israel existed merely as a
temporary foreshadowing" of the spiritual reality to come (Soulen 11).
"The dietary laws have been carnally misunderstood by the Jews, since
they really have a spiritual meaning in the overcoming of the flesh,
a meaning Christians understand but Jews do not" (Nicholls 171). It
was always thus: "the 'spiritual' church is destined from all eternity to
replace carnal Israel in God's plans" (Soulen 19). "Israel corresponds to
Christ in a merely prefigurative and carnal way, whereas the church corresponds to Jesus Christ in a definitive and spiritual way" (Soulen 29).
"The Old Testament dispensation has *redemptive power solely by virtue
of its reference to the future coming of Christ*" (Soulen 27). Yet as the
word-made-flesh, Jesus's physical presence troubles the binary in ways
that cannot easily be overcome by invocations of mystery. "Mystery" is
in effect a silencing strategy that targets ambiguity and contradiction.
Michael Wyschogrod's compelling declaration that Israel "is the carnal
anchor that God has sunk into the soil of creation" (*Body xv*) stands as
a definitive rejoinder in that debate.

It was inevitable that supersessionist theology would lead to the tri-
umphalist teaching of contempt toward Judaism. Hard supersessionism
embodies the assumption that "the stature and truth of Christianity
is founded on the rejection of Judaism" (Magid 106). Indeed, Jewish
ritual observance is declared not only dead but deadening, a destructive
force. "For hard supersessionists, the only option for Jews is conversion
to Christianity" (Novak "Supersessionism"). As Soulen writes, "supersessionism has shaped the narrative and doctrinal structure of classical
Christian theology in fundamental and systemic ways" (3). It may be
that "this idea is arguably so deeply rooted in Christianity that it cannot
easily be excised, if excised at all" (Magid 108). D'Costa argues that soft
supersessionism in some form "is necessary to Catholicism" (26). Novak
offers an explanation why: "A complete denial of supersessionism leaves
Christians unable to affirm Christianity as having brought something
new and fuller to the ancient covenant between God and Israel. Without
some kind of supersessionism, Christians have no cogent reason for not
going back to their Jewish origins" ("Supersessionism").

Thus, Novak adds, "In any realistic dialogue, Jews cannot expect Christians to jettison supersessionism altogether." Yet "genuine Jewish-Christian dialogue cannot take place until the erasure of Judaism implicit in supersessionism is somehow mitigated" (Magid 108). If soft supersessionism is inevitable in Christianity, however, hard supersessionism is not. The Catholic Church, along with mainline Protestant churches, has followed the route of theological mitigation. Founded on that historic work, both institutional and individual behavior can be reformed, substantially purged of contempt. A rapprochement of sorts can follow from the position that Christians and Jews can agree to disagree theologically. But hard supersessionism is now experiencing a resurgence in the rise of anti-Zionism, "the most seductive and plausible of the varieties of antisemitism prevalent today" (Nicholls 396).

In soft supersessionism "Judaism is still taken to be proto-Christianity" (Novak "Supersessionism"), but practical, project-oriented reconciliation between Christians and Jews becomes possible, and that difference is critical. Soft supersessionism retains a structural form of contempt, but it can be bracketed for the dual purposes of dialogue and collaboration. This residue of structural contempt need not cross the line into anti-Semitism. A soft supersessionist is not destined to be merely a tolerant anti-Semite. The reconciliation available also obviates any inclination for Jews to strike back by asserting "Christian doctrines such as the doctrine of the Trinity to be polytheistic," a reversion to paganism (Novak "Supersessionism"). Mitigation, moreover, leads to the development of interfaith relationships based in genuine affection.

These distinctions thus have dual bearing on the theological and political contexts that *Peace and Faith* addresses. The broad context is our understanding of how theology did and continues to evolve across the whole range of Christian churches. The narrower context is in how attitudes toward the Abrahamic covenant play out when Christian churches reflect on the status of the Jewish state, particularly when confronted by the Christian wing of the BDS movement. Christians are haunted, as Benjamin Ish Shalom puts it, by the possibility that the return of the Jews to Zion is "a religious event transcending accepted historical political categories." The secular wing of the BDS movement is understandably not much interested in theological issues, but they remain prominent for Christian BDS. As Gary Anderson writes in "The Return to Zion," it is difficult for Christians to avoid asking "How is one to understand the return of the Jewish people to the land of Israel in our own day theologically? The challenge for the religious believer has been whether or not to understand it as part of the eschatological fulfill-ment of scriptural promises" (unpag.). As detailed readings of a series of texts will suggest, the Christian BDS movement effectively embraces various versions of hard supersessionism. In their view, not only Israelis but also Zionists worldwide have transgressed against the moral code on which the ancient Jewish covenant was conditioned and have thus lost whatever land guarantees the covenant included. Perhaps worst of all, according to some factions of the Christian BDS movement, Zionists are essentially crucifying Jesus once more, this time in the person of suffering Palestinians. That trope leads to the demonization of the tiny Jewish state as the new Roman empire, and it revives the ancient slander of deicide.

Despite agreement over the short list of formal BDS demands and their shared anti-Zionism and comparable hostility toward Israel, secular and religious BDS movements display distinct differences in their arguments, appeal, the satisfactions they offer to their allies, and in the way they replicate traditional anti-Semitic tropes. These differ-ences include:

- the persistent presence of religious prejudices in Christian anti-Zionism, including supersessionist beliefs, in which secular anti-Zionism has no investment.
- secular anti-Zionists often revive ancient slanders, like blood libel, but they typically translate them into contemporary terms. Especially in the Islamist world, such ancient anti-Semitic slanders can be promoted unchanged from earlier incarnations.
- a difference in the span of history and the level of historical detail they reference and invoke. Secular BDS advocates commonly claim that Palestinians have been indigenous to the area for thousands of years, but, other than that, their temporal field of reference largely begins with Jewish immigration to Israel in the 1880s, the 1917 Balfour Declaration, and the original sin of the founding of the Jewish state in 1948. Christian BDS advocates ground their

political identities as well in denominational belief and in debates over biblical interpretation and its theological consequences. Some place great significance in the destruction of the second temple as an act of divine punishment.

- secular and Christian constituencies may have different ultimate solutions in mind for the Israeli-Palestinian conflict, ranging from elimination of the Jewish state to eventual conversion of the Jews. The original Hamas charter goes further, seeking literal Jewish deaths as a desideratum. There is diminishing support for a two-state solution in both secular and Christian BDS.
- there are radical differences in the nature of the communities secular and Christian BDS movements invoke, embrace, and seek to strengthen. Broadly speaking, secular and faith communities have somewhat different aspirations and self-understandings. Their terms of outreach and alliance-building differ as well. Thus, both secular and religious anti-Zionists often claim that Israel's conduct violates standards of justice, but the connotations differ for the two communities.
- there are arguably also differences in the sense of moral righteousness that secular and religious anti-Zionism confer. For both groups, for example, identification with the Palestinian cause may be "automatically to think of oneself as blessed with a higher moral consciousness" (Harrison 274). It can grant "a feeling of inner cleanliness" (Hirsh 51). But religious and political triumphalism are not interchangeable. Personal identity perceived as spiritually sanctified is not identical with identity that is politically elevated and resolute.

One obvious example is that secular BDS advocates and anti-Zionists are not likely to invoke the status of God's covenant with the Jews. Among Americans who apparently believe that covenant with the Jews is conditional upon their behavior, one of the most prominent is former US president Jimmy Carter. In his 1985 book *The Blood of Abraham*, he recalls attending a Sabbath service at the Ayelet Hashahar kibbutz in northern Galilee during his 1973 trip to Israel. He was shocked that there were only two other worshippers (25). When he meets with Prime Minister Golda Meir toward the end of the trip, the experience still troubles him. He tells her about the Sabbath service and remarks on what seems "a general absence of religious interest among the Israelis." Then he gives her a theological warning for the present: "I commented that during biblical times, the Israelites triumphed when they were close to God and were defeated when unfaithful" (29). Whether Meir was bemused or offended is uncertain, but either response was warranted. Did Carter see himself positioned to offer prophecy?

In the 1970s and 1980s, though new versions of soft supersession-ism began to appear, Jews concerned with these distinctions often experienced "soft" supersessionism as supersessionism nonetheless, even if interfaith dialogue is often facilitated by the shift to soft supersession-ism. Pope John Paul II's 1980 declaration that the covenant with the Jewish people had never been revoked effectively gave the soft superses-sionist trend a crucial boost. As Mary Boys and others have pointed out, declaring that the divine covenant with the Jews has not been revoked "leaves open . . . what the positive implication might be," since "to assert that the 'old covenant' has not been revoked carries little import if there is no theological reason for the existence of Judaism after the coming of Jesus Christ" (104, 82). "The result is the evisceration of the God of Israel in Christian theology" (Soulen 55). "The Jews were simply a vestige of an earlier age of religious consciousness, and their eventual extinction could be expected with the gradual advance of Christian civilization" (Soulen 2).

Given that soft supersessionism aims to change centuries of theol-ogy and rectify the severe human consequences it has produced, it is not surprising that the process has taken time. Nor has it been without backsliding. As Mary Boys suggests in her account of future Pope Joseph Cardinal Ratzinger's 1998 book *Many Religions—One Covenant: Israel, the Church, and the World*, even a single text can embody both trends. Thus, although "the Sinai covenant is indeed superseded," Ratzinger argues, its greater truth inheres and will be revealed for those who turn to Christ (70). Boys points out that the 1992 Catechism of the Catholic Church "gives its readers virtually no sense of Judaism as a living, vital tradition. It may speak of the covenant as not having been revoked—but that covenant seems only to play a preparatory role for the new covenant of Christianity" (70, 91). On the other hand, Michael Signer reports that some contemporary Jewish texts on the covenant issue "do not utilize the discourse of new and old covenant. They move in the direction of covenant as relationship rather than covenant as boundary marker . . . . they seem to be removed from the 'diachronic' or 'progressive' notion that 'new' is better than 'old'" (121). Boys calls progression "the positive side of discontinuity," which, as she recognizes, thus leaves discontinuity in place (95). A compromise position is that the new covenant does not break with the original nor dramatically "fulfil" it; rather in a natural evolution it explicitly extends to non-Jews, a need built into the terms of the Mosaic covenant.

In recent years, some evangelicals have qualified their convictions about the end of days and about the role contemporary history and geopolitics play in preparing for those events; in so doing they abandon the certainty of premillennial dispensationalism for what has been called the New Christian Zionism. Dispensationalists embrace a nineteenth-century belief in a broad theological periodization of history; premillennial dispensationalists like John Hagee (1940-) and Jerry Falwell (1933-2007) anticipate Christ returning to rule the earth for a thousand years. New Christian Zionism, a movement that includes both evangelical and non-evangelical Christians, espouses humility about human knowledge of history's trajectory. As Gerald McDermott writes, the movement rejects the notion that we can "plot the sequence or chronology of end-time events" ("Introduction" 14). On the contrary, for New Christian Zionists, the end of days "is a mystery we must not think we can penetrate with any precision" ("Implications and Propositions" 331). Abandoning the certainty that the end of days is readably inscribed in contemporary events may allow for both a more nuanced relationship with Israel—one in which Israeli policies can be criticized but Israel's right to exist is unquestioned—and better relations between Christians and Jews worldwide. A two-state solution becomes plausible because it is no longer considered heretical for Israel to cede part of its covenanted land to achieve peace. Embracing the Jewish state puts to rest the long-held Christian conviction that the Jews were cast aside by God for rejecting Jesus as the Messiah and are thus doomed to live in exile from the Promised Land until either they repent of their error or the Kingdom of God arrives.

Rather than give Judaism a theological and historical role that is functional but decidedly transitory, New Christian Zionism insists instead that both Christianity and Judaism will be transformed when the Messiah appears. This position partly parallels some versions of Jewish utopian messianism in which the Messiah's arrival will be heralded by transformative extra-natural events—though there are other Jewish messianic traditions, like that of Moses Maimonides, which are not comparably apocalyptic or utopian. Gershom Scholem helped draw the distinction in "Toward an Understanding of the Messianic Idea in Judaism."

Instead of thinking of Israel as a placeholder for an eventual conversion site, the existing Jewish state is seen by some New Christian Zionists to "represent a provisional and proleptic fulfillment of the promises of that world to come" (McDermott "Introduction" 27), a change in focus that makes present-day Israel "a place of spiritual testing" (McDermott "A History of Christian Zionism" 50). Israelis are to be engaged with in terms of how they live now, not on the basis of future guarantees that eliminate the need for contemporary understanding and assessment. Of course New Christian Zionism remains Christian, which means that the discomfort Jews have with its claims to a universal truth still obtains. As Darrell Bock writes, Jesus is "the one in whom covenant promises are realized . . . . the Messiah of all, both Jew and Gentile," and therefore "there is no reason for a two-covenant view of Israel that says Gentiles are saved through Jesus, but Israel is saved through the Torah" (309). But this difference is with Christianity itself, not primarily with Christian Zionism old or new.

A COVENANT FOR THE JEWISH PEOPLE

In a 1985 document issued by the Vatican's Commission for Religious Relations with the Jews, *Notes on the Correct Way to Present the Jews and Judaism in Preaching and Catechesis of the Roman Catholic Church*, hereinafter *Notes*, care is taken to strengthen the revisioning of the theological status of God's covenant with the Jews initiated by the *Dogmatic Constitution on the Church, Lumen Gentium* in 1964 and *Nostra Aetate* in 1965. The most dramatic departure from centuries of anti-Semitic hostility and consequent violence is their combined declaration that Jews cannot be held collectively responsible for the death of Christ. "This is now a magisterial teaching of what scripture says on the matter" (D'Costa 15), the highest level of Church doctrine. The covenant remains in force. Jews are still an elect and "chosen people." Reversing centuries of Catholic thought in which God's covenant with the Jews was declared null and void, superseded or displaced by a new covenant with the Church, the covenant communicated to Abraham and elaborated to Moses is treated with respect. Though that "Old Covenant" is irrevocable and eternal, however, it is also understood to have been fulfilled, realized, in the "New Covenant" with the church, which broadens the particularist covenantal promise to the Jews with a universal offer of salvation to everyone. Paradoxically, however, the universal offer of salvation through Jesus is also conditional and thus particularist, whereas Judaism makes no unique claim on salvation. Judaism's focus "is upon the sanctified *world*, not the redeemed and sanctified soul" (Harrison 323). Thus salvation as the Gospel of Paul depicted it is not really a Jewish theme or concern. At the same time, as Joseph D. Small points out, "categories of promise (Old Testament) and fulfillment (New Testament) have served to downgrade the life and faith of Israel to the status of a religious preface" (128).

As Edward Kessler wrote earlier, "fulfillment easily slides into replacement and substitution theory is alive and well in the pews" ("Reflections"). In other words, doctrinal distinctions and definitions do not necessary carry over into lay opinion. D'Costa argues that "the definition of 'fulfillment' has hardly begun to attain a settled form amongst scholars or within official Catholic teaching documents" (63). Thus one may reasonably feel that "fulfillment" carries supersessionist implications. "The Jewish priesthood and sacrificial system have been abolished by being fulfilled in Christ, the true sacrifice" (Nicholls 171). When integrated with other beliefs, including the doctrine that Christ is the source of all salvation everywhere, the supersessionist connotations are only strengthened. Thus D'Costa can write, "Many Jewish commentators felt that living Judaism was a biblical museum piece in *Nostra Aetate* (no. 4). They were right" (15). Indeed, there is an undercurrent of fear behind supersessionism: "If the original covenant is still in force,

Christ did not die for all men"; "Jews need the salvation brought by Christ as much as anyone else" (Nicholls 384, 370).

As Willie James Jennings argues, "the election of Israel has never significantly entered into the social imagination of the church. Israel's election has not done any real theological work for Christian existence" (253). One may nonetheless suggest the basis on which that work could proceed. As Joseph D. Small writes, "Everything goes back to God's promise to Abraham . . . . The church, by and of itself, cannot claim that it is the people of God . . . . Christians and Jews, synagogue and church, are bound together irreversibly, precisely as the peoples of God" (157, 158). Markus Barth is especially direct: "It is not enough to say that salvation came from the Jews; for salvation comes from the Jews" (47-48). As Karl Barth has written, "God's faithfulness in the reality of Israel is in fact the guarantee of His faithfulness to us too, and so to all men" (80). The irrevocable, unbreakable covenant with the Jews is the truth from which flows Christianity's faith in its own covenantal status.

And yet this belief in the unity of the covenantal promise has often been beyond the reach of the church. As Adam Gregerman argues in "Superiority without Supersessionism," the ongoing evolution and reversal of the Catholic Church's longtime positions comes with certain tensions and contradictions. The new perspective affirms that the Jewish covenant is still good and valid and treats the Christian covenant as an improvement or upgrade that completes what the Old Covenant could not. Recognizing that this embodies a contradiction, the Commission's 2015 *"The Gifts and the Calling of God Are Irrevocable"* (Rom 11:29): *A Reflection on Theological Questions Pertaining to Catholic-Jewish Relations on the Occasion of the 50th Anniversary of 'Nostra Aetate'"* in its section thirty-six relegates the problem to the ineffable: "That the Jews are participants in God's salvation is theologically unquestionable, but how that can be possible without confessing Christ explicitly is and remains an unfathomable divine mystery." Understandably, relegating Jewish salvation after Jesus to an unfathomable mystery leaves many Jews uneasy. Yet the theological difference is irrelevant to reconciliation efforts, as salvation is not a Jewish preoccupation. There is no Jewish yearning to abandon this world for the next one.

Comparable tensions carry over into Protestant attitudes as well, which influence the possibilities for interfaith dialogue about both theology and contemporary politics unless the tensions are resolved or managed. While I cannot hope to survey all the ways such differences play out, this section will provide some indicative examples to alert readers to the key issues that structure many of these debates.

Notes (1985) offers a crucial specification about the Old Covenant that relates directly to the Israeli-Palestinian conflict: the covenant's promise of land to the Jews is not abstract; it refers to a specific piece of land, often referred to as "the land of Canaan," though the Tanakh (the Jewish scriptures, composed of the Torah, the Prophets, and the Writings) offers a variety of implied boundaries. Yet *Notes* stops short of declaring that the State of Israel embodies that promise: "The existence of the State of Israel and its political options should be envisaged not in a perspective which is in itself religious, but in their reference to the common principles of international law." As Gregerman writes in "Is the Biblical Land Promise Irrevocable?", "The authors say, in essence, that as Catholics they think that when outside the land of Israel God wills Jews to live and to live as Jews. By contrast, Jewish life inside the land of Israel is given no religious significance." That may somewhat overstate the case, though hard supersessionism "logically entails the ontological, historical, and moral obsolescence of Israel's existence after Christ" (Soulen 30). As D'Costa writes, "In 1985, there were arguments that still opposed a Jewish homeland on supersessionist grounds. Such grounds are now dismissed in *Notes*" (135). The sentence directing how Catholics should regard the Jewish state is repeated verbatim in section five of the Commission for Religious Relations with the Jews's 2015 "*The Gifts and the Calling of God Are Irrevocable*," although *Gifts* "has no doctrinal status, even though it comes from a Pontifical dicastery entrusted to implement the Church's teaching" (D'Costa 8).Yet *Notes* goes on to say, "The permanence of Israel (while so many ancient peoples have disappeared without trace) is a historic fact and a sign to be interpreted within God's design." This is also cited in *Gifts*, paragraph 5. Thus, while the Catholic Church wants to approach the modern national state from a diplomatic/political vantage point, it cannot totally deny the perception that history—including the permanence of the Jews and their return to sovereignty—is somehow connected to God's plan. The Church approaches the day-to-day realities of Israel politically, but it does not reject the theological entirely.

The secular wing of the BDS movement is more than happy to claim that its critique of the Jewish state is already grounded in international law, not theology, but, unlike the Catholic Church, constituencies in a number of Protestant denominations believe their contemporary political stance toward Israel should instead be based partly in theology. As detailed above, evangelical Christians most prominently make a fundamental theological investment in the life and status of the Jews of Israel. For others, the status of the covenant is subject to continuing debate and discussion.

The evangelical embrace of a shared explicitly Judeo-Christian covenant to be realized through a covenanted community has proven to be a double-edged sword. On the one hand, it can erase hard supersessionism, enable interfaith dialogue, and make productive political collaboration between Christians and the Jewish State possible. As Hummel writes, "a covenant-oriented understanding of Judeo-Christianity helped organize much of evangelical political thought since the mid-twentieth century and remains central to the Christian Zionist movement" (41). Spirit-centered Christian Zionists "have expanded and built upon the theology of God's covenants and placed them at the center of Christian Zionism" (186). On the other hand, "this covenantal Judeo-Christianity was far more exclusivist and theologically circumscribed" (41). The danger was enhanced when the theological position was expanded into a Judeo-Christian mission to redeem the world that was linked with American power. That belief helped ground shared opposition to Islam after the 1979 Iranian revolution made radical Islam part of American popular and political culture, conditions dramatically enhanced thirty years later by 9/11. It underwrote shared American evangelical and Israeli government opposition to the 2015 Iran nuclear deal framework, opposition that was given political force in the Trump administration, which withdrew from the Iran nuclear agreement and imposed additional sanctions on the regime in Tehran. What all the policies of a Biden administration will be we do not yet know, though the US embassy will remain in Jerusalem, and it is likely financial support for Palestinian social services will be restored.

THE STATUS OF BEING CHOSEN

The twin subjects of chosenness and the covenant often do not have the same prominence. As reliance on theological categories and theological debate has gradually given way to political debate in many Protestant denominations, some longstanding areas of controversy have receded into the background, such as the status of the Jews as God's chosen people, which has been "the focus of so much animus in Jewish-Christian relations over the centuries" (Jospe 127). Jews, meanwhile, have continued to be ambivalent about their chosen status. Contributors throughout *Peace and Faith* discuss chosenness's theological counterpart, God's covenant with the people of Israel, but it is important here to recognize that the status of being "chosen" nonetheless lurks beneath the surface of contemporary religious disputes even when it is not overtly acknowledged.

A lingering resentment seems to permeate Christian feelings about the Jewish claim to chosenness, often based on Christian caricatures of the concept of chosenness rather than on Jewish understandings of it. While there is certainly pride in the idea of being chosen, as well as some minority Jewish interpretations of chosenness that suggest real elitism, the mainstream approach is more measured. As Raphael Jospe writes, "chosenness means neither privilege nor any innate Jewish superiority, whether explicit or implicit. Rather, what the biblical and post-biblical sources emphasize is an internally-directed Jewish responsibility to live in a certain way, based on the Torah, and the promises of divine blessing" (127). First, there is Amos 9:7, here in Robert Alter's translation, which puts the divine favor accorded to Israelites in the context of comparable justice extended to other peoples:

Are you not like the Cushites to Me,
    O Israelites? Said the LORD.
Did I not bring up Israel from the land of Egypt
    and the Philistines from Crete
        and Aram from Kir?

Some interpretations suggest that the gift of the Torah was not based on anything deserving on the part of Israel, but rather given in spite of their inadequacies and limitations. As David Novak writes in *Zionism and Judaism*, "The election of Israel is not due to any inherent properties, either biological (with their racist implications) or cultural (with their chauvinistic implications) by which Jews can claim to be inherently superior to the rest of humankind . . . . To cogently affirm that God chose the people Israel is to thereby deny that the Jews chose God" (133, 134). One might argue that the Jews did not have a choice in being chosen, so to speak, but rather that chosenness was imposed on them. "God chose the seed of Abraham, Isaac, and Jacob, a human family, neither better nor worse than others" (Soulen 5).

In any case, Christian resentment does not always overtly inform debates about the biblical covenant with Israel and whether it has been superseded by Jesus's promise of universal redemption, even though both chosenness and the Abrahamic-Mosaic covenant stoke opposition to purported Jewish "particularism." The anti-Semitic complaint about particularism cuts two ways. First, it reinforces a misreading of being "chosen" by embodying "the supposed rejection by Jews of any concern or moral responsibility for non-Jews" justified by "the absurd conceit of Jews in imagining themselves chosen by God above the rest of humanity" (Harrison 131). Then it encapsulates contempt for "the absurd and fanciful observances in diet and dress supposedly designed to placate a terrifying deity," "the painstaking obedience to the letter of petti-fogging and detailed rules of conduct" (Harrison 302, 318) and ritual observance followed most thoroughly by Orthodox Jews.

The covenant, conversely, has implications that are not exclusive and has thus provided a basis for Jewish-Christian continuity and mutuality, whereas being chosen can also more narrowly inform personal identity and the sense of self. As McDermott argues, "covenant is the main story of the Hebrew and Christian Scriptures" and is thus the primary theological category ("Covenant, Mission" 19). Michael Wyschogrod has also argued in *Body of Faith* that all subsequent individuals' ability to relate personally to God as individuals is a consequence of Abraham being chosen. As David Novak explains in *The Election of Israel*, for a time the idea of chosenness colored what it meant to be a Jew in the world. Although the historical record of Jewish residence in the Holy Land and the persistent dream of returning to it, along with the continuous fact of anti-Jewish discrimination and aggression, are major components of Zionism, the theological issues of covenant and chosenness nonetheless partly inform the status of Jewish claims to the land of Israel. The centuries-long belief that Christianity superseded and replaced Judaism seeks to nullify both:

> Everything that characterized the economy of salvation in its Israelite form becomes obsolete and is replaced by its ecclesial equivalent. The written law of Moses is replaced by the spiritual law of Christ, circumcision by baptism, natural descent by faith as criterion of membership in the people of God . . . . *carnal Israel becomes obsolete.* (Soulen 29)

It is not difficult to identify other ancient peoples who saw themselves as being chosen by their gods; in that sense, multiple convictions of chosenness could and did coexist in the ancient world. In the modern world, moreover, "the Jews are not the only nation to see themselves as distinctive and special, as being challenged with exemplary moral tasks or as being obliged to fulfill a unique historic destiny" (Jospe 128). The first important difference in Jewish status arose when the ancient Israelites committed themselves to monotheism and understood their God to be the God of all the universe, not merely a local deity. Tensions heightened when Rome converted to Christianity and Christian monotheism fused with the immense power of the Roman Empire. Jesus's message of love was then often subordinated to a harsh, absolutist faith that embodied intolerance and deadly malice, and Christians came to see themselves as the one true chosen people. Even before it acquired imperial power, emerging Christianity had to respond to why the Jews—Jesus's own people—accepted neither the Christians' claims nor their interpretation of the Jewish scripture. The early fathers used the charge of deicide and the destruction of the Temple to "prove" that the Jews' rejection of Jesus led to God's rejection of the Jews. The Roman Empire was able to take that teaching and weaponize it.

The consequences for the Jews are detailed in *Peace and Faith's* appendix. Islam also developed its own concept of being a chosen community of believers, though it maintained a more reliable, if qualified, tolerance for other monotheistic faiths. In our own time, however, radical/extremist Islamism has articulated its own Islamist version of absolute and exclusive conviction about being the chosen people, effectively importing some of the rhetoric of medieval Christianity and the Nazis. Contemporary discussion about the status of the Jews as God's chosen people often fails to acknowledge the fact that all three monotheistic faiths have a history of embracing their own chosen status.

As Reuven Firestone details, during centuries when the Jews were subjected to discrimination, violence, and exile, chosenness became partly a form of consolation, a status held in reserve during the long years when there was little material evidence to confirm it. It may be that the lack of any other palpable benefit to chosenness, which did not even assure their collective survival, led Jews to cling to belief in its theological reality more fiercely. From the Judaic perspective, only one thing mattered in that context: Jews were uniquely chosen to receive the Torah, including the Ten Commandments. As Eugene Korn writes, "the Sinai covenant provides the content, meaning, and commitment to the Jewish people's faith in God" ("The People Israel" 147). In "Covenant and Mission," David Novak calls the Torah "the constitution of the covenant" (42). Having received the Torah, the Jews were thus at least chosen to share it with the world. However, the Jews were only chosen to be its emissaries; the Torah was not withheld from others. As Korn suggests, "Sinai charged the Jewish people to be humanity's teachers, instructing all people of God's authorship of creation and his moral rules for continuing the human social order . . . . A particular people, a tiny people is tasked with the mission of bringing God's blessing to all of humanity and the light of divine morality to every corner of creation" (154-55). As Novak puts it in "Why Are the Jews Chosen?": "we are a chosen people, not a master race. We were chosen to be the trustees of God's Torah."

The belief that the Jewish people are tasked with the mission of disseminating the moral guidance of the Torah to all nations gains support from three passages in the Book of Isaiah: 42:6, 49:6, and 60:3, depending on how they are read. The second of these (in Robert Alter's translation) runs as follows:

I the LORD have called you in righteousness

and held your hand,
and preserved you and made you
    a covenant for peoples and a light of the nations,
to open blind eyes . . .

The verse is among those reinforced by the prophecy in Micah 4:2 that "from Zion shall teaching come forth / and the LORD's word from Jerusalem." As Micah and Isaiah add, the Word will lead nations to "beat swords into ploughshares" (Isaiah 2:4). But the power of the Word to produce such results does not necessarily imply a mission for the Jews. As Novak comments on Isaiah 49:6 in *Zionism and Judaism*, "When read in context, the verse does not speak of the Jews having some sort of mandate to go out and enlighten the gentiles (let alone conquer them), as the verse does not speak of the Jews extending, or being commanded to extend 'light *to* the nations' . . . . Instead, the verse speaks of what God *will* do" (132). That reading is reinforced by the fact that Judaism does not have a proselytizing mission. Unlike some other faiths, Judaism rejects "the imperialist temptation to regard the redemption of the whole world to be their own project" (147).

In *What Are Jews For?*, Adam Sutcliffe observes that "this messianic idea has been endlessly refashioned and reimagined, within both Judaism and Christianity and also in avowedly secular visions of utopian expectancy and hope," in some cases with Jews "cast as ultimately leading all humanity into a better world" (265). Yet it is not without interpretive effort that the covenant with Jews can be taken definitively to implicate that mission. Sutcliffe argues that in "God's twice-forged covenant with Abraham and Moses, God chose the Jews, but seemed to leave to them, and equally to everyone else, the task of figuring out why" (290). And so, the sense of Jewish purpose remains multivocal and embedded in the dynamics of history. And yet, as Sutcliffe writes,

this question cannot be easily evaded. The idea that Jews are bestowed with a particular historical purpose occupies a central position both in the Jewish tradition itself and in the Christian and post-Christian frameworks that have structured Western thinking about the place of the Jews as a unique minority in the wider world. The question of Jewish purpose follows inescapably from Jewish chosenness, which lies at the heart of Judaism. God chose the Jews:

but why, on what terms, and to what end? The biblical "election of Israel"—the setting apart of the Jews by God, as recipients of divine protection, and bearers of special holiness—ineluctably gives rise to a panoply of further questions. What does it mean for a universal God to single out a particular people? Where does this leave those other peoples in the eyes of God, and in relationship to Jews? Can the election of Israel be rescinded, either for all Jews, or for individuals among them? What happens if individual Jews reject their covenant with God (whatever precisely that means)? For what specific role in the world, and in the messianic denouement of human history, did God select the Jews? And why, of all people, them? (2)

For a generation after its founding, the ideals connected to chosenness were associated as well with the Jewish state, and some Christians still hope that Israel will fulfill them. After all, Israel survived even the multi-front military assault against it in its first year, and Israel's early collectivism—from the kibbutz (the Hebrew term for a community-owned and -operated settlement, traditionally a farm) to social policy—seemed to give these ideals concrete realization. But appeals to a universal covenantal mission have diminished in the wake of the occupation and of rising anti-Semitism in Europe. Sutcliffe writes again:

> The mainstream rhetoric of Zionism today, which functions as the primary binding agent both of Israeli society and of much of the Jewish diaspora, has largely dropped its early vision of itself as a fundamental positive force for the world as a whole. The "light unto the nations" argument, prominent in the speeches and writings of David Ben-Gurion up to the 1960s, has given way to an emphasis on the entitlement of Jews to collective security and an environment free of antisemitism . . . (282-3)

Of course the kibbutz itself is now likely to have become a commercial and capitalist enterprise. In both the secular and the religious BDS movements, "the universalistic, outward-oriented idea of Jewish purpose is today rallied above all in solidarity with Palestinians and in opposition to Israeli actions and policies" (Sutcliff 282). Both religious and secular wings of the BDS movement would remind us only of Israel's failure to be a light unto the nations. In that hostility, there survives a version of Jewish exceptionalism. If the founding of Israel was to make the Jewish state a nation like any other, that hope has not been realized.

Yet the tradition still provides guidance. In *The Election of Israel*, Novak points out that "it is only the Torah that instructs us that Israel is chosen and how her chosenness is to be lived," which entails embracing the "genuine dialectic between grace and merit, between election and obligation" within the framework of the Torah's concern with justice. The Torah guides us in "the transcendent standard governing Israel's relationships with the nations of the world" (254, 246, 247). Indeed, its principles have direct bearing on the first Jewish state to be established in the Holy Land in three thousand years; "The doctrine of election when rightly constituted, removes the temptation of chauvinism. It does not say Israel is somehow more human that anyone else. It does not place Israel above the nations of the world in any area of purely human interaction" (254-5). There are, moreover, extensive rabbinic teachings about the basic equality of all people.

Political Zionism, the movement to establish a homeland for the Jews also occasionally called Herzlian Zionism after its founder Theodore Herzl, was a largely secular movement from the beginning; Israel, moreover, is a predominantly secular country, albeit one whose community of hyper-nationalist, highly religious citizens has an increasingly outsized influence over politics and daily life. Unlike some of its neighbors, the Jewish state is not a theocracy run by religious elites and based on religious law. Instead, the ethical bedrock of Jewish tradition applies to secular and religious Jews alike, for all are bonded by a shared cultural heritage. To ask how that heritage applies to the Jewish state, however, places us squarely at the intersection of theology and politics. We are then burdened with thinking through how chosenness has evolved when subjected to the vicissitudes of history. It is no longer a matter that can be resolved by theology alone, which leaves us at the mercy of political bias and its pressures for self-deception.

Although some West Bank settlers and their supporters believe they have a divine right to settle anywhere within what they consider Judea and Samaria, the biblical land of Israel, many are there not for religious reasons but rather to take advantage of less expensive housing. Indeed, many Israelis simply do not personally identify with the "chosen people" narrative. Though vulgar efforts to invoke chosenness do occur, most Jews, including most Israelis, do not rely on chosenness to validate Israel's legitimacy. In his influential book *Chosen? Reading the Bible Amid the Israeli-Palestinian Conflict* (2015), Walter Brueggemann, a highly regarded Christian theologian, asserts erroneously that "Jewish Zionism is grounded in what is understood to be the nonnegotiable status of Israel as God's chosen people" (50). His book merits analysis here because it has had considerable impact on the ways BDS advocates in Protestant denominations have understood both Jewish chosenness and God's covenant with the Jews. Israelis honor the unbroken history of Jews in Palestine, but, contrary to what Brueggemann claims, they do not typically embrace a view that "compresses ancient Israel and the current state of Israel as though they were the same historical entity" (11).

A professor emeritus at the Columbia Theological Seminary in Georgia and a minister of the United Church of Christ, Brueggemann regularly advocates for the BDS movement, and his work is useful in representing the BDS wing of Protestantism. Brueggemann grounds his stance toward the Israeli-Palestinian conflict in a critique of what he considers "the brutalizing, uncompromising policy of Israel toward the Palestinian people and their political future" that has coalesced since the 1967 war (55). That policy has been supported by what he calls "a hardened Zionism that combined a desperate aspiration with an uncompromising ideology that supported the state of Israel and its security at all costs against all comers" (49). Brueggemann thereby fuses all contemporary Zionisms with the "hardnosed ideology" of the Israeli far right and concludes that there is "no realistic hope for any two-state solution" (53, 58). His book integrates these political views with his theological analysis, describing "a covenant people and a state that relies on military power without reference to covenantal restraints" (56).

There are two separate questions here, each relevant to his claim: (1) whether Israel exercises restraint in responding to military action from Hamas, the paramilitary terrorist group that has controlled Gaza since 2007, and whether that restraint involves ethical considerations; and (2) whether the government of Israel conceptualizes restraint in terms of its biblical covenant. The answer to the first question is yes, within limits, as evidenced by the care Israel has taken to minimize civilian deaths during armed conflict. The answer to the second question is no, as Israel applies the ethical principles embodied in whole centuries of Jewish tradition, rather than self-consciously trying to emulate covenantal restraints. Brueggemann wants to conflate the two questions, as his book demonstrates, so that he can bring down the wrath of the prophets upon Israel. Brueggemann and the BDS movement want us to believe the covenant has been broken anew in our own time. Their view requires that the covenant mandates exceptional behavior not just from individual Jews but from the Jewish state itself. Whether any nation state, save one surrounded by friendly nations and having no need to defend itself, could observe the commandment not to kill is doubtful.

Reviews of *Chosen?* have detailed a number of its resulting distortions. Rabbi Russell Resnik writes that "Brueggemann portrays a Zionism that doesn't represent the historical reality of the movement as much as the bogeyman of the Palestinian narrative," a perspective Brueggemann draws in part from Naim Ateek and Palestinian liberation theology. Brueggemann critiques the supersessionist tradition, "but seems unaware of the radical supersessionism of some of his ideological allies and of the impact of supersessionism on Christian anti-Zionism today" (Resnik). Peter A. Pettit decries "the casual incursion of tired antisemitic tropes into the book . . . . Jews are preoccupied with purity, claim unwanted privilege, and abuse their uncommon wealth" ("Review" 4). Gerald McDermott pointedly reminds us that "the fact that the human rights of Palestinians are violated more often by fellow Palestinians than by Israelis is conspicuously absent from this book" ("Choosing" 78). Contrary as well to Bruggemann's assertion that the Israeli government has asserted its claim to the land "without compromise," McDermott reminds us that Israel has already given up the Sinai Peninsula and the entirety of Gaza.

Once again, Brueggemann wants to use theology and biblical hermeneutics as a weapon against both the Jewish people and the Israeli state. In the anti-Zionist preface to the second edition of what is otherwise his more thoughtful book, *The Land: Place as Gift, Promise, and Challenge in Biblical Faith*, Brueggemann offers a lesson based on Israel:

Military political powers who crush opposition in order to control
more land characteristically (a) forget the warning voiced by
Yahweh, the ultimate land owner, (b) imagine that "the might of
my power has gotten me this wealth" (Deut 8:17; my translation)
and (c) therefore "choose death," both directly for those who oppose
them and for themselves in less visible but in equally inescapable
ways (xvii).

In a statement that pushes overstatement toward anti-Semitism,
he tells us Israel's "ambitions . . . are enacted in unrestrained violence
against the Palestinian population" (xv). The world saw many examples
of what actually unrestrained violence in the last century was, but
Israel did not perpetrate them either then or since. As Pettit points out,
Brueggemann "discusses traditions regarding the gift of the land in
canonical order as though it represents historical development," a violation of Brueggemann's own stated opposition to forging a direct line
from biblical prophecy to historical events ("Review" 3). Looking at
history, he declares that "the conditional if of the Torah has prevailed!"
(33). Brueggemann proclaims, "Thus, the land is *given*, the land is
taken, and the land is *losable*" (32), a sequence he regards as a divine
warning playing out in historical time, despite the fact that the unconditional grant of the land suggests the Israelites have always held title to
it and would return to it from exile. In one respect, Israelis themselves
would agree: since 1948, they have understood repeatedly that the land
could be lost to Arab military action, and more recently to potential
Iranian aggression.

Brueggemann offers no evidence to support his claim that Israelis
invoke the Torah to justify day-to-day policies in the West Bank or
elsewhere. Indeed, it would be bizarre to do so. Are we to believe that,
in trying to intercept a terrorist, Israelis declare that God has directed
them to set up a temporary checkpoint? At the same time, Israelis might
well invoke the Torah's commitment to justice in their intensified affirmative action programs for Arab citizens.

Chosen? is written as if the Israeli far right and American evangelicals were key audiences to persuade, but there is no real possibility either
group will listen to what Brueggemann has to say. The book instead is
an effort to discredit the Jewish state on fused theological and political

grounds, and its main audience is those of us—Christians, Muslims, and Jews alike—who believe there is hope for reconciliation, mutual understanding, compromise, and the realization of a two-state solution. Like most BDS-allied projects, it urges us to lose faith in any just future emerging from the Israeli polity. What a critical reading of the book and its arguments suggests instead is that the effort to deploy theology as a political weapon is fraught with grave destructive potential. As Deborah Weissman has warned, "We should consider what the blessings and the pitfalls are of seeing historical events in redemptive terms" (276). Weissman offers a cautionary lesson to all efforts to conflate theology and politics within Christian churches or Jewish synagogues. The gift of the Torah to the chosen people was not a political wager.

Despite its inherent tensions and the persistence of views that many Jews find objectionable, the Catholic Church's contemporary stance on chosenness and the Old Testament covenant has provided a basis for meaningful and ongoing interfaith dialogue. The BDS wing of the Protestant churches, represented here by Brueggemann's work, has instead undermined such conversations and often made them impossible, the consequences of which echo throughout *Peace and Faith*.

PART II CHRISTIANITY AND THE BOYCOTT MOVEMENT

BDS AND THE CHURCHES

One of the oldest traditions in both Judaism and Christianity, drawing on and amplifying exhortations by the Jewish prophets and by Jesus in the Christian Gospels, emphasizes the need to redress inequities, minister to the poor and the oppressed, and defend them against wealth and power. Once peoples in conflict are characterized as and divided into oppressors and victims, however, one group can be dehumanized and devalued, and justice can easily become justice for the oppressed alone. Over the last generation, for some Christian denominations that has meant not just championing the cause of the Palestinians but also opposing the Israeli state, which is no longer perceived as vulnerable, given that it has a powerful army that has repeatedly defeated its enemies and that oversees the administration of the West Bank. The conflict is consequently often represented as one between power and powerlessness, between the lion and the lamb. In the case of Israel alone, those with economic, political, and military power are expected to act benevolently, and those without comparable power often have their aggressive or violent actions excused. In the BDS movement—and among those church constituencies that embrace it—Palestinians are imagined not only to be powerless but also, falsely, to lack all agency. While mainline Protestant activists may recognize suffering on both sides of the Israeli-Palestinian conflict, they are often convinced, with good reason, that the Palestinians presently suffer much more. For those who feel called to address that imbalance and who believe Israel must be held accountable for it, BDS often seems the answer.

This may be an appropriate place to make a distinction applicable to the book as a whole. "Mainline" Protestantism refers to several denominations, including the United Methodist Church, the Presbyterian Church USA, the Episcopal Church, the Evangelical Lutheran Church in America, and the United Church of Christ. Evangelical Protestantism refers to a theological outlook that emphasizes the authority of scripture, a "born again" conversionary experience, the sacrifice of Jesus on the cross as making the redemption of humanity possible, and an activist orientation in missionary efforts. Evangelical Christians are more likely to belong to denominations like Southern Baptism, Pentecostalism, the Mennonite Church, or an independent/nondenominational church, though some remain members of mainline denominations. Some Catholics also self-identify as evangelical.

Some denominations also have longstanding relationships with Palestinian Christians, who understandably have a privileged voice when the Israeli-Palestinian conflict is debated in Christian spaces. The Sabeel Ecumenical Liberation Theology Center (Sabeel), a Jerusalem-based Palestinian organization founded in 1990, has been particularly influential.[4] With his preference for a single bi-national state, as opposed to two states for two peoples, Sabeel's director, Rev. Naim Ateek, has also promoted much more aggressive rhetoric. His 2001 Easter message indicted Israel with echoes of an ancient prejudice: "It seems to many of us that Jesus is on the cross again with thousands of crucified Palestinians around him." Some—ranging from Palestinian president Mahmoud Abbas to the Palestinian Authority's chief negotiator Saeb Erekat to activists like Mitri Raheb—have pressed this analogy still further, embracing the anti-Semitic claim that Jesus was actually a Palestinian, not a Jew. The damage done to public understanding by that anachronistic fiction is substantial.

Sabeel has worked within Christian denominations to transform liberation theology into a blueprint for interfaith encounters, something it was never designed to be when originally developed in Latin America. It began as a movement of self-critique within the Roman Catholic Church, one designed to correct the Church's neglect of Christ's teachings regarding the poor. As Pastor Todd Stavrakos, a convenor of Presbyterians for Middle East Peace, pointed out in a December 2020 Israel Action Network webinar on "Christian Churches And Their Challenges With Antisemitism And Anti-Zionism," Sabeel has promoted a Palestinian version of liberation theology that seeks to establish it as the means by which Christians interact with the Jewish community. The resulting logic of that effort revives ancient forms of anti-Semitism by giving them a contemporary spin. As Stavrakos put it, "If Christ's preference, if God's preference, is for the poor and the oppressed and if the Jewish community is not recognizing the plight of the Palestinians, then obviously the Jewish community is not on the side of God." The Jews have once again rejected the true God.

Jerusalem's Bethlehem Bible College echoes the Palestinian Liberation Theology trope of a new crucifixion with the title of its biennial "Christ at the Checkpoint" (CATC) conferences, though the conference is unusual in this domain in that it invites some speakers who embrace Zionism and oppose BDS. CATC has some radical anti-Zionist members; as Robert Nicholson writes, it is "a Western-facing billboard for Jesus-infused Palestinian nationalism and ground zero for a small but vocal group of Palestinian evangelicals who are working hard to undermine Christian support for Israel." But it has other members who condemn terrorism and call for peace with Israel. As Nicholson adds, "It's a fact that often gets them labeled as normalizers by their angry neighbors, which in turn forces them to talk tougher in order to reinforce their ever-precarious street cred." Sabeel's US-based affiliated group, Friends of Sabeel in North America (FOSNA), has promoted divestment resolutions both in mainline Protestant churches and on college campuses. BDS advocates in the Christian churches often call on Jewish Voice for Peace (JVP), a pro-BDS and anti-Zionist organization founded in 1996, to testify in favor of anti-Israel resolutions, thereby insulating the church from accusations of anti-Semitism by showing Jewish support for its agenda. At some church meetings, JVP spokespersons are misleadingly presented as if they are reliable representatives of the Jewish people as a whole. JVP is willing to pose as a peace group on such occasions, although it has repeatedly endorsed convicted terrorists, among them Leilah Khaled and Rasmea Odeh; Odeh received a standing ovation at a JVP national convention. JVP in reality is merely part of "an exceedingly vociferous minority of Jewish supporters of anti-Zionism" (Harrison 280). The presence of JVP at Christian meetings, moreover, demonstrates that anti-Zionism "can in principle cohabit easily with friendship toward and even a high moral regard for *individual* Jews (the cant phrase, 'Some of my best friends are Jews,' uttered by a political antisemite, may at times express no more than the truth, that is to say)." (Harrison 67).

In January 2019, JVP made its status as an anti-Zionist organization official. Although JVP has been consistently and aggressively anti-Zionist for years, the formal commitment makes it definitional. As Miriam Elman writes,

> In JVP's perspective on the Israeli-Palestinian conflict, Zionism itself is something uniquely detestable. Zionism isn't a liberation movement for a persecuted people but a manifestation of everything the left must abhor: imperialism, racism, colonialism, and apartheid . . . . JVP activists thus position themselves as the "good Jews" of the left—admitted and championed in progressive circles as the Jews who oppose other Jews. ("Left Antisemitism")

In an interview with Michael Schaeffer Omer-Man published in the magazine *+972*, JVP's director Rebecca Vilkomerson tried to justify the group's position in part by reminding us that historically "there has always been anti-Zionism within Jewish communities," a standard argument used to whitewash the quite different post-1948 meaning of

Rev. John Fife, Moderator, 204th General Assembly

Preserving the Presbyterian Commitment to Human Rights

When I chaired the MRTI committee for 11 years during South African apartheid, our church led the way in nonviolent, corporate divestment, ultimately leading to peace in South Africa. Have faith, and vote with your heart instead of your fear. Divest from Caterpillar, Motorola Solutions and Hewlett-Packard, and invest in peace. God bless you.

Divest from Violence. Invest in Peace.

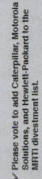

Rev. Peggy Howland

Christian Churches in Palestine are United in Asking Us for Divestment

When I was moderator of the Synod of the Northeast, I visited churches in the Middle East and spoke with our Christian brothers and sisters and Arab church leaders in several countries, including Israel and Palestine. Our brothers and sisters in Christ, the Christian Churches in Palestine, are united in asking us for divestment. They see this as a nonviolent response to the violence of a brutal occupation. Please let us help them in their commitment to nonviolence.

✓ Please vote to add Caterpillar, Motorola Solutions, and Hewlett-Packard to the MRTI divestment list.

✓ Please vote to affirm the church's continued commitment to engagement and support of peaceful pursuits in Israel/Palestine.

Nick Walrath

Palestinian Christians Need Freedom of Movement

I am a Palestinian Christian. My family in Ramallah lives under constant surveillance and fear, unable to visit Christian holy sites. We need your help to end this injustice, so they can live in peace and equality with their neighbors. Please vote to end the church's profiting from the suffering of Christians in the Holy Land.

Fig. 2—Flier designed and distributed by Jewish Voice for Peace during the 2012 Presbyterian Church USA General Assembly.

anti-Zionism. Late nineteenth- and early twentieth-century opposition to a hypothetical Jewish state is in no way comparable to the anti-Zionist determination to eliminate an actual state with seven million Jewish citizens. Vilkomerson more realistically explained that one of the motivations for the change in JVP's mission statement was to make "it easier for JVP chapters to enter into explicitly anti-Zionist coalitions." JVP has already broadcast its solidarity with the terrorist Rasmea Odeh, convicted of conspiracy in a suicide bombing, so we can expect its new anti-Zionist alliances to be equally repellant to the vast majority of Jews.

Those alliances are added to JVP's several campaigns within the Jewish community. As Elman reports,

> JVP's identity theft of Jewish heritage has been particularly visible during Passover, when its annually released Haggadah promotes BDS and it stages "liberation Seders," appropriating the holiday's rituals and texts for an anti-Israel narrative. JVP's Haggadah twists the Jewish text used during the Passover Seder—for example, by dedicating the third cup of wine to the BDS movement and featuring a section on the "Ten Plagues of the Israeli Occupation" (including the "plague" of the "denial of the right of return").

As Elman adds, JVP's organized campaign against Taglit-Birthright trips to Israel for young people represents not merely its opposition to "certain policies that they may legitimately disagree with: they are opposing the very idea of young American Jews developing an attachment to the Jewish people, to Jewish history, and to Jewish rights. They are opposing, in a word, the growth of Jewish identity." While committed anti-Zionists in Christian churches are not likely to be troubled by JVP's enhanced mission, other Christians might well take pause before accepting JVP as an adequate representative of the Jewish people, especially since JVP in January 2019 announced it is officially an anti-Zionist group. JVP's self-characterizations, moreover, include a significant amount of deception. Its overall membership claims are undocumented, and there is no evidence of what percentage is actually Jewish.

The alliance with JVP is one way that pro-BDS sentiments in some Christian denominations often run counter to the widespread reevaluation of Christianity's relationship to Jews and Judaism that gained force after the Holocaust. Critical to that process has been the effort described above to repudiate supersessionist theological narratives in which Christians have supplanted Jews to become the only legitimate heirs of God's covenant with Abraham. Unfortunately, old habits persist, and the long history of Christian anti-Jewish polemic lurks behind some anti-Zionist initiatives (Smith & Levine), among them those listed in the IHRA's examples of contemporary anti-Semitism. BDS targets religious groups because of the moral authority they wield and the high publicity value of their pro-BDS votes. Condemnation from people of faith often carries more cultural capital than opposition from opportunistic—and more overtly political—secular constituencies. As Dexter Van Zile pointed out in a 2020 online lecture, that cultural capital carries yet one more benefit: the mainline protestant churches in the anti-Zionist movement can be deployed by secular BDS groups to protect themselves from what are often legitimate charges of extremism and bigotry ("The Wages of Supersessionism").

The Christian group with the strongest anti-Zionist history is the once unequivocally pacifist American Friends Service Committee (AFSC), which actively supports BDS campaigns, trains students in BDS activism, and promotes anti-Israel rhetoric. AFSC pamphlets in the early 1970s expressed sympathy for Palestinian violence. In 1973 the AFSC called for a US embargo on military aid to Israel. Now it works through the BDS movement to realize its goals. Dalit Baum is a prominent Israeli anti-Zionist activist who directs the AFSC's Middle East Program. In 2013 the AFSC announced a "BDS Summer Institute" cosponsored with JVP; it promised training in BDS organizing strategies, media messaging, and direct action.

Some churches, especially in Europe, play a role in channeling government funds to BDS groups. The churches receive funds designed for humanitarian aid from government agencies but forward it to NGOs that sometimes have strong anti-Israel political agendas (NGO Monitor).

DIVESTMENT CAMPAIGNS IN MAINLINE PROTESTANT CHURCHES

For the most part, however, church groups in the US and Britain and international church groups with US affiliates have focused on two activities: issuing broad reports on and condemnations of Israel policy and pursuing divestment campaigns. These divestment campaigns become priorities because some churches have significant pension funds and stock holdings for which divestment from companies or international corporations doing business with Israel has material and practical consequences. In July 2004 the General Assembly of the Presbyterian Church (USA) approved a resolution setting a pathway to divestment from corporations operating in Israel. In 2005 the Central Committee of the World Council of Churches (WCC), meeting at its headquarters in Geneva, Switzerland, used similar language to encourage its 342 member churches to adopt a "phased, selective divestment from multinational corporations involved . . . in the occupation" ("WCC Endorses"). The WCC is the main global body uniting non-Catholic Christian churches. Established in 1948, the WCC "initially promoted a moderately friendly attitude toward Israel. But during the 1960s-1970s, its membership grew to include Greek Orthodox and Middle Eastern and Third World churches as well, transforming the organization's attitude toward Israel profoundly" (Ariel "Contemporary" 285). On February 6, 2021, nearly 350 church activists participating in a multi-denominational Zoom event heard one of several speakers, South African Rev. Frank Chikane, the moderator of the WCC's Commission on International Affairs, declare Israeli policies to be a "crime against humanity" and urge that "this evil cannot be allowed." He alluded to a need for violent action in saying "we need to begin to say to those who support Israel to brutalize Palestinians that the blood of the people of Palestine will be sought from them because they collaborate by allowing this system to continue" (https://www.youtube.com/watch?v=-CkiiAlT oos&fbclid=IwAR22dvIN2LAFZFw0MtyYW-tirTlmdQGnf73aJhWs y06AvCLfNsbLbbPnVtk).

In 2006 the Presbyterians' General Assembly rescinded its divest-ment language, but the denomination remained on the same pathway. Leading the effort has been the Israel Palestine Mission Network (IPMN) of the Presbyterian Church (USA). In June 2014, the General Assembly of the PCUSA passed a resolution by a vote of 310-303 to divest from Caterpillar, Motorola Solutions, and Hewlett-Packard, companies the PCUSA deemed complicit in and profiting from Israel's occupation of the West Bank and blockade of Gaza. A number of outside groups and speakers had a major impact on the PCUSA process. They included Dalit Baum, who maintains the Who Profits website devoted to "The Israeli Occupation Industry." Jewish Voice for Peace and Sabeel were active at the meeting. Jewish-American psychologist Mark Braverman, who heads the pro-Palestinian Christian group Kairos USA, has been influential within the PCUSA for some years. He warns that "Christians . . . must not be intimidated by Jews who use [anti-Semitism] to muzzle legitimate protest against injustice" (339). The self-righteous hostility a stance like his generates produces undemocratic and manipulative maneuvering at church meetings.

The votes in favor of divestment are not unanimous decisions. But the battle waged in resolution votes is for the majority, since even a slim majority vote determines church policy. Moreover, even a very close vote in favor of divestment, which should not be considered a clear mandate, is often treated as a major win by BDS advocates and the media alike. Tactics at annual church meetings can include efforts to deny equal time to opposing sides. Like academic associations, religious organizations are ill-equipped to manage controversial political issues when their membership is deeply divided. The resulting struggles often set aside respectful dialogue and opt instead for single-minded efforts to defeat pro-Israel constituencies.

At its 2005 General Synod, the United Church of Christ (UCC) passed a "Tear Down the Wall—Resolution of Witness" that helped pave the way for subsequent actions. The resolution declared the separation barrier part of the Israeli government's "de facto policy of settlement and colonization." As commonly happens, there was considerable political maneuvering both behind and during the 2005 debate. Two resolutions, one supporting and one contesting BDS were scheduled for debate. The Middle East committee approved the second resolution, which came from New England and had overt Jewish support. David Elcott of the American Jewish Committee then returned home for the sabbath. That gave Sabeel's agents an opening. They complained that the resolution signaled that the UCC was abandoning the Palestinians. On Saturday morning, they offered a new resolution that supported using economic leverages against Israel, and that resolution passed. "It denounced all forms of violence in the Middle East, 'including acts of suicide bombing by Palestinians and the use of force by Israelis in perpetuating occupation of Palestinian lands'" (Cooperman). Elcott commented that "the resolution on economic leverage expressed a deplorable 'moral equivalency between Israeli self-defense and Palestinian suicide bombing'" (Cooperman).

There were some lessons to be learned. Explicit Jewish organizational support for a resolution can be counterproductive. And every effort needs to be made to block votes on Israel-related resolutions from taking place on Shabbas and Jewish holidays when Jews are absent. Many such votes have since been scheduled to exclude or limit Jewish participation. People have also learned to be wary of resolutions like this one that include pro forma condemnations of anti-Semitism as a cover for anti-Zionism. In "Christian BDS," Giovanni Matteo Quer summarizes the relevant UCC history that frames the 2005 action:

> Already in 1999 the church synod adopted a resolution calling on the US government to stop financial aid that would support the settlements. In 2003, the synod adopted a similar resolution, condemning Israel's defense policies. Later, in 2013, the synod adopted a resolution that endorsed Palestinian liberation theology language, associating the Roman Empire with the current Israeli presence in the post-1967 territories, and called for a review of US aid to Israel and divestment initiatives. This resolution also encouraged the endorsement of the *Kairos Document*. Subsequently, in 2015, the synod confirmed its BDS policies and expressed concerns about Israel becoming an apartheid state (325).

As it happens, the UCC continues to hold investments in several securities that were targeted by a BDS resolution adopted in 2015: "The denomination's $3.2 billion retirement fund is still invested in three of the companies named by the resolution—Caterpillar ($1.7 million), Hewlett-Packard ($437,000), and Motorola ($342,000)" (Van Zile, "BDS Charade"). In 2016 the denomination issued "Promoting a Just Peace in Palestine-Israel: A Guide for United Church of Christ Faith Leaders," a 24-page document that replicates positions taken in statements by several other anti-Zionist churches. Thus it misleadingly declares that the separation barrier is "in many places, 25 feet tall" (30), a height that applies to less than ten percent of its length, describes Israel's target bombing in Gaza as "full-scale bombardments" (5), omitting any mention of Hamas military actions, endorses *Kairos Palestine* at length, urges divestment from Hewlett-Packard for developing the biometric identification system that the Palestinians demanded and that has virtually eliminated waiting times at checkpoints for those working regular jobs in Israel, rejects any effort at "'balance' between Palestinian and Israeli points of view" (19), and gives a recommended reading list limited to eight fiercely anti-Zionist books (22). It spiritualizes the covenantal promise of the land by declaring that "God does not draw political maps" (6). Denis MacEoin observed that the document naïvely takes "at face value the Palestinian statement that if Israel ended its occupation, 'Then they will see a new world in which there is no fear, no threat but rather security, justice and peace.'" In 2017 the Church passed a General Synod Resolution urging advocacy for the rights of children living under Israeli military occupation. A further statement, "The Kairos Moment Now: Toward a Human Rights Approach to a Just Peace in Palestine," was released by a network that lobbied the church in summer 2019. It declared Israel "an apartheid state," reiterated Church support for boycott and divestment, condemned the annexation of the Golan Heights, and demanded that Palestinians alone should have the power to choose between a two-state, one-state, or alternative resolution. In response to the coronavirus pandemic, the UCC's 33rd General Synod is scheduled to be held virtually in 2021.

The General Assembly of the Church of Scotland accepted the controversial Church and Society Council report on Israel/Palestine titled "The Inheritance of Abraham? A Report on the 'Promised Land'" in May 2013. The report rejects Jewish scriptural and theological claims to the land, subjects Zionism to harsh criticism, and recommends consideration of boycott and divestment resolutions. A revised version adds the qualification that the report "should not be misunderstood as questioning the right of the State of Israel to exist." In the summer of 2015, the

Christian Empowerment Council, an Israeli Christian group, released *Test the Spirits: A Christian Guide to the Anti-Israel Boycott Movement*. The 97,000-member Mennonite Church voted 418-336 to postpone consideration of similar measures until 2017. John Kampen discusses the 2017 resolutions in his chapter. Further consideration of boycott initiatives is likely in the United Methodist Church and Evangelical Lutheran Church in America (ECLA) in the near future, though at its 2019 triennial Churchwide Assembly the ECLA settled for reaffirming its existing investment screen instead of adopting a divestment resolution. An investment screen distinguishes between companies according to the criteria the organization adopts. The Methodist Church is in the process of separating into two separate denominations, a traditional denomination likely to support Israel and a contemporary denomination that may well be polarized by debates over the Israeli-Palestinian conflict like those that have roiled the Presbyterians. Expected in 2020, the decision is now delayed until August 2021. The ECLA calls its resolutions "memorials," and in 2019 several local synods put forward aggressive anti-Zionist ones, but the Church's Memorials Committee prevailed with more moderate alternatives. A timely and beneficial resolution passed urging the US government to resume funding for Jerusalem hospitals, including the Lutheran-affiliated Augusta Victoria Hospital in East Jerusalem.

Meanwhile, the 1.8 million-member Episcopal Church rejected several BDS resolutions at its 2015 General Convention and continued that pattern through 2018. The General Convention meets every three years. However, the 2018 Convention did show some movement: a resolution criticizing Israeli practices regarding Gaza passed, as did one calling on Israel to safeguard the rights of Palestinian children in police detention. Another resolution aimed to make it clear that criticism of Israeli policies and practices did not constitute a rejection of the Jewish state's right to exist; it reaffirmed Israeli self-determination and sovereignty. Two additional resolutions will await future developments before their effect can be gauged. One of these—which directed the Church to develop a "social criteria investment screen" mandating the evaluation of investments on the basis of human rights in East Jerusalem, Gaza, and the West Bank, which was taken to be a prelude to divestment—was defeated, but a version of the phrase came up in another resolution that passed, directing the Church "to avoid profiting from human rights abuses committed in Israel/Palestine." A helpful resolution advocated positive investment to benefit Palestinians. A resolution describing Israel as an apartheid state was soundly defeated. The Episcopalians have a bicameral legislature consisting of a 900-plus-member House of Deputies and a 300-member House of Bishops. The deputies are clergy and lay leaders appointed by individual dioceses and have often passed anti-Israel resolutions that are subsequently modified or defeated in the House of Bishops.

Like the debates within other denominations, those among the Episcopalians can be contentious, with passions overruling basic standards for truthfulness. In July 2018, Bishop Suffragen Gayle Harris, the second-in-command at the Episcopal Diocese of Massachusetts, testified in favor of the passage of a resolution that condemned Israel for alleged human rights abuses against Palestinian children. She declared "I was there" to see Israeli soldiers on the Temple Mount in Jerusalem attempt to put handcuffs on a three-year-old boy for bouncing a rubber ball. She declared herself witness as well to an incident when a Palestinian teenager who ran from soldiers after asking a question was shot ten times. A month later, under pressure, she issued an apology, admitting the stories were unsubstantiated rumor and that she was in fact not there to witness them ("Episcopal Diocese").

Throughout the denominations, the 2020 year embodied a pause in debates over the Israeli-Palestinian conflict, as the coronavirus pandemic forced the cancellation of face-to-face annual meetings. Abbreviated meetings held via Zoom are not likely to prove viable settings for the consideration of controversial resolutions. The PCUSA, for example, reduced its traditional week-long face-to-face meeting to two virtual days. It will meet face-to-face in 2022.

THE METHODIST ANTI-ZIONIST AGENDA

Although debates within the United Methodist Church do not have the elaborate history that they do among the Presbyterians—and although we do not have a separate essay on the Methodists in this book—it is important to show that the arc of Methodist positions on Israel follows a familiar pattern. Moreover, the sheer size of the Church, with twelve million members globally, including seven million in the US, combined with its distinctive book-length anti-Zionist study guide that I will describe in detail below, merit separate commentary here. But the United Methodist Church is diverse and decentralized. Power is concentrated both locally and in churchwide General Boards, several of which have historically been quite critical of Israel and supportive of BDS—notably the General Board of Church and Society and the General Board of Global Ministries but also, arguably, the General Board of Pension and Health Benefits. The Methodist story, as it is recounted in "Theology and the Churches: Mainline Protestant Zionism and Anti-Zionism," begins essentially with the founding of the Jewish state:

> New York Methodism in 1948 commended President Harry Truman for recognizing Israel and urged the United Nations to treat attacking Arab states as a "threat to world peace." New York Methodist bishop G. Bromley Oxnam presented an award honoring newly formed Israel's "stand for dignity and equality of opportunity." Methodist Council of Bishops president Fred Corson in 1953 joined others in urging President Dwight Eisenhower to denounce anti-Semitism in the Soviet Union. In 1954, Missouri bishop Ivan Holt of the World Methodist Council and another bishop joined prominent officials in urging Arab states to resettle eight hundred thousand Arab (i.e., Palestinian) refugees from the 1948 war . . . ."they are prevented from seeking permanent rehabilitation by these same leaders who use existence of the problem as a weapon against the West and against Israel." (Tooley 202)

By 1976, however, with opposition to the occupation growing and Palestinian liberation theology gaining influence, the balance had shifted. The Church adopted its first formal resolution on the Middle East at its General Conference, which meets every four years. The resolution observed that Israeli Jews live with "insecurity" that echoes a "long history of oppression" that culminated in the Holocaust. It also protested against Palestinian suffering, which included "arrests, tortures, and expulsions" at the hands of Israelis. It thus supported "self-determination" for both Jews and Palestinians, including a Palestinian state, while faulting the United States for dismissing Palestinian "aspirations." But it also pressed for recognition of the Palestine Liberation Organization (PLO).

In 2004, during the Second Intifada, the Church adopted "Opposition to Israeli Settlements in Palestinian Lands." By the time the 200,000-member British Methodist Church, which had endorsed the boycott of settlement products in 2010, was in the process of considering more aggressive policies, the larger church was already doing the same. Central to that effort was the book *Israel-Palestine: A Mission Study for 2007-2008*, published on behalf of the United Methodist Church's Women's Division within its General Board of Global Ministries. The book is divided in two parts: a long essay by Stephen Goldstein (pp. 6-127) and a "study guide" by Sandra Olewine (pp. 129-213). Now retired, Reverend Goldstein, a Jew who converted to Christianity, at the time was Assistant General Secretary in the office responsible for recruiting, training, and coordinating almost five hundred Methodist missionaries. Olewine, a nine-year veteran Board of Global Ministries Liaison to Jerusalem, was assigned to a ministry in Long Beach, California, at the time. Olewine is now Senior Pastor at First United Methodist Church in Pasadena, California, and one of the directors of the Methodist Hospital of Southern California.

While working in Jerusalem, Olewine made her political views clear in "The Silent Destruction of Palestine," published in *CounterPunch* in 2002, and in "As war rages to the east of us, we continue to bury the dead here" in the fiercely anti-Zionist *The Electronic Intifada* the following year. In conjunction with her commitment to Palestinian liberation theology, she served as pastor of the Evangelical Lutheran Christmas Church in Bethlehem while its regular pastor and *Kairos Palestine* coauthor Mitri Raheb was on leave. "The Silent Destruction of Palestine" reports on West Bank security measures installed by the Israelis, developments that she complains do not receive adequate coverage, telling us, "The 'prison' called Palestine gets smaller and smaller each day. The pressure builds and builds . . . . This silent destruction is the creeping hand of occupation. It is what has everyone here held in a death-grip. Without removing its stranglehold from the lives of Palestinians, Palestinians and Israelis will tragically and brutally continue to die."

Goldstein's section of the book has been faulted for its errors. As Sam Hodges reports in *The Dallas Morning News*, "a group called Christians for Fair Witness on the Middle East issued a press release announcing it was 'deeply disturbed'" by the study, criticizing its "'factual errors, misrepresentations, material omissions and distortions.'" A member of the Fair Witness executive committee, the Rev. Archer Summers of the First United Methodist Church in Palo Alto, California, called it "a blatant attempt to portray Jews and Israelis in as damning a light as possible, particularly by stereotyping Jews as aggressive, belligerent, racist, and vengeful" (Hodges).

On page seventy-two, for example, Goldstein makes the mistake of accusing Baruch Goldstein of assassinating Israeli Prime Minister Yitzhak Rabin in 1994, even though pages earlier he accurately identifies Goldstein instead as the mass murderer of twenty-nine Palestinian civilians at the Ibrahimi Mosque/Cave of the Patriarchs in Hebron in February of that year, immediately after which Goldstein was beaten to death by survivors. Rabin was killed by right-wing Israeli law student Yigal Amir in November 1995. But I am less concerned with Goldstein's factual errors than I am with the interpretations and conclusions that may have had a misleading and damaging impact on those using the book. In the end, we need to ask whether a book that relentlessly demonizes one party to the conflict can be an appropriate basis for "study," let alone a vehicle for reconciliation.

In his historical overview, Goldstein tells us "there is little in either the biblical record or the early post-biblical record that can support the proprietary claims of nineteenth- and twentieth-century European Jews to Israel-Palestine," an argument both Christians and Jews might contest, even if they would dispute some of the implications of "proprietary" (24). Jews, he continues, "were not 'returning.' They were settlers with a nineteenth-century colonial ideology," a standard BDS argument and one Methodists may debate but should not present as an unassailable conclusion in a study guide (29). The neutral term "immigrants" better captures the historical reality. The outlook of the Jews who arrived in Palestine, he insists, was "basically racist, and still is . . . they do not see Palestinians as human beings like themselves" (32), a global accusation for which there is no evidence. At that point Goldstein crosses the line into anti-Semitic slander. Later in *Peace and Faith*, for example, Michael Gizzi documents reconciliation projects that could not have functioned were this true. Goldstein's history continues by falsely telling us the 1948 war, triggered by internal and external Arab aggression that threatened the survival of the new Jewish state, was conducted solely because it "was in the Zionists' interest and offered an opportunity to further their goals of expansion beyond the United Nations partition recommendation" (65). The founding of the Jewish state was "the original sin against the Palestinians" (106), a metaphor still more dangerous in a faith context. His comments on the 1979 peace agreement with Egypt, which has likely prevented another regional war, are condemnatory: "what transpired was once again a negation of the promise for peace and a failure to pursue an honest resolution of the Palestinian-Israeli conflict"; it was a complete "sell-out" (112). Turning to more recent contexts, he cites his personal opposition to any people holding "Israeli-American joint citizenship" (96). Although joint citizenship is common worldwide, he only objects to its being held by Jews. He repeatedly urges us to see Palestinian terrorists as freedom fighters: "After the defeat of the Arab armies in 1967, the Palestinian feda'iyyin was the only group able to counter the Israeli occupation through guerilla raids into the Occupied Territories" (97). The fedayeen were Palestinian guerillas who infiltrated Israel to strike military and civilian targets after the 1948 war. Goldstein tells us at length that "Arafat was willing to do almost anything to gain a concrete agreement," a position many historians would dispute (127). Then he tells us the construction of Israel's security barrier is a "development preventing the possibility of a viable Palestinian state" (123), whereas in fact it suggests a possible border for a two-state solution. Indeed, that is why the settlers to the east of it opposed its construction. Many who have seen the barrier will find it difficult to accept the claim that it is guarded by "patrols of killer dogs most of its length" (123), though the point of the fantasy is apparent: to evoke the German shepherds used as guard dogs in German death camps.

Predictably, he is contemptuous of the 1993 Oslo Accords, using the familiar anti-Israel comparison with South Africa to suggest the Accords never offered any basis for progress toward a two-state solution:

"what we see today, a series of cantons (or Bantustans, if one uses the analogy of apartheid South Africa)" is his take on the Oslo legacy (122). One might argue instead that the fragmented areas of Palestinian territorial control in the West Bank need to be integrated into contiguous territory and still could be. Some of that process could actually begin now; it does not have to wait for a comprehensive peace agreement. That said, Oslo made it possible for the Palestinian Authority (PA), flawed as it is, to begin governing, creating policy, and developing social service institutions. The PA took responsibility for health care, for example, in 1994. It has built a responsible security force that has prevented hundreds of terrorist attacks. The West Bank land encompassing most of Areas A and B remains a foundation for an expanded Palestinian state that would encompass much of Area C, though annexation by Israel could render that option moot.

Many readers will find Goldstein's account of how the Holocaust has shaped Israeli psychology to be the single most offensive part of the book. As Dexter Van Zile points out, Goldstein argues that "Israeli attitudes toward its neighbors are not a response to the repeated multiarmy attacks against Israel or the persistent terror attacks by groups like the PLO, Hamas, and Hizballah over the past several decades . . . . Instead, Israel's suspicion of its neighbors is a delayed response to the destruction of European Jewry by the Nazis in the 1940s" (Van Zile "Mainline"). "The pain, the self-imposed sense of failure, and the attendant rage," Goldstein writes, "has infected Israeli society in terribly corrupting and unhealthy ways" (101). "To this day," he adds, "there is a latent hysteria in Israeli life that springs directly from this source. It explains the paranoiac sense of isolation that has been a main characteristic of the Israeli temper since 1948." Moreover, he concludes, "it has been the most significant factor in Israel's unwillingness to trust their Arab neighbors or the Palestinians." Pressing this claim still further, he embraces the idea that "Standing behind each Arab or Palestinian, Israelis tend to see SS men determined to push them once again into gas chambers and crematoria" (102). This hyperbolic conviction that he can read Israelis' minds and look into their souls again crosses a line into anti-Semitism.

The Israelis who work with Palestinian children, health care professionals, teachers, or security forces do not see them as SS men.

Nonetheless, there are reasons to recall the Holocaust, from Hamas's declared aim of obliterating the Jewish state to Iran's implacable hostility and its effort to build nuclear weapons. Israel actually works closely with area governments that at the same time cynically promote hostile rhetoric amongst their populations. Israelis are not preoccupied with the memory of the Holocaust, as Goldstein claims. The Holocaust generation has largely passed away. Speaking as a converted Jew who believes he retains special insight, he claims that Holocaust memory has "paralyzed us from acting" (103). But no one who visits the dynamic state of Israel would find any mass paralysis. Goldstein urges us "to live in a post-Holocaust day of healing" (102), which certainly applies to personal relations and peace negotiations alike. But the lessons the Holocaust taught us about the potential for both personal and state-level evil must not be forgotten. If we live in a post-Holocaust world, those lessons are part of the legacy we have inherited.

One of the more unusual and surprising features of *Israel-Palestine* are the study session handouts by Olewine on pages 179-213 that complete the book. Study guides about the Israeli-Palestinian conflict typically include its historical background and the whole range of relevant contemporary issues. Echoing Goldstein, her opening session tells us in loaded language that "tens of thousands of Jews poured into Palestine, the rise of Nazism in Germany having pushed them out of central Europe" (53, 179). They didn't "pour" in a deluge, they emigrated. They left not simply because of the "rise" of Nazism but because of the viciously anti-Semitic laws and regulations the Nazis put in place and the mass violence they organized against Jews. She complains that "to this day, Israel has yet to establish officially its boundaries, except for its northern border with Lebanon," considering this a failure to live up to the terms of UN Security Council Resolution 242, though Israel's neighboring states had no interest in negotiating official borders, only an armistice. She characterizes the early 1990s as a period of "negotiation, recognition, and 'reconciliation,'" the latter term in scare quotes presumably as a disparaging allusion to the Oslo Accords. In an oddly neutral sentence, she tells us "Hamas found its inspiration in the Palestinian hero Sheikh 'Izz ed-Din al-Qassim" who, Goldstein earlier told us, "had a concern for social justice and a commitment to direct action" (181,

53). She does not mention that he was a religious leader who organized attacks against the British and against Jews in the 1930s; "direct action" is a euphemism. She concludes by telling us West Bank barriers "mak[e] direct passage anywhere in the Palestinian territories impossible," which overstates the reality, and she insists that Gaza remains occupied territory despite the ostensible Israeli withdrawal. Movement in and out of Gaza is restricted by both Egypt and Israel—and Hamas imposed further restrictions during the pandemic—but Gaza itself is not occupied.

Olewine's first handouts are a mixture of standard BDS argument and more idiosyncratic political indoctrination, none of which prepares us to encounter the third handout, "Jesus is Condemned to Death" (185). When we read the introduction to her part of the book we may reasonably assume she is emphasizing a familiar analogy: "As those who strive to be faithful to following Christ, we are called to see the places where Christ is still wounded, even crucified, through the pain and struggles in people's lives today" (131). The analogy becomes somewhat odd a few sentences later: "Therefore, you are invited to 'walk' through this study as though you are walking the Way of the Cross and ultimately come to the place where you will be invited 'to roll away the stone' so that the reality of new life, resurrection, can come to all the peoples of the land where Jesus lived, loved, died and rose again."

Still expected here, one might assume, are more intricate efforts to extend the analogy between Jesus's story and Palestinian suffering. What we may not expect is that several sessions are devoted only to the story of Jesus, material that would be well known to any Methodist audience, without any comparisons to contemporary Palestine. The fifth handout is "Jesus Falls for the First Time," followed by "Veronica Wipes the Face of Jesus," "Jesus Meets the Women of Jerusalem," "Jesus Is Stripped of His Garments," and "Jesus Dies on the Cross" (191-196). We get a handout on the rights of Palestinian refugees, which predictably counts among them British, French, and US citizens of Palestinian heritage, advice about how to evaluate media coverage of Israeli premier Ehud Barak ("Was Barak's '95 percent' figure used to describe the Barak 'offers'"?), until we return to "Jesus Is Laid in the Tomb" (197-201). This is not simply an effort to sanctify her own study guide by weaving into it highlights from the life of Jesus, an impulse which some may find objectionable on its own. It is something more.

Finally, we discover where all this is heading. She is deploying tropes from the New Testament to demonize Israel. The next handout, from the fourth session, is "Who Will Roll the Stone Away?" The title is repeated for seven detailed sub-entries—except that we have leapt two thousand years from the time of Jesus's death and resurrection to the present day. Olewine is amplifying an analogy Naim Ateek had made some years earlier. "In a sermon title at Notre Dame Chapel in Jerusalem on February 24, 2001, Ateek asked 'Who will Role [sic] Away the Stone (Mark 16.3),' and went on to liken Israeli occupation policy and response to the Intifada to the stone that was placed on Jesus's grave" (Pettit "Old Whines" 208). Olewine's entry on the Sabeel Ecumenical Liberation Theology Center tells us "By learning from Jesus—his life under Occupation and his response to injustice—this theology hopes to connect the true meaning of Christian faith with the daily lives of all those who suffer under Occupation, violence, discrimination, and human rights violations" (205-6). That too is standard Palestinian liberation theology reasoning, but the repeated call to "roll the stone away" adds an anti-Semitic connotation to the lesson. Jesus is once again being prevented from rising. None of us can be redeemed while Israel has placed a boulder that blocks the entrance to his tomb and prevents the resurrection again. It is a more deeply religious and theological accusation. She has retold Jesus's story not only to give her own narrative credibility, but also to abandon analogy for identity. There are good Jews who want to move the stone, but can they? Or is Israel's national weight simply too heavy for them to bear?

As Marcia Kupfer suggested to me, Olewine's effort to use an analogy with Mark 16:3 to condemn the Jewish state adds a whole new layer of Jewish guilt for denying Jesus as the messiah and creates serious theological confusion. As the gospels have it, the boulder's removal does not occur through human intervention. A material by-product of the resurrection, it is effected through divine power. So why would we expect an earthly polity, whether the state of Israel or its opponents, to be responsible for removing today's equivalent? What use, then, is anti-Zionist activism in removing Israel from its purported role in blocking

human redemption if the task is God's? The best sense one might make
of her perplexing analogy is to revert to the notion that the solution
to the Israeli-Palestinian conflict will be divine, but then what role
does contemporary activism have? Olewine's misbegotten metaphor
points to a recurrent problem in efforts to apply biblical narratives and
theological categories to contemporary political analysis.

Despite the publication of the Goldstein/Olewine book, the General
Conference voted against divestment in 2012, though in 2014 the
United Methodist Church divested from G4S, a British-Danish firm
providing security services to private prisons. This was misreported in
the New York Times as a move related specifically to the company's
contract work with Israeli prisons holding Palestinians. Although the
UMC pension board issued a clarification, the damage was done.

Fig. 3—Demonstration at the 2012 Methodist meeting. Photo Credit: UMKR

One notable tactic at the 2012 meeting came from the key anti-
Zionist constituency within the Church, United Methodist Kairos
Response (UMKR). It leafleted the meeting with a four-page flier
printed as four panels on an 11 by 17 sheet of paper, folded in two for
easy distribution. The first page (Fig. 4) encapsulates UMKR's argument about West Bank settlements, that they are a colonialist project

that is destroying Palestinian lives. The third page (Fig.5) offers the proposed response, urging divestment from three companies accused of complicity with the occupation: Caterpillar, Motorola Solutions, and Hewlett Packard.

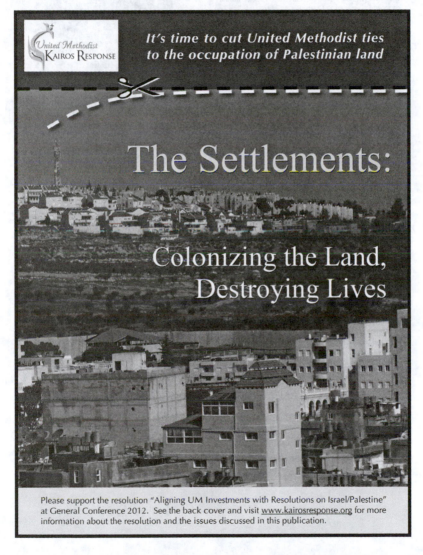

Fig. 4—United Methodist Kairos Response 2012 flier, page one (of four).

Three United Methodist Ties to the Occupation

*Some United Methodist boards and
agencies invest in companies that
help build and sustain illegal settlements
and demolish homes.*

CATERPILLAR (NYSE:CAT) An Israeli military commander referred to Caterpillar bulldozers as "the key weapon" in its military occupation of Palestinian land. The company is aware that the Israeli army uses Caterpillar equipment to destroy Palestinian homes, orchards and olive groves. This is done to clear land for illegal settlements, segregated roads and the separation wall. Caterpillar bulldozers have killed Palestinians who were not able to evacuate their homes before demolitions, which often take place with little warning. They have uprooted hundreds of thousands of olive trees and demolished water cisterns.

MOTOROLA SOLUTIONS (NYSE:MSI) Motorola developed a perimeter radar system called MotoEagle, which is used to protect at least 25 illegal settlements in the West Bank. It is installed on sniper towers as well as the separation wall, which has been ruled illegal by the International Court of Justice. Motorola also provides a mobile communications system and vehicle mounted antennae for the Israeli army in the occupied territories.

HEWLETT PACKARD COMPANY (NYSE:HPQ) HP owns Electronic Data Systems, which heads a consortium providing biometric monitoring of checkpoints, including several built inside the West Bank in violation of international law. HP provides a municipal data storage system for the illegal settlement of Ariel and has business relationships with companies in the illegal settlement of Modi'in Illit. HP also provides computers for the Israeli Army that guards the settlements, and manages information technology for the Israeli Navy, which enforces Israel's siege of the Gaza Strip.

> United Methodist boards and agencies have been engaged in shareholder advocacy with Caterpillar, Motorola Solutions and Hewlett Packard Company for years without any meaningful progress. These companies continue to profit by equipping the illegal occupation. It is time for the United Methodist Church to cut its ties with these companies until they end their support of the occupation which our church clearly opposes.

Caterpillar equipment builds settlements.

Caterpillar clears land for new settlements.

Motorola radar guards an illegal settlement.

Palestinians wait at HP-equipped checkpoint.

Fig. 5—2012 UMKR flier, page three.

The second page, which is on the settlements, does accurately represent them as illegal under international law, but then makes unforced errors like declaring that the Ma'ale Adumim settlement "cuts the West Bank in half." It does extend roughly forty percent across the West Bank in an east/west direction, but that leaves sixty percent between the settlement and the Jordanian border, certainly sufficient territory to allow for a Palestinian state, though not if Israel were to annex the Jordan Valley.

The three companies targeted for divestment present different problems. Caterpillar sells bulldozers worldwide. One of its customers is the US Defense Department, from whom Israel acquires bulldozers with congressionally appropriated funds. Caterpillar also has a Palestinian dealer. Opposing Hewlett Packard is a more serious error, because HP's biometric scanning software and technology is making Palestinian's lives more manageable and humane. The Palestinians themselves demanded greater use of biometric data as part of the 1998 Wye River Memorandum. Now biometric technology has enabled rapid transit checkpoints between the West Bank and Israel, limiting waiting to a few minutes, rather than the occasional hours that have caused much anguish and international protest. Yes, HP makes a profit; that is how capitalism works, but biometric scanning is a benefit, not an injustice.

This Methodist flier marks a shift from the emphasis on theological arguments to the rights-based political ones we saw above in their large anti-Zionist book. We would see much the same shift in emphasis between two anti-Zionist Presbyterian books, *Zionism Unsettled* and *Why Palestine Matters*. At that point, as Gunther Jikeli puts it, one may fairly wonder whether "their theology might be determined more by their political views than the other way around" (4). In part that pattern suggests awareness that the theological arguments alone had not persuaded denomination memberships. But it also reflects the fact that the theological grounds for anti-Zionism had been made, were now on record and available for continued promotion. It was now time for a new weapon to be deployed against the Jewish state.

In June 2015 at its General Synod in Cleveland the 950,000-member United Church of Christ (UCC) passed a boycott, divestment, and sanctions resolution by a vote of 508-124. Yet the same General

Synod rejected a resolution branding Israel's West Bank practices acts of apartheid 312 to 295 (with 31 abstentions), which meant that the resolution failed to get the required two-thirds majority. In 2016, the United Methodist Church, with 7 million US members and a total of 12 million worldwide, voted at its quadrennial General Conference to withdraw its membership in the U.S. Campaign to End the Israeli Occupation and defeated four divestment resolutions. Meanwhile, the unofficial United Methodists for Kairos Response (UMKR), a product of a grassroots movement of Methodist clergy and laity, still stood. UMKR was initiated in October 2010 by a group within the UMC and reaffirmed in 2018, with an accusation that Israel's 2018 "Nation-State Bill" codified an apartheid legal system. It has consistently asserted that the occupation is the major threat to the Christian presence in the Holy Land.

The United Methodist Church took the first step toward a boycott initiative in January 2016, when its pension board added five Israeli banks to a list of thirty-nine companies from several countries that failed to meet its Human Rights Investment Policy guideline. The five Israeli banks are identified as being involved in settlement construction. The denomination itself, though, at its last three quadrennial General Conferences (2008, 2012, and 2016) considered divestment resolutions and overwhelmingly rejected them. Following a pattern similar to other churches, Methodist advocacy has coalesced into competing groups. The United Methodist *Kairos* Response (UMKR) submitted two resolutions for consideration at the General Conference in May 2016, one addressing companies profiting from the occupation and another dealing with companies producing goods or services in Israeli settlements. At the same time, a member of United Methodists for Constructive Peacemaking in Israel and Palestine declared, "we are not going to participate in the continuing demonization of one side over the other or the continuation of policies that bring about fear and isolation for one side over the other" (Horowitz). In April 2018 a *Christian Today* staff writer reported that the president and vice president of the Methodist Conference "condemned the shooting of protestors in the Gaza Israel border" and accused Israel of "crimes against humanity," saying that the killing of unarmed protestors is "unacceptable in any circumstance." UMKR

maintains a website (https://www.kairosresponse.org/umkr_home.
html) that includes a long (more than 50-page two-part) 2018 report
consisting mostly of one broadside after another and a collection of links
to allied groups. There is little in the way of extended analysis. The 2020
General Conference has been postponed until 2021, when we may well
see more anti-Zionist agitation. UMKR and the Methodist Federation
for Social Action signaled as much during a January 2021 webinar
titled "A New Congress, A New Administration: New Opportunities
for Palestinian Rights!" (Lee), though any confidence they can change
US policy is likely unwarranted. Whether the willingness of some Arab
states to formally normalize relations with Israel—beginning in 2020
with the United Arab Emirates, Bahrain, Sudan, and Morocco—will
alter the attitudes of BDS advocates is impossible to say, though it may
persuade some church members that reconciliation is a better strategy
than demonization, that peace is again becoming a credible goal in
Arab/Israeli relations. The UAE/Bahrain/Sudan/Morocco agreements
will be discussed more thoroughly in Chapter 16.

PART III: THE STRUCTURE
OF *PEACE AND FAITH*

DETAILING THE HISTORICAL RECORD

As this introduction suggests, history and theology together hover over
all contemporary negotiations regarding Israel. The medieval crusades
that wantonly killed Jews and Muslims alike—suggesting to Jews that
the cross was a weapon and to Arabs that there was a fundamentally
dark side to later missionary efforts—continue to shape Middle Eastern
attitudes and memories. If the anger in some Islamic quarters is to
be addressed, the contemporary residue of that history will require
more attention from Christians. The theological quarrels between
Catholics and Protestants that played out historically in violent power
struggles remind church members as well that religious convictions
can have terrible consequences. The long history of supersessionism
which forgave and at times encouraged the murder of Jews in pogroms

and their banishment from European countries casts doubt on the motivations behind contemporary efforts to deny Israel's right to exist. And, although some church members want to leave behind any sense of personal responsibility for the past, their institutional memory is nonetheless haunted by the fact, as *Peoples and Conflict in the Middle East* puts it, that "Ever since the opening up of the death camps in 1945, Christendom has been grappling with the terrible issue they presented: was it from Christianity that so many Europeans learned hatred of Jews?" (22)

Both the questions and the historical heritage invoked above inform conversations in every denomination. The second section of the book, which uses the Presbyterian Church USA as a key example, opens with Daniel Friedman's analysis of the sociological, political, and organizational changes in the Church that have empowered its anti-Zionist wing. John Wimberly and the late William Harter, both active members of Presbyterians for Middle East Peace (PFMEP), discuss the intense debates that took place at the Church's 2014 General Assembly, while also bringing the story through 2018. Harter, notably, was active in Presbyterian debates over Israel since the early- to mid-1970s. He contributed to Presbyterian publications from that era and was influential in the National Christian Leadership Conference's actions regarding Israel. Michael Gizzi, another PFMEP member, focuses on the impact that the anti-Zionist "study guide" *Zionism Unsettled* had on the 2014 meeting. Cary Nelson traces the debates over Israel to their nineteenth century missionary roots, then does a close analysis of *Zionism Unsettled* and the other publications of the PCUSAs anti-Zionist group, including its most recent book from 2018. Two of the essays about Presbyterianism are written from inside the Church and two from outside it.

At its 2018 annual meeting the Presbyterian Church took a number of actions affecting Israelis and Palestinians. The PCUSA reaffirmed its opposition to anti-BDS legislation and formally opposed a company profiting from the sale of settlement properties. A resolution endorsing reconciliation efforts passed, despite resistance from those who oppose reconciliation initiatives on the grounds that they betray BDS's anti-normalization agenda. As *Christian Century* editor David Heim has observed, "the silencing of conversation is one of the most disturbing aspects" of the BDS movement. A resolution on human rights was amended to delete a passage opposing US economic and military aid to Israel. A resolution criticizing Israeli policies in Gaza passed as well, though with an additional passage decrying "inciteful discourse that inserts acts of violence into a massive peaceful demonstration," which clearly refers to the 2018 clashes on the Gaza border. A resolution describing Israel as a colonial project was defeated.

The third section of *Peace and Faith*, "Guideposts for the Future," examines reconciliation. Reconciliation is a complex, multifaceted concept in Christianity, with intertwining theological, political/social, interpersonal, and practical elements. Reconciliation is also important to Jews and Muslims who do not share Christian theological beliefs. The Presbyterian Church's 1974 booklet "The Middle East Conflict" quotes from the "Confession of 1967" to give direction for how reconciliation should be embodied in Middle East peacemaking:

> The church, in its own life, is called to practice the forgiveness of enemies and to commend to the nations as practical politics the search for cooperation and peace. This search requires that the nations pursue fresh and responsible relations across every line of conflict, even at risk to national security, to reduce areas of strife and to broaden international understanding . . . the church which identifies the sovereignty of any one nation or any one way of life with the cause of God denies the Lordship of Christ and betrays its calling. (7)

In warning against privileging one nation or one "way of life," the "Confession" is applicable to the Israeli-Palestinian conflict, urging Christians to seek a balance between the State of Israel and both Jewish and Palestinian ways of life. The 1974 booklet goes on in its own words to declare that "it is an ethical imperative" to "be reconciled to the conflicting peoples of the Middle East and strive to become an agent of reconciliation." Contrary to the anti-normalization agenda that would be formulated decades later, the text urges "the kind of dialogue which alone can create the understanding from which peace may evolve," which requires "a willingness to forsake polarizing formulations" (8-9). This sentiment echoes the 1973 book's statement that "the way to peace, there as here, lies not through partisanship and polarization but through reconciliation. *Shalom. Salaam*" (10).

As the first and second parts of *Peace and Faith* document, BDS-allied elements of several Christian denominations have more recently adopted precisely such "polarizing formulations." *Peoples and Conflict in the Middle East* appends a strong condemnation to its affirmative guidelines: "A self-appointed reconciler who is himself an unrepentant offender is a loathsome hypocrite" (13). The book then contextualizes this warning: "We confess that we have not yet done all that we ought to have done to be reconciled to the Jewish people, whose sufferings have been caused by the antisemitism of many Christians and in whose holocaust the churches acquiesced" (13). That is a goal that many of those committed to the BDS movement no longer include within the task of reconciliation.

The third section of *Peace and Faith* opens with Susan Andrews's inspiring account of a long-term collaboration between her Presbyterian church and a local synagogue and concludes with her reflections on a trip to Israel/Palestine and her consequent thoughts about the conflict itself and the debates within the national church. Her opening story gives us a model of reconciliation carried out not in a single encounter but rather as a continuing and evolving commitment. Her essay is a challenge to search for consensus about the Israeli-Palestinian conflict. It is also, consequently, an essay torn between joy and anguish. Seeking to establish a shared space for worship, a church and a synagogue navigate a relationship that could sour at many points. When the synagogue uses the chapel for its services, its members unsurprisingly want to cover the crucifix at the front. This request offends some church members, and the cooperation hangs by a thread as a result—until, that is, a Jewish engineer designs a pulley system to raise and lower a banner that can cover the cross with a quotation from Psalm 133. When Andrews turns to debates within the national church, she recounts a painful history of polarization, not reconciliation. The essay is a call for the PCUSA to do better.

Michael Gizzi then provides an essential guide to notable local reconciliation projects and the groups that organize them. These NGOs offer Christians, Jews, and Muslims alike opportunities to make important contributions to Palestinians' and Israelis' wellbeing, to promote dialogue between them, and to achieve better understanding for everyone involved. Sometimes working together matures into genuine friendship, affection, and love. One of us was able to attend the 2016 premiere of *Disturbing the Peace*, the film about the Israeli-Palestinian group Combatants for Peace. The film tells the story of how members of both peoples rejected their own violent pasts and chose reconciliation. At the premier, the Palestinians and Israelis who spoke on stage made it clear that their trust in each other eventually became love. I supplement Gizzi's list with a practical plan that would help prepare all parties for a successful negotiation of a two-state solution by giving examples of how to make essential progress now. I provide concise guides not only to the principles that would need to govern a final-stage agreement, but also to the work that must be done on behalf of Palestinians in Gaza and the West Bank in the present.

The impact of anti-Semitism both historically and today receives careful attention throughout the book, both in essays that take it as a main topic and others, like those by Amy Jill-Levine and Daniel Friedman, that note its relevance while addressing other topics. Detailed considerations include Edward Kessler's analysis of important early church history, followed by his accounts of the theological implications of the Holocaust and religious involvement in the BDS movement. David Fox Sandmel assesses anti-Semitic elements of the *Kairos Palestine Document*, an analysis complemented by his capsule review of the history of anti-Semitism that precedes the appendix. The book concludes with an extensive annotated timeline of Jewish-Christian relations and the history of anti-Judaism and anti-Semitism.

The twenty-first century has seen a number of Protestant churches identify with the campaign to delegitimate Israel launched at the World Conference against Racism held in Durban, South Africa, in 2001. That meeting successfully revived the "Zionism is racism" motto that the UN had adopted in 1975 but overturned in 1991. Proposals to boycott Israeli universities and divest from corporations doing business in Israel were debated in Britain and the United States in 2002 and migrated to Protestant denominational meetings by 2004. The following year the delegitimization campaign received its blessing from a group of Palestinian NGOs. The Boycott, Divestment, and Sanctions movement was under way; it had a transformative impact on a number of Protestant churches, sometimes crowding out other topics at their annual conventions. Documenting and analyzing that impact is one of this book's major aims.

DENOMINATIONAL TOPICS IN *PEACE AND FAITH*

Peace and Faith's account of evangelical beliefs and other denominational studies are interspersed with chapters on key theological and political issues and on the analysis of influential documents. Amy-Jill Levine , for example, tackles a question that has roiled Christian-Jewish relations for centuries: Does the New Testament claim that the Jewish identification with the land of Israel has been superseded by an abstract, universal notion of redemption in Jesus? Her essay reminds us that, as William Nicholls points out, "the growth of supersession was accompanied by a battle for the Bible" (382). Many Jews and Christians alike give priority instead to the Jews' historical connections to the Holy Land, which do not rely on belief in a divine covenant. The historical record was succinctly outlined by the Presbyterian Church in its 1973 book *Peoples and Conflict in the Middle East*:

> Jews have lived in Palestine since Biblical times. The Jewish presence in Palestine goes back to Abraham himself. Israel existed as a nation from 1000 B.C. until 587 B.C. when the Babylonians destroyed the Southern half of the kingdom (Judah). After that time, the region was basically under the control of other nations or empires: Persian, Greek, Roman, and the Jews existed as a vassal people within this foreign rule. Provoked by repressive acts of the Greeks, the Jews successfully revolted in 168-165 B.C., creating an independent nation for about a century. Subsequent domination by Romans resulted in the revolt of 67-70 A.D. and the Bar Kochba revolt of 132-135 A.D. These revolts were crushed by the Roman legions, however, and many Jews fled the region. Jewish population was sharply reduced in the area, but significant centers of Jewish learning persisted in Palestine under a succession of eminent rabbis. (18)

This passage gives us a capsule account of an indigenous Jewish Israeli people, an account immensely enhanced by the impressive and very detailed essay on historical background in the Presbyterian Church's 1974 pamphlet "The Middle East Conflict." But longstanding Christian tradition counters that narrative with a theological argument based partly on a selective reading of the New Testament. Levine argues that an objective reading of the New Testament in fact shows "no clear revocation of the promise of the Land, or of the covenant with the Jewish people."

As Ilan and Carol Troen detail elsewhere in their helpful essay "Indigeneity," especially in the new millennium, arguments about indigeneity have gained prominence in some debates about the Israeli-Palestinian conflict, most frequently as part of efforts to present Palestinians as the only true indigenous people in Israel: "it neatly defines Jews as invaders and the Jewish state as an intruding colonial-settler society in the service of an imperial mission" (20). The UN issued a Declaration on the Rights of Indigenous Peoples in 2007, but that failed to establish clear and legally binding definitions of the term. By contrast, the League of Nations' Mandate for Palestine, published in 1922, notably treated the Jews as re-establishing their ancient homeland in Palestine. Moreover, there is extensive textual and archeological evidence that documents the millennia-long Jewish presence in the area. Nothing comparable exists to document the shifting and often opportunistic Palestinian narratives about ancient residence, but that has not stopped exclusive claims on their behalf. The most poignant example has been the effort to claim indigeneity for the nomadic Bedouins of the Negev who ranged widely in the Middle East without establishing permanent sites of residence. Like many Palestinians, much of the modern Bedouin presence in the region likely dates to the nineteenth century. As this book will show, the claims about indigeneity surface in many anti-Zionist Christian books and essays. For those interested in reconciliation, however, those debates are counterproductive. The best route may simply be to agree that contemporary Jews and Palestinians both have legitimate claims to the land.

Since US foreign policy is often shaped at the presidential level, and since the US is Israel's major international sponsor, we include an overview by Daniel Friedman of presidential positions on Israel from Woodrow Wilson through Donald Trump and the ways they have been shaped by those presidents' Christian beliefs. A definitive account of the impact and legacy of the one-term Trump administration's policies about the Israeli-Palestinian conflict, however, will have to await events and the character of policies in the Biden administration. The new administration's policies will no doubt be partly shaped by the actions of all stakeholders though 2021 and thereafter. Nonetheless, it is clear that John Hagee and his Christians United for Israel "became the pre-ferred pro-Israel lobby group in the Trump administration," with the religious right gaining exceptional access to the White House (Hummel 209). Friedman also summarizes the state of American public opin-ion during these presidents' term of office. Robert Cathey contributes an essay that seeks to offer neutral and partly sympathetic readings of both Palestinian liberation theology, represented by Naim Ateek and Mitri Raheb, and of a thorough critique of those positions by Adam Gregerman. The index will enable readers to find other references to the same topics and writers elsewhere in the book and compare differing analyses of them.

Among the documents that receive detailed analysis here is the *Kairos Palestine Document* (2009), which has had a major influence on those Christian churches that have embraced the BDS movement. David Fox Sandmel devotes a chapter to *Kairos* that offers the most authoritative analysis it has yet received. Given the conflicting views of *Kairos Palestine* that have shaped its influence, we have in effect staged a debate about the text. Sandmel's authoritative reading is supplemented by Giovanni Mateo Quer's account of *Kairos Palestine*'s impact on Catholic groups and Robert A. Cathey's account of its role in Palestinian liberation theology. Part of what Cathey's chapter does is balance critiques of Palestinian liberation theology with an account of its self-understanding, without which our own understanding is inhib-ited. *Kairos* embodies the paradox or contradiction that shapes many anti-Zionist church documents. A fierce condemnation of Israeli policy crosses a line into a challenge to Israel's right to exist as a Jewish state. Yet its authors nonetheless feel theologically bound to say they do so while honoring Jesus's message of love, his legacy as the great reconciler, and his invitation to join a redemptive community. The same tensions structure the Methodist Church volume *Israel-Palestine: A Mission Study for 2007-2008* which will be discussed below.

As the essays about *Kairos* and everything else in *Peace and Faith* demonstrate, a church cannot address the Israeli-Palestinian conflict without simultaneously reflecting on and shaping its basic values, identity, and mission. As a result, church theory and practice call each other into question. How does one balance the project of reconciliation with the need to recognize injustices and correct them? Can condemnation and reconciliation—even love and hate—coexist in church religio-political judgments? What fundamental theological principles can or should inform a church's political projects? Do some religious principles have priority over and trump others? We cannot hope to give definitive answers to these questions, but we can raise them and try to imbue them with greater subtlety.

CONCLUSION: TOWARD DIALOGUE AND RECONCILIATION

The practical Christian goal for those participating in the dialogue is to calibrate the relationship between the core of both Israeli and Palestinian narratives so as to address Palestinian suffering without becoming anti-Israel. That opens a conversation about whether the Jewish state has failed to fulfill what many Christians see as its biblical imperative to act justly, despite there being no good secular reason why Israel should be held to a higher standard than any other nation. At this point the debate in mainline Protestant churches is confined to a conversation within the churches themselves—and often solely amongst their activist core. Their long-term strategy is nonetheless clear: to call into question whether or not there should be a Jewish state. That parallels the anti-Zionist discourses among many Islamic constituencies, a reality that must be addressed if reconciliation is to succeed.

The final supplementary opinion in *Peoples and Conflict in the Middle East* (1973) is by Wanis A. Simaan, a Fraternal Visitor to the

1972 Presbyterian General Assembly. Fraternal Visitors were representatives of the Church's missionary wing in the Middle East. "For too long," he writes, "Christian theologians as well as sentimental Christians" have "superimposed the framework of a twentieth century movement, [Zionism], . . . rooted in nineteenth century European nationalism, over the Biblical framework of the covenant . . . the two simply do not fit!" He continues, "A serious Christian understanding of the Old Testament does not expect nor does it find justification for the establishment of a Zionist Jewish state in modern Palestine" (113). He goes on to clarify that he is writing in explicit theological objection to the report's assertions that "the Abrahamic covenant is unconditional" and that the State of Israel is "a sign of the continuing relationship of God with the Jewish people" (115). "Israel may be 'a reminder of the vitality of Judaism,'" he adds, "but most of all it is a reminder of militant nationalism" (115-16). In another of the supplements, "God, Community, and Land: An Islamic Approach," Hassan Hanafi writes, "Israel is a white European implantation in the Middle East similar to the white European implantation in South Africa" (106). Hanafi ends by endorsing what we now call the one-state solution: "The only solution for the future in 'Palestine'—a secular, democratic, and free state where all humans can live without distinction of color, race, or religion. 'Palestine'—a multiracial, and multicolored state is the only possible hope for the future" (106). This utopian fantasy persists today in what Bernard Harrison calls "the absurd paradise of peace and mutual respect in a Muslim-majority successor state envisaged by protagonists of the 'one-state solution'" (293).

Included in the 1973 text, these supplements opposing the report were added as the compromise necessary to get the report published. They remind us of how long these views have circulated in the churches, and they testify to an emerging anti-Zionist wing in the Presbyterian Church (USA). James M. Fennelly, writing in opposition to Zionism in the first of the supplements, introduces a still more troubling racialized view: "The Jews claim to be the genuine people of the West Semite religious tradition, and the historical descendants, by faith, through race, of those who trysted with God on the Holy Land" (91). Writing in "Israel, The People, and The Land," R. J. Werblowsky of the Hebrew

University of Jerusalem is blunt in rebuttal: "the dissolution of the State of Israel implies, and is meant to imply, genocide" (112).

We believe reconciliation provides the theological and political context for a different way forward. Published as a manual for study, *Peoples and Conflict in the Middle East* concludes with some questions to guide local discussion. The last of these is among many that remain relevant today: "With a theological commitment to reconciliation, do you see particular opportunities for Christian mission and presence in the Middle East today? What form might it take?" (126) A revised and expanded set of questions conclude the following year's "The Middle East Conflict." There can be no better use of *Peace and Faith* than as a guide both to discussion and to decision-making.

This book overall supports an expanded interfaith engagement for the Christian mission in Israel and Palestine, one that builds on long-term interfaith dialogue projects and social services. We do believe mainline churches have a significant, if indirect, role to play in the resolution of the conflict. That role begins outside the holy land in promoting even-handed progressive thinking in the churches in members' home countries, then extends to outreach efforts to elected representatives. Faith leaders in all religions can play a mediating role in bringing people with opposing beliefs together in dialogue. That includes Christians, Jews, and Muslims, along with secular constituencies without strong religious identities. There is great need for sympathetic international promotion of productive ideas in the Holy Land itself. Distrust there is amplified by the anti-normalization agenda endorsed by the BDS movement and violently enforced by paramilitary Palestinian groups.

In the West, anti-normalization gives efforts to block Israeli speakers an aura of moral righteousness. But on the West Bank and elsewhere in the Arab world, claims that one is trying to "normalize" relations with Israel can rise to accusations of collaboration and treason. As I document in *Not in Kansas Anymore*, they can lead to assassination attempts or, in Gaza, formal executions. The campaigns against normalization predate the use of the term, dating at least to the Arab boycotts. The contemporary anti-normalization campaign got its boost when BDS adopted it as a principle and central tactic in 2005. As Giovanni Matteo Quer writes, "While the call to refrain from any cooperation with Israeli counterparts spread, peace initiatives promoting dialogue increasingly appeared on the [hostile] radar of BDS activists." Indeed, he points out that "the anti-normalization discourse unites Palestinian groups of diverse ideological orientations." The BDS anti-normalization campaign "is opposed to any form of relationship, no matter how peripheral, with Israel, rejecting its existence not just as a polity but also as a society" ("Furthering Anti-Normalization" 71, 72, 73).

There are thus real limits to the work Israelis and Palestinians themselves can do in promoting new strategies and ideas. Concerned Christians are among those who can intervene to put new thinking on the table; that begins with small group and individual efforts that encourage people to set aside hostilities and learn to think differently. But BDS-allied Christian groups commonly adopt anti-normalization principles and refuse the peacebuilding initiatives that have been fundamental for Christian practice. The projects summarized by Michael Gizzi in Chapter Fifteen have a history of success in reconciliation and offer concerned readers organized options to join that work.

In May 2010, Presbyterians Concerned for Jewish, Christian, and Muslim Relations—a group that would evolve to become Presbyterians for Middle East Peace—issued "A Critique of *A Steadfast Hope: The Palestinian Quest for Just Peace*," which had been published by the church's anti-Zionist wing the previous year.[5] "A Critique's" standards for debate among Presbyterians and its condemnation of one-sided anti-Israel publications are applicable to every denomination:

> Any policies that Presbyterians hope to advance depend upon a trustworthy rendering of both the Israeli and Palestinian experience, and no report is morally viable that allows one viewpoint to eclipse all others . . . . Without an awareness of the range of religious, ethnic, and political viewpoints, Presbyterians will pursue simplistic and misleading solutions that only deepen antipathies and undermine our credibility . . . . the Israel/Palestine Mission Network is charting a course that abandons the denomination's historic role as an impartial advocate for peace informed by the legitimate claims of both Palestinians and Israeli Jews . . . . A skewed historical reading results in a call to action that excoriates Israelis and exonerates Palestinians. There are no moral standards defined

in these materials to which both parties are held accountable . . . .
We need to hear the hopes and fears of peoples who live on opposite
sides of the separation wall. (1-3).

As this book will make clear, however, there is more than one
separation wall at stake here. There is the wall that separates Israelis
and Palestinians, but there is also the more ancient division at stake
between Christians and Jews and between Christians and Muslims. In
that context, I conclude this introduction by citing some of the recommendations for interfaith dialogue made by Rabbi James Rudin, at
the time director of the American Jewish Committee's Department of
Interreligious Affairs, and then revising a few of the core principles of
the "Dialogue Decalogue," also originally designed to address interfaith
relations, to function simultaneously for interchanges between Israelis
and Palestinians.

Rudin urged us to recognize that "dialogue is a lifelong process, not
a 'quick fix.'" We have to "seek areas of solidarity and mutual respect"
and not "try to change people's minds; concentrate on enlightenment,
explanation and clarification" (226-27). Certainly in Israel, "dialogue
is not a luxury, but rather a necessity"; it is "no longer enough . . . to
simply live side by side in a kind of de facto coexistence" (231).[6] As
Leonard Swidler has written, "dialogue is not debate. In dialogue each
partner must listen to the other as openly and sympathetically as s/he
can in an attempt to understand the other's position as precisely and,
as it were, as much from within, as possible." "Such an attitude," he
continues, "automatically includes the assumption that at any point we
might find the partner's position so persuasive that, if we would act with
integrity, we would have to change, and change can be disturbing."
Here are some principles adapted from the Decalogue:

FIRST PRINCIPLE: The primary purpose of dialogue is to learn,
that is, to change and grow in the perception and understanding of
reality, and then to act accordingly.

SECOND PRINCIPLE: Dialogue must be a two-sided project:
both between religious/ideological/national groups, and within
religious/ideological/national groups (inter- and intra-).

THIRD PRINCIPLE: It is imperative that each participant
comes to the dialogue with maximum honesty and sincerity. That

means recognizing the major elements of your own beliefs and group narratives, but also the doubts you may harbor about them.

FOURTH PRINCIPLE: The temptation to contrast your own ideals with your opposite number's practices should be resisted. Ideals should be compared with ideals, practices with practices.

FIFTH PRINCIPLE: Each participant must commit to frank and open self-description.

SIXTH PRINCIPLE: Participants should not engage in dialogue by imposing any preconceptions about where the points of disagreement lie.

SEVENTH PRINCIPLE: Successful dialogue can take place only between equals, which means that partners learn from each other, not merely seek to teach or correct one another.

EIGTH PRINCIPLE: Dialogue can only take place on the basis of mutual trust. Trust between groups or communities is based in personal trust.

NINTH PRINCIPLE: Participants in dialogue should take on a healthy level of criticism about their own traditions or national narratives. Failing to do so suggests that your own tradition has all the answers, thus making dialogue pointless.

TENTH PRINCIPLE: To understand another religion or national experience one must learn to experience it from within, to experience the other's point of view.

If the goal of dialogue is reconciliation and ultimately peace, perhaps this introduction should conclude by acknowledging how complex, multifaceted, and fraught reconciliation is in both the Holy Land and the West. As an example of dialogue at its most fraught, one may cite the rapprochement with Christian Zionism:

Not an idealistic reconciliation of radical concession and change, but a reconciliation of historical antipathies redirected toward cooperation—yes, full of half-compromises, backtracking, novelties in language, and defensive maneuvers, but producing through pressures, power struggles, alliances, and argument some observable transformations and political results. This less lofty understanding of reconciliation nevertheless captures the mix of pragmatism and idealism that animates evangelical support for the state of Israel, and evangelical existence more broadly. (Hummel 238)

In the Holy Land, moreover, reconciliation can be branded as collaboration and put its advocates at bodily risk. But it takes a certain amount of courage, even in Europe and the Americas, to resist social pressures and risk ostracization by anti-Zionist colleagues by choosing reconciliation and rejecting demonization. As we learned both in recruiting contributors to and even in inviting endorsements for the book, moreover, a willingness to speak in favor of reconciliation within your faith community does not guarantee willingness to speak to a broad interdenominational public audience. I remain astonished at what we finally saw as the need to seek contributors and endorsers who were fearless. Untenured faculty were willing to read the manuscript and comment in detail in confidence, but not one was prepared to take the risk of contributing to a collection sympathetic to the Jewish state.

Yet reconciliation has deep roots in Christian and Jewish tradition. If reconciliation is to involve both the Christian and Jewish audiences this book addresses, however, it can only do so by building on the reconciliation efforts at work since *Nostra Aetate*. But of course Holy Land projects implicate Muslim and secular audiences as well. Detailing the history of both Muslim/Christian and Muslim/Jewish relations would be the project of another book, one that would require its own timelines.[7] But that task is nonetheless essential. Only if that history is credited, however, can either Christians or Jews hope to engage the element of supersessionism in Islam with success.

Although the word "reconciliation" does not appear in the *Torah*, the *Old Testament*, as Sheldon Lewis documents in *Torah of Reconciliation*, offers numerous examples of reconciliation at work, among them Jacob returning home and reconciling with Esau, and Joseph reconciling with his brothers despite the harms they had done to him. Christians bring to this challenge both a theology and a practice of reconciliation embedded in the lesson of how Jesus lived his life. Jewish peacemaking traditions as well have long embraced principles of reconciliation as fundamental.

Christians approach reconciliation theologically as part of a particular belief system: whether between man and God or between human beings, the opportunity for reconciliation is established through the death and resurrection of Jesus Christ. Salvation through reconciliation brings to an end the estrangement, brought about through sin, between God and human beings. But reconciliation also implies a standard of human conduct, the exercise of human responsibility modeled on Jesus's teachings and his way of life. The Torah and the New Testament have important passages that guide human conduct in comparable ways. Leviticus 19:19 commands "And you shall love your fellow man as yourself," while Matthew 7:12 advises "Therefore whatever you want men to do to you, do also to them." Judaism and Christianity have long traditions that flow from these and other passages. The principle of reconciliation calls on us to abandon enmity, wrath, and war and embrace friendship, love, and peace. In that context, reconciliation empowers interfaith relations and relations between peoples. It is a path to a different future.

PART ONE:

THE HOLY LAND AND THE POLITICS OF RELIGIOUS BELIEF

CHAPTER ONE

EDWARD KESSLER

CHRISTIANITY, JEWS, AND JUDAISM

INTRODUCTION

This chapter reflects on four key moments in the history of Jewish-Christian Relations. Since the Bible establishes a fundamental connection between Jews and Christians, and since both groups lived—and continue to live—in a biblically-orientated culture, Part One reflects on changing attitudes towards Jesus the Jew, as well as Saul of Tarsus, and their implications for Christian self-understanding as well as for Jewish-Christian Relations. One of the certainties about Jesus and Saul is that they were Jews, the children of Jewish parents, brought up in

Jewish homes and raised in accordance with Jewish tradition. Jesus lived among Jews throughout his life and his followers were Jews. Indeed, no other Jew in history has rivalled Jesus in the magnitude of his influence. Of course, the death of Jesus cannot have for Jews the same significance as for Christians, and Paul's writings on its significance, particularly Romans 9:11, remain important to relations today.

Part Two explores the writings of the church fathers and the rabbis, notably polemical texts and what became known as the *Adversus Judeaos* tradition. However, these polemics—which, though unbalanced, went in both directions—are not the only story worth recounting about the patristic-rabbinic relationship. This section also reflects briefly on Jewish and Christian biblical interpretation and shows that both Jews and Christians asked the same question of the biblical text and were very close readers of Scripture. It is possible to uncover an exegetical encounter between Jewish and Christian biblical commentators in which each side was aware of the other's interpretations, for good and for ill.

Parts Three and Four explore the two issues that have dominated relations since the end of the Second World War: antisemitism and the Shoah and the significance of Zionism and that State of Israel. Both the Shoah and the creation of the State of Israel instilled an intense desire amongst many Christians and Jews to learn about their shared history, theology, and other aspects of Jewish-Christian relations. At the same time, allowing these two immense events to be the only topics for discussion between Jews and Christians brings a certain danger, which I will attend to shortly.

For example, the need to confront the Holocaust is self-evident and needs to be placed in perspective. Emil Fackenheim's proclamation in *The Jewish Bible After the Holocaust* that the Shoah resulted in a new commandment, the 614th, which stressed that it was incumbent upon Jews to survive as Jews, is a case in point. As a result, Jewish identity can easily become Shoah-centered, as can Jewish-Christian relations. While the reaction to the Shoah is an important driving force, positive relations cannot be built solely on responses to antisemitism and Christian guilt.

A similar set of concerns emerge regarding the State of Israel. After more than 70 years of sometimes perilous existence, Israel is no longer a recent creation and, since the large *aliyah* from the former Soviet Union in the 1980s and 1990s, no longer attracts comparable numbers of Jewish immigrants, though the resurgence of anti-Semitism in Europe is certainly having an impact. For much of the last decade, surveys suggest French Jews are considering emigration because of anti-Semitism and a series of violent assaults (Yardena Schwartz). While Israel will retain an important place in the Jewish-Christian relationship of the future, especially as the resolution of the Israeli-Palestinian conflict remains uncertain and the gap between Israel and the Jewish Diaspora widens, other topics of mutual interest to Jews and Christians may acquire equal status. Long-term, global warming will pose challenges to the Middle East that will alter many of the region's priorities.

One potential topic for discussion is the need for both Jews and Christians to abandon their tendency to pursue a mutually exclusive search for the one and only correct meaning of a sacred text. Rather it is essential to examine, as the rabbinic and Christian Syriac hermeneutical traditions have done, a number of different interpretations, each with its own context. The Jewish-Christian encounter should aspire to a higher degree of maturity, to allowing contradictory interpretations to co-exist, without pretending that they can be made compatible. In other words, both groups must recognize that the "plain and obvious interpretation" of the text does not hold its final meaning.

PART ONE:
JESUS, PAUL, AND JUDAISM
JESUS

Biblical scholars have spent an impressive amount of energy on the search for the historical Jesus; much of that search has revolved around his Jewishness. The identity of Jesus needs to be dealt with first because by definition Christians must take a different position on his identity than do Jews. The cleavage between Jews and Christians is determined by the fact that, from the first century CE, Christians accepted Jesus as God's Messiah. Jews did not then and never have.

"Whom do men say that I am?" Jesus once asked his disciples (Matthew 16:13). The answers varied, which reveals how little consensus over his identity there was even in his own time. A brief glance at recent scholarship indicates that many are still on this elusive trail and are as far from consensus as were the disciples. At the same time, nearly everyone agrees that Jesus was born a Jew, raised a Jew, educated as a Jew, and died a Jew. He was indicted by Pontius Pilate as "king of the Jews," and condemned to death as such.

There were many ways to be Jewish in the first century. According to Josephus, four groups existed: Pharisees; Sadducees; Essenes; and Zealots (*Antiquities* 18:1). With which did Jesus have dealings? The Gospels never mention the Essenes, although the Dead Sea Scrolls parallel some of the teachings of John the Baptist (such as the proximity of the Final Judgment and the symbolic use of ablutions to depict turning from sin). Like the Essenes, John was also an ascetic.

Jews referred to as Zealots were active from the time of the Maccabees until the last Jewish revolt against Rome in 135 CE. Josephus accuses them of destroying the Temple in the war against Rome, kidnapping Jews as hostages, and killing people they regarded as traitors during the first century CE. The Zealots are hardly mentioned in the New Testament, although Luke includes Simon the Zealot among the twelve disciples.

The Gospels make clear that Jesus's major dealings were with Pharisees and Sadducees. Both groups were in existence by the second century BCE. Josephus lists the Sadducees as one of the "three philosophies" (alongside Pharisees and Essenes). They are mentioned in the New Testament in polemics with Jesus (e.g. Mark 12:18–27 and others), and as members of the Sanhedrin that tried Paul (Acts 23:7–8). They became a powerful faction in Judean politics, but seem not to have survived the destruction of Jerusalem in 70 CE, although this may simply reflect our lack of sources for the post-70 CE period. Sadducees were mainly wealthy aristocrats, but the assumption that they were all priests or that all priests were Sadducees (a traditional extrapolation from Acts 5:17) has now been largely discarded. For example, Josephus, a priest, was a Pharisee. The Sadducees were associated with worship at the Temple in Jerusalem and collaborated with Greek and then Roman rule.

The Pharisees—other than the Jewish followers of Jesus—were the only major Jewish group to survive the Jewish rebellion against Rome. After the Temple was destroyed in 70 CE, they began to reconstruct the Jewish faith and so became known as the fathers of Rabbinic Judaism. They placed a heavy emphasis on the oral, as well as the written, Torah, and developed interpretations that laypeople could observe in whatever context they lived. The Pharisees considered themselves the authentic followers of Moses and Ezra, adapting old codes for new conditions.

Josephus claims to have chosen to join the Pharisees, but his writings always refer to the group in the third person (*Life* 12). In the New Testament, the Pharisees are prominent as the main rivals of Jesus in the gospel accounts of his ministry. The conflict between Jesus and the Pharisees generally centers on interpretation of the Torah, especially in terms of observing the Sabbath, dietary laws and issues of purity. Interestingly however, the Pharisees are notably absent from the Passion narratives.

Crucially, for all the differences between the divergent interpretations of Judaism of that time, they also had much in common. Two convictions especially bound Jews together. The first was a belief in the one and only God, who accepted no rivals. God made behavioral demands of his people, so Jewish faith could be described as ethical monotheism. The second was that God had entered into a special covenantal relationship with Jews. In the call of Abraham, the Exodus from Egypt, and the giving of the Torah on Sinai, God had elected and chosen his own people.

Naturally, the question as to why Jews rejected the Messiah became the fundamental preoccupation of New Testament writers who insisted, one way or another, on continuity between the Church and Israel. In time, the interpretation of texts became the subject of debate because, while Jews and Christians accepted that some passages referred to the coming of the Messiah, the latter believed them to be fulfilled by Jesus and the former did not. In addition, Christians referred to other texts, which had not previously been viewed as messianic, to explain why the Messiah, who had been expected to bring a Jewish triumph over Rome, suffered and was crucified. An example of this can been seen in the messianic interpretation of Psalm 118:22-3 found in Acts 4:11.

Jesus shared many of the central convictions of the Pharisees, but the beliefs of his early followers—specifically, that he was Messiah and Son of God—led to a parting of the ways with them, as well as with other Jewish groups, which helps explain why the pages of the Gospels are rife with hostility towards the Pharisees.

The New Testament shares an intrinsic problem that is common to the Tanakh (and the Qur'an), namely, that polemic against a named Other, once enshrined in documents venerated as Scripture, carries weight and authority throughout history. Moreover, it is constantly available for use or abuse, to justify the most appalling actions in the name of God. Their very existence is and remains the problem, for they cannot simply be expurgated or interpreted out of existence.

In the New Testament, the problem is increased by the fact that Jesus was a Jew who taught his fellow Jews, some of whom followed his teaching and some who did not. Most of his contemporaries, of course, had never heard of him. After his death, his Jewish followers, encouraged by their experience of the resurrection, argued for the validity of his teaching against their fellow Jews who had not been persuaded. To complicate the position further, Jesus's Jewish followers argued amongst themselves about the conditions under which Gentiles might be admitted to this new Jewish movement. In addition, some of the Jewish communities within the Jesus movement—with or without Gentile members—found themselves at odds with other Jews over issues such as halakhic observance and claims about Jesus.

The New Testament bears witness to all of this and many of the texts depict the debates and arguments taking place. These disputes were serious, vigorous, and often bitter. Yet what must not be forgotten—but which over time almost was—is that the arguments were between Jews, about a Jew and about Jewish issues (even when they concerned gentile converts).

The problem of polemic is magnified greatly when the passages are read as if they are Christian arguments against Jews. To read them this way is to misread them, and this misreading later led to what is known as the Christian "teaching of contempt" (*L'enseignement du mepris* in the words of Jules Isaac) for Jews and Judaism.

SAUL OF TARSUS

As the first Christian missionary to the Gentile world, Saul plays a unique role in Jewish–Christian relations. Convinced that God had called Gentiles to be members of his people, Paul insisted that what had happened through the death and resurrection of Christ was the fulfilment of God's promises to Israel. Tragically, later generations read his letters out of context, and so lost sight of his emphasis on continuity, misinterpreting his words as an attack on Judaism.

The passionate zeal and intellectual strength of Saul of Tarsus, who became Paul the Apostle, helped Christianity flourish. Paul's conviction that he was "in Christ" provided the spiritual energy to match his intellect. In a short space of time, Paul covered the eastern Roman Empire. In the midst of all this, his relationship to Judaism remained stronger than has often been acknowledged. Paul's identity was that of a Jew who, through a variety of circumstances, came to the conviction that Jesus was the Messiah. According to Luke, he was present at the stoning of Stephen; he himself testifies that, in his religious zeal, he did not hesitate to persecute Christians (Galatians 1:13, "how savagely I persecuted the church of God"). While on his way to Damascus, Paul had a transformative experience when he had a vision of Jesus and converted to Christianity. After a lengthy stay in Arabia, he emerged with a strong commitment to the Christian way of life.

Some scholars have tried to understand Paul on the basis of Stoic and Cynic trends, rather than from the perspective of Judaism. However, Paul writes as a concerned Jew, such as when he describes the conditions of his people by saying that "a hardening in part" has come upon Israel (Romans 11:25). He does not reject all of Israel, but laments that many Jews have rejected the Messiah. Nevertheless, he is convinced that "all of Israel will be saved" (Romans 11:26).

Paul reflects on whether the Jewish people are still the chosen people even though most Jews rejected Jesus as Messiah. With reference to Scripture, he argues this way and that. He insists, alluding to Isaiah's doctrine of the remnant, that a holy remnant remains, even though a large number have failed (Romans 11:5). Here, the remnant he envisages must be the Christians. But later in the same chapter he invokes the image of the olive tree. The old branches have been cut off to make way for the grafting in of new branches from a wild olive. Paul is quite clear that the choice of Israel by God can never be revoked: "If you, cut from what was by nature a wild olive, can be grafted unnaturally onto a cultivated olive, how much more will the branches which naturally belong there be grafted onto the olive tree which is their own?" (Romans 11:28-29) All right for the end-time. Israel remains the Chosen People and will be grafted back. But what, in Christian eyes, is the status of Judaism at the moment? The trouble is that this horticultural image does not work. Once branches are cut off, they are dead and cannot be grafted back after an interval—unless of course they develop a life of their own. It is perhaps for this reason that Paul ends by throwing up his hands in despair and proclaiming, "How rich and deep are the wisdom and knowledge of God, how incomprehensible his decisions and how unfollowable his ways!" (Romans 11:33).

Further research and reflection raise one particularly controversial question in contemporary Jewish-Christian studies: what of the ongoing validity of God's covenant with the Jewish people? A growing number of scholars reject the simple and straightforward notion of the Church as the New Israel, replacing the Old as inheritors of God's promises. They do so on the grounds of God's faithfulness. Would God renege on his word? If he has done so with regard to Jews, what guarantee is there for the churches that he won't do so again, to Christians this time?

One counterargument is that covenantal faithfulness is a two-way process: if Jews have not kept faith with God, then God has a perfect right to cast them off. It is interesting that Christians who argue this way have not often drawn the same deduction about Christian faithfulness, which has not been a notable and consistent characteristic of the last two millennia. Actually, God seems to have had a remarkable ability to keep faith with both Christians and Jews when they have not kept faith with Him, a point of which Paul is profoundly aware in Romans 9-11. There, he admits that God has temporarily suspended Israel's privileges as his chosen people, for a number of reasons, not least because "a hardening has come upon a part of Israel" (11:25). Yet he goes out of his way to deny claims that God has rejected people whom he foreknew (11:2) and asserts that their stumbling does not lead to their fall (11:11). And in 11:28, he proclaims that "the gift and the call of God are irrevocable."

PART TWO:
THE RABBIS AND
THE CHURCH FATHERS
CHURCH FATHERS

The writings of the church further illustrate a paradox which still underlies Jewish-Christian relations today. On the one hand, Jesus was born, lived, and died a Jew; the first Christians were Jews. On the other hand, Jews refused to recognize Jesus as the Messiah and attacked Christians for their misrepresentation of the Hebrew Scriptures. As far as Jews were concerned, the Messiah had not appeared, and Jesus was simply one of a number of self-proclaimed and false messiahs.

The Jewish rejection was extremely embarrassing for the early church and caused particular difficulties in its relationship with paganism. This was especially problematic because pagans were generally sympathetic to older religions and were repulsed by all things new. In their view, antiquity was equivalent to respectability, so the people of Israel were admired by a number of pagan writers on that ground. Pagan critics, such as Celsus, were quick to exploit the Jewish rejection of Christianity in their polemical writings. Celsus accused Christians of deserting Judaism even though they claimed to be faithful. In response to pagan as well as Jewish criticism, the writings of the church fathers demonstrate increasingly hardened attitudes towards Jews and Judaism. The Jew, as encountered in the pages of many of the church fathers, is not really a human being at all; at best he is an opponent and, at worst, a monster. As a result, it is often difficult to judge whether the polemical writings of the church, known as the *Adversus Judaeos* literature, illustrate a real encounter with Jews and Judaism.

The tension and growing separation between Judaism and Christianity resulted in the Early Church insisting simultaneously on the continuity as well as the discontinuity of the Old Testament and the New Testament. Continuity centered upon the claim that the God of the Hebrew Bible was the same as the God of Christ, whereas discontinuity derived from the belief that the Hebrew Bible actually pointed to a future event—to Christ.

Justin Martyr's *Dialogue with Trypho,* written around 150 CE, demonstrates the early church's view of the Scriptures. Scholars disagree as to whether there actually existed a Jew called Trypho with whom Justin debated but, at the very least, Justin records contemporary debates with Jews through the mouth of Trypho. He is also one of the first Christian authors to lay exclusive claim to the Hebrew Scriptures on the grounds that only Christians could offer correct interpretations:

> Let all of us Gentiles come together and glorify God, because He has looked down upon us; let us glorify Him by the King of glory, by the Lord of hosts. For He hath taken pleasure even in the nations, and He receives the sacrifices more gladly from us than from you. What account should I, to whom God has borne testimony, then take of circumcision? What need of that other baptism to one, who has been baptized by the Holy Spirit? I think that by these arguments I shall be able to persuade even those who are of slight intelligence. For the words have not been fitted together by me, nor adorned by human art, but they were sung by David, proclaimed as good news by Isaiah, preached by Zechariah, written down by Moses. You recognize them, Trypho? They are laid up in your scriptures, or rather, not in yours but in ours, for we obey them, but you, when you read, do not understand their sense. (Justin 29)

Others explained the Jewish relationship with the Scriptures slightly differently. For Augustine, in Enarratione on Psalm 40:14, Jews were "satchel bearers ... who carry the books for us who study them." Before then, Melito of Sardis, who lived in the second half of the second century, marked the transition toward a more accusatory relationship. Since Jews rejected Christ, he argued, they themselves were to be rejected. Indeed, not only had they rejected Christ, they had also killed him. Melito's emphasis on Jewish culpability is not unusual among early Christian writers, but one is struck by his sharp language and preoccupation with Israel's "crime." Christianity therefore is not wholly new, but it is the wholly new Israel. The synagogue gives way to the Church and the Law concedes power to the Gospel.

I will cite one further example from the church fathers, John Chrysostom, who preached in Antioch, where, according to Luke 11:26, "they first called the disciples 'Christians.'" During the lifetime of Chrysostom, in the latter half of the fourth century CE, Antioch was a pluralist city with Jews, Christians, and pagans living within its confines. Chrysostom delivered eight sermons, *Adversus Iudaeos*, in 386-87, and they demonstrate an antipathy to Jews and Judaism at an early stage of his career. They arise out of a fear of the vitality of Judaism, which threatened his authority. In his view Judaism and Christianity existed in a state of competition. He complained that Christians admired Jewish observance, participated in the Jewish festivals and fasts, and believed that synagogues were endowed with numinous aura. While his response was to attack the Christian Judaizer, the Jew became the victim.

Of course, we should remember that invective was not to be taken literally by the listeners, who would have regarded it as a form of entertainment. Nor were there angry crowds storming the synagogue as a result of Chrysostom's sermons; he simply aimed to win back Christians. He similarly attacked other groups (e.g., heretics, pagans) but the impact of Chrysostom's sermons can be seen in later generations who enjoyed his rhetoric but either did not recognize or ignored oratorical conventions of his time. Sections of the homilies were excerpted into Byzantine liturgy for Holy Week and later writers drew freely from the homilies. They were translated into Russian in the eleventh century (in the time of the first pogrom in Russian history under Prince Vladimir) and were read in medieval Europe, in Byzantium, and in Russia when Christianity was the dominant religion and Jews were subject to repressive laws. In sum, Chrysostom's *Adversus Iudaeos* sermons were used to support and encourage anti-Jewish attitudes in the Church.

Chrysostom protested that the synagogue was not an acceptable place to take an oath as it was the home of idolatry and the devil; the idea of going to synagogue was itself blasphemous. Jews, he argued, had a long history of rebellion and wrongdoing and, as a result, all the curses of Scripture were interpreted as referring to Jews and the blessings to Christians. Simply put, in the eyes of the Church fathers while Judaism languished, Christianity flourished and in particular, the responsibility for the death of Christ became firmly associated with the election of the Gentile Church. Central to the patristic argument is that Jews and Gentiles suffer a reversal of roles: the historical Israelites cease to be Israelites while the faithful Gentiles become the New Israel.

THE RABBIS

The rabbis were the successors of the Pharisees, and their success enabled Jews to survive without a homeland. Unlike other Jewish groups, it was the rabbis' ability to respond to the fall of Jerusalem and the Temple in 70 CE that enabled them, eventually, to dominate Jewish life. The date of the split between Judaism and Christianity has been the subject of much debate. Some scholars see it beginning as early as the time of Saul of Tarsus, others as late as Constantine. James Dunn has suggested that the separation between Judaism and Christianity should be described as "the partings of the ways." The view of this author is that the final separation between Judaism and Christianity was later than Constantine, demonstrated by Christian support for, socializing with, and even participating in Jewish religious activities in late-fourth-century Antioch.

There are few references to Jesus or Christianity in the rabbinic writings, and those texts that do exist rarely make direct reference. Jesus is referred to by different titles and names, which include ben Stada, ben Pandira, and Balaam. Occasionally, we find in the earliest manuscripts an explicit reference to Jeshu and/or Jeshu ha-Notzri (Nazarene). The rabbis and later editors were careful to cover their tracks and to avoid, as much as was possible, direct mention, so as to evade Christian detection and censorship. As Christianity was becoming more dominant, Jews and Judaism were becoming increasingly marginalized, and it may not be coincidental that the Jerusalem Talmud was redacted and written down at the end of the fourth century and the Babylonian Talmud at the end of the fifth—i.e., during the time Christianity was becoming more powerful and anti-Jewish legislation was being enacted.

Rabbinic knowledge about the historical Jesus is limited, based on hearsay and discussions with Jewish-Christians rather than on oral traditions linked to discussions with Jesus himself. The rabbis' understanding of Jesus is thus confused and conflicting. Their depiction, however, does tell us something about relations, especially arguments with the Jewish-Christians. The references to and stories about Jesus and the Gospel traditions indicate from the Jewish perspective the bitterness that was developing between the two communities in the early centuries of the Common Era.

In one passage (JT Ta'anit 65b) the rabbis commented on Numbers 23:19, "God is not a man that he should lie, nor the son of man that he should repent. Has he said and shall He not do it? Or has He spoken and shall not make it good?" Rabbi Abahu of the third century CE, known for his opposition to the minim [heretics], interprets this verse as a rejection of the divinity of Jesus and the claims of his followers:

> R. Abahu said: If a man says to you "I am God" he is a liar; if he says, "I am the son of man," in the end people will laugh at him; if he says, "I will go up to heaven," he says, "but shall not perform it."

Another example comes from an eighth century CE midrash, *Aggadat Bereshit*:

> How foolish is the heart of the minim, who say that the Holy One, Blessed be He, has a son. If, in the case of Abraham's son, when He saw that he was ready to slay him, He could not bear to look on in anguish, but on the contrary at once commanded, "do not lay your hand on the lad"; had He had a son, would He have abandoned him? Would He not have turned the world upside down and reduced it to tohu v'vohu. (chapter 31)

Rabbinic hostility was directed towards the figure of Jesus, but of the historical person little (if any) trace remains. His life was depicted as one of deceit and heresy and his death was fit for a criminal. In the rabbinic mind the person of Jesus and his actions caused the secession from their midst of a new and potentially life-threatening religion. When the rabbis accused Jesus of deceiving Israel, they meant it literally, for Christianity had not only resulted in some Jews "going astray," it also seemed to threaten Judaism's very existence.

EXEGETICAL ENCOUNTER

For all the polemic, both the rabbis and church fathers lived (and Jews and Christians continue to live) in a biblically-orientated culture, which resulted in similarities between Jewish and Christian approaches to Scripture. There is a joint insistence on the harmony of scripture and an emphasis on the unity of the text. Consequently, many Jewish and Christian interpretations were understandable to adherents of both religions. This explains why some church fathers, such as Origen and Jerome, turned to Jewish contemporaries for help in translating biblical texts. Although the rabbis and the church fathers developed their own distinctive methods, their approaches to the Bible would not have prevented particular interpretations from being understood in both communities.

They often asked the same questions of the biblical text because they were close readers and interested in the detail of Scripture. This is illustrated by Origen who, in Homilies on Genesis 8:1, commended his community to "observe each detail of Scripture, which has been written. For, if one knows how to dig into the depth, he will find a treasure in the details." It is not entirely by chance that Origen uses the metaphor of "digging" beneath the text. The metaphor also aptly describes the rabbinic approach, which likewise seeks to derive meaning from each detail of Scripture. For example, in *On Psalm 1:4*, Origen wrote that, "the wisdom of God pervades every divinely inspired writing, reaching out to each single letter." Similarly in the Mishnah, Avot 5:21, Rabbi Ben Bag-Bag who lived in the first century CE famously stated "turn, turn and turn it again, and you will find something new in it."

Sometimes Jewish and Christian exegesis demonstrates a live encounter. For example, note how Justin and Genesis Rabbah discussed circumcision:

> Justin (Dialogue 9): This circumcision is not, however, necessary for all men, but for you alone, in order that, as I have already said, you may suffer these things which you now suffer justly. Nor do we receive that useless baptism of cisterns, for it has nothing to do with the baptism of life. Wherefore God has also announced that you have forsaken Him, the living fountain, and digged for yourselves broken cisterns which can hold no water. Even you, who are the circumcised according to the flesh, have no need of our circumcision; but we, having the latter, do not require the former.

For if it were necessary, as you suppose, God would not have made Adam uncircumcised . . .

Genesis Rabbah (11.6): A Philosopher asked Rabbi Hoshaya: "If circumcision is so precious, why was it not given to Adam? . . . [R. Hoshaya replied]: "whatever was created in the first six days requires further preparation, e.g. mustard needs sweetening, vetches need sweetening, wheat needs grinding, and man too needs to be finished off."

Another example is the interpretation of Genesis 1:27, and the phrase, "let us make man." In *Dialogue 62*, Justin demonstrates awareness of Jewish interpretations when he complains to Trypho that

you [i.e., Jewish interpreters] may not, by changing the words already quoted, say what your teachers say, either that God said to Himself, "Let us make . . . "as we also, when we are about to make anything, often say, "Let us make" to ourselves; or that God said, "Let us make . . . " to the elements, namely the earth and such like, out of which we understood that man has come into being.

An exegetical encounter is confirmed by Genesis Rabbah 8.3:

"And God said, let us make man..." With whom did He take counsel? Rabbi Joshua ben Levi said, "He took counsel with the works of heaven and earth, like a king who had two advisors without whose knowledge he did nothing whatsoever . . . Rabbi Ammi said, "He took counsel with His own heart." It may be compared to a king who had a palace built by an architect.

PART THREE: ANTISEMITISM AND THE HOLOCAUST: ENCOUNTERING SCRIPTURE IN LIGHT OF THE SHOAH

How should Jews and Christians read the Bible after the Shoah? The significance of this question is sharpened by the fact that, in the first half of the twentieth century, Germany was one of the most biblically literate countries in the world, renowned for its highly developed biblical scholarship.

Jewish approaches fall into two categories. The first, represented by the philosopher Emil Fackenheim, the theologian Richard Rubenstein, and the novelist Elie Wiesel, argues that the Shoah resulted in a "rupture" in the relationship between Jews and God and a consequent distancing from Scripture. Richard Rubenstein offers an "atheistic" reaction in his "death of God" theology. In the first edition of *After Auschwitz* in 1966, he states that the Shoah had buried any possibility of continued belief in a covenantal God of history, but that Jews should speak in terms of an earthly existence. In the 1992 second edition Rubenstein offers a more mystical approach but, according to John Roth, Rubenstein re-affirms a view of God quite different from the mainstream view of biblical and rabbinic Judaism and spurns the notion that the Jews are in any sense a people either chosen or rejected by God.

The second approach—represented by Jacob Neusner, Eliezer Berkovits, and Michael Wyschogrod—is to view events between 1933 and 1945 like other periods of extreme Jewish suffering. Wyschogrod famously stated that "the voices of the prophets speak more loudly than did Hitler." In other words, traditional biblical interpretation provides the means by which to reflect on the Shoah.

Martin Buber holds a middle position; he calls for a struggle with the biblical text, before seeking to come to terms with it. In 1926, he wrote that: "The generations are by no means ready to listen to what the book has to say, and to obey it; they are often vexed and defiant; nevertheless, the preoccupation with this book is part of their life, and they face it in a real world." Yet in 1953 in *The Eclipse of God* Buber asks, "dare we recommend to the survivors of Auschwitz, to the Job of the gas chambers, 'thank ye the Lord for He is good, for His mercy endures forever?' (Psalm 111:1)." Adopting the phrase "eclipse of God" (*hester panim*) as a means of describing the Shoah he suggested that: "What is it that we mean when we speak of an eclipse of God which is even now taking place? Through this metaphor we make the tremendous assumption that we can glance up to the sun, and that something can step between our existence and His as between the earth and the sun."

A number of Christian scholars interpreted the Shoah in terms deliberately reminiscent of biblical language. James Moore, for example, described it as a "new revelation." Similarly, Stephen Smith, Director of the Spielberg Foundation, argued that Christians' failure to speak out against the Nazi treatment of Jews implicates the church as an accessory to Nazi actions. As a result, the Shoah is a Christian "problem" demanding a Christian response. Catholic social ethicist John Pawlikowski puts it differently, stating that "the Holocaust has made it immoral for Christians to maintain any Christology that is excessively triumphalistic or that finds the significance of the Christ Event in the displacement of the Jewish People from an ongoing covenantal relationship with God" ("Christology").

MULTIPLE INTERPRETATIONS: A WAY FORWARD

The Rabbinic Bible, the *Mikraot Gedolot*, with its commentaries spanning the centuries ranged around the biblical text, is rightly regarded as a celebration of Jewish exegesis and of the enduring, elusive nature of the debate about the meaning of Scripture. The willingness of the rabbis to accept a multitude of different possible meanings, in marked contrast to a single "authentic" meaning, backed by clerical or scholarly authority, is of great value in reading the Bible in light of the Shoah.

A rabbinic basis for asserting the value of offering different interpretations, each of which claims validity, can be found in the tractate Sanhedrin 34a in the Babylonian Talmud:

"In the School of Rabbi Ishmael, it is taught: 'See, my word is like fire, an oracle of the Eternal, and like a hammer that shatters a rock' (Jeremiah 23:29). Just as a hammer divides into several sparks so too every scriptural verse yields several meanings."

A similar approach can be found in classical Christian exegesis, notably the Syriac tradition, as the following passage from the fourth century church father, Ephrem, in his *Commentary on the Diatessaron* (I:18-19) illustrates:

> The facets of His word are more numerous than the facets of those who learn from it. God depicted His word with many beauties, so that each of those who learn from it can examine that aspect of it which he likes. And God had hidden within His word all sorts of treasures, so that each of us can be enriched by it from whatever aspect he meditates on.... Anyone who encounters Scripture should not suppose that the single one of its riches that he has found is the only one to exist; rather, he should realize that he himself is only capable of discovering that one out of the many riches which exist in it.

This approach results not only in a breadth and plurality of viewpoints but also enables Jewish and Christian readings of the Bible to deal with texts that run contrary to what we regard as fundamental values and can be read as a license for violence or bigotry. It should be applied to biblical texts, which have been (ab)used, for example, to justify slavery or second-class citizenship, to hold women in subjugation to men, Black to White, Jew to Christian and so on.

The application is dependent upon one criterion: the rejection of any interpretation that promotes hatred, discrimination or superiority of one group over another. Any such interpretation should be considered invalid, requiring reinterpretation.

This approach is based on a hermeneutical principle shared by Christians and Jews: humanity should live by the commandments and not die by their observance. This means that in light of the Shoah, biblical texts can be read in terms of the potential damage they may cause (or the real damage they have caused). Relevant to this argument is the Hebrew term, *pikuah nefesh*, which avers that the duty to preserve life takes precedence over the *mitzvoth* (commandments). Simply put, when human life is at stake the biblical text needs reinterpretation. Rabbinic interpretations of Leviticus 18:5 and Christian readings of Mark 2:27 can be used in support of this principle.

The recognition that biblical texts can have more than one meaning is significant for Jewish–Christian relations after the Shoah because Jews and Christians no longer need to discover the one "true" meaning of a biblical text; rather, they can acknowledge the validity of multiple interpretations, each located within its own context, each worthy of consideration in its own right. It also allows for the doors of interpretation to remain permanently open.

This may leave the reader feeling discomforted, because an acceptance of a multitude of interpretations arising from a single biblical passage is disconcerting. Yet, Scripture itself can exhibit an inherent ambiguity, which can result in apparently contradictory readings. Consider the following readings of Job 13:15:

Behold, he will slay me; I have no hope (RSV—Revised Standard Version).

Though he slay me, yet will I trust in him (KJV—King James Version).

The reason for the difference between the RSV and KJV is the result of a variation in the reading and spoken versions. The Masoretic vocalization (spoken reading) indicates that Job has hope while the consonantic, or written, text offers the view that Job has no hope. The Mishnah in Sotah 5:5 acknowledges the ambiguous meaning of the biblical text and recognizes that both translations are possible: "the matter is undecided—do I trust in Him or not trust?" The contradiction is meaningful as it expresses the tension of one who is torn between hope and doubt: the very tension that inhabits our mind when we read the Bible today, in light of Auschwitz. According to Andre Neher, "Job pronounces two words which signify *simultaneously* hope and hopelessness . . . I hope in Him, he shouts, but also do not hope in him."

Although such an approach may be uncomfortable because it leaves the reader with an unresolved tension, it is meaningful to those who struggle with reading the Bible after the Shoah. The presence of ambiguity can help both Christians and Jews to realize that a single interpretation is not the final or only meaning of the biblical text.

PART FOUR: ZIONISM AND THE CREATION OF THE STATE OF ISRAEL: ENCOUNTERS OF LAND

Nowhere is the subject of peace and understanding—or perhaps more realistically, violence and misunderstanding—more evident than in the Middle East, or more discussed than in the tea rooms and coffee parlors of Jerusalem, Tel Aviv, Ramallah, and Bethlehem. The apparent constant instability in Palestinian-controlled areas, combined with threats and attacks from radical religious Jewish settlers, are reminders of what seems to be an intractable conflict between Israel and the Palestinians. A story is told about an Israeli and a Palestinian leader meeting God and asking whether there will ever be peace in the Middle East in their lifetime. "Of course there will be peace," God told them. They looked relieved. "However," God continued, "not in my time." More than 130 years after the beginning of modern Zionism, a peaceful solution seems some distance away.

For Jews, the centrality of the land of the Bible, as well as the survival of 40 percent of world Jewry, is at stake. Christians, for their part, not only disagree as to the place of Israel in Christian theology, but many understandably feel particular concern for Arab Christians who live in Israel and in Palestine. Israel cannot be viewed simply as a geographical and political entity whose establishment mirrors that of any other new state. Political, social, cultural, and religious concerns all affect Israel's place in the Jewish-Christian relationship.

The land and state of Israel are intricately related to a number of subjects in that relationship. For example, it is impossible to examine covenantal theology without accounting for the importance of land. In the Bible, possession of the land of Israel was an indispensable condition of self-fulfillment both for the individual and for the community. When the destruction of the Second Temple in 70 CE created dispossession and powerlessness for the Jewish people, their response echoed both the hope of divine restoration and also the mystical idea that God was exiled along with His people. Both Jews and Christians agreed that the exile occurred partly as a result of divine punishment. Traditional Christian interpretation emphasized punishment for failing to believe in Christ, whereas Jewish interpretations explained it as a result of internal Jewish strife and argument. Nevertheless, the rabbis taught that God's Presence (Shekhinah) followed the exiles and that there were some positive consequences, such as Jewish teaching being spread far and wide.

The traditional Christian emphasis on divine punishment provided the basis for replacement theology—the belief that Christians replaced Jews as the people of God. The church fathers consistently used the historical tragedies of the Jewish people as "proof" that God had rejected them definitively because of their rejection of Jesus.

These views have changed for many reasons, one of which is the emergence of the state of Israel, in which Jews are a sovereign majority and Judaism the established religion of the land. Christianity's minority status is emphasized by the diminishing percentage of Christians living in Israel alongside an increasing and significantly larger Muslim Arab population. Yet Israel is one of the few places in the region where the absolute number of Christians has increased, from 34,000 in 1949 to over 180,000 today, many of whom are Arab-Christians and adherents of the Melkite Greek Catholic Church (Lazaroff). However, genuine contact between Arab Christians and Jews is overshadowed by the Israeli-Palestinian conflict and Jewish-Christian dialogue is often transformed into dialogue between Israelis and Palestinians or Israelis and Arabs. A Palestinian theology of liberation has developed out of the everyday experiences of Palestinian Christians living in Israel since 1948. It would not be hyperbolic to claim that the Palestinian Churches have faced a theological crisis. As Naim Ateek argues in *Justice and Only Justice: A Palestinian Theology of Liberation*, "before the creation of the state, the Old Testament was considered an essential part of Christian Scripture, pointing and witnessing to Jesus. Since the creation of the state, some Jewish and Christian interpreters have read the Old Testament largely as a Zionist text to such an extent that it has become almost repugnant to Palestinian Christians" (77-78). Palestinian Liberation theologians ask, justifiably, for their fellow Christians not to ignore the Palestinian people, their loss of homeland and struggle for liberation.

A key factor to reckon with is Christians' status as a minority in the region. Not only are Christians a minority within the State of Israel— approximately 2 percent of the Israeli population is Christian—they are also a minority within the Arab minority. On a purely psychological level, their church representatives feel under pressure. Yet the Christian Arab and the Muslim Arab, whatever their religious differences might be, live in one society, speak one language and share one culture. Dialogue with Muslims is sometimes a priority for Christians and in some dioceses it is only the dialogue with Muslims that is real, for example, in Jordan and Gaza, where there are no Jews.

Yet a wholly negative attitude towards Israel on the one hand, and an embrace of a radical Palestinian Liberation theology on the other, is unhelpful. In fact, this is as unhelpful as some extreme forms of Christian Zionism, which view any action by Israel as wholly positive. The most well-known embodiment of the extreme view is Christians United for Israel, founded by evangelical pastor and televangelist John Hagee in 2006. CUFI has been unwilling to take issue with Israeli government policies and supports West Bank annexation. The emergence of the New Christian Zionism, as detailed in this volume's introduction, has given voice to more nuanced positions. The chapter by Rynhold below takes note of more liberal trends among younger evangelicals.

For Jews, the will to survive in the Diaspora generated messianic hopes of redemption, which occasionally led to high levels of anticipation and the extraordinary claims of self-appointed messiahs such as Bar Kokhba and Shabbetai Zvi. One of the common features of times of messianic fervour was that the Promised Land became a symbol of redress for all the wrongs which Jews had suffered. Thus, modern Zionism became in part the fusion of messianic fervor and the longing for Zion. Jews took their destiny into their own hands and stopped waiting for a divine solution to their predicament. Of course, not all Jews support a Jewish state. Some ultra-Orthodox Jews today reject Zionism, arguing that Israel should be a divine and not a manmade creation. Some secular socialist Jews come to the same conclusion, albeit for different reasons.

Because land is not commonly explored by theologians, Christians have found it hard to genuinely understand mainstream Jewish attachment to the land of Israel. Biblical scholar Walter Brueggemann suggests that land should move to the center of Christian theology, arguing that Christians cannot engage in serious dialogue with Jews unless they acknowledge land as the central agenda. In his view, controversy over the state of Israel highlights the lack of a theology of place in contemporary Christianity.

Roman Catholicism's attitude towards Zionism changed greatly in the course of the 20th century. In 1904, Pope Pius X (1903-14) rejected Herzl's plea for support unequivocally stating that "The Jews have not recognised our Lord, therefore we cannot recognise the Jewish people." However, Vatican II and the 1965 document *Nostra Aetate*, while not explicitly mentioning Israel, began the process which eventually led to the Vatican's recognition of the state of Israel in 1994. Increasing awareness among Roman Catholics became noticeable during the papacy of John Paul II. His acknowledgement of its significance can be seen as early as 1984 when in his Good Friday Apostolic Letter he wrote: "the Jewish people who live in the State of Israel, and who preserve in that land such precious testimonies to their history and their faith, we must ask for the desired security and the due tranquility that is the prerogative of every nation and condition of life and of progress for every society."

Ten years later, the state of Israel and the Holy See exchanged ambassadors, and the process begun in 1965 reached another significant landmark with the Pontiff's pilgrimage to Israel in 2000. Following Jewish tradition, the Pope placed a written prayer in a crevice of the Western Wall, which read: "God of our fathers, you chose Abraham and his descendants to bring your Name to the Nations. We are deeply saddened by the behavior of those who in the course of history have caused these children of yours to suffer, and asking Your forgiveness we wish to commit ourselves to genuine brotherhood with the people of the Covenant."

Since then, John Paul II's successors Benedict XVI and Francis have visited Israel, but a resurgence of anti-Israeli attitudes, particularly in Europe, has been growing in the last few years and the feeling remains that while the Church has addressed anti-Semitism, attitudes towards the land and state of Israel continue to be problematic. Simply put, it has been easier to condemn anti-Semitism as a misunderstanding of

Christian teaching than to come to terms with the re-establishment of the Jewish State. As a result, the subject of Israel has probably caused as much disagreement and division within the Church as any other topic in Jewish-Christian dialogue.

Lutheran scholar Alice Eckhardt is one of a number who point out the contrast between Christian willingness to tackle anti-Semitism and the Shoah with reticence about Israel. She argues that Christians are more likely to think about the Shoah than the state of Israel because the former accords with the traditional stereotype of Jews as a suffering and persecuted minority. Israel, on the other hand, challenges this assumption as it transforms the victim into a victor.

The Boycott, Divestment, and Sanctions (BDS) movement, supported by a number of Protestant and Orthodox churches, has put strain on the relationship, and some Christian documents include noticeably strong criticism of Israel and equally noticeable silence, or near silence, about Palestinian failings. *Kairos Palestine* comes to mind.

For Christians and Jews to effectively discuss issues of concern, both must be prepared to listen without taking offense. Michel Sabbah, former Latin Patriach (2000-2008) commented that Christians in Israel "are called to be leaven contributing positive resolution of the crises we are passing through." Sabbah took part in a synod that started in 1995 involving the Catholic Churches of the Holy Land, comprising not only the Roman Catholic Church but also the Oriental Churches. It lasted 5 years and reflected on the changes since *Nostra Aetate*. The thirteenth Synod document was entitled "Relations with believers of other religions" and contains two sections, the first dedicated to Muslims and the second to Jews. The document makes clear that the local Church does not have the same starting point as its European counterparts, for its sees itself as free of anti-Semitic practice, policy, or responsibility for the fate of European Jewry.

Jamal Khader and David Neuhaus, the latter a Jesuit who is active in Jewish-Christian dialogue in Israel, explain further:

> Christians live as a minority face to face with a Jewish majority (those in Israel), under Israeli military occupation (those in the West Bank) or confronting a regional economic and military power (those in Jordan and Gaza). This is an absolutely unique historical situation.

Nowhere else in the world do Christians experience directly the sovereignty and power of a Jewish polity and never in history have Christians experienced Jewish sovereignty and power (these only having been reestablished in 1948 with the creation of the State of Israel). This unique situation must inform dialogue that takes place in this land between local Christians and Jews, predominantly in Israel. For many of the Holy Land faithful, unfortunately, the Jew is often first and foremost a policeman, a soldier or a settler. (70)

There are other dangers for Jews and Christians, such as the assumption that what was once an interpretation about the nature of the biblical word and promise is now concretized in a contemporary event. This emphasis on fulfilment of biblical prophecy can be seen in the writings of some evangelical Christians as well as fundamentalist Jews.

What happened a hundred years ago to Jews outside of Israel is considered by some as historically remote compared to biblical events, which are viewed as almost contemporary. The present is transformed into biblical language and geography, which leads to the danger of giving metaphysical meaning to geographical places. The fundamentalist Jew interprets the ownership of the land in terms of a divine gift. This creates a great danger of assigning divine importance to Israel and the vocation of the Jew becomes a dedication to the existence and the restoration of this cosmic state. Thus, the return to the land is a fulfillment of the divine promise and reflects a return to the original fullness. However, the biblical promises do not define the same borders and, by choosing the widest ones, fundamentalists abuse the idea of the promise itself.

There are also dangers when those who, in the name of dialogue, move from a position of commitment to the well-being of Israel to one predicated on the idea that Israel can do almost no wrong. This is not conducive to dialogue for it is not an honest and sober conversation firmly related to present realities. Although evangelical Christian Zionists strongly support Israel and especially the Settler Movement, their agenda is governed by an eschatological timetable. Their hope, as they freely admit, is that the Jewish return to Zion will be followed by the Second Coming and the acceptance of Jesus by the entire Jewish people.

Perhaps it is best to end the complex relationship between Jews and Christians with a question. David Flusser, the eminent Israeli scholar of first century Judaism, once told the following story, based on his encounter with a group of evangelical Christians visiting Israel:

"'Why should we quarrel?' I asked, 'You believe in the coming of the Messiah—so do we. So let us both work for it and pray for it. Only, when he arrives, allow me to ask him one question first: Excuse me sir, but is this your first visit to Jerusalem?'"

CHAPTER TWO

AMY-JILL LEVINE

~

THE GOSPEL AND THE LAND REVISITED: EXEGESIS, HERMENEUTICS, AND POLITICS

The New Testament is more than an historical artifact.[8] Although many biblical scholars privilege historical-critical approaches, we cannot avoid presuppositions drawn from our own cultural contexts. We also realize that the New Testament, as a text, is open to diverse interpretations from multiple fields: literary criticism in its various forms, social and cultural anthropology, Marxist and post-colonial theory, and so on. Finally, the text has a religious role: it incarnates the Christian claim that the Word was made flesh, and it is therefore the source of theological, homiletic, and soteriological teaching. It is this religious role that distinguishes the New Testament from contemporaneous literature like the works of Virgil or Philo, and it is this religious role that explains why both interreligious and political discourses so often appeal to it.

I am not a public policy specialist. I cannot read Arabic, and my modern Hebrew is weak, so I am dependent on English translations of speeches, newspapers, and charters produced by Israelis and Palestinians and their various supporters. Nor does my expertise in ancient history directly contribute to current debates on such matters as whether the nation-state of Israel should be recognized as a "Jewish" state; whether Palestinians should be granted a right to return to the homes they, their parents, or their grandparents left—or were driven from—in 1948; whether Israel committed war crimes during the most recent major incursion into Gaza; or whether Hamas is guilty of war crimes for locating rocket launchers in schools and apartment buildings or for encouraging Palestinians, including children, to blow up Jews.

I am a scholar of the Bible—the Tanakh or Old Testament and the New Testament—and its reception, and I have been tracking how various Christian stakeholders in the quest for peace in Israel/Palestine have deployed biblical text and commentary in promoting their views on such topics as the Boycott, Divestment, and Sanctions movement (BDS), the application of the covenantal promises of the land to Abraham, Isaac, and Jacob, and so on. The majority of church groups and individual Christians who cite the biblical text in promoting their views about Israel/Palestine are well-meaning. They are not, however, biblical scholars. They do not read the New Testament in Greek or their Old Testament in Hebrew, and so they will necessarily miss textual nuances, and they do not have deep familiarity with first-century history. Therefore, it is salutary to put their arguments into conversation with historical-critical biblical analysis.

This section addresses New Testament understandings of the land of Israel. The questions that churches and individual Christians committed to a biblical understanding of this topic may include: Are the promises of inheriting the land and of return to the land—promises so prominent in the Scriptures Christians and Jews share—abrogated in the New Testament? Are they transferred from Israel "according to the flesh" to the followers of Jesus? Do they remain as necessary elements of Christian soteriology (Levine "Speaking of the Middle East" 102)?

The questions have more than historical-critical implications. They have set at odds some Christian Zionists, both dispensationalists and others, who see a place for the Jewish people, as Jews, in the church and at the eschaton, against some liberation theologians. Christians with an investment in Palestinian and other Arab branches of their denominations, and religious anti-Zionists who insist that any claim the Jewish people have on the land either ended with the coming of Christ or was transferred to his followers.

These questions have become acute within broader Christendom. For example, the Anglican Consultative Council found it necessary to issue a seventy-six-page report: "Land of Promise? An Anglican exploration of Christian attitudes to the Holy Land, with special reference to 'Christian Zionism'" (2012). In a telling moment for our purposes, the document affirms, "The Jewish people have a continuing role within the purposes of God," and its denial of the claim that "Jews have forfeited any right to live in the Holy Land because of their alleged disobedience" (68). Then again, the document never cites Paul's Epistles and rarely quotes the Gospels.

The Church of Scotland in 2003 offered a position paper, "Theology of Land and Covenant," which had an explicitly theological remit: "to study what the Bible has to say about the Land [of Israel] and Covenant, and to reflect on how the biblical material has been interpreted and used in the context of the present conflict [in] Israel/Palestine" (Sect. 1:3; see also 1:5; 3:3:8; 6:2:1); in 2013, the same Church published "The Inheritance of Abraham? A Report on the 'Promised Land,'" which, by putting the phrase "promised land" in scare-quotes, signaled its anti-nationalist bias and its arguments against an "ethno-nationalist understanding" of divine promises and responsibilities (7). This publication affirms, "If Jesus is indeed the Yes to all God's promises, then for Christians the promise to Abraham about land is fulfilled through the impact of Jesus" (9). On the other hand, the document uses the expression "holy land" without definition or hesitation.

Adam Gregerman neatly summarizes the approach of this text as well as companion position papers from the Presbyterian Church (USA): "While they initially advocate a secular, non-theologized view of Israel, they then paradoxically assess, and often critique it using Scriptural texts and Christian theological concepts…. They cast Israel as a corporate religious entity by which the Jewish people might fulfill their religious obligations but criticize it for failing to properly interpret and apply Scripture in its policies" ("Israel as the 'Hermeneutical Jew'" 773).

The 2010 Presbyterian Church-USA, Middle East Study Committee (MESC) released its 172-page study of Israel/Palestine titled "Breaking Down the Walls." The report asserts: "It appears that during the first century CE, Christian authors rather fully transferred the locus of God's concrete presence in the world of space and time from the place of Zion—that is, Jerusalem—to the person of Jesus, who had been crucified and raised from the dead just outside Jerusalem" (15). The title of the report alludes not only to the concern for the separation barrier today, it also adverts, biblically, to Ephesians 2:14: "For he [i.e. the Christ] is our peace; in his flesh he has made both groups [i.e. Jews and gentiles] into one and has broken down the dividing wall, that is, the hostility between us." In the first century, readers might have picked up on the connection to the walls in the Jerusalem Temple separating the people of Israel (Jews) from the gentiles who had also come to worship Israel's God. However, in the twenty-first century, with its Christian majority, this theological removal of the wall, with Jews and gentiles united in the Christ, means the loss of distinct Jewish identity: both Jews and (pagan) gentiles all become Christians.

The view dismissing the sense of Zion as place is echoed in the PCUSA 2014 booklet, *Zionism Unsettled*, which more or less repeats the infamous UN statement equating Zionism with racism. Not surprisingly, that same year the Church's general assembly voted for a boycott/divest/sanction approach to Israel. Although that same year the PCUSA disavowed *Zionism Unsettled* as a denomination, its news bulletin states, "The Israel-Palestine Mission Network, which produced the booklet, may continue to sell and distribute it through other channels." On the PCUSA website, immediately under this notice, appears the link to

Zionism Unsettled, with advertisement, "now available for color Kindle with accompanying video episodes online." An external viewer may thus wonder what, exactly, the PCUSA would like its members to think of Zionism, understood as the self-determination of the Jewish people to live in their ancestral homeland.

Some theologians in the Middle East insist that the covenant with Israel is either defunct or transferred to the church. Fr. George Makhlour of St. George Greek Orthodox Church in Ramallah writes: "What Abraham was promised, Christians now possess because they are Abraham's true spiritual children just as the New Testament teaches" (qtd. in Burge, *Whose Land* 167), and Cyril Salim Bustros, archbishop of the Melkite Greek Catholic Church of Beirut and Byblos announced in 2010, following the Vatican Synod for the Middle East "as Christians, we're saying that this promise [of land] was essentially nullified [*abolie*] by the presence of Jesus Christ, who then brought about the Kingdom of God. As Christians, we cannot talk about a 'promised land' for the Jews. We talk about a 'promised land' which is the Kingdom of God" (Allen "Thinking Straight"). John Allen tactfully puts this quote into context in terms of both official Vatican teaching and Boustros's concern for Palestinian suffering; the bishop's point could have been better phrased.

Most recently, prominent anti-Zionist New Testament scholar Gary Burge ("You can Be an Evangelical"), decrying US President Donald Trump's decision to move the American embassy from Tel Aviv to Jerusalem, asked in the pages of the *Atlantic*, "Many of us look at modern Israel today and see a country that Amos would barely recognize. How, we wonder, can anyone build a bridge from ancient Israel to modern Israel today? Amos would hardly recognize in Tel Aviv a city based on biblical ideals." Burge then continues his well-known supersessionist reading in which "We [i.e., we evangelicals] anchor our thinking not in the Old Testament's land-based promises, but in the gospel, where the tribal or local theologies about Israel become global and universal.... Paul can refer to gentiles as children of Abraham (Romans 4:11) because it's through faith, not ethnic lineage, that one gains access to the blessings of God."

Most readers sympathetic to Burge's view would, however, have no problem identifying present-day Palestinian Christians with their first-century counterparts. One might also wonder if they would oppose present-day Greeks' objections to international recognition of the nation of Macedonia calling itself Macedonia because, they claim, the Macedonian Alexander the Great was in fact Greek. To deny the connection between Socrates and Plato to present-day Greece would be equally reifying. Nor should the issue be whether Tel Aviv is built on "biblical ideals": to judge the modern nation-state by biblical ideas is a false model; it is equally false to deny the connection of modern Jews to the land called, at one time, Judea. I would make the same argument in terms of the connection of the people who call themselves "Palestinians" to the land called by most everyone, prior to 1948, "Palestine."

Finally, some churches have substituted position statements for Bible study. The first hit under a Google search with the key terms "Bible Study" and "Palestine" yields the *"Kairos Palestine* Bible Study" from the Maine Conference of the United Church of Christ. The three-week study program addresses the *Kairos Palestine Document* and includes articles and book recommendations by noted anti-Zionists such as Mark Braverman and the aforementioned Gary Burge. Remarkably, it mentions no specific biblical passages to be discussed.

Since the Bible will be—and in Bible Studies should be—cited in debates over policy regarding Israel and Palestine, I believe that we who study this text must approach the subject with historical-critical rigor, with theological sensitivity, and with awareness that our work is not merely academic: it informs policy and peace initiatives, of both church and secular groups/organizations/institutions, and it responds to oppression and to terrorism.

Most Christians who have seminary or divinity school degrees are not prepared to address how the Bible speaks to the present-day Middle East. Indeed, most Christian seminaries and divinity schools do not offer any substantive material on Jews and Judaism, or on Jewish-Christian relations; they are thus not in a position to build upon the knowledge required to have a substantive conversation about Christian responses to conflicts in the Middle East today.

Because it is only proper that I tell you my political leanings, I am a consultant for Americans for Peace Now, the sister organization to Israel's Shalom Achshav. I have also consulted for Churches for Middle East Peace, served as an external reader on the Anglican "Land of Promise," and advised the Jewish Board of Deputies in Sydney for their dialogue with Australia's Uniting Church. I participate, throughout the English-speaking world, in Jewish-Christian dialogue about the Middle East, and I seek to say "amen" to church statements critical of the Israeli settlement enterprise. Often I cannot, because I find that the arguments legitimately criticizing Israeli policy too often bleed into raw anti-Semitism. I also consistently find that Jews and Christians have very different views of the land of Israel. New Testament study helps explain such differences.

No article can hope to completely cover the question of the New Testament and the land. W.D. Davies's *The Gospel and the Land*, for example, weighs in at over 500 print pages. Therefore, I shall address four of the questions that surface in discussions of the Bible and Israel/Palestine:

1. Why do Christians who understand their Bible from lectionaries and Jews who understand the Tanakh from the *parashah ha-shavua* receive different teachings about the land?

2. What shall one call the area in which Jesus lived, from which the Apostolic mission began, and to which Paul took his collection? Names are not merely ciphers; they cannot escape political connotations.

3. Did Paul reject Jewish nationalism and/or promote a supersessionist theology in which Israel (according to the flesh) either loses its covenant or is swallowed up in a universalizing (and anti-Judaic) Christological message?

4. Did Jesus reject Jewish nationalism or affiliation with the land?

REDRAWING THE MAP: CHRISTIAN ERASURE OF ISRAEL'S LAND THEOLOGY

Given that the promise of the land resonates throughout the Tanakh, Jewish attachment to it is understandable. Similarly, uses of "Jerusalem" and "temple" as synecdoches for the land are frequent. However, Jewish attachment to the land becomes attenuated in Christian circles through select citation, translation, and canon formation. Here are seven among many more examples, most of which concern reception history.

First, Isaiah, speaking to his exiled community in Babylon, proclaims a word of hope: "Comfort, O comfort my people, says your God; speak tenderly to Jerusalem, and cry to her that she has served her term, that her penalty is paid . . ." (40:1-2). The next verse—"A voice cries out: 'In the wilderness prepare the way of the Lord, make straight in the desert a highway for our God'" (40:3)—for Isaiah means return from exile to the homeland. Mark 1:3 applies the verse to John the Baptist, seen in his wilderness setting as preparing the way (Greek: *hodos*, cf. Acts 9:2) of Jesus. The focus on return to the land goes missing.

Second, concerning the slaughter of Bethlehem's children by Herod's soldiers, Matthew explains, "Then was fulfilled what was spoken by the prophet Jeremiah: Thus says the Lord: A voice is heard in Ramah, lamentation and bitter weeping. Rachel is weeping for her children; she refuses to be comforted for her children, because they are no more" (Matt 2:18). But Jeremiah, in the famous "new covenant" chapter, continues, "Thus says the Lord: Keep your voice from weeping, and your eyes from tears . . . there is hope for your future . . . your children shall come back to their own country" (Jer 31:15-17). Return from exile either goes missing in Matthew 2, or—if readers know the original context in Jeremiah—it is spiritualized into a hope for resurrection for the murdered children.

Such prooftexting also influences interpretation of Paul's letters. A third example appears in Romans 10:15, where Paul asks, "How are they to proclaim him unless they are sent? As it is written, 'How beautiful are the feet of those who bring good news.'" The citation is to Isaiah 52:7-10, the prophet's joyful proclamation of the end of exile and the return to a renewed and redeemed Jerusalem. Christian readers will take the proclamation to refer to the evangelists who proclaim the Christian gospel.

Fourth, appropriation of Jewish identity, perhaps by Jews themselves within the early communities of Jesus' followers, creates another separation in the imagination of Christian Bible readers between Jews and the homeland. Both James 1:1 and 1 Peter 1:1 address the "twelve tribes" (James) or the "exiles" (Peter) of the "dispersion" (Greek: *diaspora*). To live in the Diaspora requires a homeland from whence one is dispersed. For Jews, the primary addressees of both letters would be fellow Jews outside the homeland. For many Christian readers, the Diaspora indicates church members living on earth and thus apart from their heavenly king and kingdom.

None of these examples precludes Christian readers from recognizing a Jewish attachment to the land. The meaning of the antecedent verses is not exhausted by New Testament appropriations. Here scholars and theologians will need to determine if the citations in the New Testament were read, and/or should be read, in light of their original literary and historical contexts.

Fifth, along with selective appropriation in citation, translation contributes to a de-emphasis of the homeland in the New Testament and reception history. In Matthew's famous beatitude (5:5), Jesus states, "Blessed are the meek, for they will inherit the earth (Greek: *ge*). The verse draws upon Psalm 37:11: "The meek will inherit the *land* (Hebrew: *eretz*) and delight themselves in abundant prosperity." While: eretz can mean both earth (as in Genesis 1:1, the creation of heaven and "earth"), for first-century Jews in Judea and Galilee, and likely for the original readers of the Psalm, eretz most likely meant first and foremost the land of Israel. Matthew, with its universalistic focus (e.g., 28:19 with its mandate to make disciples of all the gentiles) universalizes the focus (Wilken *Land*, 48).

Canon formation adds a sixth de-emphasis. The Torah ends with Moses on Mt. Nebo; Jews could identify with him and his yearning for the land. The same yearning resounds at the very end of the Tanakh. The Ketuvim (Hebrew for "Writings" and the third part of the Tanakh) conclude with 2 Chronicles 36:23, Cyrus's edict to the Jews in Babylon:

"The Lord, the God of heaven, has given me all the kingdoms of the earth, and he has charged me to build him a house at Jerusalem, which is in Judah. Whoever is among you of all his people, may the Lord his God be with him. Let him go up." The Tanakh's last word is *v'ya'al*, in English "go up," as in the modern Hebrew term *aliyah*, the call to return to the land. In Protestant and Catholic Bibles, the Old Testament ends with Malachi's predicting the return of Elijah (Mal 4:5-6; Hebrew versification 3:23-24), effectively replacing homecoming with eschatology. The Christian Old Testament thus serves, in terms of canonical order, as a trailer for the coming of Elijah, embodied as John the Baptist; Christianity reads Elijah as predicting not just the messianic age, but also the messiah.

Finally, what Jews and Christians read liturgically also determines how each community understands the land. In the course of a year, Jews read the Torah from Genesis to Deuteronomy and so hear the promise of land repeated. For lectionary-based churches, the promises are not often heard in the Sunday readings. Likewise, Christian holidays either replace or ignore land-based pilgrimage festivals. The church ignores Sukkot (Booths/Tabernacles), replaces Passover with Holy Week and thus the Passover seder with the Last Supper (the Last Supper is apparently a seder meal in the Synoptic Gospels, but it is not in John's Gospel), and replaces Shavuot with Pentecost, a holiday that looks outward from, not inward toward, Jerusalem. Such replacement appears already in the Gospel of John, in which Jesus appropriates to himself the Jewish holidays: He is the new light of the world and so replaces Hanukkah, he is the new Paschal lamb and so replaces Passover, and so on. Where Jews then and now regarded Jerusalem as the holy city, in John's view, Jerusalem's geographical import becomes spiritualized. Jesus tells a woman from Samaria, "The hour is coming when you will worship the Father neither on this mountain (i.e., Mt. Gerizim, the mountain sacred to the Samaritans) nor in Jerusalem . . . true worshipers will worship the Father in spirit and truth" (John 4:21, 23).

These individual emphases are part of a larger conceptual distinction between how the Jewish community, generally, defines itself and how the followers of Jesus determine identity. Jews always retained an ethnic aspect to self-definition, namely, descent from or affiliation with

Abraham and Sarah, Isaac, Jacob, and Jacob's sons and grandsons (Cf. Matthew 1:1-2, 17//Luke 3:34; Matthew 3:9//Luke 3:8; Luke 1:55; 13:16; 16:24, 30; John 8:33, 39; Acts 3:13, 25; 7:2, 32; Romans 4:1; 9:7). Jewish people recognize themselves as an *ethnos*, a people sharing common ancestors and a connection to a homeland. Christians tend not to define themselves according to physical descent; they are, to use Johannine terminology, not born followers of Jesus but born anew. Similarly, to use Paul's terms, one is not born into Abraham's family but grafted in "contrary to nature" (Romans 11:24, Greek: *kata physin*) or adopted via Paul's midwifery and even labor (Galatians 4:5, Greek: *hiothesian*). If Christians think of Jews as defined by a religion and determine that religion is a matter of belief or personal choice (such a definition reveals the idea of "religion" to be a post-Enlightenment concept; it also poses a debatable proposition in terms of both psychology and theology), they may well demur from seeing Jews as having a homeland. If they recognize the ethnic aspect of Jewish "religious" identity, the idea of a national homeland becomes less alien.

Christianity is a universal religion, not tied to a homeland or parentage. The general view of the New Testament and hence of its followers is that everyone can be, and ideally should be, a follower of Jesus (preferably a baptized one). The so-called "scandal of particularity" can play no role in a universalizing religion. Judaism is not a universalizing religion, in that is has no missionary impulse. This very particularity, which is part of what connects Jews, traditionally, to the homeland, should be familiar to those Christians who remember their own connections, whether of Presbyterians to Geneva or Scotland, Lutherans to Sweden or Germany, or Anglicans to Great Britain. But especially in the United States, as ethnic churches shrink because of changing neighborhoods, the demographic leakage of memberships especially in liberal Protestant denominations, the formalizing of liturgy and hymnals, any appreciation for ethnic particularity is equally diminished. As the Western churches find themselves less ethnic and so more generic, the scandal of Jewish particularly becomes increasingly acute.

THE MATTER OF LABELING

In 1977, E.P. Sanders published his groundbreaking text, *Paul and Palestinian Judaism*. The title indicated Sanders's focus on the Jewish practices and beliefs in Jerusalem and Nazareth and Capernaum and Chorazin, rather than those in Antioch, Alexandria, or Athens. The use of "Palestinian" to refer to Paul's context was not, then, politically voluble. Times have changed.

The New Testament itself does not use the term "Palestine" and neither does the Masoretic Text nor the Septuagint. The Hebrew text mentions *Pileshet* eight times in reference to the coastal area where the Philistines settled; *Pileshet* enters the King James Version four times as "Palestina" (Exodus 15:14; Isaiah 14:29, 31; Joel 3:4). The New King James Version reads "Philistia." Following Bar Kochba's Revolt in 132-135 CE, Rome renamed Jerusalem as Aelia Capitolina and promoted the designation Syria Palaestina rather than Judea and Samaria in the attempt to erase Jewish and Samaritan identities.

Today, the term "Palestine" cannot be used, even by the most historical-critical of biblical scholars, without invoking the national aspirations of the population that claims this contested territory as their homeland. Such scholars, when teaching, should also be aware of the ignorance of twenty-first century students. The problem may be more acute in the United States, but my experiences in the UK and Australia suggest that US undergraduates are not alone in geographical ignorance. A Vanderbilt University sophomore once posed the question, "Jesus was born in Bethlehem, so why do we call him a Jew rather than a Palestinian?" It would not surprise me were someone else to retort that Jesus's family, clearly Jewish, were Israeli settlers, because these Nazareth natives were living in Bethlehem, in Palestinian territory.

The New Testament does not name the land "Palestine." Instead, it offers references to Judah and Galilee as well as Zion. In Matthew's Gospel, Herod's scribes quote from the Prophet Micah (5:2) concerning the site of the messiah's birth: "You, Bethlehem, in the land of Judah." Shortly thereafter, an angel tells Joseph, who has moved with his wife and child to Egypt to escape Herod's slaughter, "Get up, take the child and his mother, and go to the land of Israel . . ." (Matt 2:20). Joseph relocates to Nazareth in Galilee, in the land of Israel. John's Gospel also references Zion, again in a fulfillment citation: alluding to Zechariah 9:9, John 12:15 reads, "Do not be afraid, daughter of Zion."

The New Testament also uses the expression "Judea and Samaria," as found, for example, in Acts 1:8, where the risen Jesus tells his apostles, "You will be my witnesses in Jerusalem, in all Judea and Samaria, and to the ends of the earth." Writing in 1986, Harry M. Orlinsky testily observed,

> All hell broke loose the world over when the Government of the State of Israel began in the later Seventies to use the term 'Judea and Samaria' for the territory adjacent to the Jordan River on the west; after all, others had decided that the term 'Occupied West Bank' should be employed. A pity indeed—and revealing too—is the simple fact that anyone who knew something about the New Testament was aware that this term had hoary and significant tradition behind it, that it had been used already two thousand years ago, when Judea had come under the control of the Romans. Yet who drew public attention to it? ("Biblical Concept" 55)

He concluded that "Judea and Samaria" was "used by Jesus—in keeping with Jewish usage at the time—in the sense of 'Jerusalem and the rest of the country,' namely, the Land of Israel." As Peter Pettit suggested to me in an email, "Orlinsky imports an implicit claim of priority and antiquity to the discussion without ever making the case for its continuing applicability across centuries of interrupted sovereignty."

What language then should we use for the ground on which Jesus walked: Land of Israel, Zion, Judea and Samaria, or Palestine? Similar complications of identity politics impinge on whether we translate the Greek term *Ioudaios* as "Jew" or "Judean." To translate it as "Judean" serves to strip the connection of biblical history to present-day Jews (Levine *Misunderstood* 159; see Reinhartz et al *Marginalia*; Reinhartz "Jews").

PAUL AND THE LAND

Claims that Paul rejected Jewish nationalism often begin with an argument from silence: in listing the blessings given to Jews (e.g., Romans 9:4-5, "they are Israelites; theirs is the adoption, the glory, the covenant, the giving of the Law, the worship/service, and the promises; theirs the patriarchs, and from them, according to the flesh, is the Messiah," and Romans 11:28-29: "as regards election they are beloved, for the sake of their ancestors; for the gifts and the calling of God are irrevocable"), the promise of the land is not mentioned explicitly. Thus, Davies asserts, "It is surely noteworthy that the land itself is not singled out for special mention" (*Gospel* 167; Burge *Whose Land* 183). Davies continues, "In Galatians we can be fairly certain that Paul did not merely ignore the territorial aspect of the promise for political reasons: his silence points not merely to the absence of a conscious concern with it, but to his deliberate rejection of it . . . in the Christological logic of Paul, the land, like the Law, particular and provisional, had become irrelevant" (178-79). This argument from silence then expands to include much of the rest of the canon. Philip Church, for example, notes, "There is not one reference to the land of Israel in the writings of Paul, James, Peter, or Jude, or in the Book of Revelation" (49).

The argument from silence is not as strong as its proponents suggest. Here are five among a plethora of arguments against it. First, one might observe that the New Testament does not speak of loving the stranger (so Leviticus 19:34b, "You shall love the alien as yourself, for you were aliens in the land of Egypt"; see also Deuteronomy 10:19) and therefore conclude that the followers of Jesus care only for themselves. As one critic of the argument from silence trenchantly states, "One might just as well argue against the validity of repentance from the absence of the term in the Gospel of John, or against the importance of love from the term's absence in the Acts of the Apostles" (Horner 255).

Second, Paul recognizes the sanctity of the Jewish cultus and so of both the temple and of Jerusalem. In listing the advantages of the Jews, he includes "worship" or "service" (Romans 9:4, Greek: *latreia*); the cognate term would be, in Hebrew, *avodah*, which means temple sacrifice (cf. e.g., Joshua 22:27 LXX; 1 Chronicles 28:13 LXX), as Nanos ("Romans, 271) and Fredriksen ("Wright" 388) others indicate. Temple sacrifice necessarily implies the *Jerusalem* temple, and so the land of Israel.

Third, Paul may not have mentioned the land because "the right of the Jews to their land was an inarguable commonplace in his own day" (Anderson *First Things*, 7; McDermott "Covenant" 32). Whereas the gentile followers of Jesus in Rome might have questioned the permanence of the covenant, given their impression that everything had shifted over to them—a view that likely prompted Paul's writing Romans 9-11—they would not have questioned that Jews lived in, or sprang from, Judea.

Fourth, Paul's reference to "all Israel" (Romans 11:26a) may well mean exactly that—the Jewish nation, Abraham's descendants according to the flesh. In Paul's view, their salvation will occur together with the salvation of the non-Jews, as in Romans 15:10: "and again he says, 'Rejoice, O gentiles/pagans with his people'" (see Fredriksen, "Question" 197-98). Jews are not subsumed into a broader assembly, and they do not lose their ethnic identity. Since they do not lose their ethnic identity, they do not lose their connection to the land. Rather, that connection, like circumcision and kashrut and Shabbat-observance, is presupposed. The focus on the land is then reinforced in Romans 11:26b, when Paul presumes the ongoing role of Zion, whence the Deliverer will come. This place-specific reference reinforces Paul's earlier notice in Romans 9:26, where he quotes Hosea 1:10 (MT//LXX 2:1), "And it will be in the place where they were told, you are not my people, there (Greek: *ekei*) they will be called sons of the living God."

Fifth, Davies's view (Gospel 220) that Paul was free from the Law and therefore from the land proceeds from a debatable premise. In recent years, the claim that Paul saw himself, or his fellow Jews, as free from the Law has come under substantial challenge, most recently in the edited collection, *Paul Within Judaism: Restoring the First-Century Context to the Apostle*. Given that Paul recognizes that Jews still have a role to play in salvation history, that Paul sees ongoing validity in Jewish particularity, and that Paul thinks the coming of the Messiah means that both Jews and gentiles must retain their distinct ethnic identities so that the God of Israel is shown to be the God of all, then Paul would have regarded the land, as part of Jewish identity, to be of import.

One final note on Romans: the occasional claim that Paul, as a Diaspora Jew, would not have seen the land or Jerusalem as central to Jewish identity because neither Josephus nor Philo did, is a misreading of both Hellenistic authors. Robert Wilken observes that Philo uses the expression "holy land" (e.g., *Legat* 205, 330; Greek: *heiran choran*) "more frequently than any other Jewish writer of antiquity"; he also uses the expression "ancient ancestral land (*Hypothetica* in Eusebius, P.E. 8.6,355), holy city, and mother city" (*Flaccum* 46). Wilken concludes: "Just as Philo never lost the realism of the food laws even while allegorizing their details, so he never surrendered the territorial features of the land tradition" (35-37). Josephus writes in the context of the disastrous first revolt against Rome; the last thing he needs to do is to remind his readers of the people's concern for the land. The argument from Josephus's silence does not indicate general Diasporic disinterest in the land of Israel. Conversely, the broad honoring of the temple tax by Diaspora Jews displays their great interest in and loyalty to Jerusalem.

The second argument, that Paul disconnects Jews from the land, stems from Paul's comments about Abraham's heirs in Romans 4 and Galatians 3. Gary Burge summarizes, "Christian theology demands that the true recipients of these promises [to Abraham] will be found in the Christian church. Perhaps the church alone receives these promises!" (*Whose Land* 188). The argument is part of a broader perspective that finds Jewish particularity a problem to be addressed rather than a biblical teaching to be recognized or, to use the modern expression, a type of multiculturalism to be celebrated. Another term for Burge's perspective would be supersessionism.

Preferences for the (Christian) universal over the (Jewish) particular—much like theologies that prefer the spiritual or transcendent to the material or the immanent—are part of a broader Christian discourse found especially in the Epistle to the Hebrews and then taken up by several of the church fathers. However, such Platonizing, spiritualizing, or disembodied interpretations may not be the only, or the better, reading of Paul. They set up an either/or scenario when a both/and reading better fits the context. That Abraham will inherit the world (Romans 4:13; Greek: *cosmos*) does not preclude Abraham's descendants from retaining their own distinctiveness any more than it prevents them from retaining their gendered identities as male and female or their social identities as slave and free.

Paul's view of the relationship of Jews to the land of Israel can also be gleaned from several other allusions, which can only be briefly glossed here. For example, Paul self-identifies by including his tribal affiliation (Philippians 3:5), which may have included the concept of land allotment (compare the notice of the territory of Zebulun and Naphtali in Matthew 3:14-15). Similarly, his self-identification as an *Ioudaios by nature* (Greek: *physei Ioudaioi*, Galatians 2:15) or by genealogy (e.g., Romans 9:4) serves to distinguish himself and his fellow Jews from other peoples who had other homelands. Paul is speaking of blood and flesh and genealogy, not (just) cultural affiliation.

Even Paul's reference to "Jerusalem above" (Galatians 4:26) may include a hint of a *terra sancta*. Paul may have expected, as does the author of Revelation, a descent of this "holy city" onto earth, which naturally makes the land, on earth, important. Origen, citing Galatians 4:26 as well as Hebrews 12:22, railed against such material fulfillment; the promise of Jerusalem, according to Origen, does not designate a future political center but rather a spiritual vision of heavenly bliss:

> If, then, the whole earth has been cursed in the deeds of Adam and of those who died in him, it is plain that all parts of the earth share in the curse, and among others the land of Judea; so that the words, a good land and a large, a land flowing with milk and honey, cannot apply to it, although we may say of it, that both Judea and Jerusalem were the shadow and figure of that pure land, goodly and large, in the pure region of heaven, in which is the heavenly Jerusalem. (*Cels.* 7.29)

But Irenaeus and Tertullian read the Prophets, even with their words refracted through Galatians 4, as indicating a future, terrestrial Jerusalem (Wilken 65-70).

Finally, the Paul depicted in Acts firmly sees the land of Israel, and Jerusalem in particular, as part of the promises made to the Jewish people. In his speech in a synagogue in Pisidian Antioch, "after the reading of the Law and the Prophets" (Acts 13:15), Paul affirms that God, "after he had destroyed seven nations in the land of Canaan, gave them [i.e., our ancestors 'of this people Israel'] their land as an inheritance" (Acts 13:19). Paul then connects Jesus to Israel's traditions and concludes, "My brothers [and sisters], you descendants of Abraham's family, and others who fear God, to us the message of this salvation has been sent" (Acts 13:26). Paul affirms the promise of the land to the Jewish people; the coming of Jesus does not revoke it.

JESUS, THE GOSPELS, AND ACTS

Davies claims that for the Gospels, "The people of Israel living in the land had been replaced as the people of God by a universal community which had no special territorial attachment" (*Gospel* 167). Arguments for this claim are not difficult to find. Here are three that are common today:

First is the familiar but odd juxtaposition that combines the claim that Israel/the Jewish people are in exile with the assertion that Jesus dismissed any nationalistic interest in inheriting or retaining the land. For example, N. Thomas Wright insists, "The traditions which attempted to bolster Israel's national identity were out of date and out of line" and that Jesus "had not come to rehabilitate the symbol of the holy land, but to subsume it within a different fulfillment of the kingdom, which would embrace the whole of creation" (Jesus 398, 466). His summation of this view demonstrates that for him, Jews qua Jews have no eschatological future:

> Instead of Israel as a political entity emerging from political exile, we are invited in the gospel to see Israel-in-person, the true king, emerging from the exile of death itself into God's new day. That is the underlying rationale for the mission to the Gentiles: God has finally done for Israel what he was going to do for Israel, so now it's time for the Gentiles to come in. That, too, is the underlying rationale for the abolition of the food laws and the holy status of the land of Israel: a new day has dawned in God's purposes, and the symbols of the previous day are put aside, not because they were a bad thing, now happily rejected, but because they were the appropriate preparatory stages in God's plan, and have now done their work. (*Way*)

The claim determines that Christian universalism trumps Jewish particularism even as it insists that Jews as a people are particularly in exile. There is much that I find problematic here, beginning with the assertion that pre-70 CE Jews in the land of Israel found themselves in exile. The ten tribes, yes; Mary and Joseph, not so much. Nor do I see Jesus as dismissing the Jewish attachment to the land. If he had, he could easily have decamped to Damascus, or sent his followers immediately to the Diaspora rather than making them await a post-mortem commission. Had he no interest in Zion, the temple, or Jerusalem, he would not have made pilgrimage there, wept over the city, or predicted his return to it. Nor would his followers have continued to worship in Jerusalem's temple. The so-called "cleansing of the temple" does not, in its Synoptic versions, suggest an end to the temple or Jerusalem as the locus of the sacred. Instead, it points to what has been called an "eschatologically restored Jerusalem" (McDermott "Not the Zionism" 130).

Second, some interpreters read Luke 19:11 ("because he was near Jerusalem, and because they supposed that the kingdom of God was to appear immediately") and its corollary, Acts 1:6-7 ("they asked him, 'Lord, is this the time when you will restore the kingdom to Israel?' He replied, 'It is not for you to know the times or periods that the Father has set by his own authority'") as Jesus' rejection of an earthly Jewish homeland. That is not what either text says. To the contrary: Jesus affirms the presence of an earthly kingdom, and what he corrects is not the Jewish claim on the land nor the concern for nationalism, but the timing by which the Jewish presence in the land, ruled by divine will rather than Roman weapons, will be fully realized. In question is not space, but time; not if, but when.

It is the matter of timing that should determine how John's Gospel depicts its eschatological project. Although preferring Jewish to Samaritan text and practice, in John 4:23 Jesus states that "the hour is coming, and is now here, when the true worshipers will worship the Father in spirit and truth." As Burge asserts for John's Gospel, "Jesus himself becomes the locus of holy space" just as "God's vineyard, the land of Israel, now only has one vine, Jesus" (*Whose Land* 175-176). Similarly, it is Jesus who is the new temple even as he is the new and complete sacrifice. Jesus is the new Moses who leads his people in a new Exodus, not out of Egypt and into Israel, and not out of Israel and into the world, but out of darkness and into light. John's presentation may well be anti-Jewish and supersessionist (see esp. Reinhartz *Cast*); scholars are divided on the question.

Numerous other passages suggest the ongoing and positive role of the Jewish people, in their homeland, from the angel Gabriel's prediction that "the Lord God will give to [Jesus] the throne of his father David, and he will reign over the house of Jacob forever" (Luke 1:32-33;

perhaps part of an anti-Marcionite prologue), to Jesus' claim that the divine presence dwells in the temple (Matthew 23:21; the point would be contrary to Matthew's anti-Jerusalem interests), to his prediction that the Jewish people, in Jerusalem, will respond to his mission (Matthew 23:37-39//Luke 13:34-35). This is Luke's version of the prediction found also in Matthew: "Jerusalem, Jerusalem, the city that kills the prophets and stones those who are sent to it! How often have I desired to gather your children together as a hen gathers her brood under her wings, and you were not willing! See, your house is left to you. And I tell you, you will not see me until the time comes when you say, 'Blessed is the one who comes in the name of the Lord.'" This citation, which quotes Psalm 118:26, requires Jews to be present at the Parousia, the second coming. Jesus is not speaking of being greeted by German Lutherans or Peruvian Catholics. This eschatological role for Jews in the land of Israel continues throughout the tradition. Predictions that "many will come from east and west" (Matthew 8:11-12//Luke 13:28-29) would, in Jesus' own context, refer primarily if not exclusively to the return of the Jews, including the Ten Tribes, from the Diaspora to share the eschatological banquet with the patriarchs in Jerusalem. The place where the Twelve will sit on thrones and rule the Twelve Tribes of Israel (Matthew 19:28//Luke 22:29-30) presumes the ongoing existence of the Jewish people (again, a point contrary to redactional interests), and the locality of the thrones is, again, likely the land of Israel. Indeed, the only way to understand Mark 11:10—"the coming kingdom of our father David"—is to see a role yet to be played for the Jewish people in Jerusalem, which, despite all of Matthew's criticisms of it, is the "holy city" (4:5; 27:53 cf. Revelation 21:2, 10, 19; *Pace* Davies, *Gospel* 232, who insists, "There is in Matthew the awareness that the geographic dimensions of Jewish expectation, both Galilean and Judaean, have been shattered.")

For Jesus to fulfill his role as son and heir of David, there must be an Israel, a people and a land, to which he returns. In Paul's eschatological vision, Jews and gentiles worship the God of Israel together as equals. For Jews to exist eschatologically as a people, they must continue to exist as a people in the present world, and that people, for Paul, had a homeland.

ON THE ROAD...

As I read the New Testament, I see no clear revocation of the promise of the land, or of the covenant with the Jewish people. Were the covenant to be revoked, then God would be unfaithful. Nor do I see a thoroughgoing supersessionism, such that all the promises to Abraham and so to Israel are transferred to the followers of Jesus. John's Gospel allows for such a reading, as does the Epistle to the Hebrews, but the other Gospels and the rest of the New Testament, especially the letters of Paul, require Jews *qua* Jews, including their land-based ethnic identity, to have a role. Further, as I understand the Christian Bible, the Old Testament is just as much Scripture as the New and the history of Israel—that is, of those who claim physical descent from Abraham—is just as much a part of the Church's story as those who through Jesus, claim full status into the lineage of Abraham (cf. Galatians 3:7: "those who believe are the descendants of Abraham").

For me, as a liberal Zionist (despite the erasure in which this term is increasingly held), Israel is the national homeland of the Jewish people, and it has been from well before the time of Jesus to today, from ancient myth to archaeological presence. The New Testament confirms the presence of Jews in the Galilee and in Judea as well as the existence of the Second Temple.

Whatever study we make on the question of the New Testament and the land, or more broadly, the New Testament's depiction of Jews, biblical scholars will not have the last word. Christian theologians will. The biblical text will always be interpreted: as a living Word (to use Christian language), it is not restricted to a first-century readership and, therefore, it is not restricted to only one of several first-century meanings.

Some Christians may conclude that the New Testament abrogates any homeland for the Jews, and any ongoing role for the Jewish people *qua* Jews as a people, with not only a history and a genealogy, but also a geographical origin and home. That is, they may conclude that the supersessionists and replacement theologians are right. Given selective textual citation, and granting that all reading is selective, the New Testament has been, and can be read, as supporting such a claim.

Others may conclude that the New Testament regards the promise of the land as permanent, or at least they may conclude, regardless of theological views, that the New Testament attests to the presence of Jews in the land of Israel, just as it attests to the presence of Jesus's followers in Jerusalem and Joppa, today known as Jaffa. Even if one denies the existence of Abraham, the historical observations made in the New Testament support the Jewish claim to a homeland. But these Christian readers cannot stop here either, for others also claim this land, and they also require justice.

At the very least, let us look at the materials in a historically informed manner, and let us never forget that when we talk about the land, the lives of both Israelis and Palestinians, Jews and Christians, of Muslims, Samaritans, Druze, Bahais, and many others, are also at stake.

CHAPTER THREE

DANIEL FRIEDMAN

~

AMERICAN CHRISTIANITY, ISRAEL, AND THE US PRESIDENCY

Protestantism is the largest religion in America, with most Americans identifying as Christians, and most American Christians identifying as Protestant (Pew Research Center "Religious Landscape Study"). The two major subgroups within American Protestantism, evangelical and mainline Protestants, appear to have situated themselves on opposite sides of the debate over the US-Israel relationship.[9] This essay will explore the history of American Christians in the debates and advocacy over America's role in Israel/Palestine and their relationship to Jewish pro-Israel/Palestine interest groups.

In an effort to capture the Christian factor in the policymaking process of the United States, I begin with the sociotheological background for the special place of Israel/Palestine in the eyes of many Americans. I then proceed to examine each administration's major Israel/Palestine decisions from three angles. First, since every American president so far has been Christian, policymaking on Israel is unlike any other foreign policy. In order to assess the role of each president's personal convictions, I briefly examine his religious views. I have not done original research in presidential archives; my aim, rather, is to draw on a wide range of existing scholarship to make concise summaries of presidential views and actions available in one place. Second, I review the statements and political actions of evangelical and mainline Christians, seeking to contextualize the twenty-first-century Christian divide over Israel/Palestine historically. Finally, I investigate the role of Jewish advocacy groups in lobbying American Christians and motivating their political activism on Israel/Palestine.

RESTORATIONISM

The Pilgrims who arrived in America believed it was a land unlike any other. Viewed through the lens of Christianity, the journey to the New World paralleled the biblical exodus of the ancient Hebrews from slavery in Egypt and their eventual arrival in the Promised Land, leading to appellations of America as the *New Israel* (Cherry). Benjamin Franklin suggested a depiction of Moses splitting the Red Sea for the confederation seal, and then-president of Yale Ezra Stiles delivered his 1781 commencement address in Hebrew, Aramaic, and Arabic. As Herman Melville wrote, "We Americans are the peculiar, chosen people, the Israel of our time" (quoted in Grose 5).

On account of their personal affinity with biblical narrative, the restoration of the Jewish people to biblical Israel resonated with many Americans (Koplow). In 1814, Pastor John McDonald of Albany expounded upon Isaiah 18, which he interpreted as a call for America to lead the nations in returning the Jewish people to Zion. Shortly thereafter, Protestant minister Levi Parsons set off for the Holy Land, declaring that "'nothing but a miracle would prevent [the Jews'] immediate return from the four winds of heaven'" (quoted in Grose 9-10).

Such statements were not the rantings of fringe religious fanatics; in 1819, former president John Adams wrote, "'I really wish the Jews again in Judea an independent nation'" (quoted in *Fantasy* 90).

In 1878, William Blackstone (1841-1935) published *Jesus is Coming*, sales of which exceeded one million copies. Blackstone asserted therein that "the title deed to Palestine is recorded, not in the Mohammedan Serai of Jerusalem nor the Serglio of Constantinople, but in hundreds of millions of Bibles now extant in more than three hundred languages of the earth" (235). In 1891 he petitioned President Benjamin Harrison for the US to lead the way in restoring the Jews to the Holy Land, gathering hundreds of prominent signatories from the business, religious, and political spheres (Grose 35-6).

Nevertheless, this newfound Christian goodwill towards Jews and Judaism was far from universal, and traditional Christian ill-will continued to linger amongst many Americans. In addition to classic theological anti-Semitism, American gentile resentment toward Jewish self-determination in the Holy Land stemmed from Euro-American Christianity's long history of missionary engagement in the Middle East. Colonialist Christians had fomented numerous local Christian partnerships, mission churches, health facilities, and educational institutions, most notably the American University of Beirut and the American University in Cairo (Clarke 46; Korn "Divestment" 2; Makari 3). These deep bonds, as well as an American Christian mandate to pursue social justice that evolved over the course of the twentieth century, led to fierce debate amongst Americans over the issue of Israel/Palestine.

PRESIDENT WILSON AND
THE BALFOUR DECLARATION

Christians and Jews looking to restore the Jewish people to their homeland had been diligently lobbying from the late nineteenth century. Towards the end of World War I, with the break-up of the Ottoman Empire and the subsequent British mandate over the area that ancient Romans had called Palestine, that opportunity presented itself as a concrete reality. In 1917, the British government issued the *Balfour Declaration*.[10] Under President Woodrow Wilson, the US endorsed the Declaration, thereby prompting its smooth passage through the British

Cabinet and paving the way for the establishment of the State of Israel (Brog *Standing* 118).

Nevertheless, the US decision to endorse the Declaration was by no means simple. Secretary of State Lansing opposed endorsement, on the grounds that "'many Christian sects and individuals would undoubtedly resent turning the Holy Land over to the absolute control of the race credited with the death of Christ'" (quoted in Grose 70). Similarly, Samuel Edelman, director of the State Department's Near Eastern Intelligence Unit, wrote that a Jewish state would be "'polluting and intolerable'" to the "'sacredness of the Christian memorials in Palestine'" (quoted in Grose 82).[11] Ultimately, however, the president committed the US to playing an integral role in laying the groundwork for the Jewish state.

Wilson's father was a southern Presbyterian minister and his upbringing instilled in him the belief that he was in office to fulfill a higher purpose. At Princeton, he led services and once wrote, "'My life would not be worth living if it were not for the driving power of religion, for faith, pure and simple. I have seen all my life the arguments against it without having ever been moved by them'" (quoted in Merkley *Politics* 80). A daily Bible-reader, he was motivated to support the "People of the Book" (Brog *Standing* 117; Grose 66). And later, he relished the thought, "'that I, the son of the manse, should be able to help restore the Holy Land to its people!'" (quoted in Bass 18).

Yet there was Christian opposition to that goal. According to the liberal Protestant periodical *Christian Century*, Jewish nationalism was dangerous, since "it was nationalism that crucified Jesus." Indeed, the authors continued, "the Christian mind has never allowed itself to feel the same human concern for Jewish sufferings that it has felt for the cruelties visited upon [others] . . . [because they are] the judgment of God upon the Jewish people for their rejection of Jesus" (quoted in Grose 96). This claim reflected the generally lukewarm feeling liberal Protestant leaders held toward the idea of a Jewish return to Palestine (Carenen 8; Fishman 24).

Meanwhile, although fundamentalist Protestants were initially favorably disposed towards Jews, by World War I many began to resent their role in the establishment of the League of Nations, as they viewed the idea of an international superpower as the embodiment of the Antichrist. That prominent secular Jews were involved in the formation of the League appeared to confirm the existence of an international Jewish cabal, as suggested in the *Protocols of the Elders of Zion* (Ruotsila 40). Nevertheless, pro-Israel Christians across the mainline-evangelical divide won the day. When fundamentalist William Blackstone updated his earlier petition for a Jewish state, he added signatories from the leadership of the major American churches (including the Methodists and Presbyterians), which he then presented to the president in an effort to encourage his decision on the Balfour Declaration (Brog *Standing* 118).

Meanwhile, while Zionism was gaining popularity amongst European Jews, the American Jewish leadership was deeply divided. Many were concerned about the charges of dual loyalty their support might engender (AJC "Minutes"). Rabbi Isaac Mayer Wise claimed that endorsing a Jewish return to Palestine ran contrary to American Jewish aspirations, since "America is our Zion." Nevertheless, most American Jews were pro-Zionism. Indeed, while Blackstone needed no prompting when he first presented his petition to President Harrison, the second delivery came at the behest of Supreme Court Justice Louis Brandeis, the leader of the Jewish Zionist movement in America (Grose 44).

PRESIDENTS HARDING, COOLIDGE, HOOVER

While there were no major decisions impacting Israel during the interwar period, the following statements indicate the goodwill that Presidents Harding, Coolidge, and Hoover harbored toward the establishment of the State of Israel. In 1921, President Harding commented:

I am very glad to express my approval and hearty sympathy for the effort of the Palestine Foundation Fund in behalf of the restoration of Palestine as a homeland for the Jewish people. I have always viewed with an interest, which I think is quite as much practical as sentimental the proposal for the rehabilitation of Palestine, and I hope that effort now being carried on in this and other countries in this behalf may meet with the fullest measure of success. (H. 360 1922).

In 1925, President Coolidge ratified the Anglo-American Convention of December 3, 1924, which affirmed the League of

Nations' recognition of the Balfour Declaration (Anglo-American). And in 1932, President Hoover wrote:

> On the occasion of your celebration of the 15th Anniversary of the Balfour Declaration, which received the unanimous approval of both Houses of Congress by the adoption of the Lodge-Fish Resolution in 1922, I wish to express the hope that the ideal of the establishment of the National Jewish Home in Palestine, as embodied in that Declaration, will continue to prosper for the good of all the people inhabiting the Holy Land (Gilder Lehrman Institute "Hoover" 1932)

These statements and directives demonstrate the interwar presidents' fondness and support for a Jewish state. While they make no obvious reference to Christian values, the use of words like "restoration" and "Holy Land" strongly suggest the religious foundation of their endorsements.

PRESIDENT FRANKLIN DELANO ROOSEVELT AND BRITAIN'S WHITE PAPER

In 1939, Britain issued a White Paper, barring Jewish immigration into Palestine. Then-Senator Harry Truman denounced it as a capitulation to the Axis powers (Ross 6). President Roosevelt's position, however, was less clear. While he assured Jewish leaders that he did not support Britain's policy, he simultaneously sought to placate Arab leaders and members of his own administration who were opposed to a Jewish state. Roosevelt's private opposition to the White Paper was never matched either by public opposition or by US diplomatic pressure on Britain to change the policy. Indeed Roosevelt was sympathetic to the false claim that Palestine had reached its absorptive capacity by the 1930s and had no room for a major influx of immigrants (Medoff 225). He was willing to tell Rabbi Stephen Wise, perhaps the American Jewish community's foremost leader, in 1937 that Palestine had "reached the point of Jewish saturation" (Medoff 226). On account of the strong and intimate ties between the diplomatic and missionary communities, when it came to the question of a Jewish return to Palestine, the State Department vehemently and consistently objected (Grose 98-141; Preston 188).[12]

Indeed, as Rafael Medoff documents, anti-Semitism was rife in the State Department.

Franklin D. Roosevelt himself was an Episcopalian whose faith manifested itself in a commitment to ecumenism and respect for other beliefs, particularly Catholicism and Judaism (Preston 315). Yet there is considerable evidence that FDR also harbored the sort of commonplace anti-Semitism typical of his generation and social class. "A common theme underlay Roosevelt's perceptions of both Jews and Japanese Americans. Their 'blood'—that is, their innate racial characteristics—made them suspect" (Medoff 295). Both Jews and Japanese, he felt, should be spread thinly across the country, discouraged from gathering in communities. As Medoff reports in detail, Roosevelt regularly enjoyed telling jokes about Jews (291-2). Based on Roosevelt's private conversations, writers have long stated that he believed Israel was the Jewish homeland, affirming the Jews' "'unchallengeable right to Palestine'" (quoted in Grose 156). Treasury Secretary Henry Morgenthau would later recall FDR suggesting privately that Palestine be declared a de-facto Judeo-Christian country, run by a committee consisting of the Greek Orthodox Church, Protestants, and Jews. Palestinians would be transferred to a nearby Arab land, replaced by one Jewish family at a time (138-140). He offered formulaic statements supporting a "homeland" but never made policy decisions to implement one. "President Roosevelt's statements regarding Palestine after the United States entered World War II indicate he was heavily influenced by a fear that American backing for Zionism would provoke anti-American violence in the Arab world and Arab support for the Axis" (Medoff 234).

The one public action of consequence came in 1944, when the Republican national convention adopted a plank calling for "the opening of Palestine" to unrestricted Jewish immigration and land ownership and the implementation of the Balfour Declaration. It concluded: "We condemn the failure of the President to insist that the Palestine Mandatory carry out the provisions of the Balfour Declaration and the Mandate while he pretends to support them" (quoted in Medoff 245). With the Jewish vote at stake, the Democrats quickly adopted their own plank endorsing a Jewish commonwealth in Palestine (Medoff 247). "The adoption of the two party planks ensured that support for

Zionism and later for Israel, would have an enduring place in American political culture" (Medoff 249).

Meanwhile, the critical decision to be made was not whether to support a future Jewish state but whether to intervene in the present to save the Jews of Europe. On that count FDR was silent and the FDR administration failed abjectly. That failure begins with the administration's support for "the British closure of Palestine to all but a trickle of Jewish refugees" (Medoff 262) and extends to the administration's unwillingness to welcome Jewish refugees to the United States. The decision to block the refugee ship *St. Louis* from landing at a US port is but one example. "When he decided to rebuff the *St. Louis*, President Roosevelt had no reason to believe the ship would be going anywhere except back to Nazi Germany" (Medoff 88). The merchant ships that delivered weapons and supplies to Britain and Europe could have transported Jewish refugees to the US on the return trip. Portuguese liners traveled from Lisbon to the US every six weeks (Medoff 298). The Liberty ships that ferried troops and supplies to Europe returned empty. Indeed, they undertook a difficult search for sufficient ballast to make the return trips possible at all. By 1944, with knowledge of the mass murder of Jews existing throughout the allied governments, pressure to bomb the gas chambers at Auschwitz and the rail lines leading to the death camp mounted. Numerous allied bombers were in the area. Fuel factories in the vicinity of Auschwitz were repeatedly bombed (Medoff 272). No significant diversion of resources would have been required to bomb Auschwitz. But indifference to the fate of the Jews was decisive.

The mainline *Christian Century* had been swift to endorse the *White Paper* for fear of "a Jewish minority dominating the Arab majority," thereby jeopardizing Christian missionary activity (cited in Carenen 19). Similar sentiments were expressed by Henry Sloan Coffin of Union Theological Seminary and other mainline leaders (32). Nevertheless, the preponderance of mainline Protestants were favorably disposed towards the return of the Jews to Palestine. According to Carenen, the *Christian Century*'s anti-Zionism was a significant factor in Christian Realist Reinhold Niebuhr's decision in 1941 to establish a competing mainline periodical, *Christianity and Crisis* (22).

Most notably, in response to the news of the Nazi genocide taking place in Europe, New York Senator Robert F. Wagner established the bipartisan *American Christian Palestine Committee* (ACPC) to "support the Holy Land as an outpost of freedom and social justice . . . for hundreds of thousands of Jewish refugees" (Carenen 20). At its peak, two-thirds of the US Senate were members, along with distinguished Protestants nationwide. In 1944, over three thousand American civil society organizations passed pro-Zionist motions and twelve thousand letters were sent to the president and State Department (Grose 174). The most prominent ACPC victory in the mainline churches was a declaration by the Methodist Church endorsing the establishment of a Jewish state in Palestine (Carenen 28).

Meanwhile, fundamentalist Christians were generally pro-Zionist, albeit for different reasons. In contrast to mainline Christian support stemming from the Nazi genocide, fundamentalist periodicals such as *Moody Monthly* and *Our Hope* were motivated by the apparent fulfilment of biblical prophecy. Nevertheless, they refused to join forces with "secular Jews" and "nominal Christians" in their political efforts to establish a Jewish state (Carenen 30).

While the ACPC was a Protestant effort, behind the scenes it was encouraged by Jews. At its zenith, the Jewish American Zionist Emergency Council (AZEC) allocated $150,000 towards Christian advocacy efforts. In one memorandum, AZEC suggested that "'government officials in high places have indicated that strong Christian pressure . . . is needed to spur federal action on behalf of a Jewish Palestine'" (quoted in Grose 173). On the other side of the fence, however, the American Council for Judaism (ACJ) campaigned to convince Christians to oppose Zionism, contending that Judaism is a religion, not an ethnicity. While never representing the majority of Jews, it succeeded in sowing seeds of doubt among many Christians regarding Jewish attitudes towards Zionism (Carenen 31).

PRESIDENT HARRY TRUMAN AND THE FOUNDING OF ISRAEL

Within weeks of Harry Truman becoming president, allied troops liberated Buchenwald and the other death camps. The president was among those who consequently felt an increased moral urgency to create a Jewish state. In April 1946 he urged that 100,000 Jewish refugees be immediately admitted to Palestine. That October he issued a statement endorsing the establishment of an independent Jewish commonwealth there. In 1947, the United Nations proposed a plan to partition Mandate Palestine between the local Jewish and Arab populations. Secretary of State George Marshall was opposed, on the grounds that previous support for Zionism had led to a loss of American prestige in the Arab world and created opportunities for the Soviets. Yet Truman voted in favor of partition, going so far as to utilize US resources and clout to apply pressure to other countries (Ross 23). Nevertheless, the UN decision, while welcomed by the Jews living in Palestine, was rejected by the Arabs, who immediately declared war on the Jewish community. The Jews fought back, and on May 14, 1948, announced the establishment of the State of Israel. President Truman was the first to recognize the nascent country, doing so a mere eleven minutes after it came into existence. Yet Truman refused to supply Israel with arms during the war that followed.

Truman grew up in a Baptist family and evinced "an almost Fundamentalist reverence for the Bible," priding himself on having read the Bible cover-to-cover twice by age twelve, and regularly quoting Scripture to reporters (Gustafson 379; Preston 418). He once declared "Divine Providence played a great part in our history. I have the feeling that God has created us and brought us to our present position of power and strength for some great purpose" (quoted in Gustafson 384). And following his role in the establishment of Israel, Truman liked to call himself "Cyrus," a reference to the ancient Persian king who paved the way for the Jewish return to Zion in 538 BCE (Oren *Fantasy* 501).

For mainline Protestants, news of the Holocaust precipitated a period of soul-searching over American anti-Semitism, leading the ACPC to step up its efforts on behalf of Jewish immigration and Zionism. Some prominent theologians, however, continued to express opposition to Zionism, citing the potential damage to regional missionary efforts and the local Palestinian population. The *Christian Century* went so far as to demand that Jews must decide "whether they are an integral part of the nation in which they live, or members of a Levantine nation dwelling in exile" (Carenen 45; Grose 214).

By contrast, fundamentalists were mostly in favor of Zionism. *Moody Monthly* noted that the Jews' title deeds to the land were found in millions of Bibles around the world (Grose 215). Many began to call for the prosecution of Nazi war criminals, declaring that doing so would "vindicate Israel as God's peculiar people" and bring about "eternal life and blessedness for the righteous" among the gentiles. Evangelical journals unanimously rejected anti-Semitism. They nonetheless remained unwilling to join ACPC efforts, maintaining that the Jewish return to Zion should be left in God's hands (Carenen 42).

American Jewish opinion continued to be divided. Contrary to the mainstream Zionist position, Rabbi Judah Magnes, president of the Hebrew University of Jerusalem, advocated for reconciliation with the Arabs and the establishment of a binational state. Unsurprisingly, the *Christian Century* repeatedly endorsed his position (Grose 227). In 1948, a number of prominent anti-Zionist Jews and Christians formed the Committee for Justice and Peace in the Holy Land, with the stated purpose of lobbying both the US government and the UN against the establishment of a Jewish state (Marty 188). In 1951, the group morphed into American Friends of the Middle East (AFME), which consisted of previous committee members along with members of the aforementioned ACJ (Carenen 60).

Nevertheless, Zionist Jews won the day through a personal connection to the president. With Truman equivocating, Jewish leaders turned to his old friend and business partner, Eddie Jacobson. Jacobson managed to secure a backdoor meeting between Truman and Chaim Weizmann, who would become the first president of Israel. That rendezvous was pivotal in cementing Truman's support for the Zionist cause (Oren *Fantasy* 495). Domestic political considerations also played a role, given that the Jewish vote in New York was a key factor in gaining the state's support in the electoral college, but moral and geopolitical considerations loomed larger. As Douglas Little suggests, there was as well a motive that coalesced as the new state approached becoming a reality: "deeply concerned about possible Soviet inroads into the Middle

East," Truman apparently "regarded a Jewish state as a stronger bulwark against communism than anything the Arabs could muster" (87).

Reelected in 1948, Truman then faced another challenge: how to resolve the problem of the Arab refugees. Truman helped pass UN Resolution 194 which stated that refugees willing to live in peace should be allowed to return. As time passed, however, he became more sympathetic to the possibility of permanently settling most of the refugees in Arab countries, rather than in returning them all to Israel (Little 271). Meanwhile, he was finding Ben-Gurion a difficult partner. Israeli territorial ambitions had found unexpected realization in the 1948 war, and there was little Israeli impulse toward territorial concessions as part of any resettlement agreement. The Truman administration thus found reason to express frustration with the Jewish state. "As the Missouri Democrat prepared to turn the White House over to Dwight Eisenhower, relations between Israel and the United States were far cooler than they had been four years earlier" (Little 88).

PRESIDENT DWIGHT D. EISENHOWER AND THE SUEZ CRISIS

With his entry into the White House in 1953, Eisenhower assured the Arabs that the US would henceforth be more evenhanded (Ross 28). In July 1953, Eisenhower signed NSC-155/1, which called for the "reversal of the anti-American trends of Arab opinion" by declaring that "Israel will not, merely because of its Jewish population, receive Preferential treatment" (quoted Little 89). Daniel G. Hummel says, "The Eisenhower years were a low point, stemming from the U.S. administration's attempt to win over Arab states and Israel's own collusion with Great Britain and France in the Suez War in 1956" (53). As "Alice A. Butler-Smith put it concisely," for a time "'Eisenhower saw Israel as the problem rather than the potential solution.'" (Tal 25).

John Foster Dulles, Eisenhower's Secretary of State, "'spiritualized' any prophetic references to Israel" and thus discounted any covenantal commitments to actual land (Hummel 66). "After distancing the United States from European imperialism, Dulles sounded a retreat from Truman-era support of Israel" (Doran 77). Dulles remarked the "Arab fear 'that the United States will back the new State of Israel's aggressive expansion,' while the Israelis 'fear that ultimately the Arabs may try to push them into the sea'" (Tal 30). "Eisenhower's policy of becoming an even-handed broker between the Israelis and the Arabs followed, but, as Michael Doran demonstrates in detail, the policy was somewhat naively executed and failed. The problem was partly rhetorical, as the emphasis on a principle of "impartial friendship" came across as unfriendliness. As David Tal writes, "the United States would help Israel, but in the most inconspicuous manner possible" (31).

In September 1955, when Soviet Russia sent military supplies to Egypt, Israel requested arms from the US. Eisenhower refused, suggesting Israel turn to the UN for security assistance. Yet he actively encouraged the French-Israeli arms deal (Tal 36). In October 1956, when Israel—working in tandem with France and Britain—attacked Egypt in the Suez, the US threatened sanctions unless it withdrew its troops. Unable to pass a UN Security Council resolution due to a threat of veto by France and the UK, Eisenhower turned to the General Assembly to pressure Israel to withdraw (34). He appeared on national television to publicize his willingness to impose sanctions should Israel not withdraw its forces. "Eisenhower described the argument with Israel over the 1956 war not as a conflict between adversaries, but as a conflict between family members" (Tal 32), but that was not the perception in Israel. This "bitter clash during early 1957 revealed a level of reciprocal mistrust and diplomatic estrangement that would once have seemed unthinkable" (Little 93).

Nevertheless, by 1958 Eisenhower and Ben Gurion moved toward a diplomatic reconciliation. "To shut the Soviets out of the Arab world: that was Eisenhower's goal when he took office in 1953. The best method, he believed, was to broker an accommodation between the United States and Arab nationalism, and he identified Nasser as the primary partner in this effort" (Doran 245). But by the middle of 1957, the US had realized that Nasser's Egypt would not be a faithful ally and appeared prone to supporting Soviet goals in the region. At that point, Eisenhower acknowledged Israel's status as a "stable pro-Western country" in the region. Moreover, in light of Israel's role in stemming anti-US forces in Lebanon and Jordan, by the end of his term in office, Israel had become a key element of Eisenhower doctrine (Alteras), and the administration approved limited arms sales to the Jewish state. That did not, however, prevent Eisenhower from expressing his opposition to any Israeli effort to develop nuclear weapons.

Eisenhower grew up in a fundamentalist Christian home; his family were River Brethren, but they later converted to Jehovah's Witnesses. He thus "was not born into the powerful Protestant establishment, whose members still occupied most positions of cultural and political leadership in the United States during the 1950s" (Gaston 177). Most scholars aver that the president himself was not particularly religious, despite maintaining a façade of religiosity for political purposes (Preston 443). While he "grew up believing that the Jews were the chosen people, that they gave us the high ethical and moral principles of our civilization," he nonetheless considered the Zionist venture irrational, and felt no responsibility toward the fledgling state (Merkley *Presidents* 49). Postelection Eisenhower converted to his wife's Presbyterianism. Eisenhower's pastor was Rev. Edward L. R. Elson of the National Presbyterian Church. Two weeks after his inauguration, Elson baptized him and formally admitted him to the Church, which both Eisenhower and Dulles attended (Doran 10). Elson was a leading officer in the anti-Israel AFME and maintained that "Israel has no moral right to exist" (Aridan 81). "AFME, to put it bluntly, was a CIA front organization. Its official goal was to promote people-to-people exchanges between the United States and the Middle East, but its true priority was to counter the influence of the Israeli lobby in domestic American policy" (Doran 127).

The division in mainline Christian opinion came to the fore with the new administration's stated objective of exercising "neutral and impartial friendship" towards all Middle Eastern nation-states (Carenen 103). The AFME announced their approval in a *New York Times* ad; in their estimation, since Congress was susceptible to lobbying influence, "successful foreign policy-making in the United States must be concentrated in the executive." In response, the ACPC took out a full-page ad declaring that Israel's actions were due "in large measure to the inordinate provocation which, we feel, no nation in similar circumstances would have tolerated with so much patience" (103). During the 1950s, tensions between the ACPC and AFME intensified; indeed, ACPC engaged in espionage operations to keep apprised of AFME's activities (99).

Shortly prior to Israel's incursion into Sinai, the *Christian Century* criticized Israel's responses to the fedayeen (militants who crossed the border from Egypt into Israel to perpetrate acts of terror), suggesting, "The old law of an eye for an eye has apparently been supplanted in Israel's ideology by a more savage rule: a head for an eye" (107). And following the Suez crisis, the AFME applauded Eisenhower's criticism of Israel and acknowledged the president's refusal "to be cowed by Zionism and its few vocal supporters." The ACPC, for its part, responded that the AFME position "represents an insult to those thousands, if not millions, of Christians who supported the creation of the State of Israel out of genuine Christian and humanitarian motives." At the same time, they continued their clandestine operations on AFME, reporting back discussions with anti-Semitic overtones, such as the implication that the liberal pro-Israel media was controlled by the Jews (110-12).

Turning to fundamentalist thought and activity, in 1957 William Hull published *Israel – Key to Prophecy: the Story of Israel from the Regathering to the Millennium as Told by the Prophets* to warm reviews from Christian periodicals such as *Moody Monthly* and *Christian Herald*. Other fundamentalist periodicals began to stress the Abrahamic blessing, "I will bless them who bless you and curse them who curse you," with the *Sunday School Times* outlining how nations that have blessed the Jews have thrived while those that persecuted the Jews disappeared in time (Carenen 118). Nevertheless, the evangelical *Christianity Today* ran a debate between two theologians over the Jewish people's right to Israel (108) and *Bible Baptist Tribune* published a series of articles highly critical of Israel, on account of its secular foundations (120). A further feature of certain fundamentalist thought pieces was the repudiation of anti-Semitism on the one hand, but on the other, the desire to see the ultimate conversion of the Jewish people to Christianity (Carenen 121; Crouse 54).

As far as Christian debates were concerned, for mainline Protestants the question was, "Does Christianity's role in the Holocaust warrant our support for the Jewish people, to the detriment of the Arabs?" It was not a question of biblical interpretation, but a question of the application of the biblical imperative of repentance and justice. In contrast, for fundamentalists, the primary two issues were whether a *secular* State of Israel should be supported and whether God's ultimate purpose for the Jews was conversion to Christianity. Most agreed, however, that they were witnessing the unfolding of biblical prophecy. Indeed, despite their continued reticence to engage politically, evangelical leaders now called upon their brothers to pray for the Holy Land (Carenen 120).

In response to the pro-Israel ACPC's *New York Times* ad, the anti-Israel AFME wrote to each of the signatories, accusing them of "an element of misrepresentation involved in labeling [their] committee as Christian" since it received considerable funding from the Jewish Zionist Council of America (104). Given the AFME's Jewish membership (and subsequent government funding revelations, see below), the charge was a tad disingenuous.

Meanwhile, Jewish leaders sensed that weakening American support for Israel was due in part to waning Zionist fervor in the Jewish community after the State of Israel had been established. They therefore founded two pro-Israel lobbying groups, the American Israel Public Affairs Committee (AIPAC) and the Conference of Presidents of Major Jewish Organizations. These groups began engaging with Congress, where they found abundant support for Israel amongst Christian lawmakers like Republican Senate Minority Leader, William Knowland, who threatened to resign as a UN delegate if Eisenhower imposed sanctions on Israel (Crouse 70; Merkley *Presidents* 47).[13]

PRESIDENT JOHN F. KENNEDY AND THE SPECIAL RELATIONSHIP

From its very establishment, the State of Israel could never be certain of its friends in the world. That uncertainty evaporated with the election of Kennedy, who introduced the "special relationship" rhetoric employed by all future presidents, irrespective of party.[14] Kennedy was the first president to break the arms embargo on major US weapon sales to Israel and begin security consultations, ultimately leading to joint military planning (Bass 3). The sole persistent disagreement between Kennedy and Israel was over the issue of nuclear development (188). Although

Israel pledged not to develop nuclear weapons, both Kennedy and his advisors regarded the promise as suspect (Little 97).

Kennedy was the first (and until Biden, sole) non-Protestant president. He went to great pains, however, to stress that he was the president who merely happened to be Catholic. And indeed, while he was not irreligious, he was not particularly devout. Instead, he stressed that religion should be a private matter; and yet continued to appeal publicly to God's blessing (Preston 501-3). On Israel, there is little indication that his position was religiously motivated. His priest, Cardinal Richard Cushing, however, was a supporter of Israel who once noted that Israel was, for the Jewish people, "the fulfillment of prophecy, the return to the promised land, the realization of the divine covenant, the answer to the prayers of generations of the chosen people" (Feldman 217; JTA "Cardinal Cushing").

In the early 1960s, it came to light that the anti-Israel AFME was a front organization for the CIA, receiving State Department as well as oil-lobby funds. These revelations led to the swift downfall of the group (Wilford 21). With AFME no longer in the picture and American public opinion stably pro-Israel, ACPC disbanded shortly thereafter. Meanwhile, fundamentalist groups began travelling and holding conferences in Israel. After leading Southern Baptist preacher W.A. Criswell toured the Holy Land in the 1950s, he returned to America and began talking of the Jewish state as the fulfilment of biblical prophecy. In 1961, the World Conference of Pentecostal Churches held its annual convention in Jerusalem (Spector 144).

As Israeli government officials became aware of Christian interest in Israel, they began efforts to cultivate relationships with evangelicals. Prime Minister David Ben-Gurion officially received W.A. Criswell and Oral Roberts and was instrumental in hosting the Pentecostal conference. In addition, Israel's Ministry of Religious Affairs began publishing *Christian News from Israel* (144).

PRESIDENT LYNDON B. JOHNSON AND THE SIX DAY WAR

When President Johnson assumed office in 1963, Israel was clearly an underdog in the Middle East. Not only did Johnson continue Kennedy's policy of selling defensive weapons to Israel, he also began to sell offensive arms. And, while JFK delivered his message to then-Minister of Foreign affairs Golda Meir in private, LBJ publicly demonstrated his affinity for Israel, becoming the first president to host an Israeli prime minister not just to the White House but also at his ranch (Ross 77, 96). On June 5, 1967, in response to Egyptian and Syrian troops massed at its borders, Israel launched a preemptive strike. When the Soviets called the US hotline requesting support for the brokering of a ceasefire, LBJ agreed only on the condition that Egypt cooperate. After six days, however, Israel had vanquished its enemies and the war was over. Egypt's President Nasser accused the US of colluding with Israel, a claim the State Department would later call the "big lie" (95). The accusation resulted in Egypt, Syria, Algeria, Yemen, and Sudan breaking diplomatic relations with the US. Nonetheless, as Little observes, "Johnson seems to have taken vicarious pleasure from Israel's ability to thwart an Arab war of national liberation not unlike the one the United States faced in Vietnam" (101).

Johnson was born a Baptist, but at age fifteen he chose to join the Disciples of Christ, a mainline denomination, on account of its emphasis on tolerance and good deeds over the fire-and-brimstone Baptist approach (Woods 41). Johnson's father had been a Texas state legislator who opposed the KKK. His mother taught him "'the belief that the strong must care for the weak'" (quoted in Goodwin 55). Thus, according to Balmer, Johnson was driven by a commitment to Christianity's Golden Rule that he inherited from his parents (*God* 53). In LBJ's words, "'Any religion which did not struggle to remove oppression from the world of men would not be able to create the world of spirit.'" It was the job of the Church to "'reawaken the [national] conscience'" (quoted in Woods 465). This desire to protect the weak motivated his pursuit of civil rights in America and was also his impetus for America's role in Vietnam (Balmer *God* 51-3).

Indeed, Johnson was wont to compare Israel to South Vietnam, both small countries under attack from mightier external enemies (Ross 98). The clearest manifestation of Christianity as the underpinning of Johnson's commitment to Israel was his biblical belief. In a speech to the Jewish service organization Bnai Brith in 1968, he announced, "Most, if not all of you, have very deep ties to the land and with the people of Israel, as I do, for my Christian faith sprang from yours. The Bible stories are woven into my childhood memories as the gallant struggle of modern Jews to be free of persecution is also woven into our souls." To the president of Israel he declared, "'Our Republic, like yours, was nurtured by the philosophy of the ancient Hebrew teachers who taught mankind the principles of morality, of social justice, and of universal peace. This is our heritage, and it is yours'" (quoted in Ross 98). The president's pastor was the pro-Israel evangelical Billy Graham (Spector); LBJ invited him to preach and lead prayers at the National City Christian Church (Flowers 172).

Meanwhile, the dissolution of the ACPC in 1966 left a hole in mainline Protestant support for Israel. In 1967, with Israel surrounded by its enemies, Boston-area Catholic and Protestant clergymen issued a "Declaration of Moral Principle," asking Americans to recognize that Israel risked destruction. Their efforts to convince the National Council of Churches to issue a statement in defense of Israel, however, did not meet with success (Carenen 137; Merkley *Attitudes* 37). Instead, many mainline leaders publicly blamed Israel. Henry Pitt Van Dusen, president of Union Theological Seminary, criticized "Israel's assault on her Arab neighbors," and proceeded to compare Israel's actions to Hitler's blitzkrieg (Merkley *Attitudes* 38). Nevertheless, the division between the elites and the laity in the mainline was becoming increasingly apparent. Following the war, national mainline organizations such as the Lutheran Church and the NCC began to criticize Israel over its territorial acquisitions. And yet, a growing number of everyday Christians were becoming enamored by the Scriptural resonances of Israel's victories (Carenen 140).

Both fundamentalists and other evangelicals were elated at Israel's victory. On account of Israel's secularist foundations, prior to 1967 evangelicals were divided over the theological place of the modern

State of Israel. Following the war, however, fundamentalist periodicals across the board pointed to the unfolding of biblical prophecy, with some going so far as to call for the rebuilding of the Holy Temple in Jerusalem (144).

In the early 1960s, the Israeli government established a Department of Christian Affairs to galvanize American evangelical support. In 1967, the department sent a representative, Yona Malachy, to investigate American Christian attitudes toward Israel and encourage their tangible expressions of support. The Hebrew University published his findings, entitled *American Fundamentalism and Israel: The Relation of Fundamentalist Churches to Zionism and the State of Israel* (Spector 145).

PRESIDENT RICHARD M. NIXON AND THE YOM KIPPUR WAR

Nixon believed that America's position on the Six Day War had been detrimental to its relationship with the Arab nations. Thus, when he came to power, he made efforts to distance the US from Israel (Ross 125). In 1973, however, Egypt and Syria took both Israel and the US by surprise by attacking the Jewish state on their holiest day of the year, Yom Kippur. Once Nixon realized that the Soviets were providing military supplies to the Arabs, he felt compelled to deliver arms to Israel. Nevertheless, following Israel's meager victory, the president immediately pressured the country to take steps towards reconciliation with its neighbors (127, 131). But Nixon's geopolitical focus also worked to strengthen the relationship. "By the summer of 1973 the CIA and the Mossad, the chief Israeli intelligence agency were comparing notes on Palestinian terrorists and Arab radicals" (Little 106).

Nixon grew up as a Quaker, but parted ways while in college (Balmer God 63). Later, in an effort to attract evangelical support, he made overtures to Billy Graham; however, the preacher soon tired of Nixon's shallow faith commitment (Preston 541). While he admired Israel's strength and patriotism, he saw Israel as the source of instability in the region. Ultimately, he evinced no special affinity towards Israel or the Jewish people—perhaps unsurprising after the Nixon White House tapes revealed his anti-Semitism (Merkley, *Presidents* 63). Nixon's pastor during his presidency was John Huffman (Lynn Smith *Newport*), who would later be part of the PCUSA committee that authored *Breaking Down the Walls*, criticized by the Anti-Defamation League and the Simon Wiesenthal Center for its anti-Israel bias (Terry).

Though it was far from universal, Christian anti-Zionism began to cohere. In 1970, the Quakers published a report on the Israeli-Palestinian conflict entitled *Search for Peace in the Middle East*, which placed the bulk of the culpability for the 1967 war on Israel (AFSC "Search" 14-17). In January 1971, the *Christian Century* called the document "an instructive and fair-minded primer" (Forster and Epstein *Anti-Semitism* 85). On Palm Sunday 1972, Rev. Francis B. Sayre, dean of the National Cathedral in DC, likened Israel's efforts to the ancient Jews' persecution of Jesus, declaring, "even as they praise their God . . . they begin almost simultaneously to put Him to death," thus beginning what would later be called Palestinian Liberation theology (Forster and Epstein 82).

Nevertheless, mainline support for Israel persisted. In 1971, Methodist minister Franklin Littell inaugurated Christians Concerned for Israel (CCI), as a "watchdog of American Protestant attitudes toward Israel" (Carenen 60). Despite official mainline opposition toward the US-Israel alliance, Littell insisted that "once you get behind the bureaucrats in the church boards, there is a vast reservoir of goodwill toward the Holy Land" (152). CCI consisted of both mainline and evangelical Christians (158). According to Merkley, however, CCI was a one-man show that would only mobilize to garner pro-Israel support when the need arose (*Attitudes* 180).

The major pro-Israel mainline theologian of the twentieth century was undoubtedly Reinhold Niebuhr, who died in 1971. While Niebuhr's stance was expressed primarily on paper in the pages of his periodical *Christianity and Crisis*, after his passing, his widow Ursula began engaging politically. In addition to becoming the campus sponsor for the Youth Committee for Peace and Democracy in the Middle East, she was a member of the Jerusalem Committee, set up after 1967 by Jerusalem's Mayor Teddy Kollek to plan the city's development (Carenen 156).

Meanwhile, following the 1970 publication of Hal Lindsey's *The Late Great Planet Earth*, the State of Israel enjoyed growing fundamentalist support. An American best-seller, the book demonstrated the unfolding of Scriptural prophecy in Israel and throughout the world. In 1971, Pennsylvania preacher Gaylord Briley organized the Jerusalem Conference on Bible Prophecy. Fourteen hundred evangelicals descended upon Jerusalem for "a ringside seat at the Second Coming," stimulating an increase in evangelical tourism to Israel (Spector 146).

How did American Jews feel? On the anti-Israel side, the disbanded American Council of Judaism (ACJ) and Americans for Middle East Peace (AFMEP) regrouped as America-Mideast Educational and Training Services, or AMIDEAST (Wilford *Friends*). Rabbi Elmer Berger, a leading Jewish voice in the earlier group also founded American Jewish Alternatives to Zionism (Mittelman Champions). Israel importantly continued its engagement with pro-Israel Christians. Former Prime Minister Ben-Gurion was the featured speaker at the Jerusalem Conference; when he died, Hal Lindsey's work was found on his bedside table (Spector 146). And when the mainline NCC issued a statement urging the US to look to the UN "as the primary instrument for achieving and maintaining peace in the Middle East" (Forster and Epstein 323), Mayor Kollek turned to Ursula Niebuhr for help in countering international pressure for the re-division of Jerusalem (Carenen 156).

PRESIDENT GERALD FORD AND "ZIONISM IS RACISM"

Gerald Ford became president after Richard Nixon resigned. Despite his staunch support for Israel while in Congress, as president Ford largely deferred to Secretary of State Henry Kissinger in dealing with the region, and he became frustrated with Israel after Kissinger's shuttle diplomacy reached a dead end (Little 107). Living in a post-1967 world, Ford saw Israel as the mightiest state in the region and consequently questioned the need for continued American arms supplies (Ross 137). "The Israelis," he complained in his memoirs, "were always insisting that we supply them more military equipment than our own experts thought they needed" (Quoted in Little 108). He was the first president to describe Israeli settlements as illegal,[15] and at one point he threatened Israel with a "reassessment of United States policy" (Rabin 265). In response, Israel rallied Congress and produced a letter signed by seventy-six senators calling on the administration to stand firm with the Jewish state (Ross 138). Nevertheless, in anticipation of the peace deal between Israel and Egypt, President Ford signed an extensive memorandum of understanding promising $2 billion in aid, economic compensation for oil fields Israel was giving up, as well as a commitment not to recognize the PLO until it recognized Israel's right to exist (139). In a speech to the American Jewish Committee, Ford promised to "'remain the ultimate guarantor of Israel's freedom'" (quoted in Merkley *Presidents* 85).

In 1975, the United Nations issued the "Zionism is Racism" resolution. Despite US Ambassador Daniel Patrick Moynihan opposing it and declaring that "the United Nations is about to make anti-Semitism international law," it passed. President Ford responded saying that the resolution had jeopardized the credibility of the UN (Troy 171). The resolution was finally rescinded in 1991.

Ford was raised an Episcopalian; during his tenure in the White House, however, he became close with evangelical preacher Billy Zeoli (Balmer *God* 69). While he felt no religious duty towards Israel, Ford's support stemmed from a sense of America and Israel's kindred narratives, describing both as promised lands to their respective nations (Merkley *Presidents* 85). While a formal record of Zeoli's feelings on Israel/Palestine is not extant, he would later boast of meeting with chairman of the PLO Yasser Arafat (Zeoli). During that period, the US eschewed any relations with Arafat and the PLO, which it considered a terrorist organization (Christison 176).

In the 1950s, pro-Israel mainline Protestants like Niebuhr were an anomaly; by the 1970s, however, the general tide amongst Americans had shifted and Christian support for Israel was the norm. Preston attributes such support to the Holocaust, and Israel's plight in the 1967 and 1973 wars, in light of which prejudice against Jews—and by extension, Israel—was considered un-American (562). Despite the World Council of Churches' long history of criticism of Israel, the (corresponding US) National Council of Churches was more balanced. Indeed, when the UN passed "Zionism is Racism," Christian Americans of all stripes rallied together in opposition (Carenen 166; Preston 558).

At that time the pro-Israel lobby still lacked the sophistication and authority for which it would later be known. In an effort to mobilize opposition to the UN resolution, representatives of Israel's Foreign Ministry met with American Jewish leaders and urged them to solicit public support, especially from religious leaders. Given pre-existing pro-Israel Christian sentiment in America, the impact of their efforts is unclear (Troy 116).

PRESIDENT JIMMY CARTER AND PEACE WITH EGYPT

President Jimmy Carter closed the deal on one of the most important moves towards Middle East peace: the Camp David Accords between Israel and Egypt, an agreement that has withstood the test of time. Since 1979, the two countries have continued security and military cooperation and worked together to fight regional terrorist threats. Nevertheless, Carter considered Israel "a constant irritant" and was no friend of the Jewish state (Ross 145). Critical of Israel's "occupation," he would make frequent reference to UN Resolution 242, which called upon Israel to withdraw from all territories gained in 1967 (Carenen 169). "He shocked the Israelis and their U.S. supporters shortly after his inauguration by publicly endorsing the concept of a Palestinian homeland" (Little 109). "After a series of nasty diplomatic exchanges with Israel" (Little 110), the administration endorsed a 1980 UN resolution confirming Arab rights on the West Bank and in East Jerusalem. Later, writing *Palestine: Peace, Not Apartheid* (2006), he eventually became *persona non grata* in the pro-Israel community. Both there and in other writings, Carter affirms a belief that the covenantal guarantee of Israel to the Jewish people is conditional upon Israel's conduct. In *Palestine: Peace Not Apartheid* he reports telling Golda Meir that "Israel was punished whenever the leaders turned away from devout worship of God" (32). Both there and in the earlier *The Blood of Abraham* (1985) one may detect a lingering hint of supersessionist bias.

Carter came to the presidency professing his faith as a "born-again Christian" and believed that the State of Israel was the fulfilment of biblical prophecy, declaring that he "'considered this homeland for the Jews to be compatible with the teachings of the Bible, hence ordained by

God'" (quoted in Reich 10). Yet Carter is a progressive evangelical; "the messianic hope of paving the way for the Davidic kingdom was not his concern" (Ariel "Contemporary" 292). In his 1979 address before the Israeli Knesset, Carter averred that the relationship between the United States and Israel endured "because it is rooted in the consciousness and the morals and the religion of the American people themselves" (quoted in Balmer *Redeemer* 87-88).[16] But he apparently compartmentalized his biblically-derived respect for Israel, keeping it separate from any sympathy toward the Israeli government.

Despite his Baptist background, Carter's personal pastor was United Methodist Bishop William R. Cannon, who worked as a representative for the president on Arab-Israeli affairs (Brown 16; Saxon). While Cannon's views on Israel/Palestine are unclear, two points of interest should be noted: first, he was a member of an official Methodist delegation to Carter appealing for peaceful negotiations with Iran (Carter *Keeping* 523; Elliott Wright *Iran* 16); and second, during his presidency of the World Methodist Council, (1981-1986) the United Methodist Church passed a resolution, encouraging "all leaders of and participants in 'Holy Land tours' to contact indigenous Christian leaders in the Middle East, and to hear the concerns of both the Israelis and Palestinians who live there" (UMC *Resolutions* 280).

The first evangelical organization to place Israel on its formal agenda was Jerry Falwell's Moral Majority. In *Listen, America!* Falwell summed up the goals of his group as pro-life, pro-family, pro-moral, pro-American, and pro-Israel. While Christian Zionists have been accused of being overly pro-Israel at the expense of peace, in May 1978 Falwell and a number of other evangelical leaders met with Anwar Sadat and Menachem Begin to discuss peace (Liberty *Champion* 1).

Meanwhile, in response to growing evangelical support for Israel, non-Zionist evangelicals were eager to make their voices heard. In 1978, Dewey Beegle of Wesley Theological Seminary published *Prophecy and Prediction*. Beegle argued that, in contrast to Christian Zionist views, the Biblical prophecy of the Jews' return to Israel was already fulfilled following the Babylonian exile and that God's covenant was abrogated when the Jews failed to observe the commandments.

Returning to the mainline branches, in 1979, the NCC issued a Middle East policy statement calling for the curtailing of arms transfers to the Middle East, the promotion of justice and reconciliation, and the reciprocal recognition of the right of self-determination of Israel and the PLO (Findley 250). Nevertheless, mainline support for Israel continued, albeit on a much smaller scale than the new evangelical activism. In 1978, four hundred Protestant and Catholic clergy teamed up to form the National Christian Leadership Conference for Israel (Merkley *Attitudes* 180).

At this juncture the State of Israel began to acknowledge publicly the power of the rising Christian Right in America. In one "foundational myth," Prime Minister Menachem Begin established formal political ties with Christian Zionists, after being treated for a heart attack by an evangelical. Cardiologist Dr. Larry Samuels later went on to become one of the founders of the International Christian Embassy Jerusalem, an organization dedicated to supporting Israel's 1980 declaration of Jerusalem as its eternal, undivided capital (Spector 147) (ICEJ).

PRESIDENT RONALD REAGAN AND THE FIRST LEBANON WAR

Particularly in light of the 1979 Iranian Revolution, Reagan saw Israel as the US's primary stable ally in the Middle East. While Reagan was the first president to formalize strategic cooperation with Israel, he was also the first to punish Israel over divergences in policy with the suspension of aircraft deliveries. In 1982, the US joined world powers in condemning Israel for bombing the Iraqi nuclear reactor in Osirak. Nevertheless, though prime minister Menachem Begin's decision to invade Lebanon in 1982 put the relationship with the US at risk, Reagan maintained support for Israel and eventually moved past his earlier equivocation over Israel's policies entirely (Ross 180-215).

Reagan was reared in the Disciples of Christ Church. Later in life, he took up membership at Bel Air Presbyterian Church. While the Disciples and Presbyterian Churches are mainline denominations, the particular congregations Reagan attended leaned toward greater theological conservatism. Throughout his political years, Reagan surrounded himself with evangelical clergy and leaders such as James G.

Watt and Gary Bauer and sometimes referred to himself as an evangelical (Balmer *God* 110; Preston 580). His pastors were Donn Moomaw of
Bel Air and Billy Graham, from whom he sought advice regarding the
present-day fulfilment of biblical prophecies. Early in his presidency, he
invited Jerry Falwell to address the National Security Council about the
Bible and nuclear war (Katz 46-8). Concerning Israel, he later wrote,
"I've believed many things in my life, but no conviction I've ever held
has been stronger than my belief that the United States must ensure the
survival of Israel" (Reagan 410).[17]

Some American Christians echoed Reagan's thinking. Jerry
Falwell declared to Americans that "to stand against Israel is to stand
against God . . . history and scripture prove that God deals with
nations in relation to how they deal with Israel" (Falwell). Following
Israel's bombing of the Osirak reactor, John Hagee organized his first
"Night to Honor Israel," explaining that Israel's actions benefitted not
only the Jewish state, but also America and the West (Hagee *Defense*).
In 1982, the Religious Roundtable began organizing the *National
Prayer Breakfast in Honor of Israel* (Findley 244).[18] Nevertheless, anti-
Zionist evangelical voices continued to make themselves heard. In
1986, Evangelicals for Middle East Understanding was founded with
the goal of challenging the position that the Israel of the Bible is syn-
onymous with the modern Jewish state (Merkley, *Attitudes* 187).

Meanwhile, the mainline camp was becoming increasingly critical
of Israel. In 1981, United Methodist Bishop James Armstrong issued a
public letter condemning the "Falwell gospel" and arguing that "Israel
was seen as God's chosen people in a servant sense. Israel was not given
license to exploit other people. God plays no favorites" (Findley 248).
In response, Falwell accused the NCC of Marxist-Leninist leanings and
decried their shift to liberation theology and consequent rebranding
of the PLO as a champion of freedom (Crouse 156). In 1984, twenty-
four mainline denominations joined forces with several Catholic
organizations to form Churches for Middle East Peace (CMEP), with
the goal of effecting "a sound and balanced US policy" (Carenen 202).
Subsequently, CMEP issued a declaration calling on "the community of
nations and all people who love mercy to recognize and condemn this
new apartheid that oppresses the Palestinian people" (Korn *Church*).

Confronted with these divisions, Israel opted to strengthen its evangelical relationships. In 1980, Prime Minister Begin conferred the Jabotinsky Medal on Falwell in appreciation of his support for Israel. The following year Begin asked Falwell not to oppose the re-election of liberal yet pro-Israel Senator Edward Kennedy. And following the Osirak bombing, Begin called Falwell seeking his assistance in fostering American public support for Israel's actions (Spector 148). In 1983, seeing the potential for both closer ties between American Jews and Christians and galvanizing evangelical support for Israel, Rabbi Yechiel Eckstein started the Holyland Fellowship of Christians and Jews. He subsequently changed the name to the International Fellowship of Christians and Jews, responsible today for raising tens of millions of American Christian dollars annually for Israel-related causes (Chafets).

Not all American Jews, however, were convinced. Writing in the *Jerusalem Post*, a past chairman of the Conference of Presidents of Major American Jewish Organizations questioned the Israel-evangelical friendship. In his opinion, the Moral Majority's agenda was the Christianization of America, which was ultimately not good for the Jews. Others were less concerned: AIPAC's former research chief's response was, "'Sure these guys give me the heebie-jeebies. But until I see Jesus coming over the hill, I'm in favor of all the friends Israel can get'" (Merkley *Attitudes* 202, 204).

PRESIDENT GEORGE H. W. BUSH AND THE GULF WAR

President Bush entered the White House feeling neither emotional attachment to Israel nor a sense of Holocaust-induced moral responsibility. He believed that the US should display greater balance when dealing with Israel and the Arab nations. Notably, as scud missiles rained down on Israel during the Gulf War, Bush prevented the country from retaliating. Nevertheless, military and security cooperation between the two nations proceeded apace during the Bush administration (Ross 217). Ross sums up the relationship: The substance was good, the tone was difficult, and the readiness to disagree in public was clear (255).

George H.W. Bush was raised Episcopalian. While he had the electoral support of evangelicals, he required direction and education on the topic of evangelical thought and practice to understand why Israel was important to them (Martin 263). According to Merkley, nothing on record suggests President Bush harbored any religious feelings towards Israel. And while his pastor was Billy Graham, their interactions took place primarily at the president's summer home in Maine (Merkley *Presidents* 177). Indeed, according to Balmer, once they voted him in, Bush turned his back on evangelicals and slowly began to push them out of the White House. The night before the Gulf War, however, Bush invited Billy Graham to the White House, in an effort "to cloak his actions in the mantle of righteousness" (Balmer *God* 127-9).

By the late 1980s, the mainline denominations had become vocal in their criticism of Israel. In 1988, the Presbyterian Church USA called upon Israel to "cease the systematic violation of the human rights of Palestinians in the occupied territories [including] administrative detention, collective punishment, the torture of prisoners and suspects, and the deportation of dissidents" (Hopkins "Presbyterians" 163). In 1989, the mainline Evangelical Lutheran Church in America (ELCA), a group that is not "evangelical" in the familiar sense of the word, released a "social report" accusing Israel of "human rights abuses in the Occupied Territories" (Korn *Church*). And in 1991, in response to Israeli settlement building, the Lutheran and the Episcopal Churches lobbied for the imposition of US sanctions on Israel (Clarke and Flohr 69). Nevertheless, by this stage, the mainline churches' political clout had eroded substantially; in 1991, when the NCC called for the removal of all military personnel from the Middle East, the request went unacknowledged by the White House (Carenen 203).

American Jews began to establish an organized response to mainline church anti-Zionism. In 1990, Jewish Esther Levens and Christian Allen Mothersill founded the National Unity Coalition for Israel. Seeking a single voice to represent Jewish and evangelical pro-Israel organizations, they assembled a coalition of two hundred groups representing forty million people. In 1998, the group gathered over three thousand people in Washington D.C. to demonstrate support for Israel, including Ralph Reed of the Christian Coalition and Brandt Gustavson of the National Religious Broadcasters (Weber *Armageddon* 224).

PRESIDENT BILL CLINTON AND
THE OSLO ACCORDS

Given America's newfound post-Cold War strength, Clinton initially saw Israeli-Palestinian peace talks as an opportunity for America to resolve tension in the region. Following the assassination of Israeli Prime Minister Yitzhak Rabin, however, peace became a mission for the remainder of his presidency (Ross 258). While the eventual legacy of the 1993 Oslo Accords arguably remains to be seen, Clinton's greatest achievement in the region was the peace agreement between Israel and Jordan in 1994, which continues to offer security and prosperity to both countries.

Clinton's parents were not religious, and yet his mother encouraged him to attend the Park Place Baptist Church in Hot Springs. When he entered the White House, he surrounded himself with left-leaning evangelical ministers including Bill Hybels and Gordon MacDonald of World Vision, as well as Tony Campolo, the unofficial leader of "red-letter" (Evangelical Left) Christianity (Balmer *God* 139). He believed in the truth of the Bible (Merkley *Presidents* 192). At critical moments, he would call upon his faith to carry him through; the night before the Oslo Accords, for example, he read the entire Book of Joshua (Ross 268). Furthermore, Clinton would recall his first trip to Israel with his pastor, who told him that one day he would be president, instructing him, "'Just remember, God will never forgive you if you turn your back on Israel'" (quoted in Merkley *Presidents* 198).

While Dennis Ross attributes President Clinton's reticence to pressure Israel to his sensitivity to Israeli coalition politics, Spector points to the strong ties Netanyahu maintained with American Christian Zionists. Upon being summoned to Washington in 1998, Netanyahu called Jerry Falwell who arranged for fifteen hundred evangelicals to greet him upon arrival, thereby demonstrating to Clinton his strong American support and weakening the president's ability to chastise him publicly (Spector 148).

In the face of US pressure on Israel's right-of-center Likud government to continue implementing the Oslo Accords,[19] evangelicals were eager to demonstrate their support for Israel's less enthusiastic position. Jerry Falwell promised to deliver twenty thousand evangelical pastors to lobby the president against pressuring Israel (Rubin 78). And Ted Beckett started Christian Friends of Israeli Communities to provide solidarity and financial support for Israeli settlements (Merkley *Attitudes* 182).

In contrast, mainline churches took action to publicize critiques of Israel. In 1995, CMEP called on the president to recognize Palestinian rights to Jerusalem. In 1996, they ran a full-page ad in the *New York Times* insisting that Israel relinquish East Jerusalem (Rubin 76). That same year, the United Methodist Church passed two resolutions calling for reduced US aid to Israel due to settlement building (Korn *Church*).

PRESIDENT GEORGE W. BUSH AND THE SECOND INTIFADA

George W. Bush entered the White House feeling that Clinton had spent too much time on the Israeli-Palestinian conflict and placed too much pressure on Israel. Nevertheless, when Israel began engaging in targeted assassinations, the administration protested. After 9/11, however, Bush became supportive of Israel's policies, and the criticism largely disappeared except for an episode that took place as Bush sought to obtain Arab participation in an anti-terrorist coalition. He announced that the US was prepared to endorse a Palestinian state. Ariel Sharon was then Israel's prime minister. "In an emotional speech that evoked memories of the Holocaust, the Israeli prime minister likened George W. Bush to Neville Chamberlin" (Little 114). In reality, Bush was more fully committed to Israeli security than his father ever was (Little 321). In 2003, President Bush presented the two sides with a roadmap for Palestinian statehood by 2005, which led to Israel's decision to disengage from Gaza (Ross 300, 302, 324).

While Bush grew up in his parents' Episcopalian home, his personal religious journey underwent a number of stages. He first found personal faith with the cross-carrying preacher Arthur Blessitt, and then once again with Billy Graham. Despite officially joining his wife's Methodist denomination (Balmer *God* 144), he invited Franklin Graham to offer the invocation at his inauguration. The younger Graham is an avid Christian Zionist and has been publicly critical of Islam (Spector 80). Bush believed in the sanctity of Israel and even his pursuit of Palestinian statehood was rooted in his esteem for the Holy Land, once asking "Wouldn't it be amazing if democracy in the Middle East sprung first from the rocky soil of the West Bank?" (Rice 144). Making his feelings toward the Jewish state clear, in 2008, he declared, "'Some people suggest that if the United States would just break ties with Israel, all our problems in the Middle East would go away. This is a tired argument that buys into the propaganda of our enemies, and America rejects it utterly'" (quoted in Ross *Doomed* 339).

In 2002, the Episcopalians issued a statement equating "the violence of the suicide bombers and the violence of the Occupation," laying the blame for the stalled peace process on Israel. In 2004, Episcopalian Presiding Bishop, Frank T. Griswold, wrote to the president criticizing his acceptance of unilateral Israeli actions, including building the security barrier. In 2004, the Methodist Church condemned "confiscation of Palestinian land and water resources, the destruction of Palestinian homes . . . and any vision of a Greater Israel." In the same year, the Lutherans called for an end to construction of Israel's security barrier and the NCC called the barrier the "de facto imprisonment of the Palestinian population." In 2003, representatives of a number of mainline churches and other denominations came together to form the National Interreligious Leadership Initiative for Peace in the Middle East, which called on the president to put pressure on Israel and the Palestinians (Rock 110, 115). In 2004, fifty Christian leaders penned a letter to the White House, specifically calling on the president to demand that Israel remove the security barrier (Churches for Middle East Peace 82), and the Presbyterian Church (USA) proposed divestment from companies profiting from their operations in the West Bank. This motion was endorsed by the World Council of Churches, which called on churches to "work for peace in new ways and to give serious consideration to economic measures that are equitable, transparent, and nonviolent" (cited in Hallward 145).

On the other side, evangelical support for Israel reached its zenith during the Bush years. In 2006, John Hagee established Christians United for Israel (CUFI). In contrast with former evangelical pro-Israel efforts, which tended to be one agenda item amongst many, CUFI was organized solely for the purpose of Israel advocacy (Spector). CUFI today boasts of ten million members, and brings five thousand pro-Israel Christians to Washington, D.C. annually to lobby. Bush himself "relied heavily on evangelical support" and "avoided initiating diplomatic moves that might upset evangelicals with millennial convictions" (Ariel "Contemporary" 292).

In the early 2000s, recognizing growing support for Israel amongst American Christians, AIPAC began to expand its tent with outreach efforts to evangelicals and Hispanics. And shortly prior to founding CUFI, Hagee was the keynote speaker at the AIPAC convention. Either Prime Minister Netanyahu or Member of Knesset Rabbi Benny Elon is credited with motivating Hagee to galvanize pro-Israel Christians under one umbrella group. In 2004, Elon also formed the Knesset Christian Allies Caucus, a global coalition of pro-Israel Christian legislators (Clark 257).

Yet the anti-Zionist Jewish lobby, which had been quiet for many years, initiated a period of renewed activity. Jewish Voice for Peace formed in 1996, and the coalition group US Campaign to End the Israeli Occupation, in 2001, which included some Jewish affiliated groups. These activists began reaching out to mainline Churches and civil society organizations to bolster support for the Palestinians, thereby allowing Israel's detractors to provide evidence of Jewish support for their position (Bard 206).

PRESIDENT BARACK OBAMA AND THE IRAN NUCLEAR DEAL

President Obama entered the White House determined to place daylight between the US and Israel, believing that relations with Arab and Muslim countries had suffered as a result of the strong US-Israel relationship (Oren *Ally*; Ross 346). Despite his continued commitment to Israel's security, he felt that Israel could do more to promote peace efforts with the Palestinians. Consequently, he often came across as placing the greater onus on Israel and was openly critical of Israeli settlement building (Ross 392). Many Israelis felt that Obama "often supported Palestinian positions" and "mostly blamed Israel for the failure to negotiate peace" (Gilboa 16). This approach led to a good deal of friction between the White House and Israel (Oren *Ally*).

Indeed, as a result of the US's brokering of a nuclear deal with Iran and failure on the part of the Obama administration to veto an anti-Israel resolution in the UN Security Council, by the end of his term in office the relationship was particularly strained.

Prior to becoming president, Obama attended the Trinity United Church of Christ in Chicago headed by Jeremiah Wright. Equating black and Palestinian liberation theology, Wright was no friend of Israel (Richardson). During the campaign, a number of Wright's controversial proclamations and his association with "anti-Semitic" Nation of Islam leader Louis Farrakhan came to light, culminating in Obama's distancing himself from his former pastor (Powell). Despite the tense relationship between the US and Israel during his term, Obama maintained that security cooperation between the two countries improved, and that his criticism of Israel came from a place of tough love (Goodkind).

During this period, pro-Palestinian evangelicals coalesced around a biennial conference in Bethlehem called "Christ at the Checkpoint," which aimed to draw attention to the plight of Palestinian Christians (Moon). At the same time, pro-Palestinian activists in the mainline Churches began seeing success, with the passing of a number of divestment resolutions. On the pro-Israel evangelical front, CUFI expanded their activities; a lobbying office was established, headed by Gary Bauer; and the organization began working with college students and millennials.

What spheres of cooperation took place between American Jews and Christians? JVP and the US Campaign to End the Occupation continued to work closely with mainline churches, with some church groups—such as PCUSA's Israel Palestine Mission Network—signing on as official members of the US Campaign (US Campaign "Membership"). In 2013, the Israeli founder of Who Profits from the Occupation, Dalit Baum, was hired by the Quakers as Director of Economic Activism (AFSC). While these groups are on the fringes and unrepresentative of the Jewish community as a whole, their presence and participation at Church assemblies served to provide "cover" for pro-Palestinian activists to deflect charges of anti-Semitism (Plitnick 119; Yoffie; Elman).

At the same time, however, mainstream Jewish organizations also began working with members of mainline churches working to stave off attempts by the BDS movement to coopt their denominations. The Jewish Council for Public Affairs began organizing subsidized trips to Israel/Palestine for church leaders to witness the situation firsthand. Other Jewish organizations that worked with mainline churches were the Israel Action Network of the Jewish Federations of North America, J Street, and the Anti-Defamation League (Felson; Lerner). Organizations they worked with included Presbyterians for Middle East Peace and Christians for Fair Witness on the Middle East. Although the impact of Fair Witness has declined, it had an impact for several years, mostly from 2005-2008. Its impact was blunted in part because BDS constituencies in the churches put increased efforts into countering its messaging. As far as cooperation with evangelicals was concerned, CUFI's approach tended to be more hawkish and partisan than Jewish pro-Israel groups. Consequently, many of these groups chose not to work with CUFI, citing Hagee's fundamentalism as contrary to their progressive world-view (Shapiro 103; Spector 112).

PRESIDENT DONALD J. TRUMP AND THE EMBASSY MOVE

President Trump distinguished himself as the most pro-Israel president in the history of the US-Israel relationship. Early in his tenure, he declared that an Israeli-Palestinian peace agreement would be "the deal of the century" and pledged to issue a plan to make one possible. The clearest indication of Trump's own strategic intent was his awareness that Zionist evangelicals were a critical component of his political base. It was as much a gift to that base, as a gift to the Israelis and their prime minister Benjamin Netanyahu, when Trump announced in December 2017 that the US embassy would be moved from Tel Aviv to Jerusalem. The move took place in a May 2018 ceremony, an event timed to coincide with the 70th anniversary of Israel's Declaration of Independence. Trump's daughter, Ivanka, unveiled a plaque on the building, and evangelical pastor John Hagee, the founder of Christians United for Israel, delivered the benediction at the ceremony. It is said of evangelical folklore that the president was lauded for fulfilling God's will that the USA be placed in Jer-USA-lem. Trump's decision to recognize Israeli sovereignty over the Golan Heights was also important, and he took advantage of growing collaboration between Israel and the Gulf states to broker normalization agreements between Israel and three Arab states—the United Arab Emirates, Bahrain, Sudan, and Morocco—with others to follow. Agreements with first two were signed at a September, 2020, White House ceremony.

While Trump himself is not a regular churchgoer, he presented his presidency as representative of Christian America. He trumpeted his close relationship with televangelist Paula White publicly and provided unprecedented access to influential clergypersons (Jaffe-Hoffman "Kissed"). White is a pro-Israel evangelical (Duin "Led").[20] In addition, Trump is surrounded by pro-Israel Jews, and he has acknowledged publicly that his daughter and son-in-law, Ivanka and Jared Kushner, have his ear on Israel policy (Cortellessa "Hanukkah").

Less ambiguous on the personal religious front, however, was the vice-president's unabashed commitment to the Bible as the foundation for his support of Israel. Pence has referred to himself as "a Christian, a conservative and a Republican, in that order" (Hamburger "Trust"). At the inaugural White House celebration of Israel's Independence Day, he voiced the theological underpinnings for his support of Israel:

> I believe in my heart that God Himself fulfilled his promise to His people. The Lord God tells us . . . "Behold, I will cause breath to enter into you and ye shall live." And Israel lives today . . . . Today and every day, the state of Israel and her people bear witness to God's faithfulness as well as their own. How unlikely was Israel's birth? How much more unlikely has been her survival? And how confounding against all odds, both past and present, has been her thriving . . . For my part, my Christian faith compels me to cherish Israel as well as our deep alliance and historical ties (Pence "Independence").

Pence is a personal friend of CUFI lobbyist Gary Bauer, whose son is a senior aide to the vice-president. In 2014, Pence travelled to Israel with a CUFI delegation, and in 2017, Pence was the keynote speaker at the CUFI annual summit (Lake "Escape"). Indeed, after meeting with Pence on March 31, 2017, Hagee enjoyed one of the earliest scheduled meetings with President Trump, a substantive indicator of the access CUFI enjoyed (Ayala "Ties"). Furthermore, Secretary of State Mike Pompeo (who addressed the 2019 CUFI summit) often speaks of his Christian faith as an important part of his identity, and has stated, "As secretary of state and as a Christian, I'm proud to lead American diplomacy to support Israel's right to defend itself" (Wong "Rapture").

A full account of the long term impact and consequences of Trump's policies during his four-year term will take some time. Meanwhile, we await evidence of the policies the new Biden administration will adopt, along with the effect of unfolding events in the Middle East.

CONCLUSION

A number of observations emerge from this historical overview of American Christians and Israel. First, twenty-first century debates over Israel-Palestine are not a new phenomenon; the present mainline-evangelical divide has a long history. Second, while never ardent admirers of Israel to begin with, in the final decades of the twentieth century, the leadership of the mainline Churches grew gradually more and more critical of the Jewish state. Third, mainline leaders' views on Israel often have been in conflict with the general feeling of lay Christians in the pews.

Fourth, White House Israel policy had little to do with the faith of the president. While arguably a relevant factor in the early-to-mid twentieth century, the president's denominational affiliation has played less of a role in recent decades. Instead, a curious connection between the president's chosen pastor's feelings on Israel-Palestine and US foreign policy appears to be present.

Fifth, the Jewish lobby has played an important role, but not necessarily in the way those critical of American Jews' alleged disproportionate influence suggest (cf. Mearsheimer and Walt *Lobby*). Jewish Zionism and anti-Zionism were ever-present alongside Christian Israel/Palestine political activism and continue to be significant factors today as likeminded Jews and Christians work together to promote their cause on either side of the political fence.

CHAPTER FOUR

GIOVANNI MATTEO QUER

CATHOLIC ORGANIZATIONS AND THE DELEGITIMIZATION OF ISRAEL

In 2015, Pope Francis met with a delegation from the World Jewish Congress and is reported to have said that "To attack Jews is anti-Semitism, but an outright attack on the State of Israel is also anti-Semitism." He added that "There may be political disagreements between governments and on political issues, but the State of Israel has every right to exist in safety and prosperity" (Yair Rosenberg). As the story in *Tablet* puts it, with that statement "Francis drew a bright red line between critiquing Israeli policies and critiquing Israel's existence." It was the 50th anniversary of *Nostra Aetate*, the Vatican's historic declaration condemning anti-Semitism and absolving Jews of collective responsibility for the death of Jesus. In January 2020, at an event commemorating the liberation of Auschwitz, Francis condemned the "barbaric resurgence" of anti-Semitism around the world and added "I will never tire of firmly condemning every form of antisemitism" (Dahan). As Gavin D'Costa reported, Pope Benedict XVI's pontificate was "marked by an increasing use of contemporary Judaism as being the covenant of the people of God . . . in the Grand Synagogue in Rome (2006) he emphasizes the enduring of the Jewish people as a sign and witness of God's fidelity to his covenant people" (18). In a 2008 address to Israel's ambassador to the Holy See, Benedict declared that "The Holy See joins you in giving thanks to the Lord that the aspirations of the Jewish people for a home in the land of their fathers have been fulfilled, and hopes soon to see a time of even greater rejoicing when a just peace finally resolves the conflict with the Palestinians."

Francis in fact has a long history of deep engagement with the Jewish community and to Jewish-Catholic dialogue, dating to his time as Archbishop Cardinal Jorge Mario Bergoglio in Buenos Aires. As Norbert Hofman writes, "In July 2004, when the Holy See's Commission for Religious Relations with the Jews, in collaboration with the International Jewish Committee on Interreligious Consultations (IJCIC), decided to organize a conference in Buenos Aires, it availed itself of the energetic support of the local archbishop, then Cardinal Jorge Mario Bergoglio." Bergoglio gave the opening address at the 2004 conference. He had already formed "personal friendships with rabbis and members of the Jewish community, beyond those that existed at an institutional level." One distinctive project that testifies to such a relationship is *On Heaven and Earth*, the book of dialogues he coauthored with Rabbi Abraham Skorka and published in Argentina in 2010. Bergoglio continued to visit synagogues and deliver lectures there, also participating in symbolic events, such as the commemoration of the Night of Broken Glass in 2012.

Unfortunately, these sentiments have not consistently percolated down to all Catholic organizations, including both those that are and those that are not under direct Vatican supervision. Moreover, a certain ambiguity or inconsistency persists in Catholic statements. The Catholic Church, and particularly the current papacy, has often declared that antisemitism is extraneous to Christianity and, time and again, has condemned manifestations of antisemitism. Yet, the presence of contemporary antisemitism in the form also of extreme hostility toward Israel and Zionism is seldom addressed. In 2015, the Polish Episcopate published a pastoral letter marking the 50 years of the *Nostra Aetate* encyclic; the Vatican document defines new relations with Jews and also recognizes the validity of the Covenant with the Jewish people. The letter, entitled "A Common Spiritual Heritage with the Jewish People," also tackles the issue of antisemitism, defining it as "a sin against the neighbor's love, a sin that destroys the truth about Christian identity" (Polish Episcopate). In at least one public document, anti-Zionism is mentioned in connection to antisemitism. The Joint Declaration of the 18th International Catholic-Jewish Liaison Committee Meeting, held in Buenos Aires between 5 and 8 July 2004, encompasses "the total rejection of anti-Semitism in all its forms, including anti-Zionism as a more recent manifestation of anti-Semitism" (18th International Catholic-Jewish Liaison Committee). However, the Special Assembly for the Middle East convened by the Synod of Bishops in 2010 seems to hold a different opinion. On the one hand, it states that "everywhere in the Church in the Middle East the religious sentiment in anti-Judaism has been overcome, at least in theory, by the pastoral guidelines of the Second Vatican Council," and also opines that "widespread opinion seems to indicate that anti-Zionism is more a political position and, consequently, to be considered foreign to every ecclesial discourse" (Synod of Bishops). In Catholic doctrine it sometimes seems the idea of a Jewish state is merely tolerated.

Efforts continue to persuade the Vatican to take greater responsibility for anti-Zionist Catholic advocacy and activism, to exert more authority with the groups covered in this essay. To date that has not happened. If the assumption was that *Nostra Aetate* would suffice to carry the day, it hasn't. Meanwhile, whatever sunlight we can shed on these anti-Zionist efforts can help draw attention to them and may encourage Vatican intervention. Before detailing the relevant organizational agendas, I will briefly review some of the Palestinian and Christian efforts that share the anti-Zionist agenda and provide the political background for much of Catholic anti-Zionism. Further detail about that larger context can be found in several essays in the current volume.

In 2005, the Boycott, Divestment, and Sanctions (BDS) movement was endorsed by a group of Palestinian political organizations with the goal of isolating and delegitimating Israel. The call to completely isolate the Jewish state—its institutions, representatives, and all groups perceived to be associated with it—was earlier issued at the 2001 Durban Conference and characterized as a grassroots action in pursuit of justice. Ever since, manipulations of history and international law have been central strategies for Israel's detractors and the BDS movement.

Over more than a decade, while suffering many defeats, the BDS movement has nonetheless attracted substantial international support among a wide variety of groups with diverse political affiliations, including revolutionary left constituencies, human rights organizations, and various Islamic factions. A network of anti-Israel groups has developed in the Christian world, combining political and theological arguments in order to delegitimate Israel.

The *Kairos Palestine Document*, launched in 2009, was drafted by Christian Palestinian representatives of several affiliations and represents the manifesto of the Christian BDS movement. Building on liberation theology arguments and theological political documents elaborated by South African anti-apartheid activists, the *Kairos Palestine Document* defines Israel as the world's premier source of injustice and evil,[21] calls for organized resistance against it,[22] and embraces the boycott of the Jewish state as a Christian,[23] non-violent, creative response after actually condoning and praising violence.[24]

The underlying theological principles, collectively known as Palestinian Liberation Theology, build on liberationist theological arguments evolved in the 1970s and 1980s in an attempt to re-signify the Scriptures to focus on oppression and discrimination. Developed as a South American response to dictatorship and economic inequality, liberation theology emphasizes the role of the poor in history and God's love for the oppressed. Certain religious leaders have used this concept to justify armed resistance and mobilize the masses for change. Though conceptualized in a Catholic context, liberationist thought has been elaborated by Protestant churches as a theological reflection on oppressed groups, such as African-Americans, South African Blacks under the apartheid regime, LGBTQIA+ groups, and women. Notably common to these different theologies is the effort to contextualize the biblical message within contemporary situations of oppression and to elaborate on it for the oppressed themselves. Palestinian Liberation Theology is yet another form of theological reflection on conflict and human rights; its arguments, however, encompass anti-Israel political narratives. The entire Israeli polity is judged a major historical injustice. Israel's policies are deemed unreasonably unjust. Israel's originating movement, Zionism, is dismissed as a theological distortion that promotes tribal particularism rather than universal values.

Kuruvilla has analyzed the inception and development of Palestinian Liberation Theology focusing on its leaders and centers, describing it as "radical Christianity." In a previous study, the same author analyzed practical features of Palestinian Liberation theologians and communities, comparing them to the South American liberation Theology of the 1960s. He distinguishes two main differences between the two theological movements. Regarding the Palestine–Israel context and the theological response to the conflict, he describes the object of Palestinian Liberation Theology as "a form of racism where Semites are discriminating against Semites" (*Radical Christianity* 58). The political message propagated by certain Palestinian Christian centers, some of which are associated with Palestinian Liberation Theology, was also analyzed by authors who take a different stance. Nerel, for instance, maintains that the theological discourse on the conflict results in a de-Judaization of the Old Testament and a novel form of supersessionism (n. 27).

Several groups and associations as a consequence advocate for divestment both from corporations doing business in Israel and from Israel itself, campaign for boycotting Israel, and promote an anti-Israel narrative within Churches and religious institutions. In this respect, Protestant and Catholic worlds differ significantly. Protestant churches are autonomous organizations that define their own theological beliefs and agenda, while the Catholic Church is a centralized structure, in which the Congregation for the Doctrine of the Faith, the institution mandated to define the theological creed, is charged with sanctioning theological positions.[25] The Catholic Church does not endorse

Palestinian Liberation Theology. Nonetheless, some Catholic religious leaders and organizations advance some of its tenets, embrace the *Kairos Palestine Document*, and support the BDS movement.[26]

This paper does not aim to assess or measure Catholic involvement in the *Kairos* efforts or in the BDS movement as it relates to the rest of the Catholic worlds or Protestant worlds. Rather, it points to a phenomenon present in the Catholic Church. First, it analyzes recent developments in the Catholic Church's attitudes toward Zionism and Israel; second, it looks into some of the leaders that have contributed to Palestinian Liberation Theology; and, finally, it describes some of the Catholic organizations that support the call to boycott Israel.

ISRAEL, ZIONISM, AND THE CATHOLIC CHURCH

Relations between Israel and the Catholic Church have a complex history. Since their official recognition of Israel in 1993, the Holy See's policies toward Israel have evolved both politically and theologically. Politically, the Vatican has recognized Israel and its right to exist. Theologically, a degree of ambiguity still exists in the definition of Israel's existence in terms of Jewish nationhood. As Kenny pointed out in his 1993 book *Catholics, Jews and the State of Israel*, the Catholic Church "clearly recognizes the right of Jews to a homeland in Israel but it also clearly divorces the State of Israel from that recognition, treating it as being in some manner extraneous to Jewish existence, a merely political entity, the product of a political movement" (89).

After Paul VI's 1965 document *Nostra Aetate*, Catholic theology has taken major steps to establish a dialogue with Judaism and to tackle antisemitism. Yet, according to Kenny, the recognition of Israel should address "Jewish requests for existential recognition with Israel at its center" by acknowledging Israel as "the embodiment of Jewish identity, Jewish hopes, and Jewish faith" (118 -119). This ambiguity is reflected in the Catholic dialogue about antisemitism: one the one hand, the Church rejects antisemitism and has revised its teachings accordingly; on the other, it is unclear regarding contemporary manifestations of Jew-hatred, especially if directed to the State of Israel.

In 2004, during the 18th International Catholic-Jewish Liaison Committee Meeting in Buenos Aires, a group of Jewish and Catholic attendees discussed the theological components of justice and charity. On that occasion, the Committee also explored the evolution of Jewish-Catholic relations, condemning antisemitism in all its forms, including anti-Zionism.[27] This position seems to be confirmed by Pope Francis's words on the occasion of a meeting with the World Jewish Congress in October 2015, when he reportedly declared that attacks on Israel are anti-Semitic (Rowney, World Jewish Congress).

However, these positions do not reveal any doctrinal change. The official position of the Church toward Israel is formulated in the 1985 "Notes on the correct way to present the Jews and Judaism in preaching and catechesis in the Roman Catholic Church," which recognizes the historical continuity of the Jewish people,[28] and states that "the existence of the State of Israel and its political options should be envisaged not in a perspective which is in itself religious, but in their reference to the common principles of international law" (ch. VI, par. 3). This approach would enable the church to sustain a Jewish-Christian dialogue, while maintaining a certain distance from controversial positions embodied in Israeli policies, the conflict in general, and the status of Jerusalem in particular.

The Vatican has accepted political goals such as a two-state solution and Israel's disengagement from the territories while still advocating for an international status for Jerusalem, denying both Israel's and the Palestinian Authority's claims to the city as capital of the Jewish state and a future Palestinian state. According to certain authors, however, there is more than that at stake. Minerbi emphasizes that inside the Catholic Church there are voices that support a certain anti-Israeli narrative. In his book *Una Relazione Difficile* on the relations between the Vatican, Israel, and Judaism, Minerbi analyzes the position of Middle Eastern Church leaders who overemphasize the conflict as a major source of instability in the region and point to Israel as the fundamental source of instability for Christian communities (187-208). According to the author, there is a tendency among Middle Eastern Church leaders to ignore the perils of Islamic fundamentalism and, simultaneously, to champion Muslim-Christian dialogue. This is reflected in the Vatican's position on Israel, which unilaterally condemns Israeli policy and vaguely refers to extremism yet fails to address Islamic extremism.

According to Minerbi, the Vatican is "probably . . . influenced in attitudes of this sort, by the Catholic community in the Holy Land" (218).

If the extent to which Middle Eastern Church leaders influence the
Vatican's policy toward Israel is still only basis for speculation, their
impact on Catholic organizations supporting BDS is fairly evident.
A rapid look at four leaders who contributed to the *Kairos Palestine
Document* will clarify the point.

CATHOLIC LEADERS AND THE *KAIROS PALESTINE DOCUMENT*: GERIES KHOURY, MICHEL SABBAH, RAFIQ KHOURY, AND FOUAD TWAL

Several Catholic Church leaders in Israel and the Palestinian Authority
hold views on the conflict that intertwine politics with theology, as the
Kairos Palestine Document demonstrates. Some of them openly support
the BDS movement, while others are more cautious in advocating for
Israel's isolation and yet nonetheless advance a theological-political
narrative that nurtures anti-Israel views and actions. Common to
all authors is the emphasis on Zionism and the strenuous attempt to
dispute its legitimacy both politically and theologically, which results in
an uncompromising condemnation of the Jewish national movement.
Ultimately, Zionism and Israel represent evil.

The underpinnings of recent theological interpretations of the conflict can be traced to the work of the late Geries Khoury, a Melkite
Catholic and founder of the Al-Liqa'a Center, who first approached the
meaning of the Scriptures in the context of the Arab-Israeli conflict. He
started working in the 1980s, when Palestinian political consciousness
rose to become the outbreak of the First Intifada. Among the first theologians to develop a contextual reading of the Scriptures in an effort to
provide answers for Christian Palestinians torn between Arab identity
and politics, Khoury first of all aims to advance a national narrative
whereby Palestinians are a united people composed of Christians and
Muslims who are equally oppressed by the common injustice of the
"Israeli occupation." Consequently, he emphasizes Christian-Muslim
dialogue as a major tool for opposing Israeli policies and attacks
Zionism as the exploitation of Judaism for political ends. He criticizes
the "diplomatic" approach of the Vatican toward Israeli policies, and,

by and large, excludes any kind of dialogue with Judaism unless it is for the denunciation of Zionism and Israel.

In his "Christians in the Holy Land—Past, Present, and Future," Khoury enumerates the reasons for Christian-Muslim dialogue, among which is the necessity to confront Zionism and Israeli policies and argues that "the wrong exploitation of Judaism and its political interpretation serves Israel only and contributed to the emergence of Islamic currents that followed the same policy or strategy; that is, the exploitation of Islam and its political interpretation for the justification of political positions or acts." Moreover, after attacking Israel's alleged goal of dividing Palestinians along religious lines, as well as advancing Western misunderstanding of Islam and US support for Israel, he points to the existence of "conspiracies that are woven to untie our national unity and distract us by internal strife." Khoury also developed a theological opposition to Zionist claims to the Land of Israel and advanced the idea that the Palestinian people embody the life of Jesus, living under occupation and oppression, suggesting that Zionists are foreign occupiers. The aim, as he makes clear in *The Intifada of Heaven and Earth*, is both to strip Jesus of his Judaism and to support Palestinian resistance.

By juxtaposing the New Testament, which according to the author focuses on justice, with the reading of the Bible, Khoury comes to the conclusion that the Bible "rejects any Jewish politicized theology" and praises the Palestinian reading of the Bible motivated by a universalist mission in opposition to "exclusivist claims," attributed to Judaism. The charge formulated against Zionism is for portraying an exclusivist, nationalist reading of the Bible, which coupled with the sense of divine election would be the reason for Israel's alleged drive to conquer, invade, and systematically violate international law. Khoury's denunciation of the nationalist interpretation of God is supposedly directed against Israel as a Jewish State, but it is not always clear if there is a distinction between Zionism and Judaism.

In a further argument, the author explains the confusion that sometimes emerges between Zionism and Judaism. Khoury compares the Hebrew reading of the Bible to the Christian one, stressing the significance attributed to concepts such as nation and Promised Land in the two views. For the Jews, the nation means "the return to the holy land."

The author rejects that interpretation as wrong since it is based on a political reading of the Scripture. On the contrary, the Christian meaning of nation is universal and goes beyond the limits of specific peoples. Moreover, for Christians, the love of the nation is to be interpreted in the sense of serving the peoples living within one nation, evidently opposing this view to Israel, which is deemed to systematically discriminate against those who do not belong to the Jewish national group. For the author, Zionism is responsible for pursuing a plan that brought "chaos in the Middle East," and Zionist leaders for construing a sense of superiority of the Jewish race. Tellingly, the Jewish national project is deemed to be in itself exclusivist and particularistic, while the Arab nationalist project would be inclusive and universalistic. Jewish statehood is evil; it brings about oppression and hatred, while the not-yet-achieved Arab statehood will attain justice, liberation, and the triumph of love for the other.

A similar political attitude toward the conflict is reflected in the thought of Michel Sabbah, former Latin Patriarch of Jerusalem and director of the international Catholic organization Pax Christi. In his view, as he details it in *Faithful Witness on Reconciliation and Peace in the Holy Land*, Israel bears much of the responsibility for the conflict (144) for political use of the biblical narrative in regard to claims on the Land of Israel (55-60), the attacks on the Palestinian population to which Palestinians respond,[29] and a supposed lack of will to make peace despite the fact that Israel was established on the majority of what he defines as "historical Palestine" (134). His views reflect a nationalist perspective whereby he defines Christians as Arabs first and only then as belonging to different Christian denominations: "We belong to the Arab world and hence to the Arab and Muslim world" (96). Finally, Israel is considered the main source of instability in the region due to its Western-supported injustices against the Palestinian people. Peace will be possible "once the Palestinians are satisfied, once they are free and independent in their state; they will then become friendly to Israel. Once the Palestinians are friendly to Israel, the other Arab peoples will be just as friendly" (145). In this view, in which Israel is the only wrongdoer, Sabbah welcomes the anti-Israel boycott movement as a means for changing Israel, since "its aim is to help Israelis, through international pressure, to enter the right path of peace. It is the only way that can help Israelis leaders move from their political status quo" (Sabbah "Interview—Patriarch").

Sabbah's views on Israel and Zionism are better expressed in a 2013 interview with Qassam Muadi, when the campaign for Christians' integration in Israeli society and their enlistment in the IDF (Israeli Defense Forces) was commencing. Sabbah objected to Christian service in the army, claiming an inherent incompatibility between Zionism and Arabness. In Sabbah's view, Israeli society is Western, materialistic, consumeristic, individualistic, and racist because it is based in Zionism. He argues that Arabs' integration in Israeli society would necessarily lead to abandoning their national consciousness, faith, and culture. Integration policies and military service for Sabbah represent a threat to Arabness, "its spirit, identity, and consciousness."

Similarly, Rafiq Khoury, Vicar of the Patriarchate of Jerusalem, defines Arab Christian identity as almost incompatible with Israeli citizenship. He maintains that Israel, defined as a Jewish state, leaves no space for non-Jewish being. In "Arab Christians in Israel," Khoury conflates Arab Christian identity and politics, construing Jewish statehood as incompatible with the existence of minorities—as though Christians' minority status in Arab-Islamic communities provided a harmonious existence. The author defines identity as the interaction of land, people, and history, focusing in particular on how these elements forged Palestinian national distinctiveness. Ignoring how these same elements have shaped Jewish identity and their quest for statehood, Khoury argues that "the Israeli occupation forces strive to split these components from each other by distorting history and changing the geographical features of the land in order to eliminate their vital and organic relations."

The last Latin Patriarch of Jerusalem, Fouad Twal, also shares the politicized and nationalist approach to the Church's mission, overemphasizing the occupation, the wall, and other issues. On May 14, 2017, the Commission for Peace and Justice of the Assembly of Catholic Ordinaries of the Holy Land, of which Twal is member, issued a statement on normalization that ambiguously proclaimed support for dialogue but conditioned it on an anti-normalization demand to condemn injustice and the occupation: "The Church seeks and encourages dialogue with all people, including Israelis, individuals, and organizations, who recognize the need to end the occupation and eliminate discrimination" (Latin Patriarchate). Reportedly, he compared the Palestinian Christians to Jesus, who had to flee with the family from Herodian persecution (Ieraci). In an interview in 2012, asked about the difficulties of a possible agreement on the settlements, Twal commented that "With the Jews, everything is difficult" (Al-Shami).

These positions do not point to a general trend in the Catholic Church. It is, however, possible to infer that the overtly critical views of Israel, the belief that Jewish statehood is exclusivist, and the nationalist perspective on Christian identity constitute a consensus for certain Christian organizations active in the Arab-Israeli conflict.

CATHOLIC ORGANIZATIONS AND BDS

Several peace and development organizations that identify with the Catholic world are active in advocacy regarding the Arab-Israeli conflict. Many of them advocate for Israel's isolation through BDS campaigns in single countries or promote the political delegitimization of Israel through international, interdenominational Christian organizations. It is not always easy, however, to identify which activities have originated within a genuinely Catholic group. Likewise, a quantitative assessment of worldwide Catholic support for pro-BDS positions is not readily available. This section will instead examine the narratives that some of these organizations promote and their actual involvement in delegitimization campaigns.

One should understand at the outset, however, that the groups at stake here have different connections with the Church itself. Trocaire is an official organization of the Catholic Church in Ireland; its members and management are appointed by the Irish Bishops' Conference. Still more closely linked to the Vatican is the Pontifical Mission for Palestine, which is a fully functioning office of the Holy See and subject to the Vatican Secretary of State. The Associazione Papa Giovanni XXIII, which has an established presence in Jerusalem and Bethlehem, is also under papal authority. Operazione Columbia is an Associazione Papa Giovanni project. The Conference of Major Superiors of Men is found in nearly every Bishops' conference worldwide and is a canonical (as distinguished from civil) structure for the provincial superiors and Abbots of men's religious orders; the conferences are official structures of the Catholic Church. Conversely, Pax Christi and Pax Christi Belgium are independent, Catholic, lay-led organizations, though they are committed to Catholic teachings. Secours Catholique is also an independent, Catholic, lay-led organization sensitive to Catholic teachings, but its leadership is appointed subject to the approval of local bishops. Finally, CCDF—Terre Solidaire is an independent, lay-led organization without a formal affiliation with the Catholic Church. Broederlijk Delen (Belgium) also identifies as Catholic, but apparently without an official connection.

In 2016, Pax Christi released a statement supporting BDS as a means of nonviolent struggle and exerting pressure for peace (Pax Christi). In this sense, its words are reminiscent of the *Kairos Palestine Document*, which construes BDS as a nonviolent, and thus Christian, response to the Israeli occupation. The statement makes a distinction between boycotting settlements and a general boycott of Israel, rejecting the latter. Nevertheless, it also endorses several anti-Israel stances—praising the pursuit of Israel's criminalization in international forums, endorsing the right of return for Palestinian refugees, and accusing Israel of enacting racist policies against its non-Jewish population. Some Pax Christi chapters adopt harsher language and directly support BDS; for example, the Italian chapter of Pax Christi is signatory to the BDS-Italy appeal. The German chapter leads the "Besatzung schmeckt bitter" boycott campaign that targets settlement products and some international companies operating in the post-1967 territories ("Besatzung").[30] Besides the boycott campaigns, other national groups advance the *Kairos Palestine* narrative. For instance, the Austrian chapter of Pax Christi embraces the theological-political stance of separating "Biblical Israel" from the modern "State of Israel." In its 2010 "memorandum" on Israel and Palestine, the organization condemns the misuse of the Bible to perpetuate oppression ("Memorandum"). In this view, the "Jewish state" is a religious enterprise and Zionism an ideology that exploits the biblical narrative to the detriment of the Palestinian people. The disregard for the historical and political dimension of Zionism, as well as the emphasis on the Scriptures, has far-reaching consequences: Israel is attacked not for its policies but rather for its existence as a Jewish state, which is perceived as a religious distortion of the scriptures. From that perspective, Israel's Declaration of Independence asserts that the Bible and the Land of Israel have a national and cultural dimension in the role they played in forging Jewish peoplehood and nationhood. Pax Christi France also promoted BDS as a religious and political strategy to achieve a just peace. For a potent example of this rhetoric, one might reference the publication *"Qu'est-ce que BDS? Une Action Non-Violente de la Société Civile Palestinienne."*

Another French Catholic organization, Secours Catholique, in 2013 published the brochure *"Le Defi de la Paix"* in cooperation with the associations Pax Christi and CCDF-Terre Solidaire. The brochure promotes the *Kairos Palestine Document* (13) and describes Israel exclusively as a consequence of the Holocaust, established by Western powers at the expense of the Palestinian people. Tellingly, its historical review of the conflict fails to point out that what is called "the first Arab-Israeli war" was waged by Arab states, and that it resulted in two refugee crises: Arabs who fled, joined the Arab military coalition, or were expelled, and the Jewish population from Arab countries who were progressively expelled as a consequence of Israel's victory. Indeed, Jews from Arab lands are discounted as immigrants who arrived merely in consequence of "tension" resulting from the establishment of the State of Israel (6). While Israel's right to exist seems to be exclusively dependent on the Holocaust and the Jewish quest for safety, the brochure echoes the Vatican position distinguishing between historic Jewish bonds to the Land of Israel and the political project of Jewish statehood (17). Israel bears responsibility for the entire conflict, while the Palestinian people are depicted exclusively as dispossessed and justice-seeking. One year after this publication, the organization began supporting the "Made in Illegality Campaign" conducted by, among others, the pro-Palestinian organization network *"Plateforme des ONG françaises pour la Palestine"* promoted by Pax Christi Belgium (both Flemish and French communities). This campaign advocates a general boycott of Israel, condemning its presence and activities in the post-1967 territories as illegal and contrary to peacebuilding (Made in Illegality).

Among the Catholic organizations that directly support the BDS movement there is also the Italian Operazione Colombia, part of Associazione Papa Giovanni XXIII, which is a signatory to the BDS-Italy appeal. Operazione Columbia joined the BDS movement in November 2014 (Operazione Columbia). Its monthly reports of activities in the Palestinian territories consistently accuse Israel of indiscriminate violence, collective punishment, and apparent efforts to persecute the Palestinians, overlooking or denying the existence of Palestinian violence against Israelis, anti-Israel hate speech, and anti-Semitic hatred. The related blog "Tuwani Resiste" (Tuwani being the Palestinian village where the organization's activists operate) demonizes Israel by accusing it of ethnic cleansing and apartheid practices. An example of the double standard in the condemnation of violence is the description of Israel's military operation in the South Hebron area in July 2016 following the murder of the Israeli girl Hallel Yaffa Ariel in her house. There is no account of this terrorist attack and no consequent condemnation.

Certain organizations are careful not to embrace the BDS movement as a whole, although they defend it and participate in boycott campaigns. That is the case with the Belgian organization Broederlijk Delen, which indirectly supports BDS initiatives, including Made in Illegality (Goditiabois). The organization's Brigitte Herman has defended the BDS movement as a non-violent form of freedom of expression. Similarly, the Irish Catholic organization Trócaire advances the "End the Occupation" campaign, through which it calls upon the Irish government to adopt boycott policies. It also supported the controversial Irish bill banning settlement products ("Trocaire Supporting"). The appeal to the Christian world is clear in a Colm Hogan post about Bethlehem, which insinuates that the troubles of the local Christian population are entirely the result of Israel's security policies.

Other Catholic organizations support BDS within international bodies. The Pontifical Mission for Palestine, instituted in 1949 by Pope Pius XII to assist Arabs affected by the 1948-1949 conflict, and Caritas Jerusalem were among the signatories of the 2017 open letter promoted by the National Coalition of Christian Organizations in Palestine to the World Council of Churches, calling for the support of the BDS movement (World Council). This letter followed several demonstrations of hostility to Israel organized by different groups in the world under the slogan "100 years of Balfour, 70 years of Nakba, 50 years of occupation." Indeed, the letter condemns the Balfour Declaration, which is the legal core of international recognition of Jewish pursuit of statehood, as a document based on a "twisted theological premise"—referring to the Christian Zionist movement, which sees Jewish statehood as a divine sign and presage of the coming of Jesus. The same text first accuses Israel of apartheid and then calls for condemning "any theology . . . that privileges one nation over the other based on ethnicity or a covenant," referring to the supposedly distorted theological and historical assumptions of Zionism and its supporters (point 3). Interestingly, the text calls on Christian groups to condemn "any attempt to create a religious state in our land or region" (point 4) evidently referring to Israel, perceived as a religious state and not the nation-state homeland for the Jews; yet it does not urge condemnation of existing religious states built on Islamic law. Alarmingly, the letter also urges people to "revisit and challenge your religious dialogue partners" and recommends willingness to "withdraw from the partnership if needed—if the occupation and injustices in Palestine and Israel are not challenged" (point 5), apparently referring to Christian-Jewish dialogue.

In addition to political and cultural support for the boycott movement, a number of Catholic charities donate to NGOs engaged in anti-Israel work. Among its 164 chapters worldwide, Caritas Internationalis, headquartered in Rome and operating under pontifical jurisdiction, has at least ten chapters that do so. Particularly dedicated to such activities are Broederlijk Delen (Belgium), Cordaid (Caritas Netherlands), and Trócaire (Caritas Ireland), but others, including Catholic Relief Services in the US, the Catholic Agency for Overseas Development in Britain, and Secours Catholique in France, have helped fund anti-Zionist and BDS-related work (NGO Monitor "Catholic"). Other Catholic groups, including some either based in the US or with US chapters, have established their political position by signing or originating statements critical of Israel. Those include The Conference of Major Superiors of Men—headquartered in Maryland and established in 1956 as the "canonically recognized pontifical conference organized to promote the welfare of all religious priests, brothers, and candidates in the United States"—which in 2016 called for a "boycott of settlement products and companies profiting from settlements" as well as divestment from them. Other sources of such views include the Maryknoll Office for Global Concerns and Pax Christi USA.

CONCLUSIONS

Certain Palestinian organizations and their leaders combine a nationalist message with Christian discourse in order to advance an anti-Israel narrative. This discourse conflates national struggle with religious endeavor, appealing to Christian communities abroad through a religious message that advances a political agenda. It portrays Israel as the major cause of conflict, the only party rejecting peace, and an inherently violent, racist entity deserving contempt, condemnation, and international sanctions. Within this frame, boycott campaigns are non-violent struggles, in line with the Christian tenet. That helps Catholic organizations support BDS directly, through coalition appeals and open letters, or indirectly, sympathizing with the movement as a supposedly nonviolent means for achieving peace. These activities build on political misrepresentation and theological misperception of the Jewish state. Politically, Israel is supposedly the only culpable party and its very existence is incompatible with human rights. Theologically, its very being relies on purportedly fallacious conceptions of the Scriptures.

In order to overcome the potentially disruptive effects of this discourse on the relations between Jews and Christians abroad, the theological questions about Israel's existence as a Jewish state should be resolved. Nationalist propaganda exploiting Christian messages should be discontinued. The main argument is that Christians and Muslims are unsafe in a Jewish State, and that they should therefore develop a common strategy to oppose the Jewish entity. The underlying pan-Arabist model construes both Muslims and Christians first as Arab and only secondarily differing by their religious identity. Their Arabness is then conceived as incompatible with a life as a minority in a Jewish state. Politically, these stances are not a criticism of Israeli policies toward its minorities, but rather a major attempt to delegitimize the Jewish State both religiously and politically.

How should Israel invest in its minorities? How should Israel do more to promote diversity? How should Israel integrate its minorities more effectively? How should Israel promote peace in a hostile environment that calls for its destruction? These fascinating questions are not addressed. As long as these organizations believe that Christians cannot be integrated into a Jewish state because the only way to be Christians is in an Arab state, and as long as they promote a Palestinian narrative that affirms the universal right of return for refugee descendants, there is no point describing their efforts as an agenda for peace, but rather as yet another political attempt to deny Israel's right to exist as a Jewish state under the disguise of a "Christian narrative" of pursuing peace.

However minor this position may be in the Catholic world, it builds on the unresolved theological matters regarding Israel as a Jewish entity and escalates anti-Israel sentiment, which inevitably affects Jewish-Christian dialogue more widely. Given the vertical structure of the Catholic Church, it is the failure of the hierarchy to refute anti-Israel sentiment that permits it to flourish.

CHAPTER FIVE

JONATHAN RYNHOLD

—◦—

EVANGELICALS AND THE ISRAELI-PALESTINIAN CONFLICT

"I personally have a problem with trading land for peace but that's not our business. If [Israeli Prime Minister] Sharon wanted to say no to a withdrawal, okay, we would have supported him. And if he said yes, well, that's okay with me, too."

—*Jerry Falwell* (quoted in Chafets 67)

INTRODUCTION

How do American evangelicals relate to the Israeli-Palestinian conflict? Are they working to block a Palestinian state and bring on Armageddon? Or are they driven by a sense of being commanded by the Bible to support Israel irrespective of the policies pursued by the Israeli government? How important is evangelical support for Israel in political terms? Are they uniformly pro-Israel or are there important differences of approach within the evangelical community? And finally, is evangelical support for Israel poised to decline? This chapter will seek to answer these questions by surveying and analyzing evangelical approaches to the Israeli-Palestinian conflict.

This chapter begins by looking at both the demographic and political importance of American evangelicals and at the different political and theological orientations within the movement. Next, the development of Christian Zionism in America is outlined and the nature and impact of evangelical Christian Zionists' political behavior regarding the Israeli-Palestinian conflict is assessed. Subsequently, the approach of pro-Palestinian evangelicals is outlined and the question of whether they are turning the younger generation away from Israel is assessed. The attitudes of the evangelical public are then outlined and compared to the attitudes of the general public and mainline Protestants. Here, the analysis focuses on the reasons for the sharp increase in support for Israel over the Palestinians in the new millennium.

EVANGELICALS: THEOLOGY, DEMOGRAPHY, AND POLITICS

Evangelicalism is a Protestant movement formed in the eighteenth century. Today, three tenets form its core: being "born again," which involves accepting that one is saved solely by faith in Jesus; belief in the authority of the Bible as the actual word of God; and sharing faith through missionary work and charitable activities (Spector 43-45; McDermott "Evangelicals and Israel"). From World War I until the 1990s evangelicals were outnumbered and overshadowed by mainline Protestants, who dominated the worldview of the American political class. However, the past three decades have witnessed a reversal of fortunes. In the second decade of the new millennium, about sixty percent of American Protestants are evangelicals. Overall, just over a quarter of all Americans define themselves as evangelicals and they make up over a third of registered voters (Pew Research Center "American Religious").

Aside from Mormons, evangelicals are the most ideologically conservative religious group in America (Pew "A Portrait of Mormons"). Over three-quarters of white evangelicals voted for the Republican presidential candidate between 2004 and 2016 (Gregory Smith and Jessica Martinez). Exit polls suggested that between 76 and 81 percent of white evangelical Protestant voters supported Donald Trump in the 2020 election (Newport). About half of all evangelicals are traditionalists in theological terms and conservative in ideological terms; this group is often known as Fundamentalists and is also characterized by a high level of church attendance. Leading figures have included Jerry Falwell, Pat Robertson, and John Hagee. These traditionalists tend to hold to a relatively literal interpretation of Scripture, to be hostile to the theory of evolution, and to believe in a coming Armageddon. Reacting against liberalism in the 1960s, conservative evangelicals returned to politics for the first time since the 1920s. Subsequently, there was a resurgence of evangelicalism that helped make the new Christian Right a mass political movement. At the same time, there was a sizable increase in the percentage of self-identified evangelicals in Congress, from around ten percent in 1970 to more than twenty-five percent in 2004 (Mead 35).

The second group of evangelicals are centrist moderates, who make up thirty to forty percent of the evangelical population. About half identify as Republicans. The third group consists of theological modernists and ideological liberals. They comprise a little more than ten percent of evangelicals. They identify more with Democrats and few believe in Armageddon (Green "American Religious"). Leading figures in this category include Jimmy Carter, Tony Campolo and Jim Wallis, who founded the left-leaning evangelical magazine *Sojourners*, which has a circulation of 35,000 (Van Zile "Evangelical").

THE DEVELOPMENT OF CHRISTIAN ZIONISM IN AMERICA

The historical legacy of Puritan Protestantism is a major foundation of contemporary Americans' support for Israel. The Reformation led to a new emphasis on reading the Hebrew Bible. The Puritans were among the Protestants most committed to Bible study. They believed that it was important to read the Bible in the original Hebrew in order to understand it properly. Subsequently, the study of Hebrew became a core compulsory subject in early American universities.

Even today about half of Americans consistently believe that God gave the land that is now Israel to the Jewish people—including a significant percentage of Blacks, Hispanics and Catholics. This is indicative of the way in which pro-Israel elements of Puritanism have spread way beyond their original boundaries to become part of mainstream American political culture. While these attitudes are widespread, the religious group that holds these beliefs in the highest numbers and with the greatest intensity is the evangelicals (Rynhold *Arab-Israel*).

Because evangelicals tend to understand the Bible in a more literal way, they take very seriously the verse in Genesis 12:3 where God told Abraham: "I will bless them that bless thee and curse them that curse thee." This is the verse cited by most contemporary Christian Zionists to explain their support for Israel (Brog *Standing* 23-25). As Falwell put it:

> I personally believe that God deals with all nations in relation to how these nations deal with Israel ... I premise that on what God said to Abraham: "I will bless them that bless thee and curse them that curse thee." I therefore think America should without hesitation give financial and military support for the State of Israel. My political support for Israel is unconditional (quoted in Simon 64)

From the fifth century until the sixteenth century, replacement theology was dominant within Christianity. It asserted that God's covenant with the Jews was broken and all future related promises in the Bible are applicable to the Church. At the same time, the main theological position concerning biblical prophecy was *a*millennial, expecting the return of Jesus in a remote future. The Reformation changed this. Protestantism insisted that the Bible itself was a source of authority and that any believer could correctly interpret Scripture when inspired by the Holy Spirit. This led some to adopt a literalist reading of the biblical prophecies of Isaiah and Daniel, which seemed to anticipate an imminent Second Coming. In contrast to replacement theologians, Restorationists saw the Jews as the *heir* of the biblical children of Israel and thus the object of biblical prophecies about a restored Davidic kingdom. In their messianic scenarios, the return of the Jews to the Holy Land was the first step toward the Second Coming of Jesus. Restorationism flourished among the Puritans (Toon 23-26).

One particular version of Restorationism became popular in America, especially among evangelicals, in the second half of the nineteenth century—premillennial dispensationalism. It proclaimed that there will be seven years of natural disasters and terrible wars in which two-thirds of humanity will perish. Meanwhile, the Jews will return to their ancient homeland. They will establish a state there ruled by the Antichrist posing as the Messiah. The Antichrist will inflict a reign of terror. The arrival of Jesus at the end of the Great Tribulation will end the Antichrist's rule and establish the millennial kingdom. Only those Jews who accept Jesus as their personal savior will survive. Jesus will then rule, with the Jews inhabiting David's ancient kingdom. The Temple will be rebuilt, and Jerusalem will serve as the capital of the entire world (Weber *Armageddon* 20-43).

Against this background, the creation of the State of Israel in 1948 was viewed as a step toward the Second Coming of Jesus by many evangelicals. However, it was after the Six Day War in 1967 that evangelical support for Israel really took off. Not only had Israel achieved what appeared to be a miraculous victory, but it also gained control over a united Jerusalem, including the site of the ancient Jewish Temple that, according to prophecy, needs to be rebuilt before the Second Coming. Subsequently, Falwell declared that the State of Israel is "the single greatest sign indicating the imminent return of Jesus Christ" (Falwell "Twenty-First Century" 10). Other Christian Zionist leaders and activists referred often to the prophetic foundation of their support for Israel. Indeed, at least two-thirds of evangelicals believe in biblical prophecy relating to Israel (Pew "American Evangelicals").

IS IT GOOD FOR THE ISRAELIS?

If Christian Zionists are supporting Israel only as a means to bring Armageddon, which would involve the deaths of millions of Jews and the conversion of those who remain, then rather than being Israel's best friend they may actually threaten the State of Israel, since these beliefs might encourage them to support moves that would bring Armageddon closer. Indeed, there are many Christian Zionists who look forward to the rebuilding of the Temple. The Temple Mount Faithful, a very small group of Israeli Jews who want to rebuild the Temple, and the Temple Foundation reportedly receive significant funds from evangelicals. The construction of a Third Temple would presumably involve the destruction of the mosques on the Mount. This could lead to a massive war between Israel and surrounding Muslim Arab states. Hence, the Israeli security services are concerned about such activity (Shragai).

Similarly, there is speculation that Hagee and his followers support a preemptive Israeli strike on Iran's nuclear facilities which represents an attempt to trigger the end times. In his 2006 book *Jerusalem Countdown*, Hagee charts the way in which a future confrontation with Iran will lead to Armageddon. However, Hagee claims that his support for an Israeli strike is motivated solely by his concern for Israeli and US security. As he explains, "we don't believe that we can speed up the end of days one second . . . . We are powerless to change God's timetable" ("Sen. Joe Lieberman")

Indeed, despite the fact that biblical prophecy drives some evangelical extremists to undertake dangerous activities, for the overwhelming majority of Christian Zionists this is not the case. Christian Zionist pro-Israel activism is not, generally speaking, driven by a desire to hasten the end times. Of the hundreds of evangelicals interviewed by Chris Smith, not one stated that they were trying to speed up Armageddon (Spector 180-200). Moreover, when evangelicals were asked to cite their *main* theological reason for supporting Israel, fifty-nine percent said it was the Hebrew Bible's promise to bless Israel and the Jewish people, while only twenty-eight percent cited biblical prophecies (Brog *Standing* 180-200; also see Guth and Kenan).

CONSERVATIVE EVANGELICALS AND THE ISRAELI-PALESTINIAN CONFLICT

Christian Zionist organizations draw their support overwhelmingly from conservative evangelicals. The basic position of Christian Zionist organizations toward the Arab-Israeli conflict is close to that of the religious right in Israel, with whom they have forged ties, and was summed up in the proclamation of the Third International Christian Zionist Congress held in 1996. It stated that the Land of Israel has been given to the Jewish people by God as an everlasting possession by an eternal covenant. The Jewish people have the absolute right to possess and dwell in the Land, including Judea and Samaria (the West Bank), Gaza and the Golan Heights (Proclamation of the Third Christian Zionist Congress). There is thus an undercurrent among evangelicals that is theologically hostile to the idea of trading "land for peace," especially in Jerusalem. In this vein, Robertson declared that Rabin's assassination was a punishment from God for withdrawing from territory as part of the Oslo process. Later on, he declared that Ariel Sharon's stroke was a punishment from God for Israel's disengagement from Gaza in 2005. Robertson later apologized for these remarks (Pat Robertson).

In addition, Christian Zionist organizations tend to be either supportive of the settlements or at least not opposed to them. Between 2000 and 2010 more than half of the settlements in the West Bank received more than $200 million in funding from Christian Zionist evangelical organizations. However, the overwhelming bulk of the money raised by Christian Zionists is allocated within pre-1967 Israel (Frenkel; Rutenberg).

CHRISTIAN ZIONIST LOBBYING FOR ISRAEL

One leading American evangelist at the turn of the twentieth century, William Blackstone, developed the idea that the United States had a special role in the Second Coming: that of a modern Cyrus to help restore the Jews to Zion. In 1891, Blackstone organized a petition that called on President Harrison to help restore the Holy Land to the Jews. The petition was signed by 413 extremely prominent gentile Americans (Ariel "American Initiative"). Indeed, American evangelicals were excited by the rise of the Zionist movement. However, their pre-State lobbying efforts were quite limited, and were accompanied by missionary activity targeting Jews.

It was only in the wake of the Six Day War that pro-Israel sentiment translated into political support, in part because it coincided with the return of evangelicals to the American political arena for the first time in almost half a century. The relationship took off when Menachem Begin became Israeli prime minister in 1977. Begin forged links with Jerry Falwell. Support for Israel was one of the four elements that made up the founding manifesto of the so-called Moral Majority. In the 1990s, Pat Robertson's Christian Broadcasting Network donated hundreds of thousands of dollars to support Jewish immigration to Israel. Indeed, according to Rabbi Yechiel Eckstein, Robertson and Falwell were critical in the process of turning Christian Zionism from a tendency into a movement (Chafets 73). In 1983 Rabbi Eckstein founded the International Fellowship of Christians and Jews which raises money for Israel from evangelicals in America. In 2002, Eckstein organized a nationwide day of prayer for Israel in which 15,000 churches and 5 million parishioners took part (Heilman). In 2008 the IFCJ claimed contributions of $84 million (*Consolidated Statement*) and in 2015, $140 million. Eckstein estimated the average donation to be about $76, which gives a sense of the huge number of donors involved, over 300,000 (Maltz).

In the 1980s and 1990s Christian Zionists played a minor role in pro-Israel lobbying. In 1989 the Christian Israel Public Action Campaign (CIPAC) became the first registered Christian pro-Israel lobby. In 1997 Prime Minister Netanyahu worked closely with the Republican-led Congress and Christian Zionists to ease pressure that the Clinton administration put on Israel to make concessions to the Palestinians (Goldstein "Evangelicals"). Nonetheless, in the 1980s and 1990s, Israel remained a secondary issue for evangelicals. Thus, in 1996 Falwell endorsed Pat Buchanan despite Buchanan's anti-Israel positions. Moreover, in the 1990s there was no correlation between the pro-Israel activities of congresspeople and the number of evangelicals in a congressperson's district (Oldmixon et al. 407-426), which reinforces the impression that Israel was not a major political concern for most evangelicals at that time.

However, after 9/11 and the collapse of the Middle East peace process, Israel did take a more central role. Thus, at the 2002 Christian Coalition conference, foreign policy, including support for in Israel, was the main topic for the first time and there was a "Solidarity with Israel" rally at the conference (Marano). When Israel launched Operation Defensive Shield in the spring of 2002 in response to a huge wave of lethal Palestinian terrorism, Christian Zionists lobbied hard in favor of giving Israel a free hand to strike a military blow. Alongside Jewish organizations, evangelicals organized a demonstration in Washington DC attended by an estimated 100,000 people. They also organized a massive email and letter writing campaign to lobby the president (Spector 223-227). This shift in priorities was also evident in Congress. In the latter half of the 1990s, evangelical members of the House of Representatives were not especially supportive of Israel; however, from January 2001 to December 2003, evangelical conservatives in the House became strong supporters of Israel, promoting resolutions that clearly took Israel's side against the Palestinians (Oldmixon et al.)

There was also support in the Oval Office, which was then occupied by an evangelical friend of Israel. George W. Bush's underlying sympathy for the State of Israel was based on his faith. In a speech to the Knesset, President Bush stated that the State of Israel represents "the redemption of an ancient promise given to Abraham, Moses and David—a homeland for the chosen people" (The Knesset). However, end-times theology was alien to the President (Lindsay 206-209; Spector 206-209; Aikman 122-126) and key elements of his policies toward the peace process were diametrically opposed to the positions of the Christian Right. Thus, in 2003 Bush launched the "Road Map," a staged plan designed to lead to the establishment of a Palestinian state. Christian Zionists actively opposed it. Nonetheless, his administration successfully pressured the Israeli government to accept the Road Map (Rynhold *Arab-Israeli Conflict*). While in 2008 Bush personally tried to convince the Palestinian president Mahmoud Abbas to accept a peace plan that involved Palestinian statehood based on the 1967 borders (with territorial swaps) including a shared Jerusalem, Abbas rejected the offer (Bush 409-410).

Meanwhile in 2006, Hagee re-formed the Christians United for Israel (CUFI) organization as a national grassroots movement—a kind of Christian AIPAC. It has directors in every state and in more than ninety of America's leading cities and an annual conference attended by five thousand people. In July 2006, at the time of their first conference, CUFI arranged 280 meetings for their members with congresspeople (Gordon; Slater). Hagee's importance was recognized by AIPAC when he addressed its annual policy conference in 2007. In 2015, CUFI set up a new lobbying arm, the CUFI Action Fund, which lobbied against the Iran nuclear deal (Guttman). CUFI claims to have over two million members (Brog "The End of Evangelical Support").

ISRAEL RIGHT OR WRONG?

It is clear that Christian Zionist organizations tend to share the policy preferences of the ideological right in Israel regarding the Palestinians. However, the question remains as to whether these preferences guide their political behavior on the issue or whether they support Israel in a more generic sense exemplified by support for the policy of the democratically-elected government of Israel, which is the official line of AIPAC.

In the 1990s CIPAC lobbied on a variety of issues. Some of these campaigns were directed *against* the policy of Israel's left-wing government and were designed to hamper the Oslo peace process that the government was pursuing, for example opposing American aid to the Palestinian Authority. They failed in this endeavor (Kyle Smith). Meanwhile, in 1995, CIPAC, in combination with other pro-Israel organizations lobbied Congress to move the American embassy from Tel Aviv to Jerusalem. The result was the Jerusalem Embassy Act, which called for the embassy to be relocated by 1999. However, the bill contained a waiver that allowed the president to suspend implementation at six-month intervals, which is what every president has done since then until Donald Trump implemented the Act in 2018. The Israeli government did not want to proceed with the campaign, fearing that raising the issue at this stage would cause serious damage to the peace process (Rynhold "Behind the Rhetoric").

Yet things were different when the Israeli far right tried to mobilize Christian Zionists against the disengagement from Gaza that involved removing eight thousand settlers from their homes. Although most Christian Zionist activists opposed the move, they did not lobby against it. The key factor, according to the then Israeli ambassador to Washington, Danny Ayalon, was that the initiative came from the Israeli government itself and was not the result of US pressure (*personal communication*). As Falwell explained, "I personally have a problem with trading land for peace but that's not our business. If Sharon wanted to say no to a withdrawal, okay, we would have supported him. And if he [Sharon] said yes, well, that's okay with me, too" (quoted in Chafets 67). Other Christian Zionist leaders made exactly the same point (Spector 173), and this position has become central to the operational code of leading Christian Zionists in America. As Hagee explained in relation to his own lobbying organization:

> CUFI [will] never presume to tell Jerusalem how to conduct its foreign or domestic affairs. We have never, and will never, oppose Israeli efforts to advance peace. Our involvement in the peace process will continue to be restricted to defending Israel's right to make decisions free of international interference or pressure—including US pressure. (Hagee "Why Christian Zionists")

CUFI remains committed in principle to supporting an Israeli government of any ideological hew, but, unlike AIPAC has moved away from a bipartisan approach to American politics, where it clearly favors the Republican Party (Lake). This reflects the fact that Christian Zionist organizations only had influence with the Republicans; though even during the administration of George W. Bush they did not play a major role in determining policy. They had some influence but not power. Meanwhile under the Democratic administration of Barack Obama, they were completely sidelined. Obama forced Netanyahu to freeze settlement building for ten months and recognize the right of the Palestinians to statehood. Even more significantly, he obtained congressional approval for the Iran nuclear deal in the teeth of vociferous opposition from Christian Zionists, AIPAC, and Republicans in general. Their influence increased again with Donald Trump.

PRO-ISRAEL MODERATE EVANGELICALS

Like traditionalist-conservatives, moderate evangelicals generally affirm that Israel plays a special role in the Second Coming and feel a biblical duty to support the State of Israel, but not in an unconditional or uncritical way. In the 1990s they thought that biblical promises gave Israel a right to at least its pre-1967 borders and guaranteed security. At the same time, they were willing to support the peace process and a two-state solution on condition that they perceived there to be a genuine partner willing to recognize Israel and committed to peaceful coexistence (Interview with Gerald McDermott, March 30, 2011). In this vein, Richard Land, president of the Southern Baptist Ethics and Religious Liberty Commission, stated, "I would argue that nothing could be more secure for Israel than creating a viable, self-sustaining Palestinian state that agrees to live in peace and agrees to suppress terrorism" (quoted in Weber "American Evangelicals" 141-57). While for Richard Mouw, president of Fuller Theological Seminary, there was no theological reason to either require or forbid the creation of a Palestinian state: "The question for me is one of prudence, and not of theological principle."[31] In the wake of the collapse of the Oslo process and 9/11, centrists primarily blamed Arafat and the Palestinians for the failure to achieve peace (Interview with Gerald McDermott).[32] Yet like Richard Land, they tended to support the 2005 disengagement from Gaza (Strode). Still, even moderate evangelicals put Jerusalem in a different category from the rest of the West Bank. Thus, in the estimation of Richard Land, if Israel were to give the Palestinians the Temple Mount and part of the Old City of Jerusalem, evangelicals would rise up and protest—though even here Land estimated that they would ultimately acquiesce so long as it was a decision freely taken by Israel. (Spector 174-175).

"EVANHANDED" AND PRO-PALESTINIAN EVANGELICALS

As explained above, liberals are the smallest ideological group among evangelicals. Nonetheless, they have obtained political influence by making common cause with the secular left and mainline Protestants. For example, Tony Campolo was close with former president Bill Clinton, while Barack Obama chose to give his first major speech on religion in the public sphere at Jim Wallis's Sojourners' Call to Renewal conference in 2006 (Micklethwait and Wooldrige 52). Sojourners has been critical of Israel, sometimes forcefully so, but not anti-Zionist.

This group tends to advocate an evenhanded approach as opposed to the organization Evangelicals for Middle East Understanding, founded in 1986 by among others, Rev. Dr. Gary Burge. In his book *Whose Land? Whose Promise?* Burge portrays Israel's existence as a viola-tion of Christian theology, which places him in the camp of Christian anti-Semitism. Like Jimmy Carter, Burge also equates Israel with apart-heid South Africa (Van Zile "Mainline"). *Christianity Today* magazine gave the book an "award of merit," though since the early 1990s most articles about the conflict in *Christianity Today* generally adopted either a balanced or a pro-Palestinian approach to the conflict (Rynhold *The Arab-Israeli Conflict*). The balanced approach was evident in two let-ters sent to President George W. Bush by more than thirty evangelical leaders in 2002 and 2007. These letters called for the US to adopt an evenhanded approach, while expressing support for a negotiated two-state solution and condemned Palestinian terrorism and Israeli settlements (Weber "American Evangelicals").

However, since 2010 there has been an upsurge in anti-Zionist activity. This has included the production and dissemination of films such as *With God on Their Side*, as well as American evangelical par-ticipation in the "Christ at the Checkpoint" conferences in Bethlehem, including by Tony Campolo and leading lights in the megachurch movement such as Lynne Hybels, who cofounded Willow Creek, a 24,000 attendee church that also oversees a network of 7,000 churches worldwide. Hybels has also promoted evangelical tours of Israel and the Palestinian territory carried out by the Telos group. In each case, anti-Zionist speakers supporting BDS proliferate. The narrative pre-sented is one-sided: "Apartheid" Israel oppresses Palestinian victims; the Holocaust and the Nakba are morally equivalent. No mention is made of the role of radical Islamism or Palestinian rejectionism in fermenting the conflict (Van Zile "Evangelical"; Brog "The End of Evangelical").

Some of this might have had an effect. In a 2014 poll by the National Association of Evangelicals many evangelical leaders admitted to some change in their thinking about Israel and Palestine. The most common change—mentioned by about 25 percent of respondents—was greater awareness of the struggles faced by the Palestinian people (National Assoc. of Evangelicals).

EVANGELICAL OPINION TOWARDS THE ISRAELI-PALESTINIAN CONFLICT

American public opinion has been consistently pro-Israel sympathizing with Israel over the Arab states and/or Palestinians by a factor between 2:1 and 3:1. This contrasts sharply with Western Europe, where opinion has been running against Israel for some time. Moreover, in America up to 2016, majorities within all major sub-groups—conservative and liberal, Republican and Democrat, Catholic and Protestant, Black and Hispanic, young and old—have consistently preferred Israel over the other side. Nonetheless, there are significant differences between various groups regarding the degree of sympathy for both Israel and the Palestinians. There are also important divisions over policy issues related to the Arab-Israeli conflict (Rynhold, *The Arab-Israeli Conflict*). Below, the attitudes of the evangelical public are compared to the general public, the other major Protestant group in America, the mainline, and finally to those who are religiously unaffiliated, who constitute the second largest and fastest growing "religious" group in America (Pew "Religious Landscape").

White evangelicals are significantly more sympathetic to Israel than the general public, mainline Protestants, or the religiously unaffiliated (figure 1). They are also far more intensely sympathetic to Israel than the other groups, with 60 percent sympathizing with Israel "a lot" (figure 3). In parallel, the percentage of those who sympathize more with the Palestinians among evangelicals is by far the lowest (figure 2). Moreover, while sympathy for the Palestinians rose among the general public, the mainline and the religiously unaffiliated 2012-2016, among evangelicals it remained constant at 5 percent.

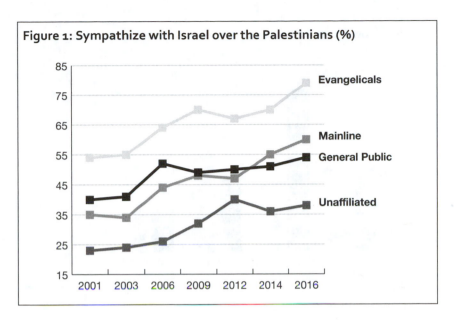

Figure 1: Sympathize with Israel over the Palestinians (%)

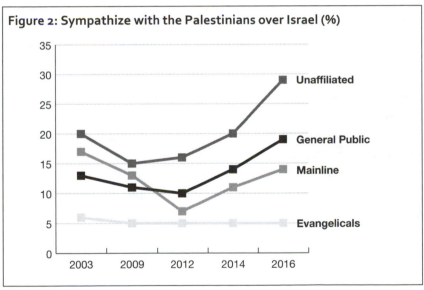

Figure 2: Sympathize with the Palestinians over Israel (%)

Data from Pew Research Center[33]

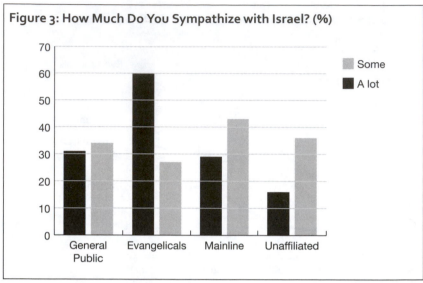

Data from Pew Research Center[34]

Although Americans have been consistently more sympathetic to Israel, when it comes to US policy throughout the twentieth century, they overwhelmingly preferred an "even-handed" approach towards the Arab-Israeli conflict (Rynhold *The Arab-Israeli Conflict*). In the twenty-first century, there has been an increase in the percentage of Americans who believe that the US should take Israel's side and many more Americans believe that the US government should support Israel rather than the Palestinians (figure 4). However, evangelicals are the only non-Jewish religious group where an absolute majority (two-thirds) believes that the US should support Israel actively over the Palestinians (figure 5).

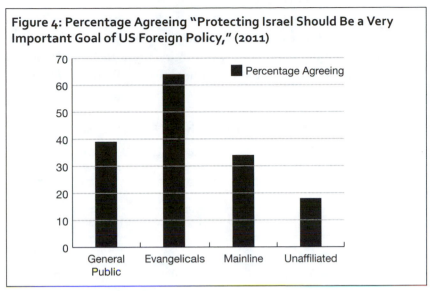

Data from Pew Research Center[35]

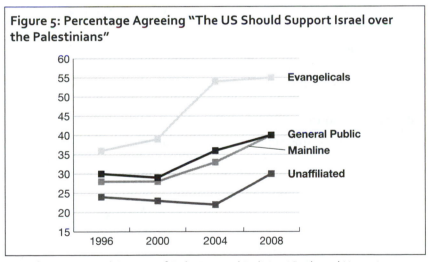

Data from National Survey of Religion and Politics (Guth and Kenan)

Among evangelicals, the most conservative traditionalist sub-group is far and away the most strongly in favor of the US government supporting Israel (table 1) and it is they who make up the core of evangelical activists lobbying for Israel. Indeed, evangelicals' attitudes to Israel tend to be very similar to the attitudes of those who identify as Republicans across the whole range of issues related to Israel and the Palestinians, which is hardly a surprise given that white evangelicals form the largest element within the base of the Republican Party (Rynhold *The Arab-Israeli Conflict*).

Table 1: Percentage Agreeing "The US Should Support Israel over the Palestinians"

Evangelicals	1996	2008
Traditionalists	50	73
Centrists	32	46
Modernists	24	36

Data from National Survey of Religion and Politics (Guth and Kenan)

Again, like most Republicans, under President Obama, most evangelicals thought US policy was not supportive enough of Israel, whereas a plurality among both the general public and mainline Protestants thought that US policy towards Israel was "about right" (table 2). Evangelicals were also more likely than any other religious group (apart from American Jews) to oppose US pressure on Israel (Jeremy Mayer).

Table 2: In relationship with Israel the US is...(%)

	Too supportive 2012/2015	Not supportive enough 2012/2015	About Right 2012/2015
General public	22/18	25/29	41/48
Mainline	25/15	26/38	41/59
Evangelicals	**12/6**	**46/55**	**41/36**
Unaffiliated	35/31	14/15	31/49

Data from Pew Research Center[36]

On core substantive issues related to the peace process, sixty-seven percent of evangelicals endorsed the building of Israeli settlements in the West Bank, about double the average for other religious groups in

America (Jeremy Mayer). Yet according to a poll conducted in 2003 by *Christianity Today,* a plurality of forty-nine percent of evangelicals were willing *in principle* to support a Palestinian state that recognized Israel and did not threaten its security, compared to thirty-nine percent who rejected the idea. The poll results for evangelical leaders were almost identical (Hertz "Evangelical" and Roadblocks"). However their support for Palestinian statehood was conditional on Israeli security and only a third of evangelicals thought that a way could be found for a Palestinian state to coexist with Israel, the majority thought otherwise (figure 6). In other words, while evangelicals have been prepared to support withdrawal in principle, since at least the collapse of the peace process in 2000, their perception that this would not bring and security to Israel means that *in practice* they continued to oppose a Palestinian state.

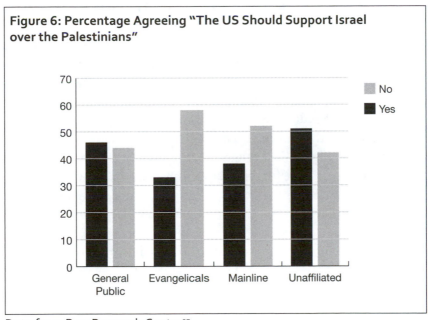

Figure 6: Percentage Agreeing "The US Should Support Israel over the Palestinians"

Data from Pew Research Center[37]

WHY HAS EVANGELICAL SUPPORT
FOR ISRAEL SURGED?

For about twenty percent of Americans religious beliefs constitute the most important factor influencing their attitudes towards the Israeli-Palestinian conflict, and most of those are evangelicals (Baumgartner et al). Clearly then, evangelical theology is critical to understanding the underlying reasons that evangelicals support Israel. Yet theology alone cannot explain the great increase in evangelical support for Israel in public opinion surveys in the new millennium. After all, the theological foundations of support for Israel were already well known to evangelicals and they have not changed. Moreover, more religiously conservative evangelicals are the strongest supporters of Israel, yet their numbers have actually declined.

In the wake of 9/11, what changed things was the centrality of radical Islamist threats to the US, whether from Al Qaeda, ISIS, or Iran. Evangelicals tend to view these threats as part of a clash of civilizations between Islam and the Judeo-Christian West. A 2002 poll indicated that more than three-quarters of evangelical leaders held a negative view of Islam, and they were far more disapproving than other Christian leaders; the same goes for the evangelical public versus the general public (Corwin Smidt). Thus, white evangelicals were far more predisposed to believe that 'Islam is more likely to encourage violence than other religions' (figure 7). Evangelicals are also much more intense in their concern regarding Islamist extremism than the American public as a whole (figure 8). Against this background many evangelicals came to support Israel as a strong frontline ally in the wider clash with radical Islamism (Brog *Standing* 78-79). From this perspective just as the U.S clashed with assorted Islamist terrorists, so too did Israel in the form of Hamas and Hezbollah.

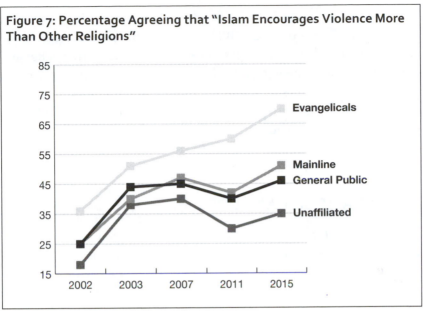

Data from Pew Research Center[38]

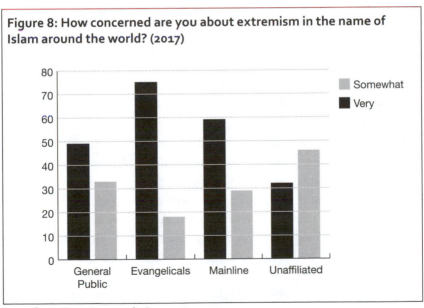

Data from Pew Research Center[39]

Nonetheless, evangelicals are hardly alone in their attitudes towards Islamist extremism. Between 2002 and 2015, the percentage of those agreeing that "Islam encourages violence more than other religions" doubled not only among evangelicals, but also among the general public, mainline Protestants, and the religiously unaffiliated. This was in sync with the upward trend in sympathy for Israel in all of these groups. Evangelicals were by far the most sympathetic to Israel and the most hostile to radical Islam, but both trends had a far wider purchase among the American public as a whole.

WILL EVANGELICAL SUPPORT FOR ISRAEL WANE?

The main target of anti-Zionist evangelicals is the younger generation. Indeed, it has been claimed that support for Israel is beginning to wane among this cohort and that over time this could lead to a reversal of fortunes (Van Zile "Evangelical"; Brog "The End"). Millennial evangelicals (those who came of age after 2000) are significantly more liberal than older generations in their attitudes toward a range of social and political issues including same-sex marriage, immigration, environmentalism and government aid to the poor (Diamont and Alper). Given that, among the general public, young liberals are the demographic group most supportive of the Palestinians over Israel (Rynhold *The Arab-Israeli Conflict*), it follows that a parallel trend may develop among evangelicals.

Indeed, there is some evidence to this effect. Pew's 2014 Religious Landscape Study found that thirty-nine percent of evangelicals under the age of 30 believe Holy Scripture is the word of God and should be taken literally, compared with sixty-four percent of those 65 or older. Other polls suggest that Israel does not rank as a top concern of younger evangelicals, as it does for older ones. Indeed millennial Christians are far less likely than older generations to believe that modern-day Israel is the fulfillment of biblical prophecy or that God has a special relationship with Israel (Pew "America's Changing"; Pinsky; Shindo).

The generational divide is highlighted by the example of Christian publisher Steven Strang and his son Cameron. Steven Strang publishes *Charisma*, a leading evangelical monthly with a consistently pro-Israel perspective. His son Cameron publishes *Relevant*, a popular magazine among millennial evangelicals, claiming to reach about a quarter of million people. *Relevant* used to be pro-Israel. However, since Lynne Hybels took Cameron Strang to visit Israel and the Palestinian territories, the magazine completely reversed its line on Israel. (Brog "The End").

Yet, despite all this it is highly unlikely that young evangelicals will completely switch allegiances and become anti-Israel. To begin with, while millennial evangelicals are more liberal than parents, they are also significantly less liberal than their non-evangelical contemporaries. A plurality is still conservative (42%) with the percentage of moderates (34%) being both much larger and growing faster more than the number of liberals (16%) (Diamont & Alper). As we know from surveys, both ideological moderates among the general public and their evangelical equivalents remain solidly pro-Israel. They may well be less supportive of Israel's far right, but they remain strongly committed to centrist positions related to US support for Israeli security (Rynhold *The Arab-Israeli Conflict*).

In one respect, support for Israel is actually growing among evangelicals. Hispanics are the largest and fastest growing ethnic minority in the US. Hispanic support for Israel is below the average for the American public, though they still prefer Israel over the Palestinians by a large margin. One group of Hispanics is far more supportive of Israel—Protestant evangelicals—and their numbers are growing fast. In the first decade of the new millennium their number increased from twelve percent of American Hispanics to twenty-two percent and the numbers continue to grow (Pew "American Religious"; Smietana). Moreover, there is now a Hispanic pro-Israel lobbying organization: the Hispanic Israel Leadership Coalition (HILC), an arm of the National Hispanic Christian Leadership Conference, which represents over forty thousand Hispanic evangelical congregations in the US.

The real challenge to pro-Israel attitudes in America is not the rise of anti-Zionism among millennial evangelicals but rather the decline in religious affiliation among the millennial generation as a whole. In 1990 about eight percent of Americans did not identify with any organized religious group; by 2017 this figure had tripled to twenty-seven percent (World Economic Forum). This was mainly a result of generational replacement. Moreover, for the first time ever, fewer than half of

Americans now identify as Protestants. This decline is of significance, because one of the main foundations of support for Israel is a widespread belief in the Bible. Indeed, the margin by which the religiously unaffiliated prefer Israel over the Palestinians is the narrowest of any ethnic or religious group in America (Rynhold *The Arab-Israeli Conflict*).

CONCLUSION

Evangelicals are more supportive of Israel than any group in America, except for American Jews, and their support is grounded in the Bible and end-times theology. However, for the overwhelming majority of evangelicals, "end times" is preordained rather than a practical program; it is primarily about being on the right side when Armageddon strikes. This is true even for the activist core of Christian Zionists who hail from the most conservative wing of the evangelical movement. Their positions on the Israeli-Palestinian conflict are similar to Israel's religious right. Though supportive of settlements and territorial maximalism, these tenets are not as central to the evangelical worldview as they are to the Jewish religious settler movement in Israel. Moreover, the thrust of evangelicals' political involvement in the Israeli-Palestinian conflict has been focused on supporting the Israeli government on issues of security regarding Palestinian terrorism and Iran, rather than opposing concessions made by Israel's government of its own free will, such as the disengagement from Gaza. As long as Israeli concessions are freely chosen, rather than a result of external pressure, the Christian Zionist lobby will not actively oppose them, whatever their preferences, with the possible exception of the division of Jerusalem.

While religious factors provide the foundation of evangelical support for Israel, the reason for the great increase in their support for Israel in the conflict with the Palestinians is a result of their perception that Israel is a very important ally in the struggle against the common threat that radical Islamism poses to the US. In this sense, evangelicals are part of a wider opinion trend in America that includes both mainline Protestants and the general public.

In terms of the political influence of Christian Zionism, there is no doubt that it has grown significantly and that it became an important part of the pro-Israel coalition in the first decade of the new millennium.

Meanwhile, when they were at the pinnacle of the political pyramid, they had some influence over policy under the Bush and Trump administrations, but they did not determine any critical decision. As per the received wisdom on lobbying, their influence was greatest when they adopted positions that had a wide resonance in public opinion – such as taking Israel's side in the war against terror. Still even then, Christian Zionist influence is limited to the Republican Party. When the Democrats are in power, they have little sway.

While evangelicals are likely to remain pro-Israel, in the long-term the relatively liberal attitudes of the younger generation may well moderate their attitudes towards the peace process. Still, their underlying support for Israeli security is bound to remain strong, especially in the face of all the Islamist threats it faces in the region—threats that they perceive as looming over both Israel and the US.

CHAPTER SIX

C. K. ROBERTSON

COMPLEXITY AND CONTENTION: FOUR DECADES OF THE EPISCOPAL CHURCH'S RESPONSES TO THE PALESTINE-ISRAEL QUESTION

During a conversation in Jerusalem in early 2015, a long-time negotiator in the seemingly endless succession of Palestinian-Israeli peace processes lamented, "Countries are not math problems to be solved."[40] His frustration is understandable, but the analogy he chose is an interesting one. Many people think of mathematics as a system of certainties and clear formulae: if only diplomatic situations could be as easy to solve as 2 + 2! And yet in many ways, the diplomatic dilemma to which this negotiator and others have devoted so much time and energy is actually similar to a specific piece of theoretical math known as Gödel's Proof, an arithmetic formula representing a meta-mathematical conclusion: "This statement is unprovable."[41] By asserting its own opposite to be true, the self-referential statement reveals an impossibly complex dilemma where success eludes any who would try to untangle it.

Success in the conversations between Israelis and Palestinians has proven similarly elusive, as participants and onlookers alike have all too often failed to take into account what that same negotiator described as the Winner's Curse, where a win/win scenario is automatically suspect. Even if a negotiated deal results in good for one side, that side will reject it *if it does not result in pain for the other side.* What is desperately needed is an investment by each party in the other's outcomes as well as its own, which requires "a passionate commitment to uncertainty, a mechanism by which I am humble in relation to the truth." As that negotiator explained, "We make space for a truth that we cannot hold on our own to become part of us." Of course, such humility does not come easily either to individuals or to groups, or even to the various churches and religious communities who have been drawn into the ongoing debate and who, as a result, have experienced tensions both between and within their constituencies.

Over the past four decades, the Episcopal Church's official responses to the Palestine/Israel imbroglio have been described by some as appropriately nuanced and by others as frustratingly inadequate. These responses have included resolutions passed by the General Convention, the denomination's bicameral governing body that meets every three years, as well as by the Executive Council, an elected board that meets three times each year between General Conventions. A brief examination of these responses, within the context of what was occurring internally in the Church at the time of each response, can help shed light on the complexity and contention with which Episcopalians have approached the untenable situation that lingers on in that land called Holy.

Gathered in Denver in 1979, the 66th General Convention of the Episcopal Church passed a resolution (1979-D089) declaring its thankfulness for the recently signed Camp David Accords between Israel and Egypt. In that resolution, the Church affirmed "the right of Israel to exist as a free State within secure borders" while also expressing support for the establishment of "a free and independent Palestinian state." The resolution furthermore recognized Jerusalem's "uniqueness" and called for "free access to the Holy City by people of all faiths." Finally, the resolution confirmed Episcopalians' "oneness in Christ with our fellow Christians in the Middle East," while also affirming that "we are engrafted in the vine of Israel," and concluded with an assurance of "love, concern and prayers for all persons in the Middle East." This resolution displays a nuanced response that clearly supports a two-state solution while also avoiding a strictly one-sided approach, with all the individual resolves falling under the umbrella of thanks for the successful Israel-Egypt peace accords. In many ways, this 1979 resolution (known as an Act of Convention) set the stage for the various statements that would follow in subsequent Conventions.

It is worth noting that this carefully crafted resolution emerged from a Convention that, along with its preceding Convention in 1976, would be known far more for approval of the ordination of women and the revision of the *Book of Common Prayer*. It was the culmination of a turbulent period of change in the 1960s and 70s that marked the end of the Episcopal Church as part of the national Establishment. That heritage could be traced all the way back to William White, first Bishop of Pennsylvania and first Presiding Bishop. White, who was in many ways the chief architect of the Church's governing structures, had previously served as chaplain to the Continental Congress, and enjoyed long conversations and lasting friendships with several of the Founding Fathers.[42] In the years that followed, despite its small size relative to other Christian denominations, the Episcopal Church continued to claim a place of national influence and political connection. Indeed, more Presidents have been Episcopalians than members of any other religious affiliation, from George Washington to George H. W. Bush.

While the Church prior to 1960 was viewed as an Establishment Church—"the Republican Party at prayer"—this image was shattered in the tumultuous years that followed, as support for Civil Rights and opposition to the war in Vietnam found strong advocates within the Church's leadership. Presiding Bishop John Hines (from Texas), who served from January 1965 through May 1974, personified the Church's new prophetic role. Many people in the pews were bewildered by the dramatic changes occurring not just in society but in the Church itself. Hines' successor, Presiding Bishop John Allin (from Mississippi), who served from June 1974 through December 1985, inherited the changes already in progress, yet took a more cautious approach to some internal matters, especially women's ordination, attempting to make room for those who disapproved. Many traditionalists stayed, albeit with reservations, while some went so far as to break away and form so-called "continuing churches" (Cf. Prichard *History* 319-60; Williams 363-66). In the midst of internal turmoil, the approach to Palestine/Israel was bold in the call for a Palestinian state yet not so bold as to speak out against what others bluntly called Israeli occupation.

The 67th General Convention, meeting in New Orleans in 1982, passed a resolution (1982-B047) reiterating support for the Camp David Accords, encouraging the recently-elected President Ronald Reagan to continue to seek peace in the Middle East, calling upon all parties in the conflict to "lay down their arms and to settle their disputes by direct negotiation and mutual recognition." The resolution concluded with a specific word of support for "the right of Palestinian people to exercise responsibility for their political future, with the proviso that the Palestinians recognize the legitimacy of the State of Israel." Three years later, the 68th General Convention, meeting in Anaheim, expressed its opposition to possible movement of the United States Embassy from Tel Aviv to Jerusalem, arguing that the status of Jerusalem should be determined "by negotiation and not by unilateral action by any one community, religion, race or nation" (1985-B017).

January 1986 witnessed the installation of Presiding Bishop Edmond Lee Browning, who spoke in his September 1985 acceptance speech in Anaheim California of the need to be both prophetic and inclusive, proclaiming that there would be "no outcasts in the Church." Browning became a strong advocate for the Palestinian people, making multiple trips to refugee camps in Gaza and the West Bank, and meeting with Yasser Arafat. As Holbrook's obituary for Browning reminds us, the Presiding Bishop eventually was awarded the Palestinian Medal of Jerusalem. During his primacy, the 69th General Convention, meeting in Detroit, passed a resolution affirming the goals of justice, peace, and reconciliation for both Israelis and Palestinians (1988-D053). The resolution spoke of the State of Israel's "right to recognized and secure borders," while lifting up the "civic and human rights of all those who live within its borders." As in 1979, this resolution affirmed Palestinians' rights "to self-determination, including choice of their own representatives and the establishment of their own state," and supported "the convening of an international conference over Palestine/ Israel under the auspices of the UN." Interestingly, this same General Convention adopted as its own a resolution passed earlier that year by the Executive Council (May 18, 1988), calling on the US government to implement diplomatic and economic sanctions against South Africa in response to that country's policy of apartheid, sanctions urged by South African Archbishop Desmond Tutu, who became a close friend of Bishop Browning. The resolution (1988-B050) was quite explicit in its recommendations of a trade embargo and boycotting of goods and called for "diplomatic persuasion" to encourage other countries to follow suit, including Israel.

During the Browning years, the Episcopal Church's leadership moved deeper into efforts for peace and justice on the global stage, even as they focused attention internally on issues of the full inclusion of gay and lesbian members. This led to increased tensions between progressive and conservative members of the Church, and further distancing from the Church's erstwhile Establishment heritage. On the one hand, Bishop Browning stood side by side with President George H. W. Bush as together they watched the last stone being placed in the Washington National Cathedral, an Episcopal church that is also the Congressionally-commissioned "national house of prayer." On the other hand, when President Bush asked Browning to come to the White

House on the eve of the First Gulf War, the Presiding Bishop declined, and instead joined the antiwar protest. The shift away from the Church's image as "the Republican Party at prayer" (whether that was ever truly the reality) moved further as the century drew to a close. While people still spoke of the Episcopal Church as a "big tent" with room for all—no outcasts, in Bishop Browning's language—some conservatives and traditionalists began to express frustration at the increasingly progressive direction taken by General Convention and Church leaders.

Moving into the 1990s and beyond, therefore, even as the Episcopal Church's official policies on Palestine-Israel issues remained fairly consistent with what had been previously articulated, the intensity of debate around these issues increased. Of course, none of this occurred in a vacuum, but rather reflected widening divisions both within the Church and between the Church and other parts of the worldwide Anglican Communion over issues of homosexuality, with many moving swiftly through the conflict spiral to a point of crisis and the threat of schism. For those who had come of age marching for civil rights for African-Americans and equal opportunities for women, the push for the full inclusion of gay and lesbian members was viewed as a comparable crusade for justice. So too was the call for boycott and divestment against the apartheid regime in South Africa. It is hardly surprising that these progressive Episcopalians also began to speak of the situation in the Middle East in similar terms. When they heard the pledge that there would be no outcasts in the Church, it was not only a black South African whom they saw in their mind's eye, it was also a Palestinian struggling in Gaza or the West Bank. Groups like the Palestine Israel Network, part of the Episcopal Peace Fellowship (EPF/PIN), began to speak out boldly against Israeli occupation of Palestinian lands. In their own words, the EPF/PIN "evolved out of a desire …. to become more actively engaged in advocacy and education and to bring concerned Episcopalians together for a more robust witness" (Episcopal Peace Fellowship). Their call for the use of economic divestment and boycott against Israel received vocal support from none other than Desmond Tutu, the South African archbishop who had championed such measures in his own homeland's struggles.

All this was occurring during a time when the Church's recently revised Prayer Book (1979) was being plumbed for fresh understandings of the spiritual life, especially in its emphasis on the baptismal covenant as the way to live out one's faith not only through individual piety but also by "striving for justice and peace…and respecting the dignity of every human being." As with other heavily debated issues within the Church, for many the battle for the rights of Palestinians was seen through that lens. The EPF/PIN spoke of their members being "mindful of the promises contained in their baptismal covenant" (Episcopal Peace Fellowship).

The 70th General Convention, meeting in Phoenix in 1991, would be remembered mainly for the record heat outside and the heated confrontation inside, as an argument over issues of sexuality in the House of Bishops became so vitriolic that Bishop Browning closed the doors and moved the House into private executive session. Yet even as leaders were reaching the first of many crisis-points in the Church's internal culture wars, careful nuance emerged in the several resolutions that were put forward, amended, and ultimately passed regarding Palestine and Israel. One that emerged from the House of Deputies, calling for a peaceful resolution to the conflict (1991-D008), affirmed the Church's prophetic role "by standing on the side of the oppressed," but was careful to express concern for both the Palestinians and the people of Israel, and to reaffirm explicitly "the existence of the State of Israel and its right to secure borders." Instead of a cry for overall divestment from Israel, the resolution urged the president and Congress "to require the State of Israel to account… for all aid in whatever form that the United States grants" but also "to hold in escrow aid to Israel by an amount equal to any expenditures by the Government of Israel to expand, develop or further establish Israeli settlements in the West Bank, Gaza and East Jerusalem and only release the aid from escrow if proof is given that settlements are not being established." This point is crucial, for it expresses unambiguous concern about Israeli settlements in Palestinian territories, and couples that concern with an almost surgical approach for how to deal with it: not the cessation of all aid, but a pause button, as it were, through the holding of funds in escrow.

Another, similar resolution (1991-A149) called for an accounting of all military assistance and sales in the Middle East, making specific mention of concern over the "*de facto* annexation of Palestinian land," and calling for "appropriate steps to ensure that no assistance provided the State of Israel shall be used to cause the relocation of Palestinian people from the homes, nor for new settlements to be located in the occupied areas of the West Bank, Gaza, and East Jerusalem." And as with the previous resolution, this one also urged a careful use of financial withholding, stating that any further resettlements should "result in the immediate curtailment of aid from the United States." With these two Acts of Convention, the Church made clear its support for Palestinians living under occupation while stopping short of a general call for boycott and divestment.

One issue on which the 70th General Convention was explicit was its support for a two-state solution (1991-A147), calling upon the United States government "(1) to assist in the creation of a Palestinian State and (2) to assist Israel to secure the human rights of indigenous Arabs within Israel." Regarding the second issue, the Convention listed several specific ways in which Israel could confirm that indigenous Arabs were being treated fairly, including the cessation of "brutalities," the restriction of military force to proportionate levels, the discontinuance of administrative detention, the permanent reopening of schools and universities for Palestinians in the occupied territories, an evenhanded approach to property rights and water rights (an ongoing concern), the opening of "candid and patient" talks between Palestinians and Israelis, and the safeguarding of Jerusalem as an "inter-religious municipality in which full respect is accorded to Christians, Jews, and Muslims." Here then was a clear statement on the political question of a two-state approach to the struggle.

Also clear was the resolution initiated by the bishops (1991-B011) calling for greater awareness of the statement made just a few months prior by the Primates of the Anglican Communion, who met in April in Newcastle, Ireland. That statement spoke of how those leaders were "saddened by the present suffering in the West Bank and Gaza Strip" and called upon the international community to respond to "the Palestinians in the Occupied Territories suffering inhumane containment, curfews and the continued denial of human rights." The Primates went so far as to call on the United Nations "to assume the administration of the West Bank and Gaza Strip from the State of Israel, and to facilitate humane policies for the people of the Occupied Territories until there is a settlement of the Palestinian/Israel issue" (Anglican Primates). By calling attention to the Primates' statement, the bishops and deputies of General Convention offered a helpful perspective for their own positions, showing how their prophetic role reflected that of global Anglicanism.

Amidst this plethora of statements of support for Palestinians struggling under occupation, the House of Deputies initiated a resolution that was careful to distinguish between "legitimate criticism of Israeli governmental policy and action, and the impropriety of anti-Jewish prejudice" (1991-D122). Such prejudice was considered deplorable and something to be eliminated from the Church's deliberations. This commitment to stand against expressions of anti-Jewish (and anti-Arab) prejudice was also mentioned in a resolution "expressing solidarity with all Christians in the Middle East, especially the members of the Diocese of Jerusalem (1991-A150). Not only did this resolution bemoan the decrease of Christian constituents in Jerusalem from twenty-four percent to two percent in just four decades, it also plainly stated the fear that "their total absence is desired by these (religious and governmental) authorities." This indictment, perhaps passed over in the middle of the detailed resolution, is possibly the most pointed and provocative word against the Israeli government in all the 1991 Acts of Convention. Much was said in that Convention, where focus had been far more on internal divisions emerging from disparate views on human sexuality so divisive in the Episcopal Church itself. In the end, time ran out and the Convention adjourned before there could be a vote on a resolution calling for a peace conference in the region (1991-A148).

The 71st General Convention, meeting three years later in Indianapolis, not only echoed the earlier indictment, but went one step further, declaring the Israeli settlements in the West Bank, Gaza, and East Jerusalem to be "illegal under international law and an obstacle to peace" (1994-D065). In the strongest possible language and with mention of the pre-1967 borders, this resolution called upon the United

States government "to withhold funds equivalent to those used by Israel for any settlement activity," and "to make those funds available to Israeli settlers leaving the occupied territories for resettlement." This resolution concluded with a note of appreciation for the "brave leadership" of Yitzhak Rabin and Yasser Arafat, while another resolution passed at that same Convention (1994-A103) specifically commended the Israeli-PLO Declaration of Principles signed one year prior.[43] The resolution reiterated the call for the United States to "condition aid and loan guarantees to Israel on its abandonment of violence as a tactic of civilian control," while also recognizing that a similar standard should be used for the newly autonomous Palestinian Authority. To emphasize the point, this Act of Convention carefully expressed that the only way to ensure a true and lasting peace would be for the United States to "adhere to a single standard of justice in its diplomatic efforts." Here then was strong, pointed language about "conditioning aid," but interestingly it was used for both Israel and Palestine, once again displaying a nuanced approach even when speaking of financial sanctions.

Meeting in Philadelphia, the site of the very first General Convention in 1785,[44] the 72nd General Convention reiterated earlier recognition of Jerusalem as the historic home to the three Abrahamic faiths and affirmed that the city "should serve as the capital for two sovereign and independent states, Israel and Palestine" (1997-A107). The resolution made specific mention of the need to remove roadblocks preventing free access to the city for Palestinians, provide for equal rights to build housing and develop institutions that had been "restricted since 1967," and count East Jerusalem as "an integral part of the occupied territories." With this single resolution, the last General Convention of the twentieth century summarized much of what had been said in the Conventions of the previous two decades, as it urged the government of the United States "to use its diplomatic and economic influence...to demonstrate a firm commitment to justice for Palestinians as it does for the security of the State of Israel." The form of economic influence to be used was unspecified, but it is noteworthy to see how American support for Israel is taken as a given while pushing for Palestinians to be granted similar support.

As the twenty-first century began, hope arose for a new iteration of the peace process, as the 73rd General Convention meeting in Denver spoke of the "final status negotiations now underway" (2000-B016). While this resolution contained familiar language about the rights of both Israelis and Palestinians, it specifically referred to the need for "the right of return for every Palestinian, as well as restitution/compensation for their loss as called for by the United Nations." An even more specific resolution called for the release of Mordechai Vanunu from Israeli imprisonment (2000-B013). Vanunu had been imprisoned in 1987 for releasing secrets of Israel's nuclear program to the British press and had spent a good deal of that time in solitary confinement. Known as a nuclear whistleblower by many outside Israel and as a traitor within Israel, he has continuously appeared on the nominations list for the Nobel Peace Prize. The 2000 General Convention resolution used the idea of the Year of Jubilee to urge the president of the United States to seek his immediate release "on humanitarian grounds."[45] By interjecting itself into this particular situation, the Episcopal Church showed its willingness to challenge Israel, in hopes that a reasonable plan between Israel and Palestine was finally within reach.

By the time of the next General Convention in the summer of 2003, the United States had experienced the worst terrorist attack in its history and subsequently initiated unprecedented and controversial national security measures while also commencing wars in Afghanistan and Iraq. Meanwhile, a war of a different kind erupted within the Episcopal Church and the Anglican Communion, as the Diocese of New Hampshire elected as its next bishop the Rev. Gene Robinson, an openly gay, partnered man who was well known within the diocese as the longtime canon to the previous bishop. Because the diocesan election was in the spring, the ensuing consent process for that election—a necessary next step before consecration can occur—took place at the 74th General Convention in Minneapolis.[46] The result was a deepening of the already-existing rift between conservatives and progressives, now to the point of schism. A relatively small but vocal minority of individuals and congregations, and even a handful of dioceses, began to distance themselves from the leadership of the Episcopal Church, and even break away altogether, often encouraged by other national churches in the

Anglican Communion.[47] Within both the nation and the Church a polarizing effect began to impose itself on every deliberation or debate.

In previous years, despite vehement disagreement, there were always opportunities for actual dialogue, even if only for pragmatic or self-serving reasons. This changed dramatically in the 2000s, as the opposing parties moved relationally from civil discourse to hostile enmity. As complexity and nuance gave way to oversimplification and caricature, opponents began to be viewed not simply as misguided, misinformed, or wrong but as evil, unpatriotic, or heretical.[48] Solutions that might have worked at an earlier stage became useless and even counterproductive, as suspicion mushroomed so that anything said by the other side was immediately discounted as a kind of sabotage: "They're just trying to trick us." Courtrooms became battlefields, as congregations that broke away from the larger Church over issues of sexuality, scriptural interpretation, and ecclesiastical authority became embroiled in property litigation ranging in the millions. A handful of other Anglican Provinces declared themselves to be out of communion with the Episcopal Church. The tendency was for every other significant issue, including the Middle East question, to be viewed through the lens of this all-consuming, polarizing conflict. Support for Palestinian rights meant being part a of left-wing, "peace and justice" agenda, while defense of Israeli policy equated to a right-wing, "biblical authority" position. Predictably, a wall went up between the opposing parties.

Following the Second Intifada that began in 2000, a very tangible 440-mile security barrier was constructed along (and in) the West Bank by the Israeli government, isolating and restricting the travel of Palestinians commuting to work. Because its border is more than double the so-called Green Line—the demarcation line that served as the de facto border of Israel from the time of the 1949 Armistice Agreements between Israel and its neighbors until the Six-Day War in 1967—and cuts significantly into the West Bank, many Palestinians describe it as an apartheid wall, while most Israelis argue that it is necessary for safety and security. The 74th General Convention passed a resolution opposing construction of the wall, then still under way, describing it as an impediment to "the implementation of the performance-based road-map leading to a final and comprehensive negotiated settlement of the

Israel-Palestinian conflict" (2003-D081). The Episcopal Church echoed
the voices of others in the international community, who said that the
wall's incursion into the West Bank violated the Geneva Convention.[49]
The Church conveyed to the president, the Secretary of State, and the
National Security Advisor of the United States the Church's support
"for their ongoing questioning of the construction of the wall."

Another Act of Convention urged Israel to end the demolition of
Palestinian homes in the Gaza Strip, the West Bank, and East Jerusalem,
which it described as "illegal under international law and a deterrent to
the peace process" (2003-D008), again citing the Geneva Convention.
Still another resolution encouraged dioceses to "assist all Episcopalians
to learn about the plight of and provide support for women and children
of all faiths in war torn areas," including Israel/Palestine (2003-A028).
However, one resolution that was rejected during that same 2003
Convention concerned the topic of an international peace zone for the
Jerusalem area (2003-D002), while two more put forward at the next
General Convention, concerning the peace process between Israel and
Palestine (2006-A011) and Israeli occupation (2006-A012) were like-
wise rejected.

Although the General Convention in 2006 failed to pass legislation
regarding Palestine and Israel—with Fair Witness among the groups
educating members about the complexity of the conflict—later that year
the Executive Council came out with two resolves outlining once more
the longstanding policies of the Episcopal Church, including support
for the two-state solution, free access to holy sites in Jerusalem, removal
of the portions of the security barrier that violate Palestinian territory,
termination of the practice of terrorism, the withdrawal of Israel from
all occupied territories, the need for Hamas to recognize the State of
Israel, and assurance that no United States tax dollars would be used,
directly or indirectly, to finance the barrier or support Israeli settlements in Palestinian territory (EXC112006.25 and EXC112006.26).
It is worth noting that 2006 also witnessed the election (at General
Convention that summer) and installation (in early November, just
weeks before Executive Council) of Nevada bishop (and former marine
biologist) Katharine Jefferts Schori as the 26th Presiding Bishop and
Primate of the Episcopal Church, the first woman to hold that office.

Meeting in Anaheim in 2009, the 76ᵗʰ General Convention crafted a prayer to be used by every Episcopalian, every congregation, and every diocese for "the divine hand" to bring down the wall around Bethlehem and for all other barriers to come down, "so all division are scattered and washed away" (2009-A037). A courtesy resolution expressing thanks for the ministry of the Rev. Canon J. Brian Grieves, a long-term staff person known for being "a fierce supporter of justice and peace for all people," notably in Palestine/Israel and South Africa, was passed (2009-D102). During twenty-one years of service on the staff at the Episcopal Church Center in New York, Grieves held a number of positions that gave him a forum for advocacy, including several years as director of Peace and Justice Ministries. Grieves had been a seminary classmate of anti-Zionist cleric Naim Ateek, who founded the Sabeel Ecumenical Liberation Theology Center in Jerusalem, and they became lifelong friends. That is significant because the Episcopalians helped give Ateek an entrée into the American mainline. Grieves was often given the opportunity to express his views in church news service releases, which promoted divestment resolutions. He also helped produce an anti-Zionist booklet for the Church. He has continued to be active in promoting BDS style resolutions. Presiding Bishop Katherine Jefferts Schori, long a supporter of reconciliation rather than hostility, was helpful in moving the Church away from BDS.

But votes were not ideologically uniform. Another resolution that included a call for unrestricted opening of borders was rejected by non-concurrence (2009-B027). Early the next year, however, Executive Council called for an end to the blockade of the Gaza Strip, allowing for free access for humanitarian assistance (EXC022010.24). And in 2011, the Council reaffirmed the Church's ongoing policies and made specific mention of its support for Palestinian statehood (EXC062011.06). Also in 2011, Presiding Bishop Jefferts Schori produced a pastoral letter in which she called all Episcopalians to both prayer and advocacy, acknowledging how the breakdown in negotiations had "brought frustrations in all quarters to new highs" and warning against "further retrenchment, further polarization masquerading as righteous anger." In the midst of a seemingly hopeless situation, the Presiding Bishop noted that though each side "believes the present moment to be untenable, nearly all agree that a future without peace is more untenable still" (Episcopal Church "Pastoral Letter").

The 77th General Convention, meeting in Indianapolis in 2012, passed a robust resolution (2012-B019) reaffirming the Church's commitment to a two-state solution "in which a secure and universally recognized State of Israel lives alongside a free, viable, and secure state for the Palestinian people, with a shared Jerusalem as the capital of both." It also commended the Presiding Bishop for her 2011 pastoral letter and called on her to develop "an interfaith model pilgrimage composed equally of Episcopalians, Jews, and Muslims," a pilgrimage which indeed took place at the start of 2015 (Matthew Davies). Perhaps the most visible, tangible resolve involved "positive investment as a necessary means to create a sound economy and a sustainable infrastructure in the West Bank and the Gaza Strip because without these measures there can and will be no viable Palestinian state and no enduring peace." In this same resolution, the Convention further encouraged Episcopalians to "give priority to investment in the institutions of the Episcopal Diocese of Jerusalem," and commended the work of the American Friends of the Episcopal Diocese of Jerusalem as well as the Good Friday Offering. As a sign of good faith in all this, the General Convention urged the Church's Economic Justice Loan Committee "to consider a loan of at least $200,000 to strengthen the economic infrastructure of the Palestinian territories." Resolution B019 marked an important response to a situation in which cynicism and despair might otherwise have won the day in the face of a deplorable political stalemate.

In its first meeting in 2013, the Executive Council affirmed the "prophetic witness" of the 77th General Convention's resolution B019 and established a B019 Coordinating Committee to assure implementation of many of the policies set out in that Act of Convention. In the same resolve (EXC022013.21), the Council celebrated the recommendation of the Economic Justice Loan Committee to invest half a million dollars in the Bank of Palestine, the first such investment by the Church in the economy of the occupied Palestinian territories. The resolve also reiterated the Church's ongoing policy that all foreign aid given by the United States government should be "comprehensively and transparently accounted to the American people" (Archives). A year later, Executive Council passed a resolve addressing the 2014 Gaza War, which had resulted in the loss of both life and livelihood for many (EXC102014.36). Here the Council reiterated calls for peaceful ways forward and specifically asked the Economic Justice Loan Committee to consider supplementing its 2013 investment in Palestine with new economic investments.

The 2015 General Convention, meeting in Salt Lake City, was particularly noteworthy for the election of the Rt. Rev. Michael Bruce Curry as the 27th Presiding Bishop and Primate, the first African-American to hold that office. Bishop Curry made history in another way, being elected by the House of Bishops on the first ballot, with confirmation of that election by the House of Deputies soon thereafter. As he has noted many times since, it was a vote for evangelism and racial reconciliation, which along with creation care became the pillars of his focus on being "the Episcopal Branch of the Jesus Movement." This marked a transition from a difficult phase of conflict involving breakaway groups, property disputes, and struggles within the Anglican Communion, in which former Presiding Bishop Jefferts Schori exercised calm, steady leadership. The internal wars of the Episcopal Church seemed, for the most part, to be over, and though some relationships remained impaired, new bridges were being built in many parts.

Sadly though, in the wake of the latest decisive breakdown of Middle East negotiations in 2014, the 78th General Convention witnessed its own internal struggle between those who called for withholding investment to the occupied territories of Palestine under Israeli control, whose resolution to that effect did not pass (2015-D016), and those who pushed for continued investment, particularly in "existing local, grassroots peace-building initiatives jointly led by Israelis and Palestinians" (2015-B013). For some Episcopalians—including members of EPF's Palestine Israel Network who in 2011 endorsed the international Boycott, Divestment, and Sanctions campaign—it appeared as if the Church was stepping back from commitments to the Palestinian cause so clearly put forward during the Browning years. Certain ecumenical partners also spoke of their frustration with the Episcopal Church's decision not to push for divestment in Israel and Israeli-occupied territory as it once had in South Africa.

Arguments against economic sanctions include the fact that since the BDS movement began three decades ago foreign investments in Israel have instead dramatically increased (Cf, Carlston 35). Unlike the situation in South Africa, economic sanctions do not appear to have been very effective. It has also been argued that such measures risk endangering Jewish-Christian relations in the US, as the National Council of Churches experienced when the American Jewish Committee and the Anti-Defamation League condemned its stance and disengaged from official dialogue (Religion News "Jewish Agencies"). And some note that while Archbishop Tutu himself had encouraged the Episcopal Church to pursue a policy of divestment against South Africa during the Apartheid Era, Jerusalem Archbishop Suheil Dawani has noticeably refrained from calling for such measures, though he has participated in advocacy efforts such as signing onto the Atlanta Statement that emerged from a summit of both Palestinian and American Christian leaders at the Carter Center in 2017. He also stood alongside other leaders in the dramatic 2018 temporary closing of the Church of the Holy Sepulchre in response to Israeli taxation.

For decades, the Palestine/Israel situation has been both complex and contentious. Episcopalians have disagreed with one another, sometimes vehemently, over questions of divestment and how to be a prophetic voice in the face of what some see as an obvious power differential between the occupier and the occupied. In 2017, with preparations underway for the 79th General Convention in Austin, Presiding Bishop Curry and the Rev. Gay Jennings, President of the House of Deputies, created a working group of five bishops and five deputies to discuss how best to shape a process for the 2018 gathering that would be open and transparent, allowing all the various voices on the issues to be heard.

Amidst the complexity and contention, amidst the rancor and resentment, what is needed now more than ever is what was described at the start as a willingness to embrace uncertainty and humility in relation to what each person or group perceives to be the truth. Quite simply, this means letting go of one's own sense of infallibility, even for a moment, long enough to listen to those on the other side, who are equally convinced of their own infallible opinion. As former Secretary of State Madeleine Albright once wrote: "Instead of seeking yet more data to defend what we already think, we need to learn what others think, and why they think it. Instead of conspiring with the like-minded, we need to spend more time learning from those we consider wrong-headed" (663). Admittedly, this is not easy, but her words reflect both a reasonableness and a tolerance that actually resonates quite clearly with the Anglican tradition from which the Episcopal Church was born.

When the monk-missionary Augustine first landed on the shores of southeast England in 597, ready to introduce the faith he had brought with him from Rome, he was surprised to find that many, including the local queen, were already Christians. To Augustine, however, their Christianity was the wrong kind, as it differed from his. Augustine wrote Pope Gregory I, who had sent him on this mission, and expressed his concern about the apparent conflict between what he knew to be true and what he was encountering there. Gregory, who rightly earned his appellation "the Great," offered a wise response that can be para-phrased as follows: "Take the best of what you bring, and also the best of what you find, and combine them into something that can build up others."[50] Here was a call to listen and learn, not just speak. Here was a humble approach to the unfamiliar, the uncomfortable. Here was a call to openness at the very start of what would eventually become Anglican Christianity.

Centuries later, during the Reformation, when some groups were disposing of Roman Catholic traditions altogether, the English reformer and Archbishop of Canterbury, Thomas Cranmer, sought a *via media* between extreme positions, retaining Catholic traditions while modify-ing them in light of the new learnings from Protestantism.[51] Similarly, the Anglican theologian Richard Hooker "thought it sad that every-thing needed to be so black and white for the extremists, for while in heaven we might hope for such clarity, here on earth we must learn to live with ambiguity, tolerating one another's differences of opinion" (Secor 183). The English Reformation was certainly not without its own bloodshed and intolerance. But the possibility was there, at least, of a more reasonable and humble approach to the truth, and it continued through the late eighteenth century when William White made his case for an American Episcopal Church with continuity and change, checks and balances. It echoed still in Archbishop Thomas Longley's call for the first Lambeth Conference in 1867, and the foundation of a worldwide Communion, carrying forward that Anglican DNA which later would be summarized by the Lambeth 1920: "It is not by reducing the different groups of Christians to uniformity, but by rightly using their diversity, that the Church can become all things to all." At its best, therefore, Anglicanism has offered the world an alternative to sectarian intolerance in the face of potentially divisive issues.

Regarding the Middle East, for four decades the Episcopal Church has called for prayer, education, and advocacy to help bring peace and clarity. It has supported the presence and ministry of Christians living in the Land of the Holy, and continuously given financial and other aid to the Episcopal Diocese of Jerusalem. It has called on the United States government to do all that it can to help, though that influence has noticeably declined since the days of the Oslo Accords. And for forty years the Church has supported a two-state solution that now appears to many to be impossible. A growing number of Palestinians, in fact, have given up on the elusive prize of two states, and are instead seeking greater civil liberties in what appears to be a seemingly permanent state of occupation.

Indeed, during a 2018 Holy Week trip to Jerusalem, Jordan, the West Bank, and Gaza, Presiding Bishop Curry and his delegation witnessed firsthand the disillusionment of many young Palestinians. Driving down the streets of Gaza City, they saw the rubble of bombed-out buildings, as well as posters and billboards on every street displaying the faces of locals who had been killed, a new group of martyrs with each fresh outbreak of violence. The result is a city where the threat of death hangs in the air and hope among the younger generation is nearly gone. They are tired of what they view as empty promises from parents, politicians, and religious leaders. Those who can leave do so, and they do not come back. But far more remain, cut off from the outside world, caught between occupiers and extremists, stuck in a system where unemployment is the norm, with no realistic way to move up or out.

Not long after that trip, Episcopalians gathered in Austin, Texas, for the 79th General Convention. It was unclear going into the meeting what decisions would be made. As noted earlier, the Presiding Bishop and President of the House of Deputies jointly appointed a working group tasked with the creation of a clearly open process, including a hearing that was held early during General Convention at which nearly fifty people spoke, most of them in favor of stronger measures, including a call for divestment. It was also determined that the House of Deputies would serve as the site of initial action for all Israel/Palestine resolutions. A total of fifteen resolutions had been submitted going into Convention, six of which passed both the House of Deputies and the House of Bishops. The most controversial resolution, D019, which spoke explicitly about the Church's financial complicity in Israeli occupation, and called for a "human rights investment screen," did not pass. Although 74 percent of the deputies voted in favor of the resolution, it was defeated in the House of Bishops, with 62 percent voting against it (Fig. 6).

Fig. 6—Episcopalian Bishops raise their hands to oppose Resolution D019. The resolution failed, 48-78. Photo: David Paulsen/Episcopal News Service

But B016 did pass, which likewise spoke of an investment screen, but without the provocative language of complicity. Interestingly, passage of this resolution was hailed by groups on completely different sides of the debate, some arguing that it was a call for divestment while others claimed just the opposite.[52] Friends of Sabeel North America applauded it as an unambiguous divestment resolution, but that is not so clear (FOSNA "Episcopal"). Whether it will result in tangible actions remains to be seen, though some companies may be screened for publicity purposes. Other resolutions were passed with far greater support, including ones dealing with the plight of Palestinian children, the disproportionate use of lethal force by both sides in the conflict, and the status of Jerusalem. It is important to note that in all this, the Episcopal Church once again spoke out for peace, for justice, even for a human rights investment screen, while stopping short of a call for boycott, divestment, and sanctions against Israel. Indeed, to the frustration of some deputies and others outside, the bishops pushed for some moderation in the use of language, being almost fully united in voting against D039, another controversial resolution that spoke of Israel as "an apartheid state." The bishops also made the decision to give these difficult issues greater attention in meetings of the House of Bishops during the 2019-21 triennium, and various resources would be made available to them and their dioceses, both from Episcopal Church staff and from groups such as Churches for Middle East Peace.

Whatever our differences on how best to proceed from this point on, Episcopalians of all persuasions can and must continue to tap into our Anglican DNA of reasonableness and tolerance and find ways to work together for a future that includes peace, security, and respect for the dignity and human rights of Palestinians and Israelis alike. None of this is as simple as 2+2=4, but some continue to cling to the hope that the seemingly insoluble problems in the Land of the Holy might one day be resolved.

CHAPTER SEVEN

ROBERT A. CATHEY

WHERE WE LIVE, WHAT WE BELIEVE: THINKING CONTEXTUALLY WITH ATEEK, RAHEB, AND GREGERMAN ABOUT ISRAEL/PALESTINE[53]

INTRODUCTION: "ON PALESTINIAN STATEHOOD"

In "On Palestinian Statehood," published in *The Wall Street Journal* in 2017, Bret Stephens asked whether the Palestinians were entitled to their own state. His answer:

> Maybe. But are they more entitled to one than the Assamese, Basques, Baloch, Corsicans, Druze, Flemish, Kashmiris, Kurds, Moros, Native Hawaiians, Northern Cypriots, Rohingya, Tibetans, Uyghurs or West Papuans—all of whom have distinct national identities, legitimate historical grievances, and plausible claims to statehood?

> Many in America claim to be experts on the Israeli–Palestinian conflict. In Jerusalem a theologian told me his interfaith center at a Midwestern church–related institution offered public programming on every major global issue with two exceptions: reproductive ethics and women's rights (i.e., abortion) and Israel/Palestine. During his decades of experience in higher education, these two sets of issues proved to be "non-dialogical." Once you open up the topic of the future of Israel and the occupied Palestinian territories (or "Palestine" as the entire region is referred to by many Arab Americans), you will get heated debate, but no illumination. [54]

Yet in January 2017, diplomats from over seventy nations gathered for a "Mideast peace conference" in Paris seeking to renew negotiations between the Israeli government and the Palestinian Authority on behalf of a future Palestinian state. And in a dramatic UN Security Council meeting on December 23, 2016, US Ambassador Samantha Power delivered a vote of "abstain" rather than "no" on behalf of the US for Resolution 2334 that condemned as illegal under international law continued Israeli settlement construction in East Jerusalem and the West Bank on Palestinian properties and lands that the Israeli Defense Forces seized from Jordanian military forces and other Arab fighters in the 1967 "Six Day War."

What role do Arab Israeli and Palestinian Christians, as historic yet challenged religious minorities in the Near East, play on the local and global stage of conflicts over the future of Israel/Palestine?

I. DISCLAIMERS AND QUALIFICATIONS

First, I am a theologian, not a political scientist or historian of the Middle East. I don't have a solution to the Israeli–Palestinian conflict, though I do conclude by offering dialogue as an alternative to contentious debate. I am also mindful of the realities of multiple vectors of conflict in the Middle East North Africa (MENA) region. If, perchance, the United Nations were able to broker a two-state compromise or "solution" between the Palestinian Authority and the Israeli government, the state of war between Israel and Hamas in Gaza, and the state of war between Israel and Lebanon would still be unresolved. Not to mention the horrific loss of life, destruction of cities, ongoing multi-pronged violent conflicts, and refugee crises in Syria, Lebanon, Jordan, and Turkey that have resulted, for example, in Syrian refugees in the University of Chicago Hospitals and Hyde Park.

Second, I am interested in how contexts shape cultural and religious beliefs and practices, and how beliefs and practices may inform and transform contexts. In this paper I don't find myself constrained to agree with, endorse, or defend all the beliefs and practices of Palestinian theologians, or of their critics.

Third, despite having spent my sabbatical in 2010-11 in Israel, Lebanon, and Syria, I am sure there is much I still don't understand, especially the rich complexities of languages, cultural and religious forms of life, nations, and political organizations, in the dynamic region of the Near East. One should apply to the topics of this paper the exegetical rule of David Barr: "Don't be too quick to understand anything."

II. UNDERSTANDING THEOLOGY IN THE "HOLY LAND(S)"

In 2004, I wasn't interested in Israel, Zionism (whether cultural, religious, or the variations in Christian Zionist movements), the Palestinians, Arab Americans, or the Christian minorities in the Middle East. My own theological interests incline toward philosophic theology and constructive revisions of the Christian doctrines of God, Christology, and ecclesiology in inter-religious perspectives informed by the natural and social sciences.

Then one day a phone call came from the Executive Presbyter of Chicago Presbytery asking me to serve on a panel of Presbyterian and Jewish speakers to address the crisis in national and local relations between established Jewish organizations and the Presbyterian Church of the USA (PCUSA). The crisis was occasioned by the decision of the Presbyterian General Assembly of 2004 to scrutinize all the denomination's investments, including the investment portfolios of the billion-dollar-plus Presbyterian Foundation in Indianapolis and the denomination's Board of Pensions in Philadelphia. The General Assembly intended to discover if the PCUSA was profiting from multinational corporations like Caterpillar, Inc. in Peoria, Illinois, that sold hardware, software, and support services to the US federal government, which in turn sold or transferred these resources to the Israeli government and the Israeli Defense Forces occupying Palestinian territories.[55]

My initial critical response to the Presbyterian General Assembly's actions and the conflicting interpretations and responses to those actions by Presbyterian leaders and laity, by American Jewish organizations, and by North American Islamic organizations, was to understand and articulate to fellow Presbyterians as best I could the concerns I was hearing from mainstream American Jewish leaders about the implications of the Presbyterian General Assembly's June 2004 decision. This was out of my concern for Christian-Jewish relations in Chicago and beyond, especially given the progress that was made in the 1980s in Presbyterian–Jewish relations in the US.[56]

I had never identified myself with Christian Zionism in any of its forms, whether Dispensational (like the "Left Behind" popular theology of novels and films), Evangelical (such as publications and films of the Billy Graham Crusade organization), Liberal Protestant (e.g., Paul Tillich and Reinhold Niebuhr in the 1940s), or post-Vatican II Roman Catholic. Certain scriptural and traditional claims that God's covenant with the ancient Israelites included promises of a "land" to them and to their descendants (however defined by future generations) in a territory between the Jordan River and the Mediterranean Sea (or some other geographic configuration), divine promises that are everlasting and binding on all future generations and the diverse peoples of the Near East, struck me as an enchanting "myth of origins." But these biblical and traditional texts are being read anachronistically and indeed abused when they are proposed in our times as constructive theological-ethical norms for adjudicating competing Israeli and Palestinian claims to territories that have been claimed and occupied by multiple empires and peoples over the millennia.

God's covenant-making activities with creatures must certainly take spatial dimensions, if there is to be space for bodies to live out the covenant's gracious provisions and life-guiding obligations.[57] But to specify the contemporary international legal boundaries of that space or "land" for today based on biblical and traditional accounts of sacred covenant promises, or biblical representations of the boundaries of the ancient kingdoms of Israel and Judah, strikes me as an example of being stuck in a state of "first naïveté" as a faithful reader. One might begin reading in this way, as many believers do, but all readings of biblical texts for constructive theological-ethical work today must pass through the "desert of historical and ideological criticism" seeking a "second naïveté," attuned to the poetic symbols, metaphors, and narrative structures of these texts.[58] To remain stuck in the literal senses of these texts may even be an act of "bad faith" or willful ignorance of the consequences of our readings over time.[59]

Since September 2004, I have participated in dialogues, debates, and committee meetings in religion-related institutional offices, churches, synagogues, theological institutions, the Israeli consulate in Chicago, the Israeli Supreme Court in Jerusalem, conferences, conference calls, webinars, study trips to Israel/Palestine and Lebanon hosted by the Jewish Council on Public Affairs, the Shalom Hartman Institute in Jerusalem, the Near East School of Theology in Beirut, Lebanon, and other communications with Jewish, Presbyterian, Palestinian, and NGO leaders and activists. Almost all of these meetings and communications were occasioned by the PCUSA's decision to scrutinize its investments in multi-national corporations in 2004 with regard to the Israeli occupation of Palestinian territories and corporate profits.

The "divestment debate" in North America, the European Union, Australia, and New Zealand, between Palestinian advocacy movements and national staff members in historic Protestant ecumenical denominations like the PCUSA, the Evangelical Lutheran Church in America, the Episcopal Church (US), the United Methodist Church, the United Church of Christ, the Anglican Church in the United Kingdom and other nations, the Church of Scotland, the United Church of Canada, the Uniting Church of Australia and New Zealand, and mainstream international and national Jewish organizations has challenged and, in some cases, fractured Christian–Jewish relations in our times.[60] In fact, Rev. Dr. John Pawlikowski, OSM, of the Catholic Theological Union—one of the founders of Holocaust Studies and an international interpreter of Vatican Council II's statement on interreligious relations, *Nostra Aetate* ('In Our Time…')—has said that we now live *after* the "golden age" of Christian–Jewish relations that occurred in the late twentieth century.

III. WORKING DEFINITIONS: "LIBERATION THEOLOGY" AND "CONTEXTUAL THEOLOGY"[61]

Since the 1960s, radically creative and subversive ways of enacting and communicating Jesus of Nazareth's message of emancipation have emerged around the planet that have become grouped under the conventional headings of "liberation theology" and the broader category of "contextual theology." In many cases, "contextual theologies" take the form of "local theologies."

Liberation theology emerged in the 1960s and 1970s out of Christian–Marxist dialogues on three continents, the Black Power movement in North America, anti-apartheid movements in South Africa and postcolonial movements in other nations, the *Minjung* Theology movement in South Korea, and feminist theology movements on four continents.[62] These theologies were distinctive in confronting "oppression and social ills" rather than limiting themselves to the cultural identity of Christian participants (Schreiter 15). They reset the methods of Christian theology, prioritizing subversive political and social action against established forces of oppression as the prime subject matter upon which theological communicators should reflect. They took aim at elites in their societies and churches that rationalized oppression, poverty, and various forms of racism, classism, and sexism. And they re-read the Bible and their theological traditions from the perspectives of the "least ones" in their social and ecclesial hierarchies.

For example, in the Western Hemisphere since the 1960s, three generations or waves of liberation theologies authored by Latinos/as have appeared: the first generation of Marxist utopians; the second generation addressing the social realities of civil wars, transnational labor and migrants, indigenous and popular religions, and globalized economies; and a third generation of dialogical Latino/as taking up issues of ecology, science and technology, interreligious dialogue and partnership, and postcolonial approaches to religions and cultures.

By the 1970s, the broad category of "contextual theologies" had emerged, overlapping significantly with subversive liberation theologies. These theologies are addressed to particular cultural contexts and peoples, including the churches and believers that indwell them, rather than the secular world in general or the global, ecumenical churches as a whole. (Think of the difference of reading Karl Barth or Paul Tillich's systematic works compared to reading James Cone, José Míguez Bonino, Alan Boesak, Kwok Pui-lan, Maria Asasi-Diaz, et al.)

According to many constructors of "contextual theologies," all Christian theologies begin as some particular people's "local theology," addressed to specific churches and believers in certain contexts at particular times and places.[63] Over time, these particularities became erased as some local theologies (and not others) were elevated by church authorities and encoded in authoritative documents like the Nicene Creed. In late Roman Christianity, the move from local theologies to binding, ecumenical, empire-wide theology was often accompanied by centuries of conflict and violence that fractured the Christian movement.[64]

Much more could be said about these overlapping categories. By analogy to debates in twentieth-century analytic philosophy and its conflicted readings of the history of Western philosophy, many modern Euro-American theologies addressed broadly to the Christian community and/or to the secular world take the form of foundational, system-building enterprises (i.e., "some white theologians think they can speak for everyone else from their privileged, pseudo-universal points of view"). By contrast, anti-foundational, neo-pragmatic contextual philosophies (cf. the late Richard Rorty and his former student, Cornel West) address the intellectual issues and social problems of particular cultures and peoples, giving up on the pretense to speak to "Reason,"

"History," "Being," "the universal human condition," "the Sacred," etc. These philosophers and theologians never forget where they came from, whom they do philosophy or theology with and for, and how much their work is embedded in and beholden to the particularities of place and time.

IV. "A PALESTINIAN THEOLOGY OF LIBERATION": NAIM ATEEK AS THEOLOGICAL PIONEER

Naim Stifan Ateek was born in Beisan (Beth Shean), Palestine, in 1937 to a Christian family. His family survived the Nakba (disaster) of May 1948 when the State of Israel was "proclaimed" and hundreds of thousands of Palestinians fled the violence or were forced to flee from their homes, businesses, lands, and communities.[65] His hometown was "occupied" on May 12, 1948 by a Zionist military unit and ordered to evacuate by a "military governor," after which the Ateeks reestablished themselves in Nazareth.

Ateek, like some other Palestinians of his generation, received his higher education in America at Hardin-Simmons University (Southern Baptist) in Abilene, Texas; the Church Divinity School of the Pacific in Berkeley, California (Episcopal); and the San Francisco Theological Seminary (Presbyterian) in San Anselmo, California. His D. Min. dissertation at San Francisco Theological Seminary was the basis for his first book, the groundbreaking work in subversive Palestinian theology: *Justice, and Only Justice* (1989).

Ordained a priest in the Anglican Church in Israel/Palestine, Ateek developed a theology that grew out of many years of pastoral care for believers and their extended families—whose lives, like his family's, were fractured by the Nakba—and his social advocacy with Israeli Arab and Palestinian Christian leaders in the region. He served as Canon of St. George's Cathedral in Jerusalem, leading its Arab-language congregation. Growing out of a series of ecumenical leadership conferences in 1989-90 co-sponsored with Mennonites in the region, Ateek and others co-founded the Sabeel Ecumenical Liberation Theology Center in Jerusalem. In Arabic, *Sabeel* means "the way," "channel," or "'spring' of life-giving water."[66] The Center functions as a meeting ground, education and conference center, publishing enterprise, and sponsor of international political advocacy between Palestinian Arab Christians in the region and Christian pilgrims, activists, and tourists from around the world, having established advocacy and fundraising chapters, the "Friends of Sabeel," in more than ten nations in North America, the European Union, and Australia. It is hard to overstate the importance of Sabeel in explaining why today so many historic Protestant denominations have active advocacy organizations that work on behalf of Palestinian Arab Christians and Muslims in Israel/Palestine, Jordan, Lebanon, Syria, and in the wider Palestinian diaspora, local organizations that over the years have widened their advocacy for Arab Christians in the wider Middle East North Africa region, and for Arab Christians and Muslims living in diaspora in global cities like Detroit, Chicago, and Los Angeles.[67]

As Ateek describes it in *Justice and Only Justice*, his hermeneutic, which has informed Sabeel, relies on a claim that the Old Testament includes three different understandings of the nature of God—nationalistic, Torah-oriented, and prophetic. The first of these Ateek considers a primitive and violent identity that has been revived in the form of the Jewish state. The Torah-oriented version is an improvement because it enabled Jewish society to be held together by religious belief, rather than political power. But it is still flawed because it is legalistic, particularist, and isolated from the larger human community. The prophetic tradition, based on the latter prophets of the Old Testament, Ateek considers a more mature and universal model. The prophetic God is now devoted to all peoples.

Samuel Kuruvilla, a political scientist at the University of Kerala in India and the first researcher to publish in English a comprehensive history of the origins, methods, and content of liberation and contextual theologies in Israel/Palestine, notes that Ateek is the only theologian in the region who consistently refers to his project as "Palestinian liberation theology." I am quoting Kuruvilla's important bullet-point enumeration of Ateek's positions. He argues for four important differences between Latin American "*teología de la libelración*" (Gustavo Gutierrez, Jon Sobrino, et al) and Ateek's theology (Kuruvilla 71-3):

- "Latin America was a continent where the vast majority of the poor were Christian. In Palestine, Christians were only a tiny minority."

Thus, there could be no simple transfer of theological method and content from Latin America to Israel/Palestine.

- "the option for the poor in Latin America was about class. In Palestine, all Palestinians were oppressed."[68]

- "the exodus paradigm did not play out in Palestine. Palestinians found themselves in the role of the dispossessed people." A crucial issue for Ateek and other Palestinian theologians is "how to read the Hebrew Bible" in a context where the Exodus narratives have already been appropriated by an increasing number of Israeli religious Zionists and influential Christian Zionists around the world, especially in North America, to rationalize the Nakba as the liberation of the Jewish people from the horrors of the *Shoah*/Holocaust carried out by the Nazis and their Christian accomplices in Europe and their Muslim accomplices in the Middle East.

- "Whereas Marxism provided tools for social analysis in Latin America, it was not well known or widely used among Palestinian theologians who looked elsewhere for their methods of social analysis." In one sense, Palestinian theology came on the local and international scene during the crises of Communism and neo-Marxism in the late twentieth century, i.e., the collapse of the Soviet Union, the end of Soviet-dominated republics in Eastern Europe, and the eclipse of Communist influence around the world. The methods, aims, and content of Ateek's theology would be much better compared to the postcolonial ideological, cultural, and literary criticism of another Palestinian born into a Greek Orthodox family in Jerusalem before the Nakba, Edward Said (1935-2003).

Recognizing key differences in context, audience, and method between Latin America and Israel/Palestine, Kuruvilla summarizes three "Concerns of Palestinian Theology" that are also exemplified in Ateek's writings (94):

- "Both Latin American and Palestinian theologians 'begin from the same place, oppression, but the different situation means they develop in a quite different way.'"

- "Uniquely, in Palestine, Christians and Muslims were both part of an oppressed people. Palestinian theologians must understand Islam not as a precondition for mission, but for survival." Palestinian

Christians and Muslims find strong points of contact in their shared Arab cultural identities, in the multifaceted concept of justice or righteousness as a central theme of both the Bible and the Holy Qur'an, and in their common experiences and resistance to the practices and policies of the Israeli government. The Israeli Defense Forces control the "security barrier" and checkpoints between Israelis and Palestinians, large sections of the West Bank, administer justice in the occupied territories, and control the borders of Gaza contiguous with Israel and, along with Egypt, the waters off the coast of Gaza.[69]

- "All of [the Palestinian theologians] took the gospel seriously and, in this situation of conflict, their emphasis was on peace and reconciliation, although they recognized the importance of their struggle to be free. For them, non-violence and dialogue was the way to liberation."

This last point is one of the most surprising and intriguing aspects of Ateek's ministry and that of other Palestinian Christian theologians, priests, and pastors: they have opted for nonviolent resistance to the Israeli occupation of their lands, to the policies and practices of the Israeli Defense Forces that control the "security barrier" and administer justice in much of their territory, and to the Israeli government that in many ways influences or controls their future as a people with a distinct identity in the Near East.

Some North American citizens in their situation would find reasons to justify taking up arms to violently resist the Israeli Defense Forces. Violent acts of Palestinian resistance to the Israeli Defense Forces and individuals, groups, and political organizations (cf. Hamas in Gaza) that target and slaughter Israeli citizens going about their daily lives in order to strike terror among the Israeli population are well documented in US and Western media outlets. Contrary to these violent forms of resistance and terror tactics, Ateek and many other Palestinian Christians appeal to the *sabeel* of Jesus of Nazareth: non-violent yet active resistance to unjust practices and policies, and economic, social, and political inequalities between Israelis and Palestinians and other Arab peoples in the region. Their theologies and ministries encourage dialogue and partnership with Israeli civil society organizations and individuals that also recognize these injustices and inequalities.

Regarding aspects of Ateek's constructive "theology of the land," he criticizes particularistic understandings of covenantal land in both Jewish and Christian forms of Zionism. His alternative land theology has been one of the most controversial themes in his work. Kuruvilla sums it up under four points and a summary statement (141-44):[70]

- In the Bible, ". . . the idea of land applied to the whole earth." ". . . God revealed himself more to the Jews when they were away from the land than when they were in it."
- ". . . occupation of a particular piece of land had moral consequences. The land was given by God to those people who were obedient to His Will and commandments."
- ". . . the concept of the Kingdom of God in the New Testament was the counterpart to the concept of land in the Old. Thus, there was certainly an imperative for working out justice and peace in a particular area . . . But this land was not just Palestine, but anywhere."
- ". . . there was good reason to cherish the land, but this applied to Palestinians as well as to Jews."
- "The land of Israel–Palestine is part of God's world. It belongs to God in the same way as does the rest of the world. God is its creator and owner–just as God is the maker and owner of the whole world. *Today, God has placed on this land both Palestinians and Jews.* They must then share it under God and become good stewards of it. It does not belong to either of them exclusively. They must share it equitably and live as good neighbors with one another. Both nations must 'do justice, love mercy, and walk humbly with God' (Micah 6:8). Once these biblical demands of justice [have] been satisfied, a good measure of peace will be achieved. The result will then be a new and deeper security enjoyed by all throughout the land. 'For the effect of justice will be peace and the result of righteousness, security and trust forever' (Isaiah 32:17)" (my emphasis).

There are other aspects of Ateek's theology and Sabeel's use of symbolism (e.g., the representation of Jesus in Sabeel's iconography and liturgies as a contemporary Palestinian tried, tortured, and executed by

Israeli authorities and soldiers) that have created enormous controversies, particularly in light of the greater awareness of Christian anti-Judaism that arose in Christian–Jewish dialogues after the Holocaust and Vatican II. We will pick up on some of those controversies when we turn to Adam Gregerman's critique of Palestinian theologies and pro-Palestinian Christian advocates around the world.

V. READING "THE BIBLE THROUGH PALESTINIAN EYES"

Mitri Raheb — Contextual Theologian for diverse peoples of the occupied Palestinian territories.

Mitri Raheb, a Palestinian Lutheran pastor and theologian from Bethlehem, likes to joke that he has attended more Presbyterian Church (USA) General Assemblies than most Presbyterians. He's right about that. Raheb is a popular, witty speaker who minces no words in confronting liberal Protestants with how our forms of discipleship in middle and upper middle class America are mired in "cheap grace." At the 2010 General Assembly meeting in Minneapolis, he warned us that too many Presbyterians wanted *"Kairos Palestine* lite." He was referring to the ecumenical *Kairos Palestine* statement written by Palestinian and Arab Israeli church leaders and published in December 2009.[71] The statement confronts the policies and practices of the Israeli occupation as a form of "apartheid" and calls for non-violent resistance through divestment by global ecumenical partner churches.

Raheb's family has lived in Bethlehem for many centuries in a community that was predominantly Christian up until the 1967 Six Day War. He was born there in 1962. Since the late 1960s the Christian percentage of the population has significantly declined, though not the actual number of Christians, as many of Bethlehem's Christians have moved to other lands where there were better opportunities for education and economic advancement. The influx of Muslims has increased their percentage in the population. Raheb achieved his Ph.D. in theology from Marburg University in Germany. He is the pastor of the Evangelical Lutheran Christmas Church in Bethlehem, which has a partner church relationship with First Presbyterian Church in Evanston, Illinois. In Bethlehem he has been a successful institutional entrepreneur as president of *Dar al-Kalima* University College in Bethlehem and former president of the Synod of the Evangelical Lutheran Church in Jordan and the Holy Land. His congregation is located in the middle of a predominantly Muslim neighborhood overlooking a marketplace. The iconography in their sanctuary inspires some and is controversial for others. Among Jesus' disciples are represented fighters of the Palestinian Liberation Organization, the revolutionary movement led by PLO chairman Yasser Arafat that preceded the Palestinian Authority, which administrates the cities and towns of Palestinians in the West Bank. He is the author of *I Am a Palestinian Christian, Bethlehem Besieged, and Faith in the Face of Empire*, and co-author of *The Cross in Contexts*.

In contrast to Ateek, Raheb gives more significance to the Old Testament in his contextual theology, since it is recognized as Scripture by Jews, Muslims, and Christians. Kuruvilla compares their uses of the Hebrew Bible:

> Whereas Ateek was theologically radical enough to advocate a selective reading of the Hebrew Bible . . . Raheb urged Palestinians to identify themselves with the God of Israel. He claimed that the crux of the Old Testament was to make the knowledge about a "Jewish God" available to all people, including the modern-day Palestinians. Raheb saw the God of both the Old and New Testament as one and the same God, a God concerned with justice . . . The only visible difference was that the New Testament God was also a God of grace who came to save all the people of the world and not just the Jewish people. The Old Testament and the New, while describing different eras and periods in human history, were still inseparably interconnected. (Kuruvilla 207-8)

Raheb also puts greater emphasis on the role of culture (in its many dimensions) in creating a contextual theology for Palestinians, in contrast to the greater focus on political issues in Ateek's liberation theology. Yet Raheb's willingness to support the "Jesus was a Palestinian" trope is one of the places where he leaves the historical and biblical record behind and crosses the line into politics.

Not shying away from controversy with either post-Vatican II Roman Catholic Popes and theologians or liberal Protestant theologians in dialogue with Jewish scholars and organizations, Raheb also criticizes post-Auschwitz theologies from Europe, North America, and Israel for becoming "trapped in the image of Jewish perpetual victimhood and refus[ing] to consider or even give space to the legitimate aspirations of the Palestinian people living under occupation in Israel or in the West Bank/Gaza for over fifty years" (Kuruvilla 204, quoting Raheb).[72]

In *I Am a Palestinian Christian*, his first book translated into English, Raheb lays out his hermeneutical principles for reading the Bible both in the context of Israel/Palestine and also with an eye to ecumenical dialogue between Christians and Christian-Jewish dialogue. They include (59-64):

1. "The Bible is God's Word in human words. The writings of the Old and New Testaments are the records and written accounts of various experiences human beings have had with the one God. They are nothing but testimonies of faith."

2. "Holy Scripture did not fall from heaven and is not timeless. It is written in history, it is history, it makes history. Every writing in the Bible originated in a specific context and relates to a context that must always be taken into consideration. This is necessary for the sake of the context itself as well as for its content, for there is no such thing as a text without a context. Typological and allegorical interpretations are neither relevant nor helpful in exegesis."

3. "The Bible is always contemporary. It is a living thing and cannot be put up in a jar. God's Spirit brings Scripture home to us; God brings it close. But this Spirit of God does not yield to our whim; it is bound to Scripture, and only faith makes it possible. No interpretation that excludes faith is possible. One can interpret Scripture correctly in any given context only when one's conscience is illuminated by faith and one's reason is permeated by love."

4. "The Bible is a great whole. The Old Testament and the New Testament form a unity. For us Christians, the Old Testament without the New Testament is not enough. But the New Testament without the Old Testament will either be misunderstood or not understood at all. The New Testament enlarges the horizon of the Old Testament and makes a correct interpretation possible. But the New Testament can be seen as a particular interpretation of the Old Testament, disclosing the correct understanding of the Old

Testament . . . The unity is grounded in God's very self, for the God of Israel is the Father of Jesus Christ."

5. "Holy Scripture is a book about a minority. The Old Testament is the faith experience of a Jewish minority in a non-Jewish world; the New Testament is the faith testimony of small Christian communities in a pagan Roman world. Persecution is a part of the experience of minorities. Thus the Bible is also a book about persecuted people, written by persecuted people."

6. "Law and Gospel are the hermeneutical keys to interpreting the Bible. Law and Gospel are the two sides of the one righteous God. The God of the Bible is simultaneously the God demanding justice and the God promising it . . . whenever we examine a controversy over justice, we must first take a look at the balance of power, for God deals differently with the powerful than with the powerless. God demands justice from the former [e.g., the State of Israel] and promises justice to the latter [e.g., the Palestinians]."

In contrast to Ateek, Raheb reads the book of Exodus as "the most holy book in the Hebrew Bible." The God of Exodus "founded the very first liberation movement on earth" (Kuruvilla 209-10). Raheb's hermeneutical principles and exegetical practice in his sermons and writings are acts of resistance against Christian Zionists and religious Jewish Zionists who claim the authority of the Bible to rationalize the status quo in Israel/Palestine, which leaves the State of Israel and its globalized economy in control of most of the wealth, resources, and weapons in the region, and the Palestinians without recognized borders, without a state, and without decisive control over their own destinies in the region. Hundreds of thousands of Palestinians still languish in United Nations refugee facilities in Gaza, Lebanon, and Syria in conditions that provide fertile ground for recruitment into violent radical organizations that sow terror in the region.

VI. "OLD WINE IN NEW BOTTLES": GREGERMAN'S CRITIQUE OF ATEEK AND RAHEB'S THEOLOGIES AS NEW FORMS OF "CHRISTIAN ANTI-JUDAISM" (THE ADVERSOS JUDAEOS TRADITION).

A few years ago, a friend emailed to me an article that included this paragraph:

Writing in the *Journal of Ecumenical Studies*, Adam Gregerman observed that theologians like Ateek "perpetuate some of the most unsavory and vicious images of the Jews as malevolent, antisocial, hostile to non-Jews." For example, Ateek wrote about "modern-day Herods" in [the State of] Israel, referring to the king who the New Testament says slaughtered the babies of Bethlehem in an attempt to murder the newborn Jesus.

In his 2004 article "Old Wine in New Bottles: Liberation Theology and the Israeli-Palestinian Conflict," Adam Gregerman shows how the categories of Christian liberation theology, first developed in Latin and North America, and Africa, have been imported into the Middle East by Christians since the First Intifada or Palestinian uprising (1987-93) to analyze and critique the State of Israel. According to Gregerman, at the same time that many Western churches and Christians are affirming their permanent "bond" with the Jewish people, some Christians in the Middle East and some of their allies in the West are recycling negative images of Jews that were common in early and medieval Christian dialogs to demonize the modern State of Israel. These theologians include, according to Gregerman, Ateek in Jerusalem and Raheb in Bethlehem.

Gregerman finds this theological and liberationist move in Christian interpretation unhelpful in understanding and analyzing the political dimensions of the Israeli-Palestinian conflict. When every conflict is analyzed in dualistic, dichotomous terms, the Israelis always come out as the evil oppressors and enemies of God and the Palestinians always turn up as the innocent oppressed who are being crucified with Christ.

In the most revealing part of his article, Gregerman takes four classic teachings of Christian anti-Judaism and shows how these doctrines and their uses of Scripture re-emerge in theological literature produced by Palestinian, American, and British Christians.[73] Ironically, the Christian theologian who identified these four teachings in the ancient literature of the Church—Rosemary Radford Ruether in her book *Faith and Fratricide*—is also the author of *The Wrath of Jonah*, a book criticizing the State of Israel in ways that recycle some of these teachings, their symbols and metaphors.

The four teachings are in italics below. After each teaching I will give one example illustrating how Gregerman identifies aspects of these anti-Jewish teachings creeping back into liberation and contextual theologies focused on the Israeli-Palestinian conflict:

> *"Classic Anti-Jewish Claim # 1: Christian Universalism vs. Jewish Particularism"*
>
>> Christianity is more moral, because it is universalistic and aims for the salvation of the gentile world, whereas Judaism is particularistic and aims for the salvation of the people of Israel alone. "All the prophetic texts saying that God will raise up salvation for Israel" apply to the "[c]hurch to prove that God intended to gather a true people of God from among the Gentiles, even in an *antithetical relation* to an apostate Israel." ("Old Wine" 318; quotations from Ruether, *Faith and Fratricide*, 1974 ed., 85-86)

When Gregerman surveyed liberation theologians, he found that "they reject an anti-Jewish supersessionism (the belief that the Bible proves that the gentiles take over Israel's place in the covenant with God) in favor of an anti-Jewish universalism (the belief that the Bible undercuts the particular promise to the Jews of covenant and land)" (320).

Part of the problem is another type of dualism: universalism vs. particularism. There are aspects of traditional Christian doctrine that are also deeply particularistic: that one particular man, Jesus of Nazareth, is the Savior of the world; that the incarnation occurred in one human being and not in a people or humankind; that there is one religious community, the Church, that mediates or proclaims salvation for all other communities. These Christian particularities are not critiqued with the same force as Jewish particularity by some of these theologians.

"Classic Anti-Jewish Claim # 2: The Canceled Covenant"
The Jewish covenant with God is only temporary and can be revoked because of disobedience. "The Jews assume the status of a people on probation who fail all the tests and finally are flunked out. The message of election refers to a believing people. The Jews proved through their history that they are not this people" (324; quotation from Ruether 137).

In liberation literature, Gregerman found a new twist on an old theme:

Judaism is no longer threatened by explicit supersessionism, in which gentiles take the place of Jews in the covenant. Now Jews risk incurring divine wrath because of acts by, or support for, the Jewish state, rather than opposition to Jesus or the prophets. Zionism the secular Jewish movement that sought to establish a nation for the Jewish people has become a modern form of faithlessness and rejection of God. Though the Jews' fault is no longer disbelief in Jesus, liberation theologians, like early Christians, indict the Jews for disobedience to God and the biblical tradition. ("Old Wine" 324)

"Classic Anti-Jewish Claim # 3: Jewish Exile"
Because of their disobedience and sinfulness, the Jews suffer the punishment of exile. "It is axiomatic in the *Adversus Judaeos* tradition that Jewish reprobation is permanent and irrevocable. The left hand of Christian victory and messianic ingathering is Jewish rejection and exile." ("Old Wine" 327; quotation from Ruether 144)
Surprisingly Gregerman discovered that "Liberation theologians are possibly alone among all modern Christian theologians in glorifying the centuries of Jewish exile and wandering. Their praise of exile is directed against the very idea of a modern State of Israel" (328). This Christian "idealization" of Jewish exile is for the most part not based on Jewish accounts, memories, or experiences of statelessness.

The "inconsistency" is that these liberation theologians are advocating for a state for the Palestinians, but not for the Jews who are deemed better off when stateless. As Gregerman explains, "No author ever suggests that the Palestinians or any other people are truer to their own traditions when residing outside their ancestral land or under the sovereignty of others. Instead, these authors continue the centuries-old Christian practice of seeing Jews as somehow different from other people, and their advocacy of Jewish weakness (but not, for example, Palestinian or American weakness) perpetuates this idea" (330).

"Classic Anti-Jewish Claim # 4: The Demonization of the Jews"
> Jews "are the type of the carnal man, who knows nothing spiritually," and they "are the very incarnation of the false, apostate principle of the fallen world, alienated from its true being in God" (333; quotations from Ruether 113).

In some of the New Testament writings and other early Christian texts, we find accusations against Jews:
> . . . Jews commit violent acts against Jesus and his followers, hinder missionary activity, spur on outside hostility to the new movement, misunderstand God and God's plan for salvation, and worship God incorrectly or not at all. In particular, the authors of texts such as Matthew, John, and Revelation are well known for penning some of the most shocking claims about Jewish malevolence, propensity for violence, faithlessness, and worldliness. In both John and Revelation, the Jews are demonized and said to be rejected by God. They serve "[their] father the devil" (Jn. 8:23, 44) and worship in a "synagogue of Satan" (Rev. 2:9, 3:9). The Jews' claim to the Bible is denied, cutting them off from their own history (for example, Jn. 5:37-40). In another famous example, the author of Matthew emphasizes the Jews' guilt at the execution of Jesus, quoting Jesus' Jewish contemporaries accepting blame for the deed upon themselves and all future Jews (27:25). Similarly, all the Gospels ratchet up the influence of Jews in Jesus' death and minimize Roman culpability, showing the Jews eager to commit a grave injustice in order to protect the Jewish community (for example, Jn. 11:50). Elsewhere, Jewish religious life is denounced as worldly and vacuous by writers

who criticize Jews' rituals as only "a shadow of what is to come" (for example, Col. 2:17) and serve paradoxically to deny rather than affirm faith in God (for example, Tit. 1:10-16). ("Old Wine" 333; quotations from Ruether 113).

The modern twist in the liberation literature is that Jews are no longer demonized as Jews per se, rather ". . . liberation theologians demonize the Jews as Zionists or Israelis" (334). These liberationists tend "to see Jews as irreligious, violent, malevolent, selfish, and indifferent to the suffering of non-Jews" and thus "the demonization of the Jews" is carried forward into the present. The end result of liberationist literature on the Israeli-Palestinian conflict is that a "political conflict" open to political critique is transformed into a deeply "religious conflict" against the backdrop of centuries of previous Christian versus Jewish hostility.

I both agree and disagree with Ateek, Raheb, and Gregerman. Ateek, Raheb, and other Palestinian theologians who contributed to *Kairos Palestine* are hopeful about the possible future of Palestinian-Israeli relations so long as justice delayed becomes justice realized. But their theologies fail to account for what Gregerman discovered in liberationist writings: the old Christian hatreds and animosities that are recycled in new conflicts.

Gregerman's critique is brilliant, but at the end of the day he wants to leave the resolution of the Israeli-Palestinian conflict up to the politicians and political analysts. Of course some faculty avoid public expression of political opinion so as to maintain their image and status as objective, disinterested scholars. Meanwhile, hundreds of thousands of Palestinian refugees and children of refugees are still living in camps in Lebanon, Jordan, Syria, and Gaza without statehood. Israeli settlements in East Jerusalem and the West Bank continue to expand. Christians in the Middle East continue to appeal to Christians in North America and Europe to engage in nonviolent action to symbolically reject the Israeli occupation of the West Bank and East Jerusalem. *How should ecumenical churches around the world assist the churches in the Middle East without falling into the old forms of Christian Anti-Judaism and modern forms of anti-Semitism?*

VII. *KAIROS PALESTINE*: A MESSAGE OF HOPE, PROTEST, NONVIOLENT RESISTANCE AND BDS

If my patient reader has arrived this close to the conclusion of this paper, let me encourage you to read *Kairos Palestine*, which is analyzed by David Sandmel elsewhere in this book. Both Ateek and Raheb were contributing authors, editors, and interpreters of this ecumenical document addressed to the diverse peoples of Israel/Palestine, and to the global ecumenical churches. As with any theology or philosophy, of course it is best not to depend solely on the second or third hand summaries of theologians like myself or political scientists like Samuel Kuruvilla. "*Take and read*" for yourself to discover whether the "crisis," the "prophetic challenge," the "time of eschatological expectation and fulfillment" that the Palestinian, Arab authors perceived in 2009 affects you in your own political and religious context.[74]

VIII: DIALOGUE AS AN ALTERNATIVE TO ANTAGONISM— CHICAGO PRESBYTERY'S STATEMENT AND PROJECT

I would like to conclude by returning to the personal narrative that opened this paper, posing a question that may offer an alternative to the theological and political disputes summarized above: How has my engagement with Presbyterian-Jewish and Presbyterian-Palestinian and Muslim dialogue in Chicago and other North American cities, along with Barcelona, Spain, Melbourne, Australia, and in Israel/Palestine affected my constructive theological contribution to efforts aimed at greater justice, peace, and a viable future for the diverse peoples of the "holy land (s)"?

In 2014-15, the Ecumenical and Inter-Religious Work Group of Chicago Presbytery prepared a local Reformed theological response to the Vatican II document on the Catholic Church's relations to other religions, *Nostra Aetate* ('In Our Time…'), on the occasion of its fiftieth anniversary. In our local document, the four primary authors sought to address the important issues facing Presbyterians and Jews in Chicago after ten years of debate over investment scrutiny and divestment, as well as dialogues over many other theological and ethical issues in Christian-Jewish relations.

The early drafts of the document were circulated among our Jewish dialogue partners and other Presbyterians in our local Work Group. A later draft was brought before the entire Presbytery meeting in Assembly in June 2015 for discussion and proposed revisions. A final draft, which can be found on CCJR's website, was presented to the November 2015 Presbytery Assembly and unanimously approved.

In this document, you will see how we proposed to keep Chicago Presbyterians and Jews in dialogue and partnership over important theological and ethical issues, while also offering guidance for how Presbyterians should address issues of "the Land" between Israelis and Palestinians. You will find our approach is different in certain ways from Ateek, Raheb, and *Kairos Palestine* as we seek to be attuned to our own context. At the same time, we encouraged further engagement by Presbyterians and Jews in the issues of justice and peace in the region.

This is a substantial document, which I urge you to read in its entirety, but I can provide a few highlights here. The Executive Summary draws attention to some of the theological principles that guided our work, among them the principle that "God has not rejected God's people, the Jews" and that "The Lord does not take back the Lord's promises." It urges us to recognize that "God calls us to dialogue and cooperation that do not ignore our real disagreements yet proceed in mutual respect and love." The document goes on to say that "the affirmation of our spiritual kinship with the Jewish community is not dependent upon a resolution of the Israeli-Palestinian conflict" (4, preface). Rather than endorsing specific solutions, "it seeks to provide a framework by which Jews and Presbyterians can discuss the conflict in an engaged, civil, and productive way" (4). But the document also seeks to "affirm the aspirations for, and the right to, self-determination by both Israelis and Palestinians," urging that we "actively work on behalf of Israelis and Palestinians, and a just and peaceful future for both, without compromising our relationship to each people" (12). It also suggests that debating Biblical claims to the land is not a productive way to proceed, that trying to apply the Bible directly to contemporary political disputes is counterproductive.

"In Our Time" includes several lists of recommended practices. I reproduce one of them here with the hope it can guide both Presbyterians and other faith communities:

Together, Presbyterians and Jews can share the most treasured aspects of our religious identity:

- By inviting, listening to and offering mutually transparent testimonies.
- By regularly discussing issues that are significant to each community.
- By sharing, through conversation or encounter, ritual practices that are especially meaningful.

Together, Presbyterians and Jews can work for the well-being of our world:

- By coming together to aid yet other religious groups who might face prejudice in their neighborhoods.
- By working together on issues of hunger, violence, poverty, immigration, and other shared concerns for the common good.
- Together, Presbyterians and Jews can create safe havens for religious diversity:
- By building relationships over time, not in reaction to crises, but in order to live out a commitment to deep hospitality and mutual respect.
- By maintaining these relationships even in (and especially in) times of crisis.
- By listening attentively and representing our Jewish dialogue partners in ways that they feel accurately represent them. (13)

Constructive theological work should seek as its audiences not only other theologians, ethicists, social scientists, and philosophers, but also congregations, churches, religious communities, and institutions looking for guidance in responding to the some of the most challenging public issues of our times.

CHAPTER EIGHT

DAVID FOX SANDMEL

THE KAIROS PALESTINE DOCUMENT, ANTI-SEMITISM, AND BDS

INTRODUCTION

On December 11, 2009, a group of Palestinian Christian clergy and laypeople released a document titled, "A moment of truth: A word of faith, hope and love from the heart of Palestinian suffering." It has come to be known as *Kairos Palestine* or the *Kairos Palestine Document* (henceforth KPD). It originally appeared with the signature of 16 Palestinian Christians, though one later withdrew his support.

The document protests what it describes as the many injustices Israel has perpetrated against the Palestinian people, and also calls to task the Palestinians themselves, the international Christian community, and the community of nations for their collective failure to advocate on behalf of the Palestinian people. It is unabashedly a Christian document; it quotes the Bible frequently and clearly shows the influence of Palestinian liberation theology, which is to be expected since several of its authors are also its leading proponents and their works are prominently promoted on KPD's website. Palestinian liberation theology is based on the liberation theologies that initially emerged in Latin America in the work of Gustavo Guttierez and others. Liberation theologies focus on aiding the poor and fighting the economic and governmental systems that oppress them. Using the Gospel accounts as a model, some liberation theologians identify the oppressive system with the Jews', rather than the Romans', persecution of Jesus.

This invocation of classical Christian anti-Judaism is troubling enough in the Latin American context, where the vast majority of people are Christian and conflicts generally lack a significant religious dimension. When this model is applied to the Israeli-Palestinian conflict, however, the Jewish authorities of the Gospels are identified with modern Israel, which has been portrayed as once again "crucifying" Jesus in the form of the Palestinians. As Naim Ateek has written,

> In this season of Lent, it seems to many of us that Jesus is on the cross again with thousands of crucified Palestinians around him. It only takes people of insight to see the hundreds of thousands of crosses throughout the land, Palestinian men, women, and children being crucified. Palestine has become one huge [G]Golgotha. The Israeli government crucifixion system is operating daily. Palestine has become the place of the skull." (NGO Monitor "Sabeel")[75]

The authors of KPD consider it to be "the word of Palestinian Christians to the world" and the founding statement of a "Christian Palestinian movement." (Kairos Palestine). It has been translated into at least 22 languages. KPD has been hailed and vilified, some viewing it as the authentic voice of Palestinian Christians crying for justice, others, in the case of the Philos Project, calling it "a theological cover for terrorism." The World Council of Churches and its Palestine Israel Ecumenical Forum (PIEF) served as a sort of incubator for its composition. WCC and PIEF have also heavily promoted the document. For example, according to the WCC:

> In the birthplace of the Lord Jesus Christ, Christians have come together from all church traditions and expressed their common word of "faith, hope and love" from the "heart of their suffering." The *Kairos Palestine Document* challenges the ecumenical family and the international community to put an end to the Israeli occupation. It is a call to the Palestinian community to remain steadfast in their land, witnessing to God's love for all, while peacefully resisting the evil of occupation. The community is a sign of hope for the ecumenical family.
>
> . . .
>
> **The Central Committee of the WCC, meeting in Geneva from 16 to 22 February 2011, therefore:**
>
> . . .
>
> 2. Urges WCC member churches to study and disseminate the Kairos Palestine Document, and to listen and concretely respond to the Palestinian Christian aspirations and calls expressed in this document.[76] [All emphases in the original.]

As we shall see, KPD has become an important weapon in the arsenal of Christian pro-Palestinian, pro-divestment activists.

KAIROS PALESTINE IN THE CHURCHES

In December 2011, representatives of Christian churches and institutions from different parts of the world met in Bethlehem.[77] The group issued "The Bethlehem Call," an affirmation of KPD that "reiterated the urgent call of the *Kairos Palestine Document* . . . and asked for a comprehensive boycott of Israel as one of the non-violent tools to end the Israeli apartheid regime." This marked the emergence of the "Global *Kairos* Network," which has branches in eleven nations (Kairos Palestine "Global"), including *Kairos* USA,[78] promoting both KPD itself and its call for boycott within local churches and denominational bodies.

Subsequent to the publication of KPD and the formation of *Kairos* USA, several church bodies have endorsed some form of boycott of Israel or investment screens, such as the United Methodist Church in 2012;[79] the Presbyterian Church (USA) in 2014; the United Church of Christ in 2015; the Evangelical Lutheran Church of America (ELCA) in 2016 (Evangelical Lutheran "Churchwide Assembly"); and the Mennonite Church USA in 2017 (Mennonite Church "Seeking"). All of these churches have promoted KPD on their websites and some reference it in their assembly resolutions or in the supporting materials (Palestine Portal). The Presbyterian Church USA produced a study guide for the KPD. In 2011, the ELCA passed a resolution ("Promoting Positive Change for Palestine") encouraging study of the document. The United Church of Christ and the Disciples of Christ jointly sponsored the Global Ministries, which calls on their members to study KPD (Global Ministries). Organizations such as the Israel Palestine Mission Network of the PCUSA, United Methodists for *Kairos* Response, the Israel Palestine Network of the Episcopal Peace Fellowship (Episcopal Peace), and Friends of Sabeel North America (FOSNA "Kairos"),[80] all of which advocate for boycott within the churches and the denominations, promote it aggressively. KPD has also been endorsed by the anti-Zionist organization Jewish Voice for Peace in a statement by its Rabbinical Council titled "Honor the courage, clarity and sensitivity of Kairos USA."

It is not possible to measure the specific effect of KPD on these churches and on the outcome of votes within their individual polities, or its reach beyond the activists on both sides and those exposed to it at national denominational meetings, but it can be said that it has become an important tool for BDS advocates within the churches. Church activists presented it as the authentic voice of Palestinian Christians calling on their Christian brothers and sisters to support them by supporting BDS. It is also impossible to ascertain how many within those churches, especially those voting in favor of boycotts, have actually read the document or studied it carefully. When it is presented as the anguished cry of Palestinians asking their Christian co-religionists to support them with a nonviolent boycott, it can be compelling and effective without actually being read and understood.

CRITIQUE OF THE *KAIROS PALESTINE DOCUMENT*

Many mainstream Jewish organizations have reacted negatively to KPD. The Anti-Defamation League called it "highly problematic" (Anti-Defamation League). The American Jewish Committee's Robert Leikind described it in a recent op-ed as a "strident, one-dimensional" document that "fuel[s] hatred and mistrust" (Leikind). NGO-Monitor is equally dismissive (Santis). The Central Conference of American Rabbis, which has not hesitated to criticize the government of Israel in general or the settlements in particular, called the document "supersessionist" and "anti-Semitic" (Central Conference). The Global Forum for Combatting Anti-Semitism, jointly sponsored by Israel's Ministry of Foreign Affairs and its Ministry of Diaspora Affairs, describes KPD as one of several "pseudo-religious formulations which promote negative stereotypes of Jews . . . which foster delegitimization of Judaism and Jews using Replacement Theology and misrepresentation of events in Israel and the region" (Ministry). The promotion of KPD, in the eyes of many mainstream Jewish communal organizations, is an expression not only of hostility to Israel, but of anti-Semitism as well.

Christian groups have also criticized KPD. Presbyterians for Middle East Peace, in a critique of the PCUSA study guide mentioned above, outlines seven shortcomings of the document and concludes: "We do both sides a great disservice by over-simplifying problems and concerns or by taking sides in ways that demonize current adversaries and future partners for peace" (PFMEP "Kairos"). The Philos Project, an evangelical, pro-Israel organization, labeled it "a theological cover for anti-Semitism."

Christians for Fair Witness on the Middle East has also critiqued the document, albeit while simultaneously affirming their sympathy for the suffering of the Palestinians: "It is their narrative, their truth and they rightfully express it." While acknowledging many of the charges leveled by KPD, Fair Witness challenges the accuracy of the document and specifically critiques it on many points. In so doing, Fair Witness "strongly encourages the US Churches to read the *Kairos Palestine Document* with an open heart but not with an uncritical mind," adding, "We also encourage our churches to seize the current opportunity to act as peacemakers—and not to fan the flames of conflict by showing contempt and punishing one side through acts of divestment and boycott" (Christians for Fair Witness).

The International Council of Christians and Jews (ICCJ) in 2010 released a carefully worded statement called "Let us have mercy on words: A Plea from the International Council of Christians and Jews to All Who Seek Interreligious Understanding" (International Council). It also affirms the legitimacy of Palestinian concerns; indeed, it praises the document on several points, even while also highlighting problems in the text:

> What strikes us as admirable is that despite the hardships that the text relates, it does not descend into rage, hatred, or even—as is sadly all too common today—empty polemic. Instead, the document manifests generosity of spirit and offers some weighty religious insights, which might not be expected from a lament.
>
> . . .
>
> This is not to say that we do not have strong differences with certain features of *Kairos Palestine*, some of which we will briefly note. However, our main purpose in so doing is to encourage open and honest conversation among religious leaders, in contrast to the widespread present tendency to misrepresent or distort different perspectives. We hope that these questions, posed to promote dialogue and clarity, might be useful to the *Kairos Palestine* authors if they ever compose a commentary or a second edition of it.[81]

ICCJ then lays out six specific critiques of the document, many of which will be taken up below. In sum, KPD has become a significant point of contention in the debate over the Israeli-Palestinian conflict and BDS among Christians and Jews, or at least among activists from both communities. In what follows, I will describe KPD and analyze those aspects that have been the object of controversy and criticism.

ANALYSIS OF KPD[82]

The official version of the KPD that appears on the *Kairos Palestine* website is prefaced with a brief statement over the signatures of the patriarchs and heads of the Christian churches in Jerusalem called "We Hear the Cry of Our Children." It is dated December 15, 2009, just after the appearance of KPD. As Malcolm Lowe has pointed out:

> With the exception of Arab Lutheran Bishop Munib Younan, the Heads of Churches played no role in the origins of this document. Some of them were taken by surprise when it appeared. They were, however, put under political pressure to toe the line propounded by the document. Four days later, consequently, they issued a brief statement of their own.

The statement of the church leaders, it should be noted, does not reference KPD nor does it call for boycotts; and, "contains nothing that would offend people of goodwill anywhere" (Lowe). Lowe writes that "We Hear the Cry of Our Children" "can be read as a mild rebuke to the authors of the document: Palestinian Christians should put their main effort into strengthening their own community rather than engaging in worldwide political agitation." Lowe then charges that the authors of KPD "exploited" the statement from the church leaders to make it seem like an endorsement. Younan, the only official church leader who originally signed KPD, later withdrew his signature. To the best of my knowledge he has not publicly explained his withdrawal, leaving others to speculate on his motivations.

The fifteen remaining authors of KPD include Michel Sabbah, who served as archbishop and Latin Patriarch of Jerusalem from 1987 to 2008 and Greek Orthodox Archbishop Atalah Hanna, the bishop of Sebastia. The latter has a history of conflict with the Patriarch of Jerusalem, and, in Lowe's words, "Far from being a leader, he is rather an opponent of the Christian leadership." There has long been tension between the patriarch in Jerusalem, who has been Greek rather than Palestinian, and Palestinian Orthodox members themselves. Prominent names among the authors are the Rev. Dr. Naim Ateek, an Anglican, and the Rev. Dr. Mitri Raheb, a Lutheran. Ateek is the founder of the Sabeel Ecumenical Liberation Theology Center in Jerusalem.[83] Both are well known and widely published theologians, and both have been accused of using classic Christian *Adversus Judaeos* tropes in their writing and lectures.[84] Several of the additional signers are closely connected to the WCC.[85] The rest are Palestinian Christian clergy and laypeople active in Palestinian Christian society.

KPD begins with a preface calling on the international community to "stand by the Palestinian people who have faced decades of oppression, displacement, suffering and clear apartheid for more than six decades . . . stand with them against injustice and apartheid." It names the occupation a "sin against God and humanity" and rejects any "theology that legitimizes the occupation," themes that are explored in more detail in the body of the document. The authors express their "hope that this document will provide the turning point to focus the efforts of all peace-loving peoples of the world, especially our Christian sisters and brothers."

In the formal introduction to KPD, the authors frame the entire document in terms of hope amid hopelessness, despite the fact that they have "reached a dead end in the tragedy of the Palestinian people." They ask what the Palestinian, Israeli, and Arab political leadership are doing, but their primary concern is how the Church locally and internationally is addressing their plight.

The first section describes "The reality on the ground." There is no peace because of the occupation. An enumeration of specific complaints about Israel follows: the "wall" (1.1.1) is dividing Palestinians from one another and Gaza, attacked by Israel in 2008 and 2009, is cut off from Palestinian territory and under a blockade. Additional charges include settlements, daily humiliations, the separation of families, lack of religious liberty (especially access to Jerusalem), the plight of refugees (including the right of return), prisoners in Israeli jails, Jerusalem being "emptied of its Palestinian citizens," Israel's ignoring international law, emigration of the best and brightest among the Christians, and Israel's use of "security" (1.1.5) as an excuse for the occupation and its evils. While almost all the complaints are targeted at Israel, the document also references internal division among Palestinians and states that the international community "bears an important responsibility . . . since it refused to deal positively with the will of the Palestinian people expressed in the outcome of democratic and legal elections in 2006."

(1.5.1)[86] This description of the 2006 elections, however, does not tell the whole story. In the elections, Hamas won a majority of seats in the Palestinian parliament, but neither Israel nor the international community would deal with a government led by Hamas, which is considered a terrorist organization. Equally relevant, though not mentioned by KPD, is that Fatah also refused to sit in a government with Hamas. When Hamas formed a government without Fatah, tensions between the groups erupted including violence and dozens of deaths. In February of 2007 a unity government was finally formed, but after Hamas took over Gaza in June 2007, Palestinian President Mahmoud Abbas dismissed that government and appointed a new prime minister, leading to split between Fatah in the West Bank and Hamas in Gaza that lasted until a fragile rapprochement was announced in 2017. But that rapprochement largely failed. Whether the multi-stage joint elections agreed to for 2021 actually take place remains to be seen.

The second section of KPD, "A Word of Faith," consists of three subsections. The first is a statement of Trinitarian faith. The second answers the question "How do we understand the word of God?" Jesus "fulfills the law and the prophets and in his light and with the guidance of the Holy Spirit, we read the Holy Scripture." Specifically, Jesus's "new teaching (Mk. 1:27)" casts a new light on "the promises, the election, the people of God, and the land." KPD accuses "fundamentalist Biblical interpretation" of turning the Scripture into "letters of stone," a "dead letter . . . used as a weapon . . . to deprive us of our rights in our own land." (2.2.2)

The final subsection is titled "Our land has a universal mission." It casts the biblical promises of land and election as a "prelude to complete universal salvation" and the "fulfillment of the Kingdom of God on earth," stating that the "promise of the land has never been a political program" (2.3). The land belongs to God and therefore must be "a land of reconciliation, peace and love" (2.3.10). It argues that Christian and Muslim Palestinians are "deeply rooted" in Palestine's history and geography and, in one of KPD's most controversial sentences, proclaims that "The West sought to make amends for what Jews had endured in the countries of Europe, but made amends on our account and in our land. They tried to correct an injustice and the result was a new injustice" (2.3.2).

The remainder of the second section is a critique of "certain theologians in the West" (2.3.3) who make use of the Bible to deny Palestinian rights. Though the term itself is not used explicitly, this is clearly an attack on Christian Zionism, a frequent target throughout KPD.

In the final paragraph of this section, KPD names "The Israeli occupation of Palestinian land" as "a sin against God and humanity." Any theology that supports the occupation is "far from Christian teachings because it calls for violence and holy war" (2.5). While Christian Zionism seems to be the primary target, it is possible that Jewish biblical interpretation is also intended. This ambiguity appears elsewhere in KPD.

The third section, entitled "Hope," begins by rehearsing the theme of hope amid hopelessness: "The clear Israeli response, refusing any solution, leaves no room for positive expectation. Despite this, our hope remains strong, because it is from God" (3.1). While realistically noting that change will not happen quickly, in a subsection called "signs of hope," the document highlights vibrant parishes and claims that "most of our young people are active apostles for justice and peace" (3.3). It mentions "local centers of theology" (probably referring to Sabeel and PIEF) and praises the "ecumenical spirit, even if still hesitant" (3.3.1). Interreligious dialogue, both Christian-Muslim and among the "three religions" is another positive sign, as is increased public awareness, including among "Jewish and Israeli voices" (3.3.4).

The following subsection is called "The Mission of the Church." KPD expresses its thanks to God that "our Church raises her voice against injustice despite the fact that some desire her to remain silent, closed in her religious devotions," possibly a dig at the heads of the churches (3.4). This church must be "prophetic"; it must proclaim the "Kingdom of God," which "cannot be tied to any earthly kingdom. . . Therefore, religion cannot favor or support any unjust political regime" (3.4.1-3). This could be taken as a rejection of all nationalist solutions, if it were not quickly narrowed only to "unjust" ones. Again, it is unclear whether "religion" refers to Christian Zionism alone or also to Jewish religious ideologies (or, again, perhaps also to the official leadership of the churches).

The fourth section, "Love," begins with four citations from the New Testament (Jn. 13:34; Mt. 5:45-46; Rom. 12:17; and 1Pet 3:9; 4.1). It then embarks on a lengthy discussion of resistance. Love "includes both friends and enemies" (4.2). In the face of aggression, "Christian love invites us to resist." Palestinians themselves bear the primary responsibility to resist, but so does the international community, which has the power to enforce international norms. Ultimately, however, it is the "perpetrators of injustice who must liberate themselves from the evil that is in them and the injustice they have imposed on others" (4.2.1).

KPD recognizes that violent resistance is a world-wide phenomenon and that Palestinians have also resorted to it. Christians, however, while they "cannot resist evil with evil," can resist with "civil disobedience." Yet, as another controversial sentence states, "We respect and have a high esteem for all those who have given their life for our nation" (4.2.5). The document then endorses "divestment and an economic boycott of everything produced by the occupation" as part of the "logic of peaceful resistance," with reference to their effectiveness in South Africa and "many other liberation movements in the world" (4.2.6). This section concludes with a vision of a "new society both for us and our opponents." Though it accuses Israel of "twist[ing] the truth of reality of the occupation by pretending that it is a battle against terrorism" and claims that "the roots of 'terrorism' are in the human injustice of the occupation," its final call is for the people of Israel to be "our partners in peace" (4.3).

Sections five through nine are addressed to Palestinians, to the churches of the world, to the international community, to Jewish and Muslim religious leaders, and, finally, to "our Palestinian people and to the Israelis." The message to Palestinians again emphasizes hope against hopelessness. It includes a statement of repentance "as individuals or as heads of Churches" (which may itself be read as a rebuke):

> For our silence, indifference, lack of communion, either because we did not persevere in our mission in this land and abandoned it, or because we did not think and do enough to reach a new and integrated vision and remain divided, contradicting our witness

and weakening our word. Repentance for our concern with our institutions, sometimes at the expense of our mission, thus silencing the prophetic voice given by the Spirit to the Church. (5.2)

It addresses Muslims with a "message of love and a call to reject fanaticism and extremism" and decries caricatures of Muslims as terrorists. To Jews, it says, "we are able to love and live together" and claims that "We can organize our political life, with all its complexity, according to the logic of this love and its power, after ending the occupation and establishing justice" (5.4.2).

To the "Churches of the World," the document first expresses its "gratitude for the solidarity," but then continues with a call to repentance for "fundamentalist theological positions [i.e. Christian Zionism] . . . . We ask our sister Churches not to offer a theological cover-up for the injustice we suffer." It encourages Christians to "Come and see," which appears to be a critique of Christian pilgrims who visit the holy sites but ignore the Christians in the land, "the living stones" (6.1-2). This section concludes by inviting churches to join the authors in condemning "all forms of racism, including anti-Semitism and Islamophobia," but at the same to time to condemn Israel's occupation of Palestinian land and to join in boycott and disinvestment.

Section seven addresses the international community, which it accuses of "double standards" and "[s]elective application of international law" that legitimizes "claims by certain armed groups and states that the international community only understand the logic of force." In its place, the document again calls for "sanctions and boycott. . . not as revenge but rather as a serious action in order to reach a just and definitive peace."

Section eight is an appeal to Jewish and Muslim religious leaders "with whom we share the same vision that every human being is created by God and has been given equal dignity . . . to rise above the political positions that have failed so far and continue to lead us on the path of failure and suffering."

Section nine is addressed to both Palestinians and Israelis. It holds that "peace is possible." It calls for a reformation of educational programs that "today are infected with hostility." Section 9.3 states:

Trying to make the state a religious state, Jewish or Islamic, suffocates the state and . . . transforms it into a state that practices discrimination and exclusion . . . We appeal to both religious Jews and Muslims: let the state be a state for all its citizens, constructed on . . . equality, liberty and respect for pluralism and not domination by a religious or numerical majority.

It then calls for Palestinians to heal their inner divisions and for the international community to support Palestinian unity and the will of the Palestinian people (9.4).

A paragraph on Jerusalem (9.5) cites the eschatological vision of Isaiah 2 in which "the nations stream" to the city. It refers both this "prophetic vision" and to "international resolutions" as the bases for a political solution and insists that "This is the first issue that should be negotiated because the recognition of Jerusalem's sanctity . . . will be a source of inspiration toward finding a solution."

KPD concludes with a final invocation of the theme of hope amid hopelessness, that God's goodness will prevail, and that "we will see here 'a new land' and 'a new human being', capable of rising up in the spirit of love each one of his or her brothers and sisters" (10).

CRITIQUE

KPD is couched in the Christian language of faith, hope, and love; and the document is peppered with references to peace, to peaceful resistance, and to the rejection of violence. The ICCJ statement describes the document's positive aspects with these words:

> What strikes us as admirable is that despite the hardships that the text relates, it does not descend into rage, hatred, or even— as is sadly all too common today—empty polemic. Instead, the document manifests generosity of spirit and offers some weighty religious insights, which might not be expected from a lament.
>
> It asserts the common humanity of everyone as made in the image of God [2.1; 8]. It sees the Land as meant to be a holy place where Jews, Christians, and Muslims can come together in love and mutual respect [5.4]. It rejects all forms of violence by anyone [5.4.3]. It insists that the Bible cannot be used to justify the violation of human rights, but must inspire faith, hope, and love [2.4].

It urges that interreligious dialogue and education occur despite its difficulties [3.3.2; 9.1]. It extends a message of love and hope to Jews and Muslims [5.4]. The Palestinian authors of the document offer a profound Christian conviction which some critics overlook: "Just as Christ rose in victory over death and evil, so too we are able, as each inhabitant of this land is able, to vanquish the evil of war" [3.5].

The spiritual encouragement that the document could offer to demoralized Christians seems to us a worthy and essential exercise in pastoral care. It seeks to bring hope to young people who could easily be tempted to hopelessness and desperation. It looks ahead to preparing Palestinian Christians to be partners with Israelis when the day comes that two independent states actually exist [9.1-2].[87]

Why, then, has it provoked such a negative response? In both explicit statements, as well as through implication and lack of clarity, KPD opens itself up to a number of possible charges. The first is the use of supersessionist themes. KPD states that "Jesus Christ came in order to fulfill the Law and the Prophets," and uses the phrase "letters of stone" (2.2.2), a reference to 2 Corinthians 3. The primary target of their theological critique, as noted above, is Christian Zionism (some forms of which are themselves supersessionist!), but the Corinthians passage has a long history of supersessionist interpretation because of Paul's juxtaposition of "spirit" and "letter." The letter, which kills, came to be identified with the law and therefore with Judaism. Therefore, it could also apply to specific Jewish theologies (e.g., certain settler ideologies) or more generally to Judaism or Zionism itself. It is not clear that, in context, this is what the authors of KPD had in mind when they referenced this passage.

There is similar ambiguity in both Sections 2.4 and 2.5. The discussion of the universality of the land in Section 2.3 can also be read as supersessionist. The Christian critique of Jewish particularism as opposed to Christian universalism is an old trope, as is the belief that the Jews lost the land because of their rejection of Jesus.

Furthermore, neither most Jews nor the state of Israel rely on theology to justify Israel's existence (see, for example, Israel's Declaration of Independence). For most Jews, the argument for the existence of the state is based on notions of Jewish nationhood and the fact that the land of Israel is their ancestral homeland. Christian critics of Israel often posit theological reasoning such as that implied by KPD as a straw man argument that can be rejected. KPD uses this tactic, and nowhere does it affirm either Jewish nationhood or any Jewish connection to the land.

Also problematic from a theological perspective is the use of the words "sin" and "holy war." As the ICCJ points out, while "such expressions may be understandable in dire straits, they are often counterproductive to the goal of significant conversation among contending forces. What did the authors seek by using such freighted terms without clear definition or explication?"

A second issue is the charge of apartheid, which is explicit both in the preamble and in the document itself (4.2.6). The invocation of the struggle against apartheid is found in the very choice of the name *Kairos Palestine* and in the repeated calls for boycott, divestment and sanctions. The attempt to describe the situation of Palestinians under Israeli authority as apartheid is highly contentious, since it is makes use of a postcolonialist critique and casts the conflict in racial terms, both of which the State of Israel and many of its defenders reject out of hand. The repeated calls for boycott, divestment and sanctions (4.2.6; 6.3; and 7) also serve to link Israel with the apartheid regime in South Africa, another well-known trope in pro-Palestinian advocacy.

KPD mentions "occupation" thirty-three times and "land" fifty, often qualified as "our land" or "Palestinian land," but it never defines what land it considers occupied. Does it intend only those lands that Israel captured in the 1967 Six-Day War, or does it refer to all of the land, on both sides of the Green Line, as the reference to "clear apartheid for more than six decades" seems to imply?[88]

This is compounded by the lack of any concrete vision of a future resolution of the conflict: the question of a one-state or two-state solution is not addressed in KPD. In this regard, the ICCJ statement cited above is incorrect; Sections 9.1-2 speak about peace but make no mention of two states. Section 9.3 talks about "the state" in the singular and insists that "the state" not be "religious, Jewish or Islamic." A case can be made that KPD anticipates a one-state solution; it never affirms the right of Israel to exist.

Further complicating this is KPD's silence about the Jewish people's connection to the land. The Christians and Muslims are "rooted" in the land, while the Jews are described as having been unjustly foisted upon them: "The West sought to make amends for what Jews had endured in the countries of Europe, but it made amends on our account and in our land. They tried to correct an injustice and the result was a new injustice" (2.3.2). This is another popular anti-Israel argument—that the Palestinians are being forced to pay for the sins of Europe, specifically the Holocaust, though again here KPD is unclear. It never uses the word Holocaust, so it could refer to the entire history of the Jews in Europe. If the Holocaust is intended, then the argument essentially ignores the history of Zionism before World War II and the Jewish people's ancestral ties to the land.

Taken as a whole, the repeated unqualified references to land, the failure to recognize Jewish connection to the land, and especially the implication that occupation and apartheid began in 1948, argue strongly that KPD is not about ending the occupation, but rather about the elimination of Israel. KPD has no choice but to admit the existence of the State of Israel, but this section appears to reject its legitimacy altogether.

With the exception of one reference to Palestinian violence (4.2.2), KPD portrays Israel solely as the aggressor and the Palestinians only as victims, and appears to suggest that any resistance, including terrorism against Israelis, is ultimately Israel's fault. It has been accused, therefore, of justifying, excusing, or downplaying such violence:

"Israel justifies its actions as self-defense . . . if there were no occupation, there would be no resistance." (1.4)

Some political parties followed the way of armed resistance. Israel used this as a pretext to accuse the Palestinians of being terrorists and was able to distort the real nature of the conflict, presenting it as an Israeli war against terror, rather than an Israeli occupation faced by Palestinian legal resistance aiming at ending it. (1.5)

We call on Israel to give up its injustice towards us, not to twist the truth of reality of the occupation by pretending that it is a battle against terrorism. The roots of "terrorism" are in the human injustice committed and in the evil of the occupation. These must be removed if there be a sincere intention to remove "terrorism." (4.3)

Placing the word terrorism in quotations marks and equating it with resistance and self-defense seems to justify not only combat with Israeli forces but violence against civilians as well. It is against this background that the following words in Section 4.2.5 provoked a storm of protest, since they can be seen to applaud terrorists, including suicide bombers: "We respect and have a high esteem for all those who have given their lives for our nation."

One of the tactics of the BDS movement is the promotion of "anti-normalization," which means that any contact or cooperation whatsoever between Palestinians and Israelis or Jews is sign of surrender.[89] Section 3.3.4 states, "we see a determination among many to overcome the resentments of the past and to be ready for reconciliation once justice has been restored." If "justice" must precede reconciliation, it can be argued that this is a call for anti-normalization.

Some of these issues, such as the charge of apartheid, and the call for boycott, sanctions, and divestment, are explicit in KPD. Others (e.g. the one-state solution) are implied by or, at the least, are plausible interpretations of ambiguities in the text. Whether these ambiguities are intentional or not is also a matter of interpretation, as is this observation. Thus, in the eyes of its critics, KPD promulgates classic Christian anti-Judaism including supersessionism and denies both the legitimacy of the State of Israel and the historic connection of the Jewish people to the land; it promotes a one-state solution, accuses Israel of racism and condones, if not encourages, terrorism. The number and variety of these grievances helps explain the negative reaction from mainstream Jewish organizations, including even the liberal CCAR.

CONCLUSION AND PERSONAL OBSERVATIONS

As the preceding discussion has demonstrated, the dramatically different responses provoked by KPD are attributable in part to the document itself, especially its failure to express its position on key issues of the Israeli-Palestinian conflict unambiguously, including issues of central concern to supporters of Israel. Those who wish to dismiss the document out of hand as both anti-Israel and anti-Semitic have ample evidence to which they can point. These grievances may not be immediately evident to supporters of the Palestinian cause (especially those unfamiliar with the history of Christian anti-Jewish rhetoric) or they may be willing to overlook them in favor of the strong articulation of Palestinian suffering and the infringement of Palestinian rights the document lifts up within a Christian theological context. For some, any criticism of the document is seen as a criticism of Palestinian Christians themselves and denial of their suffering and the legitimacy of their rights.[90]

I have Christian colleagues for whom KPD's significance is precisely because it is a Palestinian Christian statement and can rightly claim to represent a segment of the Palestinian Christian population, even if those claims are exaggerated. For them, the Palestinian Christian voice had been glaringly absent from the discourse; KPD filled that void.

I have elsewhere described KPD as a tragically flawed document. On the one hand, it calls for dialogue and repudiates violence. And it gives voice to the experience of Palestinian suffering and indignity, as Fair Witness described it: "their narrative, their truth." However, as I have said on several occasions to some of KPD's authors, though I am sympathetic to aspects of what the document presents, I am unable to say "amen" to it as whole because of its use of anti-Semitic tropes, its one-sidedness, and its distortions of history. In my view, then, KPD is a missed opportunity to bring constructive Christian witness to the discourse around the Israeli-Palestinian conflict.

This is probably an unrealistic expectation, since the primary goal of the document is neither dialogue nor reconciliation, but rather a call to action from Christians to reject Christian Zionism and end the occupation as KPD understands it, in part by supporting BDS. In this latter regard, it can be considered a qualified success, though as noted above the extent of its influence cannot be measured. It has been used in campaigns within Christian churches to promote divestment. However, while a number of churches have decided to divest from certain companies deemed to be profiting from the occupation, as yet none have expressly endorsed the BDS movement itself, which is an important distinction. For example, when the Presbyterian Church (USA) approved divestment in 2014, they made it clear that the vote should not be taken as an endorsement of the international BDS movement ("Slim Margin"). While many Christians are supportive of the use of divestment as a nonviolent tool in the campaign to end the occupation or simply because they do not, for religious reasons, want to profit from armed conflict, they do not share the goals of the international BDS movement—namely the delegitimization and ultimate dismantling of Israel—nor do they approve of some of its tactics, including anti-normalization.

In the final analysis, KPD's reach and influence have been limited, much like the BDS movement's divestment campaigns, which, despite the public attention they have garnered, have had no measurable effect on the economy of Israel or on the investment decisions of significant institutions such as universities, or on the companies BDS targets. Nonetheless, KPD continues to inspire a group of activists within the Palestinian Christian community and their allies who see themselves as part of a global "*Kairos* movement," which ensures that KPD will continue to be promoted in churches around the world.

CHAPTER NINE

JOHN KAMPEN

ASSESSING THE 2017 MENNONITE RESOLUTION ON ISRAEL/PALESTINE

On July 6, 2017, the Mennonite Church USA (MC USA)[91] adopted the resolution "Seeking Peace in Israel and Palestine" at its biennial convention held in Orlando, Florida (Mennonite Church "Seeking").[92] Of the 548 voters there were only ten in opposition to the resolution and two abstentions (Fig. 7). The persons who lined up to speak to the resolution were overwhelmingly in favor. "I could not support the resolution two years ago. It was too simplistic," Mennonite World Conference president Nelson Kraybill said, speaking in support of the motion, "I commend the committee for their thorough work"

(Mennonite Church "Third Way"). Presumably, the majority of the delegates were in agreement with the sentiment of the MC USA press release on that date, "Mennonites Choose 'Third Way' on Israel and Palestine," which suggested that the Mennonites were proposing a new way for North American Christians to enter into discussions about the Middle East. The majority of the delegates believed it to be a very evenhanded resolution, which was celebrated as a tremendous victory by many who have a particular interest in the Palestinian cause, though some felt that anything less than a full and unambiguous endorsement of BDS was inadequate. Of greater significance was the rejection of the resolution as a sincere effort to reach out to the Jewish communities of North America and Israel, as evident in the reaction of the Jewish press. Indeed, the Jewish reaction raises questions about the "third way" perspective. Does it present a genuine alternative? If not, how could so many Mennonites be thus convinced? These questions can only be answered by developing an understanding of the resolution's context and analyzing the resolution itself.

Fig. 7—98 % of Mennonites in Florida vote in favor of divestment resolution.
Photo: Medium.com

THE STRUCTURE AND CONTENT
OF THE RESOLUTION

"Seeking Peace in Israel and Palestine" begins with the expressed desire for the welfare of all peoples of the area. It uses the language of traditional Mennonite piety and practice as it is employed by more contemporary institutional representations such as the Mennonite Central Committee (MCC), the inter-Mennonite relief and service agency founded in 1920 to coordinate relief efforts for the besieged and suffering Mennonites in Russia. Today it describes itself as "a worldwide ministry of Anabaptist churches, [which] shares God's love and compassion for all in the name of Christ by responding to basic human needs and working for peace and justice" (Mennonite Church "Vision"). The MCC has offices in fifty countries and ongoing projects in at least ten more. The total income for MCC US in the 2016-17 fiscal year was $34,611,000; when combined with MCC Canada to cover its worldwide operations, the organization brought in $86,966,000 during that period. Within the confession of faith adopted by the denomination, we find additional language promulgating social justice and emphasizing the peacemaking objectives of MC USA: "As followers of Jesus, we participate in his ministry of peace and justice. He has called us to find our blessing in making peace and seeking justice" (Mennonite Church "Confession"). This perspective, moreover, provides the starting point for the July 2017 resolution: "As followers of Jesus and his gospel of reconciliation, we long for peace, security, justice, and the flourishing of all people living in Israel and Palestine" (Summary, ll. 2-3). This is immediately followed by two points of convergence that establish the parameters of the statement, "the cry of justice for Palestinians . . . living under oppressive military occupation for fifty years" and "antisemitism and violence inflicted upon Jews past and present" (Summary, ll 4-5). These two foci form the structure of the two-section resolution, the first entitled "Opposing Military Occupation and Seeking a Just Peace," the second, "Opposing Antisemitism and Seeking Right Relationship with Jewish Communities." The structure of each section consists of an introduction, a "Confession and Lament," and "Commitments." As is apparent, the desire to portray a balanced approach to the issues under discussion is echoed in the balanced two-part structure. One way of evaluating the resolution is to determine: 1) whether the intended balance is actually reflected in the resolution's text and 2) whether the intended or real impact of the resolution accomplished the balance it was designed to create.

HISTORY OF THE RESOLUTION

The present resolution has its origins in an Executive Board decision of MC USA to send "leaders from across its agencies to visit Palestine-Israel with the purpose of engaging the discussion on divestment" (MennoPIN "Brief History"). In light of what they described as "these disconcerting realities," referring to the occupation and its specific impact on Palestinian Christian life, they returned with recommendations that were circulated in a June 2007 letter to all the churches of the denomination, calling for pastors and leaders "to visit both Israel and Palestine and to deepen their understanding of the current situation in the region" (Mennonite Church "Open Letter").[93] They were also encouraged to study books such as *Under Vine and Fig Tree*, edited by Alain Epp Weaver who, with his wife Sonia, worked for eleven years on the Mennonite Central Committee's relief, development, and peacebuilding programs in the Middle East while living in the Jenin district of the West Bank, the Gaza Strip, East Jerusalem, and Amman, Jordan.

In December 2009, the *Kairos Palestine Document* was released by Palestinian Christians. This provided a new and more focused context for the denomination's interest in the area. The response came in the form of a letter dated October 5, 2011 addressed, "Dear sisters and brothers in Christ in Palestine" (Mennonite Church). The letter, signed by Ervin Stutzman, the Executive Director of the denomination, recognized the plight of Palestinians in the occupied territories: "We open our hearts when we again hear of the suffering you experience in an occupied land as homes are taken from you, families and communities are separated by walls and checkpoints, and countless large and small indignities and humiliations are visited upon you each day." Later their situation is compared to that of Christ, "We hear in your call the appeal of Christ to us." Pledges to continue sending persons to see the situation firsthand and for continued study are included in the letter.

This letter provided the genesis of the extensive and well-funded "Come and See" tours that coordinated trips to Israel/Palestine for at least 110 participants by April of 2017. For a relatively small denomination—the Mennonite Church USA now has approximately 67,000 members, in 2007 around 135,000 ("We Are Mennonites")—this included a good deal of the national and local leadership.[94]

As the result of the rather large investment of time and resources in this effort; the interest and energy level of many persons engaged in these trips; the work of Mennonite Central Committee, which will be discussed below; and the educational opportunities for travel to and study in the area supported by all Mennonite colleges and seminaries, an organization called MennoPIN (Mennonite Palestine Israel Network) was formed in 2013. According to their "four-year congregational study guide," which is available online, "MennoPIN has given particular attention to the *Kairos Palestine* call, producing a study guide for Mennonite congregations, and creating space for advocacy and action on the issue of boycott, divestment, and sanctions within Mennonite Church USA" (MennoPIN "Kairos"). The study materials are an adaptation of those produced by the Presbyterian Church, analyzed elsewhere in this book, which themselves have been a source of conflict with major Jewish organizations regarding statements about Israel/Palestine.[95] The other major connection for the leadership of MennoPIN has been Sabeel, the Ecumenical Liberation Theology Center formed by Naim Ateek, former canon of St. George's Episcopal Cathedral in Jerusalem, and the author of *Justice, and Only Justice: A Palestinian Theology of Liberation* (1989) and other books. A number of leaders in MennoPIN are also heavily involved with Friends of Sabeel North America (FOSNA), the North American arm of Sabeel, which is heavily engaged in bolstering the support of and advocating for the BDS movement in North America.

It is largely through MennoPIN's concerted planning, organizing, and strategizing that a resolution on Israel/Palestine was considered at the biannual convention of MC USA in 2015 (MennoPIN "Reflections"). Representation from the Palestinian community was present, as were leaders from MennoPIN, and both groups engaged in a number of key discussions. The resolution failed to pass due to the efforts of a few who pointed out the rather limited and simplistic view of the conflict demonstrated therein. Some procedural ambiguity within the assembly probably also contributed to its defeat. A resolution was passed requesting further work and a resubmission for the 2017 assembly.

Denominational and MennoPIN leadership perceived the need for a more extensive educational process in the directions indicated in the earlier correspondence to the denomination in 2007 and 2013. Leadership for the development of the new resolution was delegated to André Gingerich Stoner, then-director of holistic witness and interchurch relations for MC USA and an ordained minister of the denomination. Accordingly, Jonathan Brenneman—the child of a North American Mennonite father and a Palestinian mother and a recent graduate of the Master's program in Peace Studies from Notre Dame—was appointed to a voluntary service position as coordinator of the educational efforts in this field. Palestinian speakers itinerated among churches, district conferences, and schools to educate persons about the situation from the perspective of *Kairos Palestine*. For example, for two months the Jewish and Palestinian Voices for Peace tour traveled to over twenty Mennonite venues across the country. Jonathan Kuttab, a well-known Palestinian Mennonite human rights lawyer, activist, and speaker shared the stage with a member of the local Jewish Voice for Peace (JVP) chapter. (Mennonite Church "Reflections"). JVP is the only Jewish organization involved in these educational tours and invited to present at the convention. Alex Awad, described below, had been invited to speak at various events in preparation for the 2015 convention and therefore was already present.

In response to a perceived lack of balance in the 2015 resolution, the new resolution charted a different path. André Gingerich Stoner created a broader, more consultative process for the formation of the new resolution. A three-person writing team was appointed and a reference council invited to respond on a periodic basis to the drafts produced. A draft was also posted on the denominational website with invitations to comment. The structure of "confession and lament," followed by commitments to reconciliation and restoration, was rooted in an approach championed by the academic programs in restorative justice, conflict management, and peacebuilding in Mennonite colleges and universities. It was this process that resulted in the resolution adopted in 2017.

THE HISTORY OF INVOLVEMENT
IN ISRAEL/PALESTINE

The interest and experience that resulted in the level of commitment to the Palestinian cause evident in the initial 2007 letter goes back to 1949, when MCC responded to the needs of Palestinian refugees from the war of 1948 first in the Gaza Strip, and then in Lebanon and Jericho.[96] It was actively engaged in distribution of food and of "Christmas bundles," a practice continued by those MCC groups who serve refugee populations up to this very day. At that time, MCC began to coordinate the distribution of clothing for other church agencies as well. In 1954 it began distributing American surplus food through the US Title III program, so that in the space of a decade beginning in 1954 it dispensed 26,254,935 pounds of cheese, butter, oil, dried milk, and bulgur wheat. Primary distribution sites for these materials were the Mennonite schools established in Beit Jala and Hebron, as well as through women's society contacts and to welfare cases identified by the Jordanian government. Already in 1950 MCC was engaged in vocational training, opening a shoemaking school in Jericho, then one for woodworking, followed by a typing program in a community center. Of greater long-term significance was the sewing program begun in 1951 in the Ein el-Sultan refugee camp near Jericho. This rapidly was absorbed into the needlework program established in Bethlehem in 1952, which became a visible symbol throughout North American Mennonite churches of MCC's involvement in the region and a significant source of income for some Palestinian families. Here traditional Palestinian embroidery patterns were utilized in products for the North American market, still sold today in Ten Thousand Villages stores throughout North America.

Material assistance continued in Jericho until 1966. Upon the initiative and advocacy of MCC staff working in the West Bank, the organization began a rural development program that continued from 1976 to 1988. This program was initiated out of a desire "to push MCC in the direction of greater solidarity with Palestinians in the face of Israeli occupation" (XX 55). Ibrahim Matar was hired as a field worker for the program. He was chair of the Business and Economics Department of Bethlehem University and a former employee of the Lutheran World

Federation. A former colleague of his at the Federation, Ya'oub Amar, was also hired. They developed expertise in the land and water issues that posed problems for Palestinian farmers. While not under the MCC umbrella, Matar also led tours of the West Bank for foreign correspondents and developed documentaries on the Israeli settlements. As MCC worked at rural development, for example implementing drip irrigation methods into the Palestinian rural economy, workers also documented water issues and the expanding Israeli settlements in the West Bank. Other projects included supporting olive production. The MCC set up a program in which half a million olive seedlings were distributed to West Bank farmers and another million in cooperation with the Community Development Fund (later Save the Children). This program attracted more attention from the Israeli authorities and portions of it had to operate on a somewhat clandestine basis. The program permitted Matar and Leroy Friesen, country director of MCC at the time, to travel around the West Bank, documenting the details of the occupation and then disseminating them to both media and church contacts. When it came to an end in 1988 it had helped to install drip irrigation systems in eleven villages, contributed to the construction of thirty-five water systems, and dug 100 rain collection wells. It had also supported efforts to reclaim 8,000 dunams (about 1,975 acres) of arable land threatened with confiscation. Driven by the new direction among younger Mennonites toward an active role in peacemaking as opposed to the traditional stance of non-resistance, these North American staff members attracted to MCC work in the area sought opportunities to advocate for the Palestinian people and the issues they faced in Israel.

On the minds of many was the question of whether MCC had a peacemaking role in the area. Frank Epp, a historian and later president of Conrad Grebel University College, was sent to Israel and the West Bank to evaluate the potential for a peacemaking initiative and authored three volumes on the region, one more historical and the other two drawing on interviews with Palestinians and Israelis. He saw it as an attempt to give various people of the area a voice. MCC never did develop a major peace portfolio for the region. Rather, drawing attention to the occupation and documenting and challenging various aspects of it have characterized the peace efforts of MCC through the present day.

MCC workers have found this sort of effort to be more consonant with the values they bring to their mission.

The most important initiative for peacemaking was the development of a library in Jerusalem called the Peace Resource Center, which operated until 1997. As a Palestinian national consciousness began to build in the 1970s, MCC designed programming that encouraged its nonviolent expression and provided training in methods of nonviolent resistance, some of which were translated into Arabic. The impact of this work is apparent in the life of Mubarak Awad, who in 1983 founded the Palestinian Center for Nonviolence. He studied nonviolent resistance tactics during his years at Bluffton College (now Bluffton University), a Mennonite college in Ohio. His organizing attracted the attention of Israeli authorities and he was deported in 1988 to the United States, where he had become a citizen. His impact can be still seen in the nonviolent emphasis of organizations such as Sabeel and others. Volunteers from Mennonite agencies still are placed at Sabeel.

One of the factors that led to the decision to terminate the agricultural program was the increasing strength of local Palestinian organizations. Through an industrious staff and the fostering of good relationships in Palestinian communities, MCC had been an effective partner with other agencies such as Oxfam in the distribution and utilization of resources necessary for the welfare of Palestinians in the occupied territories. As time passed, their role as facilitator was no longer necessary or desirable, and supporting projects led and owned by Palestinians became the priority. While the programs have changed depending upon the political circumstances and the needs of Palestinian communities, to this day the Mennonite Central Committee has remained an engaged and active presence in these areas, including in the Gaza Strip. As the MCC reports in "MCC and Palestine and Israel: Commonly Asked Questions,"

> Through the years, MCC has accepted invitations from Palestinians to walk alongside them as they search for justice, peace and freedom. MCC has worked with Israeli partners since Israel's occupation of the West Bank, including East Jerusalem, and the Gaza Strip in 1967. MCC supports the efforts of both Palestinians and Israelis

committed to nonviolence and to a future of peace, justice and reconciliation for both peoples.

Throughout the entire period of MCC engagement in the Middle East, workers have considered their interpretive role to be very significant. MCC volunteers have made themselves available to the multiple Mennonite tourist groups and study tours organized by Mennonite agencies and educational institutions, which have impacted whole generations of students and church leaders. Though it is difficult to measure, the overall impact of these efforts has been a comparatively widespread understanding of the Palestinian situation from the perspective of the Palestinians and a good deal of empathy for their plight.

A total of 177 volunteers served in these programs from 1948 through 1999. Included in this list are many who became faculty members at Mennonite colleges and seminaries as well as serving in influential positions of denomination and Mennonite agency leadership (Weaver and Weaver 135-40). Also listed are members of the Awad and Kuttab families, Palestinians who remain connected with the Mennonite world and were leaders in the development of organizations and strategies of peaceful resistance to Israeli occupation. Alex Awad's family is one of the oldest and most celebrated Christian families in Bethlehem. His brother Bishara is the founder of Bethlehem Bible College; his nephew Sami is the director of Holy Land Trust and founder of Christ at the Checkpoint and the Bethlehem Music Festival, and his brother, Mubarak, is professor of Peace Studies at American University in Washington, DC and was recognized by Newsweek as the "Palestinian Gandhi" (Dougherty). As above, he is also the founder of the Palestinian Center for Nonviolence. Alex Awad advises the United Methodist Church's Board of Global Ministries and the Mennonite Palestine-Israel Network on issues regarding Palestine and Israel. Jonathan Kuttab is a Mennonite Palestinian human rights lawyer who was involved in the founding of the Palestinian Center for Nonviolence. With an office in East Jerusalem, he has been engaged in human rights struggles with agencies of the United Nations and has a substantive international presence. His brother Daoud is a prominent Palestinian journalist.

There is ample evidence of the tremendous impact that the time of service in Israel/Palestine had upon the lives of the volunteers and the institutional trajectory of the denomination (Weaver and Weaver 111-28). The hospitality characteristic of the Palestinian communities in which they served permitted Mennonite volunteers to gain a deep understanding of and appreciation for Palestinian life and culture, including the political realities of their plight. Careers were established and lives were changed. Examples include Merlin Swartz, who studied Islam at Harvard under Wilfred Cantwell Smith and went on to a career at Boston University, Loren Lybarger, who studied Christian-Islamic relations at the University of Chicago, and Tim Buckwalter, who became an Arabic language instructor. Others found new areas of long-time service in the Middle East, including Jordan and Egypt. The impact of this sustained engagement cultivated a climate in Mennonite churches throughout North America that countered some of the dispensationalist views and other Christian Zionist perspectives that had been influential in some segments of these churches. It nurtured a deep understanding of the issues facing Palestinians throughout the leadership structures of the Mennonite church and in many of the churches throughout the denomination as well.

A new initiative that emerged in large part from the MCC experience was the involvement of Christian Peacemaker Teams (CPT) in Israel/Palestine. This organization was begun in 1988 primarily by Mennonites with MCC or related experience, but quickly grew to include a broad range of persons and traditions who shared a commitment to Christian nonviolence. Within a few years it had a program in Israel with a continuous presence in Hebron since 1994 (Christian Peacemaker). This presence includes patrols that accompany Palestinian children to school, monitoring settler violence and soldier home invasions, and working against home demolitions. It supports Palestinian-led nonviolent resistance to Israel's military occupation and educates people in North America. It endorsed the Boycott, Divestment, and Sanctions (BDS) campaign in 2010. Itineration in Mennonite churches by present and former CPT volunteers is commonplace.

Finally, mention must be made of engagement in Israel by Mennonite mission agencies. The Mennonite Mission Network (formerly the

Mennonite Board of Missions) in conjunction with Eastern Mennonite Missions has been engaged in Israel/Palestine since the 1950s, with the Messianic Jewish movement as one primary focus (Shenk). The faculty at Israel College of the Bible, described as the seminary of Israeli Messianic Judaism, has over time included many Mennonites. During the 1970s and 1980s Mennonites became increasingly involved in the interfaith associations in Israel, primarily under the leadership of Roy Kreider. Roy and Florence Kreider were sent to Israel as missionaries by the Mennonite Board of Missions in 1953. In addition to learning Hebrew, Roy enrolled at the Hebrew University to study Jewish history and culture, as well as rabbinic literature. Their work took two forms, one with the Messianic Jewish movement in Israel, and the other organizing tours for persons to come to the holy land. Roy also brought Arab Christians into contact with the students he had among the Messianic Jews. An able scholar and leader, Roy Kreider was invited to join the Ecumenical Theological Research Fraternity, served as vice president of the Executive Committee of the Israel Interfaith Organization, and became a member of the selective Jerusalem Rainbow Dialogue, regarded as the highest-level dialogue group in Israel at the time and composed of a limited number of selected appointees. Mennonite Board of Missions involvement with Nazareth Hospital began in the 1960s and continues up to the present day. Mennonite involvement was central to the creation of Nazareth Village. It began as a project inspired by Dr. Nakhle Bishara, medical director at Nazareth Hospital, and then developed with D. Michael Hostetler its first director, who was charged with building a museum of life at the time of Jesus on the site of a wine press that was claimed to be from the first century. It opened in the year 2000. This engagement has not had as significant of an impact on the denomination as that related to the experience of MCC, CPT, and MennoPIN.

EVALUATION OF THE 2017 RESOLUTION

The 2017 MC USA resolution resulted from an internal logic within the denomination rooted in the history of its engagement with the area. As a graduate of the denominational seminary and an ordained clergyperson of the denomination, I have a certain understanding and even appreciation of this internal logic. However, in 1975, I enrolled in the Ph.D. program at Hebrew Union College-Jewish Institute of Religion in Cincinnati and thus have been privy to some of the ongoing conversations about conflict within the Jewish communities of the United States and Israel, particularly within Reform Judaism. I remain involved with Hebrew Union College in a variety of positions. My studies in Second Temple Judaism, the Dead Sea Scrolls, and the New Testament informed a growing understanding of the history of antisemitism and its implications. Regular travel to Israel/Palestine for research and academic engagement since the early 1990s also informs my perceptions. These experiences compel me to re-examine the content of the resolution and the assumptions undergirding it. While not on the writing team for the resolution, I was invited to make comments on successive drafts and made it possible for the drafters to receive a detailed evaluation from a Jewish leader in interfaith relations as well. However, this is not the place to indicate the extent to which those comments were accepted or incorporated into the final text.

The survey of the history of Mennonite involvement in the area suggests significant engagement with substantive impact on the denomination. What is missing, however, is substantive engagement with the Jewish communities of Israel and the United States about their understandings of Israel, both as a political reality and as a center of religious aspiration and imagination. While MCC materials document work with Jewish partners, it is always with regard to the situation of the Palestinians. There is no evidence of an attempt to gain further understanding of Israel's geopolitical situation, nor its implications for domestic policies related to Israel's security. Nor does one find acknowledgment of the manner in which Zion is the image at the center of so much traditional Jewish liturgy going back at least to the formation of Rabbinic Judaism as the centralizing force in the life of Jewish communities. The internal logic resulting from the history of involvement sketched above shows extremely limited evidence of substantive engagement with the issues that are at the center of Jewish life in Israel, or for that matter, in the United States. The Jewish Israeli world has not been the object of the empathetic approach that led to a deep understanding of the Palestinian world by many in the Mennonite church. The Jewish

Israeli world has rather been the object of suspicion, and sometimes hostility. For the most part, the North American Jewish community has been ignored.

After 2009, the ambiguities of the modern history of Israel and Palestine that could have informed Mennonite positions on the region were reduced to the perspectives of the *Kairos Palestine Document,* analyzed here by David Sandmel. This document thus provided the definitive interpretation of the political situation informing the resolutions of both 2015 and 2017.[97] It is recommended as the document that congregations and individuals should study in preparation for the conventions. No other sourcebooks regarding the history of the conflict are recommended. The invitation to study and to learn, then, actually introduces one to a very limited perspective. No acknowledgment has been made of the limitations of that composition within the Mennonite documentation related to its usage. Note for example the vigorous response it occasioned by the Central Conference of American Rabbis (CCAR), the official organization of Reform rabbis who adopted the "CCAR Resolution on the 2009 *Kairos Document*" on April 15, 2010 (Central Conference). Certainly elsewhere the CCAR has supported the two-state solution and continues to be engaged in a variety of human rights initiatives within Israel, including some on behalf of the Arab citizens of Israel, and arguing for fair and humane treatment of Palestinians. In its critique, the CCAR resolution notes the continuous use of supersessionist language; ambiguity regarding the nature of the occupation and, by extension, the ultimate rejection of the Jewish state as an idea; failure to acknowledge the violent Arab resistance to the establishment of a Jewish state; and failure to acknowledge the consequent violent attacks against Israeli citizens, simply regarding them as acts of resistance. While critiques of *Kairos Palestine* should not be simplistically endorsed without scrutiny, the failure to recognize that the document has been the subject of heavy critique, especially while both promoting it as the primary educational tool for the denomination and taking it as the central inspiration for the 2015 and 2017 resolutions points to the limited nature of the MC USA's discussion on Israel/Palestine. In her critique of *Kairos*, the Jewish scholar of the New Testament Amy-Jill Levine extensively engages in different aspects of Jewish-Christian dialogue, pointing out the document's weaknesses and what she terms "mistakes," while highlighting the manner in which compositions of this nature form an obstacle toward the formation of alliances between Jewish and Palestinian advocates for a peace ("Un-Christian Responses"). The denominational process of preparation did not point to or lay the groundwork for the "third way" that characterizes the official press releases issued after the passage of the 2017 resolution.

The resolution itself is structured on the basis of a false equivalence. It seems to want to put Palestinian suffering at the hands of Israel on one side of the "scale" and the history of Jewish suffering at the hands of Christians on the other. This is not a helpful way of characterizing either of these problems. Rather, there is a real conflict over land at the heart of the issue. There is a very real struggle between Israel and Palestine that has been going on since the beginning of the twentieth century and remains unresolved. By making this claim I by no means assume a simple definition of either Israel or Palestine, neither in political terms defined primarily by geography nor in the broader cultural, religious, and/or ideological terms. Emphasis on the term "occupation," while having some legitimacy with regard to land brought under the control of Israel in 1967 and assumed to be temporary, is problematic as the term used to define the issue in a more comprehensive manner. Rather, legal, historical, and religious claims to the land all are brought to bear on a present political reality in which almost all parties feel imperiled and marginalized by some segment of the international community. *Kairos Palestine* makes a claim about the land rooted in liberation theology: "Our connectedness to this land is a natural right" (2.3.4). The Mennonite resolution makes a confession of "Failing to understand the significance of the State of Israel for many Jewish people and the diversity of perspectives and understandings among Jews related to Israel and Zionism" (ll. 124-25). While one might wish for a clearer statement recognizing the failure of Mennonites to bring some understanding of "the land" in post-biblical Jewish literature and thought to bear upon the question,[98] it must be recognized that Mennonites and other Protestant academics who engage the issue of the land do so primarily from the perspective of the Hebrew Bible, and, in some instances, the

New Testament.[99] Of course, a recognition of the role of Israel in post-Holocaust Jewish life and thought also is necessary. A failure to consider the meaning of the land in Jewish religious and cultural life makes an attempt at a "third way" approach to the question impossible.

Moreover, it is possible to compile a long list of issues within the resolution that demonstrate its failure to provide a possible "third way." I will discuss only a few items to illustrate the point. Note two is an attempt to define "Israeli military occupation" and provides the justification for including Gaza in that listing. However, the withdrawal from Gaza was a major event for Israeli society, especially in that it occasioned the first abandonment and destruction of Jewish settlements and was followed by the election of Hamas and the firing of rockets from Gaza (Gordis 385-97). A very different perspective on "occupation." The use of the term "security" throughout the resolution assumes for the most part that the security of Israel can be achieved by a peaceful resolution of the Israeli-Palestinian conflict. This is clearly not the case. The security of Israel is threatened by the insecurity of all of its neighbors: Lebanon, Syria, Jordan, and Egypt. The threat that Iran poses for the security of Israel and for the remainder of the region is also very real. Security is thus a much more complicated issue than it appears in the resolution.

Listed under the "Commitments" made to address the issues of Palestinian Christians is a section entitled, "Understanding the Realities of Occupation" (ll. 76-79). The resolution states, "We urge our members who travel to Israel-Palestine to seek out diverse Palestinian and Israeli voices to better understand their experiences and perspectives." While that is a commendable injunction to seek out diverse voices, almost all Israeli Jews and North American Jews interested in Israel would find it a rather offensive starting point if the objective is to understand the occupation from diverse perspectives without gaining a more mature and comprehensive understanding of what Israel is, who lives there, and what it is trying to be. Similar questions could be raised about the assumption of the oft-cited "power imbalance." From what context does this imbalance emerge: the borders of "Israel," the surrounding region of the Middle East, the world population of Jews and Muslims?

Finally, the assumption of displacement of hundreds of thousands of Palestinians in 1947-48 receives mention and is assumed elsewhere in the document (ll. 13-15, 56-57). This is acknowledged in the lament of Yossi Klein Halevi,

> As we Israelis celebrated our reclaimed sovereignty and achieved one success after another, your people exchanged homes and olive orchards for the scorched earth of refugee camps, where you raised children without hope, the unwanted outcasts of the Arab world. I mourn the lives wasted in the bitterness of your despair against my joy. (84)

But there are a few things missing from this picture. As Halevi continues, "But I cannot apologize for surviving. What almost any Israeli Jew will tell you is that if the Palestinian and Arab leadership had accepted compromise instead of declaring a war to the death, the Palestinian tragedy would not have happened," adding, "another reason why Israeli Jews refuse to be cast as criminals in 1948. At least half of Israel's population is rooted in the Jewish communities of the Middle East." There is no acknowledgement in the resolution of the displacement of 830,000 Jews from the Arab lands of the Middle East and North Africa during those same years. This is a good example of the limited nature of the picture upon which the resolution is based and upon which it stakes out recommendations for the issues of Israel/Palestine.

We then must ask why a religious tradition is so predisposed to hear only one story. While a full investigation of this question is beyond the scope of this paper, a few cursory comments suggest some directions for consideration. The cleavage between Jewish activists and the remainder of the American left over Israel during the 1967 war had a profound impact on the new Mennonite activism that emerged in opposition to US involvement in Vietnam. Whereas previous generations had eschewed political engagement, in this new era Mennonites, along with the majority of the American left, found it easy to include Israel in critiques of US imperialism. This framework continues to influence the debate up to the present day. The inclusion of anti-Israel chants at rallies and demonstrations organized about other issues has been a commonplace occurrence throughout much of this time period.

Of course, the sensitivities of many Mennonite progressives have been formed by the assumptions and practices of the movement of which they have been a part.

Mennonites also have been an integral part of the Western Christian tradition, sharing and reproducing its anti-Semitic presuppositions in theology and practice. Mennonites have thus tended to echo the supersessionist viewpoints of their coreligionists. The extent of the rift between many politically progressive Protestant churches and the Jewish community concerning Israel is a question that bears further discussion but is beyond the scope of this paper. Where MC USA departs from many of these denominations is that it has not in any formal manner grappled with the issue of its relationship to Jews and Judaism.[100] While many of these denominations have issued statements and even adopted study guides and other such materials to provide guidance on the topic of antisemitism and other issues in Jewish-Christian relations, MC USA has no history of such engagement. Simple topics such as the portrayal and discursive use of the Pharisees or the belief in Jewish responsibility for the death of Jesus have not received sustained treatment in the publications of our theological colloquies or our meetings of biblical scholars. Yet these questions should be of particular importance to a denomination that considers the Bible as its basic authority, although, to be clear, I am not suggesting that MC USA ascribes to some theory of literal inspiration or something similar. Of equal significance is the extent to which the major trajectory of Anabaptist-Mennonite theology has highlighted its Christological center. Supersessionism has been a regular companion to Christologically-focused theology throughout Christian history. A belated attempt to make up for that lack is one explanation for what would appear to be a discordant resolution. The failure to address this issue is acknowledged in the resolution.

Some manifestations of antisemitism are very particular to a specific tradition; this is true for Mennonites, who of course have their own distinctive experiences and history. Of overweening significance for a people who have long claimed a Germanic identity is the Holocaust, although it is only very recently that this subject has begun to receive treatment by historians of the Mennonite movement. The record of Mennonite participation in the German army, complicity with Nazism, and support for the Nazi cause is rather extensive and encompasses major Mennonite population centers such as Germany, Prussia (present-day Poland), and Ukraine.[101] Extensive evidence of support for the Nazis among the Mennonite communities of Canada and South America is also apparent.[102] Addressing our own history of complicity is a necessary step in coming to terms with Jews and Judaism. The same is true for the antisemitism in our theology and religious teaching. Both of these topics require thorough treatment as we come to terms with our relationship with Judaism and the Jewish people, and with a subject of central interest to them, Israel.

There is one final question that returns us to the issue of the false equivalence between the two major sections of the resolution. Whereas the section on the Palestinian question calls for accountability, the section on antisemitism is aspirational. In this resolution we as a denomination have defined very specifically the commitments we have made to the Palestinian people and have called for accountability. The direction of this section of the resolution is very intentional and deliberate, with resources within agencies designated to carry them out. First, the resolution asks Everance, the financial services organization of the denomination, to periodically convene representatives of Mennonite-related agencies and organizations to "review investment practices for the purpose of withdrawing investments from companies that are profiting from the occupation" on behalf of MC USA (ll. 91-100). This is the one place in the resolution where the mechanisms for accountability are directly listed in the text. It is noteworthy that this is specifically with regard to the economic boycott, since, as we may recall, divestment was a major driving force in the history of the resolution discussed at the beginning of this essay. Noteworthy also is the extent to which BDS was an integral part of this history, having been formally endorsed by both CPT and FOSNA-Sabeel, and being one of three major links on the homepage of MennoPIN. This attempt to isolate Israel economically, culturally, and academically is not a strategy that can in any manner be understood as the basis for a "third way" approach to Israel/Palestine. *Kairos Palestine* also calls for economic boycott and divestment, which was understood to be an indication of solidarity with the Palestinian people. The other very specific mandate is advocating with the US government (ll. 85-89). Noteworthy is the fact that the actions emphasized in these resolutions have already been carried out. On November 20, 2017, nineteen representatives of Mennonite agencies and associated organizations met in the Everance offices in Goshen, Indiana for a consultation on investments in Israel/Palestine. Similarly, staff members and leaders of MC USA reported that they went to Capitol Hill on May 22, 2018 for a day of lobbying on these issues.

The section on antisemitism is very different. Here the church acknowledges its failure: "we confess and lament the ways we have participated in the harms against Jewish people" (l. 113-4). These misjudgments include, "Failing to recognize how these past and present threats contribute to the need for security for Jewish people" (ll. 120-1).[103] In the introductory section it is proposed that this failure is responsible for the displacement of Palestinians from their homes (ll. 11-16). Western Christians should acknowledge the failure to provide safety and security for Jews over the past two millennia; however, the displacement of Palestinians in 1948 is a much more complicated issue than these lines would suggest. The simultaneous displacement of the Jewish population from Arab countries in the Middle East and North Africa has already received mention above, but it is worth mentioning that the failure of negotiations at that point is also a complicated issue. Acknowledged in the resolution is the Mennonite Church's history of "Failing to understand the significance of the state of Israel for many Jewish people" (ll. 124-5). The willingness to advance the resolution in light of this acknowledgment might appear puzzling. It would seem advisable that a resolution on Israel/Palestine would come only *after* some attempts had been made to understand the significance of Israel to its international stakeholders.

Of the greatest importance is the much more ambiguous nature of the commitments advanced therein. The sponsorship of two conferences is commendable, and the one noted above raised awareness of the extent of Mennonite complicity in the Holocaust. In addition to one more conference, the remainder of the recommendations emphasizes building relationships with the Jewish community. There is no evidence that this will be a priority for MC USA or its Executive Board and staff. No accountability is structured into this section of the resolution and no specific actions are mandated. In other words, both the injunction to overcome historic antisemitism and its consequences and the injunction to build relationships with the Jewish people are not seen as central to church life and belief. This leaves MC USA with the same problem that it had before it began to consider the resolution—a false equivalence that people within MC USA concerned about antisemitism and our relationship with the Jewish people should find troubling. The next biennial convention (Mennocon) is scheduled for July 2021 in a form that offers options for virtual participation.

CONCLUSION

The examination of this resolution and its associated history is a particular instance of how one Protestant church connected with a progressive social agenda comes to terms with the Israeli-Palestinian question. While each mainline Christian denomination has its own particular theological traditions and history that it brings to bear on the issue, our exploration of the particular trajectory of MC USA points to several common elements. What is most apparent is that all statements tend to arrive at a similar impasse with the majority of the Jewish community in both Israel and North America. In the case of MC USA, I attempted to demonstrate that the viewpoint it brings to the question of Israel/Palestine is a logical development of its own experience and theology and the significant limitations therein. It also illustrates the manner in which a Protestant church is much more comfortable engaging in steps to confront antisemitism than it is developing a deeper and more comprehensive understanding of the meaning of the modern State of Israel for the Jewish people. Antisemitism is an important topic that Christians need to address, but it only partially covers the issues of Israel/Palestine. A Protestant church informed by a more nuanced approach to Israel would begin also to address the threats to the security and welfare of the Jewish people that are inextricably intertwined with the security and welfare of the Jewish state.

PART TWO

BOYCOTT CAMPAIGNS IN THE PRESBYTERIAN CHURCH USA

CHAPTER TEN

DANIEL FRIEDMAN

BATTLE FOR THE HOLY LAND(S): THE EVOLUTION OF AMERICAN PROTESTANT POLARIZATION ON ISRAEL AND PALESTINE

As I detail in my historical essay in this book, mainline Christian criticism of Israel is not a twenty-first century phenomenon. Indeed, as Paul Hopkins documents, the Presbyterian Church always had its fair share of adherents who disapproved of Israel's actions. What, therefore, led PCUSA to step up its pro-Palestinian activism in recent years? This essay identifies two key factors that led to the present state of affairs: first, the 2001 United Nations Durban Conference Against Racism (also known as Durban I), which singled out Israel for opprobrium and the appointment the next year of the Palestinian-born Rev. Fahed Abu-Akel as Moderator; and second, intercommunal debates over acceptance of homosexuality, which led to a mass exodus of conservatives from PCUSA. I conclude the chapter with a discussion of the consequences of these events on the polarization of American values generally.

Political ideas and interest groups often exist for considerable lengths of time before becoming salient. David Truman demonstrated in *The Governmental Process* that interest groups actualize in response to some disturbance that has occurred. Thus, interest group research seeks to identify the "disturbance" that consequently transformed the notion from an idea into an issue. As far as PCUSA statements and publications are concerned, one can point to the 2003 resolution calling on Israel to "End the Occupation Now" as the beginning of the Church's tilt in favor of the Palestinians. While the document identifies a meeting that took place in November 2002 at the United Nations as the alleged disturbance, in reality, tensions had been rising for a couple of years prior.

In fact, many suggest that the turning point was actually the World Conference against Racism in Durban, South Africa in August 2001. Convened to discuss international efforts to combat bigotry, the conference shifted its focus to criticism of Israel's policies in the disputed territories, with participants drawing comparisons between apartheid South Africa and the Jewish state (Lantos). PCUSA sent nineteen representatives to the conference, who followed up with a gathering in their United Nations office. Details of the visit are included in the PCUSA NEWS report, "Presbyterians to attend UN anti-racism conference."

Comparisons between South Africa and Israel had already begun to appear in PCUSA materials prior to Durban I.[104] In an October 2000 letter to President Clinton, Stated Clerk Clifton Kirkpatrick wrote of "the frustrations of Palestinian Christians and Muslims forced to live under a clear form of apartheid." Moreover, the Presbyterian News Service (PNS) and other agencies were becoming increasingly partial in their reporting on Israel-Palestine. For example, from January 1, 2000, to June 30, 2004, the PNS ran over ninety stories on Palestine and Israel, fifty-seven of which, according to Spotts, portrayed Israel negatively (9).[105]

In line with this growing sympathy for the Palestinian cause, the following year, at the 2002 General Assembly, Palestinian pastor Rev. Fahed Abu-Akel was elected Moderator of the Church (Makari 2). In his address to the assembly, he presented a heart-wrenching account of his youth:

> During the 1948 Arab-Israeli war, I was a 4-year-old child living in the Galilean village of Kuffer-Yassif, when Israeli troops drove my family from our home. As my father led the eight children away from our village, I looked back and saw my mother on the roof of our house, waving. She stayed behind while my father and the children journeyed to a mountain refugee camp. When we eventually returned, finding her alive, we asked her why she had not come with us. She told my father, "This is our home, our land, and our church." (Paraphrase of "Palestinian Pastor")

Coming at a time when, given events at Durban I and the then-ongoing Second Intifada, Israel's international image was at an all-time low, his moving account appears to have been decisive in earning him the post.

One of Abu-Akel's first initiatives was the convening of a Conference on the Middle East, held in March 2003 in Montreat, North Carolina, to which he invited the high-profile Palestinian activist and Lutheran minister Rev. Mitri Raheb, among others. His next step was the tasking of the Presbyterian Mission Agency's Advisory Committee on Social Witness Policy (ACSWP) with the preparation of a report on Israel-Palestine for the 215th General Assembly in 2003, culminating in the aforementioned resolution to "End the Occupation Now." Aside from the report's biased content, the title itself was indicative of the Church's new direction, which stood in contrast with the 2002 General

Assembly's resolution, "Urging Sustainable Peace between Israelis and Palestinians."

The consequences of this new perspective were manifold. First, *Church & Society*, PCUSA's official periodical, devoted the following September's issue to Israel-Palestine, including a number of controversial authors, such as Raheb, as well as Rev. Naim Ateek of the Sabeel Liberation Theology Center. In Ateek's article, he not only argued for greater understanding of Palestinian suffering but went so far as to offer a rationale for suicide bombings (51). Second, the Church commissioned the Presbyterian Mission Agency to prepare a report on socially responsible investing in Israel-Palestine. Ultimately, these initiatives culminated in the 2004 General Assembly, which can be considered the watershed moment of the Church's pro-Palestinian activism. While many previous General Assemblies proffered single resolutions relating to the Israeli-Palestinian conflict, the 2004 General Assembly produced five resolutions critical of Israel. Finally, the 2004 General Assembly established the Israel Palestine Mission Network, a Church body dedicated to furthering the Palestinian cause.

An additional sociological factor—completely unrelated to the issue of Israel-Palestine—has led to the rise of pro-Palestinian bias in PCUSA and other mainline churches. The fundamentalist-modernist controversy of the early twentieth century led to the formation of a number of conservative splinter Presbyterian denominations, including significant bodies such as the Presbyterian Church in America (PCA) and the Evangelical Presbyterian Church (EPC). Due to an important doctrinal tenet, however, most Presbyterians remained within the major northern and southern denominations, which would eventually reunite. According to Presbyterian theology, the unity of the Church must be maintained at all costs. Different viewpoints must be tolerated, and a breach should only be considered if continued membership would imply a major breach in Church doctrine and thus disloyalty to Christianity (Mackay 97). Consequently, for most of the twentieth century, the traditional body of the Church consisted of a diverse mix of member congregations and pastors, ranging from conservatives to progressives. So then what constitutes a major breach?

In 1978, the Church issued a statement prohibiting the ordination of practicing homosexuals. In 2011, however, after decades of fierce debate, that statement was overturned. Three years later, the General Assembly resolved to approve the officiating of its pastors over same-sex marriages. These debates took their toll on the Church. A significant number of conservative pastors and congregations began leaving the denomination. Between 2007 and 2015, the Evangelical Presbyterian Church inherited 350 congregations from PCUSA and, in 2012, a new Presbyterian denomination was formed, the Evangelical Covenant Order (ECO), which boasted over 350 churches as of November 2017 (Fortson and Grams 157) (ECO Presbyterian).

The departure of conservatives from the Church reverberated beyond the issue of same-sex marriage and ordination. Previously, due to the spectrum of views in the Church, doctrinal evolution was a gradual process. Once the conservatives disappeared, however, the progressive wing simply needed to convince the moderates to agree with their positions; and on a variety of issues they began to see their success accelerate. The rapid shift on the Israeli-Palestinian conflict was one of the first results of the conservatives' departure. Many of those who previously defended Israel in the face of her detractors did so on account of their belief in the biblical covenant with Israel, as well as markedly conservative political proclivities. Once that element was removed, pro-Palestinian progressives faced less difficulty convincing moderates to support their cause. Since the lingering pro-Israel advocates did not necessarily equate ancient Israel with the modern state, the only theological question remaining was one of justice. Proving the justice of Israel's actions in the face of international criticism tends to be a challenging endeavor.

This explanation is significant not merely in terms of defining the "disturbance" moment of PCUSA's shift towards the Palestinian perspective, it also contributes to a wider discussion about American values in the twenty-first century. The USA today appears to be more polarized than ever. Yet scholars continue to debate whether polarization is a widespread phenomenon amongst the general public (Abramowitz), or primarily an elite phenomenon (Fiorina). Similarly, scholars of religious sociology have challenged the notion of a polarized political culture in

American churches. Neiheisel and Djupe argued that, when it comes to religious values, individuals identify with congregations, not denominations, and are often ambivalent toward or ignorant of their churches' sociopolitical positions. Likewise, Wuthnow suggests that denominations would become increasingly irrelevant in political culture, since, as they include both conservatives and liberals, they would avoid taking a policy position and thereby alienating a significant portion of their constituency. An examination of mainline churches' pro-Palestinian activity throughout the twentieth century appears to support the proposition that churches maintained big tents and did not reflect polarized values and constituencies. While voices emanating from the churches were often critical of Israel, Protestants in the pews tended to be more favorably disposed towards the Jewish state than their leaders.

Nevertheless, the conservative exodus from PCUSA has increased its theological and political homogeneity, with the deserters founding new, more conservative denominations. With the departure of significant numbers of conservative members from the Church, the views of the leadership and the laity are becoming closer to one another on a host of issues. Indeed, emerging from this analysis is the revelation that the earlier brushstroke equations of mainline with liberal Christian and evangelical with conservative Christian were less than precise; in time, however, they are becoming more accurate depictions. As conservative and progressive Christians self-select into conservative and progressive denominations, polarization is indeed becoming a widespread phenomenon amongst elites and mass publics alike.

CHAPTER ELEVEN

JOHN WIMBERLY AND WILLIAM HARTER

WHEN THE PCUSA BEGAN TO MIRROR THE MIDDLE EAST (2004-PRESENT)

When the two of us became involved with the Palestine-Israel issue in 2004, neither of us had any idea how nasty and bitter the debate would become. We are certain that many Presbyterians, on all sides of the issues, expected the debate to be passionate, respectful, and informed and not nasty, disrespectful, and filled with misinformation. As the debate commenced, many PCUSA members had strong opinions about the proper path to peace, but few wanted Palestine-Israel to become a wedge issue further dividing our denomination at a time when other contentious issues were already causing division. How did the debate morph into something where people on both sides felt maligned and misrepresented?

For many, the Palestine-Israel peacemaking process caught our attention in new ways in the aftermath of the 2004 General Assembly in Richmond, Virginia. At that Assembly, the commissioners voted to investigate the possibility of divesting from several companies that were alleged to be supporting Israel's presence in the West Bank. The Mission Responsibility through Investment Committee was instructed "to initiate a process of phrased selective divestment in multinational corporations operating in Israel . . . and to make appropriate recommendations to the General Assembly Council for action." The motion passed with an 87% majority.

Most in the PCUSA were stunned by the immediate, united, and vehement reaction from the US Jewish community, which disagreed with the GA action in the strongest of terms. We were not. The Jewish community had been defending Israel against the foes of its existence since the state's formation in 1948. They accepted it as the norm. But the idea of boycotting selected companies doing business with Israel crossed a line in the sand.

Since the time of the Byzantine Empire, Jews have been targeted by Christians with boycotts and economic sanctions of various types. It is one thing to argue with the US Jewish community about Israel and Palestine. Jews have a dynamic, admirable tradition of debating issues. It is another thing, however, to use the weapon of boycotts and economic sanctions against the Jews. The strong reaction to the General Assembly's move should not have been surprising. The fact that it was so unexpected revealed how little many Presbyterians knew about the Jewish experience of discrimination directed against them by Christians.

In a joint letter to the Stated Clerk of the PCUSA's General Assembly, Rabbi Eric Joffe, then-president of the Union of Reform Judaism, and Rabbi Paul Menitoff, then-Executive President of the Central Conference of American Rabbis, asked, "Your support of divestment from Israel creates a worrisome double standard. Are human rights violations by Israel greater than those committed by the Palestinians? By the Syrians? By the Iranians?" ("Reform Jewish"). This is a question that PCUSA pastors would be asked time and again by rabbinical colleagues in their communities across the United States. To date, the question has not been answered to the satisfaction of a Jewish community all too familiar with being singled out for economic and other forms of discrimination by Christians.

Perhaps more typical of the reaction of many American and international Jews was a piece by Alan Dershowitz. "The Presbyterian Church (USA) has committed a grievous sin," Dershowitz thundered in an op-ed in the *Los Angeles Times*, which was published on August 4, 2004 and then widely reprinted. "Unless the church rescinds this immoral, sinful and bigoted denigration of the Jewish state, it will be 'participating in' and 'contributing to' anti-Jewish bigotry and the encouragement of terrorism" (Dershowitz).

Only a handful of General Assembly commissioners realized that they had unwittingly crossed this Rubicon.[106] The 2004 vote was held in the closing hours of the General Assembly, when everyone was packed and ready to leave. Anyone who has attended a General Assembly knows how things get pushed through in those closing hours without proper consideration. Indeed, back home in their communities, a significant number of commissioners complained that they hadn't realized what they were doing when they cast their vote and felt ill-informed by those who put forward the motion. The very narrow margins of votes on Israel-Palestine issues at all subsequent General Assemblies strongly supports the notion that commissioners were not aware of the issues or implications of their vote. There would be no more 87% margins of victory. Commissioners to future General Assemblies would have plenty of opportunities to reverse or change course on divestment.

In the years following the pro-divestment vote, the debate over Israel-Palestine intensified. Groups such as the Israel Palestine Mission Network, Presbyterians for Middle East Peace, the Presbyterian Peace Fellowship, and the National Middle East Caucus (PCUSA) devoted enormous amounts of money and time to influencing the votes of General Assemblies. Individuals who were longtime colleagues on social justice and peacemaking issues became increasingly alienated from one another over this single, unavoidably complex peacemaking issue. Congregations threatened to leave the denomination if the General Assembly voted to support or reject divestment. In a sense, while debating the issue the PCUSA began to mirror the anger and division that is present between many Palestinians and Israelis themselves.

In the fall of 2004, groups began to coalesce around divestment. Presbyterians Concerned for Jewish Christian Relations (PCJCR), which consisted of centrist and progressive Presbyterian leaders who came together to present a collective voice on behalf of Israel and Jewish peoplehood in the mid-1980s, now opposed divestment as a counter-productive peacemaking strategy. The Israel Palestine Mission Network (IPMN) and Presbyterian Peace Fellowship (PPF) became the leaders of support for the divestment decision. Both IPMN and PPF were grass-roots organizations with a significant presence in many Presbyteries. Within a few years, PCJCR ceased to exist, replaced, in large part, by Presbyterians for Middle East Peace (PFMEP), a group of conservative, centrist, and progressive Presbyterian leaders that we helped to form, and served as co-moderators of through 2018.

As the debate over Israel-Palestine unfolded, PFMEP found itself a unique position. The advocates for divestment were almost exclusively members of the PCUSA's progressive wing. They certainly convinced some centrists to vote with them, of course, but the organization was driven by progressive laity and clergy. Those who supported Israel in an almost unquestioning way and thus rejected divestment came almost exclusively from the conservative and evangelical wing. Given the departure of some conservative and evangelical congregations from the PCUSA between 2004 and 2016, it was not surprising that this faction dwindled in influence and never organized into a group like IPMN, PPF or PFMEP.

PFEMP was left as the only member in the debate that represented a theological and political cross-section of the PCUSA. Yet even though the e-blasts PFMEP sent out regularly on the issues were widely read and respected by many in the denomination who were not committed to either a pro- or anti-Israel stance, IPMN and PPF effectively painted PFMEP as an uncritical supporter of Israel.

The fall of 2004 also was a time when PCUSA denominational leaders and leaders of the US Jewish community met in an attempt to repair the breach between two groups that, historically, had a good working relationship. While the meeting was polite, it did not come close to satisfying the Jewish demands that the PCUSA end the process that could lead to divestment. If anything, the meeting simply made clear to all parties that there was going to be a long struggle over the divestment strategy being pushed by IPMN, PPF, and other activists in the PCUSA.

Several days after the joint meeting of Jewish and PCUSA leaders, the *Forward*, a prominent newspaper in the Jewish community, summarized the feelings of most American Jews regarding the PCUSA:

> The gross unfairness of the image; the desperate circumstances of Israel's struggle; the continuing efforts of its citizens, its courts and even its army to accommodate Palestinian needs despite the brutality of the confrontation—none of this appears to matter in the comic-book morality tale that has replaced reasoned discourse in too many circles. The decision last spring by the Presbyterian Church (USA) to divest from companies doing more than $1 million in annual business—however "selectively" it is to be implemented—takes this comic-book morality to a new height. It turns the coarse, abusive rhetoric of Palestinian activists and their allies into a crusade by middle-class Americans and their churches. The church's divestment resolution pays lip service to condemning the inhuman Palestinian practice of suicide bombings targeting Israel's civilian population with mass murder, but it suggests no action against Palestinian leaders or movements that perpetrate or support the murder. Only Israel is seen as culpable. As such, it represents an utter failing of moral vision on the part of a faith community that should hold moral vision aloft as its first duty ("Failure").

By the time the PCUSA gathered for its General Assembly in 2006 in Birmingham, Alabama, Presbyteries across the country had submitted 26 overtures[107] both for and against divestment:

There were 26 overtures (resolutions from presbyteries) presented to the body addressing Middle East issues, particularly involving divestment. Ten were intended to rescind what was done in 2004. Four called for a strategy of positive investment to "promote peace between the Israeli and Palestinian people," as one put it. One called for a Task Force to draft a new statement on the denomination's Middle East policy, affirming the "common Abrahamic heritage" of Muslims, Christians, and Jews. A few supported the 2004 vote (Stockton "Presbyterians").

The committee considering the overtures crafted its own motion that attempted to be a political compromise. It emphasized "engagement" with corporations doing business with Israel in ways some activists found objectionable but downplayed the divestment strategy.

The motion was interpreted by many, including many in the Jewish community, as repudiating the 2004 vote. However, PCUSA Stated Clerk Cliff Kirkpatrick quickly issued a statement denying that interpretation, saying,

"This General Assembly acknowledged that the actions of the 2004 assembly caused hurt and misunderstanding among some Presbyterians and our Jewish neighbors. However, this assembly did not rescind the previous action on divestment. Divestment is still an option, but not the goal. Instead, this assembly broadened the focus to corporate engagement to ensure that the church's financial investments do not support violence of any kind in the region (Stockton "Presbyterians")."

His statement outraged those who had worked to moderate the PCUSA position and empowered and emboldened those committed to the divestment strategy. Perhaps most importantly, it allowed the committee charged with engaging corporations, Mission Responsibility Through Investment (MRTI), to continue on a track that ultimately led to divestment. The staff person for MRTI made it clear to many, including us, that he had no intention of stopping his committee's movement toward divestment.[108] The Assembly also passed a motion offering a formal apology to the Jewish community for the hurt it caused with its 2004 action, which received a great deal of attention in the Jewish community. However, the leadership of the PCUSA appeared to ignore it in the following years.

Following Birmingham, the sense of betrayal by people committed to engagement with but not divestment from corporations was palpable. There was a strong feeling that the staff and committees of the General Assembly were bent on divestment and would interpret any action by the GA as supporting rather than stopping their efforts. In addition to MRTI, the Advisory Committee for Social Witness Policy (ACSWP) and Advisory Committee on Racial-Ethnic Concerns became leaders in promoting the divestment agenda within the PCUSA General Assembly governance structure. In one-on-one conversations we had with numerous key staffers in Louisville, they were quite clear that they favored divestment and were working to implement it as PCUSA policy. The committee staff's ideological bent served to shape the work of the GA committees.[109]

The 2008 General Assembly met in Santa Cruz, California. This Assembly was far less supportive of overtures aimed at criticizing Israel, defeating two such overtures from the Newark and San Francisco Presbyteries without even needing a tallied vote. The Assembly also took what many believed to be a significant action in declaring that the PCUSA should "not over-identify with the realities of the Israelis or Palestinians" when speaking about the Arab-Israeli conflict. This mandate was completely ignored by the GA staff and program committees in the years that followed. They considered it wrongheaded, and in any case received no instruction to obey the action of the 2008 General Assembly.

In what seemed like a fairly innocuous action, the 2008 GA created a special task force charged with developing a "comprehensive study" on Middle Eastern issues, with a special focus on Israel/Palestine, and then reporting back to the 2010 GA with recommendations. The creation of this task force set the stage for further polarization over the next two years.

Following the General Assembly, the membership of the Middle East Study Committee (MESC) was announced. The nine-member committee consisted of one person, former PCUSA Moderator Susan Andrews, who was widely acknowledged as not positioned in either a pro- or anti-divestment stance; one person, Rev. John Wimberly, who was a known opponent of divestment; and seven members who were supportive of divestment. When Rev. Wimberly attended the first meeting and heard the opening comments from the seven members who were supportive of divestment, he resigned from the committee. He said that he did not want to create the impression that the committee was in any way impartial. He felt the seven-person pro-divestment majority had already made up their minds on the issues. He also objected to the itinerary of the committee's trip to the Middle East, saying that it included visits only with anti-Israel/pro-divestment voices. The committee also expressed no interest in meeting with mainstream US Jewish leaders. Wimberly was replaced on the committee by Rev. Byron Schafer, also a known opponent of divestment. At the end of the process, Rev. Schafer was the only person who voted against recommending the committee's report to the General Assembly.

When the MESC's highly partisan report was published prior to the General Assembly in Minneapolis in 2010, there was a large negative reaction. The objections to the committee's report were summarized in a letter to GA Commissioners signed by a large number of prominent PCUSA clergy and contained in a packet sent to GA commissioners (PFMEP "Letter"). They cited the following reasons why commissioners should reject the report:

1. "[I]f Presbyterians are to speak with authority (and are to be trusted) on such matters, it is absolutely crucial that we engage all of the key parties in this discussion." The special committee had chosen not to speak even to organizations like J Street who are critical of some of Israel's policies but oppose divestment.

2. "The imbalance in this report becomes painfully obvious when one considers the space that it allots for various perspectives. It offers a 71-page 'Plea for Justice' that reflects an exclusively pro-Palestinian perspective written by two members of the committee. This is placed next to a 9-page reflection by a rabbi with whom the committee met in Jerusalem." They noted that

the rabbi who wrote the reflection later stated that he did not agree with the committee's recommendations.

3. They noted that the report is notably unbalanced in its critiques of the Israelis and the Palestinians. "[The report] fails to condemn several important and disturbing elements that prevent peace. The report does not specifically call upon Palestinian leaders to condemn violence against Israeli citizens. There is no call to neighboring nations to recognize the legitimate right of Israel to exist as a state and no affirmation of the right of Israeli citizens to defend themselves against aggression and to live in peace without the threat of terrorism."

4. The report contained significant errors in the retelling of the history of the region and theological errors such as naming terrorist acts as "violent resistance" by the Palestinians.

As the 2010 General Assembly approached, the atmosphere in Minneapolis was tense and appeared to be heading toward a bruising, toxic, and highly divisive plenary floor fight that held serious peril for both sides and for the denomination as a whole. While caucuses were meeting in separate rooms, J.C. Austin of Auburn Seminary quietly consulted with leaders of the opposing groups. Shuttling between them, he painstakingly developed a compromise. The MESC's report would be "received," not "adopted," and the parties would continue to meet after the Assembly to search for common ground that would contribute to a peaceful solution. This was crucial to PFEMP, because it meant that nothing in the report could be cemented as PCUSA policy. A floor fight avoided, the outcome was, for a brief time, known as the "Miracle of Minneapolis." After several post-Assembly meetings, however, the hope generated that summer did not come to fruition.

The failure of the MESC report to be accepted "as is" by the General Assembly deepened the polarization within the PCUSA. Increasingly, people opposed to divestment saw signs of implicit or explicit anti-Semitism at work among the advocates of divestment. They pointed to a post on the Facebook page of IPMN in which a caricature of President Obama had him wearing Jewish stars as earrings. The image was both racist and anti-Semitic. After much condemnation, IPMN removed the post from its site. Proponents of divestment increasingly saw the anti-divestment voices in the PCUSA as puppets of the American Jewish community and the Israeli government. Earlier attempts from the 2004-2008 era to bring the two sides together were not repeated.

Opponents of divestment also became convinced that they were no longer battling a group of well-intentioned Presbyterian activists so much as the international, secular Boycott, Divestment, and Sanctions (BDS) movement. The BDS movement was promoted by Palestinians to put pressure on Israel. However, the founder of the BDS movement, Omar Barghouti, made it clear that they were pushing for more than a change in Israel's policies. They sought an end to Israel's existence as a Jewish state, replaced by a secular state with a Palestinian Arab majority.

IPMN and PPF repeatedly cited the works of BDS authors on their websites and brought in speakers from the movement to their annual gatherings. Both groups disavowed BDS's goal of ending Israel's existence as a Jewish state. Yet by the General Assembly in 2016, there were overtures condemning the idea of a Zionist state (a national homeland for the Jewish people), the very reason Israel was created in 1948. Clearly, ending Israel's existence as a Zionist state had become the explicit end goal of some of the PCUSA's anti-divestment forces.

While the focus in 2008-2010 had been on the Middle East Study Committee, the MRTI committee was continuing its work, which would ultimately lead to divestment. MRTI worked in collaboration with several other denominations in a joint, concerted effort to divest from three companies doing business with Israel: Caterpillar, Hewlett-Packard, and Motorola. They brought a recommendation to divest to the 2012 General Assembly in Pittsburgh.

The committee hearings on Israel/Palestine in Pittsburgh were perceived by anti-divestment activists as totally rigged. Pro-divestment speakers were given almost two full days to present their case. Anti-divestment speakers were given one hour for twenty people to make five-minute statements each.[110] Given those disparities, it was not surprising that the committee voted overwhelmingly to recommend that the PCUSA divest.

The debate on the floor of the General Assembly was not skewed in such a one-sided manner. Both the committee chairperson and the compiler of a minority report opposing divestment were given time to speak from the podium. Officers from the Presbyterian Foundation and the PCUSA Board of Pensions both spoke against the idea of divestment. The officer from the Board of Pensions was quite clear that they would not follow the action of the GA since they had a legal fiduciary responsibility to plan-holders to invest in ways that would produce the best return at the least risk.

After comments from the podium, the debate moved to the floor of the GA, where speakers were given equal time. It was a passionate debate. It was also one in which speakers of both sides made eloquent arguments for their position. As reported in the *New York Times*,

> Arthur Shippee, a delegate from southern New England, said: "What divestment will achieve is this: We will add a whisper soon lost in the storm, but we will further the divisions in our church when we have our own serious problems to address, and we will precipitate divisions with the synagogues within our communities whom we work with frequently on a variety of issues. This will be perceived as picking on Israel, and how could it not?" ….
> [S]peaking in favor of divestment and against the pro-investment resolution, Tim Simpson, a delegate from the Presbytery of St. Augustine in Jacksonville, Fla., said: "The Palestinians aren't asking us for a check, sisters and brothers. The Palestinians are asking us for justice. They're asking us for dignity. How can you write a check to a people who don't control their own water?" (Goldstein "Close Vote")

When the vote was taken, divestment was defeated by the narrowest of margins, 323 to 321, with two abstentions. There was an audible gasp when the tally was posted on the large monitor at the front of the convention hall. In place of the divestment motion, the minority report was adopted calling upon the PCUSA to look for ways to invest positively in the Palestinian territories.

No one left Pittsburgh believing this vote would be the last. Within minutes of the tally, the BDS and pro-divestment activists proclaimed that they would return in 2014 with new overtures calling for divestment. Accepting that reality, anti-divestment activists started lobbying to create a more just system of committee hearings in which both sides would be given equal time. Both sides committed to educational efforts in attempts to inform Presbyterians of what they believed to be the true issues in the battle over divestment.

Gathering in Detroit for the 2014 General Assembly, the mood was somber. While the divisive battle over divestment grew more and more bitter, declines in membership and financial instability within the PCUSA had a demoralizing effect. Many commissioners openly expressed a desire for the divestment issue to go away so they could attend to issues that might create membership and mission growth in the denomination. But the determination of the BDS/pro-divestment activists would not go away. The commissioners to Detroit once again faced a recommendation to divest from Caterpillar, Hewlett-Packard, and Motorola.

In Detroit, IPMN and PPF introduced a new tactic in their efforts to pass divestment. They recruited a group of young Jewish women and men from the group Jewish Voice for Peace (JVP). At the GA, the JVP young people represented themselves as voices of a large segment of American Judaism. In fact, JVP is an outlier in the American Jewish community, representing voices who believe that Israel does not need to be a Zionist state. There are certainly groups, such as J Street, who are very critical of Israel's policies vis a vis the Palestinians. But even J Street is totally opposed to divestment and sent speakers to the GA to make their position known. J Street is a classic example of how it is possible to oppose specific Israeli policies yet remain committed to the existence of Israel and justice for the Palestinians.

In the committee hearings, representatives and staff from MRTI continued to claim that the companies were stonewalling them, refusing to respond to their phone calls. They had no response when anti-divestment activists revealed that they had called the main switchboard of each of the companies and been patched through immediately to the relevant company officials, despite never identifying themselves as pro- or anti-divestment. MRTI also had no response to letters from the companies saying they were more than willing to engage in continuing dialogue with the PCUSA about the issues.

The blocks of time allotted to pro- and anti-divestment speakers were once again skewed towards the pro-divestment side. At one point, a committee member even demanded, "Can we please hear from the anti-divestment side on this issue?" The Vice-Moderator responded, "I will give John Wimberly [an anti-divestment leader] two minutes to speak." Wimberly used this brief moment to inform the committee that the Methodist Church had recently refused to divest.

That evening, the Vice-Moderator sent an email to the committee with a blog post claiming that the Methodists had, indeed, divested. When Wimberly informed the Vice-Moderator the next morning that the Methodists had officially responded to that blog post saying that it was false, the Vice Moderator promised him a chance to correct the record before the committee began voting on overtures. She never gave him that chance, a fact she later acknowledged to Wimberly himself.

GA committee hearings are opened each morning with a brief devotional led by a committee member, which usually consists of a spiritual reflection on a piece of Scripture. The morning the committee was to vote on divestment and related issues, the committee's Vice-Moderator chose to lead the devotional. In it, she said that Jesus challenged the Jews and that it was time for the Presbyterians to do the same.

One of the classic anti-Semitic themes in church history is that Jesus attacked "the Jews" of his day. In this misrepresentation, Jesus's Jewish neighbors were portrayed as his antagonists rather than as the recipients of his love. It is a misrepresentation denounced by the PCUSA, as it totally ignores that, first, Jesus himself was Jewish and, second, it contradicts the Church's longstanding teaching that God sent Jesus into the world to minister first to the Jews, with the early church extending that ministry to the Gentiles.

The "devotion" in which the leader attempted to set up modern day Jews as the antagonists of the Church and of justice was perhaps the most openly anti-Semitic moment in the ten-year-long conflict over divestment. What had been lurking in the dark corners of PCUSA suddenly came bursting into the sunlight. It was a terrible thing to see. While many supporters of divestment immediately condemned the portrayal of "the Jews" as antagonists to peace and justice, a troublingly large minority agreed with the assessment.

The "devotion" reflected a tragic reality: since 2004, the PCUSA has developed a well-funded, articulate group of people who see Jews as a problem, an obstacle to justice in the Middle East, rather than as the partner in the struggle for justice that the American Jewish community has in fact always been. Of all the fallout from the divestment battle, the prominence of this group in the PCUSA is the most troubling. The PCUSA will never have healthy, productive working relationships with the American Jewish community until classic tropes of anti-Semitic thinking such as "it is the fault of the Jews" are exorcised from the Church's body.

The motion to divest was significantly amended by the committee to recognize some ugly realities in the PCUSA. It affirmed Israel's right to exist, a right that was increasingly being challenged by BDS activists in the Church. It also explicitly denied that the divestment action was in any way related to the international BDS movement. This sentiment was immediately undermined when BDS activists within and outside of PCUSA immediately proclaimed the vote as a major victory for the BDS movement.

The addition of these two statements no doubt convinced some commissioners that the vote was not anti-Israel. In fact, only four commissioners had to be convinced, because the final vote to divest was 310-303. Unlike the hushed reaction to the vote in Pittsburgh, the vote to divest was greeted with shouts of victory from many of the pro-divestment activists.

Reporting on the vote, the *New York Times* wrote,

Relations between Jews and Presbyterians soured after the Israel/Palestine Mission Network, a Presbyterian advocacy group, issued a study guide this year called *Zionism Unsettled*, which challenged the history and theological underpinnings of the Zionist movement. Jewish leaders denounced it as hateful, racist and willfully ignorant of the role of the Holocaust and violence toward Israel by the Palestinians and Arab countries in explaining the region's history. The assembly passed a measure here in Detroit saying that the study guide does not represent official church policy, but it is available for sale on the church's website (Goldstein "Presbyterians Vote").

Zionism Unsettled was an expensive piece of anti-Israel propaganda paid for and distributed by IPMN. Rabbi Rick Jacobs, head of the Reform movement in American Judaism, wrote,

In choosing one harsh narrative over all others (including over other Palestinian or Christian narratives), this new study guide is ahistorical. It doesn't introduce the totality of the issues; it includes no mention of attacks by Arab states and individuals on Israeli civilians; or the role of Hamas and Hezbollah, who consider the liberal views of the Presbyterian Church as objectionable as they do Israel. The unmistakable premise of this document is that Israel should not exist, that the Jewish people don't deserve a homeland as do other peoples and that a just compromise can't be realized. . . . As the president of America's largest Jewish denomination, I urge the leadership of the Presbyterian Church (USA) to publicly declare whether this report represents the policy and practice of the PCUSA. We ask you to stand with us to advocate for a two-state solution that will bring justice and dignity to both peoples (Jacobs).

Understanding that the extreme positions in *Zionism Unsettled* contradicted the PCUSA's positions on Israel/Palestine, the 2014 GA instructed the denomination to remove the document from all of its websites and not to sell it through the PCUSA book distribution service, without a disclaimer that *Zionism Unsettled* does not represent the views of the PCUSA.

Following the 2014 Assembly, forty of its commissioners wrote a public statement, "Reformed and Reforming," complaining about the unfair practices used in the GA committee hearings on the Israel/Palestine issue. They noted that eighteen hours were given to pro-divestment testimony while less than ten minutes were given to anti-divestment testimony. They stated that the denomination's historic commitment to "fair and open debate of crucial issues" had been set aside to pass the divestment action. They asked future Assemblies to return to the practice of balanced time for opposing opinions. It was a request that fell on deaf ears among the PCUSA's leadership.

Given the demands from the PCUSA's BDS activists, who pushed the denomination to disassociate itself from the two-state peace solution proposed by the international community, a solution that assures the continuation of a Zionist state, the 2014 Assembly sought to assuage the activists by establishing a study team to bring back a report on the two-state solution to the 2016 GA. Clearly, the commissioners had no memory of the problems created by the MESC when it was established by a previous GA. Their action threw gasoline on the fire of division in the PCUSA regarding Israel/Palestine.

As happened with the MESC, most of the team created by Louisville to study the two-state solution came to the task with predetermined opinions. Anti-divestment activists found statements by four of the five team members in which they questioned the wisdom of supporting a two-state solution. Only one person apparently came to the team with an open mind. Therefore, it was no surprise when the team wrote a report calling on the 2016 General Assembly in Portland, Oregon to terminate the PCUSA's historic support of a two-state solution (Fig. 8).

Fig. 8—2016 Portland, PCUSA GA, Presbyterians for Middle East Peace booth. Photo: Michael Gizzi

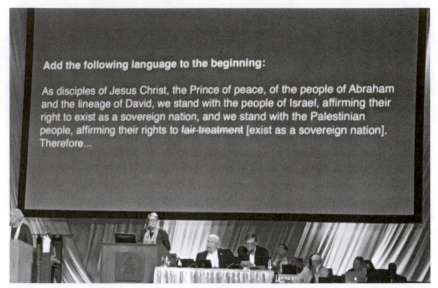

Fig. 9—The PCUSA GA debates the amended text for its 2016 report.
Photo: Michael Gizzi

When the report was debated on the floor of the 2016 General
Assembly, it was turned on its head by an amendment offered by a commissioner (PCUSA "General Assembly") (Fig. 9):

> As disciples of Jesus Christ, the Prince of peace, of the people of
> Abraham and the lineage of David, we stand with the people of
> Israel, affirming their right to exist as a sovereign nation, and we
> stand with the Palestinian people, affirming their rights to exist
> as a sovereign nation. Therefore, the 222nd General Assembly
> (2016) affirms Footnote 8, which emphasizes a preference for a
> two-state solution. The assembly also affirms our desire to stay in
> conversation with our partners in Israel who work for peace. Finally,
> the assembly expresses its opposition to any efforts to deny or
> undermine the rights of the Palestinian people or the Jewish people
> to self-determination.

In one amendment, the bulk of the team's report was neutered.
Instead of calling the two-state solution into question, the two-state
solution and Israel's right to exist as a Jewish state were affirmed. In addition, an effort to join the BDS movement's boycott of Hewlett-Packard

was rejected. In another subtle but important action, the GA Middle East Committee and the Assembly itself approved an amendment to one overture mandating that all resources coming from the denomination include anti-BDS as well as pro-BDS material and that local interfaith partners be engaged in any study process.

The actions of the 2016 General Assembly were widely viewed as a defeat for IPMN's and PPF's desire to align the PCUSA with the BDS movement's efforts to eliminate Israel as a Jewish state. However, the animus toward Israel that surfaced in 2004 clearly persisted. As commissioners left the 2016 GA, it was anticipated that more anti-Israel overtures would be considered by the 2018 General Assembly in St. Louis.

The 2018 General Assembly had a different tone and level of intensity from its predecessors in the twenty-first century. The reduced intensity was reflected in the very small number of observers watching the Middle East Committee do its work (Fig. 10). The different tone was apparent in a much more analytical approach to overtures from the Committee's members. The commissioners were not inclined to accept the work of pro-Palestinian activists in a knee-jerk manner.

Nowhere was the changed atmosphere more obvious than with the committee's rejection of the outrageous proposals from the National Coalition of Churches in Palestine. The group was a nondescript collection of anti-Israel activists who wrote a document with all the usual attacks on Israel with accompanying distortions or falsehoods regarding the facts on the ground. The Committee removed the offensive language and accepted the letter from the coalition without approving it as the overture requested.

The Committee similarly gutted an offensive overture that asked Presbyterians to have dialogues with American Jews only if far left-wing Jewish groups such as Jewish Voice for Peace were included. Since the majority of American Jews strongly reject these groups and won't participate in dialogues with them, the Committee recognized the overture for what it was: an attempt to end dialogues with the American Jewish community. The vote was 2-1 to remove the overture's offensive language and assumptions. A call to end United States aid to Israel was also easily defeated. While the committee voted to condemn ReMax for real estate transactions in the West Bank, PFME chose not to challenge it as it was largely symbolic. Ultimately this proved true; it took a year for the denomination just to send a letter to ReMax.

The Committee approved a resolution urging congregations and denominational agencies to support programs in Israel/Palestine that promote reconciliation between Israelis and Palestinians. Examples of such groups given to commissioners included one that helps bring Palestinian children to Israeli hospitals, as well as several schools with student bodies made up of both Palestinian and Israeli children. While the overture was approved, General Assembly staff are likely to ignore it. Numerous congregations, however, are looking at ways to do the work the overture recommends.

Fig. 10—PCUSA General Assembly St. Louis, 2018. Committee on Middle East Issues. Photo: Michael Gizzi

Committee members refused to hold Palestinian radicals account-able for child abuse when they defeated an overture that condemned the use of children as suicide bombers and human shields. The Committee also authorized yet another study group to bring a report to the 2020 General Assembly. It should be noted, however, that it is a limited study and there are questions as to whether it can be funded. The plenary session of the General Assembly approved all the actions of the Committee in a matter of minutes with consensus voice votes.

Why was this Assembly more moderate in its approach to Israel/ Palestine? First, the Assembly's primary issue was internal reorganization of the denomination. Second, it felt as though the anti-Israel forces had exhausted the denomination with their intense, relentless onslaught of attacks. With their conservative approach, the commissioners at the 2018 General Assembly seemed to be saying, "Enough already!"

The 2020 General Assembly was turned into a virtual meeting as a result of the COVID pandemic, and reduced to two weekends, in which social justice issues were removed from the docket. That said, the sense of fatigue with Israel-Palestine issues encountered in 2018 seemed to be proven true for 2020 as well, as there were only three overtures proposed on Israel-Palestine issues. The original General Assembly plan did not include a "Middle East Issues" committee in its structure for the first time in more than a decade. This did not prevent some anti-Israel activists from seeking to amend the agenda to include social justice issues, but they were voted down, and the only social justice issues the 2020 GA considered dealt with racism in light of the death of George Floyd at police hands. In the end, the 2020 GA was the first one with no action on Israel in decades.

CONCLUSION

What started in 2004 as a disagreement in tactics as to how best to achieve a long-lasting peace between Israelis and Palestinians continues today in the PCUSA as a much more intense struggle—to protect the existence of Israel as a Jewish state while creating a stable, independent state for the Palestinians. The issue is no longer divestment; it is the very existence of Israel as a Jewish state. Thankfully, the vote in Portland affirmed, by a near-consensus, the right of Israel and Palestine to exist as neighboring Jewish and Palestinian states. However, it would be naïve in the extreme to think that the activists who oppose Israel's existence as a Jewish state will not return to future General Assemblies with overtures opposing Israel's existence.

Indeed, naivete has been a crucial factor in perpetuating this divisive fight in the PCUSA. Commissioners in Richmond were naïve in 2004 when they thought that MRTI would simply engage corporations rather than seek to divest from them. There was plenty of information available to show that the ultimate goal was divestment, not engagement. Commissioners in Detroit were likewise naïve when they voted for divestment and thought that attaching a statement denying complicity with the BDS movement would clarify their intent. Did they fail to notice that the convention hall was filled with BDS activists applauding their vote?

The Middle East is not a place for naïve peacemakers. To be peacemakers in such a complex, complicated milieu, the PCUSA will have to apply Niebuhrian sophistication. As a young pastor, Reinhold Niebuhr tended to see the world through a right-or-wrong lens. Things were either good or evil. As he aged, he became an advocate for what has come to be called Christian realism. Christian realism seeks to apply the unchanging values of God's Word to the always-changing realities of the world. As a Christian realist, Niebuhr understood that there are few perfect solutions to life's most difficult ethical and moral issues and certainly none to a thorny issue like the Israel/Palestine conflict. Beginning in 1942, the ethicist became an advocate for the creation of a Zionist state in Palestine as the only practical way to create a safe place in the world for Jews. While he surely would condemn some of the egregious violations of human rights by both the Israeli and Palestinian governments today, it seems fairly safe to conclude that he would support the two-state solution in a less-than-perfect world where compromises are necessary. He would also be a vocal critic of the human rights abuses that sometimes redound from the policies of Israel and Palestine.

In the dispute between Jesus and Judas, a political zealot (John 12), Judas was deeply offended when Jesus chose to use an expensive oil on himself rather than sell it and use the funds to help the poor. Rejecting Judas's either/or approach to reality, Jesus claimed that there is a place for both aid to the poor and religious objects such as holy oil. Is it unreasonable to ask the PCUSA to engage in similar both/and thinking? Is not the two-state solution the ultimate both/and solution to the conflict? Both nations would achieve independence, foreign troops and terrorists would stop endangering ordinary citizens, and children could grow up filled with dreams of a wonderful life rather than a desire for vengeance.

Ironically but not unwittingly, with its actions, the PCUSA has empowered extremists, not peacemakers, on both sides of the security barrier—extremist Palestinians who want to eliminate Israel as a Jewish state and extremist Israelis who don't want the Palestinians to have a state at all. Our actions have encouraged those who reject the two-state solution in favor of a single, Palestinian-dominated state that their efforts to isolate Israel are working. Rather than negotiate with the Israelis, they hope international pressure will get them what they want. Yet PCUSA actions have also encouraged the Israeli far right to argue: the world is hostile to Israel, so why listen to the world? The world will criticize us no matter what, they insist, so let's continue to build settlements.

It is our prayer that wiser, more sophisticated and nuanced thinking on issues related to peacemaking and justice will emerge in the PCUSA in the years ahead.

CHAPTER TWELVE

MICHAEL C. GIZZI

ZIONISM UNSETTLED AND THE 2014 PCUSA BATTLES OVER DIVESTMENT

The decade-long battles over divestment in the Presbyterian Church USA were elevated to a new level in January 2014, when the Church's Israel/Palestine Mission Network (IPMN) issued its "congregational study guide," *Zionism Unsettled*. The seventy-four-page glossy booklet was intended to help Presbyterians discern the best path for peacemaking in the Israeli-Palestinian conflict. I was slated as a ruling elder commissioner to the upcoming General Assembly (GA) in Detroit that summer, but I did not anticipate how this book would impact my experience in Detroit and my ultimate role in how things played out. I had been elected by my presbytery, a group of 100 churches in

Central and Western Illinois, to be one of six representatives to the GA. I was very excited, for I assumed that the biggest thing we would do that summer was to vote to permit same-sex marriage in the Church. I was wrong. We did indeed approve same sex marriage, but the Israeli-Palestinian conflict played a much more dominant role than anyone expected.

Zionism Unsettled was issued by the IPMN, an advocacy group chartered by the GA, with the mission of promoting PCUSA's efforts at peacemaking in the Israeli-Palestinian conflict. However, in reality, the organization is solely focused on "justice for Palestinians" and is largely a front for the global Boycott, Divestment, and Sanctions (BDS) movement. As a commissioner to the GA, I knew I would have to grapple with divestment, and coming from Central Illinois, where the Caterpillar corporation (one of the three businesses targeted by BDS) is headquartered, I knew that the issue was highly contentious. Divestment was viewed by many in the presbytery as an attack on the very livelihoods of many of our members. Yet I was determined to look at the issues with an open mind and make a decision based on my read of the facts. I bought a copy of this new study guide online and sat down to read it.

It did not take ten minutes for me to realize that Zionism Unsettled was not a study guide but a one-sided piece of propaganda. It makes Israel out to be a racist state, using terms like apartheid, and demonizes the existence of Israel as a Jewish state. As a political scientist, I saw it for exactly what it was: a political polemic. Though I had not studied the Israeli-Palestinian conflict in great depth, the presentation of arguments in *Zionism Unsettled* was as one-sided and biased as anything I had seen. It was only later that I learned that the book wasn't even written by Presbyterians. Instead it was drawn from a forthcoming book authored by BDS advocates, *Zionism and the Quest for Justice in the Holy Land*, edited by Donald E. Wagner and Walter T. Davis (See Cary Nelson's critique of *Zionism Unsettled*). While I was aware of the BDS movement, it was not something I focused much on. *Zionism Unsettled* would change that irrevocably.

It is possible that I would have never purchased a copy of *Zionism Unsettled* had several things not happened during the prior eight months. In the spring of 2013, I met a local rabbi. The following winter, she offered to teach a four-week class called "A taste of Judaism" at the Presbyterian church I was attending. The class was not only educational, it extremely well-received, and made me excited about the possibility for interfaith dialogue. We had done a comparative religion class before, and I knew that our members were very much open to the possibilities of strengthening interfaith partnerships.

At about the same time that the rabbi's class ended, I learned about the controversy brewing over *Zionism Unsettled*, and decided to get a copy. I had also come across the open letter to the Church written by the Rev. Dr. Christopher Leighton, executive director of the Institute for Islamic, Jewish, and Christian Studies. Leighton published his letter in February 2014, in which he argued that *Zionism Unsettled* was the result of the IPMN's adoption of extremely polarizing tactics in its zeal to obtain support for divestment (Leighton "Open Letter). Leighton wrote that IPMN adopted an agenda that "threatens to polarize our community, betray relationships with our Jewish colleagues, and ultimately undermine our credibility as 'peacemakers.'" The publication of *Zionism Unsettled* could turn Presbyterians "from peacemakers to polemicists, and from honest dialogue partners to partisan ideologues." The letter further points out that the problem with *Zionism Unsettled* was that it takes a complex issue and applies a flawed theology to argue that the entire conflict is the fault of Zionism. Readers of *Zionism Unsettled* are told that Zionism is a doctrine that "promotes death rather than life" and leads to ethnic cleansing and "cultural genocide." In so doing, *Zionism Unsettled* revives the old claim that "Zionism is racism." According to Leighton, by "resuscitat[ing] this vicious platform," it reflects little beyond anti-Semitism.

Leighton's letter identifies both the historical and factual flaws in *Zionism Unsettled* and takes the IPMN to task for failing to realize that peacemaking "requires a venue in which hard questions can be asked, sharp disagreements explored, and shared commitments forged." "Lamentably," he explains, "this congregational study guide makes such honest engagement impossible." Moreover, *Zionism Unsettled* undermines "the grounds for honest interreligious dialogue." It does not create an opportunity for Presbyterians to explore hard questions, but instead "thrives on conspiracy and suspicion, incriminations, and a spirit of despair," and therefore "encourages congregations to retreat into their separate silos and to launch attacks on those who need to be welcomed to the table."

The IPMN never formally responded to Leighton's letter; instead, they had their ally, Rabbi Brant Rosen of Jewish Voice for Peace, write his own response. He had initially posted a blog calling it a "smart and gutsy" new church study guide. After Leighton's letter, Rosen published his own open letter in response (Rosen "Reconsidering"). Rosen challenged the characterization of Judaism's relationship with Zionism and argued that the movement to create a modern Jewish state departed from hundreds of years of rabbinical teaching. Rosen tried to downplay *Zionism Unsettled* by disputing that it ever makes the claim that the Jews' desire to return to their homeland is theologically and morally abhorrent, but instead claims that it makes the "correct distinction between a centuries-old religious tradition that spiritualized the notion of return . . . [and the] politicization of this idea by a modern nationalist movement." Rosen challenged Leighton's claims that *Zionism Unsettled* smacked of anti-Semitism, countering that anti-Zionism is not anti-Semitism. To his credit, Rosen then published a response by Leighton, which led to a meaningful debate, although that debate was more about Judaism and Zionism than *Zionism Unsettled* itself (Leighton "Guest").

There were other responses to *Zionism Unsettled*, including a statement by Rev. Dr. Catherine Henderson, president of Auburn Theological Seminary. Henderson took a similar approach to Leighton, pointing out that the "premise of the document appears to be that Zionism is the cause of the entire conflict in the Middle East and the root of all its problems. For its authors, Zionism functions as the original sin, from which flows all the suffering of the Palestinian people." In doing so, Zionism Unsettled

> [U]ndermines the legitimacy of the state of Israel and contradict policies of the Presbyterian Church (U.S.A.) over several decades. Our denomination has consistently supported the needs and aspirations of both Israelis and Palestinians; it has advocated for justice, security, and reconciliation for all, while acknowledging the complexity of the problem and the difficulty in reaching a just and lasting peace.

The Chicago Presbytery's Ecumenical and Interreligious Work Group also issued a statement on *Zionism Unsettled* focusing on three main issues (EWIG). First, they criticized IPMN's choice to argue its case outside the "bounds of the historic principles as laid down by the General Assembly over the years, equally affirming the creation and security of the State of Israel and the peoples within her, and the validity and necessity of a Palestinian state, sovereign and sustainable within negotiated and safe borders," particularly problematic as the IPMN made it appear as if it represented the policy of PCUSA. Second, *Zionism Unsettled* distorted Zionism, and "lifted up the stereotypical image of the Zionist" in a way that embodied "humanity's worst traits and motives, exhibiting long term machinations of destruction." Finally, they pointed out that, while there is nothing necessarily anti-Judaic in offering criticisms of Israeli policy, "it is unfortunate that the document is riddled with statements and allusions to Jewish people that fall under that rubric."

Criticism of *Zionism Unsettled* was certainly not limited to voices within the Presbyterian Church. American Jews were also deeply concerned. Perhaps most important amongst several statements of dissent was the op-ed published by Rabbi Rick Jacobs, president of the Union of Reformed Judaism, the largest denomination of American Jews, in the *Washington Post*. Rabbi Jacobs pointed out that *Zionism Unsettled* undermines the goals of many Christians and Jews for a two-state solution. He explains,

IPMN makes its case clearly: Zionism is at the heart of the problem, destroying both native Palestinian lives and thriving Jewish communities around the world in a supremacist misinterpretation of God's word, on par with "Christian exceptionalist beliefs that contributed to the Nazi Holocaust, the genocide of Native Americans, and countless other instances of tragic brutality." The document is profoundly disturbing for its distortion of history and theology. (Jacobs)

Jacobs also contrasted the tenor of *Zionism Unsettled* with the Jewish focus on tikkun olam ("repairing the world"). *Zionism Unsettled* emphasizes only one narrative in a way that is ahistorical. It thus ignores the totality of all the issues at play, and "makes no mention of attacks by

Arab states and individuals on Israeli civilians; or the role of Hamas and Hezbollah, who consider the liberal views of the Presbyterian Church as objectionable as they do Israel." More importantly, Jacobs argues, "the unmistakable premise of this document is that Israel should not exist, that the Jewish people don't deserve a homeland as do other peoples and that a just compromise can't be realized."

Rabbi Jacobs called on leaders of the Presbyterian Church to disassociate themselves from the policy and practice of the BDS movement represented by *Zionism Unsettled*. He alluded to the anti-Semitic elements of *Zionism Unsettled* and ended with the statement that "It was Protestant theologian Karl Barth who said, 'A church that becomes anti-Semitic or even a-Semitic sooner or later suffers the loss of its faith by losing the object of it.' For the love of God, we must do better." Rabbi Jacobs letter accurately reflected the views of the vast majority of American Jews.

TAKING ACTION

After reading *Zionism Unsettled* and the criticisms of it, I began to think about how I might raise these issues at the upcoming General Assembly. As I reflect upon my initial reaction four years later, I think I was most disturbed by the fact that the document was published under the name of a PCUSA-sanctioned mission network and was for sale on the Church's official website. It seemed to me that it was speaking, or claiming to speak, for the Church as an institution. The IPMN refutes that, declaring that it is just a study guide. To any observer, however, the reality is clear: the very use of the words Presbyterian Church USA on its cover page results in the document appearing to represent the Church. This same criticism had been levelled by both Chris Leighton and by the Chicago Interfaith group. Yet the document did not and does not have the approval of the General Assembly, the body that establishes policy for the denomination.

Had *Zionism Unsettled* been published three months earlier, I would have sought an overture in my presbytery to call for its removal, and for the General Assembly to state that *Zionism Unsettled* does not speak for the Church. But the deadlines for overtures to the 2014 General Assembly had passed, and my only option was to write what is called a "commissioner's resolution," which is the privilege of any commissioner to the General Assembly. Such a resolution would have to be co-signed by a commissioner from a different geographic region or presbytery and to satisfy several procedural thresholds to come before the assembly as business.

I reached out to a few friends and was put in contact with leaders from a group in the Church named Presbyterians for Middle East Peace (PFMEP). This group had developed in response to the IPMN's ongoing efforts to promote BDS and divestment in Church policies regarding Israel and Palestine (See John Wimberly and William Harter's essay).

Fig. 11—Rev. John Wimberly, Rev. Bill Harter, and Elder Gary Green (seated) at the PFMEP booth at the 2012 GA.

Fig. 12—A portion of the PFMEP booth at the 2014 GA. Photo: Mark Boyd.

I wrote an initial resolution, and colleagues from PFMEP helped me identify other commissioners from across the country who might be interested in co-signing the resolution. The resolution called for the General Assembly to declare that *Zionism Unsettled* does not represent the views of the Church, to direct the staff of the Presbyterian Mission Agency to stop distributing it, and to remove it from the Church's online store. Ultimately, five other commissioners from four presbyteries signed the resolution. The resolution was submitted during the first day of the 2014 General Assembly and was ultimately referred to the Committee on Middle East Issues, which was slated to consider it near the end of its business.

When the committee considered the resolution, I was given three minutes to make my arguments for it. I explained my rationale for the resolution, pointing out my background as the coordinator for adult Christian education at First Presbyterian Church in Normal, Illinois, and my professional background as a university professor. I then made my case:

> *Zionism Unsettled* is marketed as a congregational study guide on the Israeli-Palestinian conflict issued by the IPMN. A study guide should examine multiple sides of issues; provide a fair and balanced approach, asking people to think, discern, and pray about issues in

a meaningful way. After reading *Zionism Unsettled*, it became very clear that it is not a study guide, but rather a one-sided piece of political propaganda—a polemic—that demonizes Israel, describes it as being "towards a single Jewish, apartheid state." It presents a one-sided view of the conflict, distorts issues rather than educates. I was horrified by what I read in its tone and content.

To the outside world, to the press, to anyone who reads this, *Zionism Unsettled* appears to speak for the Presbyterian Church (USA). It does not matter if there is a FAQ on the website saying it does not speak for the Church. Symbolism is compelling, and this document is more than symbolic. It is being sold and distributed by the church. And to our Jewish neighbors, across America, it is an attack on not only the political state of Israel, but an attack on them, which threatens to polarize our community, betray our relationships, and undermines our role as peacemakers.

As a political scientist, I understand political propaganda. I understand why it is used. As a Christian educator, I know that a study guide should provide participants the opportunity to consider multiple viewpoints. *Zionism Unsettled* does not do that. As Christians we are to seek justice. My heart breaks over the suffering of our Palestinian brothers and sisters, but this document is destructive, and not only goes against stated General Assembly policy for a two-state solution, but damages legitimate efforts at peacemaking.

I concluded my presentation by arguing that approval of my resolution would go a long way towards eliminating further animus with our Jewish friends, and then pointed out that while the IPMN is a mission network, it does not speak for the Church as a whole, nor for the General Assembly.

There was surprisingly little opposition, although concerns were voiced that directing the Presbyterian Mission Agency to cease distribution of *Zionism Unsettled* would be censoring the freedom of expression of the IPMN. I had realized that that was a possible reaction, although my intent was not to censor IPMN, but to do whatever was necessary to distance the denomination from *Zionism Unsettled*. I remained convinced that the mere association of IPMN as a mission network of the PCUSA was enough to taint the denomination. An amendment was

Fig. 13—Mike Gizzi (standing) speaking (behind # 6) at the 2016 GA. Photo: Julie Gizzi

Fig. 14—At the 2014 PCUSA GA meeting prior to voting. Photo: Michael Gizzi.

proposed by a commissioner to delete the language on distribution, and to replace it with language that "directs all Presbyterian Church (USA) entities to express this statement in all future catalogs, print or online resources." It was a true compromise. IPMN could distribute it, but with an admonition akin to the Surgeon General's warning on a pack of cigarettes. The resolution passed the committee by a vote of 54-8, which slated it for the General Assembly's consent agenda, assuming no commissioner motioned to remove it for full consideration.

The declaration that *Zionism Unsettled* does not represent the views of the Presbyterian Church (USA) was approved on the consent agenda the next day (Fig. 14). In some ways the decision of IPMN and its allies not to pull it from the consent agenda was telling. It was obvious that the anti-Israel faction in the Church realized that they had probably gone too far with *Zionism Unsettled* and did not want to have a full plenary debate over it in front of a few thousand people. If the commissioner's resolution was given plenary debate time, it could have damaged the real goal of the IPMN, getting the denomination to vote to divest Church pension funds from the three corporations that had been targeted by the Mission Responsibility through Investment Committee. In fact, that might have actually proven beneficial to their cause, as the commissioner's resolution would have come up on the floor after the divestment vote, and perhaps could have been used as a way to mute the criticism that would come afterwards.

Indeed, within forty-five minutes of the General Assembly vote to divest, the *New York Times* reported that "Presbyterians Vote to Divest Holdings to Pressure Israel." The article began by stating that "The vote, by a count of 310 to 303, was watched closely in Washington and Jerusalem and by Palestinians as a sign of momentum for a movement to pressure Israel to stop building settlements in the West Bank and East Jerusalem and to end the occupation, with a campaign known as BDS, for Boycott, Divestment and Sanctions." The article discussed how American Jewish organizations tried to get the Church to defeat the divestment vote, referencing the open letter signed by more than 1,700 rabbis. It also discussed how relations had soured between Jews and Presbyterians after the IPMN issued *Zionism Unsettled*, which was viewed as "hateful, racist, and willfully ignorant of the role of the

Holocaust and violence toward Israel by the Palestinians and Arab countries in explaining the region's history."

The *Times* acknowledged that the General Assembly passed the resolution declaring that *Zionism Unsettled* did not represent official church policy, but also pointed out that it was available for sale on the Church's website (Fig. 15). The failure to call a halt to distribution under the imprimatur of the Church, as my initial resolution would have done, in effect exposed the hypocrisy of the Church's approach to Israel. Although the resolution went to great lengths to try to claim that the decision in no way implied that the Church was joining the BDS Movement, it only took forty-five minutes for the largest newspaper in the United States to make that connection. The General Assembly declared its support for a two-state solution and re-affirmed Israel's right to exist, yet the Church's own website featured a book that made the exact opposite claims and suggested that Zionism was a flawed theology and the cause of all oppression (Goodstein "Presbyterians Vote").

Fig. 15—The PCUSA meets in 2014. Photo: Michael Gizzi

The controversy reached a new level two days later, when newly-elected Presbyterian moderator Heath Rada was interviewed by CNN (CNN "Church Divests"). Rada was asked pointed questions about both the wisdom of the divestment vote and *Zionism Unsettled*. The moderator appeared flummoxed and completely unprepared to deal with the issues. He sought to deflect criticism of the Church by claiming that PCUSA was not against the Jewish people, but instead against elements of the Israeli government. CNN's Victor Blackwell and Lynda Kinkade took him to task about *Zionism Unsettled*, "which uses phrases like ethnic cleansing, apartheid, and cloaking secularism with messianism. It seems as if the rhetoric doesn't speak to your love of your Jewish brothers and sisters." Rada tried to counter that the Church has distanced itself by saying "we do not support the statements that were in *Zionism Unsettled*," but he was then challenged by the CNN pundits pointing out that it is still for sale on the Church website: "You either sell it or you don't." Rada fumbled around, trying to explain that it takes time to get things off the website, and implying that there are things offered by the Church's publishing company that do not represent the Church's policy. In many ways, the interview illustrated the core problem. *Zionism Unsettled* was no longer the policy of the church, but it was being sold by the Church, and it was published by an official mission network of the church.

Seven days later, the Presbyterian Church's Mission Agency issued a press release by the Church's Stated Clerk, Rev. Gradye Parsons, stating that effective immediately, *Zionism Unsettled* would no longer be sold on the Church's website. The news release repeated the language of the commissioner's resolution, but then went on to state that "The Israel-Palestine Mission Network, which produced the booklet, may continue to sell and distribute it through other channels." In light of the criticism, Parsons said, "We need to keep our focus on supporting and communicating the decisions of the General Assembly. And responding to a recent increase in feedback about the book is impacting our ability to do that."

In the months that followed, it became clear that the Israel Palestine Mission Network had little desire to advertise that its publication did not represent the views of the Church. It continues, to this very day, to sell the book on its website, and its description makes no reference to the General Assembly's statement. It is only if you click on the "BUY NOW" link that it will bring you to a page that includes the disclaimer at the very bottom. Even here, it is buried in a longer statement about the purpose and role of IPMN:

> IPMN was created by the 2004 General Assembly of the Presbyterian Church (USA) to advocate for Palestinian rights. Our mandate calls us to engage, consolidate, nourish, and channel the energy in the Presbyterian Church (USA) toward the goal of a just peace in Israel/Palestine by facilitating education, promoting partnerships, and coordinating advocacy. We to speak TO the church, not FOR the church. *Zionism Unsettled* does not represent the views of the Presbyterian Church (USA). ("Buy")

When I first saw this, I went so far as to contact the moderator of the IPMN. The response I received was curt and argued that the Presbyterian Mission Agency says this satisfies the will of the General Assembly. It was obvious that they did not intend to actually comply with the General Assembly. In 2015, the IPMN made *Zionism Unsettled* available for sale, in print and as a Kindle e-book on Amazon. Nowhere in the book's description does it include the statement that it does not represent the views of the Presbyterian Church (USA). Indeed, I actually wrote a review of the book, which included the statement required by the GA.

In the months that followed the 2014 GA vote, Presbyterians devoted to peace and opposed to divestment mobilized to make their views more visible nationally. Over one hundred signed a full-page November *New York Times* ad headed "Presbyterians: We can do better than divestment."

Presbyterians: We can do better than divestment

We, the undersigned leaders of the Presbyterian Church (U.S.A.), are deeply committed to a just and lasting peace between the Palestinian and Israeli peoples. We have watched the events of the past few months with great dismay: the murder of Israeli and Palestinian teenagers; the trauma of increasing rocket attacks by Hamas on Israeli civilians; the extensive suffering and death of Palestinians from Israel's military response; the discovery of tunnels for major terrorist attacks on Israeli civilians; and the unabated expansion of settlements. More broadly, the rise of ISIS, the persecution of Middle Eastern Christians, and a wave of anti-Semitism and Islamophobia in Europe and North America all point to the same conclusion: that the extreme elements of this conflict are gaining strength and influence.

■ To reaffirm boldly the church's commitment to a two-state solution with Israel and Palestine living side by side in peace, each with secure borders, territorial integrity, and a fair share of natural resources. We also restate our profound condemnation of the threats to a two-state solution, including: violence and terrorism, the Israeli settlements, and any denial of the legitimate aspirations of either party — including their rights to a viable and secure homeland.

■ To seek out opportunities in Palestine, Israel, and between Israelis and Palestinians for proactive investment in economic, educational, and interfaith ventures that promote understanding across ethnic and religious divides and that offer the tangible signs of a future where both Israelis and Palestinians may dwell in justice, security, and peace.

Fig. 16—2014 *New York Times* ad.

Meanwhile, those committed to the well-being of all are tempted to join in the polarization or to sink into silence and despair.

Last June, the General Assembly of our church voted very narrowly to approve the divestment of stock in three companies deemed as complicit in the occupation of the Palestinian territories. We are among the many Presbyterians all over the country who have worked against this action, believing that divestment would strengthen the extreme positions on both sides of this conflict — and further divide and discourage the vast center of the Presbyterian Church (U.S.A.) that longs for justice with love for both peoples. We continue to dissent strongly from this divestment action, and many of the Presbyterians who fill our pews on Sunday mornings share this conviction.

Yet we are more convinced than ever that those who are concerned for justice and peace in the region must reject polarization, silence, despair, or inaction — starting with ourselves. Only by working together — Muslims, Jews, and Christians; Americans, Palestinians, and Israelis — can we hope to find the true path to a just and lasting peace for both peoples. To this end, we invite Presbyterians and all people of faith and moral conviction to join with us as we commit ourselves to the following aspirations and goals:

- To reclaim the church's role as "repairer of the breach," nationally and locally, among ourselves and between Christians, Jews, and Muslims through deep and relational work that models peace and reconciliation with justice and compassion.

Most of all, we pledge ourselves anew to work with Israelis and Palestinians, with American Jews and American Palestinian Christians and Muslims, to affirm the aspirations and address the deep needs of both peoples, and to work toward the day when "they shall all sit under their own vines and under their own fig trees, and no one shall make them afraid" (Micah 4:4).

Supported by:

The Rev. Joanna M. Adams • The Rev. Dr. Paul Alcorn • The Rev. Dr. Frank Allen • The Rev. Dr. Fred R. Anderson • John L. Anderson • The Rev. Dr. Susan R. Andrews • Dr. Jon Bruce Armstrong • The Rev. J.C. Austin • The Rev. Dr. Jack W. Baca • The Rev. Dr. Anita Bell • Alison Bennett • The Rev. Dr. Earl Bland • The Rev. Mark Boyd • The Rev. Jeffrey G. Bridgeman • The Rev. Blake Brinegar • The Rev. Henry G. Brinton • The Rev. Dr. John Buchanan • The Rev. Dr. Jon Burnham • The Rev. Dr. Michael P. Burns • The Rev. Currie Burris • The Rev. Albert G. Butzer, II • Barry Byrd • The Rev. Dr. Cynthia Campbell • The Rev. Dr. Robert Andrew Cathey • Stewart Clifford • The Rev. Dr. Joseph J. Clifford • The Rev. Mike Cole • Albert Da Costa • The Rev. Dr. William P. Crawford • James Dale • Gary Davis • The Rev. Helen P. DeLeon • Ian C. Devine • Linda L. Donald • Brant J. Eelman • Shelby Etheridge • The Rev. Andrew Connors Foster • The Rev. Dr. Bryan James Franzen • John E. Gaffney, Jr • Chaplain Stin Gardner • Michael Gizzi • Mike Goodrich • The Rev. David Gray • The Rev. Dr. William H. Harter • The Rev. Dr. Stephen A. Haynar • The Rev. Larry R. Hayward • Jan Henderson • The Rev. Dr. Katharine Rhodes Henderson • Madge Huber Henning • The Rev. Dr. Mark Hostetter • The Rev. Jim Houston-Hencken • The Rev. Roy W. Howard • The Rev. Dr. Doug Hucke • Harriet Hughes • Edward W. Hummers, Jr. • The Rev. Dr. Edwin G. Hurley • The Rev. Cynthia A. Jarvis • Joan Johnson • The Rev. Dr. Scott Black Johnston • The Rev. David F. Jones • Donald G. Kilpatrick • The Rev. Craig S. King, Sr. • The Rev. Dr. Christopher M. Leighton • The Rev. Michael L. Lindvall • Jim Losey • The Rev. Dr. Arnold B. Lovell • Ms. Emily S. Lovell • The Rev. Dr. Kenneth J. Mucari • The Rev. Dr. W. Eugene March • The Rev. Dr. Lynn Gant March • Sheila Marshall • Kent McKarry • The Rev. Dr. Dave McKechnie • The Rev. Dr. Blair R. Monie • Lauzey Hartwell Murphy • The Rev. Dr. Nancy E. Muth • Barbara Nance • David Nation • The Rev. Dr. Paul Nazarian • Kathi Neubert • R. Gustav Niebuhr • The Rev. Dr. Agnes W. Norfleet • Margaret M. Obrecht • The Rev. Dr. Stephee Oglesbee • Sam Palmer • The Rev. Dr. Brian R. Paulson • The Rev. Geoffrey Pfaff • R. Mark Plumb, CRE • The Rev. Mark Plunkett • The Rev. Dean Pogue • Joe Pruehsr • Carol Pye • The Rev. Charles Pye • Rachael Rankin • The Rev. Dr. Fritz Ritsch • The Rev. Mary Rodgers • Kurt Roelofts • Garry Schoonover, RE • The Rev. Dr. Frederick N. Seay • Jim L. Shilts • The Rev. Dr. Joseph D. Small • The Rev. Jeff Smith • Anne M. Soona • The Rev. Dr. N. Graham Standish, MSW • The Rev. Todd Stavrakos • Cliff Stewart • Sylvia Washick Studenmund • Russell C. Sullivan, Jr. • Dian Duke Thomasson • The Rev. Clinton Tolbert • Joanne Walls • Jim Wallis • The Rev. Dr. Jon M. Walton • The Rev. Randolph Weber • The Rev. John Wimberly • The Rev. Dr. George B. Wirth • The Rev. Timothy R. Woodruff • The Rev. Perry Wootten • The Rev. Dr. Thomas Yorty • Elder William G. Young

Presbyterians for a Just and Peaceful Future in the Middle East | presbyterianjustpeaceful@gmail.com

Fig. 16—2014 *New York Times* ad.

It has been more than six years since the controversy over *Zionism Unsettled*. It remains for sale on IPMN's website and on Amazon. The denomination moved on from debates over divestment in the two General Assemblies since Detroit (in Portland, Oregon, June 2016; St. Louis, Missouri, June 2018) and has shifted closer and closer into the BDS camp, with a greater focus on anti-Zionism. The IPMN was emboldened by its 2014 victories, and, within a year, was declaring that it was a part of the BDS movement. *Zionism Unsettled* is no longer at the forefront of debate, but many Jews remain deeply offended by its publication, and, more importantly, the underlying argument that Zionism Unsettled presents an accurate depiction of how the majority of Presbyterian activists view the Israeli-Palestinian conflict. The deep analysis of *Zionism Unsettled* that Cary Nelson provides in chapter thirteen of this book should be required reading, as it illustrates the flawed and deeply troubling arguments that today's BDS advocates readily embrace.

On a personal note, I never would have thought of writing an essay like this one, and certainly would never have dreamed of co-editing a book on this topic, were it not for my initial reaction and response to *Zionism Unsettled*. The visceral reaction I had, and the sense of the damage that it would do to Jewish-Presbyterian relations pushed me to actively work to counter it. The work I did in Detroit in 2014, and both the satisfaction at seeing my resolution approved, and the deep disappointment at failing to stop the divestment vote, led me to want to gain more knowledge. I began focusing on alternatives to divestment, became aware of co-existence and shared society programs between Israelis and Palestinians, and completely shifted the focus of my own research. Three years later, I now have spent more than two months in Israel and the West Bank, trying to understand how actual peacemaking could come about. *Zionism Unsettled* is a terribly damaging, flawed, and deceptive document, but its existence pushed me into the frontlines of the fight against BDS.

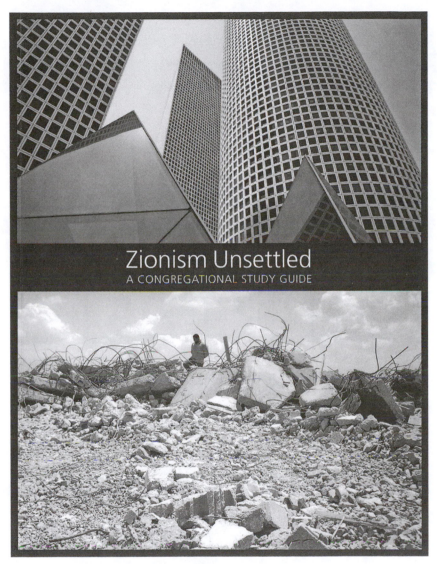

Fig. 17—contrasting images: the polemical cover to *Zionism Unsettled*.

CARY NELSON

CHAPTER THIRTEEN

⌣

A CRITICAL READING OF *ZIONISM UNSETTLED*, ITS ANTECEDENTS, AND ITS LEGACY

In their latest publication [*Why Palestine Matters*], the Israel Palestine Mission Network (IPMN) makes an outrageous claim that Palestinians are the "indigenous" people in that region while the Israelis are "colonialists." For a moment, just think about that assertion from a biblical perspective. If Israelis today are "colonialists," have Israelis always been colonialists? Do we declare the major characters in the Old and New Testaments colonialists? Were Moses and Miriam colonialists because they sought to return to their homeland after being enslaved in Egypt for generations? Was David? Were Jesus and his family members colonialists because they lived in that region as Jews?

Of course, the colonialist argument comes directly from the secular Boycott, Divestment, and Sanctions (BDS) movement, not from a group that thinks biblically or theologically about peace-making. But for Presbyterians, the Bible matters. One cannot read the Bible and declare Israel to be a "colonial project."

The Jewish presence in the region today called Israel-Palestine goes back thousands of years. There has never been a time when Jews did not live in the area we call Israel. In the middle of the 19th Century, Jerusalem was a majority-Jewish city. Even in 1936, a decade before the modern state of Israel was created, there were almost 400,000 Jews in Israel. The entire idea behind the creation of the modern Israel in its current location is rooted in the historical presence of Jews in the Israel-Palestine region. To claim that Israelis today are colonialists is, on one level, preposterous and, on another level, profoundly insulting to the Jewish experience.

—John Wimberly, from the Presbyterians for Middle East Peace
    Blog, April 12, 2018

INTRODUCTION: THE PREHISTORY OF RECENT PRESBYTERIAN DEBATES

In 2014 a volunteer advocacy group within the US Presbyterian Church (PCUSA) called the Israel Palestine Mission Network (IPMN) launched a three-pronged anti-Zionist publication campaign designed to cement opposition to Israel within the Church and promote divestment resolutions at its upcoming General Assembly, the policy-setting annual meeting. Described in greater detail below, the publications at issue comprised two books—*Zionism Unsettled: A Congregational Study Guide* (hereafter *ZU*), and *Zionism and the Quest for Justice in the Holy Land* (hereafter *Quest*), along with an elaborate nine-part open access video series. While the "study guide" model had been used by the Church for nearly fifty years as a way to address the Israeli-Palestinian conflict, IPMN by 2009 had replaced earlier published efforts to raise questions for discussion with a determination to supply answers. IPMN's projects are part of perhaps the single most extensive anti-Zionist campaign of any among Christian groups in the US. The anti-Zionist movement within the PCUSA in any case is clearly the most well-established and also the best funded campaign to emerge from a Protestant church in the US.

ZU declares its polemical thesis up front, with a cover consisting of two contrasting photographs, placed so that the top photo, representing the state of Israel, symbolically crushes the image below, in which a Palestinian stands atop the rubble of his 2005 demolished house in East Jerusalem (Fig. 17). The photograph above is of the three towers of the Arieli Center in Tel Aviv, a popular shopping mall with restaurants, a hotel, offices, and a variety of shops. The photo was taken from a low angle to eliminate any human presence and create an impression of towering, domineering, monolithic forms. Note the parallel use of angled shapes, sharp-edged above and broken below, visualizing the Manichean political contrast between faceless, inhumane mastery and abject suffering. The contrast embodies the opposition of good and evil. With its human figure atop the rubble below, the pieces of broken concrete interwoven with strands of wire stand in for ravaged human bodies overlaid with veins and arteries.

The historical roots of recent Presbyterian debates run deep, since the Church had been involved in missionary work in the Middle East for over a hundred and fifty years. While the Church never succeeded in converting Muslims, it did become part of Arab culture and ultimately allied itself with anti-colonialism in the region. The foregoing essays by Daniel Friedman, Michael Gizzi, and John Wimberly and William Harter gave us the critical background we need to follow the fierce twenty-first-century battles in the PCUSA between advocates of a two-state solution and those pro-BDS church members committed instead to delegitimizing the Jewish state. This essay will focus on a close analysis of the anti-Zionist publications issued by the latter constituency, but I will begin by providing an overview of debates within the Presbyterian Church in the US.

For five decades, beginning in 1819, Presbyterians combined forces with Congregational missionaries as part of the American Board of Commissioners for Foreign Missions. Those missionary efforts were concentrated in Syria and Lebanon in the 1820s, in Iran in the mid-1830s, in Iraq in the 1840s, and in Egypt in the 1850s. Although many countries in the area were not yet recognized nation-states and did not possess their current names or borders, these designations will help readers locate areas of missionary activity. The Anglicans and Lutherans covered Jerusalem, what is now Jordan, and the Holy Land. Although the Presbyterian Church organized its own missionary board in 1837, it did not take broad responsibility for the Levant until 1870. As Hertzel Fishman writes, "Because the (American Protestant) missionaries provided political support for the Arab cause, they inevitably became opponents of Jewish nationalism in Palestine . . . . [and] invariably supported the battle against Zionism" (179). As a consequence, the Presbyterians were often referred to as a pro-Arab church. Yet dissenting views then and now continue to divide the denomination.

Those regional commitments and experiences had both theological and organizational impacts on the Church in the US. To those experiences were added the accounts of Presbyterian missionaries who began to work with Palestinian refugees in 1948; the Board of Foreign Missions made a report critical of Israel's practices to the General Assembly the following year, citing its displacement of Palestinian refugees "too often by high handed methods" (Hopkins 149). Other reports from Presbyterian Middle East missions were more urgent in recommending action not just to ameliorate the suffering of Palestinian refugees but also to find a long-term solution to their dislocation, though there were some whose sympathies lay primarily with Israel. In the mid-1950s and 1960s, Clifford Earle, Secretary for Social Action at the Presbyterian Board of Christian Education and later first Secretary of the Advisory Council on International Affairs, expressed concern about the one-sided pro-Arab character of Church efforts and advocated expanding the mission to include help in settling Jews in Israel (Hopkins 151).

As Paul Hopkins points out in an essay essential to understanding the midcentury development of Presbyterian attitudes toward the Israeli-Palestinian conflict, a split developed between the missionaries

(at that point called "fraternal workers") and those Presbyterian leaders in the US who were focused on interfaith alliances with the Jewish
community, alliances that were strengthened by relationships built on
shared commitments to the Civil Rights Movement and to opposing
the Vietnam War. Existing divisions were exacerbated in the wake of
the 1967 war and, with it, the emergence of the occupation as an issue.
The General Assembly gradually shifted its focus toward recognizing
the needs of the refugees and making statements that aimed for balance
between Israeli and Palestinian interests. The potential for the evolution of General Assembly sentiment is evident in two major documents
approved in 1972 and 1974.

The report presented by a Middle East Task Force to the meeting in
1972, titled "Peoples and Conflict in the Middle East" and cited in the
introduction to *Peace and Faith*, was published as a paperbound book
the following year. Over 5,000 copies were distributed. The report was
not modified, but four supplementary statements were added, three of
which opposed the report's conclusions. The report confirmed that "the
Abrahamic covenant is unconditional in that it is not based on the prior
acts of the people nor can it be invalidated by any sin of the people" (32),
theological positions that IPMN would explicitly reject in later decades.
Indeed, the report emphasizes the contemporary connection: "the current state of Israel may be viewed as a sign of the continuing relationship
of God with the Jewish people." Past efforts to claim the covenant was
broken, it adds, were evidence of anti-Semitism within the church. At
the same time, the report declares what remains true in the West Bank:
"Palestinians do not enjoy rights in any degree consistent with modern
political standards" (42), which redounds from the recognition that
"Palestinians no longer lack political conceptions as they did after the
warfare of 1948-49; they have come to possess a national consciousness
and cultural identity" (28).

But that was not enough for the Palestinians' key Church constitu-
ency. The preface to the report notes that "The standing Committee on
Church and Society voted to record the dissent of the Rev James Fennelly,
Fraternal Delegate, to these recommendations" (5). The following year,
the Middle East Fraternal Workers responded in an "Open Letter to
Christians of the West" that urged their colleagues to "be sensitive and

responsive to the present Middle Eastern tragedy." As Hopkins writes, "the Fraternal Workers felt deeply that all they had given their lives to do, and their strongly held concerns for the Palestinian people, were about to be betrayed by the very church they loved and served" (158).

Two years later the balance had shifted only modestly. The Task Force's eighty-eight-page report, "The Middle East Conflict" (1974), recognized for the first time a Palestinian right to self-determination and reformulated the Church's reasoning behind the centrality of reconciliation: "To ignore injustices that have been commonplace is not reconciliation. A people 'reconciled' to its own suffering and humiliation is not truly reconciled" (8). At the same time, the report insisted that "Arab states should recognize Israel as a sovereign state, equal in political and legal status to any state in the Middle East," even adding that "Arab countries should also deal justly with Jewish claims for compensation and restoration resulting from the conflict" (22). Most importantly, however, the 1974 report added a long and quite impressive historical overview to the record. Both the 1973 and the 1974 documents merit rereading today.

At the same time, however, events in the Jewish state were leading the Church to add criticism of Israel to its otherwise balanced political commitments. The mid-1970s saw a settler movement evolve in the West Bank. The Palestine Liberation Organization meanwhile was succeeding in building political self-identification among the refugees. Then in 1988 the attendees at the General Assembly reacted to the First Intifada by urging Israel to "cease the systematic violation of human rights of Palestinians in the occupied territories." It condemned the torture of suspects and urged that US aid be contingent on "the cessation of repression against Palestinians" (Hopkins 163). A line had been crossed.

One significant consequence of the emerging dominant leadership view, despite widespread pro-Zionist sentiment among the Presbyterian laity, was the eventual election of an anti-Zionist member as moderator, the head of the denomination's General Assembly. The moderator also nominates people to committees and task forces and serves as the public face of the Church throughout his or her two-year term. Benjamin Weir, an opponent of the Jewish state, was a long time Presbyterian missionary in Lebanon until he was kidnapped by the Islamic Jihad Organization, functionally a predecessor to Hezbollah, from a Beirut street in May 1984. He was freed sixteen months later and soon elected moderator of the 1986 General Assembly. Some years later, in 2002, in the wake of two events—the 2001 World Conference against Racism in Durban, South Africa, which promoted the "Zionism is Racism" thesis, and the Second Intifada, both of which increased anti-Israel hostility in many corners—an intensely anti-Zionist Palestinian, Fahed Abu-Akel, was appointed moderator. That appointment helped lead to passage of a 2003 resolution calling on Israel to "End the Occupation Now." At the following year's General Assembly, the anti-Israel forces coalesced, established the IPMN, and pushed forward a divestment resolution. In response to the 2004 action, which took place too late for full discussion, Presbyterians who support the existence of a Jewish state came together to found Presbyterians for Middle East Peace (PFMEP), a group that was fully organized and functioning prior to the 2008 General Assembly. As Daniel Friedman elaborates in Chapter Ten, by then changes in the church's other social commitments had already begun to shift opinion on Israel still further to the left.

ZIONISM UNSETTLED AND THE 2014 GENERAL ASSEMBLY MEETING

The presence of two competing groups—IPMN and PFMEP—made for a notably contentious Assembly in June 2014. Nonetheless, the IPMN forces were able to impose one-sided procedures that blocked open debate and promoted their anti-Zionist agenda. They succeeded passing a resolution by a vote of 310-303 to divest from Caterpillar, Motorola Solutions, and Hewlett-Packard, companies the PCUSA deemed to be complicit in and profiting from Israel's occupation of the West Bank and blockade of Gaza. In response, more than forty commissioners to and observers of the PCUSA's 2014 General Assembly signed *Reformed and Reforming: A Word of Hope*, a pamphlet decrying unfair and one-sided procedures at the meeting. It notes—among numerous other examples showing that "advocates for divestment have been given, in the past five General Assemblies, enormous advantages to make their case"—that during the debate in the Committee on Middle

East Issues, pro-divestment speakers were allotted eighteen hours of testimony, while opponents were granted less than ten minutes (11). In the general meeting "peaceful local anti-divestment youth at the entrance to the assembly hall were harassed and asked to move while pro-divestment youth were given free access by GA staff" (14). The debate, they conclude, "in essence has become within the PC USA a Middle East war of proxy over the last decade" in which "the denomination's historic commitment to fair and open debate of crucial issues" has been set aside (6, 15). They plead for appropriate reform so that discussion can be refocused on "spiritual discernment of what God is calling us to do and say as peacemakers" (4). It is notable that the hijacking of the debate exhibits the same ends-justifies-the-means practices that characterized the process at the 2013 meeting of the American Studies Association (Nelson and Brahm) and the arguments we see in publications by individual BDS-allied scholars.

As I pointed out in the introduction to the book, a number of outside groups and speakers had a major impact on the PCUSA process. BDS activist Dalit Baum, director of the American Friends Service Committee's Economic Activism Program, co-founded a website titled "Who Profits: The Israel Occupation Industry" that helped the PCUSA justify divestment. Jewish Voice for Peace (JVP) and Sabeel were also active at the meeting. American psychologist Mark Braverman, a Jew who heads the pro-Palestinian Christian group *Kairos* USA, has been influential within the PCUSA for some years. The connection with the Sabeel Ecumenical Liberation Theology Center in East Jerusalem is particularly significant because Friends of Sabeel North America, one of its many national chapters, collaborates with IPMN on its publications. Founded by Anglican priest Naim Ateek in 1989, Sabeel has promoted a version of supersessionism linked with Palestinian liberation politics. Ateek writes widely on Palestinian liberation theology and promotes the idea that Palestinians are being "crucified" on the cross of Israeli policy and practices.

The partnership between IPMN and Sabeel North America that is behind *Zionism Unsettled* embodies a strong commitment to Sabeel Center politics and theology and to the beliefs promoted by its founder and others. The main coordinating center for Palestinian liberation theology, Sabeel and its allies have long been associated with efforts to emphasize the universalizing tendencies in the Old Testament as opposed to its obvious focus on one people and one land. This reflects Ateek's promotion of what he considers a more "mature understanding of God" that entails what Adam Gregerman describes as Ateek's "goal of de-Judaizing the Hebrew Bible" ("Old Wine").

Palestinian liberation theology gives great weight to prophetic denunciations of ancient Israel's misconduct without placing such writings within the overriding context of the unbroken divine commitment to the land of Israel and its people. Its project is not, however, simply one of biblical interpretation. It is aimed at delegitimizing the modern Jewish state. Perhaps its most telling element, again, is the repeated suggestion that Israel's mistreatment of Palestinians constitutes reenactments of the crucifixion of Jesus. That is the signal feature of what is consistently described as "the dark side of Zionism." Its allusion to the ancient anti-Semitic libel that Jews killed Jesus is not accidental.

The 2014 IPMN campaign and its three publication components are of interest not only in themselves but also because their anti-Zionism embodies both the ideology of the BDS movement as a whole and the sometimes-distinctive convictions that have driven divestment and boycott initiatives in other Christian denominations.[111] Addressing the campaign's arguments in the Presbyterian Church (USA) is thus also a way to respond to their use in other denominations.

Zionism Unsettled: A Congregational Study Guide, is a large-format, full color, heavily illustrated seventy-four-page publication coordinated by Walter T. Davis, an emeritus professor of sociology and religion and a former director of the Advanced Pastoral Studies Program at San Francisco Theological Seminary in San Anselmo, California. Released in January 2014, ZU was itself drawn in part from the full-length book *Zionism and the Quest for Justice in the Holy Land*, edited by Davis and Donald E. Wagner, the latter formerly a professor and director of the Center for Middle Eastern Studies at North Park University in Chicago and now the National Program Director of Friends of Sabeel-North America; both are Presbyterians and emeritus faculty members. In all likelihood, *Quest* was not widely available until the month after the June 2014 Assembly.

ZU was coordinated with the video series that has a total running time of 198 minutes.[112] Each of the guide's sections or chapters is linked to a single video that offers historical footage with further narrative and individual testimony. A supplementary video consists of excerpts from a 2012 presentation by Munther Isaac, a Palestinian faculty member at the evangelical Bethlehem Bible College in the West Bank, delivered at the college's biennial "Christ at the Checkpoint" Conference, an event launched in 2010.[113]

The entire three-part project is marketed as an integrated course on the history, theology, and current politics underlying the Israeli-Palestinian conflict. The word "unsettled" in the title has a dual meaning, expressing the aim of destabilizing the Zionist project and of stripping the Holy Land of all Jewish settlements, hence "un-settling" it. While each of the parts can stand on its own, people are urged to study all three.

In order to make it clear that the project constitutes a collective, consensual document issued jointly with Friends of Sabeel North America and not simply a collection of opinion pieces by individual authors, the names of the authors of individual chapters in the guide do not appear either in the table of contents or with the title of each chapter, but rather in a footnote in reduced type at the bottom of the opening page of each individual section. As Michael Gizzi points out in the preceding chapter, the study guide is designed so that it appears to be an official statement by the PCUSA, although it is actually an IPMN interest group project. The PCUSA logo appearing on each video reinforces the impression that IPMN speaks for the church as a whole; it is not until the end of the full series that we get an announcement that IPMN is speaking *to* the Church, not *for* it.

Each of the book's nine sections has two parts, except for the last, which has three. The second topic in each section is an unsigned "focus" page, with each focus page being printed on colored paper and placed between the numbered chapters. None of the brief published commentaries on *ZU* has addressed the structure of the book, which is one of the reasons I reproduce the table of contents here. Several of the titles highlight religious interests different from those that occupy secular BDS initiatives. But the authors of *ZU* were clearly challenged to integrate, rather than juxtapose (as with chapters two and five), religious and secular concerns. Chapter titles are in bold, followed by the focus page topics:

1. **Toward a New Framework** / Palestine, Israel, and the United Nations
2. **Political Zionism** / Constantinian Religion
3. **The Concept and Practice of a Jewish State** / A Tale of Two Villages
4. **Christian Views of Jews and Judaism** / The Covenant
5. **A Jewish Theology of Liberation** / Extremism and Intolerance in Israel
6. **Mainline Liberal Protestants and Israel** / Israel's "Image Problem"
7. **Evangelicals and Christian Zionism** / What Diaspora?
8. **A Palestinian Muslim Experience with Zionism** / Memoricide
9. **A Palestinian Christian Postscript** / Emerging from the American Jewish Cocoon / "Judaizing" the Land.

One could argue that a seamless integration of secular and theological issues would have been stronger, but the authors opt instead to appeal to different Protestant constituencies separately.

THE BIBLICAL COVENANT WITH ISRAEL

Although debates over the meaning and application of Old and New Testament texts have not had wide influence outside Christian and Jewish faith communities, in those communities at least they have long been in either the foreground or the background of the arguments people bring to their understanding of the Israeli-Palestinian conflict. With the exception perhaps of the evangelical community, however, politics has gradually displaced theology at the core of many contemporary Christian debates. Over the last generation it seems that it is increasingly those who oppose contemporary Zionism, rather than those who endorse all but the most religiously-based versions of it, who are most likely to invoke God's biblical covenant to grant the Holy Land to the Jewish people. Moreover, the fact that a small minority of Jews believe the literal biblical covenant still holds does not necessarily mean they would be unwilling to give up parts of the West Bank in exchange for peace. I will be referencing the status of the biblical covenant again in what follows, but I first want to provide some context for those references here.

Since the early history of the Church, in an argument since abandoned by most major Christian denominations, supersessionist theologians have argued that God's covenant with Israel was effectively ended by Jesus's life and crucifixion and that the Church has now inherited it. Alternatively, they have focused on the possibility that the covenant was conditional, dependent on the Jewish people adhering to God's law, an argument that survives in contemporary suggestions that Israel's current conduct means the covenant has been revoked. Still others have promoted a version of Christian universalism, suggesting that the covenant actually addressed all lands and all peoples, not some particular piece of Middle Eastern territory. Some, like Ateek, suggest the covenant is no longer about land at all:

> In other words, it is no longer the land that is significant, but Jesus Christ. The land is no longer the vehicle through which God expresses his faithfulness to people . . . . From a Christian perspective, the land no longer has any covenantal importance. The new covenant with God is based on the person of Jesus Christ. (Ateek *Cry* 60)

Gerald McDermott is forceful in condemning this "hyperspiritualist hermeneutic," which has roots that can be traced back to Origen:

> Supersessionist anti-Zionism proposes theology divorced from embodiment and physicality—a people without a land, a Jesus without his people and land and tradition, and the early church living, as it were, suspended in air above the Palestinian ground. It suggests that land, earth, and territory do not matter to embodied human existence. It would not be stretching too much to say that it is ecclesiology and eschatology without incarnation. ("Introduction" 29)

As Joseph D. Small writes, "Whatever Christians may think about current Israeli state policy in Palestine, it is essential to take considerate account of the connection of Jews to the land. The church relativizes the biblical understanding by reducing land to a placeless metaphor . . . transforming the Old Testament's earthly terrain into timeless truths" (163).

The 1973 Presbyterian report cited earlier and published by the Church as *Peoples and Conflict in the Middle East* states firmly that "The Abrahamic and Davidic covenants speak not of a spiritual bond nor of oneness based on ethical norms, but of a particular people linked to the Land as a result of God's promise" (34). This "particularism" has periodically been used as a justification for anti-Semitic violence. *Peace and Conflict* instead invokes parallel particularisms:

> Not only is Israel a reminder of the vitality of Judaism but it also reminds us of the particularism of Biblical faith. We are often inclined to assume that God reveals himself through abstract principles and universal categories. The "scandal" of particularity is manifest in Jewish identification with Israel in a way which parallels the "scandalous" claim of Christianity that the full and decisive revelation of God to man is Jesus of Nazareth. (32)

The book goes on to question the way the objection to a particularist covenant has played out in Christian belief:

> A great deal of Christian tradition and theology has claimed to go beyond this politico-nationalist covenant language and speak of an ethical-universalist covenant established at Mount Sinai and then redeemed through the atoning sacrifice of Jesus. The New Testament and the most ancient creeds teach that the Sinai covenant was fulfilled, not abrogated in Christ. They do not hold to a "replacement theology," i.e., that the New Covenant replaces the old and inferior one. (34)

Ateek and his IPMN allies disagree. The debates promoted by Palestinian liberation theology, which began to take shape in the late 1980s, have also insisted that Zionists continue to claim a divine warrant for the existence of the Jewish state. Moreover, IPMN suggests that Israelis today overwhelmingly assert the applicability of a divine covenant, which is more than misleading—it is not true. While it might seem that the fundamentally secular character of the Zionist movement presents an obstacle to this claim, it in fact makes it possible for IPMN to mount a conspiratorial theory about how secular Zionists cynically used invocations of God's covenant to promote a takeover of Palestinian land. The authors of *ZU* mention that Palestinian Christian Mitri Zaheb "refers to this practice by secular Zionists as an effort to intentionally 'brand' the State of Israel as a 'biblical entity'" (22). A *ZU* focus page on "The Covenant" expands on the Zionist conspiracy: "By linking the Zionist political project to prophetic 'promises,' many Jewish and Christian believers could be led to accept the Jewish state-building project as not emerging from the human mind, but God's" (31). A quotation from Ilan Pappé in *ZU* seals the indictment: "'they did not believe in God, but He nonetheless promised them Palestine'" (31). In other words, faithless Jews duped innocent Christians into applying an ancient religious story to contemporary life: the biblical claim "confuses many Christians who are not able to distinguish between biblical Israel and the newly created state of Israel" (22). "Yes," *ZU* emphasizes in its final paragraphs, "the Bible tells us of God's activity in covenanting with Israel, but it was ancient Israel, not the modern political State" (66).

Readers of *ZU* will look in vain if they seek evidence that this plot to deceive devout Christians and Jews ever existed, and, despite the determination in some quarters to refer to the West Bank as Judea and Samaria, IPMN does not cite examples of Israeli land policy defended with biblical justifications. But the assertion does useful work in IPMN's project nonetheless, and not only as part of an ongoing campaign to disparage Christian Zionists, though that is one of its aims. Attacks on evangelicals are one of the recurrent features of mainline Protestant BDS advocacy. The claim of false biblical self-justification makes it possible to suggest that the Jewish state is paradoxically the new pagan Rome, an embodiment of "idolatrous political nationalism" (33), an argument that University of Chicago journal *Critical Inquiry* editor W. J. T. Mitchell makes as well.[114] In this way the anti-Zionist campaign comes full circle: Zionism created a secular state that falsely claims theological warrant for its existence, but since it is in fact a community of nonbelievers—only a quarter of Israeli Jews are devout—we can understand how a faux Jewish state could betray true Jewish values of fairness and equality. No better set of false assumptions could be found to conclude that anti-Zionism is not anti-Semitic.

REPRESENTATIVE FACTUAL ERRORS
IN *ZIONISM UNSETTLED*

A whole section could be devoted to the consequential omissions in *ZU*. Most notable among these is the failure to mention the atrocities Arabs inflicted on Jewish communities from the time of the British Mandate to the most recent suicide bomber or rocket launched into Israel. There is no acknowledgment of the murderous and slanderous Hamas charter and the violence of Hezbollah. There is complete disregard for Islamic extremism, allowing all instances and examples to go unmentioned while Zionism, or, by extension, the Jews, are seen as ruthlessly violent. My first concern here, however, is with actual errors.

While the effort to lay the blame for the Israeli-Palestinian conflict at the feet of Zionist ideology is the IPMN project's main focus, that goal is grounded in a series of false historical claims frequently found in other BDS campaigns. Several such claims are deceptively offered as factual asides that casual or uninformed readers are unlikely to question. Thus, for example, the first focus page baldly informs us that in 1947 "at the time of partition Palestinian Arabs owned approximately 93 percent of the land in Palestine, Jews 7% percent" (10). This figure is a complete fabrication and should not have been endorsed and promoted by a religiously-affiliated group.

Although real estate records in Palestine were poorly documented, anyone who has read much about the matter knows that a substantial part of Palestine was not private property. It was controlled by the Ottoman Empire until its defeat in World War One. In 1922 that land fell under the administrative control of the British Mandate until the 1947 UN vote that endorsed creation of a Jewish state, at which point the state property was inherited by what would become Israel. The British *Survey of Palestine*, dating from 1945-46, reports that at least 65 percent of Palestine was such state-owned land.

Perhaps *ZU*'s editors confused Palestine as a whole with the portion that constituted private property, since in *Quest* Abu Sway claims "Arab property accounted for close to 94.5 percent of total owned land" (208), a figure that is likewise inaccurate. *ZU*'s falsification of the data is graphically reinforced when it reproduces the notorious set of maps showing what purport to be the main stages of Israeli land takeover, beginning with a 1946 "map" that shows virtually all of Palestine in green identified as "Palestinian land." Of course, the presentation of this fabricated data serves *ZU*'s argumentative interest: convincing the reader that the creation of the Jewish state was fundamentally unjust. Indeed, the effect is to suggest that the "sin of occupation" (35) begins decades before Israel conquered the West Bank in 1967, even predating the 1948 creation of the Jewish state to include fully legal Jewish land purchases since the late nineteenth century.

Did Palestinian Arabs own more land than Jews in 1948? Yes, according to a 2013 data review funded by an Arab-Jewish group generally critical of Israeli land policy, Palestinian Arabs owned between 21 and 28 percent of Mandate Palestine, but far from the exaggerated 93 percent proportion IPMN would have us accept.[115] If one combines land privately owned by Jews with that held by Jewish bodies at the time of statehood, figures range between 7.8 and 9.3 percent. In his own *Quest* essay, Don Wagner adds a disturbingly bitter element to the account by complaining that the UN's partition plan granted "most of the rich farmland and coastal region" (152) to the Jews. Much of the coastal land that Jews had in fact purchased was previously uninhabited malarial swamp land that had only become farmable and useable as a site for towns and cities when Zionist pioneers drained it in the decades prior to the founding of Israel.

A few pages later *ZU* invokes the supposed fact that "war broke out between Jewish and Arab forces when Israel declared independence in May 1948" (14). The editors apparently made a policy decision to use this neutral, both-sides-are-equally-responsible language throughout, since it is repeated in *ZU* (48). The fact that the 1948 war began when the new state was attacked by Egypt, Iraq, Jordan, Lebanon, and Syria is conveniently omitted. Matters arguably get worse when Walter Davis and Pauline Coffman state in *Zionism and the Quest for Justice in the Holy Land* that "the Arab armies never attacked Israel proper (that is, the area allotted by the UN for a Jewish state) but restricted their military activities to the defense of that portion of Palestine that the UN had allotted for an Arab state" (22).

Davis and Coffman cite Ilan Pappé's ideologically aligned *The Ethnic Cleansing of Palestine*, but the definitive study of the war is Benny

Morris's objective, revisionist *1948: A History of the First Arab-Israeli War*, which is the source behind the factual statements I make here. The Davis/Coffman passage allows us not only to suppose that some high legal principle was at issue in the Arab decision to go to war but also that the Arabs invaded both to protect the Palestinian Arabs and to defend the UN's partition standard. While popular Arab opinion was inflamed by pleas for help by Palestinian Arabs, the leaders of the Arab states each had land conquest and the expansion of their own national territory in mind. Jordan wanted to annex what we now know as the West Bank. Iraq wanted Haifa and its key oil port. Egypt wanted to block Jordan's ambitions and seize territory for itself. In the months preceding the war, with the complex exception of Jordan, the Arab states made it clear they wanted to eliminate the Jewish state. Had they been better organized and met less Jewish resistance they certainly would have succeeded.

In order to suggest that Israel's existence was never actually threatened, the coordinators of IPMN's project also tell us that the Israelis were confident of victory throughout, a claim that Ronen Berelovich echoes in the first video. Six months into the war, by October 1948, the Jews did indeed feel confident, but not in the lead up to the war or in its initial months, when fear of being overrun by the Arab armies dominated the Israeli leadership's military planning and its response to events. When an Egyptian armored column started moving northward along the Mediterranean coast on May 15, 1948, Israelis certainly understood that Egyptians aimed to eliminate the new Jewish state and that Tel Aviv was the ultimate target. Indeed, the Egyptian Air Force bombed Tel Aviv in May and June. The kibbutzim that the Egyptians attacked along the way were determined not by their location in relation to partition but rather their location on their invasion route. When the Iraqi forces attacked the Coastal Plain settlement of Geulim on May 28 they were, contrary to the fiction promoted by IPMN, within the area ceded to Israel by the UN partition plan. They were also fewer than ten miles from the Mediterranean, which put Israel in danger of being cut in two.

Jordan did halt its advance in part to honor its promise to Britain not to breach the area ceded to Israel but also because its Arab Legion, the most professional and best equipped force Israel faced, was largely led by British officers. Although Jordan had repeatedly urged the Jews to accept limited autonomy under broader Jordanian control of Palestine, rather than a Jewish state, Jordan nevertheless did violate the UN plan by occupying East Jerusalem, including the Jewish Quarter in the Old City. The UN plan designated Jerusalem as an internationally administered city. Jordan was essentially satisfied by its major territorial acquisitions. Moreover, by the end of August its forces had only five days of ammunition left.

It was military failure overall that limited the advance of the Arab armies. I have focused on IPMN's treatment of 1948 because it is the appropriate place to start. But historical misrepresentation of the seventy years since then undergirds the entire project. IPMN's authors were happy to ignore consensus by the most well-researched academic historical studies whenever they found an outlying opinion that matched their political convictions.

ZIONISM UNSETTLED'S POLEMICAL AGENDA

There are two somewhat distinct topics to address here that supplement the preceding chapter on *Zionism Unsettled* by Michael Gizzi—the project's overall aims and strategies and the numerous specific errors and misleading claims it includes. In the end, even rigorously faith-based efforts have to make strategic decisions about issues, arguments, rhetoric, spokespersons, and images if they are to produce books and videos. They must (or, at least, should) monitor their ideology and impulses so as to recognize when fact-checking is necessary to avoid succumbing to confirmation bias when deciding whether to validate a given assertion. *ZU*'s editors, I believe, failed to honor that principle fully, and the project as a result becomes a propaganda enterprise.

One way that happens is to cite a previous author's undocumented opinion as though it is now an established fact, something the authors of *Zionism Unsettled* do repeatedly. Fact checking within the echo chamber of anti-Zionist opinion will not suffice. And *ZU*'s authors did not even have the fig leaf of a university press peer review process to use as cover. *Zionism Unsettled* is structured by strategic decisions, misrepresentations, and factual errors that will not be readily apparent to those who are not dedicated students of the Israeli-Palestinian struggle.

One obviously strategic decision is the choice to make only one reference to the BDS movement in the entire *ZU* booklet (35), a decision in keeping with IPMN's wish at the time to make itself appear as independent, despite the fact that the project throughout is in harmony with and in complete support of the BDS agenda that IPMN had embraced for years. In this regard, IPMN's reluctance mirrors PCUSA's efforts to differentiate its divestment resolutions from the wider BDS movement. In *Quest*, Wagner characterizes this as merely a Protestant effort to "utilize BDS strategies (boycott, divestment, and sanctions) or similar economic leverages" (170), which, he argues, are "among the instruments of nonviolence that are capable of promoting peaceful change in societies that resist justice" (172), a global claim about Israel that draws no distinction between current government policy and the rest of Israeli society and its institutions. That one reference in *ZU*, moreover, comes in a quotation from Rabbi Brant Rosen's essay in *Quest* in which he says the BDS movement, as embodied in Jewish Voice for Peace and multiple Protestant denominations, is "challenging the American Jewish establishment's Constantinian hegemony on Israel." In a 2017 essay written for the JVP collection *On Antisemitism*, Walt Davis claims that "the Zionist ideological narrative" and its consequences for Palestinians "makes BDS necessary" (21).

The "Constantinian" modifier here, echoing anti-Zionist Mennonite theologian John Howard Yoder's description of the "Constantinian shift," invokes the merging of religion and political or state power and draws on the second focus page, "Constantinian Religion" (16). As contemporary anti-Zionist Shaul Magid writes, Yoder "saw Zionism as nothing less than a Jewish Constantinianism, which does the same danger to Judaism that Constantinianism does to Christianity" (113). That was the moment "when Christianity lost its way and succumbed to the lure of political power" (114). For Yoder, the Constantinian shift in Judaism was exemplified in the commitment to land, rather than spirituality, as the center of the religion. One might note in response that the land is a frequent topic in the Old Testament. In any case, the broader critique is directed against Jewish nationalism tout court. Nationalism occasioned a shift from religion to peoplehood as the center of Jewish identity. Like Judith Butler after him, Yoder embraces exile and the diaspora as more authentic forms of Jewishness.

This focus page cites James Carroll's powerful *Constantine's Sword*, a ground-breaking account of the Roman Catholic Church's long history of promoting anti-Judaism with anti-Semitic consequences. Carroll himself notably does not make the Constantinian indictment of Zionism. Interviews with Carroll, the first portion taken from the 2008 film based on his book, followed by excerpts from a 2011 talk at Harvard Book Store, occupy the first thirteen minutes of episode four of the companion video as well. The moment when Roman Emperor Constantine converted to Christianity, which led in turn to Christianity becoming a state religion with the power to enforce its views and sanction heretics, is transformative in Carroll's book and in the history of the Church. It is also a moment, as Carroll argues, which confirms that the cross came to double as a sword, a weapon. Here the authors find one key fault in Carroll's account: its "exposé is incomplete because it errs, like many well-intentioned partners in the 'ecumenical deal,' in failing to recognize that Israeli policies are also an expression of 'Constantinian religion'" (16). It needs to be emphasized again in response that the full range of Israeli policies are neither grounded in nor expressions of theological conviction; nor do secular Israelis necessarily see the Jewish state as the realization of a divine covenant.

Non-Christians may be surprised to find that *ZU* devotes considerable space to a review of Christianity's anti-Jewish history of "forced conversion, exclusion, execution, humiliation, caricature, ghettoization, pogroms, and genocide" (25), including especially the fourth chapter, "Christian Views of Jews and Judaism" (25-30). But *ZU* arrives in the wake of decades of Catholic and Protestant reconciliation efforts with Jews, including the Catholic Church's historic 1965 statement *Nostra Aetate*. *ZU* has a particular need to embrace that tradition, rather than seem decisively outside it, because of *ZU*'s substantially unqualified BDS-style denunciation of the Jewish state.

The reconciliation effort, however, includes several necessary components: breaking with or mitigating the nearly 2,000-year-long supersessionist tradition in which Christianity declares itself the new Israel, with its covenant replacing the one Jews traditionally have with

God; confronting the long history of anti-Semitic Christian activism, including Martin Luther's implacable hostility to Jews; embracing the core message of love Jesus preached and honoring it in contemporary relationships; recognizing the unique and universal violence done to the human capacity for compassion and the escalation of the capacity for evil manifest in the Holocaust; and recognizing the Jewish right to a homeland of their own in the Holy Land.

ZU is not altogether successful on any of these fronts. The problems with *ZU*'s engagement with the Holocaust begin in the first chapter. The authors point out that the Hebrew term for the Holocaust, *Shoah*, and the Arabic term for its collective tragedy in 1947-48 when 750,000 Arabs fled or were forced out of the new Jewish state and lost their homes, *Nakba*, both translate as "catastrophe." Treating the murder of six million as parallel to the exile of 750,000 is worse than scandalous. Yet we do not need to treat these events as either equivalent or comparable in order to recognize that they are both catastrophes in their own right, and that any given people will invest deeply in their own history and collective trauma. Palestinians, it is true, generally see the Holocaust as a fundamentally European crime, not as a violation of basic human codes and values for which we must all bear witness— though one might point out that the Palestinian Mufti of Jerusalem was a Nazi ally and sought refuge in Berlin. Many Arabs' persistent misunderstanding of the Holocaust is highlighted by the fact that, as Matthias Küntzel and Jeffrey Herf have documented, respectively, in *Jihad and Jew-Hatred: Islamism, Nazism and the Roots of 9/11* and *Nazi Propaganda for the Arab World*, contemporary Arab anti-Semitism can be traced in part to Nazi propaganda disseminated in the Arab world during the Second World War. The hatred of the new Jewish state that bloomed in 1948 thus owes something to Nazi Germany as well.

Matters are not helped in the *ZU* video series either; in the second episode Ilan Pappé minimizes the Holocaust as merely "one of the worst genocides" and crudely tells us that "for the sake of its PR and to silence its critics Israel is willing to sell the victims of the Holocaust." Underlying complaints about invocations of the Holocaust is a vulgar and anti-Semitic accusation that "Jews purposely exaggerate their sufferings in order to defraud others of the sympathy that should by rights be theirs" (Harrison 55). While Prime Ministers Menachem Begin and Benjamin Netanyahu were and are known to cite the experience of the Holocaust to justify their political decisions, sometimes inappropriately, other Israeli leaders have not. It is thus a slander to level this accusation against Israel as a whole, which is precisely what *ZU* does when it declares that "Israeli politics are driven by actual and manipulated fear of annihilation (another Holocaust)" (20). There are contexts in which fear of annihilation reasonably drives planning or policy—for example, the present concern that a nuclear-armed Iran represents an existential threat to the Jewish state. One may also fairly point out that at the outset of the 1948-49 war Israelis thought they were at risk of a second Holocaust. Now Hamas's declared intention to destroy Israel and kill Jews evokes memories of and provokes comparisons with the Holocaust. But it would be absurd to claim that Holocaust anxiety lies behind hundreds, even thousands, of Israeli policies or dominates its intricate and multifaceted political debates. There is plenty of evidence that post-Holocaust Israeli generations are not preoccupied with the *Shoah*.

ZU quotes former Israel Knesset speaker Avraham Burg's declaration that we will all be better off "when Israel frees itself from its obsession with the *Shoah* and its exclusivity" (8). Contrary to what *ZU* would like to conclude from such observations, it is important to recognize that each genocide is historically unique and exceptional. Among the components of the Shoah that, when taken together, made it a defining event both for the twentieth century and for human history as a whole were the racialized character of its extermination agenda, the distinctive mix of industrialization and individual savagery in its strategies, the number of countries that collaborated in it or remained silent, the centuries of religious hatred that undergirded it, the sheer numbers at stake in its execution, and its pervasive assault on fundamental human value. Granting that multilevel comparative specificity in no way undercuts the need to recognize what the Holocaust teaches us about human suffering or the capacity for evil generally.

ZU sanctimoniously urges that "no exceptionalist claims can be justified in our interconnected, pluralistic world" (9), but our interconnected world has not voided all historical distinctions. Contrary to the

BDS movement's efforts to convince us that Palestinian suffering has a greater moral claim on us than the suffering of any other contemporary people, one could certainly agree that "morally hazardous claims of a hierarchy of victimhood" (9) are damaging. Yet that does not mean that the treatment of the Palestinians is acceptable, or that the historically unique character of the Holocaust, the Armenian genocide, or the century's other examples of mass murder should be erased or that engagement with them should be geographically or culturally limited.

ZU then asks, "How can one compare the suffering of the African slave trade, the decimation of native peoples throughout the Americas, or the suffering inflicted upon Jews during the Holocaust?" (9). This appeal to a universal humanism makes a valid point but a deceptive one. Certainly, genocidal suffering cannot be ranked or graded, yet it is only by making such comparisons that one can identify and honor the historical specificity of these tragedies. That the Nakba was a tragedy is clear, but its more fitting comparison is with the large number of European refugees forced from their homes during World War II and with the consequent population transfers, not with the Holocaust or other genocides.

Trying to conflate claims about the unique character of the Holocaust with what amounts to a slander about the Jewish people that crosses the line into anti-Semitism, *ZU* asserts that "exceptionalism exempts the chosen from the need to conform to normal rules, laws, or general principles that we use to hold other peoples accountable" (8). That passage echoes the long history of anti-Semitic slanders attached to the idea of being chosen. As Bernard Harrison writes about anti-Zionist accusations of Israeli atrocities, we are told they "are inseparable from the nature of Jewish culture and consciousness—that they take their root in the sense Jews have of themselves as a chosen people" (152). It is then an easy step for *ZU* to add a further accusation to the exceptionalist chain of equivalences: "The dark side of Zionist exceptionalism today is the ethnic cleansing and land confiscation of Palestinians justified by an appeal to God's will derived from biblical texts" (8). While a tiny minority of Israelis would be willing to make such arguments, most Israelis are secular and would never do so. Indeed, most secular Israelis think of the concept of Jewish chosenness as an irrelevant anachronism; it remains a core belief only for religious Jews. The status of the Jewish people as "chosen," furthermore, has long been distorted to mean "superior or uniquely valued by God," rather than the authentic meaning of being chosen to bear and honor the burden of the law. As Reuven Firestone demonstrates, at various points in their history the three major monotheistic religions have all embraced versions of chosenness. For Christianity, claiming chosenness is a component of supersessionism and closely linked to the claim that Christians have replaced Jews and inherited the covenant with God. The bottom line is that there is no basis for *ZU*'s claim that Israel justifies its policies by invoking the idea of a "chosen people." *ZU*'s argument crosses the line into anti-Semitism by suggesting Jews have a sense of their own superiority that makes them hostile to other peoples.

Equally fallacious, but perhaps more painful, is *ZU*'s suggestion that the burden of responding to the Holocaust is exclusively a European one. Once you make that assumption, it is easy enough to conclude that when the Palestinians lost land they became "secondary victims of the Holocaust" (6), despite the statement's offensive effort to blur the character of the Holocaust and diminish the trauma of its true victims. Some of *ZU*'s contributors both before and since its publication have expanded on the claim that the Palestinians are also Holocaust victims. In his 2017 book *A Palestinian Theology of Liberation*, which includes an admiring foreword by respected but anti-Zionist American theologian Walter Brueggemann, Naim Ateek argues that "Palestine and its people were sacrificed on the altar of Western guilt" over the Holocaust, that "Palestinians were compelled to pay the price by their dispossession and loss of homeland," and that "One can even say that the Palestinians were the easy scapegoats" (32). Characterizing the Palestinians as "scapegoats" for the Holocaust, deliberating echoing the status of the Jews in Germany and elsewhere in World War II Europe, once again crosses a line into a fantasy unsupported by historical fact. It also implicates Jews generally, not just Israelis, in the price Palestinians supposedly paid.

For *ZU* to embrace that view on behalf of the Presbyterian Church is wholly unacceptable. It does not help that the text goes on to make an explicit comparison between Zionism and Nazism, first noting that the theologian Paul Tillich "considered Nazism a false, secular alternative to prophetic Judaism and Christianity as it was based on pagan Teutonic myths of Aryan racial supremacy and was, in essence, a closed system with no room for the prophetic critique that the Hebrew Prophets and Jesus brought to humanity" and then immediately declaring Zionism "a closed system with little room for prophetic critique" (38), an extraordinary claim in the light of the unrelenting prophetic critique that permeates the Jewish State. Here and elsewhere *ZU* unfortunately follows the standard BDS strategy of treating Zionism as monolithic, whereas from its inception in the nineteenth century to the present, Zionism has been both an evolving movement and a diverse one. One straightforward definition has, however, held throughout: Zionism is belief that, after centuries of discrimination and persecution, the Jewish people should have a homeland of their own in Israel where they can control their own destiny.

ZU's unstinting hostility to Zionism and its condemnation not merely of current Israeli policy but of the founding rationales for a Jewish state echo the views of Judith Butler, Steven Salaita, Saree Makdisi, Jasbir Puar, all detailed in my *Israel Denial*, and those of many other prominent pro-BDS faculty. It is not simply difficult but impossible to square these views with the core principle behind reconciliation: "It is time to speak the truth in love to one another" (7). This dictum is quoted in *ZU*, but it requires considerable self-deception to believe it has been honored. Even the most liberal definition of tough love can hardly account for the relentlessly antagonistic characterization of Zionism therein. "Tough love" notably is not the standard *ZU* explicitly recommends, but Donald Wagner twice recommends it in *Quest*: "It is this 'tough love' that is needed today to achieve peace and justice for both Israel and Palestine" (170). The problem for BDS and its allies is that implacable hostility is not compatible with tough love.

The challenge *ZU* faces in the context of Catholic and Protestant reconsideration and rejection of centuries of defining themselves against a demonized Jewish other is to escape similar implications when they advocate for virtuous action in opposition to the purported depravity of a demonized Jewish state. They must free their hostility of any taint of anti-Semitism, but it cannot be done, especially since they give the impression that "support for Israel is a new Jewish conspiracy" (Harrison 125). Like the rest of the BDS movement, itself overwhelmingly secular, they assume that all they have to do is bring forward several Jewish allies and, through them, point out that "some of our best friends are Jews." But it is not so easy for Christian denominations, since they came into existence and established their very identities in part through anti-Semitism. A cloud hangs over them. And *ZU* does not dispel this history by invoking "the similarities between Zionism, South African apartheid, and Jim Crow segregation in the Southern US" (18).

In chapter eight, a condensed version of Mustafa Abu Sway's essay in *Quest*, we are reminded that "Racism is the cornerstone of the Zionist project" (50). But the Anglican Reverend Naim Ateek, one of the authors of *Kairos Palestine*, gets the final word: "Zionism is a false theology" (56). "From a Palestinian Christian point of view," he argues, Zionism "is a retrogression of the Jewish community into the history of its very distant past, with its most elementary and primitive forms of the concept of God . . . a narrow and exclusive concept of a tribal God" (33). Ateek is thus reviving the historic Christian demonization of Judaism "as a primitive religion—a religion in which fear of divine vengeance, rather than the effort to emulate divine love and forgiveness, plays the principal part" (Harrison 302). More broadly, for Ateek, Zionism "commits theological injustice by its appeal to God, history and race" (57). By such reasoning, he continues, Zionism serves for fundamentalist Christians to "justify and support this ongoing humiliation and dispossession" of Palestinians (56), while for liberal Christianity it "serves as a 'price-tag' theology providing Christians a vehicle of repentance for the guilt accrued during centuries of European Christian anti-Semitism culminating in the Holocaust" (56). The "'price tag' theology" remark, suggesting that Israelis and sympathetic Christians alike have sacralized anti-Palestinian violence, is particular objectionable. Needless to say, *ZU*'s numerous and varied attacks on Zionism do not help dispel the impression that traditional supersessionist anti-Semitism underwrites the project as a whole.

ZU's third chapter, "The Concept and Practice of a Jewish State," ends with a prescription for how reconciliation and the peace process must proceed: "In Israel/Palestine, as a step that must be undertaken before forgiveness can begin: No Future Without Moral Truth. Speaking moral truth will require both courage and compassion. The time has come for us all to name the Christian theological and ethical failures that gave rise to Zionism, as well as the Jewish theological and ethical failures that Zionism has produced" (23). Christianity may have a problematic past, but Israel, IPMN argues, has a corrupt present. Thus, no dialogue should now take place except—in what is an unacknowledged echo of the BDS anti-normalization agenda—in the context of an admission of Israel's sole responsibility for contemporary injustices. What is perhaps worst about this joint BDS/IPMN agenda is that the only route forward it offers is the thoroughgoing delegitimization of the Jewish state, a tactic used to defeat a country in war, not to promote peacetime negotiations.

It is important to understand that one cannot read through *ZU* or watch the videos in search of a point-by-point critique of Israeli government policy, something, however, that millions of Zionists in Israel and worldwide engage in continually. Instead, the authors raise the long-discredited practice of claiming that supporters of Israel treat any criticism of Israeli policy as anti-Semitic. So infatuated are the organizers of this campaign that they are willing to slander organizations that regularly criticize Israeli government policy by accusing them of doing exactly the reverse. "Since Israeli statehood," they write, "the ADL has equated anti-Zionism with anti-Semitism . . . Now most if not all of the 51-member groups affiliated with the Conference of Presidents of Major Jewish Organizations are Zionist, committed to the suppression of any criticism of Israel in the mainstream American media, in American civil society, and even within their own organizations" (19). As anyone familiar with the activities and positions of the groups on the list will be aware, several of them are regularly faulted by others for attacks on Israeli government policy. Among the groups in the Conference who have argued publicly against Israeli policy or make clear that they are comfortable with such critiques are ADL, Ameinu, Americans for Peace Now, ARZA, JCPA, JLC, and URJ, among others. Of course, all these groups are Zionist in the sense that they support the existence of a Jewish state, but many of the groups on the full list also promote a two-state solution and justice for the Palestinian people.

To understand how inaccurate *ZU*'s portrayal of these groups is, all one has to do is visit their websites, which include many critiques of Israeli government policy and reflect their efforts to promote a two-state solution. Needless to say, such groups do not see themselves as anti-Semitic. Can *ZU*'s authors really be so ignorant about the groups they mischaracterize and disparage? Their false claim about the Anti-Defamation League (ADL) merits special attention because the organization's mission includes tracking, analyzing, and combatting anti-Semitism. The ADL website includes a concise and very useful set of questions and answers ("What is anti-Israel"). Some relevant examples include:

What is anti-Zionism?

Anti-Zionism is a prejudice against the Jewish movement for self-determination and the right of the Jewish people to a homeland in the State of Israel. It may be motivated by or result in anti-Semitism, or it may create a climate in which anti-Semitism becomes more acceptable.

Is criticism of Israel always anti-Semitic?

No . . . Israel is a country like any other, with some policies that are good and others that are not so good. Israel's press is often critical of its own government's policies and politicians. So are many Israeli citizens. We don't have to agree with criticism of Israeli policy. But we can't say it is beyond the bounds of reasonable discourse, and it surely isn't anti-Semitism.

ADL repeats these definitions elsewhere. The organization has also made it clear that its annual tally of anti-Semitic events "does not categorize criticism of Israel or Zionism as an anti-Semitic incident." However, "such reports are included if they cross the line from legitimate criticism to anti-Semitism by invoking classic anti-Jewish stereotypes or inappropriate Nazi imagery and/or analogies. Public expressions of anti-Israel sentiments that demonize Jews or create an atmosphere of fear or intimidation for US Jews are counted" ("Audit"). In its discussion guide to Shakespeare's *The Merchant of Venice*, the ADL reiterates that the line between anti-Zionism and anti-Semitism "is crossed when it passes from criticism of the actions or policies of the government (which is legitimate) to questioning the very existence of the Jewish state (which is a form of bigotry and anti-Semitism." One might wish that *ZU*'s authors had drawn on these careful distinctions, rather than ignoring them. I quote them here partly because it is worth asking where *ZU*'s anti-Zionism stands on this spectrum, specifically whether it crosses the line ADL draws. I would, however, rephrase the distinction between anti-Zionism and anti-Semitism to read "to argue for the elimination of the Jewish state" and characterize that as anti-Semitic, as I think scholars can, for example, debate the foundations of and justifications for a Jewish state without claiming Israel should actually be eliminated.

While attacks on Zionism have always been central to critiques of Israel, it is worth pointing out their special paradoxical status in IPMN's project. In a contradictory fashion, IPMN depicts Zionism simultaneously as a secular movement manipulating religious Christians in traditional Protestant denominations and as a fundamentalist religious movement shaping Israeli policy and appealing to evangelicals. Central to the insistence that Zionism is fundamentally a religious philosophy, a theology, is the claim that it conceives the State of Israel as a "biblical entity" established in fulfilment of God's will. Of course, there are both Christians and Jews who believe that, some with fanaticism, but there are millions in both secular and faith communities who simply do not think in those terms. While *ZU* aims to discredit those *confused* "Christians who are not able to distinguish between biblical Israel and the newly created state of Israel" (22), especially evangelicals, the focus on Zionism is also more broadly directed to *ZU*'s faith community. Framing the argument in terms of Zionism appeals to those who think in terms of spiritual essences, including all those committed to some version of Christian eschatology. Moreover, treating Zionism as a transhistorical, essentialist belief system and political imperative speaks to those who imagine it is possible to identify a nation's soul. Zionism *is* Israel, *ZU*'s authors would have us believe; everything else about a diverse and notoriously disputatious country disappears in the face of that reality.

This sort of deception is supplemented by what may be sloppiness enhanced by confirmation bias. As I pointed out above, they tell us that "war broke out between Jewish and Arab forces" in 1948, thereby sidestepping the fact that the Arab states initiated the conflict by attacking Israel. In *ZU*, unfortunately, that sort of error can be amplified to the point of slander. A large sidebar on page forty-one, which discusses the relationship between Krister Stendahl and Rabbi David Hartman, completely misrepresents an op-ed by Hartman written in response to the wave of suicide bombings carried out across Israel in 2001. With anguish, Hartman asks what message suicide bombers sent *about Israelis*: "Very simply, wipe them out. Level them." *ZU* reverses his meaning and treats this instead as a statement about what should be done to Palestinians. In a few cases, *ZU* makes statements so divorced from reality that only people who know the relevant literature could possibly understand their source. A good example is the assertion that "Jewish life is alive and well in the Islamic Republic of Iran" (48), a claim that Iranian propaganda promotes, but that has been documented as horrifically untrue. A community of over 100,000 in the late 1970s, Jews in Iran now number fewer than 9,000. The Iranian Jewish leadership is expected to condemn Israel; indeed, false accusations that Iranian Jews are Israeli or American spies have led to executions.

Equally serious is the document's promotion of the BDS affirmation of a full-scale right for millions of Palestinian descendants of those who fled or were forced out in 1948 to "return" to Israel. Since the 1978 Camp David Accords, it has gradually become clear that even many Palestinian leaders involved in formal negotiations no longer make that demand, which would imperil the Jewish majority. Instead, they ask for a frank acknowledgement of Israel's role in the Nakba, a very limited right of return for those with immediate family members in Israel, and compensation for lost property. The BDS movement continues to make it an issue two decades after some West Bank Palestinian leaders privately resolved the matter and moved on, despite public rhetoric to the contrary. It is true that Palestinian leaders have failed to educate their people about the necessity of this concession, but *ZU* is not helping matters by making a universal right of return for descendants who have never lived in Israel a necessary objective. Equally regrettable is *ZU*'s implied endorsement of the view that the existence of a *de facto* single state encompassing the West Bank means that the two-state solution is dead. Faith communities would benefit from debating that issue, but they cannot do so when, according to *Zionism Unsettled*, the matter is already decided.

At one point *ZU* makes a powerful observation that is among the few statements here that could inspire a very different engagement with the Israeli-Palestinian conflict: "With Augustine's and Anselm's perspective in mind, the traditional view (that the life, death, and resurrection of Christ is 'the most complete revelation that God has yet granted humankind') claims more than any individual can know" (30). Comparable doubt about (and willingness to question) the project's conclusions regarding the Jewish state could underwrite faith-based reconciliation efforts that would actually contribute to the search for peace.

ZU is decidedly vague about how and when reconciliation should actually play out, but key texts from the Palestinian liberation theology movement—whose arguments, as mentioned above, are central to the text—are more revealing. As Ateek writes in 2017's *A Palestinian Theology of Liberation*, "there are three essentials that must be realized in order for a genuine peace to be achieved: justice, peace, and reconciliation. The sequence is important" (142). In other words, all reconciliation efforts are invalid until Palestinians secure full justice on their own terms. Only then can peace be achieved, which is their prerequisite for reconciliation. But reconciliation is a process. It should begin now, even knowing that it may not be fully realized until years after a peace agreement is implemented. Ateek's required progression parallels BDS anti-normalization arguments against contact with Israelis on any basis that assumes equality between the parties and/or that is not based fundamentally on an Israeli admission of absolute responsibility for all injustices related to the conflict. But peace negotiations are not likely to succeed without sufficient reconciliation, without both sides striving to achieve mutual empathy and respect for one another's historical narratives. During peace negotiations themselves, sufficient reconciliation to curtail mutual demonization will also be critical. And the negotiations will need to specify forms of economic and military collaboration based on a significant degree of reconciliation. If the implementation of an agreement is to be in stages, as is almost certainly the case, reconciliation will have to proceed in stages as well.

ZIONISM AND THE QUEST FOR JUSTICE IN THE HOLY LAND

Zionism Unsettled was the product of a 14-member project committee and group of writers, editors, and image researchers headed by Walt Davis. Other than Davis himself, none of the authors of the essays in *Zionism and the Quest for Justice in the Holy Land* appear on the list of those directly responsible for *ZU*. Presumably that means none of the *Quest* authors save Davis himself condensed their own essays for publication in *ZU*. *ZU* actually appeared on January 20, 2014, five months before its source text, *Quest*, which was officially published July 1, though copies may have been available a few weeks before that. Unlike *ZU*, then, it seems likely that *Quest* had only very limited effect on the Presbyterian General Assembly's June 20 vote, which decided by a close 310 to 303 margin to divest from three companies doing business in Israel and "profiting from the occupation" of the West Bank.

It is possible that some members of the *ZU* project committee did write focus pages, while perhaps others produced edited versions of the *Quest* essays. *ZU* does not detail their individual responsibilities; some who participated in the annual meeting may have seen the entire *Quest* manuscript, but there is no way to know. In any case, *ZU* urges that groups using the guide consult *Quest* as well. The public controversy, however, as Michael Gizzi reports, focused on *ZU* and the vote.

Readers of *ZU* alone have no indication about the relationship between the two books or about what was left out of *Quest* in the process of editing it for its new life as *ZU*. *Quest* does include a highly unusual disavowal of editorial responsibility for fact checking: "The writers, not the editors, bear responsibility for the accuracy and interpretation of this [Israeli-Palestinian] history" (2). Although that disclaimer is not repeated in *ZU*, it has in effect been invisibly grandfathered into it. But a comparison of the two publications is actually instructive in more ways than one. *Quest* not only fleshes out the positions held by *ZU*'s authors; it also clarifies what strategy *ZU*'s compilers had in mind in their campaign to influence Church members and push the divestment agenda at the annual meeting.

Some differences may seem straightforward. Carole Monica Burnett's survey of Eastern Orthodox history and contemporary perspectives in

Quest may have been judged irrelevant and omitted, but the editors of
ZU may also have done so to avoid dealing with her intense anti-Israel
hostility. In her *Quest* essay, Burnett reads a series of ancient and contemporary theologians and religious leaders so as to marshal them for a
condemnation of Zionism. Burnett excuses John Chrysostom's fiercely
anti-Jewish sermons of 386-7 CE as typical of the age's rhetorical
excesses. While that is partly true, she ignores their unique, powerful
influence on subsequent violence against Jews. Meanwhile she applauds
early supersessionist arguments, such as that "Christ is the source of
meaning, the raison d'être, of the Old Testament" (97) or that "the
land grant to ancient Israel was tied to a particular era of history and
is surpassed by salvation in Christ" (98). Moreover, she finds Origen's
arguments (c. 212-215 CE) particularly instructive for contemporary
usage, writing, "the spiritual significance of the Promised Land is that
it symbolizes Christian perfection" (99). Jerome's interpretation (c. 393
CE), she claims, reinforces that reading: "the Old Testament 'land of
promise' is the heavenly kingdom of God, not Palestine" (101). Her language is carefully chosen to draw contemporary parallels. Thus Basil,
Bishop of ancient Caesarea, "condemned the practice of land seizure and
home demolition committed by the wealthy against their social inferi-
ors" (101). She concludes the historical section of her essay by invoking
the anti-Semitic trope of the greedy Jew: "the church fathers' affinity for
symbolic interpretation of the Promised Land plus their abhorrence of
greedy acquisitiveness, combined with their advocacy for the poor, add
up to a patristic tradition that offers no support for the current Zionist
perpetration of land seizure, expulsion of residents, and repopulation in
the West Bank" (102).

Other *Quest* passages absent from *ZU* reinforce the conclusion
that they were omitted in order to make the guidebook appear somewhat less aggressive in its anti-Zionism and thus more palatable to a
broad Presbyterian and interfaith audience. As Michael Gizzi's reception history of *ZU* documents, that effort was not entirely successful.
Nonetheless it is possible that some readers would, for example, have
been still more offended by the Davis and Coffman statement that "a
'Jewish state' legitimizes racism and discrimination in favor of Jews in
all areas of public life" (47), by Sway's blunt declaration that the idea of

"a Jewish democracy is an oxymoron" (204), by Wagner's insinuation that there is a contemporary lesson in his reminder that "the Prophet Elijah once challenged the people of Israel who had chosen the pagan religion of Baal over the religion of the one true God" (173), by Ateek's amplification of his characterization of Zionism as "a false theology," common to both books, with the claim that Zionism "promotes death rather than life" (219), or by wider quotation of the rhetoric in Brant Rosen's original essay, as in passages like "liberal American Christians have been theologically blackmailed into silence over Israel's human rights abuses" or his account of responses to the *Kairos* USA statement: "the Jewish Council for Public Affairs . . . hysterically condemned its 'extreme rhetoric' and referred to it as a 'false witness'" (88). What is missing from *ZU* is the charged modifier "hysterically." Rosen's key claim that Israel represents "the living embodiment of Judaism as empire" makes its way into *ZU*, but not some of the statements that amplify the claim's intensity, such as the characterization of Israel as an "overmilitarized garrison state" (67) or his belief that Israel exemplifies a "quasi-Faustian bargain we have made with political nationalism" (87). In a 2017 essay written for JVP's *On Antisemitism*, Rosen repeats the Faustian bargain claim without the "quasi" modifier, adding that Israel "commits human rights abuse at home and exports it abroad" (134). Rosen, it should be remembered, was one of the most vocal supporters of convicted terrorist Rasmea Yousuf Odeh, despite her established involvement in a 1969 Jerusalem supermarket bombing that killed two people.

The fifth episode of the *ZU* video may well be an effort to balance the harsh rhetoric of Rosen's other two contributions. Titled "Wrestling in the Daylight: A Rabbi's Journey," the first twenty minutes of the video are devoted to a more personal narrative by Rosen, one in which his voice is mild and his rhetoric comparatively moderate. It is more likely to win a hearing for his political views. Perhaps its most revealing moment comes when Rosen, in the midst of commenting critically on Israel's history and its relation to the Holocaust, advises that "if we focus on spiritual liberation and transcendent values our survival will take care of itself." Individuals can sometimes live that way, but Jews in Nazi Germany or targeted groups in many other political contexts could hardly afford to do so, and it is broadly difficult for almost any nation-state, let alone a Jewish one in the Middle East.

Brant Rosen's chapter in *ZU* is one of three, along with those by Gary Burge and Abu Sway, that is presented in the form of a third person summary, rather than as a direct condensed version of the original essay. While it would be easy for readers to miss that difference, it gives the editors greater license not to represent the original essays fully. Thus, while the summary of Burge's piece is straightforward in demonstrating his promotion of a supersessionist or replacement theology of his own, his claim that the "suspended blessing" of God's covenant with the Jews will be "restored at the end of history when Christ returns, when 'all Israel will be saved'" loses some of its aggressive edge when his assurance in *Quest* that Judaism "will join the church" is omitted (189).

For those who consult both *ZU* and *Quest*, the two texts both amplify and complicate one another. That is partly a function of format. *Quest* is a conventional, unillustrated print book that offers extended argument. Like other IPMN publications, *ZU* is a complex bricolage, a mixture of signed and unsigned contributions, chapters and inserts, illustrations with independent and argumentative captions, sidebars, and study questions. There really is nothing quite like them either in the pro-BDS or anti-BDS literature. The bricolage format, almost that of a compressed, popular coffee table book, has the effect of multidirectional critique, a kind of extrajudicial triangulation of Zionism that makes a guilty verdict inevitable.

It is almost as an aside that *ZU* tells us "there is a growing consensus—except, notably, in the US and Israel—that the existing *de facto* one-state situation/solution is irreversible" (23) and consequently that the two-state solution, the gold standard since 1947, is dead. Suffice it to say that there is no such consensus, though out of either warranted frustration or malice toward the Jewish state some maintain that only a single state from the Jordan River to the Mediterranean Sea with equality and justice for all can cure us of the disease of Zionism. As I have said before, that is a recipe for civil war, not a guarantee of equality and justice, but the appeal to a benighted humanism can seem persuasive to idealists both within and without faith communities. For readers persuaded by the *ZU* project, one thing will be clear: Israel has so betrayed humanist values that it has eliminated its very right to exist. Thus, the real problem with a two-state solution is that Israel would still be there. For BDS and IPMN, a solution that sustains the existence of a Jewish state is no solution at all.

As many advocates of a two-state solution point out, its fundamental outlines are clear: not "an end to Jewish settlements" (22), as *ZU* unrealistically declares, but incorporation of those settlement blocks near the 1967 borders into Israel and evacuation of those deeper into the West Bank; not granting a full right of return to Israel proper for millions of descendants of the original refugees, as the BDS movement demands, but return for a few thousand with relatives in Israel and full compensation for property losses for others. Two states for two peoples has been and remains the only route to justice for both peoples.

The paradox of a workable peace is that it will require not only a maximum degree of separation between the two peoples, but also a maximum degree of collaboration between them. The presence of violent agents among both Israelis and Palestinians requires boundaries, including the much-demonized separation barrier, less than ten percent of which is actually a wall, the rest being a wire fence that can easily be rerouted as necessary. Collaboration should entail working together on security and on infrastructure needs, from water resources to drip-based agriculture to sanitary systems. And tens of thousands of additional Palestinians should get legal permits to work in Israel. The full list of areas of cooperation would be longer; its implementation, over time, could make it possible to tear down that wall. But not now. Meanwhile, Israeli government policy toward Gaza and the West Bank needs change, with counter-productive practices like house demolitions eliminated, but that will most likely not happen until Israeli citizens demand it.

In the end, the key response to the *ZU* project compels us not simply to question its facts and interpretations but also to ask how it helps faith-based movements to participate meaningfully in the peace process. Foremost among these contributions are the many Christian efforts to promote empathy, mutual understanding, and reconciliation. *ZU* and *Quest* do nothing to spread those values; instead, they relentlessly castigate and demonize the Jewish state, a rhetorical tactic which only pits the parties against one another in what amounts to a war of words. Nothing good will come of such an agenda. Contrary to the BDS movement's claim, reconciliation does not lock in injustices; instead it provides the shared respect that is a prerequisite to overcoming them nonviolently. Faith-based constituencies everywhere have roles to play in promoting change from the bottom up. *ZU* and *Quest*, however, do not follow that path. One can only hope that the very clarity of their antagonism might convince some of the faithful to make a different choice than the authors.

BEFORE AND AFTER *ZIONISM UNSETTLED*

As the first section of this essay makes clear, Presbyterian debates over Israel and the Palestinians have a long history. Some of the principles underlying debates in the twenty-first century are codified in a 1980 General Assembly publication, *Peacemaking: The Believers' Calling*, which does not—except for a few sentences—directly address the Middle East, although it echoes church documents from the 1970s that do address it. There the Church highlights its central motivations for supporting Palestinians: "it is not possible to ignore the incongruous juxtaposition of affluence and arms on the one hand, and poverty and oppression on the other . . . . Our insensitivity to today's patterns of injustice, inequality, and oppression—indeed, our participation in them—denies the gospel" (5). In multiple passages, we are told that "Concern about freedom and justice may well call for policies that side with the dispossessed" (26). Belief that the Palestinians are the primary victims in the Israeli-Palestinian conflict was already present in the Church by 1948-49, although that conviction was long moderated by nascent awareness of the Holocaust. Over time, however, the Holocaust receded in centrality for some Presbyterians.

Still more directly influential was the 2010 General Assembly report *Breaking Down the Walls*, written by nine appointed members on behalf of the PCUSA's Middle East Study Committee. Among its most notable claims is its opening argument, which invokes a broad humanistic opposition to "walls" in general and links it to Israel's security barrier, the first continuous segment of which was completed during the Second Intifada, which took place roughly from 2000 through 2005. From the outset we are told, "We are called to be those who break down these walls that stand in the way of the realization of God's peaceful and just kingdom" (1). This uninformed and unrealistic opposition to all barriers to free movement has also guided the BDS movement's continuing demand that the wall be torn down, even though that would encourage violence, not peace.

The policy document is then prefaced by eight "letters to our church, partners, and engaged parties"—the ecumenical community, American Jews, American Muslims, Middle Eastern Christians, Palestinians, Israelis, and all Americans. The letter to American Jews affirms that "we support the existence of Israel as a sovereign nation within secure and recognized borders" (5). The letter to Israelis declares church members to be "strong advocates for Israel's secure existence" and says, "we are fervent in our hope that Israel would continue to be a homeland for the Jewish people" (9). The language, including the indefinite article "a," is carefully crafted to leave open the option of a one-state solution dominated by Palestinians. Yet the other letters do not repeat these assurances, which seriously undermines any political commitment they might embody. Worse still, however, is the document's endorsement and reprinting of both "The Amman Call" and *Kairos Palestine*, the latter of which is carefully analyzed by David Fox Sandmel in the present volume. *Kairos* demands an unqualified Palestinian right of return, rejects the idea of a Jewish state, and castigates the West for making amends for "what Jews had endured in the countries of Europe . . . on our account and in our land" (74). Despite the PCUSA issuing a call for a more even-handed approach to the conflict in 2008, *Breaking Down the Walls* went so far as to legitimize denying Israel's right to exist as a Jewish state. It was condemned by the Anti-Defamation League, among others.

Four years later, the IPMN issued the influential *Zionism Unsettled*, a much more expensive undertaking. *Breaking Down the Walls* was a conventional printed text. ZU was neither the first nor the last full-color, oversized book produced by IPMN in this distinctive format. Depending on how you count, it was either the second or the third, but it was certainly the one most widely publicized and debated, which is why I have concentrated on it here. The aesthetic adopted for IPMN's full color books has been largely visual; they require much less reading, being composed of short texts interspersed with pictures.

The first in the series, *Steadfast Hope: The Palestinian Quest for Just Peace*, was published in June 2009, accompanied by a DVD. A second, somewhat revised edition appeared in April 2011. The cover for the 2011 edition introduces the good versus evil dichotomy that defines the IPMN worldview (Fig. 18). A beautiful, gnarled olive tree, a defining image for the Holy Land, fills the left half of the cover. Inset on the lower right is its polar opposite, a bleak field of stumps, the ground near desert with only sparse blades of grass remaining, perhaps an area cleared for construction.

The settler assaults on olive trees are despicable, but this is something different, a comprehensive contrast between life and death, nature and desolation, and of course, as IPMN would have it, between life (Palestinians) and death (Israelis). The introduction to the 2011 edition reports that the first edition "was written in a spirit of guarded optimism," but that "those hopes were dashed." Now all "peacemakers" must confront Israel's "systematic discrimination against Arab citizens . . . a bleeding, untreated wound inflicted in 1948." The wound is not only the Nakba but the very creation of Israel as well. The authors write now with a "burning desire to speak to the Church with the unvarnished truth about this conflict." "The Church has been here before," they add, "and it is now awakening to the truth that God is calling it to be there again" (1). The following year Presbyterians Concerned for Christian, Jewish, and Muslim Relations, a group that would evolve to become Presbyterians for Middle East Peace (PFMEP), published a detailed analysis and critique of the publication. It opens with a valuable three-page statement about the principles that should guide faith-based study of the Israeli-Palestinian conflict and a condemnation of *Steadfast Hope* for violating them. Quotations from those pages, which should guide all denominations, are included in the introduction to *Peace and Faith*.

Most of the chapters in the second edition of *Steadfast Hope* remain unchanged except for minor updates, though a sidebar praising "The Amman Call" (38) is replaced by one endorsing *Kairos Palestine* (42). The major change in the text is the addition of a detailed essay, "Post-Gaza:

Fig. 18—The 2011 cover to *Steadfast Hope*

a new chapter in the quest for just peace" (36-39), which focuses on critiques of policies adopted by the second Netanyahu government. The accompanying DVD is substantially revised, with a running time increased from 78 to 120 minutes. The third video segment, "Can We Call it Apartheid?" for example, grew from nine to fourteen minutes. A new video segment on "Middle East Uprisings" is added, reflecting the hope the "Post-Gaza" essay invests in the Arab Spring heralding an era of regional democracy. That essay ends with this question: "Can we discern the hand of God in the changes now unfolding?" (39), then invites readers to "Stay tuned." But the risk of attributing divine significance to current events was made clear before long.

Two years after *Zionism Unsettled* was published, the PCUSA's Advisory Committee on Social Witness Policy (ACSWP) issued *Israel-Palestine: For Human Values in the Absence of a Just Peace* for the 2016 General Assembly. It was yet another long anti-Zionist report, this time produced by an official Church committee. Since IPMN is a voluntary interest group, the Church can claim that IPMN's publications do not represent the PCUSA or its views. The ACSWP report, on the other hand, displays the official church logo and is prefaced by the Stated Clerk of the General Assembly declaring that it was formally adopted as Church policy in June. This time the PCUSA cannot keep the text at arm's length.

Unfortunately, the authors of the report did not care to do adequate fact checking. Thus, they immediately tell us the First Intifada was "largely nonviolent" (20), despite over 800 Palestinians having been executed as suspected collaborators with Israel. Hurling stones and Molotov cocktails, moreover, was a standard demonstration tactic, which led to the loss of a hundred Israeli civilians and sixty IDF personnel. Thousands on both sides were injured, and over a thousand Palestinians died. We are further informed that "advocating for the 'two-state solution' or any other particular political arrangement has often distracted people from ongoing events and suffering," a claim that could serve as a motto for BDS politics (6), as it suggests efforts to promote political progress are an unwelcome distraction from the twin core missions of virtue signaling and condemning Zionism. The authors inexplicably declare that East Jerusalem under Jordanian control (before

1967) was "accessible by all religious groups" (18), but of course neither Israeli Christians, Jews, nor Muslims could access religious sites like the Western Wall or the Temple Mount/Haram al-Sharif. Indeed, Jordan refused to recognize any Israeli passports. The authors tell us the Israeli blockade of Gaza is responsible for the "lack of food security among much of the population," but all authorities, including Palestinians themselves, report that food supplies are adequate; the problem is that the poor cannot afford to buy food in stores, a problem exacerbated by the Palestinian Authority's decision to withhold Gazan income. When they acknowledge Palestinian hostility toward Israel, they qualify it in misleading ways, telling us, for example, that the "few" tunnels Hamas dug into Israel were only "purportedly dug to enable assault teams to attack Israeli border posts" (29); then they assert that Israeli retaliations for Hamas's rocket attacks were "unprovoked" (30), both counterfactual claims. They condemn attacks on UNRWA schools in Gaza without reporting that the schools were intentionally used as weapons depots, making them valid targets.

On behalf of PFMEP, Todd Stavrakos and Michael Gizzi produced "A Response and Rebuttal to the ACSWP Report," which is an effective and detailed rebuttal to the entire project. They begin by pointing out that the report's use of the term "Zionist Judaism" is a derogatory effort to suggest that Judaism itself has been corrupted by what ACSWP sees as political Zion's abuse of human rights. They add that "Speaking of 'tribal loyalties' with reference to Jews is code language used in the past and present to question the loyalty and fealty of the Jewish people in the states they reside" (7), a critique broadly applicable to Christian BDS movements. They point out that ACSWP "treats attacks on Israeli civilians as armed resistance, when they are really acts of terrorism" (6). In a telling rejoinder to the report's sympathetic characterization of Hamas's willingness to treat Gazans as expendable, Stavrakos and Gizzi declare that "It is disturbing to find a Body of Christ offering legitimacy for such violence" (13). One needs only to add, finally that a number of church members are active in both IPMN and ACSWP. They are intertwined political projects.

WHY PALESTINE MATTERS

Once again, the anti-Zionist forces in PCUSA struck back. The third addition to the IPMN book series, *Why Palestine Matters: The Struggle to End Colonialism*, a sequel to *Zionism Unsettled*, was issued in April 2018, just in time for PCUSA's June General Assembly. Toward the end of the book, there is a decidedly ineffective effort to extend the politics of intersectionality to include a link between Gaza and Puerto Rico in the aftermath of Hurricane Maria. The second item in "Parallels with Puerto Rico," "Letter from Gaza: 'We Are All Puerto Ricans,'" opens by declaring, "I know what it's like to struggle with shortages of vital supplies such as electricity, gas, cash, and safe water" (82).

Why Palestine Matters is a 110-page (again oversized) book consisting of thirty-nine essays, over thirty breakout supplements, and a large number of illustrations with full paragraph captions. It includes three very useful color maps, one each of Gaza, West Bank settlements, and West Bank Areas A, B, and C. The editors describe it as the third "study guide" issued by IPMN, but it is so fiercely one-sided that it would be more accurately described as an ideological and political manual for anti-Israel organizing. The volume reflects IPMN's history by once again explicitly aligning itself with the BDS movement, this time at length. Many of the essays are new, but a few are excerpts from earlier publications. In the latter category are Steven Salaita's intensely worded "Cultural Appropriation or Theft?" which warns us hyperbolically that use of the phrase "Israeli hummus" as a product label for the well-known appetizer amounts to "a project of erasure, a portent of nonexistence, a promise of genocide" (61) and Sarah Schulman's "Rebranding with Sex and Sexuality," which reprises her 2011 brief against "pinkwashing," the purported effort to distract attention from the military occupation of the West Bank by highlighting Israel's gay-friendly legal and cultural environment.

The book's political stance is signaled at the outset not only by its subtitle but also by its foreword by Richard Falk, a former United Nations Special Rapporteur on the situation of human rights in the Palestinian territories occupied since 1967 and one of Israel's most relentless longstanding opponents. He concludes his assessment of Israel's history and present prospects by insisting that "negotiation of a sustainable peace depends on the prior disavowal and abandonment of the apartheid regime that Israel relies upon to subjugate the Palestinian people" and agreement "that any legitimate state or states that emerge in Palestine formally must be neither religious nor ethnic" (8). This follows his declaration that "denying involuntary exiles a right to return to their native country is a grave violation of international refugee law" (7). He envisions a full right of return for all descendants of the 1948 Arab refugees, despite ninety-seven percent of the original refugees being deceased. If the result were to be a majority Arab state, any promise that it would be a securely secular entity would soon be forgotten. A home for the Jews it would not be.

The page devoted to Puerto Rico follows many pages devoted to more familiar "intersections," including those parallels promoted by a segment of the Black Lives Matter movement. An Israeli Defense Force/Hurricane Maria connection is a completely empty analogy, as neither the two instances of infrastructural devastation nor the human tragedies they accompanied actually have anything to do with one another. An international relief effort could address urgent requirements in both places, but what Puerto Rico needs is a serious full-scale commitment from its own country, the wealthiest country in the world, not international charity. One might have expected the editors of *Why Palestine Matters* to situate the "intersection" of Gaza City and San Juan in underlying racism as the common cause. That certainly goes a long way to explaining the Trump administration's indifference to Puerto Rico's plight, but it has little to do with the Netanyahu administration's tragic and highly dangerous neglect of Gaza.

Why Palestine Matters appropriately places the 1901 US Supreme Court case *Downes v. Bidwell* at the root of the secondary status of the island. That court decision confirmed Puerto Rican rights of liberty and property but held that the island was not part of the US for matters of revenue and administration. Yet that is not an adequate explanation of why Hurricane Maria did not provoke a new push for Puerto Rican statehood. The fact that the Island would vote reliably Democratic had more to do directly with the Republican-controlled Senate's unwillingness to address its statehood status. All this demonstrates that the specifics of history and politics can get squarely in the way of promoting "intersections" between injustices in different parts of the world. The editors are able to produce a photograph of three Puerto Rican women arm-in-arm with a Palestinian American San Francisco State University professor holding a "*Mujeres en Puerto Rico/Solidarias con Palestine*" banner and to assure us that "Palestine solidarity is an enduring feature of Puerto Rican intersectional activism." Nevertheless, it is not clear that this "enduring feature" is actually a central one.

A few pages later, Susan Landau's essay "Nonviolent Economic Action as Resistance," ostensibly a primer on the BDS movement, is illustrated with a photo captioned "The arrest of Rosa Parks on December 1, 1955, catalyzed the Montgomery bus boycott" (86). This is an equally far-fetched intersection, since not only half the planet but also half a century separates the two movements. Once again, race could be claimed as the link, however unfairly, but in fact Landau's essay doesn't invoke the US Civil Rights movement. Perhaps the editors, not the author, chose the illustration, hoping to trigger an emotional reaction in the reader. Some historical moments, I would argue, deserve their nearly sacred character as unique events. They cannot actually be honored by exploiting them for unconnected political purposes. Americans especially should not be called upon to think "Israel" when they see the moving photo of black demonstrators waving as the Alabama bus goes by in 1955. Israel's critics and supporters alike should all be able to treasure that image, in a moment of solidarity purified of irrelevant contemporary conflicts.

Notice that intersectionality—in an outreach toward the contemporary left—will now be central to IPMN's effort to appeal to American readers comes in the book's introduction, which is titled "Intersectionality and the Shared Struggle for Human Rights." The "intersection" put forward there is not between any particular social or political circumstances but rather, in the style of BDS activism everywhere, on the wholly abstract plane of universal justice: "Justice in one place is not enough without justice everywhere . . . . Scholars now use the term *intersectionality* for this interwoven web of rights and the common struggle to realize these rights all over the world" (9). In fact, these struggles have to be waged under local conditions and in the context of local politics and history. The ability to invoke a set of universal principles has genuine value in local struggles, but the struggle is not simply a universal one that can be transported intact across time and space. There is nothing scholarly about the term *intersectionality* when it is used in this way; it is merely a rhetorical platform, a polemical strategy, not a category of historical analysis. It has become a slogan, a rallying cry that tries to transform analogy into identity.

Used properly, intersectionality can be a powerful analytic tool. It helps us see how what appear to be quite separate social and political forces—like race and gender—intersect in a given place and time to produce a powerful combined impact. But claims of intersection across time and space artificially link what are typically no more than quasi-parallel phenomena, obscuring the critical details necessary to full understanding. Worse, claims that things happening in different cultures are actually identical can also undermine the specific local knowledge required for effective political action.

Contrary to what the book's editors would like us to believe, the project of human emancipation can be carried out in some places without being carried out in others. Indeed, the goal of emancipation would otherwise be impossible. The introduction concludes by claiming that the project of human emancipation "cannot proceed without Palestine," when actually, for better or worse, it can. Different struggles for human rights can inspire one another; one can learn from one struggle and try to modify its lessons so as to apply them elsewhere, but the work begins anew in every new setting, and everything has to be rearticulated as a result.

The first chapter, "Palestine Through the Lens of Colonialism and Intersectionality," and the second, "An Intersectional Approach to Justice," then follow. Whether this was a good strategy for anti-Zionist advocacy in the Presbyterian Church USA remains to be seen. It reproduces established rhetoric on campus, but it leaves behind the theological ground that has been important in the churches, thereby compounding a trend away from theology and toward politics among Protestant denominations debating the Israeli-Palestinian conflict.

Why Palestine Matters then throws its lot in with intersectionality in a far riskier and more thoroughgoing way. The next section is comprised of four double-paged color spreads, eight full pages, all in the book's oversized 8.5 by 11-inch format (Fig. 19). The four spreads— "Intersectionality: Threads of Connection," "Interconnected Struggles: Intersectional Politics Grounded in Effective Alliances," "Militarization, Repressive Policing: Unprecedented Connections Across Movements and Border," and "Cross-Movement Connections: Building a Global Movement for Justice"—do not advance arguments or make a case for particular "intersections." They simply announce a series of "intersections" by way of disconnected one-paragraph statements and an array of twenty-six color photographs and posters. At best, this tactic amounts to juxtaposition, rather than intersection, thereby jettisoning any sense of rational analysis.

A key example of mere juxtaposition is the book's repeated effort to link the Native American opposition to the Dakota Access Pipeline with organized resistance in the West Bank and Gaza. The resulting confusion has no real bearing on Israel, but it does obscure the tragic and continuing history of Native American oppression and discrimination in the Americas, effectively exploiting the Native American story for use in the anti-Zionist agenda. As my *Israel Denial* shows, that is a key damaging effect of Steven Salaita's effort to make the Israeli-Palestinian conflict central to Native American studies. The long effort first to exterminate and then to suppress and marginalize Native Americans is a story that deserves its exceptional character. The widespread willingness to discount Native American culture and values persists today. But any effort to resist the forces that conspired against American Indians in North Dakota has to focus on the political power wielded by the gas and oil industry and its Republican allies at the state and national level. Making this a story about manufactured "intersections" with Israel only dilutes and derails education and advocacy on this side of the Atlantic.

The prominence given to this purported solidarity with Native Americans in *Why Palestine Matters* is part of the BDS movement's racialized anti-Israel strategy. Like many of the views that appear and reappear in the book, there is no central, organized presentation of the claim that Jewish Israeli attitudes toward Arabs are fundamentally

The tendency has been to consider Palestine a separate—and unfortunately too often marginal—issue. This is precisely the moment to encourage everyone who believes in equality and justice to join the call for a free Palestine.

Angela Y. Davis. *Freedom Is a Constant Struggle*, 2016

…if we put identity politics ahead of the requirement to be intersectional and to connect to other struggles, we harm ourselves, our cause, as well as other causes.

Excerpt from a public talk by Omar Barghouti, delivered May 2, 2017, as told by Philip Weiss on *Mondoweiss*

Inspired J. Howard Miller's iconic "We Can Do It!" wartime poster of "Rosie the Riveter," this image was rediscovered in the '80's and used as a symbol of the feminist movement. This version has become a powerful image of feminism today as influenced by intersectionality and inclusion.

We ALL can do it!

INJUSTICE ANYWHERE Threatens JUSTICE EVERYWHERE

This quote by Martin Luther King, Jr. appears in support of the Standing Rock Sioux in a protest against the Dakota Access Pipeline, August 31st, 2016.

Like Jim Crow (and slavery), mass incarceration operates as a tightly networked system of laws, policies, customs, and institutions that operate collectively to ensure the subordinate status of a group defined largely by race.

Michelle Alexander, *The New Jim Crow: Mass Incarceration in the Age of Colorblindness*, 2010

INTERSECTIONALITY   THREADS OF CONNECTION

Islamophobia is one branch on the tree of racism. Islamophobia, homophobia, anti-Black racism, and antisemitism are all connected, and we cannot dismantle one without the other. Our liberation is intertwined, our stories are intertwined, our identities are intertwined.

"Our Liberation is Intertwined," An Interview with Linda Sarsour, *On Antisemitism: Solidarity and the Struggle for Justice*, p.33, 2017

If you have come to help me, you are wasting your time. If you have come because your liberation is bound up with mine, then let us work together.

Lilla Watson, Aboriginal activists group, Queensland, Australia

Palestinians wait to cross Qalandia checkpoint on their way to attend Ramadan Friday prayers in Jerusalem on August 3, 2012.

WHY PALESTINE MATTERS: THE STRUGGLE TO END COLONIALISM

Fig. 19—An intersectionality page from *Why Palestine Matters* (22).

racist. With roughly 100 different essays, mini-essays, essay excerpts, and argumentative photo captions offering a jumble of political assertions, *Why Palestine Matters* often operates as much by insinuation as by responsible argument. Nonetheless, when Jewish Voice for Peace's media manager Naomi Dann tells us late in the book that the white supremacist Richard Spencer sees himself as "a white Zionist" and anti-Semitically asserts he "might be right about Israel" she is drawing together threads that have been woven throughout: "There is a disturbing alliance between Zionists and white nationalists in the White House these days, and it doesn't come from nowhere. There is a shared bedrock of anxiety about demographics and racist and Islamophobic fear of 'Arabs' that goes hand in hand with both worldviews" (89). Of course, reactionary US hostility toward all peoples of color was the operative Trump White House ideology; anti-Arab sentiment is not its controlling feature.

Demographics alone should have shown this accusation to be a slander. It is critical for the editors of *Why Palestine Matters* to remind us that the Jews who returned to Palestine in the late nineteenth and early twentieth century were largely white and European; that fact is central not only to the racialized story the editors want to establish for Zionism but also to the settler colonialist narrative embraced throughout the book. The inconvenient truth that gets in the way of this story is that in the years after Israel was established as a state some 800,000 Jews fled or were expelled from often ancient communities in surrounding Arab countries to settle in Israel. The majority of Israel's Jewish population today, descendants of those exiles, are of Middle Eastern and North African, not European, descent. Socioeconomic gaps remain, but these Mizrachi Jews are critical to the coalition that brought Likud to power. Nonetheless, G. J. Tarazi insists that "the ruling elite in Israel today, are not Middle Eastern but are European settlers" (12). Just to cite a few important counter examples: In the 2018 Israeli government there were 21 ministers, of whom eight were Mizrachi, two were of mixed heritage, one was Druze and ten were Ashkenazi. Of the previous six Chiefs of the General Staff of the IDF three were Mizrachi (Shaul Mofaz, Dan Halutz, and Gadi Eizenkot) one mixed (Gabi Ashkenazi) and two Ashkenazi (Moshe Ya'alon and Benjamin Gantz).

The majority of Israelis are of Middle Eastern and North African descent, even more so when non-Jewish Israeli Arabs—who make up twenty percent of the general population—are added to the mix. If the standard marker of the socially constructed illusion of race is skin color, then Israelis and Arabs are indistinguishable. There is no lack of hostility to neighboring Arab countries in Israel, but that hostility is not racial in character. Making it seem so is nonetheless a useful anti-Zionist strategy.

Nevertheless, in *Why Palestine Matters* Israelis are accused of a "racism 'of the heart,'" an "insidious racism that cannot be changed through public policy and laws" (14): "The racial domination that took centuries to develop in the United States has been concentrated and accelerated in Israel and Palestine" (14). Here we cross the line into anti-Semitism in a dramatically new way for IPMN. *Why Palestine Matters* aims to convince us that "The treatment of African Americans in the United States and Palestinians by Israel is shockingly similar" (15). Long-time Israel opponent Pauline Coffman concludes that "The situation eerily parallels White Nationalists in the US calling for limits on non-White immigration in order to maintain the demographics they prefer" (71). "How do we connect the dots between US racism, white supremacy, and the issue of justice in Palestine" (89), asks Susan Landau? We do so, the editors of the book apparently believe, simply by repeatedly announcing they are connected.

G. J. Tarazi presses this agenda still further by suggesting that, when we examine the status of Palestinians, "parallels can be seen in the history of slavery in the United States" (13). The comparison is warranted, he argues, because they "used the Bible as a weapon" to subjugate others they considered "less than human." That view is readily substantiated in the history of American slavery but is wholly unsupportable as a characterization of Israeli attitudes toward Palestinians. Both that claim and the accusation that Israelis are engaged in genocide should have been excluded from the book. Instead, since the editors make no effort to distance themselves from any of the contributors' claims, we have to consider them generally supportive of everything the authors say.

Why Palestine Matters is on far better ground when it alerts readers to a growing crisis in Gaza, a warning both I and many Israelis have been issuing for several years. Three essays—those by Jennifer Bing, Ron Smith, and Harry Gunkel—are devoted to Gaza, the latter combining extreme hostility to Israel with an eloquent plea: "in her illness and darkness, Gaza offers us her hand. How can we refuse it?" (45) Yet excoriating Israel, the standard BDS response, will not actually help the situation by bringing relief to Gaza. Nor will Kathleen Christison's attack here on the reconciliation and dialogue initiatives that have been a hallmark of Christian peacebuilding ("Who's Afraid of Dialogue? Normalizing Oppression"). "These efforts," she writes, "tend to be feel-good projects that lull supporters and donors into an ineffectual complacency." Such "normalization," she adds, "concretizes the status quo, standardizes the dominance of the strong party over the weak party, the occupier over the occupied" (60). In fact, the mutual understanding such projects generate is essential if peace negotiations are to proceed.

When *Why Palestine Matters* confronts Gaza, it is long on condemnation and short on practical recommendations. Bing's call "to end the cruel and inhumane blockade" is no help either (42). The blockade should be moderated, but, if it were simply lifted, Hamas would bring in dangerous weapons and the military conflict would actually escalate. Instead, Egypt and Israel should combine forces to lift restrictions on exports from Gaza to help its economy. The US and other countries should press the Palestinian Authority to withdraw its effort to limit Gaza's electricity supply and put more pressure on Hamas. The fishing limit should be extended from six to at least fifteen miles. Arab countries could manage reconstruction projects directly in order to prevent Hamas from repurposing reconstruction aid to rebuild its military infrastructure, specifically its assault tunnels, as currently happens. International advocacy should focus on the practical steps that must be taken to improve conditions in Gaza.

The Presbyterian Church could play a major role there, but *Why Palestine Matters* does not point us in that direction. Detailed promotion of the existing Christian projects to build mutual empathy and understanding can make a major difference. That misdirection of Christian effort may be IPMN's most damaging legacy. It is a legacy that is ongoing. At the PCUSA's August 2019 "Big Tent" meeting in

Baltimore—an event designed to combine multiple conferences into one event and held annually since 2009—IPMN held a workshop on Why Palestine Matters. The main theme was that the Jewish state is an expression of European colonialism, which is certain to feature again at the 2022 General Assembly or thereafter.

Although the argument that Israel is a colonialist state acquired some political force not long after the 1967 war, it is really in the last thirty years that it became a lynchpin of anti-Zionism on the left. It is important to remember, as John Strawson points out, that in 1948 "the left certainly did not see Israel as a colonial state but rather saw its creation as [a] blow against Imperialism" (36), against British imperialism in particular. A generation later, the left had lost much of its definitional commitment to working class solidarity. Anti-colonialism and anti-imperialism helped fill the theoretical void created. The colonialist slander works best for Israel in the form of vehement denunciation because the actual facts do not match a responsible colonialist narrative. Neither the Jews who founded the Yishuv nor those who fled Europe after the rise of the Third Reich or in the wake of the Holocaust came as representatives of a colonial power. The Yishuv was not "the result of an Imperial power trying to move a section of its own population into the colonial territory" (Strawson 38). Moreover, they "could by no means retreat to the territory of a nonexistent colonial" state (Harrison 199). They did not aim to recreate their country of origin in the Holy Land; they sought instead to honor their ancient history by creating something new. "The Jews who arrived in Palestine from the 1880s onwards saw themselves as both pioneers and returnees" (Strawson 40). The colonialist label, however, is a spectacular brand: "Israel, seen as a triumphantly and unashamedly imperialist and colonialist state is, a fortiori, an evil state." Moreover, "as a 'colonial settler state,' it necessarily follows, *morally speaking* . . . that Israel should never have been allowed to come into existence in the first place and should cease to exist as soon as its demise can be conveniently be arranged" (Harrison 278).

The colonialist accusation serves to "transform the Jewish population of Israel from an oppressed people fleeing persecution and genocide into an aggressive colonial settler" (Strawson 41). Without the expansion of Jewish settlements into the West Bank in the 1970s and

thereafter, that transformation of Israel's image would have little plau-
sibility. And had the Arab states accepted partition in 1948 instead of
going to war the colonialist accusation would likely never have gained
traction. Projecting the accusation back in time to include the founding
of the Jewish state and turning that event into a crime is a project at
once of anti-Zionist Arab sentiment and the BDS movement within
and without Christian churches. An increasing number of Arab states,
however, are deciding that the benefits of recognizing Israel outweigh its
demonization. A portion of the BDS movement would no doubt sustain
its hostility even if two states for two peoples were to be realized. But
much of the BDS movement's purchase in Christian churches would
disappear.

CONCLUSION

Participants in the PCUSA's 2016 meeting had a comprehensive report
available that provided an objective, well-reasoned analysis of the Israeli-
Palestinian conflict. The eighty-page booklet, *Two States for Two Peoples:
A resource developed by Presbyterians for Middle East Peace* (hereafter *Two
States*) is unlike the several IPMN products in every respect (Fig. 20).
Two States is not written as a response to *Zionism Unsettled*—indeed,
ZU is only mentioned once, on page forty-one, taking exception to *ZU*'s
characterization of Zionism as a "false theology"—though the PFMEP
booklet is clearly designed to reeducate church members, counter the
IPMN campaign, and repair the damage the boycott movement had
done to the church's ability to contribute effectively toward peace and
reconciliation.

Virtually nothing in *Two States* qualifies as polemical, whereas
almost everything in *ZU* does. *ZU* bills itself as a study guide, then
provides relentless indoctrination. *Two States* takes seriously its purpose
as a resource, giving readers several historically accurate area maps and
thoroughly neutral sections, such as one listing and explaining the
various Israeli political parties and government structures. The PFMEP
document is scrupulous in its presentation of fact, evenhanded in its
treatment of Israelis and Palestinians, and consistently sound in its analysis. Contrary to IPMN's efforts to claim indigeneity for Palestinians
alone, for example, *Two States* explains that "Both Jews and Palestinians

Two States for Two Peoples

A resource developed by *Presbyterians for Middle East Peace*

www.pfmep.org

Fig. 20—The cover to *Two States for Two Peoples*

are indigenous to the land, and both Jews and Palestinians have a history of immigration to the land" (4). It does make judgments, reaching negative conclusions about both Hamas and the BDS movement, but even those judgments are measured, as when it assesses a BDS/IPMN tactic:

It is easy for an advocate to cherry-pick legal viewpoints to support a given agenda or vilify an opponent. This kind of debate does not move toward peace, rather "it would only add an insoluble element to what is already an extremely difficult problem." A reckless pursuit of "justice" rather than a negotiated peace treaty between Israel and the Palestinians is actually an obstacle to peace. (31) (attributed to Nicholas Rostow)

As PFMEP would later advise in "Two State for Two Peoples 2018 Supplement," "'justice' is a catchy term and easy to sell with little or even fraudulent information" (27). Instead, *Two States* first offers two guiding principles:

- The rights, dignity, and aspiration of both Israelis and *Palestinians must be honored and respected.*
- The course of action supported *must be consistent with principles of universal human rights*: the right of self-determination and democratic governance, the right to free expression and peaceful assembly, the right to a nationality, and the right to live in peace with neighbors.

That neither Hamas nor the Palestinian Authority honor these principles is an inconvenience IPMN simply ignores. As a way to move forward in harmony with these principles, *Two States* endorses two passages from Alliance for Middle East Peace:

- People-to-people encounters are an effective and necessary strategy to create such sustainable collective public support for peaceful mutual coexistence on equal grounds and reconciliation.
- Support for civil society programs in the Middle East is one crucial way that the international community, US Government, and private philanthropists alike can positively move the peoples of the Middle East toward peace.

BDS and IPMN predictably reject these options as examples of unacceptable "normalization." We enumerate a number of these options in Michael Gizzi's essay on reconciliation projects.

I have resisted the kind of language that would level the sort of full indictment *ZU* merits, but it is easily found elsewhere. Here is the Reverend Chris Leighton, at the time Executive Director of the Institute for Christian & Jewish Studies. He writes that *ZU*

> turns us from peacemakers to polemicists . . . and from honest dialogue partners to partisan ideologues . . . . The authors go to great lengths to document the worst expressions of Zionism and the American Jewish community, while completely exonerating the Palestinians from any ideologically driven teaching that fails to promote peace . . . . To suggest that the Jewish yearning for their own homeland—a yearning that we Presbyterians have supported for numerous other nations—is somehow theologically and morally abhorrent is to deny Jews their own identity as a people . . . . The word for that is "anti-Semitism." ("False Witness")

In 2018 PFMEP published "Two States for Two Peoples—2018 Supplement," a forty-page update and elaboration on the previous publication. Early on it describes BDS as a movement "whose leaders have called for the elimination of the Jewish state of Israel while recruiting followers on the premise that BDS is nothing more than a human rights campaign" (4). Among the important additions to *Two States* is a section describing the Palestinian assaults on freedom of speech and press in Gaza and the West Bank (7-8). *Two States* also makes a strong case for strengthening the Palestinian Authority's governing capacity as part of a nation-building process necessary to creating a viable Palestinian state. As part of that discussion, the pamphlet conducts a serious review of concepts of sovereignty and how they apply to a potential Palestinian state. The scholarly character of this analysis has no equivalent in any IPMN publication. Its citations to previous scholarship reinforce the sense of the project's objectivity.

Since I endorse PFMEP's fine work and have no reason to fault its analysis, I limit myself to brief summaries that would encourage people to visit its website and read the publications themselves, meanwhile providing detailed comments on the BDS-inspired agenda that has roiled so many Protestant denominations. Nonetheless, two things should be clear. First, PFMEP's important work gives Christians of all denominations a rational alternative to the radical disinformation that BDS allies within the churches have been disseminating. Both sides in this debate invoke longstanding Christian values in their support, but justice and reconciliation, I believe, lie more fully in the good faith PFMEP has offered than in the hostility and alienating condemnation flowing from the other side.

The Presbyterian Church has had a dual track history regarding the Israeli-Palestinian conflict for half a century, but that means some in Church leadership have long offered exemplary advice, understanding, and mutual respect. They know how to advance reconciliation directed not toward submitting to an unacceptable present but toward a future two-state solution that would assure dignity and security for both peoples. The clearest earlier evidence may be the remarkable 1973 book *Peoples and Conflict in the Middle East*, hereafter PAC, discussed above.

Offering an assurance categorically at odds with the IPMN/BDS publications, PAC concludes by reasserting to readers that the Church "does not wish to be understood as preaching moral obligations to the nations concerned with Middle Eastern issues, in the light of centuries of antisemitism and particularly of Western treatment of the Jewish people in this century, and in the light of the long history of Crusades and colonial subjugation of the Arab peoples" (51). *PAC* opens with a parallel principle, one of several that eloquently counters the BDS anti-normalization campaign: "The task force specifically rejected any attempt to judge between the parties involved in the Middle East as to which has been dealt with most unjustly. The cup of suffering caused by displacements, pogroms, crusades, and holocaust is full. Solution must be found at some level beyond the attempt to weigh the suffering of one people against that of another" (8-9).

Moving forward, they advise, "we do not believe advance can be made without conversation" (9). In an observation no less true now than it was fifty years ago, *PAC* recognizes that a productive dialogue "demands a higher respect for the faith, traditions, sufferings, accomplishments, and even the myths of the contending parties than either is now willing to grant the other . . . . It requires that all parties ask the questions that can make the future and not only those which would remake the past" (10). "The tragedies of the past cannot be ignored," they add, because "the past is a part of the blood, bone, and soul of the peoples of the present," yet "neither can the future be made of" those tragedies (10-11). The goal is productive reconciliation, which "can never succeed in winning agreement from those who believe that the definitive humiliation of one or another of these Middle Eastern peoples is essential" (11). The IPMN/BDS agenda is to delegitimate and abolish the Jewish state. Happily, the Church can use select documents from both past and present to guide it in promoting the reconciliation that is its true Christian mission. *PAC* states the matter clearly: "The way to peace, there as here, lies not through partisanship and polarization but through reconciliation. Shalom. Salaam." (10).

PART THREE

RECONCILIATION—GUIDEPOSTS
FOR THE FUTURE

CHAPTER FOURTEEN

SUSAN ANDREWS

SPIRITUAL SIBLINGS SHARING SACRED SPACE: A PASTOR'S REFLECTION

My love of Jewish rituals and stories began when I was 8 years old. My father was a Presbyterian minister, and we lived in a lovely church-owned manse, located in the middle of a Jewish neighborhood. My best friends in third grade were Gail Berman and Roberta Krieger. Gail's family were secular Jews, celebrating Hanukkah and Christmas with equal enthusiasm. But Roberta's family were practicing Jews, with a Friday evening Shabbas meal that formed the center of their spiritual life. I will never forget sitting with Roberta's family as her mother lit the Shabbas candle—and then blessed all the children with the traditional blessing prayer. I was in awe of the tenderness and the simplicity of that ritual and I felt every bit as loved as the Jewish children sitting around me.

My intellectual connection to Judaism began at Harvard Divinity School. My New Testament professor was Krister Stendahl, the great Lutheran Pauline scholar who was one of the first biblical experts to reimagine the meaning of Romans 11, Paul's lyrical tribute to the foundational identity of the Jewish people. Though the Presbyterian congregations I grew up in were not overtly anti-Semitic, there was always the subtle message that Christianity was the one sure path to salvation—and that the Jews had something to do with the death of Jesus. But the passionate lectures of Dr. Stendahl blew those biases to bits. She made it very clear that the gifts of God to the Jewish people are irrevocable and that Christians are in truth the Johnny-come-latelies to the covenant. Indeed, as Paul so vividly describes it, Christians are the small branch grafted onto the true vine of the Jewish people. This biblical awakening convinced me that both Jews and Christians are covenantal peoples, not old as opposed to new, but intertwined in God's everlasting tree of life. Though many of my Jewish friends argue against the authenticity of the Christian claim to the Covenant, I have no hesitation in proclaiming that Jews are "saved" as I am. We are spiritual siblings in this journey called faith. The epiphany I had at seminary has stoked my passion for building interfaith relationships throughout my forty-two years of ordained ministry and has led me to the most satisfying parish relationship I have experienced in my pastoral life.

Bradley Hills Presbyterian Church is a vital, open-minded congregation located in Bethesda, Maryland—three miles from the DC border and one mile from the National Institute of Health. Educated, curious, and passionate about fulfilling our mission and seeking justice, Bradley Hills has been a leader of progressive thought in the Presbyterian Church USA since 1956. It was my privilege to serve as the senior pastor of Bradley Hills from 1989 to 2006.

In 1967, a small group of agnostic liberal Jews approached the Rev. Art Hall, then the pastor of Bradley Hills, to ask if they could rent space for a weekly Hebrew school. These busy, professional people did not want to worship, they just wanted to offer liberal Jewish education to their children. The rabbi making the request was Rabbi Ed Freidman, best known for his teachings on the psychological and sociological dynamics of healthy congregations in the midst of an anxious culture. For the next twenty years the two congregations lived amicably together, while the Bethesda Jewish Congregation paid an increasing amount of rent as their Hebrew school grew. Since the BJC's Saturday schedule did not interfere with the Sunday schedule for Bradley Hills, there was little conflict—and little contact—between the two communities. But when the Jewish congregation began to request space for Shabbas and High Holy Day Services, the relationship became more complicated.

When I arrived in 1989, as the new pastor of the Presbyterian congregation, I immediately saw a golden opportunity. Why should this remain a mere rental agreement when it was clear that each congregation could learn from the other? Culturally, the members of both congregations were similar: highly educated, moderately affluent, family oriented, and often deeply engaged in the governmental and scientific life of Washington, DC. The building arrangements were becoming very complex—and potentially conflict-inducing—but I hoped that a relationship of trust and curiosity could mitigate some of the building hassles. (All the education rooms were shared by both the Jews and the Christians, with all the bulletin board issues and storage issues and extra cleaning responsibilities that such partnership can incur.)

Rabbi Reeve Brenner, who was also an NIH chaplain, was the rabbi at the time. He and I agreed to set up an inter-congregational team to meet regularly and work through these issues. We also began to plan joint worship and educational opportunities to strengthen the interfaith dynamic. A tradition was quickly established of having a joint Thanksgiving service on the Sunday morning before Thanksgiving Day. The two choirs joined forces, the liturgy and hymns were non-Christological, the children came together for the Children's Sermon and then to participate in an educational activity during the rest of the service.

The heart of the Thanksgiving service was the dialogue between the pastor and the rabbi. We would pick a topic to focus on—the Middle East, the meaning of land, etc.—and then each of us would pick a scripture from our tradition to read, with the rabbi's portion always chanted in Hebrew first. We would then discuss what we had in common and how we saw things differently, ultimately leaving the topic up in the air. Following worship we would have a kosher brunch where members of the two congregations could continue the dialogue. Over the years this service has become well-known in the Bethesda area, and continues to be well attended, with a Muslim congregation and an imam now part of the mix.

In the early 1990s a new rabbi arrived, Sunny Schnitzer, and the relationship between the two congregations simply took off. Sunny was a talented cantor and brought the gift of music to the table. The two youth groups began to meet occasionally. Together we organized a service day once a year, engaging with a family shelter across the street. We initiated a tutoring program for suspended high school students, developed in partnership with the public schools, and both Bradley Hills and BJC provided volunteers. Joint adult education was expanded, including a Bible study on Isaiah taught both by the rabbi and me, a Lenten series exploring the High Holy Days and Christian festival days, a fascinating conversation about the meaning of suffering in the two traditions, and several intense group discussions about the volatile situation in the Middle East. Through all these joint ventures deep friendships were built.

At one point, between the First and Second Intifada, the Presbyterian congregation organized a trip to the Middle East, focusing on Palestine and the occupied territories. We stayed with Palestinian families, heard from liberation theologians, and engaged with the hard realities of the occupation. When we returned home, and began to tell our stories, tension arose within the Jewish congregation. Bradley Hills decided to sponsor a young Palestinian man who was coming to the United States to earn a master's degree in rehabilitation medicine and invited him to speak. Thanks to the strong leadership of the rabbi, both congregations met with George, heard his story, and asked honest questions. And an adult education program on the history of the Middle East, taught by the rabbi, built a strong foundation for the future. We worked through the tensions, and the Jewish congregation even held a fundraiser to help with George's educational expenses.

In the mid-1990s, two things happened to deepen this unique relationship between congregations. The rabbi suggested that we "name" our relationship as something more than a building partnership. And so we wrote a covenant, calling ourselves "Spiritual Siblings Sharing Sacred Space." The Bradley Hills Session and the BJC Board unanimously voted to approve this covenant. It was signed in a joint worship session by the spiritual leaders, and during the subsequent coffee hour dozens of members from both congregations added their signatures. The signed document was turned into a ketubah and still hangs on the wall. The Covenant reads:

We, the members of Bradley Hills Presbyterian Church and the Bethesda Jewish Congregation, form together this covenant to honor the Intimate and Infinite God of Creation, the One God we both worship. Taking to heart the biblical charge to be a light to the nations, we seek to offer a prophetic vision of interfaith partnership in a pluralistic world. Continuing a relationship began in 1967, as spiritual siblings sharing sacred space, we commit ourselves to:

Acknowledge and celebrate our commonalities and differences;

Foster appreciation for the richness of our respective traditions;

Encourage curiosity and dialogue between our two communities of faith;

Bear witness to our faith in cooperative activity in the world;

Create with each other what we cannot create separately.

Recognizing the word of our great teachers, we commit ourselves to fulfill the Great Commandment: You shall love the Lord your God with all your heart, with all your soul, with all your mind, and with all you might. With deepest gratitude, we pledge to continue to celebrate the light bestowed upon us. May this union of spirit and space spark a flame of respect and understanding throughout the world.

At about the same time, the Bradley Hills building was turning forty-five years old and was badly in need of renovation and refurbishing. The church leadership approached the synagogue leadership to ask if they would support us in this effort, since they used so much of the building every week. Thus was launched "Celebrate the Light!"—a 3.5 million capital campaign to restore the building. But our Jewish friends agreed to help plan and pay for this work only if we added new space, a dedicated space for their worship, complete with a bimah, an ark, a mezuzah, and an Eternal Light.

The Bradley Hills Session spent two days in deep and tense conversation. Was it right to take this risk? Would we become "Jewish"—or water down our Christian identity? Would our Jewish friends truly carry their weight (20% of building costs and future maintenance costs for the new space)? What if BJC decided to move to their own building, or close down? Could the Christians use the new space built for the Jews, since they would still use our large sanctuary for High Holy Day services, which was the only time they had more than 100 attendees? Would they increase their annual contribution as the space they used expanded? Finally, the church leaders voted with a large majority to venture forward with the vision—and thus started a four-year-long process of consulting, finding an architect, raising the money, and supervising the whole project. Every decision took twice as long, because of the differences of opinions and styles and traditions.

The result was stunning—a Star of David shaped covenant hall built right next to our elegant cross-shaped sanctuary, with a new glass enclosed hospitality space tying the two worship spaces together. BJC immediately grew in size and spiritual strength as they strengthened their worship culture. Meanwhile the church used the new space for small weddings, contemporary worship services, meetings, and adult seminars. Through it all, the relationship of the "spiritual siblings" grew deeper with love and respect and joy. However, these transformations were not without conflict. The church lost a couple of families who felt that we were forsaking Jesus by opening up our hearts and space to Jews without trying to convert them. Growing tensions around building maintenance demanded hard conversations and clear staff accountability. Constant instability in the Middle East caused political strains between these two opinionated congregations. Three quick stories will illuminate the complexity of this journey.

When our Jewish friends used our sanctuary for High Holy Day services—and for our joint Thanksgiving service—the large cross hanging over the chancel and communion table became an obvious problem. Our Jewish partners created a banner to cover the cross during their services, but this upset the older Christian women who kept the sanctuary clean and orderly. They felt that covering the cross was sacrilegious. I gently explained to them that the cross is sacred to Christians because of the meaning and the story we attach to it but that for Jews the cross has no positive meaning, and all too often a negative meaning related to anti-Semitism. Not everyone understood, but we worked through it. That is, until the day someone put a ladder on our elegant wooden communion table in order to reach the cross with the banner! That crisis was solved when a Jewish engineer figured out a pulley system to get the banner up and down, and an artist created a stunning new banner with Hebrew words from Psalm 133: "How blessed it is when kindred dwell together in unity!"

A similar tension arose when the Building Committee designed the new space. Within the Christian community, the ignorance of and resistance to the ark, the bimah, the Eternal Light, and the mezuzot were surprisingly strong. The rabbi took the lead by finding simple designs that would not shout *Jewish*, but which still held the spiritual weight they needed for worship. It was my job to overcome the mezuzah resistance. I simply preached a sermon about the biblical scroll that rests inside each mezuzah, which, of course, are the words from Deuteronomy that Jesus refers to when he offers the first great commandment summarizing the entire Christian gospel: "You shall love the Lord, your God with all your heart, and with all your soul, and with all your might." How could good Christians object to the central teaching of Jesus?

The third example of tension between the two congregations almost broke up our relationship. In 2004, the General Assembly of the Presbyterian Church USA voted to begin a process of selective divestment from companies seen to be profiting from the violent occupation of the Palestinian territories. The complicated process of Presbyterian polity made it difficult for our Jewish friends to understand the nuance of this decision, which was really the beginning of a several year process to *study* the possibility of divestment. In any case, the angry meeting held in the covenant hall about this issue revealed deep anger and a sense of betrayal on both sides. Though BJC was a very liberal Reconstructionist congregation and had spoken forcefully against the occupation, divestment was seen as a direct threat to Israel's security and existence. For some of the Presbyterian congregants, the injustice of the occupation and its dire effect on the lives and futures of Palestinians—many of whom are Christians—was equally disturbing. A decision was made to establish a task force of leaders from both congregations to work through this issue. Intense conversations and dialogue occurred in the months that followed. The outcome was a joint overture to the next PCUSA General Assembly approved by both congregations and the presbytery. The statement called for positive *in*vestment in Palestine instead of *di*vestment and emphasized the importance of striving towards a two-state solution. The overture was passed by the PCUSA General Assembly in 2006.

EMBRACING A TWO-STATE SOLUTION

The experiences outlined above have shaped my convictions about the possibilities for and the necessity of peace in the Middle East. I consider myself both pro-Israeli and pro-Palestinian and continue to believe that a two-state solution with peace, security, and self-determination for both Palestine and Israel is God's dream for the Holy Land. As time passes, however, I find fewer and fewer Presbyterian colleagues walking by my side.

In 2008, the PCUSA General Assembly named a Middle East task force to study the changing political and spiritual dynamics unfolding in the region, which were contributing heavily to the growing divide within the Church. The purpose was to look back on all former statements related to peace in the Middle East, and to make fresh recommendations relevant to the current situation. The task force composition reflected the divergent opinions and experiences of members of the PCUSA, and included scholars, urban pastors sympathetic to interfaith relationships and history, Palestinian-born Presbyterians, and staff members familiar with our long Presbyterian presence in the Middle East. (Presbyterians were some of the first Protestant Christians to send missionaries to Lebanon, Jordan, and Syria, to Iraq and Iran. With the Lutherans, we have carried out important spiritual work within the Palestinian territories for 160 years.)

The task force listened to professors and activists from all perspectives, read voluminous reports and statements from years past, talked with national Jewish and Palestinian leaders, considered the theology of the land and traditional teachings about peace and reconciliation, and listened deeply to the stories of those directly affected by the Israeli-Palestinian standoff. Those of us who had had deep and prolonged experience engaging with Jews at the local level shared the profound meaning of that work.

The heart of our process as a task force was a two-week-long trip to Israel and the occupied territories. We talked to leaders and scholars and people living in the region, both Palestinian and Jewish. As the reality on the ground seeped into our hearts, the division within the group grew deeper and angrier. In a reflection I wrote after that trip, "Hostile Walls and Holy People," which was printed in 2010's "Breaking Down the Walls: Report of the Middle East Study Committee," I lifted up the pain and the possibilities that I experienced on that three-week sojourn, writing in part:

This time I came home depressed and anxious—sobered by the bitterness, the polarization, and the hopelessness that seems to permeate the region. Very different from my last trip to Palestine/Israel, back in 1995—in between the First and Second Intifada—when Oslo seemed promising, the Palestinian Authority had a strong voice, and Christians and Jews were building tentative bridges together. But in 2009, the situation is bleak—and the window of opportunity for peace is closing...

The first six days we met with our Christian partners in Lebanon, Syria, and Jordan—soaking in the beauty of these ancient lands, hearing the lament about the rapid diminishment of the Christian voice and presence in the Holy Land, and feeling the urgency of this moment in time.

Our final 8 days were spent in Israel/Palestine—6 days in Jerusalem and 2 days in the Galilee and Jericho. We stayed at a Christian Retreat Center in East Jerusalem, and a kosher Orthodox Jewish hotel in West Jerusalem—experiencing the cultural tension of this small, fierce and divided city. We spent a day in Hebron and a day in Bethlehem—and we talked with Christians, Muslims, Jews, Israelis, Palestinians, human rights activists, rabbis, government officials, Bedouins, scholars, settlers, and displaced refugees . . .

The historical traumas that continue to define the conflict are not just about political conflict. These traumas permeate the very essence of identity and passion and life. And they will not be healed by high sounding words in a peace agreement. They will only by healed by a global embrace of the radical grace of God . . . .

I came home hearing two messages from our journey through the Holy Land. The first was a plea from our Christian brothers and sisters to stand with them in solidarity—condemning the occupation and doing everything in our power to stop it. The second was a plea from our Israeli Jewish brothers and sisters to engage our Jewish partners here in the United States in such a way that they can hear our message—and be transformed into peacemakers with and for the people of both Israel and Palestine.

As Presbyterians continue to struggle with these issues, my prayer is that God will give us the grace and the clarity to speak the truth in love – and to further God's reign of peace and justice in the world. And my conviction is that the Living God can indeed be our peace, working to break down the dividing walls of hostility that are fragmenting this beautiful and broken world.

May it be so!

The final MESC report and recommendations submitted to the General Assembly of the PCUSA in 2010 represented a razor-thin balance between the two major perspectives of the task force. Some members wanted to recommend: 1) immediate divestment of PCUSA from companies implicated in the occupation; 2) support for the BDS movement; 3) withdrawal of all military aid to Israel; 4) endorsement of the controversial *Kairos Document* created by a coalition of Christians in Palestine; and 5) support for a one-state solution to replace the longstanding pro-two-state-solution position supported by previous General Assemblies and the American government.

Though sympathetic to these positions, I did not agree with the vehemently pro-Palestinian constituency. My reason was—and is—simple. As Presbyterians, we have deep covenantal commitments to two groups of people: the Palestinian Christians who are our brothers and sisters in Christ *and* our Jewish neighbors who have been our partners in works of justice and interfaith reconciliation for decades. I believed in 2010—and still believe in 2019—that we must honor both of those commitments by taking a both/and position instead of making an either/or decision. And a two-state solution is central to keeping both covenantal commitments strong.

Those of us on the MESC who cherish a loving friendship and partnership with our Jewish neighbors, both at the local and the national level, worked hard to come up with recommendations that embraced compromise. Among the fifty-eight points were:

1. Continued support for a two-state solution, with justice and security for both peoples;
2. Immediate cessation of settlement expansion;
3. Withdrawal of the Separation Barrier to 1967 borders;
4. Declaring Israel as a legitimate state and a homeland for the Jewish people (not a Jewish state);
5. Withholding US government aid to the state of Israel as long as Israel persists in creating new West Bank settlements;
6. Securing Jerusalem as the capital of both states;
7. Pursuing justice through shareholder resolutions and engagement with corporations involved in perpetuating the occupation, while rejecting divestment;
8. Commitment of the PCUSA to pursue positive investment in both Israel and Palestine to build an economic foundation for peace and reconciliation;
9. Encouragement for American PCUSA congregations to travel to the Holy Land, committed to interaction with Palestinian Christian and Arabs as well as Israeli Jews;

10. Increased partnership between Jewish and Presbyterian congregations in the United States, creating joint education, worship, and justice work together.

The report generated intense interest and conflict at the 2010 General Assembly. With some editing and revision, the recommendations of the task force were accepted, and the dream of a two-state solution lived to see another day in the PCUSA.

Since 2010, however, this balance of viewpoints has gone askew. I am still passionate about creating common ground, dialogue, and deep understanding between Christians, Muslims, and Jews. But I find myself increasingly isolated within the larger Presbyterian family. Conversations about divestment continue at the national level, and the pro-Palestinian voices have increased in volume and passion over the years, successfully orchestrating a vote to divest at the 2014 General Assembly. More recently, our national denominational office named a new Interfaith Staff person, who is a vocal advocate for the BDS movement. Current leadership within the denomination is vocal in their belief that a two-state solution is no longer possible or just, and there is now an official effort to study a one-state solution. This perspective seems to ignore the fact that this could end in one of two ways: the loss of a Jewish majority in the State of Israel and the end of a homeland for the Jewish people and/or a major war in the region, worsening the crisis, and unleashing catastrophic violence.

I remain convinced that we Presbyterians must honor the two commitments we have cherished throughout our long journey: 1) to advocate for justice, peace, and the human dignity of our Palestinian brothers and sisters, and 2) to maintain a dialogue and covenant relationship with our Jewish brothers and sisters and support the promise of a secure homeland made to the Jewish people following centuries of anti-Jewish hatred and the Holocaust.

As one who has experienced firsthand the rewards of Spiritual Siblings Sharing Sacred Space, my hope is that friendship and partnership can prevail. Is it possible that a free and just Palestine and a free and secure Israel could one day be covenant partners—Spiritual Siblings Sharing Sacred Space?

I believe; God, help my unbelief!

CHAPTER FIFTEEN

MICHAEL C. GIZZI

RECONCILIATION,
SHARED SOCIETY, AND
CO-EXISTENCE EFFORTS
BETWEEN ISRAELIS AND
PALESTINIANS:
AN OVERVIEW

The BDS Movement, particularly in the churches, has taken pains to avoid supporting any efforts that result in cooperative exchanges and shared social fabric between Israelis and Palestinians, or within Israel, between Jews and Arabs. They see these programs as promoting "normalization" of the Israeli occupation. Presbyterian Peace Fellowship, an interest group within the Presbyterian Church (USA), has gone so far as to create a study trip to Israel/Palestine dedicated to "co-resistance before co-existence." The trip was designed to promote resistance, not reconciliation. During the 2018 Presbyterian General Assembly, the Church's BDS advocates lobbied against a resolution that called for reconciliation and a focus on shared society. The resolution passed, although BDS activists will try to minimize its importance. The rejection of Christian churches' and activists' calls for two-state-oriented peacemaking is somewhat surprising given the centrality of reconciliation in the teachings of Jesus. Indeed, it seems likely that, were BDS activists to take such efforts seriously, they would undermine the entire effort.

This essay is intended to provide an overview of the range and scope of programs that exist to promote both reconciliation and shared society between Israelis and Palestinians. It is drawn from my experiences over seventy days in Israel between 2015 and 2018, during which I visited and interacted with a variety of programs and individuals. A list of organizations and their websites is included as an appendix at the end of this essay. The Alliance of Middle East Peace's membership roster lists more than one hundred organizations in Israel and the West Bank that are engaged in civil society work aimed at peacemaking, promoting shared society, or finding ways to end the conflict. These programs and projects are diverse in scope and have grown significantly over the past five years. Moreover, ALLMEP's membership roster isn't even comprehensive, as it only includes those organizations that have affiliated with them. The range of existing programs have a wide variety of foci and approaches. Many are focused on youth, promoting integrated public/private schools, after school programs, summer camps, sports programs, and community centers. In addition, there are programs that are centered on jobs and economic development. The third category has a policy focus, in which a particular issue drives the organization, often with a "peace dividend" and a cooperative effort that ties together Israelis and Palestinians. A fourth category is even more explicitly political, seeking to bring about an end to the conflict. These programs are also diverse; some focus on women, some are religious. A handful of such programs exist in the West Bank. While what follows is largely descriptive, it is important to understand the broad scope of programs that exist within Israel and Palestine, dedicated to reconciliation.

YOUTH PROGRAMS

By far the largest category of shared society programs targets youth. These include summer programs tied to US-based non-governmental organizations (NGOs), weekly afterschool programs, programs that build curricula within schools, programs that create partner schools, and full-fledged elementary and high schools. Some programs are religiously-based, some are entirely secular. Most programs exist within Israel proper and provide opportunities for Israeli Jews and Israeli Arabs, although some are also able to include Arabs from the West Bank, and, until a few years ago, Gaza.

SUMMER CAMP AND AFTER-SCHOOL MODELS

The "summer camp" model is perhaps the best known to those outside of Israel. Seeds of Peace is an international NGO that has operated a three-week summer camp in Maine since 1993. Its goal is to bring together cultures in conflict and promote leadership development. The summer camp model is a popular one, although the names and terminology differ. Friends Forever International is a New Hampshire-based NGO, affiliated with Rotary International, which has sponsored what it calls "lifeboat" experiences, in which delegations of ten teens— five Jews and five Arabs—from two different schools come to a US community for a two-week intensive coexistence project, in which they live, eat, do community service, and engage in a variety of programing together. The program began with a similar effort between Catholic and Protestant teens in Northern Ireland and expanded to Israel about a decade ago. Friends Forever ties two schools together and hosts meet-and-greets in Israel before the summer trip to the US, and then multiple interactions over the next year. For example, an Arab high school in the northern Galilee is paired with a Jewish school six hours to the south in Eilat. Friends Forever has very committed alumni base but is challenged by its lack of full time staff in Israel. It relies largely on teachers who are limited in the time they can dedicate to the program, and recent alumni. Moreover, its program is limited to a handful of schools.

KIDS4PEACE

Kids4Peace is also known for sending children abroad for a co-existence-oriented summer camp, but in many ways this experience is but a small part of the overall program. Kids4Peace began during the Second Intifada (2001-2005) as a small volunteer-run program sponsored by the Episcopal Church. It was created with the goal of sending groups of teens—Jews, Muslims, and Christians—to a ten-day summer camp in Texas. Like Seeds of Peace, it was an early model of a co-existence program. It had no formal organizational structure and relied entirely on volunteers. Today the camp element is merely the culmination of a year-long program that meets weekly.

The first Kids4Peace cohort began at age twelve. They wanted to continue, so, as they were got older, the volunteers simply kept creating new programs. Eventually older youth became counselors and the program continued to evolve haphazardly year after year. In 2008, the program broke away from the Episcopal Church. The Church had become fixated on "anti-normalization" issues, and the program leaders realized this was not in their best interest, since their primary goal was to promote interfaith activity. Since then the relationship between Kids4Peace and the Episcopal Church has been repaired, but the organization remains secular. Kids4Peace International, based in Washington, DC, is led by Father Josh Thomas, an Episcopal priest.

Kids4Peace incorporated as an Israeli NGO in Jerusalem in 2012. One of the first projects was to host a ten-year anniversary celebration. More than 300 people showed up, which made it clear that there was a real demand for the work that Kids4Peace had done as a summer program. Working with the community, youth, parents, and the organizational leadership team, Kids4Peace built a year-round program for

children and teens beginning in seventh grade and continuing throughout high school.

In 2014, Kids4Peace received a grant from the United States
Institute for Peace to do a ten-year evaluation of the program, focusing on measuring effectiveness in terms of youth taking action towards
peacemaking.[116] The evaluation found that after completing the program kids wanted to take actions towards peace but didn't know how.
As a result, Kids4Peace established a youth action program, focused
on community organizing and leadership development, using mentor-
practice and social action. A youth empowerment model was developed
consisting of projects ranging from community gardens to neighborhood walking tours, advocacy work related to accessibility issues in
Jerusalem, and counseling younger youth. The program is now evaluated annually.

In 2016, Kids4Peace received its first large-scale grant, an $800,000
USAID grant which funded the program through March 2019. The
grant represents about half of the program's funds. Kids4Peace applied
for a larger follow-up grant in June 2018, but the Trump administration's decision to stop giving governmental aid to programs that involve
the West Bank or Gaza make it uncertain whether this grant will be
funded. The injection of US federal aid has helped Kids4Peace expand,
but it has also placed significant requirements on the program and made
it far more dependent on external funding. Whether the Biden administration will restore all such funding remains to be seen, but significant
restored social service funding seems likely, especially given the passage
of legislation by Congress in December 2020 committing $250 million
to expand peace and reconciliation programs over the next five years.

Kids4Peace today is a robust shared society program, with over 380
kids currently involved. It is one of the few programs that cross "the
green line," serving both Israeli and Palestinian participants. Kids4Peace
begins in seventh grade, and uses a weekly afterschool program model,
with as many as twenty meetings throughout the year. Summer camps,
weekend programs, and community-wide events are incorporated into
it. Those who want their children to participate must themselves agree
to enroll in a mandatory two-year program for parents. It isn't enough
for the kids to do shared society work; the parents have to engage as

well. The summer camp for seventh graders is done locally in Israel. Eighth graders have a summer camp abroad, which is still being piloted. In 2018, it was held in North Carolina. The eighth grade curriculum explores comparative conflict and does not shy away from the political dimensions of the subject. This is different from programs like Friends Forever, which avoids overt discussions of the politics of the conflict. At the end of the ninth grade program, the students go to Washington, DC for a ten-day "global institute" focused on public policy issues. Tenth through twelfth grade participants are in the youth action program, and are focused on community organizing and leadership. The youth empowerment program is being continually evaluated. The underlying goal of building a resilient community resonates throughout all elements of the program. Kids4Peace provides the foundation for long-term commitment to shared society and does something that few programs do by directly bringing East Jerusalem's Palestinians together with Israeli Jews.

JERUSALEM INTERNATIONAL YMCA

The Jerusalem International YMCA offers a wide range of shared society programs within Jerusalem itself. It is located in an iconic building across the street from the King David Hotel. The YMCA's "peace kindergarten" began in 1933 and was the first bilingual kindergarten in Israel. In 1982 the kindergarten was expanded to include a preschool for children aged six months to five years old. The preschool is also bilingual and serves both Jewish and Arab children. Each classroom has both a Hebrew- and Arabic-speaking teacher so that the children learn to speak both languages fluently. At the end of each day, parents are invited to a storytelling session in Hebrew and Arabic, which allows them to get to know each other. The entire program seeks to promote the values of equality, multiculturalism, and tolerance among children and their parents. For several years the program served as a feeder for the Hand in Hand Jewish-Arab School discussed below.

In addition, the YMCA has a full range of children's and youth programs, all of which are designed to bring together young people from around Jerusalem in a variety of creative endeavors. All programs have three staff members: two teachers, one an Arabic speaker and the other a Hebrew speaker, and a translator to assist with dialogue. The children's programs include activities like cooking, jujitsu and taekwondo, photography, swimming, origami, Zumba, chess, and arts and science projects. The youth programs are focused on music and theater, documentary filmmaking, and a leadership training program for local university students interested in work as youth counselors. The youth program also includes a bilingual and multicultural summer camp focused in the same core areas. All of the programs are designed to provide Jewish and Arab children the opportunity to interact and learn how to see beyond otherness.

In 2017 the YMCA opened the largest underground sports center in the Middle East, complete with basketball and squash courts, a swimming pool, and a complete gymnasium, and offering more than fifty exercise classes each week. The fitness center includes 100,000 square feet of programming space, is open to all residents of Jerusalem regardless of age, neighborhood, or family status, and has a range of price options. Like the YMCA itself, the facility is designed to ensure that Palestinians and Israelis can work out in the same space.

For a long time, the Jerusalem International YMCA was funded by grants from the American YMCA system, but it recently became completely independent. The preschool, youth, and children's programs are all nonprofit. The Three Arches Hotel, however, is a for-profit enterprise, and the fitness center is intended to be self-sustaining through membership fees. The NGO elements rely entirely on financial support from individuals and organizations. Most contributors are individuals, and as yet the YMCA has not sought grant funding through programs like USAID.

AFTERSCHOOL PROGRAMS

There are other year-round youth programs that function within public and private schools. A New Way, for example, is a program based outside of Tel Aviv that has also been in existence since the Second Intifada. A New Way is premised on the understanding that tensions between Israeli Jews and Arabs are an ongoing threat to the stability and resilience of Israeli society and seeks to help children break free from stereotypes. Unlike Kids4Peace, A New Way runs programs in Jewish and Arab schools. In Israel, Jewish children attend Hebrew-language schools, while Arab children go to Arabic-language schools. A New Way has thirty-two partner communities and works with sixty schools. According to the program director, in 2017 A New Way reached over 5,000 children, teachers, parents, and community members.

A New Way is very much tied to schools and teachers. For example, one partnership program connects one school in Taibeh and another in North Tel Aviv, about 20 miles apart. Under the auspices of A New Way, two teachers spent a year developing a curriculum that would break down barriers between Taibeh's Arab students and North Tel Aviv's Jewish ones. The project involved thirty students from each school and began with each of the teachers traveling to the other's school to give a presentation on the respective group's history, religion, culture, customs, and norms and values. After the teachers' presentations, A New Way coordinates a series of student visits between the two schools. The ultimate goal of the organization is to create a "civic society" of Jews and Arabs who know and understand each other.

Recently, A New Way has expanded beyond schools themselves, working to implement a community-wide model and bring in more participants. They work not only with teachers and principals, but also with municipal leaders and mayors in order to develop programs that go beyond the classroom to accomplish the same goals in the community at large. Indeed, demand for programming has begun to outstrip A New Way's resources, and there are waiting lists for schools and communities to participate. A New Way relies on a central staff in Ramat HaSharon, just north of Tel Aviv, including 8 paid coordinators, each of whom organize in a designated region, and a growing number of volunteers. What is perhaps most interesting about A New Way is how it has developed its work over seventeen years largely under the radar. It has not attracted the same international attention that programs like Kids4Peace or Seeds of Peace have garnered, although this may be due in part to the fact that A New Way is an Israeli NGO and not tied to a US-based NGO.

COMMUNITY YOUTH PROGRAMS

Other programs target both youth and adults. In US terms, the Arab-Jewish Community Center in Jaffa is a crossover between a local YMCA or JCC chapter and the Boys & Girls Club of America. Jaffa is a mixed community with approximately 35,000 Jews and 20,000 Arabs. The Community Center provides a gathering place, hosting afterschool programs, dance classes, martial arts classes, a library, a gymnasium, a women-only gym, and a focus on programming that promotes tolerance (Figs. 21, 22).

Fig. 21—Arab-Jewish Community Center in Jaffa signage. Photo: Michael Gizzi.

The Center sponsors a youth parliament for high school students and is tied to the Jewish-Arab Citizens Accord Forum, an NGO located in Jerusalem, which coordinates youth parliaments all over the country. It also sponsors a classroom exchange program between third and fourth graders enrolled in Jewish and Arab public school. The kids do joint programs twice a month at the Community Center and visit each other's school at the end of the year. The teenagers in the youth parliament also organize a summer camp for the younger children. There is a youth camp organized by the teenagers as well. There are also programs

Fig. 22—The Arab-Jewish Community Center in Jaffa. Photo: Michael Gizzi

aimed for women in the community. Similar programs occur in Haifa, at a community center sponsored by the same Citizens Accord Forum.

About a quarter mile from the Jewish-Arab Community center in Jaffa is the headquarters of the Peres Center for Peace and Innovation, which was created by the late Prime Minister Shimon Peres to promote reconciliation between Israelis and Palestinians and between Israeli Jews and Israeli Arabs. One of the core missions of the Peres Center is peace education, focused on youth and young adults. The peace education program is multifaceted; it is based on the idea that within conflict resolution it is easy to take on and reproduce stereotypes. Their programs thus seek to breakdown those stereotypes. They do this in a variety of ways, often by adding in a peacemaking component to recreational activities. For example, when children play soccer at the Peres Center, they have to pass the ball to a member of the other ethnocultural group on their mixed team. They have also developed a partner-school program, where two schools are paired together. They work with communities in Arab villages in Israel and on the West Bank. The Peres Center used to do similar programming in Gaza, but that has not been possible since 2014 due to increased tensions and violence.

The YaLa program targets 18-35 year-olds. YaLa is a movement developed through Facebook with the goal of integrating people across Israel, the West Bank, and other nations in the Middle East and North Africa. They administrate private groups and include online courses provided by American universities. It has approximately 300 participants, who meet regularly online using Facebook, and other technology tools like Google Hangouts, then have face to face meetings. Participants are mostly in their twenties and come from the West Bank, Gaza, and Israel. They even had a participant from Gaza who lost two family members in the 2014 war but felt that it was essential to participate in the program.

PUBLIC SCHOOLS

In Israel, public education is largely segregated into Jewish and Arab schools. There are both public and private schools. There are also religious schools for Jews and religious Muslim schools. In Arab schools, students learn Arabic, Hebrew, and English. Jewish schools do not require Arabic. This makes interaction between kids harder and poses a significant challenge to co-existence. But there are efforts today to bridge those gaps, including a series of private schools that are bilingual, and integrated. The Hand in Hand Center for Jewish-Arabic Education is perhaps the largest.

Hand in Hand was created by a group of families who wanted to build a shared society and a shared community in the late 1990s (Fig. 23). They started with a pre-kindergarten program, and today the Max Rayne School in the Pat neighborhood of Jerusalem has 600 students, pre-K through twelfth grade (Fig. 24). There are four other campuses across Israel, all pre-K or elementary schools, reaching as far north as Haifa.

Hand in Hand schools are focused on bilingualism and biculturalism. Up through the sixth grade, one Jewish and one Arab instructor are paired up to teach students. Classes are split evenly between Jews and Arab. Most of the Jewish students are secular Jews. Few of the female Arab students wear a hijab, along with some of the female teachers. After sixth grade, the teachers are not paired, but half of the junior and senior high school teachers are Jewish and half are Arab, and each teaches their subject in their own language. The school also includes Arab Christians, and students are taught about all three religions' traditions. They also are cognizant of bifurcated cultural and political touchstones. For example, on May 14-15, they will celebrate Yom HaAtzmaut, or Israeli Independence Day, but will also commemorate the date known to Palestinians as Nakba Day, when Palestinians lost their homeland.

Hand in Hand has well-organized programs that engage students in dialogue and train community members to deal with conflict. The school does not hide from controversy, but instead acknowledges the tensions that exist, and works to overcome them. 2014 was a particularly hard year, as there were several instances when the school was defaced with racist anti-Arab graffiti. Each time, the students cleaned it up and worked to show their solidarity. During the July 2014 war in Gaza, students, parents, and as many as 250 community members engaged in weekly peace marches beginning at the school.

Fig. 23—A Hand in Hand classroom at the Max Rayne School, Jerusalem. Credit: Michael Gizzi

Fig. 24—Multilingual signage at the Max Rayne School. Photo: Michael Gizzi.

Hand in Hand's worst day—and perhaps its best— was in late November 2014, when three extremist Jews broke into the school at night, entered a first-grade classroom, sprayed messages of hate on the walls and used books as kindling to set the room on fire. The fire was put out quickly, with only minor damage and eventually the 3 perpetrators were arrested. The upside of this crisis, however, was a striking increase in global awareness of Hand in Hand and its mission. Two of the school's students were even flown to Washington, DC, to light the White House Chanukah menorah and meet President Obama.

Another example of the Max Rayne Campus's impact is how the neighborhood where it is located has changed in response to the school. Initially there was a "NIMBY" or "Not in My Backyard" reaction to bringing Arab children to a poorer, predominately Jewish neighborhood. Over the years, however, the school has done a lot of outreach in the neighborhood, and tensions have eased. After the fire in 2014, the neighbors wrote a note saying, "We are ashamed of the racism and violence, and are glad you are here."

Hand in Hand is largely funded as a public school; it receives about forty percent of its funds from the state, parents pay approximately $1500 per year (currently about 6000 Israeli shekels), and the rest comes from philanthropy. They hope to build up to ten schools over the next decade.

There are other bilingual schools, as well as a bilingual kibbutz— Wahat al-Salaam/Neve Shalom, or Oasis of Peace—that has existed since the 1970s. Neve Shalom also includes a peace school and is populated by a group of Jews and Arabs who have committed to living together. The kibbutz specifically tries to address the challenges that all of the aforementioned youth programs face. When Israeli Jewish and Druze students graduate high school, they are required to complete a period of military service, generally two years for women and three years for men. Arabs and ultra-Orthodox Jews are exempted from this service. This quasi-universal conscription is often a roadblock to maintaining cross-cultural connections after high school, as half of the graduates enter the military and half become its primary targets.

CROSS-OVER PROGRAMS

In 2017, a new program began in Akko, near Haifa, also known as Acre or Akka: the Akko Center for Arts and Technology (A-CAT). A-CAT is the brainchild of a Mark Frank, a lawyer from Pittsburgh (Fig. 25). Frank was inspired by Bill Strickland, who developed a series of urban economic and learning centers in the US in order to foster strong learning environments in low income and racially stratified communities, empower disadvantaged people for economic success, and nurture close bonds across racial and ethnic divides. Mark Frank took Strickland's model to Akko, chosen both for its diverse community of Jews and Arabs and its peripheral location far north of Tel Aviv and Jerusalem. Akko is similar to Haifa and Jaffa, cities known for being home to diverse cultures and a mix of Jewish and Arab citizens. Yet Akko is also a community where there is still considerable de facto segregation. People live in the same community but separate themselves ethnically, culturally, and religiously. A-CAT was intended to help overcome some of those differences.

A-CAT provides locals with a space to develop both personal and economic ties and holds classes that teach professional and trade-based skills, thus improving the general quality of life in the Western Galilee. The Center was built in an old parking garage, which was gutted and transformed into a state-of-the-art facility serving teenagers and adults. Unlike many shared society programs in Israel, A-CAT is housed in a modern facility, with high ceilings, up-to-date equipment, and bright colors with inspirational quotes on the walls.

A-CAT offers programs for both teenagers and adults. The adolescent programs provide enrichment for 14- through18-year-olds focused on 3D printing and photography. The Center's afterschool program uses technology and art not only to teach teens new skills but also to help them connect with students from other backgrounds. In the words of A-CAT's director taken from a personal interview, "The language is technology, which leads them to art. They like technology, indeed, it is state of the art. We bring them here, we get them life skills."

Fig. 25—Multilingual signage at the AKKO Center. Photo: Michael Gizzi

The youth program is split 50-50, Jewish and Arab, so that no one feels like a minority. There are two instructors for each class, one Jewish, one Arab. The program starts in Hebrew but offers full support for students who don't speak the language. This is an issue particularly for kids that come from Arab villages, who are more hesitant and often less proficient in Hebrew. They don't teach Hebrew, but by the third or fourth meeting, the kids find ways to communicate and gain self-confidence. Each class has eighteen students who are bused to A-CAT from their respective schools. There is always food waiting for them when they arrive. A small lunch provides social time, and then they split into programming groups (3D printing and photography). The program lasts for twelve sessions, after which there is a big ceremony for "graduation." The kids can continue on for another twelve-week session in the other program.

The photography classes use advanced digital SLR cameras. They want the kids to realize they are being trusted with expensive equipment. They take field trips, sometimes only a few blocks away, into the predominately Arab old city. Typically, Jewish kids would not go there by themselves, but when they travel together, they feel safe. The two groups integrate and become A-CAT's ambassadors. The 3D printing program is more vocationally focused, as the students are learning how to use highly advanced tools that have the potential to translate into jobs in manufacturing, all while learning about art, science, and themselves.

The adult programs are focused on hospitality management and quality assurance in industry. The latter program provides adult students with knowledge and tools that will prepare them for entry-level industrial jobs in Northern Israel. A-CAT works with local factories to meet industry requirements, offering both professional training and practical experiences in the field. The program is co-sponsored by the Akko municipality and Erez College, which is also located in Western Galilee. Graduates receive certificates from all three organizations. The entrepreneurial and management track focuses on the tourism and hospitality field. The curriculum is designed to educate and train tourism operators in the specifics of how to run a business, including creating business plans, legal aspects, branding, and marketing on social media. The program is run in conjunction with the School of Tourism at the University of Haifa, which provides a certificate of completion upon graduation.

In A-CAT's first academic year, there were 465 participants, 230 Arabs and 235 Jews. The youth program had 383 participants, 192 Arabs and 190 Jews. The adult programs—which were intentionally made smaller to suit the nature of the training programs—had 82 participants, 37 Arabs and 45 Jews. In 2018, the program had almost doubled in enrollments. While A-CAT had to work hard to recruit schools to participate initially, now schools are approaching them, and they are considering expanding the afterschool program to two years. Teachers report a change in behavior and attitudes in their students. Much of the financial support for A-CAT still comes from the US, but they are using their success to build relationships with both the local governments and the Israeli Ministry of Education, the Ministry of Tourism, and the Ministry of Economy, which oversees industry and labor. A-CAT has recently sought additional funding from USAID to further develop programs focused on conflict management. A-CAT ultimately hopes to spread its mission and build other centers throughout Northern and Central Israel.

CROSSING THE GREEN LINE

It is true that much of the shared society work takes place in Israel proper, where close to 2 million Arab citizens live amidst over six million Jews. In part this is because it is practically easier to organize within these borders. This does not mean that important programming does not take place across the Green Line, bringing together Israeli Jews and Arabs living in the West Bank or even Gaza. The discussion of Kids4Peace provides an example of a program that seeks to build positive relationships between Arab residents of East Jerusalem and their Jewish neighbors. The Friends of Roots program in Gush Etzion, which lies south of Bethlehem, is an example of a program that operates entirely within the West Bank, working with Jewish settlers and Palestinians living in the same region. Roots is dedicated to co-existence, building empathy, and shared living. It offers dual narrative programs, leadership development opportunities for both Jews and Palestinians, language courses in Hebrew and Arabic, summer camps for area children, and pre-conscription academies for Jewish high school students, so they can learn and understand the Palestinian narrative before they enlist in the Israel Defense Forces (IDF). Friends of Roots began in 2014 and claims to have reached more than 13,000 people within the next four years. Friends of Roots, however, could be considered an outlier. Gush Etzion was established on land purchased by Jews long before the 1948 War for Independence. Jews were forced to abandon it after the war, when the areas east of the Green Line came under Jordanian control but returned after the Six Day War in 1967. The Jewish ties to the land in "the Gush" are longstanding. The area has also been home to many Palestinians and has been one of the flash points of conflict. The fact that some Jews and Arabs have found a way to promote shared society there is a testament to how effective reconciliation efforts can be.

There are other programs that cross the Green Line. One of those is the environmental public policy interest group EcoPeace, formerly known as Friends of the Earth Middle East. EcoPeace is primarily dedicated to water policy. Water is a scarce resource in the region, and there are major environmental issues that touch both Israelis and Palestinians. The organization takes a unique approach to water sustainability issues, operating under the theory that "good waters make good neighbors."

EcoPeace has built programs that pair Israeli communities with neighboring Palestinian communities as well as communities that cross the international border with Jordan. People engage in projects aimed at water sustainability, but there is a "peace dividend" which comes from working together. Today twenty-eight communities in eleven water basins participate in EcoPeace's work projects.

The aforementioned Peres Center for Peace and Innovation also has a variety of programs focused on business and medicine that directly impact Palestinians in the West Bank and Gaza. Their business and environmental programs encourage economic development and business exchanges between Israeli and Palestinian businesses on the West Bank. In 2014, in the midst of Operation Protective Edge, the Peres Center organized a Palestinian Product Exhibition in Nazareth, where more than one thousand "Business to Business" (B2B) meetings were facilitated. Forty Palestinian companies attended. There, meetings were part of the Peres Center's ongoing efforts to promote regional economic cooperation and partnerships by explicitly targeting West Bank businesses. Many of the Peres business and environment projects also seek to strengthen relations between Jewish and Arab businesses within Israel through programs like a start-up business accelerator. They also offer mentoring and a variety of services found in business incubators.

The Peres Center's third focus is on medicine and health care. They provide medical training for Palestinian doctors and medical staff in the West Bank and Gaza. The Palestinian Authority has been separated from the Israeli government's health care system since 1999, but their medical resources are nowhere near the same level as Israel's. To ameliorate this discrepancy, the Peres Center has trained more than 300 doctors. They have also provided assistance for sick children in the occupied territories. Fifty percent of the Palestinian population in the occupied territories is under the age of fourteen, and their Saving Children program has treated more than 10,500 children. The Peres Center works with both Hadassah Medical Center in Jerusalem, the largest Hospital in Israel, and with Save a Child's Heart Hospital in Tel Aviv.

The Peres Center's training for Palestinian doctors and nurses is significantly enhanced by its partnership with Hadassah. The Ein-Karem

campus of the Hadassah Medical Center is well known for its focus on
shared society (Figs. 26, 27). As you walk through the hospital, it is
clear that, when it comes to medicine, the social boundaries that nearly
always separate Jews from Arabs disappear. The hospital's nursing staff
is integrated, and the nursing and medical school trains Jews and Arabs
alike. Patient common areas are equally integrated. Religious and ethnic
divisions seem to disappear. It is hard to imagine that one would find its
like anywhere else in the Middle East. Hadassah works hard to develop
partnerships with its Palestinian counterparts, providing resources for
Palestinian hospitals and medical staff, which often lack the facilities
and expertise.

Fig. 26—Group display of handprints, Hadassah Ein Kareem. Photo: Michael
Gizzi.

Fig. 27—Arabs and Jews together at Hadassah Ein Kareem. Photo: Michael Gizzi.

Hadassah's pediatric cardiac department treats at least three Palestinian children every month and works with a variety of other NGOs and the IDF to provide medical care not only for Palestinians, but for children from other Arab countries as well. Hadassah participates in the Israel Defense Force's "Operation Good Neighbor" program that provides emergency medical care for Syrians displaced by the Syrian Civil War. Operation Good Neighbor began in 2016, and has provided food, supplies and basic medical treatment to Syrians, all the while maintaining a policy of non-intervention in the conflict. More than 1200 children have received treatment. The army also facilitates transportation into Israel for ailing Syrian children and their parents. Once inside Israel, most of the children are treated at the Poriya Medical Center in Tiberias or at the Galilee Medical Center in Nahariya. The most critical cases are transported to Hadassah Ein Karem in Jerusalem. Every two months doctors from Hadassah travel the two hours north to Tiberias to triage children brought from Syria for treatment. As I learned in a June 2018 interview with Hadassah doctors, on one triage visit in spring 2018, doctors treated seventeen children brought across the border.

Hadassah also works with other NGOs engaged in the same type of humanitarian work. One of its major partners is the Christian NGO Shevet Achim, which provides free housing for families of sick children from places like Syria or Iraq who have come to Israel for medical treatment. Shevet Achim not only provides a place for family members, it also actively seeks out children needing care, helps with the logistics of transporting then to Israeli hospitals, and raises funds to cover the cost of medical expenses. At Hadassah, non-Israeli children are given a fifty percent discount, and sometimes the doctors even provide services pro bono. While Shevet Achim's primary focus is international, it also helps Palestinian children.

CONCLUSION

This overview can in no way be considered comprehensive. There are simply too many organizations doing shared society and reconciliation work within Israel and Palestine. Even the Alliance for Middle East Peace membership, which lists more than one hundred organizations, does not cover all of them. There are always new programs, like A-CAT, which emerge on the scene, and others that fade away. One such program, which I visited in 2016, was a business to business organization called Breaking the Impasse, which sought to use economic leverage between 300 Israeli and Palestinian business leaders to push action on the conflict. It never seemed to gain traction, and, by 2018, its website had disappeared. There are other programs that function under the radar and don't seek widespread attention, realizing that their work can best be accomplished in the shadows. One such program is the Shades Negotiations Project, which brings together young leaders from both the Palestinian Authority and the Israeli government and provides staffing to politicians. Through the intervention of several embassies, Shades teaches these up-and-coming leaders to work together and see beyond the stereotypes, in order to hopefully push their parties' leadership to ease tensions and reduce conflict. There are also numerous programs that exist within larger organizations, be they private schools like the

Leo Baeck High School in Haifa, which commits funds for students to participate in a variety of shared society efforts, or a research institution like the Shalom Hartman Institute in Jerusalem, whose scholars promote shared society through their writings and public speaking. In recent years, the Center for a Shared Society at Givat Haviva has done remarkable work promoting bilingual education in Israeli schools and has worked closely with the Israeli Ministry of Education to put Arab teachers in Jewish schools and vice versa, with the goal of improving students' language skills (Figs. 28, 29).

Fig. 28—Entrance to Center for a Shared Society at Givat Haviva. Photo: Michael Gizzi

The Abraham Initiatives (also known as the Abraham Fund) is an NGO that focuses on the status of Arab citizens of Israel. It focuses on ending racial profiling by Israeli police and facilitates exchange programs intended to improve the status of women across each ethnic group. Sikkuy is an NGO focused on promoting civic equality between Jews and Arabs within Israel and attempts to improve coverage of Arab

issues in Israeli media. There are also programs that are explicitly political, such as Combatants for Peace, which brings together former Israeli
soldiers and Palestinian fighters who are committed to ending the occupation and effecting political change.

Undeniably, the majority of programs exist within Israel proper
and target Israeli Jews and Arab citizens. Most of the major exceptions
to this rule are those based in Jerusalem. The programs that cross the
Green Line into the Palestinian territories face additional challenges,
including the ability of participants to travel from Palestine to Israel and
vice versa. This is not an insurmountable issue, but it does complicate
programming. Friends of Roots is probably the most significant organization that seeks to build relationships between Israeli settlers and local
Palestinians, a model that is worth trying to replicate elsewhere.

There has been one glaring omission in the discussion of programs
in this essay: Gaza. Prior to Operation Protective Edge in July 2014
there were more groups attempting to bridge the gap between Israelis
and Palestinians living in Gaza and significant efforts by organizations
like the Peres Center to provide services for individuals living in Gaza.
The nature of the ongoing conflict and near-constant acts of terrorism committed by Hamas have all but eliminated most face to face
interactions. Medical and humanitarian aid still gets through, but most
programs are not able to reach Gaza.

The BDS Movement consistently belittles and ignores many of the
programs I have described here. Any effort that promotes cooperation,
cultural understanding, and person-to-person exchanges contradicts
their goal of delegitimizing Israel. Yet, if a solution to the conflict,
short of eliminating the Israel as a Jewish state, is going to succeed, it is
absolutely essential that shared society and reconciliation efforts be promoted and not discouraged. Christian churches considering how they
can impact Middle East peacemaking would be wise to fully investigate
the numerous ways in which they could assist those who work, day in
and day out, across Israel and in parts of the West Bank, to foster true
reconciliation.

APPENDIX: SHARED SOCIETY PROGRAMS

The following organizations have been referenced in this essay. A more complete listing of shared society programs can be found on the website of the Alliance for Middle East Peace, http://www.allmep.org/

Abraham Fund Initiatives, https://www.abrahamfund.org/
A-CAT, https://www.acatcenter.org/
A New Way, https://www.anewway.org.il/
Arab-Jewish Community Center in Jaffa, http://ajccjaffa.weebly.com/
Combatants for Peace, http://cfpeace.org/
EcoPeace, http://ecopeaceme.org/
Friends Forever International, https://www.ff.international/
Friends of Roots, https://www.friendsofroots.net/
Hadassah Medical Center, http://www.hadassah-med.com/
Hand in Hand Center for Jewish-Arabic Education, https://www.
    handinhandk12.org/
Kids4Peace, http://www.k4pjerusalem.org/
Jerusalem International YMCA, http://ymca.org.il/
Jewish-Arab Citizens Accord Forum, http://www.caf.org.il/
Oasis of Peace: Wahat Salaam-Neve Shalom, https://wasns.org/
Givat Haviva Center for a Shared Society, http://www.givathaviva.org/
Peres Center for Peace and Innovation, https://www.peres-center.
    org/en/
Seeds of Peace, https://www.seedsofpeace.org/
Sikkuy, http://www.sikkuy.org.il
Shalom Hartman Institute, https://hartman.org.il/
Shevet Achim, https://shevet.org/

CHAPTER SIXTEEN

CARY NELSON

A RECONCILIATION ROADMAP

INTRODUCTION

From a Christian perspective, reconciliation builds on mutual empathy and understanding to correct injustices, expand peoples' opportunities, and improve the quality of their lives. True reconciliation is not designed to stabilize and reinforce the status quo. It does not settle for that. Reconciliation is aimed at changing the status quo, at substituting love and understanding for hatred and distrust and thus preparing both peoples to negotiate in good faith. With more than a century of experience in building reconciliation projects in the Holy

Land, Christians of many denominations are uniquely well positioned to make timely and deeply necessary contributions toward peace.

While the end goal of the peace process is a formal agreement between Israelis and Palestinians, the decades-long exclusive focus on final stage negotiations has left many, including many Christian groups and institutions, without a practical agenda to advocate for the changes that would help make that goal achievable. The continuing Christian and Jewish investment in organizations that build productive relationships between Israelis and Palestinians has borne fruit not only in strengthening the constituency for peace but also in establishing the trust necessary for both negotiating and implementing an agreement. Michael Gizzi has provided us with a valuable overview of reconciliation-oriented organizations to which people can commit time and resources. But trust in the willingness and ability of the primary parties to achieve an agreement has largely evaporated. To publish a book addressing Christian views of the Israeli-Palestinian conflict without at least a concise guide to practical routes forward would, we believe, leave readers with a basic question unanswered. We all need a roadmap for tangible progress toward justice for both peoples, a list of practical steps that would that could turn skeptics and opponents into believers. This chapter outlines such a roadmap in four sections. Beginning with an account of the likely components of a two-state solution and proceeding to a list of solutions to two-state challenges, suggestions for improving the lives of Palestinians living in the West Bank, and an agenda for addressing urgent economic and humanitarian needs in Gaza.[117]

Practical steps to build trust, improve lives, and establish conditions favorable to formal negotiations necessarily occur at the intersection between political and technical issues. Unfortunately, a sense of political hopelessness too often leaves people unwilling to recognize that some problems have straightforward technical solutions. And that in turn means that the potential to improve the political climate by pursuing technical solutions is ignored. The recommendations to follow include some that are primarily political, others that are mainly technical, but a strict separation between the two categories never obtains.

Traditional reconciliation projects commonly build personal relationships between members of different religious or ethnic groups by

establishing social and institutional contexts in which those relationships can flourish. Many take place in intimate settings like a classroom,
a church, a workshop, or a theater that are small in scale by definition.
As Gizzi documents, the Jerusalem International YMCA has been
bringing young Jews and Palestinians together since 1933. Over time,
such programs can reach many hundreds of people, but they are unable
to impact tens of thousands and thereby motivate entire populations to
seek reconciliation. They are often genuinely transformative for those
involved, however, and many have lifelong effects on participants. They
can change peoples' basic understandings of one another and change
how people live their lives. Hand in Hand, for example, runs several
bilingual schools in Israel that educate Jews and Palestinians together.
It is not unusual to find that some of the graduates years later return
to teach in the programs. Reconciliation programs also create critical
constituencies for peace, and some prepare people to contribute toward
a peace process. Thus a confidential Israeli NGO trains fifteen Jews and
fifteen Palestinians together each year in how to conduct peace negotiations; should negotiations begin in earnest, they will be ready to assist.
Many reconciliation programs could be expanded if they had increased
donations from abroad, something interested people of faith can do.

By their very nature and focus, small scale reconciliation programs
are not designed to directly produce changes in national policy and
practices. They are an essential strategy and must continue to be part of
any plan, but they cannot independently produce comprehensive social
change. The larger project of national reconciliation requires additional
initiatives that address both short-term and long-term needs and redress
actual inequities to establish trust, create the conditions necessary for
negotiations, and persuade all parties to make the sacrifices that will
be required. This chapter is designed to identify actions that will help
fill that need. It draws on and condenses hundreds of pages of think
tank proposals to offer about fifty practical steps that would change the
status quo, improving Palestinians' lives while actually strengthening
Israeli security.

Among the changes in policy and practice that could be initiated immediately and would not depend on final stage negotiations
would be a permanent extension to the approved fishing limit in the

Mediterranean off the coast of Gaza. Israel should stop increasing and decreasing the permitted fishing range in a reward and punishment system. Israel should also immediately begin facilitating increased agricultural and light manufacturing exports from both Gaza and the West Bank. Building a new solar array near Gaza to supply it with increased electricity, on the other hand, would take months, but it would not require years to complete. Meanwhile, Israel could follow the lead of the manufacturer of the Watergen machine—a device that successfully produces drinking water by condensing moisture in the air—by providing the device for key buildings like hospitals and sewage treatment plants (Associated Press "Israeli billionaire").

For years Palestinians have documented the frustrating delays at checkpoints both internal to the West Bank and at transit points into Israel. In spring 2019 Israel finally constructed new Bethlehem and Qalandiyah checkpoints with smart card readers using biometric data that allow for rapid passage (Hass). The architecture was made far more friendly and attractive as well. The same technology is in use at Ben Gurion airport. Converting more checkpoints into these rapid transit facilities should begin immediately and many could be completed within a year. At least 50,000 more Palestinians should rapidly be approved for work in Israel. The amount of anger and bitterness that would be eliminated by these two actions is considerable. It is a completely practical and straightforward form of reconciliation. Israel would continue to control its security, but Palestinians approved to work there would cross into the country unhampered. Developing a natural gas field off the Gazan coast, on the other hand, would take several years, as would building an offshore Gaza port based on an artificial island and constructing better communication infrastructure in the West Bank, but visibly starting construction within the year would promote reconciliation as well. People of faith could initiate campaigns around these and other projects and draw secular communities into supporting them. Public advocacy can make the difference in whether policies and practices are changed.

Some projects, like establishing a Palestinian airport in the West Bank and enhancing security infrastructure in the Jordan Valley, would not be practical outside a formal peace agreement and a resolution of all outstanding issues, but many projects, such as those above, could be initiated and completed in the near term and without a broader agreement. That said, despite the fact that some are convinced otherwise, large scale international economic investment in Gaza and the West Bank, which would seriously help reconciliation, is unlikely outside the framework of a political resolution and serious progress toward achieving it. Some of the more modest recommendations that follow, however, such as the establishment of small business loan funds, are realistic mid-term goals.

There is one action, however, that could permanently scuttle the option of a two-state solution and likely any chance for peace—Israeli annexation of substantial portions of the West Bank. Both the Jordan Valley and the settlements deep into the West Bank fall into this category. It is impossible to say with any certainty whether a new Israeli government will have acted on any annexation pledges by the time this book appears in print, though the 2020 normalization agreements with the United Arab Emirates (UAE), Bahrain, Sudan, and Morocco and the election of Joseph Biden make widespread annexation after January 20, 2021, unlikely. If annexation has not occurred, all faith groups should continue to agitate against it, since the Israeli government insists it has only been postponed. If annexation does occur, it is unlikely to meet with international approval and all faith groups should agitate for its reversal. But a distinction can also be drawn between formal, legal *de jure* annexation and the *de facto* annexation built into settlement expansion, infrastructure construction, and the exclusion of Palestinians from designated areas. There may be a tipping point where settlement expansion especially could derail progress in the normalization process. Although the progress of de facto annexation can be accelerated or decelerated as political calculations seem to dictate, those calculations remain guesses at best. Shaul Arieli, who has long studied the geographical and political implications of the occupation of the West Bank, has written compellingly about the costs of further annexation, focusing especially on the Jordan Valley. His general conclusions offer a stark warning:

> The aim of those wishing to annex is clear. It is to annul the Oslo Accords and to foil any chance for a two-state solution for two peoples, in violation of international law and of treaties Israel has

signed. It's obvious that their wish is to displace the Palestinians eastward to Jordan at an opportune moment, and fulfill their messianic ultra-nationalist dreams . . . . The price Israel will have to pay in the short term for this messianic adventure, which is feeding on a sense of intoxication with power, will be intolerable for Israeli society. In the long run it will destroy the Zionist vision.

Given that eventual Jordan Valley annexation has been firmly endorsed by the Netanyahu government, it is important for proponents of a two-state solution to redouble efforts to oppose it and educate the public accordingly. Since annexation has at least been postponed by the September 2020 Abraham Accords with the UAE and Bahrain, followed by agreements with Sudan and Morocco, one may also ask what impact the Accords will have on delegitimation efforts in the near term. Committed BDS leaders will not stand down; they will likely redouble their efforts, with no hesitation in condemning wealthy Arab regimes for betraying the Palestinians by normalizing relations with Israel. But church members not committed to BDS may feel the traditional religious goal of reconciliation has now become more plausible and actions to encourage it imperative. Those are arguments to advance before and during church discussions and debate. That said, events are rarely reliably predictable, perhaps especially so in the Middle East. I would not invest unqualified faith in the notion that peace will break out everywhere and lead to a resolution of the Israeli/Palestinian conflict any time soon. One may recall the exaggerated hope many invested in the outcomes heralded by the Arab Spring. On the negative side, the transactional elements of the new agreements and the arms sales expected will intensify the regional arms race already under way and further harden the Sunni/Shia divide. On the other hand, Israel's anxieties should be lessened, and Arab leaders have been given an opportunity to teach reconciliation to hostile populations. Business transactions and cultural exchanges between Arabs and Israelis will surely have positive impact well beyond the less public security cooperation that laid the groundwork for normalization. Should they choose to exercise it, the Arab states who sign these agreements will have sufficient leverage to press Israel to implement some of the practical improvements in daily life detailed in the following pages. The Accords are a very good development. Time will tell what further progress they make possible. Though establishment of an independent Palestinian state is no longer a precondition for normalization with Arab countries, neither the Israeli-Palestinian conflict nor the two-state solution to it has been taken off the table.

In its December 2020 report *A New U.S. Strategy for the Israeli-Palestinian Conflict*, coauthored by Ilan Goldenberg, Michael Koplow, and Tamara Cofman Wittes, the Center for a New American Security offers its recommendations for ways the Biden administration should reset its policies toward Israel and the Palestinians. The report is directed not only toward policy makers themselves but also toward those willing to advocate for such changes. Believing, as I do, that conditions do not suggest final stage negotiations could succeed at present, the authors concentrate on combining long-term guiding principles with practical steps to take now. They believe, as I do, that improving the lives of Israelis and Palestinians will help "rebuild support within Israeli and Palestinian society for coexistence and negotiations" (5): "the United States must focus on taking tangible steps, both on the ground and diplomatically, that will improve the freedom, prosperity, and security of all people living between the Mediterranean Sea and the Jordan River while also cultivating the conditions for a future two-state agreement negotiated between the parties" (2). Religious groups might well consider a similar change of focus, shifting emphasis from promoting comprehensive negotiations toward tangible achievements that could lead to such negotiations.

The report includes as well a number of policy and practice reforms both for Israel and the Palestinian Authority. Israel should, for example, "end its demolitions of attackers' homes, which serves as a form of collective punishment." The PA/PLO should "shift the payments for families of the deceased [terrorists] to the main social security and welfare programs implemented by the PA" (38). All families should be treated the same, assisted on the basis of their needs, not because a relative has died as a celebrated martyr. Both the US government and religious groups can "offer incentives and support mechanisms aimed at marginalizing extremist voices, to root out incitement from official discourse and to promote a culture of tolerance and coexistence on both sides" (5).

To deter the special dangers built into creeping annexation, the CNAS report urges the US to explain to Israel that

Four kinds of Israeli actions will trigger a particularly strong U.S. response: (1) building or advancing plans to build in areas particularly relevant to the viability of a two-state outcome, like E-1, Givat HaMatos, E-2, and Atarot; (2) transferring or expulsing Palestinian communities from any of these or other areas; (3) constructing major new infrastructure such as roads inside the West Bank that are meant to strengthen the connection between the settlements and Israel; or (4) making any change to the historic status quo on the Haram al-Sharif/Temple Mount reaffirmed by Israel in 2015. (4)

Both secular and religious advocacy groups can reinforce these very specific recommendations. They can educate both their members and elected politicians about such matters.

Finally, readers may feel that the recommendations that follow include more tasks for the Israelis than for the Palestinians. That is partly based on the realities of unequal power and resources. But the greater reason is that the key requirements for Palestinians, like adopting transparent finances and eliminating incitement are difficult, transformational requirements.

1. GOVERNING PRINCIPLES FOR A TWO-STATE SOLUTION

Although realistic final stage negotiations are likely a few years in the future, discussions about the principles that should guide them are widespread. These suggestions are intended to inform resulting dialogue and debate. Indeed, the aspirational goal of the two-state solution has little political purchase without efforts to confront the doubts and reservations that have accumulated over the last hundred years. It is essential, meanwhile, that steps be taken to move in the right direction when possible and steps not be taken to block implementation of these principles.

(A) One potential guiding principle for negotiations is that any solution must combine separation and collaboration. Physical separation into two states, with a physical barrier, must be bolstered by cooperation in security, infrastructure, and economic development. That will make it possible over time to relax security constraints. In that spirit, both parties must make key concessions. As part of a workable two-state agreement, Israel must (1) explicitly abandon all ambitions to establish a "Greater Israel" encompassing the West Bank; (2) commit to a modified version of its pre-1967 borders; and (3) agree to the permanent division of Jerusalem and to recognize East Jerusalem as the capital of a Palestinian state. The Palestinians, in turn, must (1) specify that a final status agreement would settle all issues and end the conflict; (2) recognize Israel as a homeland for the Jewish people and agree that the right of return for Palestinian refugees is limited to returning to the Palestinian state and not Israel, excepting only those refugees whose immediate family members are Israeli citizens; and (3) accept a form of non-militarized sovereignty consistent with restrictions to guarantee Israel's security. Despite their public posturing, both parties have already more or less consented to a basic agreement on these terms.

(B) Even with a final agreement in hand, achievement of a Palestinian state could not be fully realized overnight. Full implementation could take a decade. Progress toward its realization, however, should begin now, even before formal negotiations commence.

(C) Implementation of any final status agreement would occur as "a conditions-based, performance-dependent area-by-area phased redeployment of Israeli security forces with target timetables, benchmarks, and an effective remediation process" (Goldenberg *Advancing* 4). The first area targeted for redeployment might be the northern area of the West Bank between Jenin and Nablus, especially given the relative lack of Israeli settlements to be evacuated and the economic and political practicality of anchoring the area with Palestinian cities at each end.

(D) The Palestinian Authority would maintain an enhanced security force equipped with mutually-agreed-upon weapons, including an elite counterterrorism unit capable of handling internal threats both to its own security and that of Israel. That security force would be composed of

vetted and protected personnel, including intelligence officers to detect terrorist activity, counter-terrorism forces to raid sites and arrest perpetrators, forensics experts for site exploitation, pretrial detention officers to ensure prisoners do not escape, prosecutors and judges to conduct trials and issue warrants, and post-trial detention officers to ensure prisoners are not released early; and stand-alone detention facilities (Goldenberg *Advancing* 5).

The security force would be equipped to handle potential terrorist attacks by spoilers opposed to an agreement and strong enough to prevent the overthrow of the legitimate governing authority by force. Although cooperation between Israeli and Palestinian security forces has generally been effective for some time, the full spectrum of Palestinian capacities listed here does not yet exist; it would have to be developed and strengthened over time.

(E) Israel would cease limiting Palestinian mobility within the established Palestinian state and would not intrude on Palestinian territory with ground forces short of a grave emergency such as an invasion. An agreement might establish conditions in which Palestinians could request Israeli military assistance, but it is highly unlikely the Palestinians would sign one providing for Israeli re-entry. Israel, however, "is a sovereign state that enjoys the right of self-defense," and it could invade another state if necessary (Goldenberg *Advancing* 7, also see pp. 17 and 22).

(F) Israeli settlers would be financially rewarded for willingly leaving areas east of the security barrier and, in a staged process, those refusing to leave would be physically removed by the IDF. They would be given new housing in exchange for the loss of their homes and be reimbursed for moving costs. The Israeli government needs to pass legislation to enable the first of these goals. Settlers would also have incentive to move because the loss of IDF troops stationed near their settlement would make them and their property more vulnerable.

(G) The overall goal is the creation of a single Palestinian state composed of both the West Bank and Gaza and governed by the Palestinian Authority, but a condition for its realization is a complete dismantling of Gaza's offensive military capacities, including all rocket and missile systems.

(H) Israeli, Jordanian, and Palestinian security forces would share data from a detailed traveler database encompassing watch lists and biometric data for secure identification. This would ease the transit across borders for pre-approved travelers.

(I) In the interim period prior to the establishment of the Palestinian state, Israel would be responsible for law enforcement in the West Bank, prosecuting violations by both Israelis and Palestinians under the same legal standards.

(J) In the interim period prior to the establishment of a Palestinian state, Israel must take responsibility for policing Palestinian neighborhoods in East Jerusalem and villages nearby, while upgrading municipal and welfare services to a level comparable to those in West Jerusalem. Economic investments in East Jerusalem should be encouraged both regionally and internationally. A continuous police presence is needed to eliminate illegal weapons and curtail criminal activity. The goal is to increase personal security for both East and West Jerusalem, while giving economic opportunity to those who presently lack it.

(K) There must be no formal Israeli annexation of any West Bank territory prior to a negotiated settlement.

2. SOLUTIONS TO TWO-STATE CHALLENGES

This is not intended to be a comprehensive or fully detailed list of problems and solutions, but rather a representative list of frequently raised issues. The sources I list in the notes and bibliography provide further detail.

(A) PROTECTING BEN-GURION AIRPORT. Border areas near Ben-Gurion airport would not transition to Palestinian control until some years into the implementation of a two-state agreement. Development would be restricted in sensitive areas, including limitations on building and even agricultural crop height.[118] Confidence in the enhanced counter-terrorism capacities of the Palestinian security forces would be a precondition for the final phase of Israeli withdrawal from areas near Israel's main international airport.

(B) THE JORDAN VALLEY. The rise of ISIS—the self-styled Islamic State of Iraq and Syria, also sometimes known as ISIL or Daesh—and Iran's intrusion into Syria have increased Israeli concern about the security of the Jordan Valley were it to revert to Palestinian control. The territorial defeat of ISIS did not convince Israelis that other regional security threats had been similarly neutralized. Proposals to answer these concerns include the establishment of a two-kilometer-wide security zone along the Jordan River. It would parallel and be comparable to the security zone Jordan has established on its side of the Jordan Valley. Palestinian security forces would monitor their side of the border but with mandatory assistance from American military personnel and a contingent of non-uniformed Israelis. Given Israel's lack of confidence in the United Nations, American military representatives would be the most palatable substitute. A physical barrier and electronic surveillance would supplement the monitoring personnel.[119] However, discussions with Palestinians suggest that they would not find construction of such a barrier to be politically acceptable until a final status agreement was signed.

(C) INTERNAL SECURITY OF THE PALESTINIAN AUTHORITY (see the GOVERNING PRINCIPLES section above)

(D) A PALESTINIAN AIRPORT. It would be a matter both of pride and economic opportunity for the Palestinian state to have its own airport. Despite restrictions necessary to maintain Israel's security, arrangements for both a Palestinian airport in the Jordan Valley and an offshore Gaza port facility are both possible and desirable. The airport would be restricted to licensed commercial carriers, as well as medevac flights, helicopter airlifts, and counterterrorism units. Private civilian flights would be prohibited. Palestinians could exercise sovereignty from the ground to 10,000 feet, with Israeli Air Force planes free to traverse Palestinian territory above that level. Palestinian pilots and air traffic controllers would be carefully vetted and monitored for security thereafter. Regional coordination of flights would be maintained, with provision for Israel taking temporary control of Palestinian airspace in the case of a national defense emergency.(see Goldenberg Advancing pp. 37-40)

(E) JERUSALEM. Israel must revise its policy by stating clearly and unequivocally that it has no sovereignty over the Palestinian neighborhoods and villages of East Jerusalem. In 1967, Israel annexed these areas surrounding Jerusalem to the city's municipal jurisdiction, despite the fact that they had not previously been part of the city. This hasty and coercive move was an error of historic proportions and must be rectified.

3. *IMPROVING WEST BANK PALESTINIANS' LIVES*

Both for humanitarian and strategic reasons Israel must move efficiently to improve the quality of daily life and increase economic opportunity in the West Bank. The Israeli NGO Gisha listed the WB unemployment rate at 14 percent in the first quarter of 2020.[120] As in other countries and communities, high unemployment has an unmistakably deleterious effect on the social fabric. Reducing resentment, tension, friction, and antagonism can counteract the impulse toward violence and help build the trust and sense of hope necessary to reconciliation. Crucially, however, a short-term decrease in tensions will not reduce Palestinians' determination to achieve statehood. Improving the prospects for statehood, however, depends on an internationally supported project to improve the Palestinian economy by developing concentrated industrial zones, including zones near the border with Israel. Over the past decade, international priorities have shifted, in part because of the Syrian refugee crisis, and West Bank economic growth has declined. It should be noted that there is strong support in the Israeli military for making improvements to West Bank infrastructure. The following are steps Israel can take to reduce conflict and foster increased support for a two-state solution:

(**A**) Announce a formal policy decision ending settlement expansion east of the security barrier.

(**B**) Issue a firm declaration that Israel has no permanent territorial ambitions east of the security barrier.

(**C**) Strengthen the formal commitment to maintaining the status quo on the Temple Mount/Haram al-Sharif.

(**D**) Expand the collection of biometric data for Palestinians seeking to work in or visit Israel and use that data to vet and pre-approve thousands of Palestinians for rapid entry into Israel. Establish separate fast lanes at checkpoints to make transit for those Palestinians much easier and more efficient.

(**E**) Issue 50,000 additional work permits for Palestinians seeking employment in Israel proper on top of the 30,000 and 20,000 announced in 2016 and 2018 respectively. Unemployment is a major source of suffering and discontent, and the West Bank economy is intricately bound up with that of Israel. Those Palestinians who want to work in Israel should be able to do so. Unlike the 50,000 Palestinians who work in Israel without proper documentation, Palestinians with work permits can easily return to their homes at the end of the day.

(F) Complete the missing sections of the security barrier, making adjustments in its route as appropriate, and implement a strict border control regime along its full length. Violence is typically perpetrated by Palestinians passing through gaps in the security barrier, not by those Israel approves for passage from the West Bank through checkpoints. Gaps in the security fence also allow Israelis to smuggle weapons onto the West Bank. Reducing Palestinian violence would disincentivize punitive actions like house demolitions and increase overall confidence in the peace process. Reducing the flow of weapons into Israeli settlements should help curtail Israeli violence as well. If the fence and those monitoring it can assume more responsibility for security, it should be possible to reduce the level of Israeli intrusion into Palestinian life. (See "Security First" by Commanders for Israel's Security)

(G) Assist with laying down new water lines in the West Bank to help further develop Palestinian agriculture. Increase water allotments for Palestinian farmers, and encourage use of recycled water, a practice that works very well for Israeli agriculture.

(H) Make it easier to ship Palestinian agricultural products and manufacturing goods into Israel and to port facilities for shipment elsewhere, including to countries that do not trade with Israel. To this end, additional paved roads should be constructed in Palestinian areas.

(I) Make financial exchanges between Israeli and Palestinian banks easier and improve internet connections and wireless communications in the West Bank. A November 2015 agreement between Israelis and Palestinians was designed to enable Palestinian telecom companies to provide 3G service to the West Bank, but this does not go far enough. Palestinians should have immediate access to a 4G broadband mobile network.

(J) Establish an international small business loan fund to support initiatives in the West Bank.

(K) Facilitate approval of Palestinian building permits and begin planning for the transfer of ten percent of Area C to Palestinian control under Areas A and B, thereby linking many of the fragmentary segments of Areas A and B—demarcations designated by the 1993 Oslo Accords—into continuous territory before an agreement is reached. Transferring this small amount of territory to Palestinian Authority control will strengthen the PA's ability to secure law and order, strengthen the Palestinian economy, and legalize thousands of homes currently under threat of demolition. Even designating tiny portions of Area C as Area A could create "territorial contiguity between certain Palestinian villages and towns"; it could "provide the PA with a major deliverable in solving the housing demolition threat hanging over thousands of illegal housing units which are home to over 250,000 Palestinians" (Commanders "Gaza" 26). Approve new West Bank Palestinian cities, including a second model city similar to Rawabi.

4. WHAT THE PEOPLE OF GAZA NEED NOW

A group of over 280 former Israeli generals, security officials, and high-level police officers a and a number of international sources have echoed the United Nations' recent warning that, without significant interventions, the Gaza Strip may soon be largely unfit for human habitation. In its 2018 book, *The Crisis of the Gaza Strip: A Way Out*—which is one of the best guides both to Gaza's needs and to the multinational political maneuvering that curtails any effort to meet them—Israel's Institute for National Security Studies (INSS) confirms Gaza's humanitarian crisis. Israel Policy Forum's online summer 2018 project, "50 Steps Before the Deal," adds further detail and numerous supporting videos. "Gaza: An Alternative Strategy," issued by Commanders for Israel's Security in November 2019, echoes these suggestions and adds a number of its own.

Nearly 20,000 apartments and houses were destroyed during the summer of 2014; as of May 2017, 30,000 people still had only temporary housing. The electrical grid is disintegrating and is currently only intermittently functional, having been limited to ten hours service per day. A November 2018 agreement brokered by Egypt, Israel, Qatar, and the UN arranged for Qatar to fund $10 million in fuel for Gaza from

Israeli suppliers each month; though there is no guarantee it will not collapse, it increased the daily electrical supply to twelve hours or more (Halbfinger). Sewage treatment is essentially nonexistent, with substantial raw sewage flowing in the streets, which is ultimately deposited in the Mediterranean, contaminating coastal areas in Gaza, Egypt, and Israel. The risks to health are substantial and epidemics a real possibility. The shortage of drinkable water is acute, with almost all of the water in Gaza's coastal aquifer now contaminated and undrinkable.

According to the Israeli NGO Gisha, the unemployment rate in Gaza reached forty-eight percent in the third quarter of 2020, up from a rate of forty-five percent in 2019. Unless averted, this humanitarian crisis is likely to produce a political crisis of considerable dimensions. Hamas seems largely uninterested in improving residents' lives, the Palestinian Authority is reluctant to enhance Hamas's status by doing so, and Egypt is unwilling to either open the Rafah crossing on Gaza's southern border permanently or assume any responsibility for Gaza's humanitarian needs. Israel, on the other hand, has a vested humanitarian and security interest in ameliorating this impending disaster. Although Israel formally withdrew from Gaza in 2005, it still controls access by sea, supplies much of the area's energy needs, and oversees its northern and eastern borders. A coordinated effort to improve conditions in both the West Bank and Gaza simultaneously should help persuade people that Hamas is not being rewarded for its violent tactics. Meanwhile the humanitarian crisis in Gaza opens opportunities for still more malevolent actors to seek advantage there, including ISIS offshoots and Palestinian Islamic Jihad. Israel should help achieve these short-term needs and long-term goals:

(A) Increase the number of trucks delivering basic goods from Israel into Gaza through the Kerem Shalom and Erez crossings, located at Gaza's southeast corner and northern border respectively. Encourage Egypt to permanently reopen the Rafah crossing on Gaza's southern border and implement appropriate vetting procedures to prevent travel to Iran for military and arms manufacture training. Eliminate the smuggling of weapons, many of which are supplied by Iran, through remaining underground tunnels between Egypt and Gaza. Establish an additional commercial crossing point between Israel and Gaza to help Gaza's economy and relieve the overburdened Kerem Shalom crossing.

(B) Urge the Palestinian Authority to accept and cooperate with the necessity of humanitarian aid to Gaza.

(C) Expand Gazan fishing rights in the Mediterranean from nine to at least fifteen miles, which would produce both economic and nutritional benefits.

(D) Issue thousands of additional permits for Gazans to work in Israel, with thorough security vetting, and activate those permits. Ease entry restrictions on travel to Israel for medical services.

(E) Proceed expeditiously to build the planned large solar field in Israel near the Gazan border to supply Palestinians with additional electricity.

(F) Assemble an international coalition to meet Gaza's acute sewage treatment needs.

(G) Expand opportunities for Gazans to study abroad. Work with Egypt, Jordan, and the Palestinian Authority to enable more Palestinians to exit through the Rafah crossing and travel through Cairo or Amman for that purpose. Institute a pilot program for carefully vetted Gazans to study in the West Bank.

(H) Curtail Hamas's diversion of materials and resources into tunnel-building and military stockpiling. Encourage internationally supervised expenditures on reconstruction of Gaza housing, medical facilities, and infrastructure. The UN has so far failed to enforce the 2014 Gaza Reconstruction Mechanism that was designed to prevent repurposing materials for military use. Explicit sanctions should be put in place to prevent Hamas from repurposing aid, and reconstruction work needs to be internationally monitored. These moves should enable Israel to relax its restrictions on movement of dual-purpose items into Gaza. International willingness to fund reconstruction, however, will be limited so long as there is reasonable certainty it will be destroyed in a forthcoming conflict. A ceasefire needs to be stable and reliable. That will require a firm Hamas commitment to end all active aggression, including rocket attacks and tunnel construction.

(I) Encourage additional agricultural and manufacturing exports from Gaza to Israel and elsewhere. Imports and exports do not present significant security risks for Israel. Although transport of goods from Gaza has been substantially increased since 2011-2014, the 2016 level was still only 15% of that in 1999.

(J) Call on international aid organizations to help fund and carry out the reconstruction of Gaza's electricity infrastructure, including upgrading transmission lines, expanding the capacity of Gaza's power station, and facilitating the Gaza power station's transition to natural gas. Israel on its own should increase the electrical power it supplies to Gaza and connect Gaza to its natural gas transmission network. Gaza's small power plant is supplemented by Israeli and Egyptian electricity, but even this joint effort supplies only half the necessary supply.

(K) Make completion of a new water pipeline from Israel to Gaza an urgent priority. Help establish substantial desalinization capability in Gaza. The European Union and USAID are scheduled to fund the second stage of the Deir al-Balah desalinization plant, work on which began in 2018. Israel has been charged with coordinating this effort, but substantially more desalinization capacity will be necessary to meet Gaza's long-term water needs. Moreover, desalinization plants cannot operate without adequate power. Gaza would further benefit from an additional, internationally-financed water reservoir.

(L) Continue upgrading the security barrier along the border with Gaza and continue to develop and apply tunnel detection technology. Successful interdiction of Hamas's violence should decrease the occurrence of Israeli military responses that put ordinary Gazans at risk.

(M) International organizations like the United Nations Relief and Works Agency (UNRWA) should eliminate anti-Israel incitement from textbooks supplied to Gaza schools and substitute arguments favoring coexistence.

(N) Establish an international small business loan fund to support private initiatives in Gaza.

(O) Construct a rail line from the Erez crossing to Israel's Ashdod port to facilitate exports from Gaza.

(P) Move forward on the widely discussed offshore Gaza port to be constructed on an artificial island in the Mediterranean. Israel would monitor and inspect all shipping and approve all human entry. The Israeli government has also proposed establishing a dedicated floating pier in Cyprus as an alternative, which would probably be less expensive and could be established more rapidly. Whether it would be as versatile or have the same capacity as an offshore port is less clear, but it could be a good interim option.[121]

(Q) Begin plans for foreign development of a natural gas field off the Gaza coast, which could be completed in three years.

(R) There is huge potential for the development of a tourism industry along the Gaza coast, but not without international confidence in long-term peace. In order to create this assurance, Hamas would have to establish and honor a coastal demilitarized zone as a first step and then move to publicly and comprehensively reject violence.

APPENDIX

APPENDIX:

INTRODUCTION (CN)

A substantial portion of this book has been devoted to the half century in which a number of Christian churches have struggled with their long history of anti-Semitism, sought to reconceive the theological status of Judaism, and negotiated the influence of anti-Semitism on their relationship with the Jewish State. The worldwide increase in anti-Semitic incidents over the past decade has made these issues still more urgent. All the world's interfaith relations are burdened with historical legacies that remain alive and relevant today, nowhere more so, however, than when the Israel-Palestinian conflict is at stake. There is an immense (and increasing) body of scholarly literature about the history of anti-Semitism, but it would be unrealistic to imagine that most readers of this book will have that literature readily in mind. To make it available with as much detail as practical, a brief preface and annotated timeline on anti-Semitism as it has shaped church history and Christian relations with Jews concludes this book. The entries for expulsions of the Jews from European countries, accusations of blood libel, and massacres of Jews are included to signal a pattern. A complete list would add literally hundreds of entries to the timeline.

Readers of this appendix might keep in mind the distinction Bernard Harrison draws on throughout *Blaming the Jews* (2020) between social anti-Semitism (which targets individuals) and political anti-Semitism ("a body of pseudo-explanatory theory capable of directing the political outlook of believers," 19). Social anti-Semitism is thus "the form of antisemitism that can reasonably be regarded as a version of racism . . . a *state of mind*." Political anti-Semitism "is not a state of mind at all but rather a *cultural formation*" (143), or an ideology. "Social prejudice justifies itself by appeal to a range of contemptuous stereotypes to which individuals of the despised group are held to conform" (67). Political prejudice is initially directed "not against *individuals* but against *collective entities*, real or imagined" (66). "Against the Jewish collectivity, it asserts (in their most general form consistently over the past two millennia) a range of entirely delusive accusations, among them an absolute commitment to evil, conspiratorial organization of an essentially impenetrable kind and vast power to harm any non-Jewish society that harbors Jews" (79). "Antisemitism as a structured system of mutually supporting beliefs offers a powerful illusion of political understanding" (241).

The modern apotheosis of political prejudice was to be found in the Third Reich, but since then, in both secular and Christian demonization of Israel—in such tropes as accusations of Israeli genocide, claims that Israel's crimes outweigh those of any other nation, assertions that that Zionism threatens peace and security worldwide, and in conspiratorial warnings about the immense and sinister but hidden powers of the Israeli lobby—we find that political anti-Semitism remains a contemporary force. "It is *political* antisemitism that possesses the power to revive again endlessly, now on this side of politics, now on that, bringing the old hatreds with it" (137). A key strategy in both secular and Christian BDS "is to attempt to prevent discussion from focusing on political antisemitism by pretending that social antisemitism is the only form that antisemitism can take" (162).

"Masquerading as a universally explanatory worldview," political anti-Semitism renders its devotees "unable to recognize their antisemitism for what it is: not an antisemitism of emotional dislike and contempt but rather an antisemitism of *belief*, and thus an antisemitism of the most potentially lethal kind" (70, 400). Political anti-Semitism "allows believers to persuade themselves that their hatred of Israel—and Jews—arises not from any *personal* dislike of Jews but rather from moral impulses of a generously altruistic and humanitarian character" (400). Yet political anti-Semitism "is the kind of antisemitism that burns synagogues" (162). Both historically and in the present, political anti-Semitism can be a substantial part of how people understand the world. It often proceeds not through rational debate but by way of "the violent and belligerent repetition of a small range of entirely factually ungrounded but profoundly defamatory charges to the effect that Israel is a racist, apartheid, or Nazi state" (439).

For much Western history, it is unnecessary to distinguish between political and religious anti-Semitism; they are the same. Christian anti-Semitism always had a distinctive theological component, but, after Constantine, it was integrated with and implemented by state power. As the Enlightenment progressed, religious and secular anti-Semitisms began to diverge. In both contemporary Christian and Islamic hostility toward the Jewish state, however, the relevant explanatory systems combine politics and religion, though secular anti-Zionism mostly ignores theological arguments. Sometimes intertwined and sometimes conceptually separate, political and religious anti-Semitism now also appeal to different constituencies and develop within different organizations.

DAVID FOX SANDMEL

PREFACE TO A TIMELINE: A BRIEF HISTORY OF ANTI-SEMITISM

DEFINITION OF ANTI-SEMITISM

Anti-Semitism refers to prejudice and/or discrimination that is directed toward Jews. Anti-Semitism can be based on stereotypes and myths that target Jews as a people, their religious practices and beliefs, and/or the Jewish State of Israel. The International Holocaust Remembrance Alliance (IHRA) adopted this definition in 2016: "Antisemitism is a certain perception of Jews, which may be expressed as hatred toward Jews. Rhetorical and physical manifestations of antisemitism are directed toward Jewish or non-Jewish individuals and/or their property, toward Jewish community institutions and religious facilities." It added these examples:

- Calling for, aiding, or justifying the killing or harming of Jews in the name of a radical ideology or an extremist view of religion.
- Making mendacious, dehumanizing, demonizing, or stereotypical allegations about Jews as such or the power of Jews as collective—such as, especially but not exclusively, the myth about a world Jewish conspiracy or of Jews controlling the media, economy, government or other societal institutions.
- Accusing Jews as a people of being responsible for real or imagined wrongdoing committed by a single Jewish person or group, or even for acts committed by non-Jews.
- Denying the fact, scope, mechanisms (e.g. gas chambers), or intentionality of the genocide of the Jewish people at the hands of National Socialist Germany and its supporters and accomplices during World War II (the Holocaust).

- Accusing the Jews as a people, or Israel as a state, of inventing or exaggerating the Holocaust.
- Accusing Jewish citizens of being more loyal to Israel, or to the alleged priorities of Jews worldwide, than to the interests of their own nations.
- Denying the Jewish people their right to self-determination, e.g., by claiming that the existence of a State of Israel is a racist endeavor.
- Applying double standards by requiring of it a behavior not expected or demanded of any other democratic nation.
- Using the symbols and images associated with classic antisemitism (e.g., claims of Jews killing Jesus or blood libel) to characterize Israel or Israelis.
- Drawing comparisons of contemporary Israeli policy to that of the Nazis.
- Holding Jews collectively responsible for actions of the state of Israel.

Historically, what began as a conflict over religious beliefs evolved into a systematic policy of political, economic, and social isolation, exclusion, degradation, and attempted annihilation. Anti-Semitism did not begin in the Nazi era, nor did it end with the close of World War II. Its continuance over the millennia speaks to the power of scapegoating a group that is defined as the "other."

ANTIQUITY

According to the book of Genesis, Abraham, who is revered by the three major monotheistic religions (Judaism, Christianity, and Islam), led his family to Canaan around 1,800 years before the Common Era (BCE), where a new nation—the people of Israel—eventually came into being. During the centuries before the rise of Christianity, the Israelites (the early Jewish people) experienced intermittent persecution because they refused to adopt the religious practices of the people in whose territory they dwelled, or those of the regimes that conquered the land. Their refusal to worship idols was seen as stubbornness, which came to be known as a characteristic Jewish trait. Some Greco-Roman writers mocked the Jews because of their "strange" practices—such as Sabbath observance or dietary regulations—but they also critiqued other peoples on similar grounds. There were incidents of anti-Jewish violence, especially in Egypt, such as the destruction of the Jewish temple at Elephantine c. 410 BCE and anti-Jewish riots in Alexandria in 38 C.E.

THE RISE OF CHRISTIANITY

After the advent of Christianity, a new anti-Judaism evolved. Initially, Christianity was seen as simply another Jewish sect, since Jesus and the Disciples were Jewish and preached a form of Judaism. During the first few hundred years after the crucifixion of Jesus by the Romans, adherents of both Judaism and Christianity co-existed—sometimes peacefully, sometimes with animosity—as they sought to practice their faiths in the same lands. However, as Christianity developed, it attracted primarily Gentile converts. What began as a form of Judaism eventually became a separate religion. Christianity had to explain how it differed from Judaism and often did so in the polemical style common in that era. Since both religions based their legitimacy on the Old Testament, Christians sought to establish the validity of their religion by claiming it was the continuation of biblical Israel and had superseded Judaism and the Jews. The refusal of Jews to accept Jesus as the Messiah was viewed as another manifestation of their stubbornness and later as a sign of their supposed hatred of Jesus and Christianity. The primary example of this was the idea that the Jews were responsible for the death of Jesus, known as "deicide." Jews and Judaism occupied a unique place in the Christian theology and imagination; no other people or tradition posed the same questions or challenges.

THE MIDDLE AGES

After the conversion of Emperor Constantine I, Christianity became the sole official religion of the Roman Empire. During the next three centuries (300–600 C.E.) a new pattern of institutionalized discrimination—that is, discrimination integrated into legal and/ or economic systems—against Jews emerged. To name but a few examples: Jews were forbidden to marry Christians (399 C.E.), were prohibited from holding positions in government (439 C.E.) and were barred from bearing witness against Christians in court (531 C.E.).

As Jews were officially being ostracized, certain bizarre fantasies about Jews arose in Northern Europe that foreshadowed the anti-Semitic conspiracies of later centuries. It was alleged that Jews were in league with the Devil, had horns and tails, and routinely murdered Christians in order to reenact the murder of Jesus and to collect Christian blood for their religious rituals. The latter allegations, referred to as "blood libels," were devised by Thomas of Monmouth in 1150 to explain the mysterious death of a Christian boy. This theme recurs in English and German myths.

During this same period, a theological view, articulated by Augustine of Hippo (354-430 C.E.) taught that the Jews "must be allowed to survive, but never to thrive" so that their debased position in society could serve as "proper punishments for their refusal to recognize the truth of the Church's claims" and as a living warning to faithless Christians.

In 1095, Pope Urban II made a general appeal to the Christians of Europe to take up the cross and sword and "liberate" the Holy Land from the Muslims, beginning what was to be known as the Crusades. The religious fervor that drove men, and later even children, on the Crusades had direct consequences for Jews. The Crusader army, which more closely resembled a mob, swept through Jewish communities looting, raping, and massacring Jews as they went. Thus the pogrom—the organized massacre of a targeted group of people—was born. It should be noted that popes and other Church officials ostensibly opposed violence against the Jews but were generally unable or unwilling to control public sentiment.

During the mid-fourteenth century, the bubonic plague spread throughout Europe, killing an estimated one-third of the population in a period known as the Black Death. Fear, superstition, and ignorance cried out for someone to blame. Jews were a convenient scapegoat, in particular because of the myths and stereotypes about them that many already believed. Though Jews were also dying from the plague, they were accused of poisoning wells and spreading the disease. In Germany and Austria it is estimated that 100,000 Jews were burned alive for this and other false accusations, including using the blood of Christian boys to make matzah (unleavened bread that is eaten during the Jewish holiday of Passover) and for desecrating the host (the sacramental wafer used in the Christian Eucharist). Christian art depicting anti-Semitic stereotypes in grotesque detail was displayed in churches to inflame the masses.

Martin Luther, who catalyzed the sixteenth-century Protestant Reformation, wrote a pamphlet in 1545 entitled *The Jews and Their Lies*, claiming that Jews thirsted for Christian blood and calling for them to be slayed en masse. The Nazis reprinted it in 1935. Some scholars feel that these scurrilous broadsides mark the transition from anti-Judaism (attacks motivated because of the Jews' refusal to accept Christianity) to anti-Semitism (hatred of Jews as a so-called race that would contaminate the purity of another race). Others trace this idea to the concept of "purity of blood," which was used during the Spanish Inquisition to impugn the faith of Jews who converted to Christianity and their descendants, alleging that Jewish unfaithfulness was transmitted biologically from one generation to the next.

Increasingly throughout the medieval period, Jews were subjected to political, economic, and social discrimination, and deprived of their legal and civil rights. Beginning in the thirteenth century, Jews in many countries were required to wear a distinctive symbol (a badge and/or a pointed hat) so that they could be immediately recognized, a tradition that was revived in Nazi Germany. In the sixteenth century, many Jews were officially restricted to certain areas, which came to be known as "ghettos," after the section of Venice known as the "ghetto nuovo," (literally, "the New Foundry"), the first such example.

Since Jews were not allowed to own land, employ Christians, or join certain guilds, and because the Church did not allow Christians to loan money for profit, Jews had few alternatives but to become moneylenders. Once they became associated with the forbidden trade of usury—the practice of lending money and charging high interest—a new set of stereotypes evolved around the Jews as money-hungry and greedy. As moneylenders, Jews were frequently useful to rulers who used their capital to build cathedrals, outfit armies, and engage in international commerce. As long as the Jews benefited the ruler, either through finance or by serving as convenient scapegoats, they were tolerated. When it suited the ruler, they were expelled, driven out—from

England in 1290, France in 1394, and Spain in 1492, to name but a few examples.

MODERN ANTI-SEMITISM

The term "anti-Semitism" was coined in 1879 by the German political agitator Wilhelm Marr (1819-1904) in his pamphlet, *Victory of Judaism over Germanism*. He claimed that Jews were conspiring to run the state and should be excluded from citizenship. Anti-Semitism, in Marr's conception, was linked to the Jews as a people, rather than to Judaism as a religion. In 1903, the Russian secret police published a forged collection of documents that became known as *The Protocols of the Elders of Zion*. It told of a secret plot by rabbis to take over the world. Racism and anti-Semitism were also facilitated by the development of Social Darwinism and pseudo-scientific theories of racial superiority and inferiority.

In 1894, Alfred Dreyfus, a Jewish captain in the French army, was falsely accused and convicted of selling military secrets to the Germans. When evidence was discovered that Dreyfus was innocent, it was quickly covered up by the Officers of the General Staff, who wanted to blame the crime on a Jew. Although Dreyfus was eventually vindicated, "The Dreyfus Affair," as it became known, showed how deeply-rooted and pervasive anti-Semitism was in France.

In Russia, Jews were routinely blamed for all the problems of the Russian peasantry, despite the fact that most Jews were peasants themselves. Pogroms were instigated by the czarist secret police in part to deflect anger from the regime—another case of scapegoating. The Russian Orthodox Church often abetted the police through anti-Jewish sermons. In 1905, for example, Russia's loss in the Russo-Japanese War moved the government to incite a bloody pogrom in the Bessarabian capital, Kishinev. Between 1917 and 1921, after the Russian Revolution, more than 500 Jewish communities in the Ukraine were wiped out in pogroms. About 60,000 Jewish men, women, and children were murdered.

THE HOLOCAUST

Why was it in Germany that anti-Semitism turned into genocide, the deliberate extermination, of the Jewish community? After all, France, England, and Russia all had longstanding anti-Semitic traditions. Germany, however, was more deeply saturated with anti-Semitic culture in the nineteenth and early twentieth century than any other area of Europe. Concepts of German exceptionalism were based on pseudo-scientific racial theories, such as the one proposed by the aforementioned Marr, who also popularized the term "antisemitismus." Following its defeat in World War I, Germany was a deeply troubled country. The victorious countries, including the United States, France, and England, also forced them to sign the Treaty of Versailles, which compelled Germany to give up territory and to pay large-scale reparations. Adolph Hitler was a demagogic leader, and obedience to authority was a strong cultural norm in Germany. Hitler called upon remembered myths of the "blood libel" from the Middle Ages and combined it with racial anti-Semitism to evoke fear that the Jews would contaminate what he referred to as the superior Aryan race. Therefore, according to Hitler's doctrine, all Jews must be eliminated.

There may be no more succinct description of the Holocaust than the statement issued by the Vatican on March 12, 1998:

This century has witnessed an unspeakable tragedy, which can never be forgotten — the attempt by the Nazi regime to exterminate the Jewish people, with the consequent killing of millions of Jews. Women and men, old and young, children and infants, for the sole reason of their Jewish origin, were persecuted and deported. Some were killed immediately, while others were degraded, ill-treated, tortured and utterly robbed of their human dignity, and then murdered. Very few of those who entered the [concentration] camps survived, and those who did remained scarred for life. This was the Shoah (the Holocaust).

POST-HOLOCAUST JEWISH-CHRISTIAN RELATIONS

The post-war era saw the emergence of Jewish-Christian dialogue, including numerous publications, conferences, and the establishment of centers of Jewish-Christian relations. The revelation of the genocide of European Jewry shocked the Christian world. How was it possible that such a horrendous crime could be carried out by so many people who considered themselves Christians? This resulted in a profound crisis among Christian theologians and provoked a difficult examination of Christian teachings about Jews and Judaism. Prominent theologians and church bodies acknowledged the direct connection between the historic Christian teaching of contempt for Jews and Judaism and the Nazis' "Final Solution." This revisioning led to the development of new, non-supersessionist theologies, perhaps the most famous of which is *Nostra Aetate* (1965), one of the documents produced by the Catholic Church's Second Vatican Council. *Nostra Aetate* repudiated the charge of deicide and implied that the Jewish covenant with God remained in effect. It also denounced anti-Semitism and called for dialogue.

Speaking to sixty theologians and clergy from around the world at a Vatican symposium October 30–November 1, 1997, Pope John Paul II recognized that "erroneous and unjust interpretations of the New Testament regarding the Jewish people and their alleged culpability have circulated for too long" and "contributed to a lulling of many consciences" at the time of World War II, so that, while there were "Christians who did everything to save those who were persecuted, even to the point of risking their own lives, the spiritual resistance of many was not what humanity expected of Christ's disciples."

CONTEMPORARY ANTI-SEMITISM

After the Holocaust, after the world witnessed the horrors of Auschwitz, anti-Semitism became far less accepted. Seeing what anti-Semitism could lead to made peoples and nations ashamed of openly expressing anti-Semitism.

Anti-Semitism did not completely disappear, but the events of World War II significantly inhibited its expression. As the decades passed, as memories faded and criticism of the Jewish State of Israel mounted, many of these inhibitions weakened. In recent years, there has been a concerning upsurge of anti-Semitism around the world. Some is directly connected to Israel—accusing Israel of age-old anti-Semitic charges, such as blood libels and using evil power to control the world.

Some manifestations of anti-Semitism are more indirect. The excessive criticism of Israel leads some people to feel more comfortable attacking Jews and Jewish institutions around the world. Historically, Islam has viewed Jews and Judaism as a "people of the book," a second-class status that often brought with it certain legal restrictions, but which was higher than the status of "idolaters." Whereas the persistence of Jews and Judaism was a central theological concern for Christianity, it was not nearly as important for Islam. Thus, by and large, Jews experienced less oppression under Muslim rule than under Christian rule. However, since the establishment of the state of Israel, anti-Semitism has grown significantly in the Arab world, in part in reaction to the Israeli-Palestinian conflict, but also because of the exploitation of that conflict by autocratic rulers to deflect popular anger over repression—another example of scapegoating.

Others are expressing anti-Semitism in more traditional ways. For example, Anti-Defamation League (ADL) polls have shown that large numbers of Europeans believe that their Jewish citizens are not loyal to the countries in which they live, and that they have a disproportionate amount of political and economic power. Coinciding with the spread of ethnic nationalism, the explosion of online white supremacist communities demonstrates that anti-Semitism is still a significant problem.

This resurgence of anti-Semitism is a great concern, especially as we move further and further away from the lessons of the Holocaust. The Jewish people do have allies in the United States and around the world, however, who remember the lessons of history and are ready to stand against this very old and very sinister hatred.

CARY NELSON

⌣

ANNOTATED TIMELINE OF JEWISH/CHRISTIAN RELATIONS AND THE HISTORY OF ANTI-JUDAISM

c. 33 Jesus is crucified.

c. 58 Paul, who did not know Jesus personally, writes his last letter to the Romans. Contemporary scholarship generally agrees that, of the thirteen Epistles in the New Testament attributed to Paul, only seven were written by Paul himself. The role his letters have played in Jewish-Christian relations has been unique. Thus, for example, Galatians 1:15-16 describes an experience on the road to Damascus that Paul likely understood as a call to a new spiritual understanding. But the later Gospel of Luke, reflecting the growing split between Judaism and Christianity, has long led Christians to see Paul's experience as one of conversion, which has powerfully shaped the Catholic and Protestant churches' sense of their identity and mission. However, most scholars now believe that Paul lived and died thinking of himself as a Jew and that the debates he engaged in constituted conflicts within Judaism. Romans 9-11 is the longest New Testament discussion of the Jews' relation to Christian beliefs and reflects Paul's struggle with how Jews who rejected the good news of Jesus fit in to God's plan. In these chapters, however, Paul states unequivocally:

> *They are Israelites, and to them belong the adoption, the glory, the covenants, the giving of the law, the worship, and the promises; to them*

belong the patriarchs, and from them, according to the flesh, comes the
Messiah, who is over all, God blessed forever. Amen. (9:4-5)

I ask, then, has God rejected his people? By no means! I myself am an
Israelite, a descendant of Abraham, a member of the tribe of Benjamin.
God has not rejected his people whom he foreknew. (11:1-2)

It is to Romans 9-11 that Christians turned after the Holocaust to
develop a new, positive theology of Jewish-Christian relations.

66-73 Jews in Israel revolt against Rome. In response to initial
victories in which the Roman garrison in Jerusalem was destroyed and
a Roman force sent from Syria was routed, Rome sent 60,000 troops to
suppress the Jewish revolt. Perhaps as many as a million Jews died in the
resulting catastrophe.

70 Titus destroys the Second Temple in Jerusalem; the golden menorah
that resided in the Temple, the only one of its kind, is brought to Rome
as a trophy.

c. 70 The Gospel of Mark is completed. All four gospels were composed
over a period of years, using both oral traditions going back to the time
of Jesus himself as well as various written records. Each Gospel reflects
the perspective of the community in which it was written.

c. 80-90 The Gospels of Matthew and Luke are completed. They
reflect the disputes and conflicts of the era in which they are composed.
Matthew 27:24-25 has had a particularly vexed history in Christian-
Jewish relations. At this version of Jesus's trial Pilate washes his hands
before the crowd and announces "'I am innocent of this man's blood; see
to it yourselves.' Then the people as a whole answered, 'His blood be on
us and on our children!'" The "blood cry" citation is unique to Matthew
and "was used by some Christians through the centuries to claim that
all Jews in all times and places were collectively responsible for the
death of Jesus. More likely, the phrase reflects Matthew's interpretation
of the tragic events of 70 CE, when Rome destroyed Jerusalem and

burned the Temple: the 'children' of the Jerusalem crowd were the ones to witness that destruction" (Gale 10). Most of the New Testament was written before Christianity had separated from Judaism, although later generations of Christians believed that the separation had taken place with Jesus' crucifixion, or at least no later than the destruction of the Second Temple. Thus, what were in reality intra-Jewish debates came to be seen as conflicts between Jews and Jesus (as if Jesus was not Jewish!) or between Jews and Christians, setting the stage for the development of Christian anti-Judaism.

c. 70-130 The Gospel of John and the Epistle to the Hebrews are composed. According to Adele Reinhartz, "John is highly disturbing in its presentation of 'the Jews". . . . [They] are the archenemies of Jesus and his followers; they are oblivious to the truth and relentless in pursuit of Jesus to the point of masterminding his demise. Their behavior towards Jesus and their failure to believe demonstrate that they have relinquished their covenantal relationship with the God of Israel and show them to be instead the children of the devil [8:44]. For this reason, John's Gospel has been called both the most Jewish and the most anti-Jewish of the Gospels" ("Introduction" 168).

c. 132 The first *Adversus Judaeos* text, the *Epistle of Barnabas*, is composed. The Epistle, which ultimately was not included in the canon of the New Testament, asserts that Christians are the only true covenant people and that the Jewish covenant with God has ended. Though not yet named, supersessionism—the logic that Christians have replaced Jews as God's chosen community—solidified during the second and third centuries as the Church's dominant perspective. It would be equally defining in Protestant denominations after the Reformation. Negative portrayals of Jews begin to become a way to define Christian identity and the meaning of Christianity against Judaism, as Christianity relies on an imaginary version of Judaism to define itself as Judaism's polar opposite.

132-5 The Bar Kochba revolt in Judea against Rome. After the Jews are defeated, many are sold into slavery. Judea is renamed Syria Palestina, an attempt to erase the Jewish connection to the land.

c. 140 The heretical Marcion (c. 90-155), who moved to Rome from Sinope on the Black Sea, aims to eliminate any vestige of Judaism from Christianity by rejecting the Old Testament and drawing "a sharp distinction between the Creator God of the Jews, characterized by a spurious justice, deceitfulness, and inconsistency, and the eternal, distant 'stranger' God, revealed as the Father of Jesus Christ" (Lieu 284). "Marcion held that the God from whom Jesus came was a different and far higher deity from the creating and law-giving God spoken of in the Jewish bible" (Harrison 304). We know Marcion's arguments only from the record of those who sought to refute him and ultimately named him a heretic. Despite the fact that he was excommunicated for his radical theology, elements of his views are fundamental to supersessionist history. "Marcion systematically expressed his rejection of material creation in terms of a rejection of letter, law (meaning Jewish scripture) and above all, Judaism" (Nirenberg 98). In his 1924 monograph on Marcion, German Protestant theologian Adolf von Harnack (1851-1930) would agree with him that the Hebrew scriptures should be removed from the Christian canon altogether.

c. 160 Justin Martyr (c. 100-165) completes his *Dialogue with Typho*, which consists of his imaginary dialogue with a Jew in which he tries to prove that Jesus is the Jewish Messiah. According to Kessler, "For Justin, the divine rebuke should be applied to contemporary Jews, not just biblical Israel; likewise he applies the divine blessings to Christians only . . . Justin is the earliest exponent of the teaching that the Church appropriated the Old Testament. Only Christians could offer true interpretations for they are the heirs to all God's promises and are the true Israel" (53). The land granted to ancient Israel was merely a temporary gift; it is superseded by the eternal heavenly dwelling place offered through salvation in Christ.

165 Melito (c. 140-185), the Bishop of Sardis, sometimes called the first poet of deicide, composes Peri Pascha ("On the Pascha") between 160 and 170 C.E:

> This one was murdered. And where was he murdered? In the very center of Jerusalem! Why? Because he had healed their lame, and had cleansed their lepers, and had guided their blind with light, and had raised up their dead. For this reason he suffered . . . Why, O Israel did you do this strange injustice? You dishonored the one who had honored you. You held in contempt the one who held you in esteem. You denied the one who publicly acknowledged you. You renounced the one who proclaimed you his own. You killed the one who made you to live. Why did you do this, O Israel? . . . It was necessary for him to suffer, yes, but not by you; it was necessary for him to be dishonored, but not by you; it was necessary for him to be judged, but not by you; it was necessary for him to be crucified, but not by you, nor by your right hand . . . O lawless Israel, why did you commit this extraordinary crime of casting your Lord into new sufferings—your master, the one who formed you, the one who made you, the one who honored you, the one who called you Israel? . . . O ungrateful Israel, come here and be judged . . . .

Melito was not alone in claiming that the Jews killed Christ, but the forceful rhetoric of his long poem made it memorable, and helped inaugurate the supersessionist tradition and root the deicide charge in the Christian imagination.

c. 180 Irenaeus of Lyons (c. 130-c. 200) produces his *Adversus Haereses*, disputing Marcion's arguments but showing "little sympathy for the Jews. Notwithstanding their special election by God, they have not heeded the prophets and have connived in the crucifixion of Christ (and indeed in later anti-Christian persecutions)" (Plested 214).

c. 198-208 Tertullian (c. 155 – c. 240), a Christian theologian and lawyer from Carthage, issues the anti-Jewish *De Adversus Iudaeos*, thus giving a name to the genre. His "treatment of the problems of the Trinity effectively defined the terminology for succeeding western theology up to the present" (Nicholls 181). How much he actually knew about

Judaism is in doubt, but he codified "Christian ideas concerning the radical inferiority of Jews and Judaism" (Harrison 305). He established rhetorical conventions for anti-Jewish invective that persisted until *Nostra Aetate* (1965). Thus he promoted the theological claim that "Jews were always unworthy of divine election, and now that their long trail of crimes has culminated in the murder of their Messiah, they have finally lost it" (Harrison 306). That helped him argue that Christianity, not Judaism, was Israel's true heir.

212-215 During these years, Origen (c. 185-c. 254), bishop of Alexandria and biblical scholar, likely composed his *De Principiis*, his single most comprehensive theological treatise. A complex figure who knew the Jews of Alexandria and Palestine well, his respect for Jewish scholarship was combined with disdain for Jewish theology. He believed Jews read the Bible with excessive literalism and that this lack of spiritual understanding led them to deny Jesus as the true Messiah. "His derogatory rhetoric and supersessionist remarks place him among the emerging *Adversus Judaeos* thinkers of the early Church" (Kessler 57).

306-373 Ephrem the Syrian, a Christian deacon and theologian, composes a series of hymns that include disparaging and condemnatory references to Jews. Several are paeans to Jesus Christ; others castigate Jewish practices and observance: "In their heart dwells deadly poison . . . In fresh matza they secretly offer the old leaven of unbelief . . . whoever takes some of that matza takes the lethal drug of Judas Iscariot."

312-313 The Roman Emperor Constantine I converts to Christianity. He then collaborates in issuing the Edict of Milan, which removes penalties for practicing Christianity and ends the Roman persecution of Christians. From 380 on, Christianity becomes increasingly linked with state power and is thus itself influenced by a different kind of triumphalism.

315 A Roman edict makes it illegal for Jews to proselytize. In 388 it becomes a crime punishable by death.

c. 315 Eusebius, bishop of Caesarea's (c. 260-339) influential history of the early Church, *Ecclesiastical History*, helps sustain Christian anti-Jewish attitudes for centuries.

380 Christianity becomes the Roman Empire's official religion by way of the Edict of Thessalonica, as issued by three reigning Roman emperors.

386 John Chrysostom (c. 350-407) of Antioch (a city located in modern Turkey), later to become Archbishop of Constantinople, delivers *Adversus Judaeos*, eight bitter and highly aggressive sermons from 386 to the following year. The rhetoric—calling Judaism a disease, disparaging fasting as a sin and a form of drunkenness, castigating synagogues as places for "whores, thieves, and the crowd of dancers"—was partly theatrical and partly expressive of a competitive environment in which Christianity's authority was still in doubt. Its later impact proved both material and unmistakable after Chrysostom's works were read aloud in the Middle Ages in Europe and were translated into Russian during the country's first pogrom. Promoted by the Nazis, his works "have perhaps been the most damaging and influential in the popular imagination, and his denunciations of Judaism gave the Church for centuries a pseudo-religious basis for persecuting Jews . . . with a divine seal of approval" (Kessler 61). But his writings are also permeated with consuming hatred. About the Jews, he wrote, "although such beasts are unfit for work, they are fit for killing"; "Do you see that demons dwell in their souls and that these demons are more dangerous than the ones of old" (Homily I).

388 A Christian mob attacks and burns a synagogue in the city of Callincus on the Euphrates. The Roman authorities order it to be rebuilt, but Ambrose (337-397), the bishop of Milan and mentor of St. Augustine, intervenes. Addressing a letter and sermon to Emperor Theodosius urging him not to rebuild the synagogue, Ambrose describes synagogues as "a haunt of infidels, a home of the impious, a hiding place of madmen, under the damnation of God himself" and thus advocates their destruction "that there not be a place here Christ is denied."

c. 393 Jerome (c. 342-420), a Christian ascetic and scholar, completes his *Hebrew Questions on Genesis*, in which he demonstrates notable respect for Jewish learning. He produces a Latin translation of the Hebrew Bible known as the Vulgate, which becomes the standard biblical text of the Catholic Church for more than a millennium. His respect for individual Jewish scholars, however, does not extend to Judaism as a whole. Under attack for his use of Jewish sources, he responds, "If it is expedient to hate any people and to detest any nation, I have a notable hatred for the circumcised; even now they persecute our lord Jesus Christ in the synagogues of Satan."

414-415 Jews expelled from Alexandria, Egypt, the world's largest Jewish community at the time.

429 Augustine (354-430), bishop of Hippo in North Africa, writes *Adversus Judaeos*, one of his many post-conversion works that address the status of Judaism. His overall position is that Jews serve as "witnesses to the victory of the Church as the true Israel, to the mercy of God who preserves them in spite of all adversity, and to the truth of the Hebrew scriptures as foretelling the coming of Christ" (McManus 42). They thus have a special role in the salvation of the world. But in *Contra Faustum Manichaeum*, a polemic against the Manichean leader Faustus (c.340-before 400), Augustine "depicts Jews as children of Cain whose dispersion and woes were God's punishment. Just as the blood of Abel called out to God from the earth, so did the blood of Christ; just as Cain was cursed but lived under divine protection, so did Jews—they served as witnesses to their own evil and the Christian truth. Even so, they were not to be harmed but preached to with love. Their blindness to the acceptance of Christ marked them as no longer the elect of God . . . God preserved them in their adversity to demonstrate the truth of the Old Testament as foretelling the coming of Christ. This theology continued until the sixteenth century" (Kessler 51). That preaching of course aimed at conversion. Immensely influential, Augustine's views helped keep Jews alive in some contexts, but they also established a status that imperiled Jews in others. "Augustine's relatively benign attitude toward Jews is rooted still in assumptions of supersessionism that would prove to be deadly. The 'witness' prescription attributed to him—Let them survive, but not thrive!—would underlie the destructive ambivalence that marked Catholic attitudes toward Jews from then on. Ultimately, history would show that such a double-edged ambivalence is impossible to sustain without disastrous consequences" (Carroll 219).

438 The *Theodosian Code*, a collation of imperial legislation initiated in 312 and thereafter, is promoted by the Roman Emperor Theodosius II. It establishes a standard of reluctant toleration, upholding freedom of worship while prohibiting Jews from proselytizing, holding public office, marrying Christians, or owning Christian slaves. The Code's treatment of Christian heretics is notably harsher still.

535-53 The *Justinian Code* in the Eastern-Byzantine Empire under the Emperor Justin I removes many of the rights granted Jews in earlier proclamations. New rules include a prohibition against heretics or Jews testifying against Christians in court. In the newly acquired North African province Jews and heretics were forbidden to worship, with synagogues and heretical places of worship reassigned to the Church.

614 Emperor Heraclitus forbids the practice of Judaism in the Byzantine Empire, triggering a wave of forced conversions throughout Europe.

638 The Islamic conquest of Jerusalem. Jews are allowed to return to the city. The Diaspora was fundamental to Augustine's theology of universal witness by the Jews; thus the Jewish return to Jerusalem amounted to a desecration of the city in Christian eyes.

820-827 Agobard (c.779-840), archbishop of Lyon, issues a series of pamphlets attacking the Jews, among them "On the Insolence of the Jews," "On the Superstition of the Jews," and "On Avoiding the Fellowship and Society of the Jews."

1095-6 Despite resistance by some local bishops, the First Crusade kills 5,000-10,000 Jews in Europe as crusaders ravage Jewish communities on their way to the Holy Land. "The attack on the Jews set a disastrous precedent, depositing a fatal poison in the European psyche and imagination" (Mayer 25). In 1099 the crusaders take Jerusalem and eliminate the Jewish community there.

C. 1120 *Sicut Judaeis* ("As the Jews"), a Papal bull laying out the Church policy toward the treatment of Jews, is first issued by Callixtus II and subsequently reaffirmed by more than a score of later popes. It prohibits violence, forced conversion, and property confiscation, though it ambivalently warns against illegal practices in synagogues. It has only limited success in controlling violence, and is undermined by the contradiction between papal prohibitions against violence and the continuing teaching of contempt in Christian worship and study.

1144 The death of the twelve-year-old tanner's apprentice William of Norwich in England occasions the first generalized accusation of blood libel. A generation later, the Benedictine monk Thomas of Monmouth writes *The Life and Passion of the Martyr St. William of Norwich*, completed around 1150. The blood libel accuses Jews of ritually reenacting Jesus's crucifixion by murdering a Christian child and using his blood in satanic rituals that mock the consumption of the Eucharist. Blood libel gives ammunition to punish Jews not just for an ancient crime but also for its contemporary reenactment. The perverse claim and the impulse to kill Jews in retribution spread to the Rhineland in 1147, to another English city in 1168, to France in 1171 (when thirty-one Jews were burned at the stake), and throughout Europe. The charge of "host desecration," that Jews would steal and ritually "murder" the communion wafer that represents the body of Christ, led to forty Jews of Breslau in Lower Silesia being burned at the stake in 1453. "The earliest recorded account of Jewish murder," writes Marc Saperstein, "is embellished with the suggestion of an international Jewish conspiracy, sanctioned by ancient Jewish texts, which Christians ought to fear" (21). The Nazis were to revive blood libel charges that Jews killed children and used their blood.

1146 Bernard of Clairvaux (1090-1153) endorses attacks on Muslims but ceases anti-Jewish preaching during the Second Crusade. He urges that Christians follow the Church policy protecting Jews from physical assault, despite faulting Jews for their stubborn disbelief and inability to reason properly. The main preacher of the Crusade, he issues a proclamation condemning anti-Jewish violence and traveled the Rhineland promoting the argument that "the Jews are not to be persecuted, killed, or even put to flight." Yet he repeated such slanders as the claim of extreme Jewish carnality and emphasized that their dispersal through the world demonstrated their complicity in the crime of crucifixion. He thus "plants the seed of the very violence he abhors" (Carroll 271). "To label a group the most heinous of enemies and then to demand for them tolerance (albeit limited) and safety is probably to make demands that the human psyche, over the long run, must have difficulty making" (Chazan 144). "When Jews are blamed for the event that makes possible Christian salvation, a new, more pernicious layer is added to the Augustinian framework of ambivalence" (Carroll 289).

1187 Jerusalem is captured by Saladin, returning it to Muslim control.

1190 While Richard I is engaged in the Third Crusade, the entire Jewish community of York, England, about 150 people, is massacred on March 16.

1215 The Fourth Council of the Lateran headed by Pope Innocent II rules that Jews and Muslims must wear distinguishable dress. At different times and places a specific but varying identifying mark for Jews was mandated. In Narbonne in 1227 it was an oval badge in the center of the breast. In 1269 Louis IX of France imposed a fine on Jews appearing in public without a badge. In 1274 Edward I of England mandated a badge of yellow felt designed to resemble the tablets of the law. In German-speaking areas, the badge requirement was less common than the *Judenhut*, a conical hat. The Lateran Council systematized anti-Jewish practices, adding that they were prohibited from taking public office, must pay special taxes to local clergy, and were forbidden to go outside during Holy Week.

1236 Pope Gregory IX receives detailed charges against the Talmud, among them the claim that it blasphemes against Jesus and is replete with hostility toward non-Jews. King Louis IX of France complies with a papal order that copies be seized. In 1240, following a public debate about the Talmud known as a "disputation," twenty-four wagonloads of rabbinic manuscripts and all the copies of the Talmud that could be found are burned in Paris. His successor Innocent IV, who served as Pope from 1243-54, said of the Talmud that "in it are blasphemies against God and His Christ, and against the blessed Virgin, fables that are manifestly beyond all explanation erroneous abuses, and unheard of stupidities—yet this is what they teach and feed their children" (qtd. in Synan 112).

1242 King James I of Aragon requires all Jews in the kingdom to attend the conversionist sermons of the Dominicans and Franciscans.

1260 Thomas Aquinas (c. 1225-1274) publishes *Summa Contra Gentiles*, a synthesis of the faith as it can be presented by those seeking to convert unbelievers, emphasizing that Christ is "the absolutely necessary way to salvation." According to Carroll, "It was Thomas who overturned the idea of the Jew's 'invincible ignorance' . . . Thomas concluded that Jews, confronted with the truth of Jesus, had not been ignorant at all. They knew very well that Jesus was the Messiah, Son of God, but they murdered him anyway. 'The disbelief of Jews derived, therefore,' the scholar Jeremy Cohen summarizes Aquinas, 'not from ignorance, but from a defiance of the truth'" (305-6). Perhaps unsurprisingly, therefore, Aquinas endorsed forced conversions and the requirement that Jews wear an identifying badge, though he opposed more violent measures.

c. 1280 Spanish Dominican Raymond Martini's (c. 1220-1285) *Pugeo Fidei* ("The Dagger of Faith") supports the truth of Christianity and the falsity of Judaism by citing biblical and Talmudic texts, abstracted from their contextual meaning.

1290 Edward I expels the Jews from England. They are subsequently expelled from France in 1306, from Austria in 1421, from Spain in 1492, from Portugal in 1496, and from Provence in 1498.

1304 In Florence, on November 9, Giordano da Rivalto, a noted Dominican friar, delivers a sermon that claims the Jews "would, were they able, crucify him anew every day," successfully rallying the local population to slaughter 24,000 Jews (Cohen 239).

c. 1330 Abner of Burgos (c. 1270-1340), a Jewish convert to Christianity who became an anti-Jewish polemicist, often wrote in Hebrew and became a major source for Spanish Christian anti-Semitism. He presses for conversionist preaching and the separation of Jews from Christians.

1341 Hundreds of Jews are killed by rioters in Seville in June, followed by similar numbers the next month in Valencia and again in Barcelona in August. The massacres then spread to other cities in modern-day Spain.

1348 In what constitutes the first international Jewish conspiracy theory, the plague is attributed to Jews deliberately poisoning Europe's water in order to cause the Black Death. The rumor had it that a native of Toledo initiated the plot, supplying poison to Jewish agents throughout Europe. Under severe torture, Jews in Geneva confessed. That triggered the slaughter of thousands of Jews in the Rhineland and elsewhere, perhaps as many as twelve thousand in the city of Mainz alone. Whole Jewish communities are massacred. Officials in plague towns wrote to others warning them that the Jews were poisoning wells. Pope Clement VI, who lived in Avignon, was able to prevent the burning of Jews there, but elsewhere his orders were ignored. In effect, "the mob merely enacted, in practice, a hatred which the Church taught in theory and enforced in social degradation whenever possible" (Reuther 206).

c. 1390 English poet Geoffrey Chaucer (c. 1340-1400) includes "The Prioress's Tale," a blood libel narrative, in *The Canterbury Tales*. However, there were no known Jews in England at the time, and Chaucer writes of Jews with at least some respect elsewhere, so Chaucer's views are ambiguous.

1391 Hundreds of Jews are massacred throughout Spain, encouraged by anti-Semitic sermons.

c. 1460 Alonso de Espina (d. 1469) composes his five-volume *Fortalitium Fidei* ("Fortress of the Faith"), which consolidates much of the previous *Adversus Judaeos* literature and later became a resource for preachers and anti-Jewish writers. De Espina promoted the Spanish Inquisition.

1478 Responding to a request from Spanish monarchs Ferdinand and Isabella, Pope Sixtus IV establishes the Holy Office of the Inquisition in Spain, which had previously operated in France, Germany, and elsewhere. In Spain it focused initially on the Church's hostility toward *conversos*, Jews who had converted to Christianity either willingly or under duress but subsequently were accused of having relapsed. Any Jew accused of "consorting" with a *converso* could also be prosecuted, so the Inquisition effectively amounted to an assault on Judaism itself. In 1483 Ferdinand and Isabella appointed Dominican friar Tomás de Torquemada as president of a state council to administer the inquisition. As the *Justinian Code* had defined it earlier, heresy was a state crime, not merely a religious one, and a capital offense. Already a feature of judicial proceedings, torture was adopted by the Inquisition to obtain confessions. Secret or crypto-Jews could confess and do penance, though those who relapsed or who were suspected of relapsing were burned at the stake. Accusations were often based on the barest of pretense, for example, absence of chimney smoke on Saturdays was considered a sign that a family might be honoring the Sabbath. "The savagery of the onslaught against the *conversos* was without equal in the history of any tribunal in the western world" (Kamen 41). Perhaps two thousand were burned in the first eight years alone. The most intense period of assaults on *conversos* lasted until 1530, but as the inquisition spread to other Spanish territories trials and executions continued. Thirty-seven *conversos* were burned in Majorca in 1691. The last trial of a *converso* took place in Córdoba in 1818. It is notable that the assault on *conversos* demonstrated that the Church was more threatened by an enemy within than by a decisively external religion. But it also helped compound European Christians' view that Jews were fundamentally inferior.

1516 The Venetian Senate establishes the first Jewish ghetto. Jewish ghettos are then opened in Rome in 1555 and in Florence in 1570. By the end of the century the Tuscany port of Leghorn is the only large Italian city without a closed ghetto.

1523 Martin Luther (1483-1546), the most powerful voice of the Reformation, issues *That Jesus Christ Was Born a Jew*, followed later by *Against the Sabbatarians* (1538) and *On the Jews and Their Lies* (1543). At his most polemical, he indulged in crude invective: "One must beware of the shit of Rabbis, who have in a sense made the Holy Scripture into a latrine of sorts, into which they may introduce their shameful pursuits and utterly stupid opinions." The Jews "are a pest in the midst of our lands." Luther produced new interpretations of about a hundred of the Psalms in which he recast them as foretelling Jesus' suffering. "Wherever the voice of the psalmist cries out, it is the voice of Jesus crying out against his tormentors, the Jews" (Nirenberg 253). This was part of his fundamental effort to disparage both Catholic and Jewish devotional practice and ceremony in order to transform Christianity into a religion based on personal faith in Christ achieved through a literal reading of scripture, one guided by his own accounts of what such a literal reading entailed. His early emphasis on conversion to Christianity as a tactic, one that made him willing to denounce blood libel, was eventually supplemented by recommendations to expel those who refused to convert, seize rabbinical texts, prohibit rabbis from teaching, and burn down synagogues and Jewish homes. Jews should be "forbidden on pain of death to praise God, to give thanks, to pray, and to teach publicly." Luther was convinced that "ever since Christ's appearance on earth, the Jews have had no more future as Jews" (Oberman 46). Foreshadowing the grisly mission of Nazism, "The ambivalence that had mainly characterized Roman Catholicism's attitude toward Jews would not be a feature of politicized Lutheranism. Luther wanted Germany to be *judenrein*" (Carroll 368).

1545-48, 1551-52, 1562-63 The Council of Trent meets in northern Italy and assigns responsibility for Jesus' death to all sinners, not the Jews, but the view does not prevail in the Church and does not end accusations of Jewish responsibility in practice.

1546 The archbishop of Toledo rejects Pope Paul III's appointment of a *converso* priest to a clerical position on the grounds that he had impure blood. The Pope withdraws the appointment. The following year the archbishop issues the Statute of Toledo setting the standard of *limpieza de sangre*, or blood purity, for appointments in the cathedral. The Pope rejects the decree, but the Inquisition begins applying the criterion in other areas, barring people of Jewish ancestry from university and other appointments. Then in 1555, when grand inquisitor Gian Pietro Caraffa (1476-1559) becomes Pope Paul IV, he ratifies the blood purity statute. He issues the papal bull *Cum Nimis Absurdum* which goes further: Jews cannot attend a Christian university; they are prohibited from owning real estate or hiring Christian servants; the requirement to wear a yellow conical hat is to be enforced; Jews must pay for the construction of a walled ghetto at the foot of Vatican Hill with only one entrance, and they must live in it. The blood purity principle was soon extended to several Catholic institutions in Rome, this time by Pope Paul V in 1611 (Baron 68-69). Blood purity regulations remained on the books in Catholic religious orders, including the Jesuits, until the twentieth century. "The Spanish 'purity of blood' legislation was an ominous venture into new conception of Jewishness" (Saperstein 27). "They are the ancestor of the Nazi Nuremberg Laws" (Ruether 203).

1553 Pope Julius III burns thousands of volumes of the Talmud in Rome.

1554 John Calvin (1509-1564), one of the major leaders of the second generation of the Reformation, issues *Defense of the orthodox faith*, which makes it clear that punishing heretics is a state responsibility, though he never advocates violence against Jews. Indeed, his *Ad quaestiones et objecta Judaei cuius Responsio* ("Response to Questions and Objections of a Certain Jew") takes the form of a relatively sympathetic dialogue with a Jew. Calvin rejected the supersessionist claim that Christianity had actually replaced God's covenant with the Jewish people but echoed the longstanding belief that Jews have suffered deservedly as punishment for rejecting Jesus as the Messiah, thereby breaking the covenant.

1559 The Dominicans seize and burn all copies of the Talmud throughout Italy.

1567 The Jews are permitted to return to France. Oliver Cromwell readmits them to England in 1656.

1634 The most famous passion play, performed once a decade at Oberammergau in the Bavarian Alps, debuts. Medieval passion plays inaugurated a tradition that continues in some areas to the present day, and they can have a significant impact on popular understanding of the suffering and death of Jesus. Often these dramatizations exaggerate Jewish responsibility for Jesus's death and present the Jews in a highly stereotypical fashion, while downplaying the Roman role. They can as a consequence be damaging to Jewish-Christian relations. The Roman Pontius Pilate has sometimes been treated in these plays as a weak but noble figure, whereas the historical record shows he was quite ruthless. In 1984 a joint Jewish-Christian set of recommendations was issued with stipulations to correct the Jewish stereotypes at Oberammergau; a 2010 report notes many improvements, but some problems still remain. James Carroll recalls passion plays from the late 1950s or early 1960s: "I remembered . . . the Rabbis with their robes and hooked noses, I remembered the Jews with their conical hats and unsubtle horns, which made them like devils . . . When the chorus of 'Jews' cried out their 'Crucify him!' I understood" (33).

1648 The Cossacks massacre thousands of East European Jews.

1670 French philosopher and scientist Blaise Pascal's (1623-1662) unfinished *Apologie de la religion Chrétienne* ("Defense of the Christian Religion") is published posthumously as *Pensées* ("thoughts"). Though he recognized Jews for their courage in honoring Mosaic Law, Pascal also argued that God had rejected the covenant and repeated a number of traditional anti-Jewish stereotypes, including characterizations of Jews as wretched, blind, and accursed.

1764 The Enlightenment writer Voltaire (1694-1778) publishes his *Philosophical Dictionary*, which describes superstition, avarice, and hatred of others as Jewish characteristics. While Voltaire often wrote as a satirist, many contemporary scholars assert that these caricatures contributed to a rationalist anti-Semitism that continued to be influential for some time. His *Treatise on Tolerance* (1763) preaches liberty of conscience and religious tolerance, which he opposes to fanatics who, in Nirenberg's description, "harm others in pursuit of their own beliefs and therefore should not be tolerated . . . unsurprisingly, his paradigmatic fanatics are the Jews, whom for the purpose he paints very darkly indeed . . . the use of Judaism to represent the existential danger posed by intolerance is a fantastic distortion of reality" (354-5). As Sutcliff reminds us, Voltaire is often seen as "the key 'link' between medieval and modern Jew-hatred, remoulding the long-standing religious animus against Jew as killers of Christ into a new, secular rejection of them as enemies of reason" (78). For Voltaire, Judaism was "the definitional opposite to Enlightenment rationality" (79).

1789 The US Constitution grants all citizens, including Jews, nominal equality. Article VI of the Constitution of the United States declares that "no religious test shall ever be required as a qualification to any office or public trust under the United States." States, however, were not bound by this federal statute. Thus, for example, it was not until 1826 that Jews were allowed to hold office in Maryland. The First Amendment to the Constitution, adopted on December 15, 1791, aims to ensure separation of church and state. But the Naturalization Act of 1790 limits citizenship to "free white persons," which would complicate immigrant Jews' legal status for the next century and a half.

1790 Moses Seixas, the warden of the Hebrew Congregation of Rhode Island, writes a letter to the newly elected president George Washington, welcoming him on his visit to the city. Washington writes a response, with a concluding paragraph that borrows some of Seixas's own language: "The Citizens of the United States of America have a right to applaud themselves for giving to Mankind examples of an enlarged and liberal policy: a policy worthy of imitation. All possess alike liberty of conscience and immunities of citizenship. It is now no more that toleration is spoken of, as if it was by the indulgence of one class of people that another enjoyed the exercise of their inherent natural rights. For happily the Government of the United States, which gives to bigotry no sanction, to persecution no assistance, requires only that they who live under its protection, should demean themselves as good citizens."

1791 Catherine II of Russia (1762-1796) mandates that Jewish residence is restricted to towns and cities within a defined geographical area, the Pale of Settlement. The Pale would survive until the Russian Revolution of 1917. France approves an emancipation act that grants Jews civil rights as individuals but restricts their privileges as a community.

1793 Immanuel Kant (1724-1804), a German philosopher central to both the Enlightenment and modern philosophy writ large, issues *Religion with the Bounds of Reason Alone*, followed by *The Conflict of the Faculties* (1794). Kant sought to redefine the relationship between the human mind and nature or the material world, in a dualistic model that defined a capacity for reason grounded in a morality free of bondage to material determination. Like a number of other thinkers, he overlaid this project with an opposition between Judaism and Christianity. As Bernard Harrison writes, for Kant "Judaism supposedly works to prevent its adherents from becoming fully responsible and self-directing moral agents, through its subordination of individual moral responsibility to communal observance of law" (335). As Nirenberg explains, Kant offered a "founding distinction between a Jewish 'slavery' based on fear of the law, self-love, and formal ritual, and a Christian 'freedom' based on love of God and neighbor and an inner yearning for morality . . .

[Kant] was calling for a thorough de-Judaization of Christianity . . .
This de-Judaization was a principle task of Kant's writings on rational
religion . . . Insofar as 'reason has wrested itself free from the burden" of
faith corrupted by Judaism, the 'invisible kingdom of God on earth' is
close at hand . . . Kant envisions the '[e]uthanasia of Jews and Judaism'
in messianic terms . . . 'Strictly speaking Judaism is not a religion at all
. . . Judaism as such, taken in its purity, entails absolutely no religious
faith,' demanding only obedience to law and political hatred of all other
peoples" (Nirenberg 358-9).

1796 The Netherlands grants Jews full equality and citizenship.

1840 In the Damascus blood libel affair of 1840, thirteen notable
members of the Jewish community are arrested, accused of murdering a
Christian monk for ritual purposes. The nine who survived torture and
imprisonment were later freed.

1843 Despite being of Jewish ancestry, Karl Marx (1818-1883)
publishes two essays on the "Jewish Question," the second of which
bundles together a series of traditional anti-Semitic tropes: "What is
the basis of Judaism? Practical need, self-interest. What is the secular
cult of the Jew? Haggling. What is his secular God? Money . . . The
emancipation of the Jews is in the last analysis the emancipation of
humankind from Judaism . . . Money is the jealous god of Israel before
whom no other God may stand . . . Exchange is the true God of the
Jews . . . The chimerical nationality of the Jew is the nationality of the
merchant . . . As soon as society succeeds in abolishing the empirical
essence of Judaism—the market and the conditions which give rise to
it—the Jew will have become impossible." Marx would soon enlarge this
polemic into a general critique of capitalism, but that general critique
is first drawn out of the legacy of anti-Judaism, despite his support for
Jewish emancipation elsewhere (Fine & Spencer 35).

1870 The Jews of Italy are "emancipated," and no longer required to
live in ghettos. Up to this point, the restriction of Jews in Rome to a
ghetto had been repeatedly abolished and reinstated. When the Roman

Republic was formed in 1798 the requirement was abolished, but when the Papal States were reinstated in 1799 the ghetto was reestablished. Pope Pius IX allowed Jews to live outside the ghetto in 1848 but reversed himself two years later. He had complained that some Jews were disturbing the city like dogs barking. "For three hundred years, the keeper of the keys of the Jews' first and, until modern times, last and most squalid concentration camp was the keeper of the keys of Peter" (Carroll 449). The Roman ghetto was the last remaining ghetto in Western Europe until the Nazis reestablished them. After the Rome ghetto was abolished, many Jews continued to live there, which made them especially vulnerable when the Nazis raided the area to deport Jews in October 1943.

1877 Benjamin Disraeli's "The Jewish Question is the Oriental Quest" predicts that fifty million Jews would live in Palestine within fifty years.

1879 Wilhelm Marr (1819-1904), a German journalist and politician, coins the term antisemitism. Marr developed pseudo-scientific theories of race to argue that Jews were inferior to Europeans, especially German "Aryans." In *Der Weg zum Siege des Germanenthums über das Judenthum* ("The Way to Victory of Germanism over Judaism") he warns that Jews would take over the world if they could. He founded the League of Anti-Semites to combat the Jewish threat. The League prepared the country for the creation of the Anti-Semitic Party, which won seats in the Reichstag in 1882.

1880 German historian and Reichstag member Heinrich von Treitschke (1834-1896) publishes *Ein Wort über unser Judenthem* ("A Word About our Jews") which coined the phrase *Die Juden sind unser Unglück!* ("The Jews are our misfortune!") which was later adopted as a motto by the Nazi publication *Der Stürmer.*

1880-1881 Prominent German anti-Semites launch a petition campaign demanding that the 1869 legal emancipation of the Jews be reversed.

1881-84 Pogroms and anti-Jewish riots take place in the Ukraine and southern Russia. Both individual Jews and entire families are murdered. Mass Jewish emigration to the US and elsewhere follows through 1921.

1882 On May 3, 1882, a series of anti-Semitic regulations that became known as the May Laws are enacted by Tsar Alexander III of Russia on the advice of Count Nikolay Pavlovich Ignatyev. Intended to be temporary, they were periodically expanded and remained in effect until the 1917 revolution. The laws barred Jews from leaving towns and cities to settle in new areas, a regulation designed to assure rural communities that "the inhabitants of the countryside may know the government is protecting them from the Jews." Jews were denied rights to own mortgages or exercise power of attorney. In subsequent months, quotas were put in place for Jewish participation in various social institutions and Jews were prohibited from running for elected office.

1886 The Catholic writer and journalist Edouard Drumont (1844-1917) publishes his widely popular anti-Semitic book *La France Juive*.

1891 Following a Chicago conference of Christians and Jews in 1890, Methodist leader William E. Blackstone submits the Blackstone Memorial, a petition with hundreds of business, political, and religious leader signatories, to President Benjamin Harrison urging US support for restoring Jews to the Holy Land. In 1917 Blackstone submits the Second Memorial, this time urging support of the Balfour Declaration, to President Woodrow Wilson.

1891-92 20,000 Jews, most of the Jewish population, is expelled from Moscow.

1894 Captain Alfred Dreyfus (2859-1935), the only Jewish member of the French General Staff, is arrested and tried for treason, having been accused of passing military secrets to the German military embassy in Paris. Convicted on fabricated evidence in 1895, Dreyfus was publicly stripped of his rank before a crowd shouting "Death to the Jews!" and became a symbol of the eternal Jewish traitor. After being held in extremely poor conditions on Devil's Island, Dreyfus was retried in 1899. However, the military was unwilling to admit its error and ignored substantial evidence against one Major Ferdinand Esterhazy, so Dreyfus was re-convicted.. Convinced of Dreyfus's innocence, the novelist and journalist Emile Zola (1840-1902) famously wrote his expose *J'Accuse…!* (1898). The publication of Zola's essay occasioned anti-Semitic riots in France; Zola was tried and convicted of defamation, then escaped to England to avoid imprisonment. According to Kessler, "The debate about Dreyfus split France. To the French nationalistic and religious right, Dreyfus the Jew symbolized all the liberal, alien, and de-Christianizing pressures on the traditional Christian order in the country. The Catholic Church through its media gave considerable support to the anti-Dreyfus sentiment sweeping France" (127). For example, the Vatican newspaper *L'Osservatore Romano* fulminated that "Jewry can no longer be excused or tolerated." Priests gave hundreds of anti-Semitic speeches and sermons (Bloy 247). The French president pardoned Dreyfus in 1899. The French army officially declared him innocent in 1995.

1896 Theodor Herzl (1860-1904) publishes *Der Judenstaat* (The Jewish State) inspired in part by the Dreyfus case. In the pamphlet, Herzl predicts creation of a Jewish state. He then founds the World Zionist Organization, which hosts the First Zionist Congress in 1897, thus launching the movement to establish a Jewish state in the land of Israel known as "political Zionism" or occasionally "Herzlian Zionism."

1903 *The Protocols of the Elders of Zion* is published in Russia and migrates to the West in 1917. Entirely fabricated, it purports to expose a Jewish plot to take over the world. It continues to be widely available and influential in a number of Arab countries.

1903-06 A series of pogroms sweep the Ukraine and Bessarabia in Russia, impacting 64 towns or cities and 626 villages. The 1905 pogrom in Odessa leaves as many as 2,500 Jews dead.

1916 D. W. Griffith's *Intolerance* inaugurates a tradition of cinematic depictions of the life of Jesus and the role of the Jews either in his crucifixion or in accepting or resisting his divinity. These films have had a significant impact on popular understanding of Jewish/Christian relationships, particularly such films as *The Robe* (1953) and *Ben-Hur* (1959). Pier Paolo Pasolini's *Il vangelo secondo Matteo* [The Gospel According to St. Matthew] (1966) is more a parable about the present than a historical film, but it nonetheless places blame for the crucifixion on the Jews, whereas Franco Zeffirelli's *Jesus of Nazareth* (1977), influenced by Nostra Aetate, absolves the Jews of any collective guilt for Christ's death. The most controversial of recent films is Mel Gibson's *The Passion of the Christ* (2004), which some critics felt promoted anti-Semitism.

1917 The Balfour Declaration is issued, announcing British government support for a Jewish home in Palestine. A British Mandate to establish a home for the Jewish people in Palestine is confirmed by the League of Nations in 1922.

1918-20 Tens of thousands of Jews are killed by Ukrainian nationalists, Polish officials, and Red Army soldiers in Belarus and in Poland's Galacia Province (now western Ukraine).

1920 American industrialist Henry Ford funds printing 500,000 copies of *The Protocols of the Elders of Zion*.

1923 Jewish philosopher Martin Buber (1878-1965) publishes perhaps his most famous work, *Ich und Du* (*I and Thou*). In a famous 1933 dialogue with Protestant scholar Karl Ludwig Schmidt (1891-1956), Buber presses for an admission that the Jewish covenant had not been terminated. A unique and influential proponent of Jewish-Christian dialogue, he describes Jesus as his "great brother."

1933 Adolph Hitler (1889-1945) is appointed Chancellor of Germany. Hitler made clear his intent to blame all of Germany's ills on the Jews in his personal autobiography and manifesto, *Mein Kampf* (*My*

Struggle). *Mein Kampf* was published in 1925, having been completed during Hitler's imprisonment for his role in the 1923 Beer Hall Putsch, a violent riot and attempted coup d'état in Munich. After his release, Hitler immediately began rebuilding the Nazi Party, which gained a handful of seats in the Reichstag in the 1924, 1926, and 1928 elections. The Nazis' rise to power was dramatically accelerated by the onset of the Great Depression in 1929, which caused acute economic hardship for an already-overburdened German populace. By making Jews the scapegoat for this and other calamities, Hitler galvanized an overwhelming amount of public support. Moreover, the February 1933 Reichstag fire, which was falsely blamed on communists, created a rationale to suspend civil liberties and normal government functions and thus to consolidate Nazi power.

Once Hitler overpowered his political rivals to become Chancellor, the Nazis began putting anti-Semitic practices in place. On April 1, 1933, a nationwide boycott of Jewish businesses went into effect, although it was quickly abandoned. Two weeks later Jewish government workers, including teachers in public schools and universities, were fired. Books by Jewish writers—among them Brecht, Einstein, Freud, Heine, Hesse, Kafka, Mann, Marx, and Proust—were branded as degenerate. The burning of Jewish books in Germany begins on May 10 in Berlin, echoing earlier Church practice. German students and faculty took part. Joseph Goebbels declares, "The age of rampant Jewish intellectualism is now at an end."

The Nazis also draw at least obliquely on Christian eschatology, projecting a glorious future time for Germany. As Carroll argues, "However modern Nazism was, it planted its roots in the soil of age-old Church attitudes and a nearly unbroken chain of Church-sponsored acts of Jew hatred. However pagan Nazism was, it drew its sustenance from groundwater poisoned by the Church's most solemnly held ideology—its theology . . . Nazism, by tapping into a deep, ever-fresh reservoir of Christian hatred of Jews, was able to make an accomplice of the Catholic Church in history's worst crime, even though, by then, it was the last thing the Church consciously wanted to be . . . When Nazism defined Jews as the negative other, in opposition to which it defined itself, it was building on a structure of the European mind that was firmly in place before Hitler was born . . . [Hitler's] program of elimination of Jews as a people was unprecedented, but not unprepared for" (Carroll 476, 478, 521).

That spring, the Vatican's Secretary of State, Eugenio Pacelli, began negotiations with Hitler to reach an agreement, the *Reichskonkordat*, which was concluded on July 8. The year before, Germany's Catholic hierarchy had banned Nazi Party membership for Catholics and prohibited anyone wearing the swastika from receiving communion. By March 1933, however, the Catholic hierarchy had already reversed itself at the Fulda Episcopal Conference, expressing "a certain confidence in the new government, subject to reservations concerning some religious and moral lapses." Those reservations never came. While the Church declared that the concordat should not be taken as a moral endorsement of Nazism, it purportedly guaranteed the Church authority over its own affairs by effectively making any real political opposition to Hitler out of bounds and thus gave some moral cover to Hitler at a critical moment. The Vatican never repudiated it.

In July 1933, the Reichstag announced a new "Reich Church" incorporating all Protestant denominations under the leadership of Reich Bishop Ludwig Mueller (1883-1945), a well-known anti-Semite and friend of Hitler.

1934 The fiercely anti-Semitic newspaper *Der Stürmer* (1923-1945), published by Julius Streicher (1885-1946), begins to give special prominence to a contemporary form of blood libel, featuring broadsheets describing alleged crimes by so-called Jewish degenerates. The newspaper urged the extermination of the Jews from its founding. Its peak circulation reaches nearly half a million copies. Streicher was tried and convicted at Nuremberg and then executed.

1935 The Nuremberg Laws are introduced in September. The first law, the Reich Citizenship Law, deprived Jews of German citizenship and defined Jews as a racial, instead of a religious, group. The second law, the Law for the Protection of German Blood and Honor, banned marriage between Jews and non-Jewish Germans and criminalized sexual relations between them. Persecution could now be firmly based on a racial definition of identity, rather than a religious one. The laws also applied to black people, Romani people, and people of mixed racial heritage.

1937 The Peel Commission, a British Royal Commission of Inquiry, recommends the partition of Palestine into separate Jewish and Arab states and suggests population transfers will be necessary.

1938 In March, Germany annexes Austria in an action known as the *Anschluss*. The Nazis begin to arrest both German and Austrian Jews and deport them to the Dachau, Buchenwald, and Sachsenhausen concentration camps, all located in Germany. *Kristallnacht* (Night of the Broken Glass), occurs on November 9-10 in Germany. Nearly 300 synagogues are burned; many Jewish homes and 7,000 Jewish businesses are damaged or destroyed; 30,000 Jewish men are arrested and taken to concentration camps.

1939 Germany invades Poland on September 1, and the Second World War begins. The SS St. Louis, a ship carrying 936 German Jewish refugees, is turned back by Cuba and the US. While the US would denounce Nazi violence against Jews, it continued to bar entry for Jewish refugees. Several countries agree to accept passengers, including 288 that were taken in by Britain, but between 225 and 250 were killed during the Holocaust. Eugenio Pacelli, who had negotiated the Reichskonkordat, becomes Pope Pius XII. Britain issues its White Paper blocking Jewish immigration to Palestine.

1940 The Nazis establish the Jewish ghetto in Lodz, Poland, on February 8, 1940.

1941 Reviving a medieval practice, the Nazis require Jews in Germany to wear a yellow badge. The following fall the *Judenstern* (literally "Jew's star") is introduced to Belgium, France, and the Netherlands. The Nazis had introduced the requirement in Poland in November 1939.

1941 Since Germany had invaded Poland in 1939, special mobile killing units of the Security Police and the SS, or Einsatzgruppen, had begun killing civilians perceived as enemies, recruiting collaborators, and murdering Jews. These were not combat operations; the Einsatzgruppen operated in the wake of the Wehrmacht's offensive.

With the start of Operation Barbarossa, the campaign against the Soviet Union in June 1941, as the US Holocaust Museum writes, "the scale of Einsatzgruppen mass murder operations vastly increased"; they "organized and helped to carry out the shooting of more than half a million people, the vast majority of them Jews, in the first nine months of the war." "On any given day in the second half of 1941, the Germans shot more Jews than had been killed by pogroms in the entire history of the Russian Empire" (Snyder 227). Local collaborators joined the killing squads, which were also assisted by the Wehrmacht. Entire Jewish villages, or shtetls, in the Ukraine were eliminated. "An Einsatzkommando painted Stars of David on their trucks to broadcast their mission of finding Jews and killing them" (Snyder 235). In Belarus, SS Special Commando Oskar Dirlewanger's "preferred method was to herd the local population inside a barn, set the barn on fire, and then shoot with machine guns anyone who tried to escape" (Snyder 242). In the Minsk ghetto, "German soldiers would force Jewish girls to dance naked at night; in the morning only the girls' corpses remained" (Snyder 230). A German (Austrian) policeman wrote home to his wife, "Infants flew in great arcs through the air, and we shot them in pieces in flight, before their bodies fell into the pit and into the water" (quoted in Snyder 205-6).

In the fall of 1941 the Nazis institute Operation Reinhard (Einsatz Reinhard), the code name for the plan to murder two million Jews in German-occupied Poland. Three killing sites—Belzec, Sobibor, and Treblinka—operate between 1942 and 1943, using carbon monoxide gas to kill about 1.7 million Jews, along with Poles, Roma, and Russian prisoners of war.

1941-1944 The Vichy government in France freezes Jewish bank accounts, begins mass arrests of Jews in 1941, and in 1942 begins shipping 76,000 Jews to Nazi death camps.

1942 At a villa in the Berlin suburb of Wannsee, senior Nazi officials and SS leaders meet on January 20 to plan and coordinate the extermination of the Jews that had begun six months earlier. By the time of the Wannsee Conference tens of thousands of Jews had already been murdered all over Eastern Europe. More than 50,000 Jews were shot in massacres such as the one at Ia i in Romania and Babi Yar in the Ukraine—sometimes collectively referred to as "the Holocaust by bullets"—executed as part of Operation Barbarossa, the Nazi invasion of the Soviet Union. From May 6-11 some 600 delegates and Zionists from eighteen countries meet at the Biltmore Hotel in NYC. They issue the Biltmore Program, which formally calls for the creation of a Jewish Commonwealth in Palestine. Over 300,000 Jews are deported from the Warsaw Ghetto, most to the Treblinka death camp and the rest to forced labor camps in Poland and Germany. In October, SS chief Heinrich Himmler orders the liquidation of the Warsaw Ghetto.

1943 The Warsaw Ghetto Uprising takes place in occupied Poland between April 19 and May 16, the largest and perhaps most symbolically significant act of Jewish resistance during the Holocaust. Despite early successes, however, the rebels are defeated, and the majority of the remaining Jews are deported to both Treblinka and the Majdanek concentration camp.

1943 Demark distinguishes itself by being the only Nazi-occupied country to resist the deportation of its Jewish citizens. In October, the Danes organize a program that ferries 7,200 Jews and their non-Jewish family members to neutral Sweden. The same month over a thousand Jews are seized from the ghetto area in Rome and taken to Auschwitz without public protest from the Vatican. However, some Catholic institutions in Rome did offer aid and shelter to Jews.

1945 Auschwitz-Birkenau is liberated by the Red Army on January 27, Buchenwald by the US Army on April 10, and Bergen-Belsen by the British Army on April 15. Over a million Jews and tens of thousands of Roma, Poles, and Soviet prisoners of war were killed at Auschwitz; at the camp's peak operation, 6,000 Jews were gassed daily.

1946 In Kielce, Poland, on July 4, a mob of Polish soldiers, police, and civilians murder at least forty Jews and injure still more after a false blood libel spreads that a temporarily missing Polish child had been ritually murdered by Jews. The incident helped persuade many Jews that a return to Poland was impossible.

1947 The Second Conference of the International Council of Christians and Jews takes place at Seelisberg, Switzerland, from July 30 through August 5. It issues "An Address to the Churches," which includes The Ten Points of Seelisberg:

1. Remember that One God speaks to us all through the Old and the New Testaments.
2. Remember that Jesus was born of a Jewish mother of the seed of David and the people of Israel, and that His everlasting love and forgiveness embraces His own people and the whole world.
3. Remember that the first disciples, the apostles and the first martyrs were Jews.
4. Remember that the fundamental commandment of Christianity, to love God and one's neighbor, proclaimed already in the Old Testament and confirmed by Jesus, is binding upon both Christians and Jews in all human relationships, without any exception.
5. Avoid distorting or misrepresenting biblical or post-biblical Judaism with the object of extolling Christianity.
6. Avoid using the word Jews in the exclusive sense of the enemies of Jesus, and the words "the enemies of Jesus" to designate the whole Jewish people.
7. Avoid presenting the Passion in such a way as to bring the odium of the killing of Jesus upon all Jews or upon Jews alone. It was only a section of the Jews in Jerusalem who demanded the death of Jesus, and the Christian message has always been that it was the sins of mankind which were exemplified by those Jews and the sins in which all men share that brought Christ to the Cross.
8. Avoid referring to the scriptural curses, or the cry of a raging mob: "His blood be upon us and our children," without

remembering that this cry should not count against the infinitely more weighty words of our Lord: "Father forgive them for they know not what they do."

9. Avoid promoting the superstitious notion that the Jewish people are reprobate, accursed, reserved for a destiny of suffering.

10. Avoid speaking of the Jews as if the first members of the Church had not been Jews.

1948 Pursuant, in part, to the 1947 vote to approve UN Resolution 181 (II), a partition plan that proposed carving both a Jewish and an Arab state out of Mandatory Palestine, the State of Israel is proclaimed by its first Prime Minister, David Ben-Gurion, on May 14. Meeting in Amsterdam that year, the World Council of Churches (WCC) describes anti-Semitism as "sin," but recommits itself to the effort to convert Jews.

1949 Though no one was ever excommunicated for being a Nazi, Pope Pius XII excommunicates all Communist party members.

1958 Angelo Giuseppe Roncalli (1881-1963) becomes Pope John XXIII. During World War II, when he was papal nuncio for Turkey and Greece, he had provided baptismal certificates to thousands of Hungarian Jews in an attempt to protect them from the Germans.

1959 Pope John XXIII removes the word "perfidious" from the "Good Friday Prayer for the Perfidious Jews." He also announces the convening of the Second Vatican Council, which opens in 1962. In 1960, the pope tasks Cardinal Augustin Bea with writing a Declaration on the Jews.

1961 SS Commander Adolph Eichmann (1906-1962), who organized Jewish deportations to the extermination camps, is captured in Argentina, brought to Israel, tried and convicted, and executed by Israelis. Eichmann's trial is one of the first in history to be widely televised, and is watched all over the world. The trial includes the testimony of 112 witnesses, many of them Holocaust survivors.

1963 German dramatist Rolf Hochhuth's (1931-2020) play *The Deputy* premiers in Germany; it charges Pope Pius XII with a key role in condoning the Holocaust. President Kennedy breaks the arms embargo and becomes the first US President to approve the sale of advanced weaponry to Israel.

1965 *Nostra Aetate* ['In Our Time"], which evolved out of Cardinal Bea's original "Declaration on the Jews," is promulgated by the Catholic Church as one part of the Second Vatican Council. It declares that Jews should not be represented as having been rejected by God and that Christ's crucifixion "cannot be blamed upon all the Jews then living, nor upon the Jews of today." Fisher highlights the gravity of this shift: "With this simple statement an entire theological edifice, built over centuries, collapsed" . . . . It is easily the most significant document concerning Jewish-Christian relations in Church history since Paul in Romans 9-11. In 15 sentences it rejected anti-Judaic theological polemics and condemned antisemitism, and replaced them with the foundations for a renewed vision of the continuing role of the Jewish people in God's plan of salvation for all humanity" (320).

1973 The American Friends Service Committee (AFSC) calls for a US embargo on military aid to Israel.

1980 The Synod of the Evangelical Church of the Rhineland issues "Towards Renovation of the Relationship of Christians and Jews." It declares that "the continuing existence of the Jewish people, its return to the Land of Promise, and also the foundation of the state of Israel, are signs of the faithfulness of God towards his people" and confesses "with dismay the co-responsibility and guilt of German Christendom for the Holocaust."

1982 The World Council of Churches (WCC), the main global body uniting non-Catholic Christian churches, issues "Ecumenical Considerations on Jewish-Christian Dialogue," acknowledging that "It should not be surprising that Jews resent those Christian theologies in which they as a people are assigned to play a negative role. Tragically, such patterns of thought in Christianity have often led to overt acts of condescension, persecutions, and worse." The text points to the destructive effects of supersessionist convictions and acknowledges that "Teachings of contempt for Jews and Judaism in certain Christian traditions proved a spawning ground for the evil of the Nazi Holocaust," but it remains committed to proselytizing to the Jews. Notably the Central Committee of the WCC in 2005 urged its 342 member churches to adopt a "phased, selective divestment from multinational corporations involved . . . in the occupation" of the West Bank.

1985 The Vatican Commission for Religious Relations with The Jews issues "Notes on the Correct Way to Present Jews and Judaism in Preaching and Catechesis in the Roman Catholic Church (June 24, 1985)" acknowledges that "The Gospels are the outcome of long and complicated editorial work. The dogmatic constitution *Dei Verbum* [November 18, 1965], following the Pontifical Biblical Commission's Instruction *Sancta Mater Ecclesia*, distinguished three stages: 'The sacred authors wrote the four Gospels, selecting some things from the many which had been handed on by word of mouth or in writing, reducing some of them to a synthesis, explicating some things in view of the situation of their Churches, and preserving the form of proclamation, but always in such fashion that they told us the honest truth about Jesus' (no. 19). Hence, it cannot be ruled out that some references hostile or less than favorable to the Jews have their historical context in conflicts between the nascent Church and the Jewish community. Certain controversies reflect Christian-Jewish relations long after the time of Jesus."

1986 Pope John Paul II speaks at Rome's central synagogue on April 13, the first recorded papal visit to a synagogue.

1987 The Presbyterian Church of the USA produces a study guide, *A Theological Understanding of the Relationship Between Christians and Jews*, rejecting the belief that Christ's coming ended God's covenant with the Jews or made it obsolete.

1988 Anglican Church circulates "Jews, Christians, Muslims: The Way of Dialogue," guidelines which acknowledge that "the Jewish people have been misrepresented and caricatured" through centuries of Christian preaching and pedagogy and declares that Christians "must develop programmes of teaching, preaching, and common social action which eradicate prejudice and promote dialogue and sharing among biblical peoples."

1989 The Anglican Communion priest Naim Ateek (1937-), a founding figure in the Palestinian Liberation Theology movement and founder of the Sabeel Ecumenical Liberation Theology Center in Jerusalem, publishes *Justice and Only Justice, a Palestinian Theology of Liberation*, eventually followed by *A Palestinian Christian Cry for Reconciliation* in 2008. In 2009, Sabeel will endorse the *Kairos Palestine Document*, which urges Christians worldwide to support all three strategies of the Boycott, Divestment, and Sanctions movement. In his 2001 Easter message Ateek declared that "the suffering of Jesus Christ at the hands of evil political and religious powers two thousand years ago is lived out again in Palestine. The number of innocent Palestinians and Israelis that have fallen victim to Israeli state policy is increasing. Here in Palestine Jesus is again walking the via dolorosa. Jesus is the powerless Palestinian humiliated at a checkpoint, the woman trying to get through to the hospital for treatment, the young man whose dignity is trampled, the young student who cannot get to the university to study, the unemployed father who needs to find bread to feed his family; the list is tragically getting longer, and Jesus is there in their midst suffering with them. He is with them when their homes are shelled by tanks and helicopter gunships. He is with them in their towns and villages, in their pains and sorrows . . . Jesus is on the cross again with thousands of crucified Palestinians around him. It only takes people of insight to see the hundreds of thousands of crosses throughout the land, Palestinian men, women, and children being crucified. Palestine has become one huge Golgotha. The Israeli government crucifixion system is operating daily. Palestine has become the place of the skull."

1994 The Vatican recognizes the State of Israel. The "Declaration of the Evangelical Lutheran Church in America to the Jewish Community" acknowledges "Luther's anti-Judaic diatribes and the violent recommendations of his later writings against the Jews" and states that it rejects "this violent invective, and yet more do we express our deep and abiding sorrow over its tragic effects on subsequent generations."

1996 The Southern Baptist Convention revises its charter to state that "we believe in the lost condition of every of every human being, whether Jew or Gentile, who does not accept salvation by faith in Jesus Christ, and therefore in the necessity of presenting gospel to the Jews."

1997 The Protestant United Church of Canada publishes *Bearing Faithful Witness*, which calls for repentance for theological anti-Judaism and characterizes the Church's rejection of Jews as an act of disobedience to God.

1998 The Roman Catholic Church issues *We Remember: A Reflection on the Holocaust*, which serves as a profound statement of repentance, but maintains that anti-Semitism's roots lie outside Christianity. It acknowledges that individual members of the Church collaborated with the Nazis or committed crimes but exonerates the Church as such.

2000 In March Pope John Paul II visits Jerusalem, including the Holocaust memorial Yad Vashem, the Holocaust museum, and the Western Wall. According to Carroll, "For the pope to stand in devotion before that remnant of the Temple, for him to offer a prayer that did not invoke the name of Jesus, for him to leave a sorrowful *kvitel*, a written prayer, in a crevice of the wall, in Jewish custom, was the single most momentous act of his papacy . . . an unmistakable act of affirmation of the Temple, and of God's unbroken covenant with the Jewish people today" (109-10). In August, the Vatican statement *Dominus Iesus* "reiterates that all salvation ultimately comes through Christ and that those who do not acknowledge him stand in considerable peril in terms of their salvation" (Kessler 181). The same year the American

Christian Scholars Group on Christian-Jewish Relations promotes the idea that God's redemptive power continues to work within Judaism. In September more than 200 Jewish scholars and rabbis sign *Dabru Emet: A Jewish Statement of Christians and Christianity* (the Hebrew *dabru emet*, a phrase from Zechariah 8:16, means "speak truth" in Hebrew); the statement welcomes recent Christian witness to "God's enduring covenant with the Jewish people." It also declares that "Without the long history of Christian anti-Judaism and Christian violence against Jews, Nazi ideology could not have taken hold," but that "Nazism itself was not an inevitable outcome of Christianity."

2001 The World Conference Against Racism, Racial Discrimination, Xenophobia and Related Intolerance is held in Durban, South Africa during August and September. An effort to revive the claim that Zionism is racism fails and is deflected to a parallel event, but the conference nonetheless effectively triggers the Boycott, Divestment, and Sanctions movement.

2004 The General Assembly of the Presbyterian Church USA approves a pathway to divestment from certain corporations operating in Israel. In 2006 the General Assembly rescinds that language.

2005 The Central Committee of the World Council of Churches (WCC), the main global body uniting non-Catholic Christian churches, encourages its 342 member churches to begin "phased, selective divestment from multinational corporations involved . . . in the occupation."

2010 The British Methodist Church votes to endorse the boycott of West Bank settlement products. In 2016 the United Methodist Church identifies five Israeli banks in which it will not invest.

2013 The American Studies Association becomes the first of several small academic professional organizations to call for a boycott of Israeli universities.

2014 The Israel Palestine Mission Network of the Presbyterian Church (USA) issues the fiercely anti-Zionist booklet and video series, *Zionism Unsettled*. In 2016, Presbyterians for Middle East Peace (PFMEP), a group of lay members and clergy critical of BDS, issues a substantial report endorsing the fundamental route to peace, "Two States for Two Peoples." In June the General Assembly votes to divest from Caterpillar, Motorola Solutions, and Hewlett-Packard.

2015 A group of seventy Orthodox rabbis sign "To Do the Will of Our Father in Heaven: Toward a Partnership between Jews and Christians," which states that "the emergence of Christianity in human history is neither an accident nor an error, but the willed divine outcome and gift to the nations. In separating Judaism and Christianity, G-d willed a separation between partners with significant theological differences, not a separation between enemies." It promotes the belief that "Both Jews and Christians have a common covenantal mission to perfect the world under the sovereignty of the Almighty, so that all humanity will call on His name and abominations will be removed from the earth" and confirms that "We Jews and Christians have more in common than what divides us: the ethical monotheism of Abraham; the relationship with the One Creator of Heaven and Earth, Who loves and cares for all of us; Jewish Sacred Scriptures; a belief in a binding tradition; and the values of life, family, compassionate righteousness, justice, inalienable freedom, universal love and ultimate world peace." It is important to note that most, if not all, of the rabbis who have endorsed the document are identified with the progressive or liberal segment of the modern orthodox world; in other words, the authors represent a subset of a subset of the diverse world of Orthodox Judaism.

A few days later in December, on the 50th anniversary of *Nostra Aetate*, the Vatican issues "The Gifts and the Calling of God Are Irrevocable." It declares that "The dialogue with Judaism is for Christians something quite special, since Christianity possesses Jewish roots which determine relations between the two in a unique way (cf. 'Evangelii gaudium', 247). In spite of the historical breach and the painful conflicts arising from it, the Church remains conscious of its enduring interconnected-ness with Judaism. Judaism is not to be considered simply as another religion; the Jews are instead our 'elder brothers (Saint Pope John Paul II), our 'fathers in faith' (Benedict XVI). Jesus was a Jew, was at home in the Jewish tradition of his time, and was decisively shaped by this religious milieu (cf. "Ecclesia in Medio Oriente," 20). His first disciples gathered around him had the same heritage and were defined by the same Jewish tradition in their everyday life . . . One cannot understand Jesus' teaching or that of his disciples without situating it within the Jewish horizon in the context of the living tradition of Israel; one would understand his teachings even less so if they were seen in opposition to this tradition." While arguing that "Since God has never revoked his covenant with his people Israel, there cannot be different paths or approaches to God's salvation" and concluding that "The theory that there may be two different paths to salvation, the Jewish path without Christ and the path with the Christ, whom Christians believe is Jesus of Nazareth, would in fact endanger the foundations of Christian faith," it concludes that "the Catholic Church neither conducts nor supports any specific institutional mission work directed towards Jews."

The result is a reasonable foundation for sympathetic coexistence and indeed for partnerships on many fronts. The document rejects the hard supersessionist model that had prevailed through the second half of the twentieth century, a position that a number of Protestant denominations also took after the Holocaust.

2015 On January 7, two gunmen force their way into the offices of the *Charlie Hebdo* magazine in Paris, killing twelve and wounding eleven. "On that day, the executioner showed us that he had decided we were all Jewish," the magazine's editor would later write. Two days after the massacre, on January 9, a gunman pledging allegiance to the Islamic State enters a Hypercacher kosher supermarket in Paris, killing four Jews and holding nineteen people hostage. The police storm the building and eliminate him. These were among an increasing number of other assaults on French Jews. The murders left many feeling that France is no longer a safe place for Jews to live.

2016 The Mennonite Church USA takes a vote that BDS groups described as a call for divestment, but is in actuality a motion that urges its members not to buy products produced in West Bank settlements and "asks" their investment body to review any holdings that might profit from occupation.

2017 In August the Conference of European Rabbis, the Rabbinical Council of America, and the Commission of the Chief Rabbinate of Israel, representing significant Orthodox institutions, issues the detailed statement "Between Jerusalem and Rome: Reflections on 50 Years of *Nostra Aetate*," which observes that "Despite the irreconcilable theological differences, we Jews view Catholics as our partners, close allies, friends and brothers in our mutual quest for a better world blessed with peace, social justice and security," and calls upon "all Christian denominations that have not yet done so to follow the example of the Catholic Church and excise antisemitism from their liturgy and doctrines, to end the active mission to Jews, and to work towards a better world hand-in-hand with us, the Jewish people," It further urges the Church "to join us in deepening our combat against our generation's new barbarism, namely the radical offshoots of Islam, which endanger our global society and does not spare the very numerous moderate Muslims."

2018 The US moves its embassy from Tel Aviv to Jerusalem. The May 14th opening ceremony features several prominent US evangelicals.

2018-2019 On October 27, 2018, eleven Jews are murdered and six wounded at the Tree of Life synagogue in Pittsburgh, Pennsylvania. The shooting attack, carried out by a lone gunman during Sabbath services, is the deadliest attack on American Jews in the country's history. On April 27, 2019, a gunman opened fire during services at the Chabad of Poway synagogue in Poway, California, killing one and injuring three. Jewish facilities in the US were no longer safe places.

NOTES

NOTES TO THE INTRODUCTION

1   See Gerald Steinberg's "Uncivil, Society: Tracking the Funders and Enablers of the Demonization of Israel" for a concise summary of the funding pattern. It includes numerous citations useful in finding further information.

2   AJC, "Inside Vatican Diplomacy: Anti-Semitism, Israel, and the Middle East." July 6, 2020.

3   I quote from Goosen's "Real History" because it more easily available, but the version published as " How to Catch" includes a valuable series of notes not reprinted in *Tablet*.

4   For a detailed critique of Ateek's theology and Sabeel's impact on mainline churches, see Dexter Van Zile. "Updating the Ancient Infrastructure of Christian Contempt: Sabeel."

5   As William Harter wrote to us, "Presbyterians Concerned for Christian, Jewish and Muslim Relations was an outgrowth of Presbyterians Concerned for Jewish-Christian Relations, formed in the early '80's to address issues, monitor statements, and mobilize at General Assemblies. We were very active in promoting the 1984 PCUS Statement on Christians and Jews, developed by Dave Taylor and Jorge Lara-Braud (an excellent document), which hit such heavy weather generated by the bureaucracy and ME missionaries that Jorge moved that it be tabled until 1987, when it became" A Theological Understanding of the Relationship Between Christians and Jews." (1984 was the merging north-south GA, so proposals from both denominations were considered.) We continued to function under that name until the divestment controversy erupted (2004) when Chris Leighton

suggested to the ad hoc group Katherine Henderson had gathered (Summer, 2004, at Auburn) that we rename the group to (hopefully) include reconciliation-oriented Muslims. Chuck Henderson, editor of Cross Currents was the chair/convenor. Soon after, however, we formed PFMEP, which meant that much we would have focussed on was now directed by the PFMEP Executive Committee."

6   James Rudin was my rabbi during high school in a Bucks County synagogue founded by my father.

7   For an important overview of the latter, see Meddeb and Stora, eds., *A History of Jewish-Muslim Relations.*

AMY-JILL LEVINE NOTES

8   An earlier version of this paper was presented as a plenary at the 70th general meeting of the Studiorum Novi Testamenti Societas in Amsterdam (July 2015).

DANIEL FRIEDMAN NOTES

9   What is the difference between an evangelical and mainline Protestant? Revelations 20 speaks of the messiah's return at "a thousand years." Beginning in the eighteenth century, American premillennialists and postmillennialists began to debate whether the Second Coming would occur prior to, or subsequent to, the Millennium. Simply put, the debate concerned whether the world must achieve perfection as a prerequisite to Jesus' arrival, or whether he first would return and then bring perfection to the world. Postmillennialists, those of the former perspective, were generally optimistic about the state of the world, viewing history as essentially linear, with an evolutionary progress that would culminate in the Second Coming. As such, many Americans viewed their country as the representation of such an epoch. In contrast, premillennialists viewed the world pessimistically, and saw the corruption and degeneration of society as proof of the imminent arrival of the messiah, who would usher in the messianic era in a revolutionary manner (Marsden 49). This theological divide played out in the modernist-fundamentalist debate at the end of the nineteenth century, when "new winds of liberalism, Darwinism, biblical criticism, and secularism began to blow" (Ahlstrom 811). Postmillennialists welcomed these new ideas and incorporated them into their weltanschauung, viewing religion in terms of an evolutionary development that adjusts to the standards and needs of modern culture.

Premillennialists were opposed to such foreign influences (Marsden 25), and in 1906, Milton and Lyman Stewart published a series of twelve pamphlets entitled *The Fundamentals*, which outlined the doctrines that are 'fundamental' to traditional Christianity, including the literal understanding of the Bible and the inerrancy of Scripture. Liberal Protestants were also gaining ground over their coreligionists with a new idea: the Social Gospel, an approach that placed greater emphasis on Christianity's obligation to social justice. The movement became the tangible expression of postmillennialism, as adherents felt that the manifestation of the kingdom of God required their active involvement (Rauschenbusch). During this time, Social Gospel ministers began to reframe Jesus as a powerful pursuer of social justice, and America as the God-incarnate (Wills 385). Such beliefs were adopted by the Congregationalists, Episcopalians and Methodists (Preston 240) and culminated in the establishment of the Federal Council of Churches "to advance the Social Gospel" (264). In the years following WWII, all of the major modernist denominations decided to focus on unifying their political efforts. They thus joined forces, coalescing around the term 'mainline,' which represented progressive politics, middle-to-upper social class and minimal tension with evolving American culture (Coffman 5, 147). And for reasons relating to marketability, most conservative Protestants eventually replaced the fundamentalist appellation with the softer sounding 'evangelical.'

10   "His Majesty's Government view with favor the establishment in Palestine of a national home for the Jewish people, and will use their best endeavours to facilitate the achievement of this object, it being clearly understood that nothing shall be done which may prejudice the civil and religious rights of existing non-Jewish communities in Palestine, or the rights and political status enjoyed by Jews in any other country" (cited in Grose 65).

11   In an attempt to shift American support away from the Declaration, Lansing proposed an independent investigation into Palestinian feelings on the ground. The King-Crane commission concluded that "'the places which are most sacred to Christians--those having to do with Jesus—and which are also sacred to Moslems, are not only not sacred to Jews, but abhorrent to them. It is simply impossible, under these circumstances, for Moslems and Christians to feel satisfied to have these places in Jewish hands'" (cited in Grose 88).

12   While FDR left little in the way of an Israel legacy, his widow, Eleanor was a member of the US delegation to the UN. She was in favour of supporting the UN; since the body had recommended the establishment of a Jewish state, she conveyed her recommendation for US support to Truman (Grose 242).

13   For Knowland's fundamentalist Christian associations, see Schafer (130).

14   In a meeting in Palm Beach, JFK said to then-foreign minister of Israel, Golda Meir, "'The United States has a special relationship with Israel in the Middle East really comparable only to that which it has with Britain over a wide range of world affairs. But for us to play properly the role we are called upon to play, we cannot afford the luxury of identifying Israel—or Pakistan, or certain other countries—as our exclusive friends, hewing to the line of close and intimate allies (for we feel that about Israel though it is not a formal ally) and letting other countries go. If we pulled out of the Arab Middle East and maintained our ties only with Israel this would not be in Israel's interest'" (quoted in Spiegel 106).

15   This claim was continued by Carter. Reagan, however, pulled back and preferred to refer to the settlements as obstacles to peace. It wasn't until President Obama that the question of the legality of settlements was brought up again in America (Ross 140).

16   How are we to account for his evangelicalism on the one hand, and his ultimate distance from the evangelical and Jewish communities, on the other? According to Preston, Carter's religion was often divorced from public policy, summonsed only in criticism of the nation, but never as a source of inspiration (576).

17   In his memoirs, he links Israel's security to moral responsibility for the Holocaust (as opposed to biblical motives).

18   Prayers at the event included a call for strategic cooperation with Israel, an affirmation of the divine right of the Jews to the Land of Israel, a rejection of charges of dual loyalty levelled at Jewish Americans, a call for the transfer of the US embassy to Jerusalem, and an exhortation that "the Scripturally-delineated boundaries of the Holy Land never be compromised by the shifting sands of political and economic expediency" (Findley 244).

19   Following the assassination of Rabin, his left-of-centre Labor Party lost the Israeli elections to Benjamin Netanyahu's Likud Party.

GIOVANNI MATTEO QUER NOTES

20   http://www.ifcj.org/who-we-are/endorsements/paula-white.html, accessed Feb 5, 2018.

21   In 2.3.2, the Kairos Palestine Document states that: "It was an injustice when we [meaning Palestinian Arabs] were driven out. The West sought to make amends for what

Jews had endured in the countries of Europe, but it made amends on our account and in our land. They tried to correct an injustice and the result was a new injustice." Later in 2.5, the Document declares that "the Israeli occupation of Palestinian land is a sin against God and humanity because it deprives the Palestinians of their basic human rights, bestowed by God. It distorts the image of God in the Israeli who has become an occupier just as it distorts this image in the Palestinian living under occupation." See the Kairos Palestine Document.

22   In 4.2.1, par. 2, the Kairos Palestine Document States: "The aggression against the Palestinian people, which is the Israeli occupation, is an evil that must be resisted. It is an evil and a sin that must be resisted and removed. Primary responsibility for this rests with the Palestinians themselves suffering occupation. Christian love invites us to resist it." Later, in 4.2.3, the Document declares that: "our option as Christians in the face of the Israeli occupation is to resist. Resistance is a right and a duty for the Christian. But it is resistance with love as its logic."

23   In 4.2.6, the Document declares: "We understand this to integrate the logic of peaceful resistance. These advocacy campaigns must be carried out with courage, openly sincerely proclaiming that their object is not revenge but rather to put an end to the existing evil, liberating both the perpetrators and the victims of injustice;" in 6.3, the Document emphasizes: "we see boycott and disinvestment as tools of non-violence for justice, peace and security for all."

24   In 4.2.5, the Document emphasizes: "We do not resist with death but rather through respect of life. We respect and have a high esteem for all those who have given their life for our nation. And we affirm that every citizen must be ready to defend his or her life, freedom and land."

25   For instance, Joseph Ratzinger, in his capacity as Prefect of the Congregation drafted in 1984 the "Instruction on Certain Aspects of the 'Theology of Liberation,'" in which he criticizes the use of Marxist doctrines (Congregation).

26   Tellingly, among the signatories of the Kairos Palestine Document, there are: the former Latin Patriarch of Jerusalem Fouad Twal, the former Custodian of the Holy Land Pierbattista Pizzaballa, as well as the leaders of Eastern Catholic affiliations Archbishop Paul Nabil Sayah of the Maronite Church, Archbishop Joseph-Jules Zerey of the Greek Catholic Church, Bishop Gregor Peter Malki of the Syrian Catholic Church, and Bishop Raphael Minassian of the Armenian Catholic Church. Among the drafters of the Document and leaders of the international movement of support for Kairos, there are: Geries

Khoury, Rafiq Khoury, Jamal Khader, and the former Latin Patriarch of Jerusalem Michel Sabbah.

27 The Joint Declaration states: "These past forty years of our fraternal dialogue stand in stark contrast to almost two millennia of a 'teaching of contempt' and all its painful consequences. We draw encouragement from the fruits of our collective strivings which include the recognition of the unique and unbroken covenantal relationship between God and the Jewish People and the total rejection of anti-Semitism in all its forms, including anti-Zionism as a more recent manifestation of anti-Semitism (Joint Declaration)."

28 Notes, chapter VI, par. 4 states: "The permanence of Israel (while so many ancient peoples have disappeared without trace) is a historic fact and a sign to be interpreted within God's design" (Vatican Commission).

29 *Faithful Witness on Reconciliation and Peace in the Holy Land*, pp. 97-98 and 145, where he states that "manifestations of Palestinian hostility today are not due to inborn hostility against the Israeli people; they are, rather, the expression of the resistance of the Palestinian people to what they consider a drive to dispossess them from their land."

30 As reported in the organization's website, the company Heidelberg Cement is deemed to violate international law and the 2011 OECD (Organization for European Cooperation and Development) Guidelines for Multinational Enterprises on business and human rights. See Pax Christi, "Heidelberg Cement." Tellingly, this strategy was used against the company CRH in Ireland, where the organization Ireland Palestine Solidarity Campaign filed a complaint with the OECD National Contact Point on similar grounds. The proceedings have not advanced. A similar proceeding has been initiated against the company G4S for its services provided to Israel's security system in UK. The findings of the proceedings recognized that the company has limited capacity to address impacts on human rights (G4S). In general, CSR (Corporate Social Responsibility) is the novel field of anti-Israel focus, where the legal discourse is twisted in the attempt to inculpate any activity in the post-1967 territories as a violation of Geneva Law. Interestingly, Israel is the only state targeted on these grounds, while CSR elaborates standards for international companies based on labor law, environmental law, anti-corruption law, and respect of indigenous rights in terms of access to ancestral lands. Moreover, the international humanitarian law standard applied to Israel is rejected by tribunals, which have not yet recognized the applicability of international humanitarian law to private actors.

JONATHAN RYNHOLD NOTES

31   Other leading evangelicals who take a moderate approach include Albert Mohler Jr.,
president of Southern Baptist Theological Seminary; and Craig Blaising, executive vice
president and provost at Southwestern Baptist Theological Seminary. See. Blaising, Craig
A ., "The Church and the Present State of Israel: A Progressive Dispensational View,";
Foust, Michael. "Mohler: Christians Should Support Israel, Yet Hold It Accountable";
"Prayer Is the Only Solution to Middle East Crisis."

32   See also the comments of Franklin Graham, president of the Billy Graham Evange-
listic Association, in the *Charlotte Observer*, October 16, 2000.

33   Pew Research Center, "Modest Backing for Israel in Gaza Crisis"; Smith Samantha
and Carroll Doherty. "5 Facts About How Americans View The Israeli-Palestinian Conflict."; Pew, "As Mideast Violence Continues, a Wide Partisan Gap in Israel-Palestinian
Sympathies"; Pew, "Public Says U.S. Does Not Have Responsibility to Act in Syria"; Pew,
"American Evangelicals and Israel."

34   Pew, "More Approve Than Disapprove of Iran Talks, But Most Think Iranians Are
Not Serious."

35   Pew, "Goal of Libyan Operation Less Clear to Public: Top Middle East Priority:
Preventing Terrorism."

36   Pew, "More View Netanyahu Favorably than Unfavorably"; Pew, "As Hagel Fight
Begins, Wide Partisan Differences in Support for Israel."

37   Pew, "Public Divided over Whether Israel, Independent Palestinian State Can Coexist."

38   Pew, "Religion and Politics: Contention and Consensus: Chapter 4"; Pew, "Public
Expresses Mixed Views of Islam, Mormonism"; Pew, "Continuing Divide in Views of Islam
and Violence"; Pew, "Views of Government's Handling of Terrorism Fall to Post-9/11 Low."

39   Pew, "In First Month, Views of Trump Are Already Strongly Felt, Deeply Polarized.";
Gregory Smith.

C. K. ROBERTSON NOTES

40   From a conversation during an interreligious pilgrimage to Palestine and Israel in January 2015. For a reporter's first-hand account of the pilgrimage, cf. Davies "No Zero-Sum Solution."

41   Although similar to the so-called Liar's Dilemma, which says, "This statement is false," Gödel applied mathematical rigor to create a formulaic proof that by definition cannot be proven. Cf. Hawking 258. For more, see Nagel and Newman, and Robertson *Archetypes*.

42   White wrote that the new Church should "contain the constituent principles of the Church of England and yet be independent of foreign jurisdiction or influence." Cf. White, Case.

43   Another resolution that passed acknowledged the leadership of former President George H. W. Bush and former Secretary of State James Baker, "both active Episcopalians," for their work in initiating the peace process that was still continuing at the time of the Convention.

44   The gathering in 1785 consisted of the House of Deputies only, as William White and others set about establishing an organizational structure first, and then at the Convention addressed the question of bishops and apostolic succession. Philadelphia also hosted the second General Convention in 1786, and the third in 1789, at which the Constitution of the Episcopal Church was drafted, a House of Bishops was formed, and the first American *Book of Common Prayer* was authorized.

45   Vanunu would eventually be paroled in 2004, and housed in St George's Anglican Cathedral with numerous restrictions placed upon him. In the years since, he has been arrested and convicted many times.

46   The consent process following the election of a bishop usually involves the Registrar of General Convention mailing consent forms to both bishops with jurisdiction and diocesan standing committees, and they send back their response. A simple majority of consents from each group is needed. So, the formula is: a diocese elects, and the Church at large confirms that election. The bishop-elect can then move forward toward ordination and consecration. When an election occurs within a certain number of weeks before a General Convention, then the usual consent process gives way to a vote at Convention in both the House of Bishops and the House of Deputies, which creating a far more public scenario, which clearly had an impact in the case of Gene Robinson.

47   A whole new set of acronyms emerged, each with its own foreign connection: AMiA, or the Anglican Mission in America, linked with the Province de L'Eglise Anglicane au Rwanda; CANA, or the Convocation of Anglicans in North America, a missionary body of the Church of Nigeria; ACNA, or the Anglican Church in North America, connected largely with the Province of the Southern Cone, now called the Anglican Church of South America.

48   One way of understanding these internal struggles is through a tool called "the spiral of unmanaged conflict." (Cf. Carpenter and Kennedy 11–17.) This spiral depicts the relational process between individuals or groups when dealing with a conflicting issue, X, that is left unresolved. If the parties involved do not adequately resolve, or at least manage, their differences, then the next time they face X, it will be in a different guise, as X^2, X^3, and so on. With each new manifestation of X over time, the intensity of anxiety, anger, or tension that the parties bring to the disagreement increases dramatically. This process can be viewed as follows:

X^1 – Presenting issue / problem arises

X^2 – Sides form along the lines of the issue

X^3 – Positions harden

X^4 – Communication between parties breaks down

X^5 – Resources are committed to the cause

X^6 – Conflict spills outside the parties

X^7 – Perceptions of reality become distorted

X^8 – Sense of crisis emerges

For a view of the property litigation in light of scripture, see Robertson, "Courtroom Dramas."

49   These groups included the United Nations, the International Red Cross, Amnesty International, the World Council of Churches, and several nations.

50   From the *Libellus Responsionum*: "You know, my brother, the custom of the Roman church in which you were trained. If you have found anything in either the Roman or the Gallican or another other church which may be more acceptable to Almighty God, I am willing that you carefully make choice of the same and diligently teach the English church, which is as yet new in the faith, whatever you can gather from the several churches."

51   Cranmer's *Book of Common Prayer* represented both change and continuity, retaining the ordained orders of bishops and priests while allowing them to be married, keeping the service of Holy Eucharist while putting it in the English vernacular.

52   Compare the July 13, 2018 statement by the American Jewish Committee commending the Episcopal Church for "once again rejecting divestment directed against Israel" (AJC Commends) with a tweet on that same day by Friends of Sabeel North America that said, "The Episcopal Church voted today to divest" (https://twitter.com/fosnalive/status/1017892738685997057).

ROBERT CATHEY NOTES

53   This chapter was originally prepared as a paper presentation for the Global Christianities Workshop, University of Chicago Divinity School, January 24, 2017. My thanks to So Jung Kim, Elsa Marty, and Prof. Angie Heo for the invitation to present my research.

54   On the conflicting narratives told by Israelis, Palestinians, and historians about their overlapping histories in the region of the Near East, see Robert I. Rotberg, ed. *Israeli and Palestinian Narratives of Conflict: History's Double Helix.*

55   Contrary to what was initially reported by Presbyterian Church (USA)'s own news agency and by mainstream media after the General Assembly's vote, the denomination did not divest its holdings from any multi-national corporations in 2004. Its General Assembly triggered an official process of investment scrutiny and engagement with specific corporations to discover how and whether the corporations were profiting from Israeli occupation and settlements on Palestinian properties and lands. This process, called Mission Responsibility Through Investment (MRTI), is aimed at convincing corporate stockholders and executives to terminate corporate practices resulting in profits that violate basic human rights, international law, and denominational ethical guidelines that govern all Presbyterian investments. In the 1980s, the denomination's MRTI process was applied by the Presbyterian Church (USA) to IBM and other corporations that profited from the sale of hardware and software to the government of South Africa during the regime of apartheid. The General Assembly of the Presbyterian Church (USA) voted in June 2014 to divest from Caterpillar, Inc. and two other corporations that profit from the sale of goods and services to the Israeli government after ten years of corporate engagement through stockholder resolutions, communications, and meetings with denominational executives. The vote and decision to divest occurred only after years of conversations and debates at the local and national levels by Presbyterians in their own governing bodies, and in communication with Christian, Jewish, Muslim, and governmental institutions, including members of Israeli civil society, and mainstream Jewish organizations engaged in advocacy for the State or peoples of Israel, and Jewish organizations engaged in advocacy for the Palestinians.

56   For example, see 199th General Assembly (1987) of Presbyterian Church (USA) study document addressed to Presbyterians and their Jewish neighbors in America, "A Theological Understanding of the Relations between Christians and Jews."

57   Walter Brueggemann, *The Land: Place as Gift, Promise, and Challenge in Biblical Faith.* In a more recent and controversial book and study guide, Brueggemann applied his biblical theology of place in *Chosen? Reading the Bible Amid the Israeli-Palestinian* Conflict.

58   I refer to Paul Ricoeur's three interpretive stages of reading sacred texts in The Symbolism of Evil and his essays on biblical interpretation in *The Conflict of Interpretation: Essays in Hermeneutics; Essays on Biblical Interpretation; and The Philosophy of Paul Ricoeur: An Anthology of His Work Figuring the Sacred: Religion, Narrative and Imagination.*

59   See Regina Schwartz, *The Curse of Cain: The Violent Legacy of Monotheism* for her contrast between traditional and majority readings of biblical texts under principles of scarcity (the covenant is closed; God's people are carefully bounded and membership is exclusive; there is not enough 'holy land' and divine manifestation to go around, etc.) and historic and minority readings of those texts under a principle of plenitude (the covenant is open and inclusive; there is 'holy land' and 'holy places' accessible to many peoples; divine manifestations occur to a variety of peoples, etc.).

60   For contrasting views of the international BDS campaign, see Omar Barghouti, *BDS: Boycott, Divestment, Sanctions: The Global Struggle for Palestinian Rights and Cary Nelson, Dreams Deferred: A Concise Guide to the Israeli-Palestinian Conflict and the Movement to Boycott Israel.* Barghouti refers to the Presbyterian Church (USA) on pp. 55 and 141 and Nelson addresses BDS and Christian churches on pp. 66-72. For an analysis of Israeli history and politics very different from Barghouti's see Ben-Dror Yemini, *Industry of Lies.*

61   Benjamin Valentin, Jean-Pierre Ruiz, and other Latino(a) theologians in the US, stipulate there are "liberation *theologies*," not one essential "liberation *theology*." Thus Valentin:

> Generally put, liberation theologies are modes of theological discourse that rethink the meaning and purpose of human existence, social life, faith, and religious thought and practice by paying attention to those ignored by history—that is, those who have generally been denied voice, positive identity, and an adequate material standard of living. In sum, these are theological colloquies that take the problem of oppression and injustice seriously and seek to advance enhancing self-images and communal

images, enable coping techniques and sociopolitical adjustments that could foster greater social justice as a whole.

Valentin continues:

> Besides their characteristic concern for injustice and suffering, and besides their ameliorative impulse, liberation theologies are also generally marked by two other keynotes: first, the understanding that theological treatises are shaped by and should look to respond to the historical, sociocultural, and socioeconomic contexts from which they originate; second, the desire to reach into and draw from the particular experiences, life circumstances, and expressive cultures of a specific people, community, or social group (Benjamin Valentin, 'Hispanic / Latino(a) Theology," in *Liberation Theologies in the United States: An Introduction*, ed. Stacey M. Floyd-Thomas and Anthony B. Pinn, 98.

Cited by Jean-Pierre Ruiz, "Where We Live, What We Believe: Thinking Contextually about Israel, Palestine, and the Churches," 6-7.

62   Very accurate overview chapters on Latin American liberation theologies, Feminist theology, and US Black theology are in James C. Livingston, Francis Schüssler Fiorenza with Sarah Coakley and James H. Evans, Jr., Modern Christian Thought: Volume 2, The Twentieth Century, second ed., chaps. 9, 13, and 14.

63   For example, compare form- and redaction critical readings of the four Gospels and the book of Acts in the New Testament.

64   For a popular account of this process, see John Philip Jenkins, *Jesus Wars: How Four Patriarchs, Three Queens, and Two Emperors Decided What Christians Would Believe for the Next 1,500 Years.*

65   For a fictional representation of one day in the Nakba by an Israeli author who was a contemporary witness of the forced evacuation of Arab villages, see S. Yizhar (pen name of Yizhar Smilansky), *Khirbet Khizeh*, 131. According to the publisher of the English trans., this "Hebrew masterpiece," offers a "wrenchingly honest view of modern Israel's founding."

66   Samuel J. Kuruvilla, *Radical Christianity in Palestine and Israel: Liberation and Theology in the Middle East*, 122. Kuruvilla's published dissertation is the most detailed account in English I am aware of regarding the origins, methods, and contents of liberation and contextual theologies among Palestinian and Arab Israeli Christians. Its structure and con-

tents cover many of the most important topics. The book version was only lightly edited by the publisher, if at all. I found a number of its sentences and paragraphs were difficult to comprehend what the author was trying to say, and at times it is repetitious. Someone, perhaps Kuruvilla or someone else, needs to write a brief introduction to liberation and contextual theologies in Israel/Palestine for students, pilgrims, activists, and others traveling to the region for the first time.

67   On the global diaspora of Palestinians, see Mark Levine and Gershon Shafir, eds., *Struggle and Survival in Palestine/Israel.* The "social biographies" of twenty-four Palestinians over time and space are reconstructed by an international group of social scientists.

68   The 'option for the poor' refers to the subversive transition by Latin American theologians from 'doing theology' for the audience of the elites and upper classes of society and church to embracing preferential perspectives, methods, themes, and actions on behalf of the 'least ones' in society.

69   For important issues regarding justice, human rights, and prisons that contain Palestinians in the region, see Lisa Hajjar, *Courting Conflict: The Israeli Military Court System in the West Bank and Gaza.* Hajjar is a social scientist at University of California at Santa Barbara. For a global interpretation of the larger aims of Israeli government and Israeli Defense Forces policies and practices regarding the Palestinians and other peoples in the region, see Jeff Halper, *War Against the People: Israel, the Palestinians and Global Pacification.* Halper is an Israeli-American anthropologist who lives in Jerusalem and directs the Israeli Committee Against Home Demolitions (ICAHD).

70   The quotations are Kuruvilla's summaries of Ateek's points and are accurate to the best of my knowledge.

71   For the history and theologies of the prior *Kairos* documents, see Robert McAfee Brown, ed. *Kairos: Three Prophetic Challenges to the Church.*

72   For another controversial critique of Post-Holocaust Christian theology by an American Jewish author with family roots in Palestine, see Mark Braverman, Fatal Embrace: Christians, Jews, and the Search for Peace in the Holy Land, esp. "Part Two: Beyond Atonement," Chaps. 5-8 where Braverman critiques Paul van Buren, Clark Williamson, R. Kendall Soulen, and other Christian theologians deeply engaged in revising Christian teachings and practices in light of Christian-Jewish dialogue and partnership.

73   On the origins in Egypt in the Hellenic Age of anti-Judaism and the transmission of the stereotypes, tropes, categories, and arguments of this ideology by Christian exegetes

and theologians, Muslim scholars, modern philosophers, political ideologists, et al., see David Nirenberg, *Anti-Judaism: The Western Tradition*. Nirenberg's thesis is that anti-Judaism is hard wired into western civilization, neither a peripheral ideology to western cultures nor marginal to Christian exegesis and doctrine. It functions even in times and places when there are no Jews or very few Jews around to be the target of its animus. In light of Nirenberg's structural argument and careful collection of textual evidence across the centuries, we should not be surprised to find tropes, exegetical moves, and theological arguments in the Near East region among Palestinian and Arab Christians that replicate the deep structures of anti-Judaism. Nor should we be surprised to discover them in N. American Christian discourse, e.g., in the popular *Left Behind* novels and films and in Mel Gibson's *Passion of the Christ*, an internationally successful film that premiered with a very positive review from the Pope and was first shown in the Midwest region on the campus of Willow Creek Community Church in Barrington, IL, one of the largest mega-churches in N. America with a network of hundreds of congregations in its sphere of influence.

74   Follow the link below to an online recording of "Where We Live, What We Believe: Thinking Contextually about Israel, Palestine, and the Churches," a public program at St. Joseph University, Philadelphia, PA on October 9, 2016, sponsored by The Institute for Jewish – Catholic Relations that is co-directed by Prof. Phil Cunningham and Prof. Adam Gregerman. You can view my presentation on *Kairos Palestine* along with that of Rev. Dr. Jean-Pierre Ruiz (St. Johns University, NY) on Latin American liberation theology and Pope Francis and our discussion with an audience at St. Joseph University: http://www.sju.edu/int/academics/centers/ijcr/ [accessed January 18, 2017.]

DAVID FOX SANDMEL—KAIROS NOTES

75   See also Amy-Jill Levine, T*he Misunderstood Jew: The Church and the Scandal of the Jewish Jesus*, 167-70, 183-85 and Giovanni Matteo Quer, "The Jews, Israel, and Palestinian Replacement Theology."

76   https://www.oikoumene.org/en/resources/documents/central-committee/2011/report-on-public-issues/minute-on-the-presence-and-witness-of-christians-in-the-middle-east. Accessed Nov. 11, 2017. Other references can be found here: https://www.oikoumene.org/en/resources/documents/other-ecumenical-bodies/kairos-palestine-document ; https://www.oikoumene.org/en/resources/documents/other-ecumenical-bodies/south-african-response-to-kairos-palestine-document; https://www.oikoumene.org/en/resources/documents/wcc-programmes/public-witness/peace-building-cf/wcc-policy-on-

palestine-and-israel-1948-2016-summary; https://www.oikoumene.org/en/resources/
documents/wcc-programmes/public-witness/statement-from-the-peacebuilding-and-
reconciliation-consultation; https://www.oikoumene.org/en/resources/documents/central-
committee/2016/statement-on-the-israeli-palestinian-conflict-and-peace-process; https://
www.oikoumene.org/en/resources/documents/central-committee/geneva-2014/statement-
on-economic-measures-and-christian-responsibility-toward-israel-and-palestine

77   The Kairos Palestine website states that the representatives came from "over twenty
countries;" the document itself refers to "fifteen."

78   ". . . a group of clergy, theologians and laypersons founded Kairos USA in 2011 and
soon after published *Call to Action: U.S. Response to the Kairos Palestine Document.* The
Call to Action document is a 25-page statement that takes a bold, prophetic stand for justice in the Holy Land and advocates for nonviolent resistance to oppression of Palestinians
and Israeli civil society and joining the international grassroots movement to break the
current political stalemate" (Kairos USA). "Call to Action" has garnered no more than 600
signatures. The website, which offers study and worship materials related to KPD, a blog,
and an events calendar, appears not to have been updated since November 2016.

79   At its 2016 convention, however, the UMC took several actions in the direction of a
more balanced approach to the Israeli-Palestinian issue. See my article "What the United
Methodist Church Got Right."

80   The Sabeel Ecumenical Liberation Theology Center describes itself as "an ecumenical
grassroots liberation theology movement among Palestinian Christians. Inspired by the life
and teaching of Jesus Christ, this liberation theology seeks to deepen the faith of Palestinian Christians, to promote unity among them and lead them to act for justice and peace"
(Sabeel).

81   No such clarification or second edition has been forthcoming, though in private
conversations I and others have had with authors of KPD, several have acknowledged that
some of the critiques, at least, are valid.

82   This analysis is based on the official English version of the KPD, as found on the
KPD website.

83   Another author, Cedar Duaybis is also affiliated with Sabeel, http://www.kairospales-
tine.ps/index.php/about-us/leadership/33-kairos-palestine-co-authors/25-cedar-duaybis.
Accessed Nov. 12, 2017.

84   See, for example, Melanie Phillips, "'Jesus was a Palestinian': The Return of Christian Anti-Semitism."

85   Rifat Kassis, http://www.kairospalestine.ps/index.php/about-us/leadership/33-kairos-palestine-co-authors/20-rifat-kassis (accessed Nov. 12. 2017); Yusuf Daher, http://www.kairospalestine.ps/index.php/about-us/leadership/33-kairos-palestine-co-authors/21-yusef-daher; and Nidal Abu Zuluf, http://www.kairospalestine.ps/index.php/about-us/leadership/33-kairos-palestine-co-authors/23-nidal-abu-zuluf

86   In those elections, Hamas won a majority of seats in the Palestinian parliament, but neither Israel nor the international community would deal with a government led by Hamas, which is considered a terrorist organization. Many Palestinians also objected to Hamas led government and internal tensions eventually led to a split between Fatah controlled West Bank and Hamas controlled Gaza.

87   Sections 9.1 and 9.2 do not explicitly mention two-states.

88   KPD appeared in the 61st year after the establishment of the state.

89   Rifat Odeh Kassis, one of the authors of KPD, defines normalization in these terms: *"Normalisation means to participate in any project or initiative or activity, local or international, specifically designed for gathering (either directly or indirectly) Palestinians (and/or Arabs) and Israelis, whether individuals or institutions; that does not explicitly aim to expose and resist the occupation and all forms of discrimination and oppression against the Palestinian people."* (Kairos South Africa).

90   When I offered a critique of the document as part of a broader presentation on the persistence of anti-Semitism, to the Central Committee of the WCC in June 2016, my presentation was subsequently repudiated by the General Secretary, who referred to it as propaganda. My talk can be found here, beginning at 1:00:00, https://youtu.be/XQuP IODpoNQ?list=PLI22eVXX9FYmJohFrHZaIV3Qivgr18RYh. The Secretary General's response can be found here, at 1:00, https://www.youtube.com/watch?v=puwB1hTPu-I.

JOHN KAMPEN NOTES

91   Mennonite Church USA was formed in 2001 with the union of two former denominations, the Mennonite Church and the General Conference Mennonite Church. In the process of union it was formed into two independent national bodies, one for the United States and the other for Canada.

92   References to the resolution in the following text will include the line numbers according to this version on the denomination website.

93   I responded to this letter already at that time: "Mennonites, Judaism." It is no longer available on the web-site but is cited in the blog post by Nafziger, "Window into Anti-semitism."

94   If one includes all denominations derived from Anabaptist traditions, including the Amish, then the numbers are much larger (*Mennonite World Review*).

95   Note the critique by Smith and Levine, "Habits of Anti-Judaism."

96   This history is available in greater detail in the volume by Weaver and Weaver, *Salt and Sign.*

97   The central document recommended for study by Mennonite Church USA in preparation for both conferences was *Kairos Palestine* and remains the definitive document recommended by the denomination for congregational and individual study.

98   This question was already addressed in Schechter, Aspects. See the classic studies by Davies, Gospel and the Land and Territorial Dimension. See also Gafni, Land.

99   Jeschke, *Rethinking.* See also the influential works by Brueggemann, *The Land and Chosen?*

100 Kampen, "We Need to Engage"; Kampen, "Mennonites, Jews"; Kampen, "Our Commitment."

101 Goossen, *Chosen Nation.* Reports of a recent major conference on the subject include: Schrag, "Scholars Uncover Hidden Stories"; Houser, Schrag, and Zuercher, "Neighbors, Killers, Enablers, Witnesses"; Schirch, "How Mennonites Reckon."

102 Epp, "Analysis of Germanism"; Thiessen, *Mennonite and Nazi?*

103 It is interesting to observe the lack of reference throughout the statement to "the Jewish people," a common designation in Jewish literature. While it might be assumed that the absence of the definite article represents some attempt to acknowledge the differences in belief and practice throughout the Jewish community, the inability to recognize the collectivity is indicative of the manner in which Protestant individualism has determined how religious groupings are defined in Western culture and has been inadequate as a basis for understanding Jewish identity. It also overlooks the definitions employed by the Nazis which did not use categories of individual belief and practice to determine the status of who a Jew was.

DANIEL FRIEDMAN NOTES

104   See "How to be an Effect Advocate" (Presbyterian Church USA) for a June 2001 appeal to Church members to unite in solidarity with other Christians with the goal of applying similar pressures upon Israel as were placed on South Africa. The first group to explicitly call for divestment was Students for Justice in Palestine at Berkeley (Clarke 45).

105   A glance at the list of titles found in Spotts's appendix support his claim of institutional bias.

106   General Assembly commissioners are the elected members of the GA. They are split 50-50 between pastors (teaching elders) and lay persons (ruling elders). Each geographical presbytery sends a set number of commissioners to the GA based on the proportionate to the number of Presbyterian church members within the presbytery. The GA also includes non-voting Young Adult Advisory Delagates (YAADs) theological seminary advisory delegates (TSADs). Before each vote that the GA commissioners take, the YAADs and TSADs cast an advisory vote, which is immediately shared with the commissioners.

107   Overtures are resolutions put forth by regional organizations of churches (presbyteries) that form the basis of the General Assembly's work. A presbytery approves an overtue to be considered at the next General Assembly. It must be approved ("concurred") by a second presbytery in order to be considered on the docket of the next GA.

108   The influence that Louisville staff play over GA committees is substantial. They work with the elected commissioner's who are slated to chair the relevant GA committees; shape the way the agenda will proceed, and by the rules of the GA are given numerous opportunities to speak before the commissioners. During a GA committee meeting, non-commissioners are not allowed to speak except during periods of public comment, but this does not apply to PCUSA staff. The end result is that when staff members are determined to implement a specific policy, such as divestment, they have privileges which bias the process.

109   This is a good example of how staff are able to shape committee processes to advantage one side.

110   PCUSA staff wield considerable discretion during the two years in between GA's. The vote calling for a letter to ReMAX is instructive. The 2016 GA approved the sending of the letter, but the staff took a year to do it. Staff members realize that a letter to ReMAX is largely symbolic, and will not be acted upon. Thus, the GA action itself is more important for its symbolism than the substance of what the Church is purportedly seeking to accomplish. Staff know this, and allocate their time appropriately.

CARY NELSON—*ZU* NOTES

111　BDS movements in other denominations have mostly been reluctant to cite *Zionism Unsettled* since it was seriously criticized when it was published. But it does occasionally get endorsed, as with the Episcopal Peace Fellowship's 2017 online "Palestine Israel Tool Kit" The Episcopal Peace Fellowship is a group that explicitly supports the BDS movement.

112　While the claim is not part of ZU, it is important to note that Don Wagner has made a particularly unscrupulous accusation against the IDF, namely, as Buffalo faculty member Ernest Sternberg reports, that at an October 22, 2010, SUNY Buffalo lecture Wagner claimed "that Israeli soldiers dressed up as Lebanese Phalangist militiamen to massacre Palestinians in Beirut in 1982." Wagner was asserting that the IDF not only allowed Lebanese troops to enter the Sabra and Shatila refugee camps but actually disguised itself and joined the massacre. There are no reputable sources echoing Wagner's accusation. See Sternberg's "Israelis Dressed Up as Christian Militiamen to Kill Palestinians!"

113　Munther Isaac has continued his campaign against Israel. See "Munther, Isaacc" for his website with a video about the theology of the land and other publications and presentations.

114　See the chapter on Saree Makdisi in my *Israel Denial* for a summary and analysis of Mitchell's views.

115　For detailed data on land ownership see Yitzhak Reiter, "Sugiyat Hs-Karka'ot." Also see Ruth Kark, "Planning Housing and Land Policy." For a detailed account of the issues and the data, see Kenneth W. Stein, *The Land Question in Palestine, 1917-1939.*

MICHAEL GIZZI—RECONCILIATION NOTES

116　Such evaluations appear to be rare in the world of shared society programs in Israel. Of all the programs I visited between 2015 and 2018, Kids4Peace had done more structured evaluation work than any. Some programs also are reluctant to share evaluation data if they have it. Friends Forever International claimed to have done numerous studies of the impact of its programs, but refused to share the data beyond its board, considering it to be proprietary information.

CARY NELSON—RECONCILIATION ROADMAP NOTES

117   Adapted in part from a series of recent reports: *Security First: Changing the Rules of the Game* and *Enhancing West Bank Stability and Security: Reducing Friction between Israelis and Palestinians* by Reshef et al, both issued by Commanders for Israel's Security; *New thinking on the Israeli-Palestinian peace process: towards a hybrid approach*, issued by BI-COM; *Advancing the Dialogue: A Security System for the Two-State Solution* by Goldenberg et al from the Center for a New American Security; *Advancing Two-State Security* from Israel Policy Forum; and from Anat Kurz, Udi Dekel, and Benedetta Berti, eds., *The Crisis of the Gaza Strip: A Way Out*. Most pro-boycott "anti-normalization" constituencies oppose the dialogue and collaboration between Israelis and Palestinians necessary to achieve the goals above.

118   See Ilan Goldenberg et al, "Advancing the Dialogue," p. 32: "areas adjacent to Ben Gurion International Airport would need to be designated 'exceptional security zones.' In these areas, zoning restrictions would limit the height of structures that could otherwise be used by terrorists to fire on air traffic or the airport itself. There could also be restrictions on agriculture in these zones to ensure crops remain below a certain height that could otherwise be used by potential attackers as cover."

119   See Ilan Goldenberg et al, "Advancing the Dialogue," for a detailed discussion of what would be required: "a comprehensive border security system far superior to today's border fence; the new system would include redundant physical barriers, motion sensors, long-range aerostat-borne sensors, tunnelling detection systems, and border control towers" (17). See further details on p. 30.

120   For comparative figures see the CIA *World Factbook*. Area comparisons include Jordan, with an official rate of 18.5% and an unofficial one of 30%, Egypt 12.2%, and Syria 50%.

121   See Ilan Goldenberg et al, "Advancing the Dialogue," for a general discussion of maritime security issues, pp. 40-41.

BIBLIOGRAPHY

18th International Catholic-Jewish Liaison Committee. "Joint Declaration" (July 5–8, 2004), online at http://www.vatican.va/roman_curia/pontifical_councils/chrstuni/relations-jews-docs/rc_pc_chrstuni_ doc_20040708_declaration-buenos-aires_en.html

Abramowitz, Alan I. *The Disappearing Center.* New Haven: Yale University Press, 2010.

Advisory Committee on Social Witness Policy. *Resolution on Israel and Palestine: End the Occupation Now.* 2003.

AFSC (American Friends Service Committee), "Search for Peace in the Middle East" (1970), available online at https://www.afsc.org/document/search-peace-middle-east.

_____, "Dalit Baum," available online at https://www.afsc.org/media-kit/bios/dalit-baum.

Ahlstrom, Sydney E. *A Religious History of the American People.* New Haven: Yale University Press, 1972.

Aikman, David. *A Man of Faith: The Spiritual Journey of George W. Bush.* Nashville: Tenn: W. Publishing Group, 2004.

Albright, Madeleine. *Madam Secretary.* New York: Miramax Books, 2003.

Allen, John L., Jr. "Thinking Straight about Israel, the Jews and the Archbishop," *All Things Catholic/National Catholic Reporter*, Oct. 27, 2010. (https://www.ncronline.org/blogs/all-things-catholic/thinking-straight-about-israel-jews-and-archbishop).

Al-Shami, Ghassan, Interview (in Arabic) with the Patriarch Fouad Twal (August 5, 2012), Weekly program "Ajras al-Mashriq" [Bells of the Orient] of the Lebanese Al-Mayadeen, available online at http://www.almayadeen.net/episodes/535140/البطريرك-فؤاد-طوال---بطريرك-القدس-اللاتين.

Alter, Robert. *The Hebrew Bible: A Translation with Commentary* (Three-Volume). NY: W. W. Norton & Company, 2018.

Alteras, Isaac. Eisenhower and Israel: *US-Israeli Relations, 1953-1960.* Gainesville, FL: University Press of Florida, 1993.

American Jewish Committee (AJC) Executive Committee) "Minutes" (February 2, 1918), available online at http://ajcarchives.org/ajcarchive/DigitalArchive.aspx?panes=2.

_____, "AJC Commends Episcopal Church Rejection of Israel Divestment, Expresses Concern on Other Issues" (July 13, 2018), available online at https://www.prnewswire. com/news-releases/ajc-commends-episcopal-church-rejection-of-israel-divestment-expresses-concern-on-other-issues-300680804.html.

Anderson, Gary A. "Zionism and the Covenant." *First Things: A Monthly Journal of Religion & Public Life*, no. 155 (August 2005): 7.

_____, "The Return to Zion as the Fulfillment and Non-Fulfillment of Biblical Promises." In Robert W. Jenson and Eugene Korn, eds. *Returning to Zion: Christian and Jewish Perspectives.* (unpaginated e-book).

Anglican Communion Network for Interfaith Concerns. *Land of Promise? An Anglican exploration of Christian attitudes to the Holy Land, with special reference to 'Christian Zionism.'* London: Anglican Consultative Council, 2012. http://www.anglicancommunion. org/media/18907/land_of_promise.pdf).

Anglican Primates, "Statement from the Anglican Primates Meeting 11 April 1991, Newcastle, Northern Ireland," available online at https://www.anglicancommunion.org/ media/288368/statement_primates_meeting_1991.pdf.

Anglo-American Convention (December 3, 1924), available online at http://www.allied-powersholocaust.org/wp-content/uploads/2015/03/1924-Anglo-American-Convention. pdf.

Anti-Defamation League (ADL), "Anti-Semitism and The Merchant of Venice: A Discussion Guide for Educators" (2006), available online at https://www.adl.org/sites/ default/files/documents/assets/pdf/education-outreach/Merchant_Venice_Discussion_Guide.pdf.

_____, "Presbyterians Avoid Rupture with Jewish People, But Bias Against Israel Continues" (July 9, 2010), available online at https://www.adl.org/news/press-releases/ presbyterians-avoid-rupture-with-jewish-people-but-bias-against-israel.

_____, "ADL Audit: Anti-Semitic Incidents Declined 19 Percent Across the United States in 2013" (April 1, 2014), available online at https://www.adl.org/news/press-releases/adl-audit-anti-semitic-incidents-declined-19-percent-across-the-united-states.

_____, "What Is… Anti-Israel, Anti-Semitic, Anti-Zionist?" available online at https:// www.adl.org/resources/tools-and-strategies/what-is-anti-israel-anti-semitic-anti-zionist.

Archives of the Episcopal Church, "Implementation of General Convention Resolution B019," Resolves of the Executive Council, EXC022013.21, available online by searching at https://www.episcopalarchives.org/cgi-bin/executive_council/EXCsearch.pl.

Aridan, Natan. *Advocating for Israel: Diplomats and Lobbyists from Truman to Nixon.* Lanham, MD: Lexington Books, 2017.

Ariel, Yaakov., "An American Initiative for a Jewish State: William Blackstone and the Petition of 1891." *Studies in Zionism* 10:2 (1989), 125-137.

_____, "An Unexpected Alliance: Christian Zionism and Its Historical Significance." *Modern Judaism* 26: 1 (2006), 74-100.

_____, "Contemporary Christianity and Israel." In S. Ilan Troen and Rachel Fish, eds. *Essential Israel: Essays for the 21ˢᵗ Century*, pp.280-310.

Arieli, Shaul, "This Will Be the Heavy Price of Annexation for the Israelis," *Haaretz* (May 24, 20), online at https://www.haaretz.com/opinion/.premium-this-will-be-the-heavy-cost-of-annexation-for-the-israelis-1.8868955.

Associated Press. *Lightning Out of Israel: The Six-Day War in the Middle East.* New York: Prentice Hall, 1967.

Associated Press, "Israeli billionaire hopes to bring water to parched Gaza," *Haaretz* (May 7, 2020), online at https://www.haaretz.com/middle-east-news/palestinians/israeli-billionaire-hopes-to-bring-water-to-parched-gaza-1.8830093.

Ateek, Naim. *A Palestinian Christian Cry for Reconciliation.* Maryknoll, NY: Orbis Books, 2008.

———. *A Palestinian Theology of Liberation: The Bible, Justice, and the Palestine-Israel Conflict.* Maryknoll, NY: Orbis Books, 2017.

———. "Suicide bombings: a Palestinian Christian perspective," *Church & Society* 94, no. 1 (2003).

Ayala, Elaine. "Hagee meets with Trump, Pence on U.S.-Israel ties," *San Antonio Express-News* (April 4, 2017).

Balmer, Randall H. *God in the White House: A History.* New York: HarperOne, 2008.

———. Redeemer: *The Life of Jimmy Carter.* New York: Basic Books, 2014.

Bard, Mitchell. *The Arab Lobby: The invisible alliance that undermines America's interests in the Middle East.* New York: Harper Collins, 2010.

Barghouti, Omar. *BDS: Boycott, Divestment, Sanctions: The Global Struggle for Palestinian Rights.* Chicago: Haymarket Books, 2011.

Baron, Salo Wittmayer. *A Social and Religious History of the Jews. 9 14: Late Middle Ages and Era of European Expansion, 1200 - 1650 Catholic Restoration and Wars of Religion.* 2. ed., rev. and enlarged. New York: Columbia Univ. Press [u.a.], 1969.

Barth, Karl. *Dogmatics in Outline*, trans G. T. Thompson. London: SCM, 1952.

Barth, Markus. *The People of God.* Eugene, OR: Wipf & Stock, 1983.

Bass, Warren. *Support Any Friend: Kennedy's Middle East and the Making of the US-Israel Alliance.* New York: Oxford University Press, 2003.

Baumgartner, Jody, Peter , and Jonathan Morris., "A Clash of Civilizations? The Influence of Religion on Public Opinion of U.S. Foreign Policy in the Middle East." *Political Science Quarterly*, 61:2, 171–179.

Bergoglio, Jorge Mario, and Abraham Skorka. Trans. Alejandro Bemudez and Howard Googman. O*n Heaven and Earth*. NY: Image/Random House, 2013.

Berḳovits, Eli'ezer. *Faith after the Holocaust*. New York: KTAV Publishing House, 1973.

"The Bethlehem Call: Here We Stand – Stand with Us" (December 14, 2011). Southern Africa. https://kairossouthernafrica.wordpress.com/2011/12/14/the-bethlehem-call-here-we-stand-stand-with-us/.

Blackstone, William. *Jesus Is Coming*. Chicago: Fleming H. Revell, 1908.

Blaising, Craig, "Then You Will Know that I am the Lord." In Robert W. Jenson and Eugene Korn, eds. *Returning to Zion: Christian and Jewish Perspectives.*

_____, "The Church and the Present State of Israel: A Progressive Dispensational View," *Moore to the Point* (May 1, 2002), available online at http://cdn1.russellmoore.com/documents/russellmoore/israel-church.pdf.

Bloy, Leon. *Pilgrim of the Absolute*. Edited by Raissa Maritain. Translated by John Coleman and Harry Lorin Binsse. London: Eyre and Spottiswoode, 1947.

Bock, Darrell, "How Should the New Christian Zionism Proceed?" In Gerald R. McDermott, ed. *The New Christian Zionism: Fresh Perspectives on Israel & The Land*, pp. 305- 317.

Boyer, Paul. *When Time Shall Be No More: Prophecy Belief in Modern American Culture*. Cambridge, United Kingdom: Belknap Press, 1992.

Boys, Mary C., "The Covenant in Contemporary Ecclesial Documents." In Eugene B. Korn and John T. Pawlikowski, eds. *Two Faiths, One Covenant? Jewish and Christian Identity in the Presence of the Other*, pp. 81-110.

Braverman, Mark. F*atal Embrace: Christians, Jews, and the Search for Peace in the Holy Land*. Austin: Synergy Books, 2010.

Brenneman, Jonathan. "MC USA Leaders visit Capitol Hill to advocate for Peace in Palestine and Israel," *The Mennonite*, June 27, 2018. https://themennonite.org/daily-news/mc-usa-leaders-visit-capitol-hill-advocate-peace-palestine-israel/.

Britain Israel Communications and Research Centre. "New thinking on the Israeli-Palestinian peace process: towards a hybrid approach" Last modified March 31, 2017. http://www.bicom.org.uk/analysis/new-thinking-israeli-palestinian-peace-process-towards-hybrid-approach/.

Brog, David. Standing *With Israel: Why Christians Support the Jewish State*. Lake Mary, FL: Charisma, 2006.

_____, "The End of Evangelical Support for Israel?" (2014), Available online at http://www.meforum.org/3769/israel-evangelical-support.

Brown, Robert McAfee, ed. *Kairos: Three Prophetic Challenges to the Church*. Grand Rapids, MI: Eerdmans, 1990.

Brown, Shelly V. "No Ordinary Chapel." *Emory Magazine*, October 1981.

Brueggemann, Walter. *The Land: Place as Gift, Promise, and Challenge in Biblical Faith*, second ed. Minneapolis: Fortress Press, 2002.

———. *Chosen? Reading the Bible Amid the Israeli-Palestinian Conflict*. Louisville, KY: Westminster John Knox Press, 2015.

Buber, Martin. "The Man of Today and the Jewish Bible," in *Israel and the World: essays in a time of crisis*, 89-102. New York: Schocken, 1948.

———. *The Eclipse of God: studies in the relation between religion and philosophy*, London: Gollancz, 1953.

Burge, Gary M. "You Can Be an Evangelical and Reject Trump's Jerusalem Decision." *The Atlantic*, Dec 6, 2017. https://www.theatlantic.com/international/archive/2017/12/evangelical-trump-jerusalem-embassy/547643/.

———. *Whose Land? Whose Promise: What Christians are Not Being Told about Israel and the Palestinians*. Cleveland: Pilgrim Press, 2003.

Burnett, Carole Monica., "Zionism Unsettled: A Congregational Study Guide." *Washington Report on Middle East Affairs* 5:1 (2014), 47-48.

Bush, George W. Decision Points. New York City, New York: Crown, 2010.

Central Conference of American Rabbis, "CCAR Resolution on the 2009 Kairos Document." Available online at https://www.ccarnet.org/ccar-resolutions/ccar-resolution-2009-kairos-document/.

Carenen, Caitlin. *The Fervent Embrace: Liberal Protestants, Evangelicals, and Israel*. New York: New York University Press, 2012.

Carlstom, Gregg. "The Permanent Occupation? Fifty Years after Israel Seized Control of the West Bank, the Palestinians May Have Finally Lost their Bid for Independence," *Newsweek* 189, no. 8 (Sept 8, 2017): 20-35.

Carpenter, Susan L., and W. J. D. Kennedy. *Managing Public Disputes: A Practical Guide for Government, Business, and Citizens' Groups*. San Francisco, CA: Jossey-Bass, 2001.

Carroll, James. *Constantine's Sword: The Church and the Jews*. New York: Houghton Mifflin, 2001.

Carter, Jimmy. *The Blood of Abraham*. Boston: Houghton Mifflin, 1985.

_____, *Keeping Faith*. Fayetteville, AR: University of Arkansas Press, 1995.

_____. *Palestine: Peace Not Apartheid*. NY: Simon and Schuster, 2006.

Central Intelligence Agency (CIA), *World Factbook*, available online at https://www.cia.gov/library/publications/the-world-factbook/.

Chafets, Ze'ev. *A Match Made in Heaven: American Jews, Christian Zionists, and One Man's Exploration of the Weird and Wonderful Judeo-Evangelical Alliance.* New York: Harper Collins, 2007.

Chazan, Robert. *In the Year 1096: The First Crusade and the Jews.* Philadelphia: Jewish Publication Society, 1996.

Cherry, Conrad. *God's New Israel: Religious interpretations of American Destiny.* Upper Saddle River, NJ: Prentice-Hall, 1971.

Christian Peacemaker Teams Palestine, available online at http://cptpalestine.com.

Christian Today, "Methodists accuse Israel of 'crimes against humanity' at Gaza protests," (April 4, 2018), available online at https://www.christiantoday.com/article/methodists-accuse-israel-of-crimes-against-humanity-at-gaza-protests/128085.htm.

Christians for Fair Witness on the Middle East, "The Kairos Palestine Document," available online at http://wfsites.websitecreatorprotool.com/christianfairwitness.com/PalestinianKairos.pdf (Part I) and https://0201.nccdn.net/4_2/000/000/056/7dc/KairosPalestinianDocument2.pdf (Part II).

Christison, Kathleen. *Perceptions of Palestine: Their Influence on U.S. Middle East Policy.* Berkeley: University of California Press, 2001.

Church, Philip, "'Here We Have No Lasting City' (Heb 13:14): The Promised Land in the Letter to the Hebrews," in *The Gospel and the Land of Promise: Christian Approaches to the Land of the Bible,* edited by Philip Church, Peter Walker, Tim Bulkeley, and Tim Meadowcraft, Eugene, OR: Wipf and Stock, 2011.

Church of Scotland, "Theology of Land and Covenant," 2003 (http://www.churchofscotland.org.uk/__data/assets/pdf_file/0009/13230/Theology_of_Land_and_Covenant.pdf).

———. "The Inheritance of Abraham? A Report on the 'Promised Land,'" 2013.

Churches for Middle East Peace, "U.S. Ecumenical Leaders' Letter to President Bush." *Church & Society* 95, no. 1 (September 2004): 82–84.

Clark, Victoria. *Allies for Armageddon: The Rise of Christian Zionism.* London: Yale University Press, 2007.

Clarke, Duncan L. "Mainline Protestants Begin to Divest from Israel: A Moral Imperative or "Effective" Anti-Semitism?" *Journal of Palestine Studies* 35, no. 1 (2005): 44-59. doi:10.1525/jps.2005.35,44.

Clarke, Duncan L., and Eric Flohr. "Christian Churches and the Palestine Question." *Journal of Palestine Studies* 21, no. 4 (1992): 67-79.

Clinton, Bill. *My Life.* London: Hutchinson, 2004.

CNN (Cable News Network), "Church Divests Over Israeli Politics" (video), New Day (June 21, 2014), available online at http://cnnios-f.akamaihd.net/i/cnn/big/

bestoftv/2014/06/22/exp-pcusa-israel.cnn_ios_,440,650,840,1240,.mp4.csmil/master.
m3u8?__b__=650.

Coffman, Elesha J. *The Christian Century and the Rise of the Protestant Mainline.* New
York: Oxford University Press, 2013.

Cohen, Jeremy. *The Friars and the Jews: The Evolution of Medieval Anti-Judaism.* Ithaca,
NY: Cornell University Press, 1982.

Commanders for Israel's Security. *Enhancing West Bank stability and Security: Reducing
Friction between Israelis and Palestinians, Improving Palestinian Authority Governance.*
Jerusalem: Commanders for Israel's Security, 2017. http://en.cis.org.il/wp-content/
uploads/2017/06/Enhancing-West-Bank-Stability-and-Security.pdf.

———. *Regulating Israeli and Palestinian Construction in Area C.* Commanders for
Israel's Security, 2017. http://en.cis.org.il/wp-content/uploads/2017/05/Regulating-
Construction-in-Area-C.pdf.

———. *Security First: Changing the Rules of the Game.* Jerusalem: Commanders for
Israel's Security, 2016. http://en.cis.org.il/wpcontent/uploads/2016/05/snpl_plan_eng.
pdf.

_____, "Gaza: An Alternative Israeli Strategy" (November 2019). http://en.cis.org.il/
wp-content/uploads/2019/11/GAZA-AN-ALTERNATIVE-ISRAELI-STRATEGY.pdf.

Commission Proche-Orient. "Qu'est-ce que BDS ? (Boycott, Désinvestissement,
Sanctions) Une action non-violente de la société civile palestinienne." Penser et vivre
la paix, n°10 (Feb 2017). http://www.paxchristi.cef.fr/v2/wp-content/uploads/CollPX-
2017-n%C2%B010-BDS-proche-orient-1.pdf.

Commissioners to and Observers of the 221st General Assembly of the PCUSA,
Reformed and Reforming: A Word of Hope.

Congregation for the Doctrine of the Faith (The Vatican), Instruction on Certain
Aspects of the "Theology of Liberation," available online at http://www.vatican.va/
roman_curia/congregations/cfaith/documents/rc_con_cfaith_doc_19840806_
theology-liberation_en.html.

Cooperman, Alan, "United Church of Christ Urges Economic Pressure on Mideast,"
The Washington Post (July 6, 2005), online at https://www.washingtonpost.com/archive/
politics/2005/07/06/united-church-of-christ-urges-economic-pressure-on-mideast/
cc057709-3bcf-42d7-b318-6ba50c54e43f/.

Cortellessa, Eric. "At Hanukkah party, Trump signs controversial executive order on
anti-Semitism," Times of Israel (Dec. 12, 2019).

Crouse, Eric. *American Christian Support for Israel.* Lanham, MD: Lexington Books,
2015.

Cunningham, Philip A., ed. *Christ Jesus and the Jewish People Today: New Explorations of
Theological Interrelationships.* Grand Rapids, MI: Eerdmans, 2011.

D'Souza, Dinesh. *Jerry Falwell: Before the Millennium: A Critical Biography.* Chicago: Regnery, 1984.

Dahan, Deborah, "Pope Francis condemns resurgence of antisemitism around the world," *The Jerusalem Post* (January 21, 2020), online at https://www.jpost.com/ diaspora/antisemitism/pope-francis-condemns-the-resurgence-of-antisemitism-around-the-world-614716.

Danby, Herbert. *The Mishnah.* Oxford: Oxford University Press, 1933.

Davies, Matthew. "No Zero-Sum Solution to Israeli-Palestinian Conflict: US Interfaith Leaders Dedicated to Being Partners in Building Peace." *Episcopal News Service*, January 27, 2015. http://episcopaldigitalnetwork.com/ens/2015/01/27/ no-zero-sum-solution-to-israeli-palestinian-conflict/.

Davies, William D. *The Gospel and the Land: Early Christianity and Jewish Territorial Doctrine.* Berkeley: University of California Press, 1974.

———. *The Territorial Dimension of Judaism.* Berkeley: University of California Press, 1982.

D'Costa, Gavin. *Catholic Doctrines on the Jewish People after Vatican II.* Oxford: Oxford University Press, 2019.

Dershowitz, Alan, "Presbyterians' Shameful Boycott," *Los Angeles Times* (August 4, 2004), available online at https://www.latimes.com/archives/la-xpm-2004-aug-04-oe-dershowitz4-story.html.

Diamant, Jeff and Becka Alper, "Though Still Conservative, Young Evangelicals Are More Liberal Than Their Elders On Some Issues," Pew Research Center (May 4, 2017), available online at http://www.pewresearch.org/fact-tank/2017/05/04/though-still-conservative-young-evangelicals-are-more-liberal-than-their-elders-on-some-issues/.

Dockser Marcus, Amy. *Jerusalem 1913: The Origins of the Arab-Israeli Conflict.* New York: Penguin, 2007.

Doran, Michael. *Ike's Gamble: America's Rise to Dominance in the Middle East.* NY: Free Press, 2016.

Dorrien, Gary J., "Evangelical Ironies: Theology, Politics and Israel". In Mittleman, A., B. Johnson, and N. Isserman, eds., *Uneasy Allies? Evangelical and Jewish Relations.* Lanham, Maryland: Lexington Books, 2007, pp. 103-126.

Dougherty, Terry, "Rev. Alex Awad," Indiana Center for Middle East Peace (February 22, 2017), available online at http://indianacmep.org/awad/.

Douglas, Ian T. "The State of Play for the Anglican Covenant: General Convention 2009." *Anglican & Episcopal History* 78, no.1 (2009), 1-8.

Duin, Julia. "She led Trump to Christ: The rise of the televangelist who advises the White House," *Washington Post*, Nov 14, 2017.

Dunn, James. *The Partings of the Ways: between Christianity and Judaism, and their significance for the character of Christianity.* London: SCM, 1992.

Eckardt, Alice. L. and R. A. Eckardt, "The Place of the Jewish State in Christian-Jewish Relations," *European Judaism,* 2:1 (1992), 3-14.

ECO Presbyterian (A Covenant Order of Evangelical Presbyterians), available online at http://cptpalestine.com.

Elman, Miriam F., "Left Antisemitism: The Rhetoric and Activism of Jewish Voice for Peace." In Andrew Pessin and Corine E. Blackmer, eds. *Poisoning the Wells: Antisemitism in Contemporary America.* NY: ISGAP/Routledge, 2001, in press.

Episcopal Church, "A Pastoral Letter on Israeli-Palestinian Peace" by Presiding Bishop Katherine Jefferts Schori (October 3, 2011), available online at https://www.episcopal church.org/posts/publicaffairs/episcopal-church-presiding-bishop-issues-pastoral-letter-israeli-palestinian.

Episcopal Diocese of Massachusetts, "Bishops issue statement of apology" (August 17, 2018), online at www.diomass.org/news/diocesan-news/bishops-issue-statement-apology.

Episcopal Peace Fellowship, "Palestine Israel Tool Kit," available online at https://epfnational.org/pin/palestine-israel-tool-kit/.

_____, "Palestine Israel Network," available online at https://epfnational.org/pin/.

_____, "Episcopal Church Adopts Human Rights Investment Screen" (July 13, 2018), online at https://epfnational.org/pin/episcopal-church-adopts-human-rights-investment-screen/.

Epp, Frank H. "An Analysis of Germanism and National Socialism in the Immigrant Newspaper of a Canadian Minority Group, the Mennonites, in the 1930's." PhD diss., University of Minnesota, 1965.

———. *The Israelis: Portrait of a People in Conflict.* Harrisonburg, VA: Herald Press, 1980.

———. *The Palestinians: Portrait of a People in Conflict.* Harrisonburg, VA: Herald Press, 1976.

———. *Whose Land is Palestine? The Middle East Problem in Historical Perspective.* Grand Rapids, MI: Eerdmans, 1970.

Epstein, Isidore, and I. W. Slotki, and M. Ginsberg. *The Babylonian Talmud.* London: Soncino Press, 1938.

Evangelical Lutheran Church in America, "Promoting Positive Change for Palestine" (2011), available online at http://download.elca.org/ELCA%20Resource%20 Repository/Promoting_Positive_Change_Palestine_SPR11.pdf?_ga= 2.172849703.547674716.1510424307-1572002079.1510424307&_gac= 1.159565519.1510442339.

CjwKCAiA3JrQBRBtEiwAN7cEGgTjuBXj0qHzmer53CpOnQvl6O80s-
NAAH0NtSftdJI8VYZ3XU3YVnBoCUvIQAvD_BwE.

_____, "ELCA Churchwide Assembly addresses human rights concerns in
Israel and Palestine" (August 9, 2016), available online at https://www.elca.org/
News-and-Events/7855?_ga=2.210638353.547674716.1510424307-1572002%20
079.1510424307.

"EWIG Statement on 'Zionism Unsettled,'" Ecumenical and Interreligious Work
Group of Chicago Presbytery (2014), available online at https://www.pfmep.org/
press-releases/137-eiwg-statement-on-zionism-unsettled.

Fackenheim, Emil, "The Holocaust and the State of Israel: Their Relation." In Eva
Fleischner, ed. *Auschwitz: Beginning of a New Era?* NY: KTAV Publishing, 1977, pp.
205- 215.

_____. *The Jewish Bible after the Holocaust.* Manchester, UK: Manchester University
Press, 1992.

"Failure of Moral Vision, A," Forward (October 1, 2004) (Editorial), available online at
https://forward.com/opinion/editorial/4262/a-failure-of-moral-vision/.

Falwell, Jerry. *Listen, America!* New York: Bantam Books, 1981.

_____, "The Twenty-First Century and the End of the World," *Fundamentalist Journal*
(May 1988).

Feldman, Egal. *Catholics and Jews in Twentieth-century America.* Urbana: University of
Illinois Press, 2001.

Felson, Ethan. "Fight to Overturn Divestment Call Can Provide Lessons for Activists."
Jewish Telegraphic Agency (June 26, 2006). https://www.jta.org/2006/06/26/archive/
fight-to-overturn-divestment-call-can-provide-lessons-for-activists.

_____, "'On the Road': The Jewish Community Relations Encounter with Evangeli-
cals." In Alan Mittleman, Byron Johnson, and Nancy Isserman, eds. U*neasy Allies?
Evangelical and Jewish Relations.* Lanham, MD: Lexington Books, 2006.

_____, "Evangelical ad was wrong," *Jewish Telegraphic Agency* (April 4, 2008),
available at https://www.google.com/amp/s/www.jta.org/2008/04/04/opinion/
evangelical-ad-was-wrong/amp.

Fiorina, Morris, Samuel Abrams and Jeremy Pope. *Culture War? The Myth of a Polarized
America.* New York: Pearson Longman, 2005.

Findley, Paul. *They Dare to Speak Out.* Chicago: Lawrence Hill, 1985.

Fine, Robert, and Philip Spencer. *Antisemitism and the Left: On the Return of the Jewish
Question.* Manchester, UK: Manchester University Press, 2017.

Firestone, Reuven. *Who Are the Real Chosen People?* Woodstock, VT: Skylight Paths,
2008.

Fisher, Eugene J., "Nostra Aetate." In Kessler, E. (Ed.), *A Dictionary of Jewish-Christian Relations*. Cambridge: Cambridge University Press, 2008, pp. 320-21.

Fishman, Hetzel. *American Protestantism and a Jewish State*. Detroit: Wayne State University Press, 1973.

Flowers, Ronald B. "Disciples in the White House," in *Restoring the First-century Church in the Twenty-first Century*. Edited by Haymes, Don, Warren Lewis, and Hans Rollmann. Eugene, OR: Wipf and Stock Publishers, 2005.

Forbes, Bruce David. "How popular Are the *Left Behind* Books…and Why? A Discussion of Popular Culture." In Bruce David Forbes and Jeanne Halgren Kilde, eds, *Rapture, Revelation, and the End Times: Exploring the "Left Behind" Series*. New York: Palgrave Macmillan, 2004, 5–32.

Forster, Arnold and Benjamin Epstein. *The New Anti-Semitism*. New York: McGraw Hill, 1974.

Fortson, S. Donald and Rollin G. Grams. *Unchanging Witness: The Consistent Christian Teaching on Homosexuality in Scripture and Tradition*. Nashville, TN: B&H Publishing, 2016.

FOSNA—Friends of Sabeel North America: A Christian Voice for Palestine, "The Kairos Palestine Document, a prayerful call of Palestinian Christians to end the occupation," available online at https://www.fosna.org/content/kairos-palestine-document-prayerful-call-palestinian-christians-end-occupation.

FOSNA, "The Episcopal Church Votes to Divest!" (July 13, 2018), online at https://www.fosna.org/episcopal-church-votes-divest.

Foust, Michael. "Mohler: Christians Should Support Israel, Yet Hold It Accountable," Baptist Press (April 25, 2002), available online at http://www.bpnews.net/bpnews.asp?id=13230.

Fredriksen, Paula, "The Question of Worship: Gods, Pagans, and the Redemption of Israel," in *Paul within Judaism: Restoring the First-Century Context to the Apostle*, edited Mark D. Nanos and Magnus Zetterholm, 175-201. Minneapolis: Fortress Press, 2015.

———. Review of N.T. Wright, *The Faithfulness of God. Catholic Biblical Quarterly* 77 (2015): 387-91.

Freedman, H., Maurice Simon, S. M. Lehrman, J. Israelstam, Judah J. Slotki, J. Rabbinowitz, A. Cohen, and Louis I. Rabinowitz. *Midrash rabbah: translated into English with notes, glossary and indices*. London: Soncino Press, 1961.

G4S, "Final Statement After Examination of Complaint" (Lawyers for Palestinian Human Rights (LPHR) & G4S PLC (March 2015), available online at https://assets.publishing.service.gov.uk/government/uploads/system/uploads/attachment_data/file/431972/bis-15-306-lawyers-for-palestinian-human-rights-final-statement-after-examination-of-complaint-uk-national-contact-point-for-the-oecd-guidelines-for-multinational-enterprises-r1.pdf.

Gafni, Isaiah M. *Land, Center and Diaspora: Jewish Constructs in Late Antiquity*. Journal for the Study of the Pseudepigrapha Supplement Series 21. Sheffield: Sheffield Academic Press, 1997.

Gale, Aaron M. Introduction to The Gospel According to Matthew. In *The Jewish Annotated New Testament: New Revised Standard Version Bible Translation*. Edited by Amy-Jill Levine and Marc Zvi Brettler. Second edition. 9-10. Oxford: Oxford University Press, 2017.

Gaston, K. Healan. *Imagining Judeo-Christian America: Religion, Secularism, and the Redefinition of Democracy*. Chicago: University of Chicago Press, 2019.

General Assembly, PC (USA). *Peoples and Conflict in the Middle East—A Preliminary Report for Study*. Philadelphia: General Assembly, 1973.

———. *The Middle East Conflict, A Presbyterian Report*. New York: General Assembly, 1974.

Gilboa, Eytan, *The American Public and Israel in the Twenty-First Century*. Ramat Gan, Israel: BESA Center for Strategic Studies, Bar-Ilan University, 2020.

Gish, Arthur, *Hebron Journal: Stories of Nonviolent Peacemaking*. Scottdale, PA: Herald Press, 2001.

Global Ministries, "Palestinian Christian Kairos," available online at https://www.globalministries.org/palestinian_christian_kairos.

Goditiabois, Julie, "Actualiteitsnota over Israël en de Palestijnse gebieden," Broederlijk Delen (2018), available online at https://www.broederlijkdelen.be/nl/actualiteitsnota-over-israel-en-de-palestijnse-gebieden.

Goldenberg, Ilan, and Gadi Shammi, Nimrod Novik, and Kris Bauman. *Advancing the Dialogue: A Security System for the Two-State Solution*. Washington, D.C.: Center for a New American Security, 2016. http://twostatesecurity.org/new/wp-content/uploads/2017/03/CNASreport.pdf.

Goldenberg, Ilan, and Michael Koplow, and Tamara Cofman Wittes. *A New Strategy for the Israeli-Palestinian Conflict*. Washington, DC: Center for a New American Security, 2020. https://www.cnas.org/publications/reports/a-new-u-s-strategy-for-the-israeli-palestinian-conflict.

Goldman, Shalom. *God's Sacred Tongue: Hebrew and the American Imagination*. Chapel Hill, NC: University of North Carolina Press, 2004.

Goldstein, Stephen R., and Sandra Olewine. *Israel-Palestine: Mission Study for 2007-2008: Study Guide*. New York, NY: Women's Division, General Board of Global Ministries, The United Methodist Church, 2007.

Goodkind, Nicole. "Obama Says He's 'Basically A Liberal Jew,' Is Not Optimistic About Israeli-Palestinian Peace Talks," *Newsweek*, January 26, 2018. https://www.yahoo.com/news/obama-says-apos-apos-basically-221431351.html

Goodstein, Laurie, "In Close Vote, Presbyterian Church Rejects Divesting in Firms That Aid Israeli Occupation," *New York Times* (July 5, 2012), available online at https://www.nytimes.com/2012/07/06/us/presbyterian-church-wont-divest-in-firms-aiding-occupation.html?mcubz=1.

_____, "Presbyterians Vote to Divest Holdings to Pressure Israel," *New York Times* (June 20, 2014).

Goodwin, Doris K. *Lyndon Johnson and the American Dream*. New York: St. Martin's, 1976.

Gordis, Daniel. *Israel: A Concise History of a Nation Reborn*. New York: Harper Collins, 2016.

Gordon, Jerry, "What a 'Night to Honor Israel': The CUFI Washington Summit Dinner in DC," *Israpundit* (July 20, 2006).

Gorenberg, Gershon. *The End of Days: Fundamentalism and the Struggle for the Temple Mount*. Oxford, United Kingdom: Oxford University Press, 2000.

Goossen, Benjamin W. *Chosen Nation: Mennonites and Germany in a Global Era*. Princeton: Princeton University Press, 2017.

_____, "Mennonites and the Holocaust: An Introduction," *Annabaptist Historians* (February 7, 2018), online at https://anabaptisthistorians.org/2018/02/07/mennonites-and-the-holocaust-an-introduction/.

_____, "Five Myths about Mennonites and the Holocaust," *Anabaptist Historians* (June 14, 2018), online at https://anabaptisthistorians.org/2018/06/14/five-myths-about-mennonites-and-the-holocaust/.

_____, "Mennonites and the Waffen-SS," *Anabaptist Historians* (June 20, 2019), online at https://anabaptisthistorians.org/2019/06/20/mennonites-and-the-waffen-ss/.

_____, "How to Catch a Mennonite Nazi," *Anabaptist Historians* (October 29, 2020).

_____, "The Real History of the Mennonites and the Holocaust," *Tablet* (November 16, 2020).

Green, John C., "The American Religious Landscape and Political Attitudes: A Baseline for 2004" www.uakron.edu/bliss/research/archives/2004/Religious_Landscape_2004.pdf.

_____, "The American Public and Sympathy for Israel: Present and Future. *Journal of Ecumenical Studies*, 44: 1 (2009), 107-121.

Gregerman, Adam, "Israel as the 'Hermeneutical Jew' in Protestant Statements on the Land and State of Israel: Four Presbyterian Examples," *Kirche und Israel*, 2015; Israel Affairs 23.5 (2017): 773-93 (https://doi.org/10.1080/13537121.2017.1343786).

———. "Old Wine in New Bottles: Liberation Theology and the Israeli – Palestinian Conflict," *Journal of Ecumenical Studies* 41, no. 3-4 (Summer-Fall 2004), 313-40.

Grose, Peter. *Israel in the Mind of America*. New York: Knopf, 1983.

Gross, Marissa, "The Salute to Israel Parade" (2008), available online at http://jcpa.org/article/the-salute-to-Israel-parade/.

Grossman, Lawrence, "The Organized Jewish Community and Evangelical America." In Alan Mittleman, Byron R. Johnson, and Nancy Isserman, eds. *Uneasy Allies? Evangelical and Jewish Relations*. Lanham, Maryland: Lexington Books, 2007, pp. 19-72.

Gustafson, Merlin. "The Religion of a President." *Journal of Church and State* 10, no. 3 (October 1, 1968): 379–87. https://doi.org/10.1093/jcs/10.3.379.

Guth, James, "The Bush Administration, American Religious Politics, and Middle East Policy," Chicago, Illinois: American Political Science Association, September 2004.

_____, "Religious Leadership and Support for Israel: A Study of Clergy in Nineteen Denominations," New Orleans, Louisiana: Southern Political Science Association, 2007.

Guth, James, and Kenan, W., " *Religious Factors and American Public Support for Israel: 1992–2008*. Seattle, Washington: American Political Science Association, 2011.

Guttman, Nathan, "Are Christian Zionists the 800-Pound Gorilla in the Pro-Israel Room?" *Forward* (July 16, 2015).

Hagee, John. *Final Dawn over Jerusalem*. Nashville, Tennessee: Thomas Nelson, 1998.

_____. *Jerusalem Countdown*. Lake Mary, Florida: FrontLine, 2006.

_____. *In Defense of Israel*. 1st ed. Lake Mary, FL: FrontLine, 2007.

_____, "Why Christian Zionists Really Support Israel," *Jewish Daily Forward* (May 21, 2010).

Hajjar, Lisa. *Courting Conflict: The Israeli Military Court System in the West Bank and Gaza*. London: University of California Press, 2005.

Halbfinger, David M., "Tensions Ease in Gaza, Allowing Money and Fuel to Roll In." *New York Times*, November 9, 2018. https://www.nytimes.com/2018/11/09/world/middleeast/gaza-hamas-israel-bordermoney-fuel.html.

Halevi, Yossi Klein. *Letters to my Palestinian Neighbor*. New York: Harper, 2018.

Hall, S. G.. *Melito of Sardis: on Pascha and Fragments*. Oxford, United Kingdom: Clarendon Press, 1979.

Hallward, Maia C. *Transnational Activism and the Israeli-Palestinian Conflict*. New York: Palgrave, 2013.

Halper, Jeff. War *Against the People: Israel, the Palestinians and Global Pacification*. London: Pluto Press, 2015.

Halsell, Grace. *Prophecy and Politics: Militant Evangelists on the Road to Nuclear War*. Westport, Connecticut: Lawrence Hill, 1986.

Hamburger, Tom. "How Pence gained — and then tested — the trust of many conservative activists," *Washington Post* (July 15, 2016).

Harkins, P.W. *Prophecy and Politics: Militant Evangelists on the Road to Nuclear War.* Westport, Connecticut: Lawrence Hill, 1979.

Hass, Amira, "Renovated Checkpoints Mean Palestinians No Longer Feel Like Cows Being Led to the Slaughter," *Haaretz* (May 25, 2019).

Hawking, Stephen. *God Created the Integers: The Mathematical Breakthroughs that Changed History.* Philadelphia, PA: Running Press, 2007.

Haynes, Stephen R. *Reluctant Witnesses: Jews and the Christian Imagination.* Louisville, Kentucky: Westminster/John Knox Press, 1995.

Hebb, Ross N. "The Americans at Lambeth." *Anglican & Episcopal History* 78, no.1 (2009), 9-29.

Heilman, Uriel, "US Churches Pray for Israel," *Jerusalem Post* (October 18, 2004).

Heim, David, "Boycotting the boycott: The problem with the BDS movement," *Christian Century* (July 2015).

Henderson, Katherine, "Auburn Seminary Statement on *Zionism Unsettled*" (February 18, 2014), reprinted at https://www.jta.org/2014/02/18/united-states/auburn-seminary-head-on-presbyterian-zionism-guide-demonization-distortion-imbalance.

Herf, Jeffrey. N*azi Propaganda for the Arab World.* New Haven: Yale University Press, 2009.

Hertz, Todd, "The Evangelical View of Israel," *Christianity Today* (June 9, 2003).

_____, "Roadblocks and Voting Blocs: Today's Evangelicals Are Committed to Peace–Not Just Security–for Israel," *Christianity Today* (July 1, 2003).

Herzl, Theodor. *The Complete Diaries of Theodor Herzl*, volume 4, ed. Raphael Patal. NY: Herzl Press., 1960.

Heschel, Abraham J. *Israel: An Echo of Eternity.* NY: Farrar, Straus & Giroux, 1969.

Hessel, Dieter T., ed. *The Church's Public Role: Retrospect and Prospect.* Grand Rapids, Michigan: Eerdmans, 1993.

Himmelfarb, Gertrude. *The People of the Book: Philosemitism in England from Cromwell to Churchill.* New York City, New York: Encounter, 2011.

Hirsh, David. *Contemporary Left Antisemitism.* NY: Routledge, 2018.

Hodges, Sam, "United Methodist Women's study of Israel-Palestine prompts complaints," *The Dallas Morning News* (April 7, 2008), online at https://www.dallasnews.com/news/faith/2008/04/07/united-methodist-women-s-study-of-israel-palestine-prompts-complaints/.

Hoffman, Norbert, "With Francis' Friendship," *L'Osservatore Romano* (February 7, 2014), p. 15, online at https://www.ewtn.com/catholicism/library/with-francis-friendship-1333.

Hogan, Colm. "Bethlehem: The Capital of Christmas." *Trócaire News*, December 20, 2016. https://www.trocaire.org/news/bethlehem-christmas.

Holbrook, Sheryl Kujawa, "'There will be no outcasts': Official obituary for Edmond Lee Browning," Episcopal News Service (July 12, 2016), available online at https://www.episcopalnewsservice.org/pressreleases/there-will-be-no-outcasts-official-obituary-for-edmond-lee-browning/.

Hopkins, Paul A., "American Presbyterians and the Middle East Conflict," *American Presbyterians* 68, no. 1 (Fall 1990): 143-65.

Horner, Barry E., *Future Israel: Why Christian Anti-Judaism Must Be Challenged*. New American Commentary Studies in Bible and Theology. Nashville: B&H Academic, 2007.

Horowitz, Richard. "U.S. Church Puts 5 Banks From Israel on a Blacklist." *Jewish Business News*, January 14, 2016. http://jewishbusinessnews.com/2016/01/14/u-s-church-puts-5-banks-from-israel-on-a-blacklist/.

Houser, Gordon, Paul Schrag, and Melanie Zuercher. "Neighbors, Killers, Enablers, Witnesses: Conferences Looks at the Many Roles of Mennonites in the Holocaust." *The Mennonite*, March 19, 2018. https://themennonite.org/daily-news/neighbors-killers-enablers-witnesses-conference-looks-many-roles-mennonites-holocaust/

Hughes, Richard T. *Myths America Lives By*. Urbana, Illinois: University of Illinois Press, 2003.

Hummel, Daniel G. *Covenant Brothers: Evangelicals, Jews, and U.S.-Israeli Relations*. Philadelphia, PA: University of Pennsylvania Press, 2019.

ICEJ (International Christian Embassy Jerusalem, "History: The ICEJ's story and purpose," available online at https://int.icej.org/history.

Ieraci, Laura. "Patriarch: Holy Land Christians 'pray, weep, suffer and wait' with Jesus." *The Catholic Sun*, September 29, 2015. http://www.catholicsun.org/2015/09/29/patriarch-holy-land-christians-pray-weep-suffer-and-wait-with-jesus/.

Inbari, Motti, "American Evangelicals and Israel," paper presented at the 2019 annual meetings of the Academic Engagement Network and the Association for Israel Studies.

Inbari, Motti, and Kirill Bumin, "The Attitudes of Evangelicals towards the Arab-Israeli Conflict," *Journal of State and Church* 62:4 (2020): 603–629.

Inbari, Motti, and Kirill Bumin, and M. Gordon Byrd, "Why Do Evangelicals Support Israel?" *Politics and Religion* 14:1 (2021): 1-36.

International Council of Christians and Jews, "Let Us Have Mercy Upon Words" (July 26 2010), available online at https://ccjr.us/dialogika-resources/documents-and-statements/interreligious/iccj/iccj2010july26-2.

Isaac, Jules, *The Teaching of Contempt.* New York: Holt, Rhinehart and Winston, 1964.

Isaac, Munther, "Munther Isaac: Articles, Sermons Videos," available online at http://muntherisaac.blogspot.com.

Israel/Palestine Mission Network of the Presbyterian Church (USA). *Steadfast Hope: The Palestinian Quest for Just Peace*, 2nd ed. 2011.

_____, "Home," available online at http://new.israelpalestinemissionnetwork.org/.

_____, "Buy Zionism Unsettled," available online at http://new.israelpalestinemission-network.org/component/content/article?id=281.

———. *Why Palestine Matters: The Struggle to End Colonialism.* 2018.

———. *Zionism Unsettled: A Congregational Study Guide.* 2014. http://new.israel palestinemissionnetwork.org/component/content/article/70/256-zionism-unsettled.

Israel Policy Forum. *50 Steps Before the Deal.* New York: Israel Policy Forum, 2018. http://50beforethedeal.com/about/.

———. *Advancing Two-State Security — 2017.* New York: Israel Policy Forum, 2017. http://twostatesecurity.org/file/2017/03/IPFBriefingBook.pdf.

Jacobs, Rick, "What the Presbyterians Got Wrong on Israel," *Washington Post* (April 1, 2014), available online at https://www.washingtonpost.com/national/religion/commentary-what-the-presbyterians-got-wrong-on-israel/2014/04/01/b1a314dc-b9b6-11e3-80de-2ff8801f27af_story.html?utm_term=.dca6783808ce.

Jaffe-Hoffman, Maayan. "Evangelicals see Trump plan as proof 'Israel kissed by God' – analysis," *Jerusalem Post* (Jan 27, 2020).

Jantzen, Mark, and John D. Thiesen, eds. *European Mennonites and the Holocaust.* Toronto: University of Toronto Press, 2020.

Jenkins, John Philip. *Jesus Wars: How Four Patriarchs, Three Queens, and Two Emperors Decided What Christians Would Believe for the Next 1,500 Years.* NY: HarperOne, 2011.

Jennings, William James. *The Christian Imagination: Theology and the Origins of Race.* New Haven: Yale University Press, 2010.

Jenson, Robert W. and Eugene B. Korn, eds. *Covenant and Hope: Christian and Jewish Reflections.* Grand Rapids, MI: William B. Eerdmans, 2012.

Jenson, Robert W., "Afterword: Where Do We Go from Here? Future Theological Challenges for Christians and Jews." In *Covenant and Hope: Christian and Jewish Reflections*, pp. 284-88.

_____, "The Prophet's Double Vision of the Return to Zion." In Robert W. Jenson and Eugene Korn, eds. *Returning to Zion: Christian and Jewish Perspectives.*

Jenson, Robert W. and Eugene Korn, eds. *Returning to Zion: Christian and Jewish Perspectives* (*Essays from the Institute for Theological Inquiry.* Efrat, Israel: Center for Jewish-Christian Understanding and Cooperation, 2015 (unpaginated eBook).

Jeschke, Marlin. *Rethinking Holy Land: A Study in Salvation Geography*. Scottdale, PA: Herald Press, 2005.

Jewish Telegraphic Agency. "Cardinal Cushing Contributes $500 for Jewish Education in Israel," *Jewish Telegraphic Agency*, July 24, 1962, accessed 7 Nov 2016.

Jewish Voice for Peace, ed. *On Antisemitism: Solidarity and the Struggle for Justice*. Chicago: Haymarket Books, 2017.

Jewish Voice for Peace Rabbinical Council, "Honor the courage, clarity and sensitivity of Kairos USA," available online at https://kairosusa.org/endorsements/jewish-voice-for-peace-rabbinical-council/.

Jikeli, Gunther, "Is Religion Coming Back as a Source for Antisemitic Views? *Religions* 10:8 (May 2020).

Joint Declaration (The Vatican), The 18th International Catholic-Jewish Liaison Committee Meeting (July 5-8, 2004), available online at http://www.vatican.va/roman_curia/pontifical_councils/chrstuni/relations-jews-docs/rc_pc_chrstuni_doc_20040708_declaration-buenos-aires_en.html.

John Chrysostom. *Discourses against Judaizing Christians*. Translated by Paul W. Harkins. FC 68. Washington, D.C.: Catholic University of America Press, 1979.

Jones, Robert P. and Daniel Cox. *Clergy Voices: Findings from the 2008 Mainline Protestant Clergy Voices Survey*. Washington, D.C.: Public Religion Research, 2009.

Josephus, Flavius, and H. St. J. Thackeray. *Josephus: with an English translation by H. St. J. Thackeray: in nine volumes*. Cambridge, MA: Heinemann, 1926.

Jospe, Raphael, "The Concept of the Chosen People: An Interpretation," *Judaism: A Quarterly Journal of Jewish Life and Thought* 43:2 (Spring 1994), 127-48.

Justin, and A. Lukyn Williams. *Justin Martyr, the dialogue with Trypho*. London: S.P.C.K., 1930.

Kairos Palestine, available online at http://www.kairospalestine.ps.

_____, "Kairos Document," available online at http://www.kairospalestine.ps/index.php/about-us/kairos-palestine-document and at http://www.kairospalestine.ps/sites/default/files/English.pdf.

_____, "Global Kairos," available online at http://www.kairospalestine.ps/index.php/about-us/global-kairos.

Kairos South Africa, "What does 'normalization' mean in the Palestine-Israel conflict?" (May 19, 2011), available online at https://kairossouthernafrica.wordpress.com/2011/05/19/what-does-normalisation-mean-in-the-palestine-israel-conflict/.

Kairos USA, "Call to Action: U.S. Response to the Kairos Palestine Document," available online at https://kairosusa.org/wp-content/uploads/2013/12/Kairos-USA-Call-to-Action.pdf.

Kamen, Henry. *Inquisition and Society in Spain; In the Sixteenth and Seventeenth Centuries*. Bloomington, IN: Indiana University Press, 1985.

Kampen, John. "Mennonites, Jews, and the Land: Preparing for a Discussion," *The Mennonite*, June 10, 2016. https://themennonite.org/opinion/mennonites-jews-land-preparing-discussion/.

———. "Mennonites, Judaism, and Israel-Palestine." *The Mennonite*, July 23, 2007.

———. "Our Commitment to Jewish Dialogue." *The Mennonite* 21, no. 3 (March 2018): 32.

———. "We Need to Engage the Jewish Community." *The Mennonite* 19, no. 5 (May 2016): 31.

Kaplan, Esther. *With God on Their Side: How Christian Fundamentalists Trampled Science, Policy, and Democracy in George Bush's White House*. New York City, New York: New Press, 2004.

Kark, Ruth, "Planning Housing and Land Policy: The Formation of Concepts and Governmental Frameworks." In Ilan Troen and Noah Lucas, eds. *Israel: The First Decade of Independence*. Albany: State University of New York Press, 1995, pp. 461-494.

Katz, David S. "Magic and the Millennium." In *The Meanings of Magic: From the Bible to Buffalo Bill*. Edited by Amy Wygant, 33-54. New York: Berghahn, 2006.

Kellstedt, Lyman A., and Corwin E. Smidt, John C. Green, and James L. Guth, "A Gentle Stream or a 'River Glorious'? The Religious Left in the 2004 Election." In Campbell, D. E. ed., *A Matter of Faith: Religion in the 2004 Presidential Election*. 232-256. Washington, D.C.: Brookings Institution Press, 2007.

Kenny, Anthony. *Catholics, Jews and the State of Israel*. Mahwah, NJ: Stimulus Books, 1993.

Kessler, Edward. *An Introduction to Jewish-Christian Relations*. Cambridge: Cambridge University Press, 2010.

_____, " Reflections from a European Jewish Theologian," *Council of Centers on Jewish-Christian Relations* (2015), online at www.cjr.us/dialogika-resources/documents-and-starements/analyses/crj-2015dec10/kessler-2015dec10.

Kessler, Edward and James Aitken, eds., *Challenges in Jewish-Christian Relations*, New York: Paulist Press, 2006.

Kessler, Edward and Neil Wenborn, eds., *A Dictionary of Jewish-Christian Relations*, Cambridge: Cambridge University Press, 2005.

Khader, Jamal, and David Neuhaus, "A Holy Land Context for Nostra Aetate." *Studies in Christian-Jewish Relations* 1, no. 1 (2005), 67-88, available online at. https://doi.org/10.6017/scjr.v1i1.1360.

Khoury, Geries, "Christian-Muslim Arab Dialog in the Holy Land" (Bethlehem: Al Liqaa Center, 2006), English translation available at: http://www.al-liqacenter.org.

ps/eng/p_materials/Christian-Muslim-d.php . The original is part of, Geries Khoury, *Arab Masihiyun wa-Muslimun—Madian, Hadiran, Mustaqbalan*, (Bethlehem, Al Liqaa Center, 2006), 111-166, in particular 132-8.

———. *Intifadat Asama' wa Intifadat al Ard* [The Intifada of Heaven and Earth]. Nazareth: Al-Hakim, 1990.

_____. Arab Masihiyun wa-Muslimun—Madian, Hadiran, Mustaqbalan. Jala, Palestine: Bethlehem, Al Liqaa Center, 2006.

Khoury, Rafiq, "Arab Christians in Israel: in Search of an Identity," published on the site of the Latin Patriarchate in Jerusalem (April 29, 2009), available at: http://en.lpj.org/2009/04/29/chretiens-arabes-en-israel-a-la-recherche-dune-identite/.

_____, "Identity: Meaning, Components and Dimensions," Al Liqa Center, see note 2; available at: http://www.al-liqacenter.org.ps/eng/p_materials/Identity.php.

Kommoission Israel/Palästina von Pax Christi Österreich, "Memorandum" (March 13, 2010). Available at http://w3.khg.jku.at/pax/blog/wp-content/uploads/2010/05/Memorandum-Israel-u.-Pal%C3%A4stina-13.03.2010.pdf.

Koplow, Michael J. "Value Judgment: Why Do Americans Support Israel?" *Security Studies* 20, no. 2 (April 1, 2011): 266–302. https://doi.org/10.1080/09636412.2011.572 690.

Korn, Eugene. *Church Attitudes Toward the Israeli-Palestinian Conflict*. New York: Anti-Defamation League, 2002.

———. "Divestment from Israel, the Liberal Churches, and Jewish Responses: A Strategic Analysis." *Post-Holocaust and Anti-Semitism*, no. 52 (2007): 1–8.

_____, "The People Israel, Christianity, and the Covenantal Responsibility to History." In Robert W. Jenson and Eugene B. Korn, eds. *Covenant and Hope: Christian and Jewish Reflections*, pp. 145-72.

Korn, Eugene B. and John T. Pawlikowski, eds. *Two Faiths, One Covenant? Jewish and Christian Identity in the Presence of the Other*. NY: Rowman & Littlefield, 2005.

Küntzel, Matthias. *Jihad and Jew-Hatred: Islamism, Nazism and the Roots of 9/11*. Telos Press, 2007.

Kurtz, Lester, and Kelly Goran Fulton, "Love Your Enemies? Protestants and United States Foreign Policy." In Wuthnow R. and J. H. Evans, (Eds.), *The Quiet Hand of God: Faith-Based Activism and the Public Role of Mainline Protestantism*, 364-380. Berkeley: University of California Press 2002, pp. 364-380.

Kuruvilla, Samuel J., "Theologies of Liberation in Latin America and Palestine-Israel in Comparative Perspective: Contextual Differences and Practical Similarities," *Holy Land Studies* (2010), 9: 51–69.

_____. *Radical Christianity in Palestine and Israel: Liberation and Theology in the Middle East*. London: I. B. Tauris, 2013.

Kurz, Anat, and Uri Dekel and Benedetta Berti, eds. *The Crisis of the Gaza Strip: A Way Out.* Tel Aviv: Institute for National Security Studies, 2017.

Lake, Eli, "Pro-Israel Evangelicals Escape AIPAC's Shadow," *Bloomberg* (January 10, 2017).

Lantos, Tom. "The Durban Debacle: An Insider's View of the UN World Conference against Racism," Fletcher Forum of World Affairs 26, no. 1 (Winter/Spring 2002): 31-52.

Latin Patriarchate of Jerusalem, "Commission for Justice and Peace of the Assembly of Catholic Ordinaries of the Holy Land: The Question of Normalization" (May 14, 2017), available online at https://www.lpj.org/commission-justice-and-peace-question-of-normalization/.

Lazaroff, Tovah, "Ten things to know about Christians in Israel," *The Jerusalem Post* (December 25, 2018), online at https://www.jpost.com/Israel-News/Ten-things-to-know-about-Christians-in-Israel-575354.

Lee, Kennedy, "Anti-Israel Christian Left Sees 'New Opportunities' in Congress, Administration," *Juicy Ecumenicism* (January 28, 2021), online at https://juicyecumenism.com/2021/01/28/anti-israel-christian-left/.

Leighton, Christopher M., "False Witness: A misguided study guide," *The Christian Century* (May 2, 2014).

_____, "Open Letter to the Presbyterian Church," *Institute for Islamic, Christian, Jewish Studies* (Feb 6, 2014).

_____, "Guest Post: Rev. Chris Leighton responds to my Open Letter," *Shalom Rav: A Blog By Rabbi Brant Rosen* (February 23, 2014).

Leikind, Robert, "Kairos Palestine and the Unholy Crusade Against Israel," American Jewish Committee, available online at https://www.ajc.org/news/kairos-palestine-and-the-unholy-crusade-against-israel-0.

Lerner, Rachel. "Time To Prove Two-State Solution Isn't Just Rhetoric." *New York Jewish Week*, July 17, 2012.

Levine, Amy-Jill, *The Misunderstood Jew: The Church and the Scandal of the Jewish Jesus.* San Francisco: Harper San Francisco, 2006.

———."Speaking of the Middle East: Jews and Christians in Dialogue and Dispute," in *Post-Holocaust Jewish–Christian Dialogue After the Flood, before the Rainbow,* edited by Alan L. Berger, 57-76. Lanham, MD: Lexington, 2015.

———. "Un-Christian Responses to the Middle East." *ABC Religion and Ethics,* July 21, 2010. https://www.abc.net.au/religion/un-christian-responses-to-the-middle-east/10102228.

Levine, Amy-Jill, and Marc Zvi Brettler, eds. *The Jewish Annotated New Testament: New Revised Standard Version Bible Translation.* Oxford: Oxford University Press, 2011.

Levine, Mark and Gershon Shafir, eds. *Struggle and Survival in Palestine/Israel*. Berkeley, CA and London: University of California Press, 2012.a

Lewis, Sheldon. *Torah of Reconciliation*. NY & Jerusalem: Gefen, 2012.

Liberty University. *The Journal Champion* 1, no. 1 (1978).

Libreria Editrice Vaticana, "Address of His Holiness Benedict XVI to His Excellency Mr. Mordechay Lewy Ambassador to The Holy See" (May 12, 2008), online at http://www.vatican.va/content/benedict-xvi/en/speeches/2008/may/documents/hf_ben-xvi_spe_20080512_ambassador-israel.html.

Lieu, Judith, *Image and Reality: The Jews and the World of Christianity in the Second Century*. Edinburgh: T & T Clark, 1996.

Lindner, Eileen, ed. *Yearbook of American and Canadian Churches 2006*. Nashville, Tennessee: Abingdon Press. 2006.

Lindsay, D. Michael. *Faith in the Halls of Power: How Evangelicals Joined the American Elite*. Oxford, United Kingdom: Oxford University Press, 2007.

Little, Douglas. *American Orientalism: The United States and the Middle East Since 1945*. Chapel Hill: University of North Carolina Press, 2002.

Livingston, James C., and Francis Schüssler Fiorenza. *Modern Christian Thought: Volume 2, The twentieth century*, 2nd ed. Minneapolis: Fortress Press, 2006.

Lowe, Malcolm, "The Palestinian "Kairos" Document: A Behind-the Scenes Analysis," *New English Review* (April 2010), available online https://www.newenglishreview.org/Malcolm_Lowe/The_Palestinian_%22Kairos%22_Document%3A_A_Behind-the-Scenes_Analysis/.

MacEoin, Denis, ""A 'Guide' to the Israeli-Palestinian Conflict by the United Church of Christ," Gatestone Institute" (September 15, 2019).

Mackay, John A. *The Presbyterian Way of Life*. Upper Saddle River, NJ: Prentice-Hall, 1960.

Made in Illegality, available online at http://www.madeinillegality.org/accueil?lang=fr#body.

Magid, Shaul, "Christian Supersessionism, Zionism, and the Contemporary Scene: A Critical Reading of Peter Och's Reading of John Howard Yoder," *Journal of Religious Ethics* (2017), 104-141.

Makari, Victor E. "Israel and Palestine: The Quest for Peace." *Church & Society* 94, no. 1 (September 2003): 1–4.

Maltz, Judy, "Evangelical aid was once taboo in Israel. Now it's on the rise. Why?" *Haaretz* August 16, 2016).

Marano, Lou, "Christians Rally for Israel in Washington," *United Press International* (October 13, 2002).

Marcus, Amy Dockser. Jerusalem 1913: The Origins of the Arab-Israeli Conflict. New York City, New York: Penguin, 2007.

Marsden, George M. *Understanding Fundamentalism and Evangelicalism*. Grand Rapids, Michigan: Eerdmans, 1991.

_____. Fundamentalism and American Culture. New York: Oxford University Press, 2006.

Martin, William. *With God on Our Side*. New York: Broadway Books, 1997.

Marty, Martin E. *Modern American Religion: Under God, Indivisible, 1941-1960*. Chicago: University of Chicago Press, 1996.

Mason, Steve et al, "Jew and Judean: A Forum on Politics and Historiography in the Translation of Ancient Texts" (August 26, 2014), available at http://marginalia. lareviewofbooks.org/jew-judean-forum/.

May, Melanie. *Jerusalem Testament: Palestinian Christians Speak, 1988-2008*. Grand Rapids, MI: Eerdmans, 2010.

Mayer, Arnold. *Why Did the Heavens Not Darken? The Final Solution in History*. New York: Pantheon, 1988.

Mayer, Jeremy D., "Christian Fundamentalists and Public Opinion toward the Middle East: Israel's New Best Friends?. *Social Science Quarterly*, 85:3 (2004), 695–713.

McDermott, Gerald R., "Evangelicals and Israel." In Mittleman, A., B. Johnson, and N. Isserman, eds. U*neasy Allies? Evangelical and Jewish Relations*. Lanham, Maryland: Lexington Books 2007, pp. 129-132..

_____, "Covenant, Mission, and Relating to the Other," in *Covenant and Hope: Christian and Jewish Reflections*, edited by Robert W. Jenson and Eugene Korn, pp. 19-40.

———. "Not the Christian Zionism You're Thinking Of." *Christianity Today*, April 17, 2015. https://www.christianitytoday.com/ct/2015/april-web-only/not-christian-zionism-youre-thinking-of.html.

_____, "Choosing to Misread? Review of Brueggemann's Chosen?" Providence (Spring 2016), 78-81.

_____, ed. *The New Christian Zionism: Fresh Perspectives on Israel & The Land*. Downers Grove, IL: InterVarsity Press, 2016.

_____, "Introduction." In *The New Christian Zionism*, pp. 11-29.

_____, "A History of Christian Zionism." In *The New Christian Zionism*, pp. 45-75.

_____, "Implications and Propositions." In *The New Christian Zionism*, pp 319-334.

_____. *Israel Matters: Why Christians Must Think Differently about the People and the Land*. Grand Rapids, MI: Brazos Press, 2017.

McManus, Dennis D. "Augustine of Hippo." In *A Dictionary of Jewish-Christian Relations*, edited by Edward Kessler and Neil Wenborn, 42. Cambridge: Cambridge University Press, 2005.

McMichael, Steven J., "The Covenant in Patristic and Medieval Christian Theology." In Eugene B. Korn and John T. Pawlikowski, eds. *Two Faiths, One Covenant? Jewish and Christian Identity in the Presence of the Other*, pp. 45-64.

Mead, Walter Russell, "The New Israel and the Old: Why Gentile Americans Back the Jewish State," *Foreign Affairs* (2008) 87:4, 28–46.

Mearsheimer, John and Stephen Walt. *The Israel Lobby and US Foreign Policy*. NY: Farrar, Strauss and Giroux, 2007.

Meddeb, Abdelwahab, and Benjamin Stora, eds., *A History of Jewish-Muslim Relations: From the Origins to the Present Day. Princeton*, NJ: Princeton University Press, 2013.

Medoff, Rafael. *The Jews Should Keep Quiet: Franklin D. Roosevelt, Rabbi Stephen S. Wise, and the Holocaust*. Phila., PA: Jewish Publication Society, 2019.

Melito, and Stuart George Hall. *On Pascha and Fragments*. Oxford Early Christian Texts. Oxford: Clarendon Press, 1979.

Mennonite Central Committee, "MCC and Palestine and Israel: Commonly Asked Questions," available online at https://mcc.org/sites/mcc.org/files/media/common/documents/palestine_israel_booklet_web_us.pdf.

Mennonite Church USA. *Confession of Faith in a Mennonite Perspective*. Scottdale: Herald Press, 1995.

_____, "Vision and Mission," available online at https://mcc.org/learn/about/mission.

_____, "An Open Letter to Mennonite Church USA congregations: Becoming Peace-makers in Israel/Palestine, June 2007," available online at http://mennoniteusa.org/wp-content/uploads/2015/03/2007OpenLtrAndResourcesIsraelPalestine2007June.pdf.

_____, "Dear sisters and brothers in Christ in Palestine" (letter from Ervin Stutzman, Executive Director of the Church, endorsing the Kairos Document, October 5, 2011), available online at http://mennoniteusa.org/wp-content/uploads/2015/03/KairosLtr_2011Oct5.pdf.

_____, "Seeking Peace in Israel and Palestine: A Resolution for Mennonite Church USA" (January 2017), available online at http://mennoniteusa.org/wp-content/uploads/2017/01/IP-Resolution.pdf.

_____, "Confession of Faith In a Mennonite Perspective—Article 22. Peace, Justice, and Nonresistance," available online at http://mennoniteusa.org/confession-of-faith/peace-justice-and-nonresistance/.

_____, "Reflections on the Jewish and Palestinian Voices for Peace Tour" (June 19, 2017), available online at http://mennoniteusa.org/menno-snapshots/reflections-jewish-palestinian-voices-peace-tour/.

_____, "Mennonites choose 'third way' on Israel and Palestine" (July 6, 2017), available online at http://mennoniteusa.org/news/mennonites-choose-third-way-israel-palestine/.

———. "MC USA Consultation on Investment and Israel/Palestine." *The Mennonite*, January 28, 2018. (https://themennonite.org/daily-news/mc-usa-consultation-investment-israel-palestine/).

_____, "We Are Mennonites," online at http://mennoniteusa.org/who-we-are/structure/.

Mennopin, "Mennonite Church USA Kansas City 2015 Resolution on Israel-Palestine" (February 27, 2015), available online at https://mennopin.org/2015/03/22/resolution/.

_____, "Kairos" (2016), available online at https://mennopin.files.wordpress.com/2016/04/kairos_studyguide_mennopin.pdf.

_____, "Brief History of Mennonite Involvement in Israel-Palestine" (2017), prepared by Timothy Seideland Andre Gingerich Stoner, available online at https://mennopin.org/brief-history-of-mennonite-involvement-in-palestine-israel/.

Mennonite World Review, "Broad census counts more Anabaptists" (May 27, 2019), online at http://mennoworld.org/2019/05/27/news/broad-census-counts-more-anabaptists/.

Mercati, Silvio Giuseppe. *S. Ephraem Syri opera*. Romae: Pontifical Biblical Institute, 1915.

Merkley, Paul Charles. *American Presidents, Religion, and Israel*. Westport, CT: Praeger, 2004.

———. *Christian Attitudes Towards the State of Israel*. Montreal: McGill-Queens University Press, 2001.

———. *The Politics of Christian Zionism, 1891-1948*. New York: Taylor & Francis, 1998.

Micklethwait, John, and Adrian Wooldridge. *God Is Back: How the Global Revival of Faith Is Changing the World*. London, United Kingdom: Penguin Press, 2009.

Minerbi, Sergio. *Una Relazione Difficile—Vaticano, Ebraismo, Israele*. Rome: Bonanno, 2016.

Ministry of Foreign Affairs (Israel), "The Action Plan for Combatting Antisemitism 2015 and Beyond and Final Statements," available online at https://mfa.gov.il/MFA/ABOUTTHEMINISTRY/CONFERENCES-SEMINARS/GFCA2013/Documents/GFCA2015Booklet.pdf.

Mitchell, W.J. T. "Holy Landscape: Israel, Palestine, and the American Wilderness." *Critical Inquiry* 26, no. 2 (Winter 2000): 193-223.

Mittelman, Sheba. "Champions of the Arab Cause in USA." *Patterns of Prejudice* 13, no. 5 (January 1, 1979): 1–4. https://doi.org/10.1080/0031322X.1979.9969534.

Mohammed, H. "Behind the Rhetoric: President Bush and U.S. Policy on the Israeli-Palestinian Conflict," *American Diplomacy* (2015) 22:1, 79-92.

Montgomery, Ray, and Bob Odell. *The List: Persecution of Jews Throughout History*. Jerusalem: Root Source Press, 2019.

Moon, Luke. "In Bethlehem, the Wrong Kind of Christian Festival" *The Tower*, no. 13 (April 2014.) http://www.thetower.org/article/in-bethlehem-the-wrong-kind-of-christian-festival/.

Morris, Benny. *1948: A History of the First Arab-Israeli War*. New Haven: Yale University Press, 2008.

Muadi, Qassam, "Kalimat al-Masihiyyin Wahida: La lil-Tajnid," interview with Michel Sabbah (September 2013), Quds Network, available online at www.qudsn.ps/article/27302.

Nafziger, Tim. "A Window into Antisemitism and Nazism among Mennonites in North America, Part 1." *The Mennonite*, July 27, 2007. https://themennonite.org/window-antisemitism-nazism-among-mennonite-north-america-part-1/.

Nagel, Ernest, and James R. Newman. *Gödel's Proof, Revised Edition*. New York: NYU Press, 2008.

Nanos, Mark, "The Letter of Paul to the Romans," in *Jewish Annotated New Testament*, 2d edition, edited by Amy-Jill Levine and Marc Z. Brettler, 285-320. New York: Oxford University Press, 2017.

_____. *Paul within Judaism: Restoring the First-Century Context to the Apostle*. Minneapolis, Minnesota: Fortress Press, 2015.

Nanos, Mark, and Magnus Zetterholm (eds.), *Paul within Judaism: Restoring the First-Century Context to the Apostle*. Minneapolis: Fortress Press, 2015.

National Association of Evangelicals, "Evangelical Leaders Reflect on Israel, Palestine" (July 2014), available online at https://www.nae.net/evangelical-leaders-reflect-on-israel-palestine/.

The National Coalition of Christian Organizations in Palestine. "Open letter from The National Coalition of Christian Organizations in Palestine." *World Council of Churches*, June 21, 2017. https://www.oikoumene.org/en/resources/documents/general-secretary/letters-received/open-letter-from-the-national-coalition-of-christian-organizations-in-palestine/.

Naveh, Eyal, "Unconventional 'Christian Zionist': The Theologian Reinhold Niebuhr and His Attitude toward the Jewish National Movement," *Studies in Zionism* (1990) 11:2, 183–196.

Nehr, Andre, *L'Exil de la parole: du silence biblique au silence d'Auschwitz*. Paris: Editions du Seuil, 1970.

Neiheisel, J. R. and Djupe, P. A. "Intra-Organizational Constraints on Churches' Public Witness," *Journal for the Scientific Study of Religion* 47 (2008): 427–441.

Nelson, Cary. *Israel Denial: Anti-Zionism, Anti-Semitism, and the Faculty Campaign Against the Jewish State.* Bloomington: Academic Engagement Network/Indiana University Press, 2019.

Nerel, Gershon, "Anti-Zionism in the 'Electronic Church' of Palestinian Christianity" ACTA (Analysis of Current Trends in Anti-Semitism) (2006).

Neusner, Jacob. *Jews and Christians: The Myth of a Common Tradition.* London, SCM Press, 1991.

Newport, Frank, "AP Votecast survey shows that 81% of white evangelical Protestant voters went for Trump in 2020," *Gallup* (November 13, 2020).

NGO Monitor. *Catholic Aid Societies and Political Campaigns Directed at Israel.* Jerusalem: BDS In the Pews (2014-2015), available online at http://www.ngo-monitor. org/data/images/File/Catholic_Jun_2015.pdf.

_____, "Sabeel's Theology of Contempt: Injecting Anti-Israel and Antisemitic Activism into Churches" (June 2015), available online at https://www.ngo-monitor.org/ data/images/File/NGOMonitor_Sabeel_June_2015.pdf.

———. "Government Funding for NGOs involved in BDS," available at https://www. ngo-monitor.org/data/images/File/BDS_Table.pdf.

Nicholls, William. *Christian Antisemitism: A History of Hate.* Northvale, NJ: Jason Aronson, 1993.

Nicholson, Robert, "Islam, Christianity, & the End of Palestine," *Providence: A Journal of Christianity & American Foreign Policy* (September 13, 2016), available online at https://providencemag.com/2016/09/islam-christianity-end-palestine/.

Nirenberg, David, *Anti-Judaism: The Western Tradition.* New York: W. W. Norton, 2013.

Novak, David. *The Election of Israel: The Idea of the Chosen People.* Cambridge: Cambridge University Press, 1995.

_____, "The Covenant in Rabbinic Thought." In Eugene B. Korn and John T. Pawlikowski, eds. *Two Faiths, One Covenant? Jewish and Christian Identity in the Presence of the Other,* pp 65-80.

_____, "Why Are the Jews Chosen?" *First Things* (April 2010).

_____, "Covenant and Mission." In Robert W. Jenson and Eugene B. Korn, eds. *Covenant and Hope: Christian and Jewish Reflections,* pp. 41-57.

_____. *Zionism and Judaism: A New Theory.* NY: Cambridge University Press, 2015.

_____, "Supersessionism Hard and Soft," *First Things* (February 2019).

Oberman, Heiko. *The Roots of Anti-Semitism in the Age of Renaissance and Reformation.* Philadelphia: Fortress, 1984.

Ochs, Peter, "Meantime and End time Theologies of the Return to Zion." In Robert W. Jenson and Eugene Korn, eds. *Returning to Zion: Christian and Jewish Perspectives.*

Oldmixon, Elizabeth A., and Beth A. Rosenson, and Kenneth. D. Wald, "Conflict over Israel: The Role of Religion, Race, Party, and Ideology in the U.S. House of Representatives, 1997–2002," *Terrorism and Political Violence,* (2005) 17:3, 407–426.

Olewine, Sandra. "As war rages to the east of us, we continue to bury the dead here." *The Electronic Intifada,* March 26, 2003.

———. "Dark Gethsemane: A Lenten Message from the Holy Land," *Crossings,* March 24, 2001.

———. "The Silent Destruction of Palestine," *CounterPunch,* May 31, 2002.

———. "Snow in Jerusalem." *Washington Report on Middle East Affairs,* April 2000, 11, 83.

———. "*The Sorrow Unseen, the Story Untold...*" September 13, 2001. http://groups. colgate.edu/aarislam/olewine.htm.

Operazione Columbia, "Adesione all Campagna BDS" (December 15, 2014), available online at http://www.operazionecolomba.it/italia/2282-adesione-alla-campagna-bds. html.

Oren, Michael B., *Ally: My Journey Across the American-Israeli Divide.* New York: Random House, 2015.

———. *Power, Faith and Fantasy.* New York: Norton, 2007.

Orlinsky, Harry M., "The Biblical Concept of the Land of Israel: Cornerstone of the Covenant between God and Israel," in *The Land of Israel: Jewish Perspectives,* edited by Lawrence A. Hoffman, 27-64. Notre Dame, IN: University of Notre Dame Press, 1986.

Origène of Alexandria. *Homélies sur la Genèse.* Edited by Louis Doutreleau. SC 7. Paris: Cerf, 1976.

Palestine Israel Ecumenical Forum (PIEF), "Calls to Action" (Kairos Palestine Document), available online at https://pief.oikoumene.org/en/calls-to-action.

Palestine Israel Network, "Palestine Israel Toolkit," available online at http://muntherisaac.blogspot.com.

Palestine Portal, "Opposition to Israeli Settlements in Palestinian Land (#6111, 2012 BOR), available online at http://www.palestineportal.org/wp-content/uploads/2016/10/ UMC_OppositionToIsraeliSettlements_Adopted2012_Res6111_BOR2016.pdf.

"Palestinian pastor elected moderator of the US Presbyterian Church" (June 17, 2002), available online at http://www.comeandsee.com/view.php?sid=314.

Pappe, Ilan. *The Ethnic Cleansing of Palestine.* London: Oneworld Publications, 2006.

Pawlikowski, John T. *Christ in the Light of the Christian-Jewish Dialogue.* Eugene, OR: Wipf and Stock Publishers, 2001.

————. "Christology after the Holocaust," *Encounter* 59 (Summer 1998): 345-368.

Pax Christi International. *Call for a new Israeli-Palestinian peace process: the moment for renewed commitment.* Brussels: Pax Christi International, December 1, 2016, available at https://www.paxchristi.net/sites/default/files/december_2016_israel-palestine_statement. pdf.

————. "HeidelbergCement muss Völkerrecht und OECD-Leitsätze einhalten," available online at https://www.paxchristi.de/meldungen/view/5857631100993536/ HeidelbergCement%20muss%20Völkerrecht%20und%20OECD-Leitsätze%20 einhalten.

PCUSA NEWS. "Presbyterians to Attend UN Anti-racism Conference." News release (August 22, 200), available online at https://archive.wfn.org/2001/08/msg00224.html.

Pence, Mike. https://www.whitehouse.gov/the-press-office/2017/05/02/remarks-vice-president-pence-israel-independence-day-commemoration-event.

Pettit, Peter A., "Old Whines With New Spins." In Jesper Svartik and Jacob Wiren, eds. *Religious Stereotyping and Interreligious Relations.* NY: Palgrave, 2013, pp. 207-220.

_____, "Review of Walter Brueggemann, Chosen?" *Studies in Christian-Jewish Relations* No. 10 (2015), 1-5.

_____, "How New is the New Christian Zionism?" *The Christian Century* (August 14, 2017).

Pew Research Center, "Religion and Politics: Contention and Consensus: Chapter 4" (July 24, 2003), available online at https://www.people-press.org/2003/07/24/iv-changing-perceptions-of-islam/.

_____, "American Evangelicals and Israel" (April 15, 2005), available online at https://www.pewforum.org/2005/04/15/american-evangelicals-and-israel/.

_____, "Public Expresses Mixed Views of Islam, Mormonism" (September 25, 2007), available online at https://www.pewforum.org/2007/09/26/public-expresses-mixed-views-of-islam-mormonism/.

_____, "Modest Backing for Israel in Gaza Crisis" (January 13, 2009), available online at https://www.people-press.org/2009/01/13/modest-backing-for-israel-in-gaza-crisis/.

_____, "A Portrait of Mormons in the U.S." July 24. 2009), available online at http://www.pewforum.org/2009/07/24/a-portrait-of-mormons-in-the-us-social-and-political-views/.

_____, "Continuing Divide in Views of Islam and Violence" (March 9, 2011), available online at https://www.pewforum.org/2007/09/26/public-expresses-mixed-views-of-islam-mormonism/.

_____, "Goal of Libyan Operation Less Clear to Public: Top Middle East Priority: Preventing Terrorism" (April 5, 2011), available online at https://www.people-press. org/2011/04/05/goal-of-libyan-operation-less-clear-to-public/.

_____, "As Hagel Fight Begins, Wide Partisan Differences in Support for Israel" (January 8, 2013), available online at https://www.people-press.org/2013/01/08/ As-Hagel-Fight-Begins-Wide-Partisan-Differences-In-Support-For-Israel/.

_____, "Public Divided Over Whether Israel, Independent Palestinian State can Coexist" (April 29, 2014), available online at https://www.people-press.org/2014/04/ 29/public-divided-over-whether-israel-independent-palestinian-state-can-coexist/.

_____, "As Mideast Violence Continues, a Wide Partisan Gap in Israel-Palestinian Sympathies" (July 15, 2014), available online at https://www.people-press.org/2014/07/15/ as-mideast-violence-continues-a-wide-partisan-gap-in-israel-palestinian-sympathies/.

_____, "More View Netanyahu Favorably than Unfavorably" (February 27, 2015), available online at https://www.people-press.org/2015/02/27/more-view-netanyahu-favorably-than-unfavorably-many-unaware-of-israeli-leader/.

_____, "More Approve Than Disapprove of Iran Talks, But Most Think Iranians Are Not Serious" (March 30, 2015), available online at https://www.people-press.org/2015/ 03/30/more-approve-than-disapprove-of-iran-talks-but-most-think-iranians-are-not-serious/.

_____, "Religious Landscape Study" (2015), available online at https://www.pewforum. org/religious-landscape-study/.

_____, "Views of Government's Handling of Terrorism Fall to Post-9/11 Low" (December 15, 2015), available online at https://www.people-press.org/2015/12/15/ views-of-governments-handling-of-terrorism-fall-to-post-911-low/.

_____, "In First Month, Views of Trump Are Already Strongly Felt, Deeply Polarized" (February 16, 2017), available online at https://www.people-press. org/2017/02/16/3-views-of-islam-and-extremism-in-the-u-s-and-abroad/.

Phillips, Melanie "'Jesus was a Palestinian': The Return of Christian Anti-Semitism." Commentary Magazine, June 1, 2014. https://www.commentarymagazine.com/articles/ jesus-was-a-palestinian-the-return-of-christian-anti-semitism/.

"*Philosemites or Antisemites? Evangelical Christian Attitudes toward Jews, Judaism, and the State of Israel*" (2002). Available at http://sicsa.huji.ac.il/20Ariel.htm.

Pinsky, Mark, "Will Evangelicals Abandon Israel?," *Moment* (October 12, 2017).

Plested, Marcus. "Irenaeus of Lyon." In *A Dictionary of Jewish-Christian Relations*, edited by Edward Kessler and Neil Wenborn, 213-14. Cambridge: Cambridge University Press, 2005.

Plitnick, Mitchell. "National Jewish Group Applauds Presbyterian Church's Historic Stand against Occupation." *Church & Society* 95, no. 1 (September 2004): 119–20.

Polish Episcopate, "WspólneduchowedziedzictwochrześcijaniZ˙ydów– ListpasterskiEpiskopatuPolski

z okazji 50. rocznicy 'Nostra Aetate'" (October 2015), online at https://episkopat.pl/ wspolne-duchowe-dziedzictwo-chrzescijan-i-zydow/.

Powell, Michael. "Following Months of Criticism, Obama Quits His Church," *New York Times*, June 1, 2008.

"Prayer Is the Only Solution to Middle East Crisis," *Come and See* (May 9, 2002), available online at http://www.comeandsee.com/view.php?sid=299.

Presbyterian Church USA (PCUSA). "A Theological Understanding of the Relations between Christians and Jews" (1987), available online at http://www.pcusa.org/site_media/media/uploads/_resolutions/christians-jews.pdf.

_____, "Presbyterian Church (USA) Letter on the Middle East." Presbyterian Church (USA) Office of the General Assembly to President Bill Clinton (October 14, 2000).

_____, "How to be an Effective Advocate," (June 2001), available online at https://web.archive.org/web/20040804131108/http://www.pcusa.org/pcusa/wmd/ep/resources/mideast/conflict/6-advocacy.pdf.

_____, "Breaking Down the Walls." *The Report of the Middle East Study Committee as Approved by the 219ᵗʰ General Assembly* (2010).

_____, "Kairos Palestine Document and A Study Guide for the Presbyterian Church (U.S.A.) (2011), available online at https://www.pcusa.org/site_media/media/uploads/oga/pdf/kairos-palestinestudy-guide-final-6-14-11.pdf.

_____, "By slim margin, Assembly approves divestment from three companies doing business in Israel/Palestine" (June 20, 2014), available online at https://www.pcusa.org/news/2014/6/20/slim-margin-assembly-approves-divestment-three-com/.

_____, "Zionism Unsettled No Longer Sold on PC(USA) Website" (June 27, 2014), available online at https://www.pcusa.org/news/2014/6/27/zionism-unsettled-no-longer-sold-pcusa-website/.

_____, General Assembly (2016), "Middle East Issues," available online at https://www.pc-biz.org/#/committee/567/business.

Presbyterians for Middle East Peace (PFMEP). "Letter" (Breaking Down the Walls, 2010), available online at https://www.pfmep.org/docs/PFMEP_Packet.pdf.

_____, "A Response and Rebuttal to the ACSWP Report" (by Todd Stavrakos and Michael Gizzi, 2016), available online at https://www.pfmep.org/163-222nd-general-assembly/184-a-response-and-rebuttal-to-the-acswp-report-israel-palestine-for-human-values-in-the-absence-of-a-just-peace.

_____. Two States for Two Peoples, A resource developed by Presbyterians for Middle East Peace. PFMEP, 2016.

https://www.pfmep.org/images/stories/PDFs/TwoStatesforTwoPeoples.pdf.

_____, "The Kairos Palestine Document and PCUSA's Response Time for a Candid Discussion" PFMEP (2018), available online at https://ngo-monitor.org/data/images/File/christmas%20perverted.pdf.

_____. *Two States for Two Peoples 2018 Supplement 2018*. PFMEP, 2018. https://docs. google.com/viewer?url=https%3A%2F%2Fwww.pfmep.org%2Fimages%2FPFMEP_ Homepage%2FTwo_States_2018.pdf.

Presbyterian Mission Agency. "Zionism Unsettled No Longer Sold on PC (USA) Website." June 27, 2014.

Presbytery of Chicago - PC (USA). „"In Our Time" - A Statement on Relations between the Presbytery of Chicago and the Jewish Community in Metropolitan Chicago." Council of Centers on Jewish-Christian Relations. November 21, 2015. Accessed August 06, 2019. https://www.ccjr.us/dialogika-resources/documents-and-statements/ protestant-churches/na/presbyterian/pc-usa-chicago-2015nov21.

Presler, Titus. "Listening Toward Reconciliation: A Conversation Initiative in Today's Anglican Alienations." *Anglican Theological Review* 89, no. 2 (2007), 247-66.

Preston, Andrew, *Sword of the Spirit, Shield of Faith*. New York: Knopf, 2012.

Prichard, Robert W. *A History of the Episcopal Church*, Third Edition. New York: Morehouse, 2014.

———. "Courts, Covenants, and Canon Law: A Review of Legal and Canonical Issues Facing the General Convention." *Anglican & Episcopal History* 78, no.1 (2009), 30-66.

Procario-Foley, Elena G., ed., *Righting Relations after the Holocaust and Vatican II: Essays in Honor of John Pawlikowski*, New York: Paulist Press, 2018.

Quer, Giovanni Matteo, "The Jews, Israel, and Palestinian Replacement Theology." In *Anti-Judaism, Antisemitism, and Delegitimizing Israel*, ed. Robert Wistrich. Lincoln, Nebraska: University of Nebraska Press, 2016.

_____, "Christian BDS: An Act of Love?" In Alvin H. Rosenfeld, ed. *Anti-Zionism and Antisemitism: The Dynamics of Delegitimization*, pp. 302-38.

_____, "Israel and Zionism in the Eyes of Palestinian Christian Theologians," *Religions* 10:8 (August 2019).

_____, "Behind the BDS Discourse: Furthering Anti-Normalization," *The Israeli Journal of Foreign Affairs* 14:1 (2020), 69-79.

Rabin, Yitzhak, *The Rabin Memoirs*. Boston: Little, Brown & Company, 1979.

Raheb, Mitri. *Bethlehem Besieged: Stories of Hope in Times of Trouble*. Minneapolis, MN: Fortress, 2004.

———. *Faith in the Face of Empire: The Bible Through Palestinian Eyes*. Maryknoll, NY: Orbis Books, 2014.

———. *I Am a Palestinian Christian*. Minneapolis: Fortress Press, 1995.

Raheb, Mitri, with Suzanne Watts Henderson. *The Cross in Contexts: Suffering and Redemption in Palestine*. Maryknoll, NY: Orbis Books, 2017.

Rauschenbusch, Walter. *A Theology for the Social Gospel*. New York: Macmillan, 1917.

Reagan, Ronald. *An American Life: The Autobiography*. New York: Simon and Schuster, 1990.

"Reform Jewish Leaders Criticize Presbyterian Church (USA)'s Actions on Israel, Prose-lytization," Union for Reform Judaism (July 27, 2004), available online at http://urj.org/blog/2004/07/26/reform-jewish-leaders-criticize-presbyterian-church-usas-actions-israel.

Reich, Bernard. *Securing the Covenant: United States-Israel Relations after the Cold War.* Contributions in Political Science 351. Westport, CT: Praeger, 1995.

Reichley, James A. *Religion in American Public Life*. Washington, D.C.: Brookings Institution, 1985.

Reinhartz, Adele. "Introduction to The Gospel According to John." In *The Jewish Anno-tated New Testament: New Revised Standard Version Bible Translation*. Edited by Amy-Jill Levine and Marc Zvi Brettler. Second edition. 168-74. Oxford: Oxford University Press, 2017.

———. "'Jews' and Jews in the Fourth Gospel," in *Anti-Judaism and the Fourth Gospel: Papers of the Leuven Colloquium, 2000*, edited by R. Bieringer, Didier Pollefeyt, and F. Vandecasteele-Vanneuville, 341-56. Assen: Royal Van Gorcum, 2001.

———. *Cast Out of the Covenant: Jews and Anti-Judaism in the Gospel of John*. Lanham, MD: Lexington Books, 2018.

Reinhartz, Adele, Steve Mason, Daniel R. Schwartz, Annette Yoshiko Reed, Joan Taylor, Malcolm F. Lowe, Jonathan Klawans, Ruth Sheridan, and James G. Crossley, "Jew and Judean: A Forum on Politics and Historiography in the Translation of Ancient Texts." *Marginalia: A Los Angeles Review of Books Channel*, August 26, 2014 (http://marginalia.lareviewofbooks.org/jew-judean-forum/).

Reiter, Yitzhak, "Sugiyat Hs-Karka'ot." In Yitzhak Reiter and Orna Cohen, eds., *Ha-Hevra Ha'Aravit Be-Yisrael: Ogdan Meida*. Neve Han: 2013, Ch. 5.

Religion News Service, "Jewish agencies condemn church groups' resolution on Israel" (September 15, 2016), available online at https://religionnews.com/2016/09/15/jewish-agencies-condemn-church-groups-resolution-on-israel/.

Rempel, Gerhard, "Mennonites and the Holocaust: From Collaboration to Perpetua-tion," *The Mennonite Quarterly Review* (October 2010), 507-549, online at https://www.goshen.edu/wp-content/uploads/sites/75/2016/06/Oct10Rempel.pdf.

Resnik, Rabbi Russell, "Review of Walter Bruggemann, *Chosen?*" *Kesher Journal* No. 29 (2015).

Rice, Condoleezza. *No Higher Honor: A Memoir of My Years in Washington*. New York: Crown, 2011.

Richardson, Bradford. "Jeremiah Wright: 'Jesus was a Palestinian'." *TheHill.com*, October 10, 2015.

Ricoeur, Paul. *The Conflict of Interpretation: Essays in Hermeneutics*. Edited by Don Ihde. Evanston, IL: Northwestern University Press, 2007.

————. *Essays on Biblical Interpretation.* Edited and translated by Lewis Mudge. Philadelphia: Fortress Press, 1980.

————. *Figuring the Sacred: Religion, Narrative and Imagination.* Edited by Mark I. Wallace. Translated by David Pellauer. Minneapolis: Fortress Press, 1995.

_____. *The Philosophy of Paul Ricoeur: An Anthology of His Work.* Edited by Charles E. Regan and David Stewart. Boston: Beacon Press, 1997.

————. *The Symbolism of Evil.* Translated by Emerson Buchanan. Boston: Beacon Press, 1986.

Robertson, C. K. *Conflict in Corinth: Redefining the System.* New York: Peter Lang, 2001.

————. "Courtroom Dramas: A Pauline Alternative for Conflict Management." *Anglican Theological Review* 89, no. 4 (2007), 589-610.

————. "The Challenge of Definition: Conflict and Concord in Anglicanism." *Anglican & Episcopal History* 78, no. 4 (2009).

Robertson, Robin. *Jungian Archetypes: Jung, Gödel, and the History of Archetypes.* York, ME: Nicolas-Hays, 1995.

Rock, Stephen R. *Faith and Foreign Policy: The Views and Influence of U.S. Christians and Christian Organizations.* New York: Continuum, 2011.

Rosen, Brant, "Reconsidering *Zionism Unsettled*: An Open Letter to Reverend Chris Leighton," Shalom Rav: A Blog by Rabbi Brant Rosen (February 22, 2014), available online at https://rabbibrant.com/2014/02/19/reconsidering-zionism-unsettled-an-open-letter-to-reverend-chris-leighton/.

Rosenberg, Joel C., "Evangelical Attitudes Toward Israel," LifeWay Research (2017), available online at http://lifewayresearch.com/wp-content/uploads/2017/12/Evangelical-Attitudes-Toward-Israel-Research-Study-Report.pdf.

Rosenberg, Yair, "Pope Francis: Anti-Zionism is Anti-Semitism," *Tablet* (October 29, 2015), online at https://www.tabletmag.com/sections/news/articles/pope-francis-anti-zionism-is-anti-semitism.

Rosenfeld, Alvin, ed. *Anti-Zionism and Antisemitism: The Dynamics of Delegitimization.* Bloomington: Indiana University Press, 2019.

Rosenson, Beth A., Elizabeth A. Oldmixon, and Kenneth D. Wald. "U.S. Senators' Support for Israel Examined Through Sponsorship/Cosponsorship Decisions, 1993–2002: The Influence of Elite and Constituent Factors." *Foreign Policy Analysis* 5, no. 1 (2009): 73–91

Ross, Dennis. *Doomed to Succeed.* New York: Farrar, Straus and Giroux, 2015.

Rostow, Nicholas, "Are the Settlements Illegal?" *The American Interest* (March 1, 2010), available online at https://www.the-american-interest.com/2010/03/01/are-the-settlements-illegal/

Rotberg, Robert I., ed. *Israeli and Palestinian Narratives of Conflict: History's Double Helix*. Bloomington, IN: Indiana University Press, 2006.

Rowney, Jo-Anne, "Pope Francis says 'attacks on Jews are anti-Semitic, as are attacks on Israel'" *Catholic Herald* (October 29, 2015), available online at https://catholicherald.co.uk/news/2015/10/29/pope-francis-says-attacks-on-jews-are-anti-semitic-as-are-attacks-on-israel/.

Rubin, Neil. *American Jewry and the Oslo Years*. London: Palgrave Macmillan, 2012.

Rubenstein, Richard. *After Auschwitz: history, theology, and contemporary Judaism*. 2nd ed. Baltimore: John Hopkins University Press, 1992.

Rudin, Rabbi James. *Christians & Jews Faith to Faith: Tragic History, Promising Present, Fragile Future*. Woodstock, Vermont: Jewish Lights Publishing, 2011.

Ruether, Rosemary Radford. *Faith and Fratricide: The Theological Roots of Anti-Semitism*. New York: Seabury, 1974.

Ruether, Rosemary Radford, and Herman J. Ruether. *The Wrath of Jonah: The Crisis of Religious Nationalism in the Israeli – Palestinian Conflict*, 2nd ed. Minneapolis: Fortress Press, 2002.

Ruiz, Jean-Pierre. "Where We Live, What We Believe: Thinking Contextually about Israel, Palestine, and the Churches." Paper presented at St. Joseph University, Philadelphia, PA, October 9, 2016.

Ruotsila, Markku. *The Origins of Christian Anti-Internationalism*. Washington, DC: Georgetown University Press, 2008.

Ruthven, Malise. *Fundamentalism: The Search for Meaning*. Oxford: Oxford University Press, 2005.

Rynhold, Jonathan, "Labour, Likud, the 'Special Relationship,' and the Peace Process, 1988–96," *Israel Affairs* (1997) 3:3–4, 239–262.

_____. *The Arab-Israeli Conflict in American Political Culture*. Cambridge, United Kingdom: Cambridge University Press, 2015.

Sabbah, Michel, *Faithful Witness on Reconciliation and Peace in the Holy Land*. New York: New City Press, 2009.

_____, Interview: "Patriarch Emeritus Michel Sabbah speaks from Jerusalem," *Live Encounters* (March 2016), available online at https://liveencounters.net/2016-le-mag/03-march-2016/patriarch-emeritus-michel-sabbah-speaks-from-jerusalem/.

Sabeel Ecumenical Liberation Theology Center, website at https://sabeel.org.

Saldarini, Anthony J. *Pharisees, Scribes and Sadducees in Palestinian Society*, Edinburgh: T. & T. Clark, 1989.

Sandeen, Ernst. R. *The Roots of Fundamentalism: British and American Millenarianism*, 1800–1930. Chicago, Illinois: University of Chicago Press, 1970.

Sanders, E. P., *Paul and Palestinian Judaism: A Comparison of Patterns of Religion.* Philadelphia: Fortress Press, 1977.

Sandmel, David Fox, "What the United Methodist Church Got Right" (June 5, 2016), available online at http://blogs.timesofisrael.com/what-the-united-methodist-church-got-right/.

Santis, Yitzhak, "Christmas Perverted: Western governments fund religious incitement as a political weapon against Israel," *The Jerusalem Report*-NGO Monitor (January 26, 2015), available online at https://ngo-monitor.org/data/images/File/christmas%20perverted.pdf.

Saxon, Wolfgang. "William R. Cannon, 81, Methodist Theologian," *New York Times*, May 13, 1997.

Schäfer, Axel R. *Countercultural Conservatives: American Evangelicalism from the Postwar Revival to the New Christian Right.* Studies in American Thought and Culture. Madison: The University of Wisconsin Press, 2011.

Schäfer, Peter. *Jesus in the Talmud.* Princeton: Princeton University Press, 2009.

Schechter, Solomon. *Aspects of Rabbinic Theology.* 3rd ed. Woodstock: Jewish Lights, 1993.

Schirch, Lisa. "How Mennonites Reckon with our History in the Holocaust." *The Mennonite*, March 26, 2018. https://themennonite.org/?s=holocaust.

_____, "Mennonites, Nazism, White Supremacy and the Holocaust: A Summary," online at https://lisaschirch.wordpress.com/2018/05/09/mennonites-nazism-white-supremacy-and-the-holocaust-a-summary/.

Scholem, Gershom. *The Messianic Idea in Judaism.* NY: Schocken Books, 1971.

Schrag, Carl, "American Jews and Evangelical Christians: Anatomy of a Changing Relationship," *Jewish Political Studies Review*, (2005) 17: 1-2, 171–181.

Schrag, Carl, S. Bayme, and H. T. Shapiro, "Ripples from the Matzav: Grassroots Responses of American Jewry to the Situation in Israel." NY: American Jewish Committee (2004).

Schrag, Paul. "Scholars Uncover Hidden Stories of the Holocaust: Conference Explores Mennonite Complicity, Wartime Experiences Ranging From Atrocity to Mercy." *Mennonite World Review*, March 18, 2018. http://mennoworld.org/2018/03/19/news/scholars-uncover-hidden-stories-of-the-holocaust/.

Schreiter, Robert J. *Constructing Local Theologies.* 30th anniversary rev. ed. Maryknoll, NY: Orbis Books, 2015.

Schwartz, Regina. *The Curse of Cain: The Violent Legacy of Monotheism.* Chicago: University of Chicago Press, 1998.

Schwartz, Yardena, "'Things Have Only Gotten Worse': French Jews are fleeing their country," *National Geographic* (November 20, 2019), online at https://www.national geographic.com/history/2019/11/french-jews-fleeing-country/.

Secor, Philip B. *Richard Hooker: Prophet of Anglicanism.* Tunbridge Wells: Burns & Oates, 1999.

Secours Catholique. *Le Defi De La Paix.* CCFD-Terre Solidaire, 2013.

Shalom, Benjamin Ish, "A Theology of Sovereignty: Judaism at the Crossroads." In Robert W. Jenson and Eugene Korn, eds. *Returning to Zion: Christian and Jewish Perspectives.*

Shapiro, Faydra. *Christian Zionism: Navigating the Jewish-Christian Border.* Eugene, OR: Cascade Books, 2015.

Shenk, Marie. *Mennonite Encounter with Judaism in Israel: An MBM Story of Creative Presence over Four Decades, 1953-93.* Mission Insight 15. Elkhart, IN: Mennonite Board of Missions, 2000.

Shindler, Colin, "Likud and the Christian Dispensationalists: A Symbolic Relationship," *Israel Studies* (2000) 5:1, 153–182.

Shindo, Nick, "Apocalypse Later: Millennial Evangelicals, Israel-Palestine, and the Kingdom of God," *Religion & Politics* (January 3, 2017), available online at https://religionandpolitics.org/2017/01/03/apocalypse-later-millennial-evangelicals-israel-palestine-and-the-kingdom-of-god/.

Simon, Merrill. *Jerry Falwell and the Jews.* Middle Village, New York: Jonathan David, 1999.

Signer, Michael A, "The Covenant in Recent Theological Statements." In Eugene B. Korn and John T. Pawlikowski, eds. *Two Faiths, One Covenant? Jewish and Christian Identity in the Presence of the Other*, pp. 111-124.

Slater, Wayne, "Protecting Israel is San Antonio Pastor John Hagee's Mission," *Dallas Morning News* (October 28, 2007).

Small, Joseph D. *Flawed Church, Faithful God: A Reformed Ecclesiology for the Real World.* Grand Rapids, MI: Wm. B. Eerdmans, 2018.

Smidt, Corwin, "Religion and American Attitudes toward Islam and an Invasion of Iraq," *Sociology of Religion*, (2005) 66:3, 243–261.

Smietana, Bob, "On Israel, Most Hispanic Christians Are Ambivalent," *Christianity Today* (June 2017), available online at www.christianitytoday.com/news/2017/june/on-israel-most-hispanic-christian-zionism-ambivalent-nhclc.html.

Smith, Gregory, "Most White Evangelicals Approve of Trump Travel Prohibition and Express Concerns About Extremism," Pew Research Center (February 27, 2017), https://www.pewresearch.org/fact-tank/2017/02/27/most-white-evangelicals-approve-of-trump-travel-prohibition-and-express-concerns-about-extremism/.

Smith, Kyle M.. *A Congruence of Interests: Christian Zionism and U.S. Policy toward Israel, 1977–1998*. Bowling Green, Ohio: Bowling Green State University, Graduate College, 2006.

Smith, Lynn. "Newport Pastor Was a Nixon Confidante in the Watergate Era," *Los Angeles Times*, October 29, 1989.

Smith, Robert O. *More Desired than Our Owne Salvation: The Roots of Christian Zionism*. NY: Oxford University Press, 2013.

Smith, Samantha, and Carol Doherty, "5 Facts About How Americans View the Israeli-Palestinian Conflict, Pew Research Center (May 23, 2016), https://www.pewresearch.org/fact-tank/2016/05/23/5-facts-about-how-americans-view-the-israeli-palestinian-conflict/.

Smith, Ted A., and Amy-Jill Levine. "Habits of Anti-Judaism." *Christian Century* 127, no. 13 (June 29, 2010): 26–29. http://middle-east-analysis.blogspot.com/2010/06/habits-of-anti-judaism-critiquing-pcusa.html.

Snyder, Timothy. *Bloodlands: Europe Between Hitler and Stalin*. NY: Basic Books, 2010.

Soulen, R. Kendall. *The God of Israel and Christian Theology*. Minneapolis, Minnesota: Fortress Press, 1996.

Spector, Stephen. *Evangelicals and Israel: The Story of American Christian Zionism*. New York: Oxford University Press, 2009.

Spiegel, Steven L. *The Other Arab-Israeli Conflict: Making America's Middle East Policy, from Truman to Reagan*. Middle Eastern Studies 1. Chicago: University of Chicago Press, 1991.

Spotts, Will. *Pride and Prejudice: The Presbyterian Divestment Story*. September 28, 2005. https://web.archive.org/web/20060618181200/http://www.bearing-witness.org/spotts/pride.pdf, 2005.

Stein, Kenneth W. *The Land Question in Palestine, 1917-1939*. Chapel Hill: University of North Carolina Press, 1984.

Steinberg, Gerald M., "Uncivil Society: Tracking the Funders and Enablers of the Demonization of Israel," *Israel Studies* 24:2 (Summer 2019), 182-205.

Sternberg, Ernest, "Israelis Dressed Up as Christian Militiamen to Kill Palestinians!: A New Blood Libel Debuts at the State University of New York at Buffalo," *SPME* (February 2, 2011).

Stemberger, Günter. *Jewish contemporaries of Jesus: Pharisees, Sadducees, Essenes*. Minneapolis: Fortress, 1995.

Stephens, Bret. "On Palestinian Statehood." *The Wall Street Journal*, January 9, 2017.

Stockton, Ronald R., "Christian Zionism: Prophecy and Public Opinion," *Middle East Journal* (1987) 41:2, 234–253.

_____, "Presbyterians, Jews and Divestment: The Church Steps Back," Middle East Policy Council (Winter 2006), available online at http://www.mepc.org/presbyterians-jews-and-divestment-church-steps-back.

Strawson, John, "Colonialism," "Word Crimes," special issue of *Israel Studies* 24:2 (2019), 33-44.

Strode, Tom "Land: Evangelical Majority Supports Israel's Gaza Withdrawal," *Baptist Press* (September 26, 2005).

Sutcliffe, Adam. *What Are Jews For?* Princeton, NJ: Princeton University Press, 2020.

Swidler, Leonard, "The Dialogue Decalogue : Ground Rules for Interreligious, Interideological Dialogue" *Journal of Ecumenical Studies* 20:1 (Winter 1983), available online at https://static1.squarespace.com/static/5464ade0e4b055bfb204446e/t/5c6eff08 0d9297feece59829/1550778120399/DIALOGUE-DECALOGUE%2BEDITED%2BW ITH%2BSKIT%2B%26%2BAIR%2B5-5-18.pdf.

Synod of Bishops, "The Catholic Church in the Middle East: Communion and Witness–Instrumentum Laboris" (Vatican City: 2010, Libreria Editrice Vaticana) par. 90. p. 34, online at http://www. vatican.va/roman_curia/synod/documents/rc_synod_doc_20100606_instrumentum-mo_en.pdf.

Tal, David, "United States-Israel Relations (1953-1957) Revisted," *Israel Studies* 26:1 (2020), 24-46.

The Talmud of Jerusalem as printed in the first Venetian edition of 1522, with a marginal commentary following the Krakow edition of 1609. Krotoschin, 1866.

Terry, Edward. "Israel-Palestine debate rages long before General Assembly." *The Layman*, March 16, 2010.

Teugels, Lieve M. *Aggadat Bereshit: Transl. from the Hebrew with an Introd. and Notes*. Jewish and Christian Perspectives Series 4. Leiden: Brill, 2001.

Theissen, John D. *Mennonite and Nazi? Attitudes Among Mennonite Colonists in Latin America, 1933-1945*. Studies in Anabaptist and Mennonite History. Kitchener, ON: Pandora Press, 1999.

Tooley, Mark, "Theology and the Churches: Mainline Protestant Zionism and Anti-Zionism." In Gerald R. McDermott, ed. *The New Christian Zionism: Fresh Perspectives on Israel & The Land*, pp. 197-219.

Toon, Peter. ed. *Puritans, the Millennium and the Future of Israel: Puritan Eschatology, 1600 to 1660*. Cambridge, United Kingdom: James Clarke & Co. Ltd., 1970.

Trócaire, "Trócaire Supporting Settlement Goods Ban Bill" (January 29, 2018), available online at https://www.trocaire.org/news/ban-trade-with-israeli-settlements.

Troen, S. Ilan, and Rachel Fish, eds. *Essential Israel: Essays for the 21st Century*. Bloomington: Indiana University Press, 2017.

Troen, S. Ilan, and Carol Troen, "Indigeneity," *Israel Studies* 2: 24 (Summer 2019), 17-32.

Troy, Gil. *Moynihan's Moment: America's Fight Against Zionism as Racism*. New York: Oxford University Press, 2013.

Truman, David. *The Governmental Process*. New York: Knopf, 1951.

"Tuwani(R)Esiste." Tuwani(R)Esiste. http://tuwaniresiste.operazionecolomba.it/.

United Church of Christ, "United Church of Christ votes to divest from companies that profit from Israeli Occupation" (June 30, 2015), available online at http://uccfiles.com/pdf/Middle-East-Resolutions-Release.pdf.

_____, "Promoting a Just Peace in Palestine-Israel: A Guide for United Church of Christ Faith Leaders" (September 2016), available online at https://irp-cdn.multiscreens-ite.com/1c33daec/files/uploaded/UCC%20Guide%20-%20Promoting%20Peace%20in%20Pa.pdf.

_____, "The Kairos Moment Now: Toward a Human Rights Approach to a Just Peace in Palestine" (Summer 2019), available online at https://irp-cdn.multiscreensite.com/1c33daec/files/uploaded/2019%20HR%20Statement%20FinalBW3.pdf.

United Methodist Church (U.S.). *The Book of resolutions of the United Methodist Church, 1984.*

"United Methodists for Kairos Response—Peace And Justice Advocacy For Palestine And Israel." United Methodist Kairos Response. Accessed August 06, 2019. https://www.kairosresponse.org/umkr_home.html.

US Campaign for Palestinian Rights, "Membership Groups," available online at https://uscpr.org/membership/membership-groups/.

Valentin, Benjamin, "Hispanic / Latino(a) Theology." In *Liberation Theologies in the United States: An Introduction*, edited by Stacey Floyd-Thomas and Anthony B. Pinn. New York: New York University Press, 2010.

Van Zile, Dexter , "Mainline Churches Embrace Gary Burge's Harmful Mythology," *Camera* (September 11, 2007), available at http://www.camera.org/index.asp?x_print=1&x_context=2&x_outlet=118&x_article=1371.

_____, "The Mennonite's Mission," *Camera* (February 20, 2008), online at https://www.camera.org/article/the-mennonites-mission/.

_____, "Key Mennonite Institutions against Israel," Jerusalem Center for Public Affairs (July 6, 2009), online at https://jcpa.org/article/key-mennonite-institutions-against-israel/.

_____, "Mainline Christian 'Peacemakers' Against Israel," *Think-Israel* (Nov-Dec 2009), online at http://www.think-israel.org/vanzile.christianpeacemakers.html.

_____, "Updating the Ancient Infrastructure of Christian Contempt: Sabeel," *Jewish Political Studies Review* 23:1 (Spring 2011), online at https://jcpa.org/article/updating-the-ancient-infrastructure-of-christian-contempt-sabeel/.

_____, "Evangelical Anti-Zionism as an Adaptive Response to Shifts in American Cultural Attitudes," *Jerusalem Center for Public Affairs* (2013) 25:1-2, 39-64. Available at http://jcpa.org/article/evangelical-anti-zionism/.

_____, "BDS Charade: United Church of Christ's 'Divestment' From Israel," *The Algemeiner* (January 3, 2019), online at https://www.algemeiner.com/2019/01/03/bds-charade-united-church-of-christs-divestment-from-israel/.

_____, "Hypocrisy, thy name is mainline Protestant," *The Jerusalem Post* (Aug 28, 2019), online at https://www.jpost.com/Opinion/Hypocrisy-thy-name-is-mainline-Protestant-600023.

_____, "The Wages of Supersessionism: BDS and The Decline of the American Mainline," Zoom presentation: Scholars for Peace in the Middle East (October 20, 2020).

Vatican Commission for Religious Relations with the Jews, "Notes on the Correct Way to Present the Jews and Judaism in Preaching and Catechesis of the Roman Catholic Church (1982), available online at http://www.vatican.va/roman_curia/pontifical_councils/chrstuni/relations-jews-docs/rc_pc_chrstuni_doc_19820306_jews-judaism_en.html.

Vince, Warren Lang. *Pulpit Politics: Faces of American Protestant Nationalism in the Twentieth Century*. Albany, New York: State University of New York Press, 1997.

Voss, Carl Hermann, and David A. Rausch, "American Christians and Israel, 1948–1988," *American Jewish Archives* (1988) 40:1, 41–81.

Wagner, Donald E., Walter T. Davis, eds. *Zionism and the Quest for Justice in the Holy Land*. Philadelphia: Casemate Publishers, 2014.

Wald, Kenneth D., and Allison Calhoun-Brown. *Religion and Politics in the United States*. 4th ed. Lanham, Maryland: Rowman and Littlefield 2003.

Wald, Kenneth D., J. L. Guth, C. R. Fraser, J. C. Green, C. E. Smidt, and L. A. Kellstedt. (1997). "Reclaiming Zion: How American Religious Groups View the Middle East." In Sheffer, G., ed., *U.S.-Israeli Relations at the Crossroads*. 147-168. London, United Kingdom: Frank Cass, 1997.

"WCC endorses divestment from Israel," *The Christian Century* (March 22, 2005), online at https://www.christiancentury.org/article/2005-03/wcc-endorses-divestment-israel.

Weaver, Alain Epp. *Inhabiting the Land: Thinking Theologically about the Palestinian-Israeli Conflict*. Cascade Companions 39. Eugene, OR: Wipf and Stock, 2018.

———, ed. *Under Vine and Fig Tree: Biblical Theologies of Land and the Palestinian-Israeli Conflict*. Telford, PA: Cascadia, 2007.

Weaver, Alain Epp, and Sonia K. Weaver. *Salt and Sign: Mennonite Central Committee in Palestine, 1949-1999.* Akron: Mennonite Central Committee, 1999.

Weber, Timothy P. *On the Road to Armageddon: How Evangelicals Became Israel's Best Friend.* Grand Rapids, MI: Baker Academic, 2004.

_____, "American Evangelicals and Israel: A Complicated Alliance." In Frankel, J. and E. Mendelsohn, eds., The Protestant-Jewish Conundrum. *Studies in Contemporary Jewry*, vol. 24 (2010) 141-157. New York City, New York: Oxford University Press.

Weissman, Deborah, "Zionism as Jewish Hope and Responsibility." In Robert W. Jenson and Eugene B. Korn, eds. *Covenant and Hope: Christian and Jewish Reflections*, pp. 263-83.

White, William. *A Case of the Episcopal Churches in the United States Considered.* Philadelphia: David C. Claypoole, 1782.

Who Profits: The Israeli Occupation Industry, available online at https://whoprofits.org.

Wiesel, Elie, *The Night Trilogy.* New York: Hill and Wang, 1987.

Wilford, Hugh. "American Friends of the Middle East: The CIA, US Citizens, and the Secret Battle for American Public Opinion in the Arab–Israeli Conflict, 1947–1967." *Journal of American Studies* 51, no. 1 (February 2017): 93–116.

Wilken, Robert, *The Land Called Holy.* New Haven: Yale, 1994.

Williams, Peter W. *America's Religions: From their Origins to the Twenty-First Century* (fourth edition). Urbana: University of Illinois Press, 2008.

Wills, Garry. *Head and Heart: American Christianities.* New York: Penguin, 2007.

Wong, Edward. "The Rapture and the Real World: Mike Pompeo Blends Beliefs and Policy," *New York Times* (March 30, 2019).

Woods, Randall B. *LBJ: Architect of American Ambition.* New York: Free Press, 2006.

World Council of Churches, "Open letter from The National Coalition of Christian Organizations in Palestine" (June 21, 2017), available online at Open letter from The National Coalition of Christian Organizations in Palestine.

World Economic Forum, "More Americans than ever before say that they aren't religious," (September 2017), available online at https://www.weforum.org/agenda/2017/09/more-americans-than-ever-before-say-that-they-arent-religious.

World Jewish Congress, "'Attacks on Jews are anti-Semitism, as are attacks on Israel,' Pope Francis tells Jewish leader" (October 28, 2015), available online at https://www.worldjewishcongress.org/en/news/attacks-on-jews-are-anti-semitism-as-are-attacks-on-israel-pope-francis-tells-jewish-leader-10-3-2015.

Wright, Elliott. "Excursus: Iran and the United Methodists," *Worldview Magazine*, July 1980.

Wright, N. Thomas, *Jesus and the Victory of God.* Minneapolis: Fortress Press, 1997.

————. Wright, N. T. *The Way of the Lord: Christian Pilgrimage Today.* Grand Rapids, MI: Eerdmans, 2014.

Wuthnow, Robert. *The Restructuring of American Religion.* Princeton: Princeton University Press, 1990.

Wyschogrod, Michael. "Faith and the Holocaust." *Judaism* 20 (Summer 1971): 286-294.

_____. *Body of Faith.* Lanham, MD: Rowman & Littlefield, 1996.

Yemini, Ben-Dror. *Industry of Lies: Media, Academia, and the Israeli-Palestinian Conflict.* New York: Institute for the Study of Global Antisemitism and Policy, 2017.

Yizhar, S. *Khirbet Khizeh.* Translated by N. R. M. De Lange and Yaacob Dweck. First Farrar, Straus and Giroux edition. New York: Farrar, Straus and Giroux, 2008.

Yoder, John Howard, "Is There Such a Thing as Being Ready for Another Millennium?" In Jurgen Moltmann, Miroslav Volf, and Thomas Kucharz, eds. *The Future of Theology: Essays in Honor of Jurgen Moltmann.* Grand Rapids, MI: Eerdmans, 1996.

_____. *The Jewish-Christian Schism Revisited.* Ed. Michael G. Cartwright and Peter Ochs. Harrisonburg, PA: Herald Press, 2008.

Yoffie, Eric H. "How a Radical anti-Israel Jewish Group Colluded With the U.S. Presbyterian Church," *Haaretz*, June 23, 2014.

Zeoli, "Billy Zeoli—About Me," available online at http://billyzeoli.blogspot.com/p/about-me.html.

ABOUT THE CONTRIBUTORS

Susan Andrews is a semi-retired Presbyterian pastor who has served parishes in Pennsylvania, New Jersey, Maryland, and Missouri. She also served as General Presbyter of Hudson River Presbytery, overseeing the mission and ministry of ninety-one parishes for nine years. In 2003 she was elected Moderator of the 215th General Assembly of the Presbyterian Church, USA. The partnership with the Bethesda Jewish Congregation, described in her essay, continues to be strong under the leadership of the Rev. David Gray and Rabbi Sunny Schnitzer. In the last few years, this interfaith collaboration has been enriched by the participation of a local Muslim community.

Robert A. Cathey is professor of theology at McCormick Theological Seminary, Chicago, and the author of *God in Postliberal Perspective: Between Realism and Non-Realism* (Routledge, 2009). With Elena G. Procario-Foley, he edited and contributed to *Righting Relations After the Holocaust and Vatican II: Essays in Honor of John T. Pawlikowski, OSM* (Paulist Press, 2018). He is a member of the Christian Leadership Initiative of the American Jewish Committee and the Shalom Hartman Institute, Jerusalem, and a coauthor of *"…In Our Time…" A Statement on Relations between the Presbytery of Chicago and the Jewish Community in Metropolitan Chicago* (November 21, 2015). He is an elected member of the Christian Scholars Group on Jewish-Christian Relations, and former president of the American Theological Society, Midwest.

Currently he is researching the deep awareness of nature and place in Reformed theology and literature.

Daniel Friedman is a doctoral candidate in International Relations at the University of Alberta, Canada. His research examines American Christian interest group competition over US foreign policy on Israel. He is the rabbi of Hampstead Garden Suburb Synagogue in London, UK, and was previously appointed by the Government of Canada to chair the National Holocaust Monument Council.

Rev. Dr. Bill Harter, pastor emeritus of Falling Springs Presbyterian Church in Chambersburg, Pennsylvania, was inspired to study Judaism by his very close family ties from childhood with Jewish families in Titusville, PA and Clarence, NY. His doctoral work in Jewish and Christian origins lead him to academic work in Holocaust studies; in the Soviet Jewry movement; in peacemaking in the Middle East; in alleviating the persecution of Christians and other minorities in the Middle East and elsewhere; and in affirming the legitimate rights and aspirations of both Israelis and Palestinians, and to participate in activism working to counter anti-Semitism. He attended all but four General Assemblies since 1970 at which he has helped mobilize formal and informal coalitions to counter anti-Judaic and anti-Israel resolutions; served on numerous editing teams; and helped write and edit the UPUSA *Task Force Report on the Middle East* (1974), *A Theological Understanding of the Relationship Between Christians and Jews (1978), Reformed and Reforming* (2015), and *Two States for Two Peoples* (2016). He and his late wife and lifelong co-pastor, the Rev. Linda B. Harter, lived and studied in Jerusalem in 1965 and 1966. They have since directed, co-directed, or participated in forty-five tours to Israel as well as the PA, Jordan, Sinai, Turkey, Lebanon, Greece, and Rome. Bill Harter passed away in 2020.

John Kampen is the Van Bogard Dunn Professor of Biblical Interpretation at the Methodist Theological School in Ohio, specializing in the Dead Sea Scrolls, the New Testament, and Jewish history of the Greco-Roman period. His most recent book is *Matthew within*

Sectarian Judaism from Yale University Press. He earned his Ph.D. from Hebrew Union College in Cincinnati, which awarded him its Founders Medallion for his academic achievements. His research first took him to Jerusalem in 1992 and he has returned on a regular basis since that time. A deep understanding of the history of antisemitism informs his speaking and teaching. He is ordained as clergy in Mennonite Church USA and served as Academic Dean of Bluffton University, a denominational college, for seven years. Before that he was professor and academic dean at Payne Theological Seminary in Wilberforce, Ohio affiliated with the African Methodist Episcopal Church.

Edward Kessler, MBE, is founding director of the Woolf Institute and a leading thinker in interfaith relations, primarily Jewish-Christian-Muslim Relations. In 2002, he was elected as a fellow of St Edmund's College, and in 2011 he was awarded an MBE by Queen Elizabeth II for his contributions to interfaith relations. He has written or edited 12 books, including the standard undergraduate textbook, *An Introduction to Jewish-Christian Relations* (Cambridge, 2010). His most recent books are *Jews, Christians and Muslims* (SCM, 2013) and *Jesus* (The History Press, 2016). As a principal of the Cambridge Theological Federation, and affiliated lecturer at the Faculty of Divinity, much of his academic work has examined Scripture and explored the significance of sharing a sacred text to Jewish-Christian relations.

Amy-Jill Levine is University Professor of New Testament and Jewish Studies and Mary Jane Werthan Professor of Jewish Studies at Vanderbilt Divinity School and College of Arts and Science. She has been awarded honorary doctorates from the University of Richmond, the Episcopal Theological Seminary of the Southwest, the University of South Carolina-Upstate, Drury University, Christian Theological Seminary, and Franklin College, and grants from the Mellon Foundation, the National Endowment for the Humanities, and the American Council of Learned Societies, Professor Levine works in the areas of Biblical Studies, Christian Origins, Jewish/Christian Relations, and Religion, Gender, and Sexuality. Her numerous publications include *The Misunderstood Jew: The Church and the Scandal of the Jewish Jesus; Short Stories by*

Jesus: The Enigmatic Parables of a Controversial Rabbi, and *The Jewish Annotated New Testament* (co-edited with Marc Z. Brettler). A member of an Orthodox synagogue and a life member of Hadassah, Professor Levine also studies how Christian individuals and churches use biblical material to talk about present-day Middle Eastern politics.

Giovanni Mateo Quer is a researcher at the Kantor Center for the study of Contemporary European Jewry, and was a postdoctoral fellow at the Komper Center for the Study of Antisemitism and Racism at the University of Haifa. He has also worked for nongovernmental and international organizations. His recent publications include "The Jews, Israel, and Palestinian Replacement Theology" in *Anti-Judaism, Antisemitism, and Delegitimizing Israel*, edited by Robert S. Wistrich and "Christian BDS: An Act of Love" in *Anti-Zionism and Antisemitism: The Dynamics of Delegitimization* edited by Alvin H. Rosenfeld. His interests include diversity management, human rights, and Israel Studies.

Rev. C. K. Robertson, Ph.D. is Canon to the Presiding Bishop for Ministry Beyond the Episcopal Church, and a Distinguished Visiting Professor at General Theological Seminary in New York City. He has served on the governing board of the National Council of Churches USA and is a member of the Council on Foreign Relations. Dr. Robertson is the author of over a dozen books as well as general editor of the "Studies in Episcopal & Anglican Theology" series through Peter Lang Publishing.

Jonathan Rynhold is the director of the Argov Center for the study of Israel and the Jewish People in the political studies department at Bar-Ilan University. His research focuses on US-Israeli relations, and Israeli foreign policy. He has authored many academic articles on, for example, the rise and fall of the Oslo peace process, and the role of peace and security in Israeli elections. His book, *The Arab-Israeli Conflict in American Political Culture*, won the Israeli Association for Political Science prize for the best book in 2015. Professor Rynhold, also took a leading role in combatting the academic boycott of Israel in the

UK, and has served as an advisor to diaspora Jewish organizations on combatting the BDS movement.

Rabbi David Fox Sandmel, Ph.D., has served as Director of Interreligious Engagement at ADL since 2014. From 2003-2014, he held the Crown-Ryan Chair in Jewish Studies at the Catholic Theological Union in Chicago. He was the Judaic Scholar at the Institute for Christian & Jewish Studies in Baltimore (now the Institute for Islamic, Christian & Jewish Studies), where he managed the project that produced "Dabru Emet: A Jewish Statement on Christians and Christianity." He is an editor of *Christianity in Jewish Terms and Irreconcilable Differences? A Learning Resource for Jews and Christians*. His commentary on First Thessalonians appears in *The Jewish Annotated New Testament*. Rabbi Sandmel represents ADL and is an officer of, the International Jewish Committee on Interreligious Consultations, a consortium of Jewish organizations that serves as the official dialogue partner of the Vatican, the World Council of Churches, and the Greek Orthodox Church. He holds a B.A. in Jewish Studies from Ohio State University, received Rabbinic Ordination and Masters in Hebrew Literature from the Hebrew Union College-Jewish Institute of Religion in Cincinnati, and completed his doctorate in Religious Studies at the University of Pennsylvania.

John Wimberly has been a Presbyterian pastor since 1974. Interfaith relations and the pursuit of justice have been focal points of his ministry. His interest in the Israeli-Palestinian issue is rooted in his belief that boycotts, divestment and sanctions are counter-productive tools in this particular conflict. Since the PCUSA began aligning itself with BDS, he has maintained that this strategy would simply exacerbate and deepen the divisions between these two neighbors rather than move either party toward reconciliation. As a person involved in grassroots movements throughout his life, he believes that, ultimately, the Israel-Palestine conflict will be resolved from the bottom up, not the top down.

ABOUT THE EDITORS

Michael C. Gizzi is professor of criminal justice at Illinois State University, where he teaches classes on constitutional law (criminal procedure), courts, criminal law, corrections, and introduction to criminal justice. He is coauthor of *The Web of Democracy: An Introduction to American Politics* and *The Fourth Amendment in Flux: The Roberts Court, Crime Control, & Digital Privacy*. He has published widely on search and seizure law, the war on drugs, and Supreme Court decision-making. He has been active in Presbyterians for Middle East Peace for a number of years, writing on the group's behalf and participating in the denomination's debates. He has researched reconciliation projects on several trips to Israel and Palestine.

Cary Nelson is Jubilee Professor of Liberal Arts and Sciences and Professor of English at the University of Illinois at Urbana-Champaign and an affiliated professor at the University of Haifa. He is the recipient of an honorary doctorate from Ben-Gurion University of the Negev. He is a former president of the American Association of University Professors and is current chair of the Alliance fior Academic Freedom. His work is the subject of an edited collection, *Cary Nelson and the Struggle for the University: Poetry, Politics, and the Profession*. He is the author or editor of thirty-five books and has written 300 essays and reviews. Among his authored books are *Manifesto of a Tenured Radical; Revolutionary Memory: Recovering the Poetry of the American Left; No University is an Island: Saving Academic Freedom; Academic Keywords: A Devil's Dictionary for Higher Education* (with Stephen Watt); and *Recommended Principles to Guide Academy-Industry Relationships* (with Jennifer Washburn). His edited and coedited books include *Theory in the Classroom; Higher Education Under Fire; Marxism and the Interpretation of Culture; Cultural Studies; Madrid 1937: Letters of the Abraham Lincoln Brigade From the Spanish Civil War; Will Teach for Food: Academic Labor in Crisis;* and *Anthology of Modern American Poetry.*

Peace and Faith completes a linked series of five books dealing with the Israel-Palestinian conflict and its intersections with anti-Semitism:

Cary Nelson & Gabriel Brahm, coed., The Case Against Academic Boycotts of Israel (2015).

Cary Nelson, *Dreams Deferred: A Concise Guide to the Israeli-Palestinian Conflict & the Movement to Boycott Israel* (2016).

Cary Nelson, *Israel Denial: Anti-Zionism, Anti-Semitism, & the Faculty Campaign Against the Jewish State* (2019).

Cary Nelson, Not in Kansas Anymore: Academic Freedom in Palestinian Universities (2021).

Cary Nelson & Michael C. Gizzi, coed., *Peace and Faith: Christian Churches and the Israeli-Palestinian Conflict* (2021).

INDEX*

*The Annotated Timeline is not included in the index.